OXFORD JUNIOR ENCYCLOPAEDIA

VOLUME VII
INDUSTRY AND COMMERCE

OXFORD JUNIOR ENCYCLOPAEDIA

GENERAL EDITORS
LAURA E. SALT AND ROBERT SINCLAIR
ILLUSTRATIONS EDITOR: HELEN MARY PETTER

VOLUME VII

INDUSTRY AND COMMERCE

OXFORD UNIVERSITY PRESS

Oxford University Press, Amen House, London E.C.4

GLASGOW NEW YORK TORONTO MELBOURNE WELLINGTON
BOMBAY CALCUTTA MADRAS KARACHI
CAPE TOWN IBADAN NAIROBI ACCRA SINGAPORE

FIRST PUBLISHED 1951
REPRINTED WITH CORRECTIONS 1955, 1957

PRINTED IN GREAT BRITAIN

PREFACE

IN authorizing the preparation of this work the Delegates of the Oxford University Press had foremost in mind the need to provide a basic book of reference for school libraries. In form it was to be a genuine encyclopaedia, in treatment and vocabulary suitable for the young reader. To many children (and indeed to many adults) reading is not a natural activity: they do not turn to books for their own sake. But they can be trained to go to books for information which they want for some particular purpose—and thus, very often, to form a habit which will be of lifelong value. Their capacity to read continuously for any length of time being limited, they can absorb knowledge better if they get it in small quantities: therefore they will often read reference books when they may reject the reading of more extended matter. Again, it is probably true to say of such readers that their approach is from the particular to the general, and from the application to the principle, rather than the reverse, that their main interest is in the modern world around them, and that since they are not very good at conceiving things outside their own experience, their capacity for grasping abstract ideas is limited. On the other hand, once their interest is aroused, they will often pursue a subject to remarkable lengths, so long as its development is logical and the treatment avoids dullness.

But such generalizations can easily be overdone: many children using the books will not be of this type. Moreover, it was evident from the first that a project involving so great an amount of work, however exactly it might meet its principal mark, would be fully justified only if it could be of service to a far wider circle of readers. Even for the age-group first in mind, anything like 'writing down to children' must plainly be taboo—but clear exposition and simple language are no bad qualities in writing for any audience. Here, then, it seemed was the opportunity to provide a work of reference suitable for many readers to whom the large, standard encyclopaedias are too heavy and technical, and the popular alternatives for the most part neither sufficiently complete nor authoritative. The fact that the plan allowed for an exceptionally large proportion of illustrations to text (between one-quarter and one-third of the total space) is an advantage to any reader, since pictures may, in many instances, save whole paragraphs of involved explanation. With these secondary aims well in mind, therefore, the General

Editors have ventured to hope that the encyclopaedia may find usefulness not only among certain younger children, but also among older students in clubs, libraries, and Young People's Colleges, and even to no small extent among their parents and other adults who may wish for a simple approach to some unfamiliar or forgotten subject.

SCOPE AND EMPHASIS. Within certain limits the OXFORD JUNIOR ENCY-CLOPAEDIA purports to be reasonably comprehensive, though (in common with all general encyclopaedias) not exhaustive. Chief among these limits is that matter already easily available in school text-books is included only so far as its presence is necessary for the proper understanding of the subject under discussion. Thus, although an immense field of history is surveyed, it will be found mainly under headings dealing with its effects, or in the biographies of those who lived to make it. Purely technical or scientific subjects, also, are omitted except when they have some general interest. In natural history and kindred studies the immense variety of forms necessarily led at times either to their treatment by groups or to their omission on purely arbitrary decisions as to which species would, in all probability, never be looked for, or because there was nothing particularly interesting to say of them. In point of general balance the stress is laid rather on the modern world, though due space is given to the factors which have shaped it, no less than to those which are changing it.

ARRANGEMENT. The encyclopaedia is planned to consist of twelve volumes. Each is arranged alphabetically within itself, and each deals with a particular range of related subjects. Within its terms of reference, then, each volume is virtually self-contained, and, owing to the great number of single-line cross-references, can well be used alone. This arrangement, which has several incidental advantages (as of production, in difficult times, and of prompt revision later), arose mainly from one consideration. If articles were to be kept really short—and, in fact, few approach and almost none exceeds 2,000 words—many subjects could be dealt with comprehensively only by referring the reader to other relevant articles—itself a desirable thing to do. It was clearly preferable for these to be under his hand, rather than be dispersed through any of the twelve volumes at the caprice of the alphabet. This the present arrangement achieves to a great extent. If it has led to a small amount of overlapping, that again is not without its advantages.

The cross-references play an indispensable part in the make-up of the encyclopaedia. They are of two kinds: references in the text to further articles amplifying the particular point under review, and references at the end of an article to others taking the whole subject farther. Therefore, a reader looking up any wide subject, such as MONEY, and following up its cross-references either in the text or at the end of the article, can discover under what main headwords the subject is treated. These, again, will refer him to any subsidiary articles, as also, in many cases, to those of a complementary nature. Thus he may be guided either from the general to the particular or vice versa. It is believed that the titles of the twelve volumes (see p. x), in conjunction with their sub-titles, will usually lead the reader straight to the volume containing the information he wants. In selecting headwords, the rules generally followed have been to prefer the familiar, or even the colloquial, reserving the technical alternative for a single-line entry, and to group narrow subjects under a headword of wider scope. Thus, for COOPERING, *see* CASK-MAKING; for ACCOUNTANCY, *see* BOOK-KEEPING, for PIECE WORK, *see* WAGES; for CHEQUE, *see* BANKING; and for JOURNEYMEN, *see* CRAFT GUILDS.

L. E. S., R. S.

OXFORD, 1951

LIST OF CONTRIBUTORS

VOLUME EDITOR

H. V. R. GEARY, M.C.

CONTRIBUTORS

B. ALWYN JAY, Director, Timber Development Association, Ltd.

T. R. BARNARD, B.Sc.Tech., M.I.Min.E.

DORA BILLINGTON, A.R.C.A., President, The Arts and Crafts Exhibition Society.

G. M. BOUMPHREY.

ASA BRIGGS, M.A., B.Sc. (Econ.), Fellow of Worcester College, Oxford.

MARTIN S. BRIGGS, F.R.I.B.A.

PETER BRYAN.

E. A. CARPENTER, B.A., Lecturer at the City of London College.

J. C. CHASTON, Ph.D., A.R.S.M., A.Inst.P., F.I.M.

ERNEST J. CLYNE.

SYDNEY M. COCKERELL.

G. D. H. COLE, M.A., Professor of Social and Political Theory, Oxford.

J. G. COOK, Ph.D.

J. G. DAVIS, D.Sc., Ph.D. (Lond.), F.R.I.C.

G. DILLEY, Ph.C.

STUART H. HASTIE, O.B.E., M.C., B.Sc., F.R.I.C.

R. W. HAYMAN, F.Z.S.

C. H. HAYWARD.

LESLIE HERMAN.

G. HORNER, A.R.I.C., M.Sc.

S. A. HORWOOD, M.B.E.

GORDON HUGHES.

A. S. IRVINE, M.A. (Oxon.).

T. M. JONES.

C. KISBY, A.R.C.A., A.T.I.

J. KORN, F.B.S.I., A.M.I.I.A., Principal, The Cordwainers Technical College.

J. S. LINDSAY, F.S.A.

GORDON LOGIE, A.R.I.B.A., A.M.T.P.I., A.A.Dip.

C. G. McAULIFFE, B.A.

GEORGE MacINTYRE McLEAN, of British Ropes Ltd., Doncaster.

E. C. J. MARSH, B.Sc. (Lond.), F.R.I.C., F.I.M.

S. R. W. MARTIN, Ph. D., A.R.C.S., F.R.I.C., D.I.C.

T. E. METCALFE, M.B.E.

J. H. BERNARD MOORE, B.Com., Lecturer in Commerce at the City of London College.

D. DYLAN PRITCHARD, M.A. (Wales).

A. B. PURBRICK, A.I.C.S.

A. HINGSTON QUIGGIN.

R. A. ROSSER, B.A., B.Sc., A.R.I.C.

MARGARET SIMEON, A.R.C.A.

RICHARD J. SMITH, F.T.I.

FRANCIS SPEAR, A.R.C.A.

CLAUDE H. SPIERS, M.A., Ph.D. (Cantab.).

E. N. TIRATSOO, Ph.D., D.I.C., B.Sc., A.R.S.M., F.G.S., F.R.G.S., M.Inst.Pet.

P. A. WELLS, M.A., M.Sc., F.Inst. P., formerly Director of Education to the International Wool Secretariat.

GORDON WEST.

Assistant Editors—W. F. JEFFREY, STELLA M. RODWAY

COLOUR PLATES

ACKNOWLEDGEMENTS

THE EDITORS wish to thank all those who have freely contributed material for the text and have lent photographs. Special thanks are due to Dr. John Johnson, C.B.E., for his help in the selection of material from the collection of ephemeral printing at the University Press, Oxford. Acknowledgement to the owners of photographs is given beneath the illustrations. The hall-marks on p. 22 are reproduced by permission of the Executors of the late Frederick Bradbury, F.S.A., from his book *Guide to Marks of Origin on British and Irish Silver Plate and Old Sheffield Plate Makers' Marks*, published by J. W. Northend, Sheffield. Others who have given assistance include:

Achille Serre, Ltd.; George Allen & Unwin, Ltd.; Bank of England; Batchelors Peas, Ltd.; Bowater Paper Corporation, Ltd.; The Brewers' Society; Lieut.-Colonel H. S. Bristowe; British Aluminium Company, Ltd.; British Ropes, Ltd.; The Cornish Mining Development Board; The Distillers Company, Ltd.; The Goldsmiths Company; Hudson's Bay Company; Imperial Chemical Industries, Ltd.; The Institute of Quarrying; The International Wool Secretariat; The Irish Linen Guild; The Linoleum Manufacturers' Association; London & Cambridge Economic Service; The Mining Association of Great Britain; Petroleum Information Bureau; Royal Exchange Assurance; The Scotch Whisky Association; Sir Francis Towle, C.B.E.; Walpole Bros. (London), Ltd.

PLAN OF VOLUMES

HOW TO USE THIS BOOK

THIS VOLUME is one of twelve, each on a separate subject, the whole set forming what is called an encyclopaedia, or work from which you can find out almost anything you want to know. (The word comes originally from the Greek *enkuklios*, circular or complete, and *paideia*, education.) Each of the twelve volumes is arranged alphabetically within itself, as twelve dictionaries would be.

The difference between a dictionary and an encyclopaedia is that, while the first gives you no more than the meanings and derivations of words, the second tells you a very great deal more about their subjects. For instance, from a dictionary you could find that COPRA is the dried kernel of the coconut, from which coconut oil is obtained, and you would learn little more; but an encyclopaedia will tell you that the principal producing countries are Indonesia, Malaya, Ceylon, and the Philippine Islands; that copra is an important ingredient in the manufacture of soap; that it is used for making margarine, salad oil, and cooking oils; and you will also learn how the copra is separated from the nut and how it is dried. Then a dictionary contains nearly every word in the language; but an encyclopaedia deals only with words and subjects about which there is something interesting to be said, beyond their bare meanings. So you should not expect to find every word in an encyclopaedia—every subject is there, but not every word.

To find any subject, you have first to decide in which of the twelve volumes it comes. Each of these has a title as well as a number, and also a list of general subjects to make the title clearer. All these are set out in the Plan of Volumes on the opposite page. Very often you will be able to tell from the title alone which volume contains the information you need; but if not, the list of sub-headings on the plan opposite will help to direct you. For example, if you want to read about people, the way they have lived at different times and places, and the things they have believed and worshipped, you would turn to Volume I. If, however, you want to find out about an animal or plant, you would look it up in Volume II, Natural History; but if you wanted to know how that animal or plant is used in something like farming, fishing, or trapping, you would find it in Volume VI. If your subject were something in nature that does not have life—such as the sun, or a particular country or river, or a kind of stone—you would find it in Volume

III, with tides, earthquakes, the weather, and many other things. Matters connected with communication of any kind—of people or goods, or even of ideas—are in Volume IV. So you would look there for languages, and printing, and broadcasting, as well as for ships, and trains, and roads. But if it is the engineering side of any of these things that interests you, Volume VIII, Engineering, is the place to try. Recreations are in Volume IX, which includes games and sports, entertainment, clubs, animal pets, and sporting animals. How we are governed and protected by the State, the law, and the armed forces is told in Volume X. Volume XI deals with almost everything connected with our homes, from the building and furnishing of the house to the clothes and health of those who live in it. The titles of Volumes V and XII, Great Lives and The Arts, explain themselves. A rather fuller account of the volume you are now reading, on INDUSTRY AND COMMERCE, is given on page xiii opposite.

To find your subject in the volume, think of its ordinary name, and then look it up just as though you were using a dictionary—the As on the first page and the Zs (if there are any) on the last. If you cannot find it, try a more general word. For instance, if you want to read about Negatives, and cannot find them under that name (as you cannot), try either PHOTOGRAPHY, HISTORY OF or PROCESS REPRODUCTION—either of which will lead you to it. As you read any article, you will probably come across the titles of other articles in some way connected with what you are reading. You will know that they are titles of other articles because they will be printed in capital letters. Either they will be followed by (q.v.) in brackets (this is short for the Latin *quod vide*, and means 'which see'), or else they themselves will be in brackets, with the word *see* in front of them. You can look up these other articles at once if you want to know more about the particular point dealt with, or you can save them up until you have finished the article you are reading. At the end of any article you may find the words 'See also', followed by one or more titles in small capital letters. If you look these titles up, they will tell you still more about the subject that interests you. These last 'cross-references' are very useful if you want to look up a particularly wide subject (such as MINING or TRADE), because they show you at once the titles of all the main articles dealing with it. You can then decide for yourself which to read.

WHAT YOU WILL FIND IN THIS VOLUME

THIS VOLUME IS ABOUT HOW THINGS ARE MADE, AND THE ORGANIZATIONS
WHICH ARE NECESSARY TO ENABLE MEN TO MAKE, TO SELL, AND TO BUY THE
THINGS THEY USE

RAW MATERIALS. This volume tells how the minerals needed for manufactures are extracted from the earth. Metals and coal are obtained by MINING, stone by STONE-QUARRYING, and oil from OIL WELLS. Some raw materials have to be converted into other products before they can be used in industry. You will read how petrol and other substances are prepared from MINERAL OILS by DISTILLATION, how chalk and clay are made into CEMENT and BRICKS AND TILES, and how use is made of BY-PRODUCTS from manufactures. The CHEMICAL INDUSTRY gets its raw materials from the air as well as the earth to make ACIDS and ALKALIS and countless chemical substances which form the basis of many manufactures, such as PLASTICS and RAYON.

MANUFACTURES. You will read how the great industries of the world, such as SHIPBUILDING and the BUILDING INDUSTRY, are organized. In many industries, such as POTTERY and GOLD AND SILVER WORK, the hand craftsman still does much of the work, while in the others, such as PRINTING, the machine has almost taken the place of the hand worker. Articles on the COTTON and WOOL INDUSTRIES explain how these materials are spun and woven into fabrics. Other articles describe how our food is made—how FLOUR MILLING grinds the grain ready for BAKING, how SUGAR REFINING extracts pure sugar from cane and beet, and how BREWING is done.

ORGANIZATION OF INDUSTRY. To make production run smoothly in modern industries, FACTORY ORGANIZATION is necessary. In the Middle Ages masters and workmen were organized in CRAFT GUILDS, which controlled WAGES and APPRENTICESHIP. But since the INDUSTRIAL REVOLUTION things have changed. Businesses are controlled by LIMITED COMPANIES and PUBLIC UTILITY COMPANIES, while LABOUR is organized in TRADE UNIONS. Managers must follow the rules of BUSINESS ORGANIZATION, and must study the science of STATISTICS when calculating how best to act.

MARKETING. The history of TRADE is a long story, from the early barterings of primitive peoples, to the medieval organization of the MERCHANT ADVENTURERS and the HANSEATIC LEAGUE, the later merchant explorers of the CHARTERED COMPANIES, and finally to the elaborate organization of modern INTERNATIONAL TRADE. Manufacturers use the services of WHOLESALE TRADING and RETAIL TRADING to distribute their goods to the people who want them. They make known their goods by TRADE FAIRS and EXHIBITIONS and by all the many devices of ADVERTISING AND PUBLICITY; and they find out what the public want by various methods of MARKET RESEARCH.

MONEY. Trade cannot advance very far without a medium of exchange. Here you can read about the strange things used as PRIMITIVE MONEY to pay for goods, and how gradually our modern MONEY system has evolved, using not only COINS but other more convenient methods of PAYMENT. As trade developed, so did the business of BANKING, and the methods of financing trade by CAPITAL, subscribed in the form of STOCKS AND SHARES. Important safeguards against misfortune in business are now provided by INSURANCE.

The words in capitals are the headings of some of the articles

A

ACCOUNTANCY, *see* BOOK-KEEPING.

ACCOUNTING, MACHINE. There are many objections to keeping the accounting records of a business in ordinary handwriting. Figures, from INVOICES (q.v.) or other documents, may be copied into the books wrongly. Columns of figures may be wrongly totalled. Mistakes may be made in calculating the balances of the accounts: that is, the differences between their debit and credit sides (*see* BOOK-KEEPING). Unless the book-keeping is done by clerks whose writing is not only clear and legible, but also rather good to look at, the records will lack neatness and sometimes will even be difficult to read. Handwritten records also require a large staff of clerks, which is wasteful as clerical labour is not directly productive.

The keeping of accounts by means of accounting machines gets over these objections; but the machines themselves are fairly expensive, and, like other machines, will not pay for themselves unless they are regularly used. Machine accounting, even by the simplest and cheapest machines, is therefore hardly possible for the very small firm; and the more expensive machines are used only by the very largest organizations, such as leading industries, public utility corporations, and important local authorities like the London County Council.

The earliest accounting machines were the adding machine and the cash register. The cash register, in its less elaborate forms, merely gives a duplicated list of individual sales and the total, although it can also be designed to give totals for different classes of sales. It is therefore not, in a strict sense, an accounting machine.

The adding machine was really the forerunner of the modern accounting machine. It has two forms. The first merely delivers a total of the items to be added up. The operator presses down the keys of the machine for each item, and then presses another key which causes the machine to show the total of the items. Some of these machines are small and compact enough to be used on the counters of retail stores, and they are generally useful whenever columns of figures have to be added up or checked. The other form of adding machine not only delivers a total but prints a list of all the items; this list is made on a continuous roll of narrow paper, which can be torn off as required. By using rolls of papers interleaved with carbon paper, duplicate and triplicate lists can be obtained. Most of these machines not only calculate and type a total, but also a series of sub-totals. They were first used in large numbers by the big London bankers, and the London Bankers' Clearing House, for listing and totalling immense numbers of cheques. Other firms soon discovered the value of these machines, and by the beginning of the present century they were in general use. The early machines were operated entirely by hand. About 40 years ago they were adapted for electrical power, and their working speed was greatly increased. But whether hand or electric machines were used, the keys of the machine had to be depressed by the hand of the operator for each separate item. As in all machines, a human limit was thus set to the speed at which these adding machines could be made to work.

The adding machine has rather limited uses for accounting purposes, as book-keeping involves not only addition but also subtraction. Several machines are now in regular use which perform both these operations. The ledger-posting machine has a keyboard containing not only figures but also letters; it is really a combination of a simple TYPEWRITER (q.v. Vol. IV) and an adding and subtracting machine. These machines do not, of course, write records on to the bound pages of an ordinary ledger; loose sheets, or thin cards, are used instead. As in the

Barclays Bank
OPERATORS AT WORK ON ACCOUNTING MACHINES IN THE FENCHURCH STREET BRANCH OF BARCLAYS BANK
Those in the background are preparing customers' statements

adding machine, the record can be typed and calculated in duplicate or triplicate. The duplicate record can be posted to the customer as his statement of account, and thus the clerical labour of making out a separate statement is avoided.

In the simpler forms of ledger-posting machine, the balance of the customer's account, brought forward from the previous month, has to be put in by the operator, who may possibly put in the wrong balance by mistake. A more complicated and rather expensive form of ledger-posting

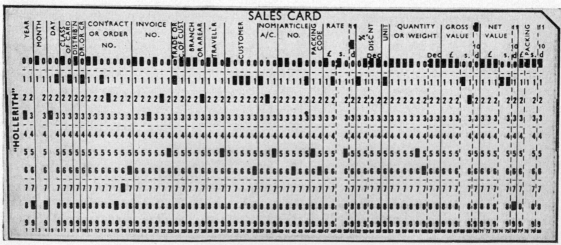

British Tabulating Machine Co.
A 'HOLLERITH' SALES CARD PUNCHED WITH DETAILS OF A SALE
The information is recorded on the cards by means of the holes which are punched in the appropriate columns. From these sales cards are prepared the invoices for dispatch to customers, and a subsequent analysis of sales which may be required under a variety of headings.

machine automatically memorizes, for each one of a series of accounts, the balance that was last calculated. Each customer's account is given a number, and, when the keyboard is set to this number, the last balance is automatically brought forward and typed in.

Many business calculations involve multiplication and division, as well as addition and subtraction. Machines have been invented for such calculations; they perform all the normal operations of arithmetic, but do not type out the separate figures of each calculation. They add, subtract, multiply, and divide, in numbers or in money, or in weights and measures; and their keyboards can be adapted for all kinds of money systems or systems of weights and measures, decimal or other. These machines can work out interest, discount, and percentages, and also foreign-exchange calculations.

The most elaborate machines of all use what is generally known as the 'punched card system'. This is comparatively expensive, and would only be found profitable by the larger firms and corporations. It is usual for the manufacturers of the machines to supply them, and maintain them in efficiency and repair, for a fixed annual rental. There are two main forms of these machines now used in Britain; although one differs slightly from the other, the principle of each is the same. Small cards, about half the size of a postcard, are used, and holes are punched in them; the firm using the cards works out a standard code, by which a hole punched in a particular place means a particular letter, or figure, or sum of money. To avoid the mistakes that all human beings are liable to make, all holes are punched twice. The first operator will punch holes in a card from, say, a pay-sheet; they are then passed on to a second operator who repeats the process on a slightly different machine called a verifier. If the second operator depresses a key not corresponding to a hole in the card the machine will lock, thus detecting an error. As it is unlikely that two operators would make the same error, the possibility of mistakes is thus reduced to a minimum, and mistakes that do occur can be put right at an early stage. Once the cards have been punched, other machines can sort them out into any conceivable groupings or arrangements. Totals and calculations are done in another machine, called the tabulator. This reproduces, on a continuous roll of paper, all the details on the punched cards, translating the punched holes into typed letters and figures, and giving sub-totals and grand totals. Such tabulators are responsible for some of the electricity and gas accounts that are sent out to British householders.

The accounting machine saves a business much clerical labour and many clerical errors, and therefore reduces considerably the routine tasks of the chief accountant. But his trained intelligence and judgement are still necessary, for accounting machines are unable to select for themselves the figures they are to deal with.

See also BOOK-KEEPING.
See also Vol. IV: COUNTING INSTRUMENTS.
See also Vol. VIII: CALCULATING MACHINE.

ACETATE, *see* PLASTICS; RAYON.

ACETIC ACID, *see* ACIDS, Section 2.

ACIDS. 1. These play a vital part in providing the necessities of everyday life. The man in the street may only meet sulphuric acid, as such, in the battery of his car or radio set. But much of his food depends on fertilizers; explosives help to win the coal for his fire, and 'pickling' is needed during the manufacture of his bicycle frame: all these need sulphuric acid. His car tyres may have a link with formic acid; his suit and the jelly he eats may be linked with hydrochloric acid; his tie with acetic acid. In fact, it is possible to trace back most of the things used by modern mankind to one or other of these important acids.

The word 'acid' is derived from the Latin *acidus* meaning sour, and was applied by the early chemists to substances having certain qualities in common with sour wine or vinegar. It is a name loosely applied to any sour substance. Acids are chemically distinct from ALKALIS (q.v.), and each neutralizes the effect of the other. Acids are either organic or inorganic (*see* CHEMISTRY, Vol. III). In the main the organic acids, which are compounds of carbon, are weak acids, and the inorganic acids, such as sulphuric and hydrochloric, are strong acids. The inorganic acids rarely occur in the free state in nature, but their salts (a chemist's term for certain compounds) are found widely distributed, as constituents of mineral and salt deposits, and as soluble salts in natural waters such as seas and lakes. For example, sodium chloride (common salt as used for food) is present in sea-water, in springs and lakes, and as rock-salt in large deposits in Cheshire and many other parts of the world. From this common salt, industrial hydrochloric acid is produced. Various acids, mostly organic, are formed during the life processes of animals, plants, and other living organisms: the lactic acid of sour milk is an example; and carbonic acid, the carbon dioxide of the atmosphere, is a waste product of living things.

The most important acids in industry are sulphuric acid, hydrochloric acid, and nitric acid, which are inorganic; and acetic acid and formic acid, which are organic. Sulphuric acid is probably the most important manufactured raw material of INDUSTRIAL CHEMISTRY (q.v.); as long ago as 1843 it was said that the commercial prosperity of a country could be judged from the amount of sulphuric acid it consumed.

2. INORGANIC ACIDS. Sulphuric Acid (Oil of Vitriol) was probably known to the ancients, but its first mention is generally ascribed to Geber, an Arab chemist about the 8th century A.D., who refers to the 'spirit' which can be expelled from ALUM (q.v.) and which possesses solvent powers. In early times small quantities were produced either by the distilling of ferrous sulphate (green vitriol) or by the burning of sulphur and saltpetre in moist vessels in the presence of air. Early in the 18th century an English quack doctor named Ward produced acid at Richmond by the second of these methods,

using glass vessels which held 66 gallons. In 1846 Roebuck, of Birmingham, replaced the fragile glass vessels by lead chambers, and was soon supplying acid made in this way to linen bleachers in England and Scotland (see LINEN INDUSTRY). This early work laid the foundations of the modern sulphuric acid industry, and a modified form of the lead chamber process is still widely used.

The first stage in sulphuric acid manufacture is the production of sulphur dioxide by burning sulphur or sulphurous materials; the second stage is, broadly speaking, to combine the sulphur dioxide with water and more oxygen from the air. The raw materials used include sulphur from the U.S.A. and Sicily; pyrites from Spain and Scandinavia; anhydrite, a mineral found in the British Isles, the European continent, the U.S.A., and Canada; and spent oxide, a by-product from gasworks. Sulphur is an element; pyrites is a form of metal ore. Two methods are used for the second stage. In the chamber process, sulphur dioxide and air, mixed with oxides of nitrogen, react chemically with water or steam in the large lead chambers to produce sulphuric acid. The other process, the contact process, dates back to a British patent taken out in 1831 by Peregrine Phillips, a Bristol vinegar manufacturer. This method depends upon the combination of sulphur dioxide and oxygen from the air in the presence of a solid catalyst such as platinum or vanadium. (A catalyst is a substance which helps

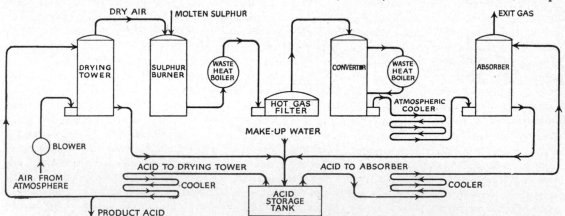

DIAGRAM OF THE CONTACT PROCESS FOR PRODUCING SULPHURIC ACID FROM SULPHUR

First stage: molten sulphur is burnt in the burner (top left) in the presence of air which has been made very dry by an acid treatment in the drying-tower. Second stage: the burning has produced sulphur dioxide gas, which is then filtered and passes to the converter; there it combines with air in contact with a catalyst (see article above) and becomes sulphur trioxide gas. Next, in the absorber (right), the gas is absorbed in acid and becomes sulphuric acid. Spare heat is used to warm boilers

Simon Carves

PLANT FOR PRODUCING SULPHURIC ACID BY THE CONTACT PROCESS

Low on the left is the hot-gas filter with the converter next to it. The exit chimney for waste gases rises from the
absorber. To the right is a cooler

chemical reaction without being altered chemically itself.) It was not used to any great extent until the end of the 19th century; but it can produce stronger acid than the chamber process, and it has been widely adopted.

Sulphuric acid, first used in bleaching and tinning, is now used in enormous quantities for making ARTIFICIAL FERTILIZERS (q.v. Vol. VI). Other important uses are in the descaling or 'pickling' of metals in certain stages of production, in the manufacture of explosives, dyes, drugs, metal sulphates, and plastics including rayon, in petroleum refining and electro-plating, and in crop-spraying. Few industries do not depend at some stage, directly or indirectly, on sulphuric acid.

Hydrochloric Acid (Muriatic Acid) is a solution of hydrogen chloride gas in water. The gas is sometimes found in nature in the free state or dissolved in water—for example, in gases coming off volcanoes, in springs, and in some rivers. The Arabian alchemists were well acquainted with *aqua regia*, a mixture of hydrochloric acid and nitric acid; but pure aqueous hydrochloric *spiritus salis* (spirits of salt) is first heard of in the 15th century. Glauber, a German chemist, produced the acid in 1648 by the action of sulphuric acid on common salt. Since then there have been several improvements, but the production of hydrochloric acid from salt is still an important manufacturing process. A method of production developed comparatively recently is the making of the acid from its elements, hydrogen and chlorine. These are burned together to form hydrogen chloride gas, which is absorbed in water to give a pure grade of acid.

The main uses of hydrochloric acid are in metal descaling (removing the tarnished surface from metal); decomposing the bones used in the manufacture of gelatine; as a 'sour' after the alkaline scouring and bleaching of TEXTILES; in the production of glucose from starch and casein (the basis of cheese) from milk; in the manufacture of DYES (qq.v.); and for the preparation of metallic chlorides.

Nitric Acid (*aqua fortis*) occurs in nature chiefly as the nitrates of potassium and sodium (Bengal saltpetre and Chile nitre). Some nitric acid is formed by electrical discharges in the atmosphere, and is washed down by rain. The ancient Egyptians are believed to have used nitric acid to dissolve silver. It was well known to the early alchemists, and in the 16th century it was used to part gold and silver (see CHEMISTRY, HISTORY OF). About 1658 Glauber prepared it by heating saltpetre with sulphuric acid. This process was used for many years, Chile nitre taking the place of saltpetre, and has only recently been abandoned. In 1785 Cavendish showed that the acid could be produced by passing electric sparks through moist air, the oxygen and nitrogen of the air combining. More than 100 years later this method was adopted on a large scale in Norway, where air was passed through an electric arc furnace and absorbed the nitrogen oxides in water to form nitric acid. The second modern method of preparation dates back to the Rev. Isaac Milner, of Cambridge, who found in 1788 that ammonia could be oxidized to gases which formed nitric acid with water. To-day, this principle has been adopted commercially.

Large quantities of nitric acid are used in the manufacture of explosives, dyestuffs, metallic nitrates, and fertilizers.

3. ORGANIC ACIDS. Acetic Acid is present in certain fluids, in living creatures, and as calcium or potassium salts in the juices of plants. It is most popularly known as a constituent of vinegar, a small percentage of which is acetic acid. Vinegar is produced from dilute alcohol solutions (alcohol with much water). The dilute alcohol may be wine, which gives 'wine vinegar' which is still used in France; cider (a form used mainly in the U.S.A.); or a mixture prepared by the fermentation of malted grain to give 'malt vinegar'. Vinegar is also supplied to-day which contains pure acetic acid made by other methods and coloured with caramel (a kind of burnt sugar). Acetic acid can be obtained by the chemical treatment of wood or sawdust. It can also be made from alcohol or acetylene gas.

The largest use for acetic acid is in the manufacture of cellulose acetate (acetate RAYON (q.v.)), a form of artificial silk. Large amounts are also used for making other chemicals and solvents, in dyeing, for the pickling of fish and vegetables, in artificial vinegar manufacture, leather tanning and finishing, and oil refining.

Formic Acid occurs in stinging nettles, and in many fluids of animal origin, such as sweat. It was discovered in 1760 by Rey, who obtained it from the bodies of red ants. *Formica* is the Latin for ant, and from this the acid got its name. Its modern industrial manufacture is based, in principle, on the combination of carbon monoxide and water.

Formic acid is used in certain textile dyeing and printing processes. It is also used for coagulating into rubber the milky white fluid, called latex, that is collected from the rubber tree (see RUBBER, Vol. VI). For this purpose formic acid has replaced the acetic acid formerly used. The acid is also used in TANNING (q.v.), in the rayon industry, and for making many inorganic and organic formates. The latter are used as solvents in preparing varnishes and lacquers.

See also ALKALIS; CHEMISTRY, INDUSTRIAL; CHEMISTRY, HISTORY OF.

See also Vol. III: CHEMISTRY.

ACTUARY, *see* INSURANCE.

ADVERTISING AND PUBLICITY. 1. Advertising is a way in which merchants and manufacturers increase the sales of goods, and has become an important and specialized branch of modern economic life. The word 'advertising' comes from a French word meaning 'to bring to notice'. Advertising does two things. It tells would-be buyers that a certain article is on sale, and where they can buy it; and, when many firms supply the same article, it tries to encourage people to buy the advertiser's own brand. In fact, brands and advertising have developed together. A manufacturer of a standard commodity, such as floor polish, would only lose business to his competitors if he did not advertise his own floor polish under some striking name, or 'brand'.

'Publicity' means much the same thing as advertising, although the word is more often used in a rather special sense. For example, if a manufacturer is about to open a new factory, he may advertise in newspapers and put up posters. But he may also give publicity to the opening of the factory by inviting a famous film star to attend as well as the mayor of the nearest town. Crowds would collect to watch their arrival, while press photographers and newsreel cameramen recorded the scene. Business men also talk of a 'publicity campaign' when, for example, the wool industry draws attention to the superiority of wool, or when the government of a country such as Switzerland encourages travellers to visit it. In the same way the Buy British and the Festival of Britain (1951) publicity campaigns are intended to draw attention to British goods.

Advertising and publicity both really date from an early stage in man's economic life. Every TRADE SIGN (q.v.) over a shop is a kind of advertisement, and trade signs certainly go back at least as far as the days of ancient Rome. An actual display of the goods is another old form of advertising. In medieval times a good deal of such advertising took place at the regular TRADE FAIRS (q.v.) held in important centres. Fairs and EXHIBITIONS (q.v.) are still held to-day.

2. ADVERTISING SPECIALISTS. Most firms spending money on advertising use advertising agents or contractors. An advertising agency is often itself an important firm with staffs of writers and artists. The agent who is asked to conduct an advertising campaign must first be told for what market, that is, for what kind of people, the goods to be advertised are intended. Sometimes the seller of the goods is not himself quite clear what his market will be. In that case the advertising specialist may be asked to discover what kinds of people are likely to buy the article offered, where they live, and in what quantities they are likely to buy it. Investigations of this kind are called MARKET RESEARCH (q.v.). This is usually carried out by most advertising firms as a branch of their own business, but there are firms that specialize in this alone. When the nature of the market has been studied, it is then decided what means shall be used for the advertising campaign. This depends upon the nature and extent of the market, and the kinds of people likely to be interested in the goods. The medium, or media (*see* Section 3), must be chosen and used to attract the attention of the public. The public is not a single public, all with the same ideas and reactions, but several widely differing groups of people with minds working very differently from each other's. An advertising specialist must know what people

BILL-POSTERS OF THE EARLY 20TH CENTURY

buy and the reasons why they buy it. Some people can be convinced by exaggeration or over-statement, particularly if these are repeated long enough; other people can only be convinced by under-statement or restraint.

It is often said that it is the buyers of the goods who really pay for the advertisement. This is true, for the cost of advertising is one of the costs of producing the article, and the selling price must be fixed to cover all costs. But a successful advertising campaign may so broaden the demand for a product, and increase the quantity produced, that the cost of producing each item may fall, and the selling price may then be lowered. This may not always happen, but it sometimes does.

3. ADVERTISING MEDIA. These are the various ways of advertising. Direct advertising includes not only circulars, booklets, and pamphlets sent through the post, but also handbills distributed in the street, or to people's homes. Advertising at trade fairs and exhibitions may include other forms of advertising than display; posters may be used on the exhibitor's stand, and pamphlets may be handed to any inquirer. Cinema advertising can be done in two ways: either short

The Times

PICCADILLY CIRCUS AT NIGHT WITH THE BUILDINGS LIT UP BY ADVERTISEMENTS IN COLOURED LIGHTS

films which work up to a climax disclosing the advertiser's message, or what are really posters thrown on to the screen. In the United States and other countries, where broadcasting is a matter for private enterprise (*see* BROADCASTING CORPORATIONS, Section 2, Vol. IV), the radio programmes are interrupted with advertising messages. Loudspeaker vans can hardly be included in radio advertising; they are really a modern revival of the 'bellman' or 'crier' of medieval days, who used to walk through the streets telling the time and giving the news.

4. PRESS ADVERTISING. The development of the modern newspaper and magazine, and of press advertising, have marched in step with one another. Press advertisements are either 'classified' or 'display'. Display advertisements do not differ much from outdoor posters; they are reproduced on a small scale in black-and-white and perhaps a colour instead of on a large scale in many colours. Classified advertisements are non-displayed announcements grouped under a general heading, such as 'Articles for sale and wanted' and 'Houses for sale and to let'. Measured by the money paid for them, press advertisements are now the most important form of advertising. In the late 19th century newspaper proprietors, such as Alfred Harmsworth (later Lord Northcliffe), found that they

could lower the price of their papers and increase circulation by developing revenue from advertisements. Circulation and advertisement revenue were closely linked; as circulation increased, there would be more readers of any given advertisement, and the advertiser could be asked to pay more; increased advertisement revenue could be used to reduce the newspaper's price, and this would increase circulation still further. Until the 1930's, the *Daily Mail* (one of Lord Northcliffe's newspapers) often devoted the whole of its front page to an advertisement by a single firm, and at one period the price charged for one day's use of this front page was £1,000. The circulations of the popular newspapers have since been greatly increased, and sums of this kind are now obtained for a smaller allocation of space (*see* NEWSPAPER INDUSTRY).

The success of any advertisement depends on getting the public to pay attention to it. Most newspapers still use part of their front page for advertisements; it is argued that the front page will first catch the reader's eye. The publishers of the earlier magazines did not like to spoil the look of their reading matter by advertisements, and these were placed before and after the reading matter, so that the reader could avoid the advertisements, unless he wanted to read them. The Americans, who have always led the world in advertising methods, were the first to decide that there were advertising disadvantages in this separation of advertisements and reading matter, and the modern system of mixing reading matter and advertisements is now general.

The purpose of every advertiser is to bring his message before those people who are interested in what he is trying to sell. The big, popular newspapers, which are read by all classes of people, usually carry advertisements of goods which are in general demand. The professional and trade journals generally carry more specialized advertisements. For example, an advertiser who wished to reach medical men only would advertise in the *Lancet* or the *British Medical Journal*. There are also many publications dealing with religious, ecclesiastical, intellectual, professional, sporting, or other interests, and it is rarely that an advertiser fails to find the right journal for his needs.

Firms conducting MAIL-ORDER TRADING (q.v.) often want to know which press media are the best for advertising. They can often get this information by including 'keying' devices in their advertisements. Keying can take many forms, the most usual being that advertisements in different papers give different addresses to which replies should be sent, or may ask the reader to write to a department with a special number. Thus the advertiser can see at once which newspaper was read by the person who answered the advertisement.

5. OUTDOOR ADVERTISING. The poster is a very early form of outdoor advertising. Many examples still survive, such as the theatre playbills of the 16th century and later. In the late 18th and early 19th centuries there were no laws controlling bill-posting. Teams of billposters would stick their bills on any prominent site, walls, lamp-posts, even the doors of public and private buildings, and they often took care to cover up the bills of their rivals. This was called 'fly-posting', and is now illegal if done without the permission of the owner of the site. Hoardings, walls, and other places where permission to post has been given, are now rented by large firms of bill-posting contractors, who have replaced the adventurous fly-posters of the early 19th century. Such places are given the trade name of 'sites'. Advertisement by poster has never been confined to outdoor sites; a great deal of it is done in buses, in railway carriages, and some shops (*see* COLOUR PLATE

OPPOSITE PAGE 80). Poster advertising is not so selective as press advertising. It is, however, possible to select outdoor sites to a limited extent, and, in railway advertising, to discriminate between first-class and third-class carriages, according to the product advertised. Poster advertising is now restricted by law where there is danger of its spoiling the countryside.

6. DIRECT ADVERTISING. By this method the advertiser can choose the exact public he wishes to reach. It is much used in mail-order trading, lists of likely addresses being drawn up from classified directories or similar publications. Direct advertising is much used in the financial world. There is at least one firm in the City of London which specializes in the preparation of classified lists of shareholders; a prospectus for a new issue of shares in, say, a mining venture (*see* STOCKS AND SHARES) will be sent only to those who are already shareholders in mining

London Transport

POSTER BY REX WHISTLER

Today it is the practice to commission first class artists to design posters companies. Many devices are used by direct advertisers: one is the use of the 'Births' column of a newspaper to obtain addresses of likely buyers of babies' requirements. Direct advertising can be followed up by a letter, or by a personal call from a representative.

7. OTHER PUBLICITY METHODS. Window-dressing has now become highly specialized, and for every important trade there are window-dressing specialists who can arrange much better displays than the shop-keeper himself. The larger firms and the DEPARTMENT STORES (q.v.) have window-dressing experts on their permanent staff.

The invention of sound-broadcasting, and later of television, gave new opportunities to advertising contractors: millions of listeners could be reached quickly. Until Independent Television was permitted, Britain was able to prevent an art useful to society from being exploited for commercial purposes. Broadcasting by private enterprise has this in common with the newspapers: that it cannot be made profitable without advertising. In countries where commercial broadcasting is allowed, it is possible to 'time' advertising announcements. For example, tennis racquets could be advertised in the middle of a running commentary on an international tournament, or selected books after a critical or literary discussion.

AGENT. This is a person who represents individuals or firms in business. His work is generally to introduce the buyer to the manufacturer or merchant, though some agents are employed by merchants to buy goods for them from the producers or manufacturers. As the agent is buying and selling not for himself but on behalf of someone else, he does not run the same trading risks as the merchant, nor does he make the same profit. Most agents receive from their employers COMMISSION (q.v.) on the goods they sell.

Agents vary greatly in status and importance. At one extreme stands the person who happens to hear that a friend of his is going to buy a wireless set, introduces him to a shop, and then draws a COMMISSION (q.v.) on the price of the set. At the other is the firm owning a large showroom, with the exclusive district or national agency for the distribution of a certain make of car. Between these two extremes lie many classes of agent. Commercially, the most important are the manufacturers' agents: some are sole agents in a given territory for all the products of one manufacturer, and others are agents for many different lines of goods turned out by several manufacturers.

Most agents work continuously for one firm, or for a group of firms in the same industry. Firms of theatre-ticket and travel agents are excellent examples of this class (see ENTERTAINMENT INDUSTRY). But many firms called by the name of agent should rather be called BROKERS (q.v.): house and estate agents are examples, as are the so-called commission-agents who buy and sell produce on the various MARKETS (q.v.). The other kind of commission-agent, the bookmaker or turf accountant, is rather a speculator than an agent. Patent agents, as they are called, are hardly agents at all: they are really experts in the law and practice of patenting inventions (see PATENTS). But advertising agents are true agents, working mostly for the firms regularly employing them (see ADVERTISING AND PUBLICITY). Some agents are concerned with selling the services of an individual: a literary agent, for instance, introduces an author to a publisher, and a theatrical agent introduces an actor to a company or a producer.

Agents and agencies fill a useful place in the world of commerce. They assist the buyer or consumer as well as the seller. A traveller saves time by dealing with a travel agency instead of making the round of the shipping offices for a vacant berth. But it also saves time and expense for shipping offices to deal with a few travel agencies instead of hundreds of passengers. In fact, the agent, without bearing the same risk, performs many of the useful functions of the wholesaler or warehouseman (see WHOLESALE TRADING). Some agents, from small beginnings, become so wealthy and influential as to be able largely to dictate the policy of their manufacturers or producers.

AIRCRAFT INDUSTRY. This began in a small way at about the same time as successful flying itself, in the years just before the First World War (see FLYING, HISTORY OF, Vol. IV). Most of the leading firms in the British aircraft industry to-day were already in existence in those early days, although on a much smaller scale. Before that war France and America were ahead of Britain in making aircraft and aero engines. During the war the need for aircraft

De Havilland Aircraft Co.

BUILDING 'COMET' JET AIRLINERS
In the foreground men are assembling a wing

for the fighting forces caused the tiny British aircraft industry to become large and efficient (*see* AIR FORCES, Vol. X).

It was the practice then for some firms to manufacture engines, working quite separately from firms which manufactured the rest of the aircraft. Engine production was at first almost entirely a Government responsibility; most of the engines that were British throughout were made either at the Royal Aircraft Factory at Farnborough or by outside firms, such as Beardmore, under Government licence. There were a few engines from other sources, but these were mostly imported from Continental firms—the Gnome, Le Rhône, Clerget, and Hispano-Suiza engines. Shortly after the outbreak of war in 1914 British firms in the MOTOR INDUSTRY (q.v.)—notably Rolls-Royce, Napier, Armstrong-Siddeley, and Wolseley Motors—began to produce engines. Some of these were foreign models made under licence: for instance, the Wolseley Viper was a modified Hispano-Suiza.

The separation between the aircraft and the engine firms lasted throughout the First World War. Most of the aircraft firms were small, and in those days the Hendon district of north-west London was the most concentrated centre of the industry. In Hendon itself were Claude Grahame-White and Company and the Aircraft Manufacturing Company; a few miles away at Cricklewood was Handley-Page Ltd., and at Stag Lane, Edgware, there was a small concern called the London and Provincial Aviation Company. Outside London the most prominent firm was the Bristol Aeroplane Company, with works at Filton. All these firms possessed not only their own constructional and erecting shops, but also aeroplane hangars and private aerodromes.

The important post of test-pilot to an aircraft company originated during this period. It was the test-pilot's job to judge in the air itself the suitability of the aircraft turned out, and to report whether or not they measured up to the behaviour and performance specified or promised by their designers. In spite of the great effort made by British designers and industrialists, the young British aircraft industry could not in the early years of the war keep pace with the demands of the Services. Even in 1917 the French-built and French-engined 'Spad' was being purchased abroad for the fighter squadrons, then called 'scout' squadrons; in 1918 the American 'Liberty' engine was being used for what were then medium-bombers (*see* AIR WARFARE, HISTORY OF, Vol. X). After the First World War, CIVIL AVIATION (q.v. Vol. IV) began to develop, and long before the Second

World War the aircraft industry had become a leading industry in Britain.

There is now a growing tendency to manufacture an aircraft and its engine within one firm, although there are a few firms, particularly Rolls-Royce and Napier, who build engines only. The most important reason for this policy has been the change from wood to metal construction. Wood was the only material used for aircraft bodies during the First World War; the methods of working it, and the craftsmen employed, differed greatly from those that would have suited metal construction. Hence some of the important aircraft manufacturing firms at that time were peace-time manufacturers of constructions in wood—Boulton and Paul of Norwich, for instance, whose speciality was portable or sectional wooden buildings. Metal construction, on the other hand, lends itself to the use of the same materials, the employment of the same trades, and often to the same type of factory layout, as for the making of engines.

The British aircraft industry now builds for the world market, and its export trade section is vitally important. For many firms the civil side is now more important than the R.A.F. side. During the First World War, and afterwards, the Bristol Aeroplane Company used almost exclusively to turn out aircraft for war service, notably the famous 'Bristol Fighter'. By 1950 its aircraft were mostly built for civil flying.

Some modern aircraft firms have come into existence through the amalgamation of engine and aircraft firms into a single company. The Hawker-Siddeley Company is an example. An important development between the First and Second World Wars was the increasingly important part played by such heavy-engineering firms as Armstrong-Whitworth, Vickers-Armstrong, and the English Electric Company in the aircraft industry. Many of the older firms in the industry still exist, although most of them are now part of larger concerns. The Hawker-Siddeley Company, for instance, includes the once independent firms of Sopwith, Fairey, and Gloster Aircraft.

See also Vol. VIII: Aeronautical Engineering.

ALABASTER, see Marble and Alabaster.

ALCHEMY, see Chemistry, History of.

ALCOHOL, see Industrial Alcohol.

ALKALIS. 1. The word 'alkali' is the name which chemists give to a number of substances, including soda, potash, and ammonia, which in some ways can be regarded as being the opposite of Acids (q.v.). An alkali and an acid neutralize one another when brought together, and lose their chemical identity and form a salt.

More than 400 distinct trades in the United Kingdom use alkali products, but over half the output is absorbed by four trades: paper-making, glass manufacture, soap manufacture, and the production of artificial silk or rayon. Without alkali products we could have no glass for windows or bottles, and no aluminium for kitchenware or aircraft. There would be neither soap nor soap-powders for the laundry or the household. Clothes could only be made from rough cotton; greasy, grey, homespun wool; or raw, gummy, yellow silk. The only paper which could be made in any great quantity would be newsprint, which would be quite unsuitable for writing on; and all dyes and the non-mineral drugs would have to be boiled out of plants or animals. Also high-grade steel could not be made in any quantity from the low-grade

EARLY PRODUCTION OF POTASH

L.C.I.

LOADING SODA ASH BY NIGHT

Soda ash is stored in the silos on the right and packed into bags for transport

ores available in Britain. The alkali consumption of a nation may be said to indicate its degree of industrialization, and without alkalis the complicated economic life of modern mankind would be impossible.

The English word 'alkali' is practically the Arabic *al-qaliy*, which means, roughly, 'the burned'; the name was probably given because wood ashes have been used as a source of alkali from very early times. Records of the use of alkali go very far back. A glass bead, well over 5,000 years old, found in Egypt was probably made from trona, an alkali which is the 'nitre' of the Bible. Trona was also used for embalming, bodies being soaked in solutions of it for long periods. On a tablet from Tello in Babylonia it is recorded that in 2800 B.C. soap was made from oil and vegetable ash. The properties and uses of alkali were well known to the Greeks and Romans. Pliny the Elder, who wrote in the 1st century A.D., gives a very full account of them

in his *Natural History*. He was the first to distinguish broadly between the two commonly occurring alkalis—soda and potash. In fact, little was added to his knowledge of the subject until the 18th century.

To-day several alkaline substances are made in enormous quantities by the chemical industry. These are the sodium and potassium alkalis, and AMMONIA (q.v.) and quicklime. The three most common sodium alkalis are sodium bicarbonate (mild), sodium carbonate or soda ash (medium), and sodium hydroxide or caustic soda (strong).

2. POTASH ALKALIS. These have many specialized uses in industry. In earlier days they were extracted from wood ashes. In 1820 a more profitable vegetable source of potash was found in the residue left after distilling fermented beet-sugar molasses (*see* DISTILLATION). But already vegetable sources were being replaced by mineral sources. The Germans were mining

potash mineral salts from deposits in Saxony. During the First World War, since the Allied nations could no longer get German potash, other sources were developed in the Dead Sea, in Spain, and in the U.S.A. Years later, during the Second World War, deep drilling for oil in Yorkshire showed the presence of beds of salt containing potash salts. Britain's regular supplies of home-produced potash alkalis, however, are manufactured from imported potassium chloride (sylvite). About 200,000 tons of this are imported every year; most of it goes on to the land as ARTIFICIAL FERTILIZERS (q.v. Vol. VI), and about 12,000 tons a year are converted into potassium hydroxide. Of this, about 3,000 tons are made into potassium carbonate. The hydroxide is used mainly in the dyestuffs trade (see DYES) and to make special soaps such as shaving-cream; the carbonate is used for special optical glasses.

3. SODA ALKALIS. Just as potash alkalis were manufactured earlier from wood ash, so soda alkalis were once made from the ashes of seaweed and sea-shore plants. Many of these plants came from the marshes along the coasts of France and Spain, but artificial salt marshes were also made for growing the plants. When the plants were burned, the ashes were fused together into blue-grey lumps. Many chemists tried to find a way of converting salt into soda, and by the end of the 18th century salt (sodium chloride) was being treated with sulphuric acid (see ACIDS) to form sodium sulphate and hydrochloric acid. On heating the sodium sulphate with charcoal and limestone, and boiling the 'black ash' so formed with water, a solution of soda was obtained. This process was widely used for many years because it was a cheap method of producing bleaching-powder and chlorine as BY-PRODUCTS (q.v.). But chlorine can now be produced much more cheaply by ELECTROLYSIS (q.v. Vol. VIII) and to-day all sodium carbonate in Britain is made by the ammonia-soda process. This process causes the two components of salt (sodium chloride) and of limestone (calcium carbonate) to change places so as to produce sodium carbonate and calcium chloride. British soda alkali is manufactured by this process entirely from raw materials obtained within the country. The limestone comes from Wales and Derbyshire, and brine is drawn from the salt deposits deep below the fields of Cheshire and Lancashire; the coal is mined locally, and the ammonia and coke used come from the surrounding gasworks and coke-ovens.

Caustic soda is made by several processes. In the lime-soda process soda ash is dissolved. The resulting soda liquor is mixed with milk of lime, and a mixture of chalk and caustic soda is produced. The chalk is removed, and the clear caustic soda liquor is then evaporated. A great deal of caustic soda is sold industrially as a solution containing about 50% of the solid. Caustic soda can also be made directly from brine by electrolysis, with chlorine and hydrogen as by-products. Most of the world production of chlorine is obtained by this method, and the caustic soda simultaneously produced now exceeds the total world output by the lime-soda process.

What is called 'washing-soda' by the housewife is really crystallized soda ash. The crystals contain about one-third soda ash, the rest being water of crystallization, that is, the water which makes the soda ash take a crystalline form. They are crystallized from lukewarm soda solution after bleaching and filtering. Bicarbonate of soda is made by carbonating a solution of soda ash, and is one of the purest industrial chemicals made, containing only about $1\frac{3}{4}$ oz. of salt and other insoluble matter in every ton. Sodium silicate is known to the housewife as 'water-glass' for preserving eggs. It is made by fusing together in a furnace very pure sand and dense soda ash. The bright blue clear glass, which results when the mass is cooled, is dissolved in water, and filtered or settled to free it from insoluble impurities. Sodium silicate is used in the soap trade, and also as an adhesive in making corrugated cardboard and cardboard boxes and containers.

See also ACIDS; CHEMISTRY, INDUSTRIAL; CHEMISTRY, HISTORY OF.
See also Vol. III: CHEMISTRY.

ALUM occurs in mineral form in many parts of the world, mostly where volcanic action has taken place in the past (see VOLCANOES, Vol. III). Its natural mineral forms are generally alunite, alumstone, or alum-rock. There are fairly extensive deposits in Italy and Hungary, in some of the Greek islands, and in various parts of North and South America. These mineral deposits are usually a mixture of aluminium and potassium sulphates.

Alum was well known to the ancients, and

in his *Natural History* the Roman, Pliny the Elder, mentions it as a mordant, a fixing chemical which is used with DYES (q.v.) Although the Italian and Hungarian deposits are still mined, the uses of natural alum are now much more restricted than they were, and in recent years aluminium sulphate, manufactured from CHINA CLAY (q.v.) or bauxite (*see* ALUMINIUM INDUSTRY), has replaced the natural rock material for most industrial purposes. Alum has many uses in modern industry, principally as a mordant for the more sensitive colours, particularly the synthetic dyes, as well as in leather dressing (*see* TANNING), and for sizing the better quality papers in PAPERMAKING (q.v.).

ALUMINIUM INDUSTRY. Aluminium is the third most abundant element in the world.

It accounts for some 8% of the earth's crust, a figure which is only exceeded by oxygen and silicon. It has a great affinity for oxygen, and is not therefore to be found naturally in its metallic state (*see* METAL ORES, Vol. III); most aluminium-bearing ores consist of the oxide, alumina, mixed with other compounds, mainly of iron and silicon. For the same reason, aluminium is not easily separated from its associated oxygen, and the metal cannot be obtained by direct reduction with heat in the presence of carbon, as in the SMELTING of iron (q.v. Vol. VIII).

While most common rocks, clays, and various soils contain substantial amounts of aluminium silicate and oxides, the only material so far used on any large scale for aluminium production is bauxite, a reddish-brown rock, so called after

International News Photo

BAUXITE FROM AN AMERICAN MINE BEING CARRIED BY CONVEYOR-BELT TO THE HAMMER MILL TO BE CRUSHED

Les Baux, a small town in the south of France where it was discovered. Bauxite is essentially a mixture of oxides, principally those of aluminium, silicon, and iron, in proportions varying according to locality. A workable bauxite may contain 50–60% of alumina. Large deposits occur in the south of France, the British and Dutch Guianas, the Gold Coast, Greece, and in several areas of Central Europe and North America.

Aluminium has many important industrial uses. Possibly its earliest application was to the handling of food, and it is now used for pots and pans, food-processing plant, brewing equipment, milk pasteurizing plant, and other dairy equipment. It is also used to make aluminium foil for a wide range of wrapping purposes, and also kitchen and labour-saving household equipment. The present day chemical industry uses aluminium extensively, both for stationary plant and installations such as storage tanks and reaction vessels, and also for the bulk transport of liquids by large-capacity tankers.

The use of aluminium alloys is common in all forms of transport. Air transport owes its modern development almost entirely to the high-strength aluminium alloys (see AERONAUTICAL ENGINEERING, Vol. VIII). In road transport, both passenger and commercial vehicles make wide use of aluminium sheeting for roof and side panels; and aluminium sections, castings, and forgings are used extensively for underframes and power components. It is likely that the metal will be used to a greater extent in the development of the railways, as is happening already in America and on the Continent. Aluminium-magnesium alloys are being used more and more for marine purposes, ranging from small boats and powered craft to deck superstructures of cargo vessels and large passenger ships.

In structural work, too, aluminium alloys are rapidly increasing their scope because their lightness and durability save material, time, and labour, not only during actual erection, but also in transport and in maintenance. Bungalows, school buildings, and factory roofs can be made of aluminium. There is an all-aluminium twin-leaf bascule-type bridge at Sunderland; and travelling cranes, excavators, and huge sliding hangar doors are now made of this light, strong material.

Because it is a good conductor of electricity, aluminium is widely used for electrical equipment. Thousands of miles of steel-cored aluminium cables of the 'Grid' system take electric current over the country, whilst aluminium circuits distribute current throughout film studios and big office buildings.

Aluminium granules and powder are used in metal smelting and refining and also in the fireworks industry. For paint, aluminium paste is in general use as a basis with exceptional protective qualities and durability.

See also Vol. VIII: METALS.
See also Vol. III: MINERALS; METAL ORES.

AMMONIA was first discovered and prepared by Joseph Priestley, the famous chemist, in 1774. Certain compounds of ammonia occur in nature in mineral form, but these deposits are small, and for modern uses ammonia is manufactured, directly or as a BY-PRODUCT (q.v.). In the early 19th century gas companies looked upon it as a useless by-product, which had to be extracted from the crude gas coming from the retorts before the purified gas could be passed through the mains. It was not long, however, before industry found many uses for it, mainly in the preparation of industrial ALKALIS (q.v.) and ARTIFICIAL FERTILIZERS (q.v. Vol. VI).

Chemically, ammonia is a compound of nitrogen and hydrogen, nitrogen being one of the main constituents of the air. Ammonia is produced mainly in two ways—either synthetically from hydrogen and the nitrogen of the air, or by the 'destructive distillation' of coal or of lignite—the lignite being a form of 'brown' coal of which there are extensive deposits in Germany. Destructive distillation is the heating of a material in a closed vessel without access to air, and is the treatment to which coal is subjected in a gas-works (see DISTILLATION). The air is really the source of all ammonia, even of that contained in coal, for coal is decomposed vegetable matter, which has absorbed nitrogen from the atmosphere during the process of decomposition (see COAL, Vol. III). In modern days the quantity of ammonia produced synthetically is much greater than that coming from gas-works and coke-ovens, and it can be produced so much more cheaply that many of the smaller gas-works and coke-oven installations have found it unprofitable to recover their ammonia at all. A small quantity of ammonia is still produced in Scotland from the distillation of shale (see SHALE

COMPRESSORS FOR THE PRODUCTION OF AMMONIA BY SYNTHESIS FROM NITROGEN AND HYDROGEN

I.C.I.

OIL), and in some iron and steel plants a little is recovered from blast-furnace gas.

See also CHEMISTRY, HISTORY OF; CHEMISTRY, INDUSTRIAL. See also Vol. VI: ARTIFICIAL FERTILIZERS.

ANILINE DYES, *see* DYES.

APPRENTICESHIP. The training of skilled workers has always been vital to a country's efficiency. In earlier days in England the CRAFT GUILDS (q.v.) were responsible for this training, and it took the form of a long period of apprenticeship during which a boy who wished to learn a trade was 'bound' to an employer who was a master of it. The fact that the master took the apprentice in to live as one of his own family led to this kind of apprenticeship being called 'domestic'. In former days an apprentice became a journeyman when he had finished his training (*see* CRAFT GUILDS).

Queen Elizabeth tightened up the earlier rules concerning apprenticeship, which were beginning to be disregarded in some trades as the craft guilds declined. One of the Acts of Parliament made in her reign, the Statute of Apprentices of 1563, laid down a period of seven years' training between the ages of seventeen and twenty-four as the rule for all trades, and made the local JUSTICES OF THE PEACE (q.v. Vol. X) responsible for administering the Act. As new industries arose during the INDUSTRIAL REVOLUTION (q.v.) and the guilds continued to lose their influence, the Justices applied the Act of 1563 only to crafts named in it or being practised when it was passed, and apprenticeship began to lose ground. When industry was expanding still further and becoming mechanized in the early 19th century, many of the old apprenticeship rules were thought to be a hindrance to enterprise, and in 1814 Parliament passed an Act abolishing the more important parts of the Act of 1563.

The Industrial Revolution and the Act of 1814 did not destroy apprenticeship as an institution, but changed its nature. Apprentices were still admitted to various trades, but they lived in their own homes and no longer in those of the masters responsible for them. By the beginning of the 20th century the decline of hand CRAFTSMANSHIP (q.v.) and the rise of big mechanized industries, had reduced the number of trades in which employers thought apprenticeship necessary. The skilled TRADE UNIONS (q.v.), however, considered the continuance of apprenticeship to be in their own interests, as it helped them to insist on a reasonable wage-gap between the skilled and the unskilled worker. But during the First World War apprenticeship fell to a very low ebb, and in fact there was little formal training of tradesmen at all. There was far more work to be done than people to do it, and in the engineering and allied industries turning out munitions of war the 'dilution' of skilled labour by unskilled had to be accepted. The wages of unskilled workers rose considerably, and boys and young men preferred to earn immediately a full wage as an unskilled worker rather than to bind themselves to a long period of training at mere pocket-money wages. At the end of the war the Government realized

The OATH to be administred to every Apprentice of the Company of APOTHECARIES, *London*, at their Binding.

YOU shall swear to be good and true to Our Sovereign Lord King GEORGE, and well and truly you shall serve your Master for the Term of your Apprenticehood, and in all lawful and honest Causes you shall be obedient unto him, and unto the Master, Wardens and Assistants of this Company, and have them in due Reverence. The lawful Ordinances and Secrets of the said Fellowship you shall keep, and give no Information or Instruction thereof to any Person but of the said Fellowship. In all these Things you shall well and truly behave you, and surely keep your Oath to your Power.

So help You, GOD.

And if it happen that you depart your Master's Service, you shall not serve any Person out of the said Fellowship, without Licence of the Master and Wardens for the Time being, upon pain to forfeit and pay to the Use of the Company such Penalty as shall be assessed upon you by the Master, Wardens and Assistants for the Time being.

God save King GEORGE.

AN 18TH-CENTURY APPRENTICE'S OATH

that this situation was against the country's interests, and, in consultation with many of the leading trade unions, they took vigorous action. As a result, about 100,000 young unskilled workers were reclaimed as apprentices. Government training grants, supplementing the low wages of apprentices, encouraged this movement. The Second World War created much the same kind of situation, and it was met in the same way, by increasing training and maintenance grants.

Apprenticeship is still an important feature of British industry, although in many branches it has become an arrangement by word of mouth, and not by a written contract. In earlier days a formal agreement in writing was invariably made between the apprentice's parent or guardian and the employer. Such agreements were called 'indentures', and had to be completed before a magistrate. Indentured apprenticeship survives nowadays mainly in trades where skill with the hands is still essential: for example, it survives in the various branches of the building industry, in bespoke tailoring, the fur trade, ship repairing, surgical and scientific instrument making, studio photography, cabinet-making, the jewellery and precious metals trades, saddlery and harness-making, printing, coopering or cask making, hairdressing, and many of the branches of engineering. Many of these trades take on 'learners' under a merely spoken agreement, as well as indentured apprentices. In most trades the original period of seven years' apprenticeship has been reduced to five, and training now runs from the ages of sixteen to twenty-one To serve one's apprenticeship is 'to serve one's time', and when the period of apprenticeship is over one is said to be 'out of one's time'. Apprentices out of their time have not yet acquired the skill of experienced tradesmen, and they usually spend some time in their trade as 'improvers'. In some trades a distinction is made between the different classes of apprentices. This is particularly true of engineering, which recognizes two distinct classes of apprentice: the 'pupil' apprentice who will eventually be a trained engineer (in the sense of a professional man who makes plans for others to carry out), and the 'trade' apprentice who will become a skilled artificer (that is, a mechanic, often highly skilled, who carries out the designs). The 'trainee' system of informal apprenticeship, for those whose educational and other qualifications are likely to fit them for executive rank

Keystone

CADETS GOING ALOFT ON THE 'CHINDWARA'

in industry, is a modern form of the pupil apprentice system. Sea apprentices, or cadets, are really in the pupil apprentice class, as they are destined to be executive 'deck officers' when out of their time. Apprenticeship has always been a vigorous growth in the Merchant Navy, and in 1950 the British India Steam Navigation Company sent to sea the *Chindwara*, specially fitted out as a training ship for thirty cadets.

A form of apprenticeship is necessary before entry into many professions, notably the law, accountancy, and the architects' and surveyors' professions, but the agreements entered into are called 'articles' and not 'indentures'.

See also DOMESTIC SYSTEM; CRAFT GUILDS.

ARTIFICIAL FERTILIZERS; *see* ARTIFICIAL FERTILIZERS, Vol. VI.

ARTIFICIAL SILK, *see* RAYON.

ASBESTOS. The word 'asbestos' is Greek, and means something that will not burn. It is the general name given to a group of minerals of differing chemical composition, but all having the same general properties. Of the different varieties, chrysotile asbestos is commercially the most important, and accounts for over nine-tenths of the present production of the world.

Although it is chemically a mineral, asbestos has many of the characteristics of a textile fibre. In fact, the French Canadians who first discovered it in Quebec called it *pierre à coton*—cotton stone. It can be spun into thread and woven into fabric in the same way as cotton, wool, hemp, rayon, and silk. It can also be felted into thin or thick masses of pliable material (*see* FELT).

Asbestos was well known to the ancients, if we can believe certain records. From it the Chinese are said to have made cloth for the cuffs or ruffles of sleeves, and when they got dirty the dirt could be burned off instead of washed. The Vestal Virgins of Rome, who had charge of the 'sacred fire' on the hearth of the temple of Vesta, were supposed to have lamps that never went out, and it is probable that these had asbestos wicks. Charlemagne, the Frankish Emperor, is said to have used an asbestos table-cloth for important banquets, and to have amused his guests after dinner by throwing it into the fire and bringing it out clean.

Asbestos occurs in nature in crystalline form, as veins running through ROCKS (q.v. Vol. III). When extracted, these veins are silky to the touch, and separate easily into individual fibres, rather like those of the cotton-plant. Asbestos is found in most parts of the world, but Canada and Rhodesia produce most of what is used to-day in the world's industries. The principal Canadian deposits are in Quebec and Ontario. Russia has extensive deposits in the Ural Mountains mining regions. In the early 19th century the Italians, who had local deposits of asbestos, began to work it on a large scale. But they did not foresee its many uses, perhaps because the Italian variety could not be spun on ordinary textile machinery. An invention of this period was an asbestos paper which, it was suggested, might be used for making bank-notes.

About 1860, important deposits of asbestos were found in Quebec. This Canadian asbestos was a great improvement on the Italian, and could be spun on the ordinary spindles used in the Lancashire cotton mills.

Canadian National Film Board

ASBESTOS FIBRES BEING PROCESSED IN A QUEBEC PLANT

Wood of any kind must be kept out of asbestos mines and quarries, because the asbestos fibres attract to themselves small particles and splinters of wood, which may severely damage the spinning machinery. 'Wood discipline' in asbestos mines is therefore very strict; matches are prohibited, the mine-workers being supplied with lighters. In spite of the fact that asbestos can now be spun alone, cotton is usually mixed with it to provide additional strength, but the proportion of cotton rarely exceeds one-fifth of the whole.

The industrial importance of asbestos lies in its fireproof qualities. Most people have seen it in one of its most frequent uses—the fireproof curtains which, under the theatre regulations, must be lowered and raised at least once during every public performance. In the brakes of road and rail vehicles, the blocks which are pressed against a moving part to stop the vehicle are faced with asbestos or rubberized asbestos, since the friction causes heat. Asbestos has important uses in engineering, for the packing of various joints that have to be resistant to great heat or to corrosion by acids. The thin leaves, or gaskets, that are used to make a gas-tight joint, between the cylinder block and the cylinder head of a motor engine, are made of asbestos faced with copper; similar gaskets are used to fill the joints between the car engine and the exhaust pipe (*see* INTERNAL COMBUSTION ENGINE, Vol. VIII). Asbestos is used to line filters in the manufacture of acids. Conveyor belts that have to convey hot materials are usually made from asbestos.

Mixed with rubber, it has many uses as an insulating material in electrical work; flex for lamps and other household articles contains a good deal of asbestos. It is also greatly used for the lagging or wrapping of boilers and steam-pipes, so that heat will be retained inside the boiler or the pipe, and will not be radiated into the air surrounding it. A modern use of this kind is for heat-insulating covers for enclosing hot-water tanks in a house. These covers are not unlike a large tea-cosy in appearance, and have the same effect—that of keeping the heat in, and preventing its radiating outward.

Mixed with cement, asbestos enters into the composition of various types of fireproof board used in the building trade. These boards can be used, not only for walls and other structures, but also for backing pieces of furniture that have to be put up against radiators.

Asbestos is also used for fireproof clothing, including the fireproof gloves with which workers can lift out bodily, without injury, red-hot crucibles of molten metal from furnaces. In wartime, asbestos clothing of this sort is much used, particularly by men operating flame-throwers or trying to destroy those used by the enemy.

Some fire brigades supply asbestos suits for firemen who have to face intense heat in chemical fires. The fire squads of airports and warships are fitted with them.

See also Vol. III: MINERALS, Section 3.
See also Vol. X: FIRE BRIGADE.

ASSAYING. 1. This was originally the testing of ores and alloys (*see* METAL ORES, Vol. III) to determine their content of gold and silver; but the term (derived from the French verb *essayer*, to test) is now used in a wider sense to denote the analysis of ores, alloys, and metallurgical products of all kinds. All trade and industry in metals and metal products, including metal smelting and refining, depends on accurate and rapid assaying.

The prospector who searches for minerals must make tests to identify those he discovers. Later his samples are assayed independently to establish the richness of his finds. In all mining operations the value and the selling price of the ores which are shipped are settled on the basis of assay values determined from carefully selected samples. In smelting operations, such as the production of pig-iron or crude copper, the furnace charges of ore, coke, and limestone can only be calculated if assay values are already known; and for the control of steel-making and all refining processes it is necessary to rely on information provided by the assay laboratory. Assaying is used industrially to check the composition of alloys and to make certain that there are no harmful impurities in them; and in the markets of the world the prices paid for both the base and the precious metals are settled in terms of assay values. Gold, for instance, must assay more than 99·6% gold to be acceptable on the bullion market; and aluminium ingots are marketed in two grades, assaying either 98 or 99% of aluminium.

There is now no basic method of assay, and any method that will give an assay figure rapidly and with sufficient precision may be used. Most assay work involves the examination of large numbers of samples, all of similar composition.

One of the oldest methods of assay (often illustrated in 'Western' films) is the miner's concentration or 'panning' test, which is still in use for the examination of gold or tin ores (see GOLD-MINING). The ore is crushed, to ensure that the particles of gold or heavy tin mineral are all broken away from adhering earth and rock; and a weighed sample is stirred with water in a miner's pan—a flat-bottomed, sheet-iron pan with sloping sides. The heavier metallic concentrate settles to the bottom, and the lighter material, remaining in suspension, is carefully poured away. More water is repeatedly added and further light rock dust washed away, the pan being shaken with a jerky, circular motion. Eventually a clean residue of nearly pure gold or mineral, which can be weighed, is left in the pan.

Many of the older methods of assaying ores reproduce on a small scale the operations used in industrial SMELTING (q.v. Vol. VIII). The 'fire-assay' of gold and silver is essentially a smelting operation, and is still capable of pro-

ducing accurate results. In its simplest form, as used for very rich gold concentrates or silver ores, the process is known as 'scorification'. It consists in heating the sample with about 200 times its weight of lead on a saucer-shaped fire-clay dish to a temperature of about 1,100° C. The heating is done in a small fire-clay chamber called a muffle furnace. This receptacle is heated by flames which pass round the sides and never come into contact with the objects inside. The molten lead dissolves the gold and silver: on top of this molten metal there forms a slag-like layer of molten litharge (lead oxide), in which is gradually collected any rocky matter and most of any base-metal impurities. The whole lot is then poured into a mould, and the lead sinks to the bottom before cooling and hardening. The lead is later broken away from the slag and cleaned. This lead button, which contains all the gold and silver in the original ore, is now placed on a small dish, known as a 'cupel', made of bone ash, compressed magnesia, or some

LONDON HALL-MARKS OF THE STUART AND GEORGIAN PERIOD

London Edinburgh Dublin   MAKER'S MARK

Glasgow Sheffield Birmingham   ASSAY MARK
MARK OF ORIGIN

1544 1558 1578 1598 1618   DUTY MARK
DATE LETTER

HALL-MARKS

similar absorbent material, and put back in a muffle furnace. The lead melts and again starts to oxidize, and as fast as the molten litharge is formed it is absorbed into the cupel. Provided that air is allowed to circulate freely through the furnace, the lead button rapidly decreases in size, until finally all the lead (together with any base metals in it) has been converted into oxide and only the gold and silver are left as a small, bright, metallic bead of alloy gleaming on the surface of the cupel. The bead, when cool, is weighed; and the proportion of gold and silver (together) in the original sample of ore can be calculated. It remains only to determine how much of each precious metal is present. The bead is flattened and dropped into boiling nitric acid; this dissolves the silver (provided that there is 4 to 10 times as much silver as gold) and so 'parts' it from the gold, which remains as a heavy powder at the bottom of the glass 'parting flask'. The pure gold is washed and weighed; and the original weight of silver—all of which has now been dissolved away—is easily calculated by subtraction.

Assays of base metal ores and alloys now usually involve 'wet' methods of analysis. The sample is first dissolved in a solution, usually by attack with ACIDS (q.v.). Sometimes a metal can then be separated by an ELECTRO-PLATING operation (q.v. Vol. VIII). Whichever method is used, the assayer must be alert to detect the presence of unsuspected impurities; and he must always be sure that the sample he is examining is a good sample of the whole.

2. HALL-MARKS. A further branch of assaying is the work of the assay offices in hall-marking gold and silver articles. The law of hall-marks dates from the time of Edward I. All gold and silver wares (with a few exceptions) must now be submitted before sale to one of the assay offices for examination and stamping. Samples are taken from each article by scraping or cutting; if the assay is satisfactory, the work is stamped with a hall-mark comprising symbols denoting the city of test (a leopard's head for London, an anchor for Birmingham, and so on), the standard of quality, and the year. Originally all hall-marking was done at Goldsmiths' Hall, London, but Assay Offices are now also established at Birmingham, Chester, Sheffield, Dublin, Edinburgh, and Glasgow. Gold content is expressed in terms of carats or twenty-fourth parts (pure gold is 24 carats), and the standards recognized are 9, 14, 18, and 22 carats. Standard silver contains 92·5% of silver, the balance being usually copper. Articles which are deficient in precious metal and 'do not pass the hall' (Goldsmiths' Hall) are broken up.

See also GOLD MINING; SILVER MINING; COINING; GOLD AND SILVER WORK.

See also Vol. III: METAL ORES.

ASSETS, see BOOK-KEEPING.

AUCTIONS. These are public sales of goods, conducted by an auctioneer, who is required by law to have a licence for the purpose. He

NOTICE OF THE SALE OF A SHIP BY AUCTION

AN AUCTION OF PICTURES AT CHRISTIE'S, 1808
Coloured aquatint by Rowlandson and Pugin from Ackermann's *Microcosm of London*

asks the crowd of buyers assembled in the auction-room to make offers, or 'bids', for the various items on sale. He tries to encourage buyers to bid higher figures, and finally names the highest bidder as the buyer of the goods. This is called 'knocking down' the goods, for the bidding ends when the auctioneer bangs a small hammer on a table at which he stands. This is often set on a raised platform called a rostrum.

The ancient Romans are believed to have invented sales by auction, and the English word comes from the Latin *auctio*, meaning 'increase'. The Romans usually sold in this way the spoils taken in war; these sales were called *sub hasta*, meaning 'under the spear', a spear being stuck in the ground as a signal to collect a crowd. In England, in the 18th and 19th centuries, goods were often sold 'by the candle': a short piece of candle was lighted by the auctioneer, and bids could be made while it stayed alight.

The EAST INDIA COMPANY (q.v.) sometimes used this method, and it was also used in the timber trade until quite late in the 19th century.

Practically all goods whose qualities vary from parcel to parcel, and from season to season, are sold by auction. Among these are wool, tea, coffee, cocoa, hides, skins, furs, spices, fruit and vegetables, and wines. Auction sales are also usual for land and property, antique furniture, pictures, rare books, old china and porcelain, and similar works of art. The auction-rooms at Christie's and Sotheby's, in the West End of London, are famous for such sales.

An auction is usually announced beforehand by an advertisement containing full particulars of the articles stating where they can be seen by prospective buyers. But if the advertisement cannot give all the details, catalogues are printed, and each group of goods to be sold together, called a 'lot', is usually given a number.

The auctioneer need not begin with Lot 1 and go on in numerical order; he may wait until his experienced eye sees certain people in the room whom he knows, and he will then produce the lots in which they are most likely to be interested. The auctioneer's services are paid for in the form of a percentage COMMISSION (q.v.) on the actual value obtained by the selling of the goods. The auctioneer therefore has a direct interest in pushing up the bidding as high as possible.

An auctioneer must know fairly accurately the current market values of the goods he is selling, and he should be acquainted with the regular buyers of such goods. He will not waste time by starting the bidding too low, and waiting while it climbs slowly. He will also play on the jealousies and rivalries among his buyers, and will often succeed in getting a high price because he manœuvres two business rivals into bidding against each other. It is largely on his advice that a seller will fix 'reserve' prices, that is, prices below which the goods must not be sold. But even the best auctioneers find it very difficult to stop a 'knock-out', whereby dealers illegally arrange beforehand not to bid against each other, but to nominate one of themselves as the only bidder, in the hope of buying goods at extremely low prices. If a knock-out is organized on these lines, the real auction sale takes place privately afterwards, among the dealers themselves.

See also RETAIL TRADING.

AUDITING. This means checking the accuracy of business accounts in a thorough and systematic manner. In most well-ordered businesses the accounts are ruled off and balanced at regular intervals, and they are checked by persons other than those who have written them up. Such checks are not true audits; if they are thorough, they may be called internal audits, and in many large firms internal audit is regularly going on.

The word audit usually means external audit by an outside professional auditor. This is usually done shortly after the end of the trading year. The auditors first go through the day books and vouchers, check the routine posting of the ledgers, and take out a trial balance, to make sure that the two sides agree (*see* BOOK-KEEPING). They check the cash balance, ascertain the bank balance and reconcile it with the bank's own passbook or statement, and count and value the securities, stock-in-hand, and other assets. They make sure that the customers' ledger balances are agreed as correct by the customers themselves. They then proceed to draw up the Trading and Profit and Loss Accounts for the year, and finally the Balance Sheet.

One-man businesses and PARTNERSHIPS (q.v.) are not obliged to employ outside auditors, although this is a wise precaution against fraud and embezzlement. But LIMITED COMPANIES (q.v.) are compelled by law to employ them, and the Balance Sheet of a limited company must bear an auditor's certificate.

There are three principal professional bodies recognized by law and custom in England for audit purposes: the Institute of Chartered Accountants, the Society of Incorporated Accountants and Auditors, and the Association of Certified and Corporate Accountants.

See also BOOK-KEEPING.

B

BAKING INDUSTRY. **1.** The professional baker has a long history. There were public bakehouses in ancient Rome from the 2nd century B.C. There is a good deal of evidence that bread was largely baked outside the home in medieval England: from the 13th century onwards there are several laws for the 'assize' of bread, that is, for the fixing of what we should nowadays call 'controlled' prices, which would be fair to both baker and buyer (*see* USURY). CRAFT GUILDS (q.v.) were formed in the baking trade early in the Middle Ages, and two separate London companies of bakers received charters of incorporation in the early 14th century: the Company of White Bakers, and the Company of Brown Bakers.

The products of the baking industry fall into two classes—bread, and flour confectionery: this is the trade term for sweetened flour products, such as cakes and biscuits. Most of the processes are the same in both classes of products; they are blending and mixing the flour, dough mixing, loaf-making or shaping, baking, cooling, and packing.

2. BREAD. Most large bakers have a special flour-room where flour of various qualities is mixed by machinery. Small bakers usually buy their flour ready blended, and the proprietary flours used in the much-advertised special breads must always be bought ready blended. Kneading or mixing the dough was done by hand until the middle of the 18th century. A Frenchman then invented a machine to do this, and the machinery has since then been considerably improved. Modern dough-mixers copy very faithfully the action of the human arm as it travels from end to end of the mixing trough and handles and turns over the material. There are two main methods of mixing dough: the 'straight' method, and the 'sponge and dough' process. By the first method the flour, yeast, and other ingredients used are all mixed together at the same time. By the second the yeast is first prepared by mixing it with warm water and a small quantity of flour, and the resulting mixture is worked up into a kind of sponge. This mixture is then put aside and 'rested' for a short time; more flour is then added, and all the ingredients are mechanically mixed and become dough. Whichever process is used, the dough is allowed to 'rest' after mixing, to promote 'ripening' or FERMENTATION (q.v., Vol. II).

The next process is to shape the dough into loaves. Until the end of the 19th century there was no satisfactory way of shaping loaves by machinery; all the machines devised had treated the dough too severely and upset its rather delicate chemical stability. A successful machine invented at the turn of the century has now been improved upon, and there are few large bakeries where loaves are still shaped by hand. In fact, most processes in the industry are now fully mechanized. After being shaped, the loaves pass to the ovens. The earlier ovens were heated internally; later the heat—usually from coal or wood—was applied externally, and passed around the oven through flues. In the mid-19th century the Perkins steam-pipe oven was introduced, which used superheated steam and could raise oven temperatures to 500° F. In the Victorian

Records Office, Guildhall

A BAKER PUNISHED FOR FRAUD
14th-century manuscript (*Assisa Panis*)

MIXING THE DOUGH

Hovis

THE LOAVES RISING

Hovis

PUTTING THE LOAVES INTO THE OVEN

Hovis

days in Britain an up-to-date baker would advertise his 'steam' bakery. Small bakers to-day use ovens heated internally or externally, or sometimes both, by gas, oil, or electricity, and the loaves are put into and taken out of the ovens on trays. In the larger bakeries continuous conveyor ovens are used. Some of these are as much as 100 feet long; an endless chain conveyor carries the loaves slowly through them, and the period of baking is on the average just under an hour. When baked, the loaves are stacked on wooden racks in the cooling room; if they are to be wrapped in waxed paper or cellophane they travel on a conveyor through an automatic wrapping machine. Many bakers in the U.S.A. cut their loaves into slices by machinery, then wrap the sliced loaf in airproof paper to keep it moist for the customer; some modern British bakeries have adopted this system of 'pre-slicing'.

In Britain and North America the most popular shape of loaf is the oblong tin or pan loaf with its rounded top; the English cottage loaf (round, with a second lump of dough on top) is not often seen now. In Scotland the tall, white-sided batch loaf with its thick bottom crust has a wide sale, and in France the long, thin, 'baton' slashed on top. In the bakery trade the term 'quartern' is generally used of a 4-lb. loaf and 'half-quartern' of a 2-lb. loaf.

3. Biscuits and Confectionery. Making cakes and pastries is much like making bread, except that various mechanical sponge and batter mixers and shaping and chopping machines are used. In biscuit making the mixed dough is passed through a 'brake' machine which rolls it into smooth sheets. These sheets are then stamped out by another machine into the shape required, and the 'scrap' dough is sent back to the 'brake' machine. In a modern biscuit factory the ovens are of the long continuous type, and the biscuits pass through them on trays, carried on chain conveyors. The maximum length of a biscuit oven is usually 90 feet, and the time taken for baking varies from about 5 minutes to half-an-hour. Biscuit ovens are usually fired by gas, with burners above and below the trays. The coating of biscuits with sugar, chocolate, or other mixtures is done after baking by hand or machine; the making of 'sandwich' biscuits (with a sweet filling between) is mechanical. After cooling, biscuits are weighed and packed into tins, cartons, and

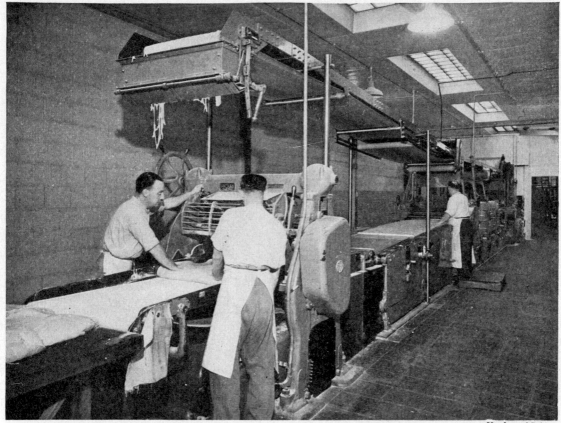

Huntley and Palmers

BISCUIT DOUGH BEING PASSED THROUGH A 'BRAKE' MACHINE

packets, usually by hand. Assorted biscuits are generally assembled by hand according to a pre-arranged plan.

4. ORGANIZATION. The baking industry has greatly developed during the present century. There has been much amalgamation, as in other industries. Some large firms have made much headway, particularly in large towns, and various MULTIPLE SHOP firms (q.v.) operate from central factories. But the typical unit in the industry is still the small personal business. The small man manages to compete with the large concerns because most of the machines used are available on a small scale as well as on a large scale. A recent survey stated that nine out of every ten bakers used mechanical aids to the fullest extent possible. Most bakers claim that there is little profit in bread, and that the chief profit of any bakery business comes from sales of cakes, or flour confectionery. In recent years the trade has been taken up by large firms such as Lyons, which produce on an immense scale and have the advantage of a widespread distributing organization. Slab cake, made on mass production lines by continuous processes, has become an important branch of the industry.

See also FLOUR MILLING; SUGAR CONFECTIONERY.

BALANCE OF TRADE, *see* INTERNATIONAL TRADE.

BALANCE SHEET, *see* BOOK-KEEPING.

BANK ACCOUNTS. Few people nowadays keep large sums of spare money in their own possession. To do so would be to risk losing it by burglary or fire; in any case, money so hoarded would not earn any INTEREST (q.v.) for its owner. So most people with spare money open an account with a bank, and they may choose between two sorts of account. Money put into a 'deposit' account is, so to speak, lent to the

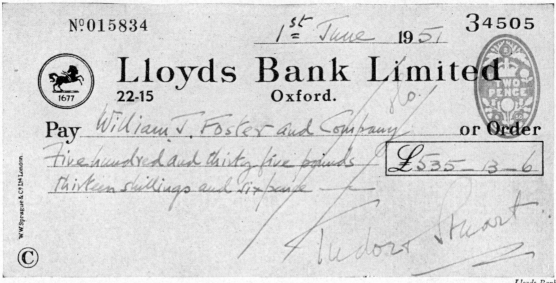

A CROSSED CHEQUE

Lloyds Bank

bank for a fixed period, and the bank credits the depositor's account with interest at so much per cent. per annum. In Britain the rate of interest usually changes with the BANK-RATE (q.v.). If depositors wish to withdraw their money, they are expected to give the required notice—generally 14 days. The other kind of account is the 'current' account, such as most people keep for their day-to-day receipts and expenses. Sums may be withdrawn from current accounts without notice, by means of cheques (*see* illustration), but a banker will insist that a minimum balance be kept, the profit on which will compensate him for his clerical and overhead expenses in keeping the account. If the balance falls below the minimum, the banker will usually make a charge for keeping the account, and this is 'debited' to the customer every half-year. Interest is not usually paid on current accounts kept with the London branches of the big British banks, but a small rate is paid by country branches and by foreign and colonial banks.

In exchange for their services bankers expect a certain standard of conduct from their customers. Account holders are expected to take all possible care of cheque-books, and not to give blank cheque forms to strangers; they are also expected to use crossed cheques for greater safety whenever possible (*see* PAYMENT). Customers must comply with certain legal require-ments. The amounts in words and in figures, for which cheques are drawn, must agree. Cheques over 6 months old are regarded as out of date, and bankers will refuse to pay them. If cheques are made out in a person's name, followed by the words 'or Order', they must be signed on the back by this person, who is called the 'payee'. This signature is called an 'endorsement', and it has to be exactly as written on the face of the cheque. Thus a cheque payable to Edward F. Jones would not be properly endorsed if the payee signed as 'E. F. Jones'. Cheques made payable to firms or companies must be endorsed by officials who have full authority to do this.

A customer may not 'draw' cheques (that is, write out cheques) in excess of his balance unless he has previously arranged with the bank to pay or 'honour' such cheques. Bankers will nearly always allow their customers to overdraw their accounts (that is, to draw cheques in excess of the balance), against SECURITY (q.v.). Most bankers will allow temporary overdrafts against no special security, provided that they trust the customer. Cheques drawn in excess of the permitted limit of overdraft, or in excess of the customer's balance if no overdraft arrangements have been made, may be returned unpaid, or 'dishonoured'. The word 'dishonour' used here is a technical term used by bankers; but in fact, a customer's reputation will be seriously damaged if cheques given to his business connexions are returned to their own bankers, with such words as 'Refer to Drawer', 'Insufficient Funds', or 'In Excess of Arrangements', written in red ink in the top left-hand corner.

Cheques are 'cleared', or their value collected from the paying banker, in the following way. All cheques in England and Wales have the letters T, M, or C in the bottom left-hand corner, which stand for Town, Metropolitan, and Country Clearing. The letters differ according to the location of the branch on which the cheques are drawn. T is for bank offices within walking distance of the Clearing House in the City of London; M is for offices in the London area outside the Town Clearing radius; C is for country offices in England and Wales. Cheques paid in by customers are sorted and sent to the CLEARING HOUSE (q.v.), thence to the Head Offices of the banks on which they are drawn, and thence to the branch where the account is kept, and this branch must be given time to return cheques in excess of arrangements or incorrectly drawn or endorsed. In the Town Clearing all these operations can be carried through the same day, and it is therefore usual for Town Clearing offices to allow their customers to draw the following day against any Town Clearing cheques paid in. But Town Clearing offices will not allow customers to draw that day against Metropolitan or Country Clearing cheques paid in; and a delay of 2 days for Metropolitan cheques, and of 3 for Country cheques, is usually required before customers are allowed to draw against them. A longer interval may be required if the customers paying in keep their accounts at Metropolitan or Country branches. The intervals necessary for the 'clearing' of Scottish and Irish cheques are longer still.

Some of the advantages of a bank account may be obtained by having an account with the Post Office Savings Bank, but broadly speaking the Post Office runs 'deposit' and not 'current' accounts. Interest at $2\frac{1}{2}\%$ per annum is allowed on such accounts, and amounts of £3 may be drawn out on demand without notice at any Post Office, and larger sums if notice is given. If a Post Office depositor wishes to pay some person at a distance by cheque, he may obtain, by giving notice, a 'warrant'—which is really a cheque—for the amount. But the use of the Post Office for such 'current' account pur-

poses involves a certain amount of delay, and the commercial banks are much better organized for this type of banking service.

See also BANKING; PAYMENT.

BANK CREDIT, see CREDIT.

BANK DRAFTS, see PAYMENT.

BANK FAILURES. Although these are now largely things of the past, they were a serious problem to people 100 and more years ago. They were caused because people who had deposited money in a bank were frightened that the bank would not be able to pay back their money. A 'run' on a bank is an attempt by large numbers of the bank's customers to withdraw all their deposits in coin at the same time, or to change the bank's notes for coin. But the business of banking cannot be really profitable unless customers' deposits are lent out or invested, a small amount of coin being retained as 'till money'. If, therefore, a 'run' on a bank continues until no more coin is left, the bank is forced to stop paying out. A bank which issues its own bank-notes is more likely to experience a 'run' than one that does not. Banking is an ancient practice, but in English history there is little mention of bank failures until the time of the goldsmith bankers of the 17th century. They were the first English bankers to issue bank-notes. They were therefore very badly placed when in 1672 Charles II, who had borrowed heavily from them, refused to pay back his loans. This led to a run on the goldsmiths, who became unable to pay all their customers.

In the 18th century the SOUTH SEA BUBBLE (q.v.) brought down several small banks, but banking in those days was not as widely spread over the country as it was later on, and the first real outbreak of bank failures in Britain did not develop until the time of the French Revolution. It was the habit in those days, as it is now, for country bankers and merchants to keep big accounts and money reserves in London, and in 1793, when war broke out between England and France, the collapse of a big London banking house started a general panic, first in Newcastle and then all over the country. Out of about 400 country bankers then in business, 100 closed completely, and others were badly shaken. In 1797 Newcastle again led a general panic, and soon the BANK OF ENGLAND (q.v.) itself was forced to ask the Government for permission to suspend its legal obligation to give gold for its notes. In 1810, and again in 1812, the same kind of thing happened; between 1780 and 1820 nearly 1,000 banks must have closed their doors. The worst year of all for the country bankers was 1825, and a general panic followed the failure of two big London banking companies.

Such books as E. M. Craik's *John Halifax, Gentleman*, Mrs. Gaskell's *Cranford*, and especially Stanley Weyman's *Ovington's Bank*, give a vivid picture of the effect of bank failures on the life of the people in the early 19th century.

The chief reason for the many failures at this time was that every small country bank issued its own notes. When the rumour went round that a bank was in difficulties, immense queues of customers formed outside its offices, all eager to change their notes for gold or (if that could not be paid) for the notes of some other bank in which the public had not lost confidence.

When this kind of 'run' on his bank developed, a banker was put into a very difficult position. His bank would probably weather the storm if he could rapidly turn some of his investments—usually BILLS OF EXCHANGE (q.v.)—into gold or Bank of England notes; but to do this someone had to travel to London and back again by stage-coach or post-chaise, and by the time the gold or notes arrived the bank might have been forced to close its doors. In 1825 a record journey was made by post-chaise from London to Birmingham, in less than 8 hours, to bring gold

and Bank of England notes to a Birmingham banking house, which thus managed to survive the crisis. At this time the fastest stage-coach took 18 hours to cover the 110 miles.

The decrease in bank failures after 1825 is generally thought to be the result of changes in the law, which deliberately encouraged large joint-stock banks, owned by many shareholders and having immense reserves which the earlier country partnerships could not build up (*see* LIMITED COMPANIES). The building of railways must also have helped bankers, for many bank failures in the early 19th century were due just as much to the difficulty of transporting stocks of gold coins quickly enough as to bad banking or bad management. Bank failures later than 1825 were of rather a different pattern, and were often quite local. The European political revolutions of 1848 brought down over 100 banks in France, Belgium, and Holland, but British concerns were not much affected. In 1857 a most spectacular failure was that of the City of Glasgow Bank which caused so much disturbance that troops were called out to keep order. In 1866 the failure of the big London house of Overend, Gurney and Co. brought about general financial panic. In 1890 the big London merchant banking house of Baring nearly suspended payment, but with the help of the Bank of England and other City institutions it managed to survive.

By the turn of the century the new joint-stock banks in Britain had grown big, and were unlikely to be disturbed by a 'run'. But smaller private banks were not so fortunate; nor were foreign countries which had not followed the British example of the powerful bank with many branches. Abroad, one of the biggest failures of the early 20th century was that of the Knickerbocker Trust Company of New York, which caused as great a panic in that city as had the failure of Overend, Gurney and Co. in London 40 years earlier. In 1911 the Birkbeck Bank in Holborn suspended payment, and those

Lloyds Bank

SAVING THE BANK IN 1825 BY BRINGING BANK-NOTES AND COIN FROM THE BANK OF ENGLAND TO TAYLORS AND LLOYDS, A PRIVATE BANK IN BIRMINGHAM

A BANK-NOTE OF THE NORWICH AND SWAFFHAM BANK WHICH FAILED IN 1826
It is stamped to show that the bank had failed and that two dividends were subsequently paid by the bankers

who were present on the last afternoon before this bank closed its doors will remember the immense crowd of tensely quiet and nervous depositors gradually edging their way towards the cashiers. The aftermath of the First World War led to many small failures, none of them of great importance. Farrow's Bank, which had built up a popular business by advertising methods which were not traditional in British banking, failed for a considerable sum. There were several failures abroad.

The last important bank failures were catastrophic in their effects. The world crisis of 1931 was ushered in by the failure, in May of that year, of the Creditanstalt of Vienna. The Darmstädter Bank in Germany—as large as one of the British 'Big Five' banks—very shortly followed suit.

Since the First World War British banking has been remarkably free from failures. Apart from the size and strength of the banks themselves, this is largely due to the disuse of gold coins as actual money, and the complete disappearance—except in Scotland and Ireland—of any form of bank-note other than those issued by the Bank of England. There is no longer any purpose in besieging the counter of a bank merely to change one's notes into other notes like them; and modern banks are so intimately linked with the life of the people that no Government would permit a 'run' upon them to be successful.

See also BANKING; BANK OF ENGLAND.

BANKING. The English word 'bank' comes from the Italian *banco* or *banca*, which meant originally a shelf or bench. The word came to be used in Italy for a tradesman's stall or counter, or a money-changer's table. The Greek word for table, *trapeza*, was used for a bank in Ancient Greece, and is still used in modern Greece. When the Italians introduced banking into other countries, the word bank came into general use. Although banks to-day are important institutions, without which business could scarcely continue, the general principles of banking have changed little throughout the centuries.

In Great Britain organized banking began when the Lombards, or men from Lombardy in northern Italy, set up branch houses in London, and from them the famous street in the City of London took its name. The money of those days was of metal (*see* COINS) and the Lombards were goldsmiths and silversmiths as well as bankers. In the 16th and 17th centuries British goldsmith-bankers began to become more prominent and important.

These goldsmith-bankers began by taking in coin from private and commercial customers for safe keeping, because they could provide the necessary strong-rooms, watchmen, and guards. They issued receipts for these deposits, and the owners of the coin then began to pay debts by asking the bankers to make the payments, and by handing in their receipts for alteration. This was the first step towards modern banking. The bankers soon discovered that a lot of the coin deposited with them never left their custody: they were merely asked to change its ownership from one person to another. Another move forward was made when the bankers, instead of issuing a single receipt for coin deposited with them, issued a set of receipts, in round figures, which could be handed by the holders to their creditors, in settlement of commercial transactions. Very soon these receipts, or bank-notes as they came to be called, passed from hand to hand, each holder in turn being satisfied that he could go and collect hard coin if he wanted to, and finding the passing of a piece of paper a more convenient way of doing business than cashing the paper for coin. A more advanced stage was reached when the bankers were asked to lend money, and they discovered that the borrowers would be quite content if loans were made in bank-notes instead of in actual coin.

When this stage was reached, we had the basis of modern banking. The notes simply represented claims to coin. There were more notes put in circulation by each banker than he possessed in actual coin; but he relied on two factors to enable him to meet his liabilities. Firstly, it was unlikely that everybody to whom he owed money would ask for it at the same time. Secondly, if such depositors did unduly press him for coin, he trusted in his ability to call in his loans fast enough to be able to satisfy those who wanted to draw coin out. Banking was seen to be a business of owing people more cash than one possessed at the moment, and of having one's assets, other than actual coin, so organized that it would be a fairly simple process to convert them.

It was obviously necessary that any LOANS (q.v.) or other investments, made with the cash originally deposited, should be well secured or have good SECURITY (q.v.) behind them, and should be made only for short periods. But some loans could be made for longer periods if some of the depositors agreed not to ask for their money within a certain fixed time. This arrangement enabled the bankers to lend money not only for longer periods but also against less perfect security, and therefore to charge higher rates of INTEREST (q.v.). But to tempt the depositor to agree to his part in the arrangement, he was offered a rate of interest by the bankers. Thus, the modern distinction arose between current accounts, which are withdrawable on demand, and deposit accounts, which earn a moderate rate of interest and are withdrawable only after proper notice has been given (see BANK ACCOUNTS). The PROFITS (q.v.) of a banker obviously came from the difference between the rate of interest he paid to depositors, and the rate he could charge on his loans and advances to borrowers, or could earn by investing in BILLS OF EXCHANGE, Government SECURITIES (qq.v.), or similar kinds of investment (see MONEY MARKET).

In the early 17th century the London goldsmith-bankers, in addition to issuing bank-notes and making loans, started the beginnings of our modern system of accounts withdrawable by cheque. A banker would open for a customer what was called a 'running cash'. This meant that he would arrange for his customer to issue orders on him in favour of other merchants up to an agreed limit; and he would either pay out notes or coin to persons presenting the orders, or would open a similar running cash for them if they so wished. It was only necessary for these written orders on bankers to be printed, in small books of perforated cheque-forms, for the running cash to develop into the modern current account as we now know it. But for many years London and country bankers not only went in for deposit-banking, as the running cash system soon came to be called, but also continued to issue bank-notes. No interest had to be paid on these, and they represented the most profitable line of operation for any banker. The business of issuing notes gradually became concentrated in the hands of the BANK OF ENGLAND itself (q.v.). In this way the ordinary business of banking took on more and more of a deposit-banking character, until it became that and nothing else.

By this time bankers had to a large extent forgotten that they had originally started up as

GEORGE GISZE, A GERMAN MERCHANT IN LONDON
Painting by Hans Holbein, 1532

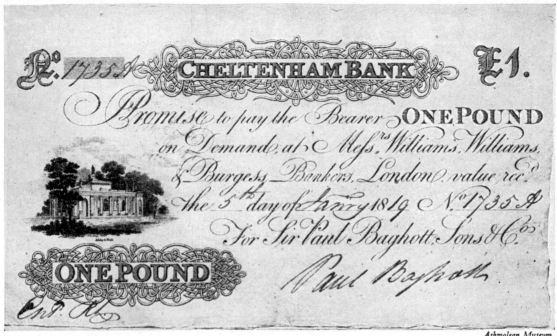

Ashmolean Museum

A BANK-NOTE OF THE CHELTENHAM BANK, DATED 1819
The date and signature were written by hand when the note was issued

safe deposits for their customers' coin. By issuing notes, and making loans, they were really creating a new and extra kind of money, and the only limit to this was set by the quantity of coin or Bank of England notes they thought it necessary to keep as a cash reserve. Roughly, the proportion of cash to their current and deposit account liabilities to customers, which experience taught them was reasonably satisfactory, was 1 to 10, or 10%. If one of his customers wanted to borrow, in order to pay the money borrowed to another customer, a banker would merely debit the account (*see* BOOK-KEEPING) of the borrower when his cheque was presented, and credit the account of the customer who paid it in. If we consider the system of banks in Great Britain as a whole, any banker lending money would debit the account of the borrower, and any banker receiving the cheque drawn would credit the account of his depositor, and so the modern saying that 'every loan creates a deposit' is seen to be true.

Two institutions have helped British banking to reach its present highly developed stage. The first are the Bankers' CLEARING HOUSES (q.v.) in London and the big provincial towns, where cheques drawn on the banks are totalled daily,

taken to the head offices, and distributed to the various branches. Every evening a general balance is struck, which is settled by a mutual exchange of special cheques, or 'tickets' as they are called, on the Bank of England.

The second institution is the BANK OF ENGLAND (q.v.), where all other banks keep accounts in order to settle their clearing-house transactions. Nowadays British banks regard a balance at the Bank of England as equivalent to actual cash. To some extent the Bank of England can control the size of these balances, and thus control the use of bank credit in the whole country.

A banker must invest his customers' deposits in such a way that they can be easily turned again into money. The 'assets' side of the balance sheet of any of our big British banks shows how this is done, and how customers' deposits are invested, the rate of interest earned increasing as the investment becomes more difficult to turn rapidly into cash. First comes the item 'cash in hand and at the Bank of England', on which no interest at all is earned; then comes 'money at call and short notice', earning in 1951 not less than $\frac{1}{2}$% per annum; then comes 'bills discounted', on which the average rate of interest is slightly higher; then come various classes of

Westminster Bank   Barclays Bank

Lloyds   Bank

1677

National Provincial Bank   Midland   Bank

COATS OF ARMS AND CRESTS OF THE 'BIG FIVE' BANKS

they draw up income-tax returns and claims; and act as TRUSTEES and executors under WILLS and settlements (qq.v. Vol. X). Finally, they are in a position to obtain good information concerning the credit and standing of private individuals and merchants all over the world, and with reasonable safeguards for discretion they will let their own customers have this information (*see* CREDIT).

Including the Bank of England, there are twelve members of the London Bankers' Clearing House, of whom the most important are the 'Big Five': Barclays, Lloyds, Midland, National Provincial, and Westminster. Scotland and Ireland have several banks, and most of them have London offices. There are several banks with London head-offices, and branches in the Dominions, Colonies, and dependencies. Likewise, many banks with head-offices in Commonwealth territories have offices in London. London is also the headquarters of many British banks operating in foreign countries, and all the important purely foreign banks have London offices. With the exception of the Midland Bank, which confines its interests to the United Kingdom, the Big Five control subsidiaries operating in the British Commonwealth and in certain foreign countries. No list of British banks would be complete without mention of the MERCHANT BANKERS (q.v.), specializing in international trade and finance, of which the house of Rothschild is a famous example.

See also BANK OF ENGLAND; BANK ACCOUNTS; MONEY MARKET; BANK FAILURES; SECURITIES.

securities, on which the return is higher still; and finally there is a large item, 'loans and advances', on which the interest-rate may average between 4 and 5% per annum. British banks restrict such loans to short-term transactions, and this custom has helped in freeing the British banking system from the failures and crises which have so frequently affected foreign banks.

British banks also deal with other types of business. They transfer money, by their own drafts or cheques, or telegraphically, between any towns in Britain, and between London and cities overseas. This means that they are dealers in foreign CURRENCY, which is subject to RATES OF EXCHANGE (qq.v.). They issue travellers' cheques and documents called 'letters of credit', by which British tourists and travellers can obtain funds at any town in the world big enough to have a bank. They open credits in favour of exporters and importers, and thus help international trade. They open small savings accounts for depositors of modest means; they advise on, and buy and sell, government securities and other STOCKS AND SHARES (q.v.);

BANK OF ENGLAND. In earlier days, when kings were often short of money, private business men were able to gain some advantage for themselves in exchange for lending them money. For instance, in return for a loan of £1,200,000 to William III in 1694, a London merchant named Paterson, and some friends, obtained a Royal Charter to form themselves into a company with the name of the Governor and Company of the Bank of England. Since the days of Charles II bankers had discovered that more profit was made by issuing their own bank-notes, and making loans and advances in these notes, than by lending actual gold coin (*see* BANKING). One of the privileges given to Paterson and his friends was that of being the only banking company, as distinct from a partnership, within a radius of 65 miles from the City of London,

Graphic Photo Union

THE ENTRANCE TO THE BANK OF ENGLAND IN THREADNEEDLE STREET
This building was completed in 1937 replacing the earlier one built in the 18th century

Bank of England

A BANK OF ENGLAND BEADLE

issuing bank should be allowed to open in any part of the United Kingdom; that only those banks which then lawfully issued notes might continue to do so; and that, if such banks for any reason ceased to issue notes, the Bank of England might increase its own 'fiduciary' issue (that is, that part of its issue covered only by SECURITIES (q.v.) and not by gold) by two-thirds of the lapsed amounts.

During the second half of the 19th century the larger banks, organized as LIMITED COMPANIES (q.v.), gradually absorbed the smaller country banks. Under the 1844 Act these large joint-stock banks lost the right to issue notes, and the Bank of England took over their note issues. The result was that throughout the rest of the 19th and the early part of the 20th century the Bank of England gradually became the only bank able to issue notes. By 1921 the last country note-issuing bank (Fox, Fowler and Co., of Wellington, Somerset) amalgamated with Lloyds Bank Limited, and the Bank of England found itself the sole note-issuing bank in England and Wales. In Scotland and Ireland no such amalgamations took place, and thus independent note issues of banks in those countries are still made.

Between 1844 and 1921 the Bank gradually realized that, while it wished merely to be an ordinary commercial bank (though on a large scale) working for the profit of its shareholders, it was being forced to act in the general interests of the country. It possessed the country's largest individual stock of gold, and the defence of this stock of gold was a great responsibility. It was already the leader of the British banking community, and it was increasingly looked upon by other bankers as a place where they could always borrow in time of need. So, whenever its gold stock was threatened, either by an ordinary commercial or political panic which caused a lot of people to exchange their bank-notes for gold (*see* BANK FAILURES), or by an unbalanced state of international trade, it would put up its BANK-RATE (q.v.) in order to prevent borrowing and to lower prices, and also to encourage foreign bankers to send gold to London because of the higher rates of interest to be earned there.

The First World War caused London to lose to some extent its position as the world's international banking centre. As at the time of the Napoleonic Wars, the Bank's note issue from August 1914 onwards ceased to be exchangeable

allowed to issue its own bank-notes. In return for the loan the Bank was to receive £100,000 yearly from the Treasury. It soon became the leading banking company in the United Kingdom. In 1797 it ran into serious difficulty because William PITT (q.v. Vol. V), the Prime Minister at the time, although promising not to borrow money from it, continually did so to finance the war against Napoleon. The Bank had to suspend gold payments and appealed to the PRIVY COUNCIL (q.v. Vol. X), who supported the Bank's decision.

In the early 19th century many people thought that throughout the country there were too many banks that issued notes. Just before 1844 the Government of Sir Robert Peel decided to pass legislation that would gradually bring the issue of all bank-notes into the hands of the Bank of England. The Bank Charter Act of 1844 therefore laid down that, above an agreed limit of £14 million, the Bank was only to issue notes up to the value of the gold coin or gold bullion that it actually held; that no new note-for gold sovereigns. The problem of maintaining the value of the British pound note with no fixed exchange value in gold (*see* GOLD STANDARD, Vol. X) was so serious that the Bank and the Treasury had to work closely together. By the end of the war, therefore, the Bank realized that it was in fact, although not in name, a State or Central Bank, whose chief responsibility was to safeguard the internal and foreign-exchange value of our money.

When the Second World War broke out, the Bank of England worked closely with the British Treasury, the United States Treasury, and the President of the Federal Reserve Banking System (which is the American equivalent of the Bank of England) to manage the world's monetary affairs, to encourage international trade, to keep world prices steady, and to promote the fullest possible employment.

By the end of the Second World War, the Bank was acting as a true State Bank, linking its financial policy to that of the Government; but it was still owned by private shareholders, and had a Governor and Court of Directors not legally subject to control by the Government. In 1946 an Act of Parliament made it a true State Bank, owned and controlled by the Government, although still operating more on the lines of a public corporation than as an actual government department.

> See also BANKING; MONEY MARKET.
> See also Vol. X: NATIONAL FINANCE; GOLD STANDARD.

Bank of England

A BANK MESSENGER POSTING UP THE BANK-RATE NOTICE IN THE BANK OF ENGLAND

BANK-RATE. This is the Bank of England's official minimum rate at which it will discount BILLS OF EXCHANGE for, or make loans to, the members of the London MONEY MARKET (qq.v.).

Although Bank-rate is an emergency rate, and although the members of the Money Market can nearly always borrow more cheaply among themselves, movements in Bank-rate are important because all money rates throughout the country move in the same direction. For example, the rate of interest allowed by the ordinary commercial banks on deposit accounts (*see* BANK ACCOUNTS) is usually quoted at so much per cent. below Bank-rate. Similarly, their rates for loans, overdrafts, and other advances are usually quoted at so much per cent. above Bank-rate. Also, these banks are regular lenders of what is called day-to-day money, or call-money, to the other members of the London Money Market; if Bank-rate rises, and they have

to increase the rate of INTEREST (q.v.) on deposits, they must charge higher rates for call-money. Rates for call-money therefore tend to go up and down with Bank-rate. Moreover, the Money Market is constantly engaged in discounting, or buying, bills of exchange; and, as many of the bill-discounting houses borrow call-money to do this, they must naturally charge higher rates of discount, or interest, on their bills if they have to pay higher rates for call-money. Therefore when the Bank-rate rises, all money rates, bill rates, and loan rates rise with it; and a fall in Bank-rate has the opposite effect.

The reasons for changes in Bank-rate are explained in the article on the BANK OF ENGLAND (q.v.). In 1939, after the outbreak of war, Bank-rate came down to 2%, at which it stayed until 1950. Since then it has been frequently changed, and early in 1957 stood at 5%.

> See also BANKING; MONEY MARKET; CURRENCY.

BARRELS, *see* CASK-MAKING.

BARTER, *see* EXCHANGE AND TRADE.

BASKET-MAKING. This is one of the oldest crafts, and one of the few which can still face the competition of machines, for the successful shaping and weaving of willow or cane has not been widely done by machinery. Baskets were made by primitive man before the art of the potter was discovered; and before the potter's wheel had been invented, POTTERY (q.v.) was made by modelling the clay on a mould of basket-work. Again, it was almost certainly the practice of intertwining grass, rushes, or canes to make baskets, which led, later, to weaving, and so to all the textile arts. In early times baskets were used more widely than now. The ancient Egyptians sometimes made their coffins of basket-work, and the American Indians used baskets in religious ceremonies. In Britain basket-work was an important craft in the Middle Ages. The records of the Company of Basket Makers in London date from the 17th century, though the Company was in existence long before that date.

To-day baskets are used for packing goods in textile mills and other factories, and for carrying fruit and vegetables. The fishing industry uses baskets for traps, such as lobster-pots, as well as for packing fish. Baskets vary in shape and size from the shopping basket to the huge 'skeps' used in dye-works. As new methods of transport and packing are introduced, other kinds of containers are replacing baskets; but there are many purposes for which they are still needed.

In Britain the basket-maker generally works on his own, in a small workshop. He does not need any elaborate or expensive equipment, and he can do the whole process single-handed. It is a craft that is particularly suitable for blind people, who work either on their own or in workshops. During the First World War blind basket-makers made gun-mats and shell-baskets, and in the Second World War they made the parachute panniers used in airborne engagements. They also make all types of industrial baskets. Basket-making is a simple craft to learn, and the materials are cheap.

Until the 19th century baskets were made of

FIG. I. WEAVING A BAKER'S BASKET ON A LAPBOARD

locally grown materials, which in Britain were usually willows, osiers, and hazel. Now, rattan or other cane is imported from Singapore, sea-grass from China, and raffia from Madagascar. Willows need a great deal of water, and they usually grow where the beds can be flooded or irrigated in the low moors of Somerset, the Trent valley, and East Anglia, and in Belgium, Holland, Siberia, and the Argentine. The long thin shoots of the willows, 'withies' as they are often called, are harvested in the autumn and winter, when the leaf has fallen, and before the sap begins to move. If they are required to be 'buff', they are cut as early as possible and, before being peeled, are boiled in large open boilers for 6 to 8 hours. This stains them a golden-brown shade. For white willow the withies are cut later, and are left to stand in pits in at least 18 inches of water till May or June. They are peeled when they are in full leaf. Hazel has a thicker stem; it is not stripped, but is often split.

Before a basket can be made, the willows or cane must be soaked in water for from 1 to 5 hours according to size, and then laid down to mellow for a few hours. Next, they are sorted or 'cut over': that is, trimmed to the sizes needed. The basket-maker works on a slightly raised platform, and the basket he is making stands on a 'lapboard' (Fig. 1). His tools are a 'shop knife' for cutting over the willows, a 'picking knife'

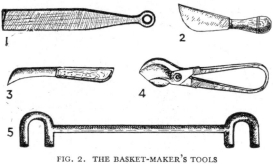

FIG. 2. THE BASKET-MAKER'S TOOLS
1. Beating-iron. 2. Picking knife. 3. Shop knife.
4. Shears. 5. Commander

for trimming long ends when finished, a 'beating iron,' for closing up the weaving as he works, shears for cutting thick sticks, and a 'com-mander' for straightening crooked sticks by a levering movement (see Fig. 2). For small work lighter tools are used. Baskets are usually begun at the bottom. For a square basket the bottom is made in a screw block (Fig. 3); round and

oval bottoms are begun by forming a cross with sticks, and then opening the crossed sticks and weaving round them (Fig. 4). When the bottom is made, the uprights, or stakes, are put in, and

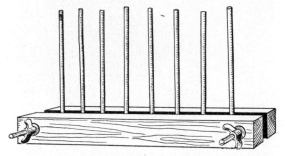

FIG. 3. SCREW-BLOCK FOR MAKING SQUARE-BOTTOMED BASKETS
Fine willows or cane are woven between the uprights

the sides filled in by weaving until the top is reached. Various forms of plaiting or twisting are used to form a finishing border.

Different methods are used for different materials and purposes. Feeding baskets, used

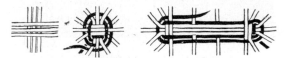

FIG. 4. THE START OF ROUND AND OVAL BASKETS

on farms, are made of split hazel or oak. The Lancashire basket-makers make light baskets in peeled buff willow. Their shopping-baskets are often called 'Southports' after the Lancashire town. The Cornish fishermen make lobster-pots of green willows. Basket chairs are made by weaving in cane or willow and strengthening the work with wooden frames, which are often nailed together. The small boat called the Welsh coracle is a large oval basket covered with waterproofing material, made of split ash inter-woven with willow twigs. It has hardly changed in form since it was used 2,000 years ago by the ancient Britons, and is still used to-day by fisher-men for salmon and sea-trout in the West Wales river estuaries (see also CANOE, Vol. IV).

See also CRAFTSMANSHIP; WOOL WEAVING.
See also Vol. VI: RURAL CRAFTS.

BATCH PRODUCTION, see PRODUCTION.

BAUXITE, see ALUMINIUM INDUSTRY.

BEARER BOND, see BOND.

Whitbread & Co.

PUTTING HOPS INTO THE COPPER

BEER BREWING. 1. HISTORY. The history of brewing goes back some 10,000 years to ancient Egypt—almost to the beginning of agriculture itself. The art of brewing was known to the ancient Greeks, and had established itself 2,000 years ago in Britain, for it was discovered and appreciated by the Roman invaders in 54 B.C. To the Saxons and the Danes the drinking of ale was a tradition, and they brought with them their own ideas on brewing it; but it was under the Normans that brewing was first properly organized, especially in abbeys and monasteries all over the country. The abbeys of those days looked after travellers as a duty, and the real origin of English INNS (q.v. Vol. IV) was the guest-house attached to the abbey. Here, beer brewed by the monks was provided. Brewing was also associated with the farmhouse; the term 'brewster' (still used to-day to describe the February sessions of the Justices to deal particularly with liquor licences) no doubt derives from the activity of the medieval farmer's wife in producing beer for her family and for those employed about the farm. As recently as 1881

there were 71,000 farmer-brewers; to-day there are only 3,000.

Brewing on a wholesale scale began during the 18th century. Important centres were London, where there were large numbers of inns and taverns, and Burton-on-Trent, where the 'hard' water was peculiarly suitable for brewing beer. But from the Dissolution of the Monasteries in the 16th century, until quite recent times, brewing was still extensively carried on in the inn itself, although there are probably no more than 200 publican-brewers left to-day, among the 625 holders of brewers' licences. Beer brewing is an important industry in many other countries, especially in Germany and Czecho-slovakia.

2. MATERIALS. Beer is brewed to-day from the same materials, and by the same principles, as have been used continuously for 5 centuries, ever since the introduction of HOPS (q.v. Vol. VI) altered the medieval 'ale' into the beer of to-day. Science has supplanted rule-of-thumb methods, as it has in many other food industries.

The chief of the materials used is malted barley (*see* MALTING), supplemented in more recent times by sugar, roasted barley and malt (for colouring the dark beers), flaked barley (barley rolled out flat and partly cooked, rather like porridge oats) and flaked oats, rice, and maize. Hops are added to flavour the beer and to give it good 'keeping' qualities. YEAST is used to introduce the natural process of FER-

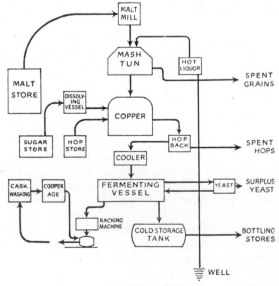

CHART SHOWING THE PROCESSES IN THE MAKING OF BEER

MENTATION (qq.v. Vol. II). All these materials are used under the supervision of the officers of CUSTOMS AND EXCISE (q.v. Vol. X), and everything that enters into the brewing process must be carefully entered by the brewer into the official brewing book, at least 2 hours before the process starts.

3. TECHNIQUE. The impression gained from a visit to a modern brewhouse is of a large, lofty building, containing at various levels rows of huge vessels of different shapes—mash-tuns, boiling-coppers, hop-backs, fermenting-vessels, and storage tanks—and with few employees about. Plenty of human activity is, however, to be seen in the other departments outside the brewhouse: the cask shed where incoming empties are scalded, the cooperage where they are repaired, the racking room where they are filled, and the loading stages where they are sent off on their journey to the public houses.

The first operation in brewing occurs in the milling-room at the top of the building. Here the malt is screened or sieved to remove any particles of root, foreign seeds, and dust. The grains are then crushed into small particles called 'grist'. The grist passes down through tubes to the mash-tuns—squat-shaped cylindrical iron vessels with domed covers provided with sliding inspection doors. The function of the mash-tun is rather like that of a teapot. Here the 'liquor' is introduced, hot but well below boiling-point, and the work is begun of converting the starchy particles of malt into sugars which are soluble and fermentable. The brewer never refers to 'water', but always calls it 'liquor'; he is very particular about its absolute purity, and he generally prefers a very 'hard' water. After about 2 hours in the mash-tun, this liquor, now called 'wort', is drawn off by taps at the bottom of the vessel. At the same time, more hot liquor is spread over the grist by means of revolving arms known as 'sparges' inside the mash-tun, to get the final extract from the malt.

The wort now passes to the coppers, where the hops are added, and sugar, too, if it is to be used. Here the wort is boiled for about 2 hours, and then run off through a vessel known as the 'hop-back', an enormous strainer which removes the spent hops from the wort. This is usually the end of the first descent by gravity from the top of the building. The wort is pumped up to the top of the brewery again to pass through the refrigerators, batteries of pipes cooled by cold

Whitbread & Co.

PITCHING YEAST INTO THE WORT

water passing through them. The wort passes on to the fermenting vessels, large open tanks formerly built of wood, but nowadays usually of stainless steel, copper, aluminium, or concrete with a special lining material. It is at this point that the excise officer assesses the duty on the beer by measuring its volume by the 'dip', and its strength, or 'original gravity', with a HYDROMETER (q.v. Vol. VIII). Yeast is now introduced. Fermentation begins as the yeast grows and multiplies and throws up the familiar 'head' of foam, which at first may rise several feet high. This process lasts for some days, and as it goes on the head settles and is eventually skimmed off for further use or for sale.

The wort has now become beer, and passes to huge cylindrical storage tanks, where it is kept at a low temperature for varying periods, and sometimes for many weeks. If it is to be bottled it will be pumped through a pipe-line to the bottling depot close by (*see* BOTTLING (BEER)), or carried by road or rail tank-wagon, or in casks, to a distant depot. Otherwise its next passage is to the racking-room, where it is run into the familiar oak casks in which it will be taken to the cellars of public-houses. In the cellars it is clarified with 'finings' made from isinglass and, after a short period in which to settle, it is ready to be drawn up through tubing, now generally made of glass or stainless steel, by the beer-engines mounted on the bar counter.

4. FINANCE AND ORGANIZATION. Of the 400 brewery companies and firms now existing, a large number are still family concerns; but many have developed into LIMITED COMPANIES (q.v.). Only a quarter of the capital of the average company is represented by the brewery and its plant; the remainder is invested in the ownership of the licensed premises in which its beers are mainly sold (*see* Section 5). Out of the price the customer pays for a glass of beer, about two-thirds goes directly to the Treasury in beer duty. The remainder represents the cost of labour and materials in manufacture, the expenses of distribution, the profit of the brewery and the retailer, as well as the cost of maintaining, rebuilding, and improving licensed premises, which has been estimated to be £15 million a year. Over 8,000 million pints of beer are drunk in Britain annually, and in addition British beer finds its way to many other parts of the world. The beers which may be bought on draught from the cask are generally bitter beer, mild ale, and stout; other kinds are more usually bottled (*see* BOTTLING (BEER)).

5. INNS AND TAVERNS. Under what is called the 'tied house' system, most inns and public-houses are owned by brewing companies. By the end of the 19th century they were buying inns and taverns; within 50 years they had acquired the majority of those in England and Wales. Many were rebuilt, and others renovated. The brewery owns and maintains the building, and usually also the equipment of the public rooms. It is let to a tenant at a fixed rent which is seldom more than 1% of the capital value of the house. This system allows adequate supervision of the conditions under which the brewery's beer reaches the consumer, and it facilitates long-term planning, and therefore economy of production. The well-known national brands of beer are stocked by almost every licensed house, whether 'tied' or not.

In some parts of the country the brewery retains full control of the 'tied house', which is run by a resident manager. This, too, is the practice in the State-managed houses in the Carlisle district. Of every 100 licensed premises in England and Wales, nearly 80 are let by breweries to 'tied' tenants, about 6 are directly managed by breweries, and the remainder are 'free', as are most of the houses in Scotland.

See also MALTING; BOTTLING (BEER); WHISKY DISTILLING; CIDER-MAKING.
See also Vol. VI: HOPS.
See also Vol. II: FERMENTATION; YEAST.

BILL, *see* INVOICE.

BILLINGSGATE, *see* FISH TRADE.

BILL OF LADING. In the first place, this is a contract to convey goods from one port to another, made between a shipping company and a shipper (the person or firm which arranges for the shipping company to carry the goods). The contract states what risks will be accepted by the shipping company and what risks the shipper must insure against. Secondly, it is a receipt given by the master of a ship for the goods or cargo named in the bill of lading. The bill is one of the most important documents used in international trade, and the system by which bankers lend money 'against' ships' cargoes depends entirely on it. Bills of lading are usually made out in three copies, because they are posted about the world from one banker or merchant

AN OLD BILL OF LADING

to another, and mails sometimes get damaged or destroyed.

In the third place, a bill of lading is what is called by business men a 'document of title'. The bill may be 'endorsed', like a cheque, having on its back the signature of the consignor (the person who sent the goods) or consignee (the person to whom they are sent), according to the way in which it has been drawn up. Provided that the bill is thus endorsed, the person who is in possession of it is the only one to whom the ship's AGENT (q.v.) at the port of destination will deliver the goods; without production of the endorsed bill of lading no goods will be delivered. A banker in London who is asked, say, by an exporter in London to advance money against the cargo shipped will insist upon all three copies of the endorsed bill of lading being handed to him as security. The banker then sends the bill of lading—which is usually attached to a BILL OF EXCHANGE, an insurance policy, an INVOICE (qq.v.), and other relevant documents —to his agent in the port of destination, in, say, Australia, who will arrange that the documents will only be handed to the importing merchant in Australia in exchange for the necessary cash.

Bills of lading are printed forms usually bearing the crest or coat of arms of the shipping company. They have been used for centuries, and their rather out-of-date language is left unchanged because the words and phrases used have been argued about before the law courts and have been given by judges a very definite meaning. Most bills of lading have a lengthy and picturesque list of all the risks of navigation for which the shipping line will not be responsible, such as: 'The Act of God, the King's Enemies, Pirates, Robbers, or Thieves by Land or Sea, arrests or restraints of Princes, Rulers, or People . . . barratry, jettison . . .' and so on.

See also OVERSEAS TRADE.

BILL OF EXCHANGE. This is a promise to pay a definite sum of money on a future date. A bill of exchange is a 'negotiable instrument': that is, it may be passed from one person to another; in this way VALUE (q.v.), either in goods or money, may be transferred from one person to another without the actual exchange of money. There are other documents which promise to pay money, but they are not true bills of exchange. The simplest of these is the IOU: the letters obviously representing the words 'I owe

you'. An IOU is simply an acknowledgement of a debt, and cannot be bought and sold, or 'negotiated'. Between the IOU and the true bill of exchange comes the 'promissory note'. This is a negotiable promise to repay money. The difference between these three documents is seen in the examples given below of a debt of £1,000 owing to James Robinson by Thomas Perkins.

IOU

To James Robinson

    IOU

    £1,000

                   THOMAS PERKINS

                       1 Jan. 1951

Promissory Note

£1,000   London, 1 Jan. 1951

Three months after date I promise to pay to James Robinson or his order the sum of One Thousand Pounds.

                  THOMAS PERKINS

Bill of Exchange

£1,000   London, 1 Jan. 1951

Three months after date pay to me or my order the sum of One Thousand Pounds value received.

                  JAMES ROBINSON

To: THOMAS PERKINS

(overprinted: Accepted 1.1.51 Payable at Midland Bank Ltd. Poultry, E.C.2 THOMAS PERKINS)

A special Act of Parliament, called the Bills of Exchange Act, lays down the rights and duties of persons whose names appear on bills of exchange; so in Great Britain it is more usual for promises of this kind to be drawn up in the true bill-of-exchange form. In Canada and the United States the promissory-note form is more usual, and in those countries the simple name 'note' is generally used.

A true bill of exchange is drawn up in the form of an invitation by the person claiming the money to the person owing it, and it does not become negotiable until the debtor signifies his 'acceptance' of the invitation, as in the illustration given. He is then called the 'acceptor', and the bill is called an 'acceptance'.

N. M. Rothschild & Sons

BILL OF EXCHANGE DRAWN BY NATHAN MAYER VON ROTHSCHILD IN 1804
Nathan Mayer opened the London house of the Rothschild banking business founded in Germany by his father

The interval of time between the drawing of a bill and its date of payment, or 'due date', is called the 'usance' of the bill. In calculating the due dates of bills in Great Britain 3 'days of grace' are allowed by law in addition to the normal period of the bill. Thus Thomas Perkins's acceptance in the illustration is due 3 months and 3 days from 1 January 1951: that is, on 4 April 1951. Days of grace do not apply to the Treasury Bills issued by the British Government.

Money in one's pocket now, and money promised for the future, are not quite the same thing. A bill of exchange due 3 months ahead will not be worth its full face value when it is 'accepted'. The difference between the present and future value of bills is called their rate of 'discount'. It is generally stated at so much per cent. per annum. Thus, if the rate of discount were 2% per annum, a bill for £1,000 due exactly 3 months ahead would have a present value of £995. Bankers and others buy and sell bills of exchange as part of their ordinary business, and this is called 'discounting' bills. There are firms in the City of London who specialize in bill dealings and are called 'bill brokers' (*see* MONEY MARKET).

BLACKLEAD, *see* GRAPHITE.

BLEACHING takes place in the making of TEXTILES (q.v.), either to give a white finish or to give a fabric a neutral colour before it is dyed. Wool and linen were the most important fabrics in the early days of the English textile industry. Wool, when well washed and scoured, was al-most white, and any further bleaching was not attempted. Unbleached linen, however, had a brownish and unattractive appearance, and in the 18th century linen fabrics were regularly sent for bleaching to Holland. There were three stages in the Dutch process: steeping the fabrics for some time in alkaline liquor; repeated washings in buttermilk; and finally the spreading of the fabrics on the grass in sunshine and air for several months. This process was expensive, largely because of the long time taken. In 1756 Dr. Francis Horne of Edinburgh used a solution of weak sulphuric acid instead of buttermilk, and his process reduced the time from months to days.

Modern substances used are chlorine, hydrogen peroxide, and sulphur dioxide. The possibilities of chlorine were discovered in 1785, but it was some time before anyone invented a convenient compound. At the end of the 18th century a Glasgow chemical manufacturer introduced what is now called bleaching powder, or chloride of lime. This is the general substance used for most modern fabrics, and particularly for cottons. Silks do not respond well to treatment by ordinary bleaching-powder, and certain kinds, particularly tussore, are usually bleached in a solution of hydrogen peroxide, which is sometimes used for woollen fabrics. The latter are also often bleached by sulphur dioxide; they are exposed when damp to the fumes of burning sulphur. This process is known as 'stoving'.

See also LINEN INDUSTRY; CHEMISTRY, INDUSTRIAL.

A DUTCH BLEACHING-GROUND
Painting by David Teniers the Younger, 1610–90

Barber Institute of Fine Arts

BLOCK-PRINTING, *see* TEXTILE PRINTING.

BOND. This is a paper stating that a government or firm has borrowed money at a certain rate of INTEREST (q.v.). It gives anyone who holds it (and who is known as the 'bearer' of it) the right to receive an annual income in interest. Bonds are therefore generally called 'bearer bonds'. They are bought and sold on the Stock Exchanges, and are usually artistic-looking documents, printed on stout paper of high quality and folded in two. The first fold states the amount borrowed, the rate of interest payable, the dates on which interest will be paid, and the date on which the money borrowed will finally be repaid. At the bottom is the signature of the official signing the contract on behalf of the government or firm. The second fold is a sheet of small coupons, serially numbered, and dated with the successive dates of payment of interest. Whoever happens to possess the bond, at any date when interest is due, cuts the proper coupon from this sheet, and forwards it to his banker who arranges to collect the interest on his behalf.

Although bearer bonds of this type are still popular in North America, they are issued less often than before in Great Britain, because they might fairly easily be smuggled out of the country in order to evade the laws prohibiting the export of property or capital.

See also STOCK EXCHANGES.

BONDED WAREHOUSE, *see* WAREHOUSES.

BONUS, *see* WAGES.

BOOKBINDING. The purpose of binding a book is to hold the pages together in such a way that it can be opened for reading and closed to protect the pages from damage.

1. HISTORY. Flat books replaced written rolls in the early Christian era (*see* BOOKS, HISTORY OF, Vol. IV), and the leaves of parchment were then placed between wooden boards to keep them flat. The first bound books, with

BIBLE BOUND IN 1935 FOR WORCESTER CATHEDRAL BY
DOUGLAS COCKERELL

It is bound in morocco leather with silver gilt clasps,
corners, and nails

the boards covered with leather, appeared in the
4th century. From that time magnificent book-
bindings were made, some with decorated
leather covers, some overlaid with gold set with
precious stones, others with carved ivory plaques.
During the 15th century gold tooling on leather
was introduced from the East and was used,
particularly in Venice, for manuscripts and early
printed books. Other materials were also used;
velvet and embroidered covers were popular in
Stuart England.

Until the 19th century books were not usually
bound before being sold; the customer bought
them with paper wrappers or even in sheets, and
had them bound himself by a binder. The
owner of a book would have his own particular
style of binding, the tooled leather being perhaps
decorated with his coat of arms. Towards the
end of the 18th century books began to be issued
with boards attached as covers. At first these
were not lettered, for they were intended to be
temporary cases to be replaced by leather bindings. Soon books came to be sold with the
boards covered with paper, sometimes decorated
with marbling, and with the title printed on
stuck-on labels.

Cloth was used as a cheap substitute for
leather in the early 19th century. It was often
stamped to imitate leather, and the stuck-on
labels of the older style persisted until a cloth

was introduced which would take coloured
lettering. Throughout the century, as the
technical difficulties were overcome, the cloth
was decorated more and more with colour,
embossing, and gold. At the end of the century
there was a reaction towards greater simplicity,
while the immense increase in the output of
books led to the production of cheap book-
covers or 'cases' by mechanical methods.

2. BINDING PROCESS. Most books are printed,
a number of pages at a time, on a large sheet of
paper which is folded into Folio, Quarto, Octavo,
and so on (see BOOK SIZES, Vol. IV) up to as
many as 32 or 64 leaves at a time (see Fig. 1).
Thus sections are formed of a number of folded
leaves inside each other. A very thin booklet,
consisting of only one section of this kind, may
be held together by being sewn through the fold,
or 'spine'. A proper book will be made up of a
number of sections; these are held together by
stitches through the back of the sections, and
over tapes or round cords stretched at right

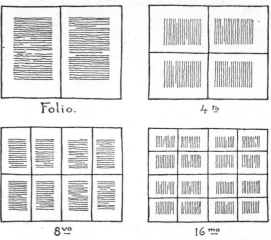

FIG. 1. HOW SHEETS ARE FOLDED

(Figs. 1 and 4 from Douglas Cockerell's *Bookbinding and the
Care of Books*, Pitman, and Figs. 2, 3, 5 drawn by J. R.
Tebbutt)

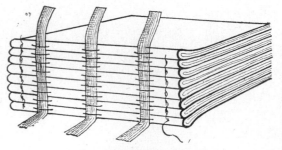

FIG. 2. THE STITCHED SECTIONS

angles across the spine of the book (*see* Fig. 2). An additional 'endpaper' section (generally a piece of stouter paper) is sewn or stuck on at the beginning and end of the book. The ends of the tapes or 'slips' are usually pasted down on to the endpapers to make a secure fixing for the boards of the book-cover. The spine of the book

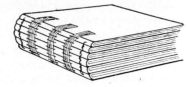

FIG. 3. THE ENDPAPERS ADDED AND THE BACK ROUNDED

is brushed with thin glue and, while the glue is still soft, the book is 'rounded', either by gently tapping the spine into a convex form with a

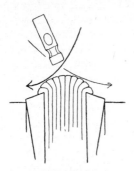

FIG. 4. BACKING THE BOOK

hammer (Fig. 3) or by a machine. This 'rounding' causes the sections to slide over each other, and when the glue sets the book is held in shape. Rounding is followed by 'backing'; this process forms joints for the hard cover; the book is gripped between wedge-shaped backing boards in a press, and the sections are fanned out (in hand binding) with the stroking motion of a hammer (Fig. 4).

The book may be covered with leather, vellum, or cloth or paper. A leather cover is stuck direct to the spine. If the book is sewn on cords, the slips are laced into the boards (Fig. 5), and the book is covered with leather stuck direct to the spine, so that the cords stand out as raised bands on it. Instead of covering the whole book with the same material, it may be 'half-bound', with a piece of leather, cloth,

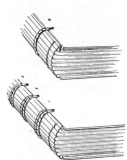

FIG. 5. CORDS LACED TO THE BOARDS

or vellum covering the spine and part of the boards, and sometimes the corners, the rest of the boards being covered with cloth or paper.

3. MACHINE BINDING. Nowadays nearly all books (this Encyclopaedia for instance) are produced by machine binding, and ingenious machines have been invented to replace the old hand-methods. The printed sheets are first folded inside each other by machines which can give almost any combination. Then the endpapers are attached by machine to the first and last section of the book. The folded sections are then 'gathered' into their correct order. The books are then sewn by semi-automatic machines which can sew at the rate of 90 sections a minute. The sewn books are then taken to the nipping or smashing machine which has taken the place of the hammer. This machine was invented about 1890, and can inflict a pressure of about 10 to 15 tons on the book. The books are cut to their right size by a guillotine, and fed first over a glueing roller and then over a hard brush which scrapes the glue between the sections. The books are then 'rounded' and 'backed'. A second coat of glue is applied to the backs of the books and a strip of mull (a kind of gauze), slightly shorter than the length of the books, fixed to it. When the books are dry they are ready to be 'cased in', that is, enclosed in book-covers.

The cases are made entirely by machinery. First, boards of the right size for the book are

Common Ground Film Strip

MACHINE BINDING OF BOOKS

The sewn book enters the machine at the lower left and comes out at the top with its case stuck on

made by an electrically-driven cutting machine. Cloth covers are made in rectangular sheets so that they overlap the boards by about ½ in. Hot glue is next applied to the upper surface of the covers, and a pair of boards is lifted by air suction and placed correctly on the glued fabrics. The whole case is then put into a press where it is subjected to pressure. The case can now receive its title and any ornamentation which is required.

If the book is to be lettered in gold and tooled with a pattern, heated brass tools are pressed on the cover. The impression is painted with a mixture called 'glair', made of white of egg. When the glair is dry, the cover is lightly greased, and gold leaf is laid on. The hot tool is then pressed through the gold; this fires the glair, so that it holds the gold in the impression of the tool; the surplus gold round the impression is removed with a gold rubber and benzine. 'Blind tooling' is done by using the hot tools on damp leather, when they leave an impression darker than the surrounding leather. This blind tooling can be very effective, and may be satisfactorily combined with gold tooling.

See also Vol. IV: BOOKS, HISTORY OF.

BOOK-KEEPING, or Accountancy, is the keeping of records of money transactions, a practice as old as the transactions themselves. Modern double-entry book-keeping dates from the merchants and bankers of the Italian Renaissance, which began in the 15th century. Until then merchants had always distinguished in their records between their assets (what they possessed and what they were owed by others) and their liabilities (what they themselves owed to others). But the Italians discovered that if the difference between assets and liabilities, which was what a merchant was worth, was put on to the liabilities side of the records as a balancing item, both sides of the records added up to the same amount; and they discovered also that every transaction would cause a change in two items of the records, and that these changes would cause the total of the assets still to equal the total of the liabilities. For example, if raw materials were bought for cash, the asset 'cash' would be diminished, and the asset 'raw materials' would be correspondingly increased, leaving the total of assets unchanged; while, if a liability to a merchant for goods bought on credit were paid off in cash, total liabilities and total assets would be diminished by equal amounts. As the years passed, the new accountancy became a standardized technique.

The most important rule is that records of different things must not be jumbled together. The records, or 'accounts', must aim at giving the maximum of information; and this would not be secured if a mixed collection of assets,

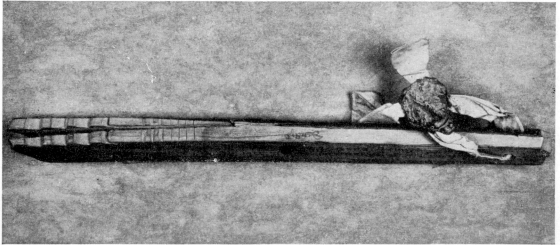

Public Record Office

STOCK AND FOIL OF A PRIVATE TALLY: A PRIMITIVE FORM OF BOOK-KEEPING

Tallies were used for receipts, the amount being indicated by notches. After these had been cut the shafts were split, the longer piece (the stock) being given to the payer, and the shorter piece (the foil) being kept for reference (compare the counterfoil of a cheque). When the accounts were audited, the two pieces were fitted together to see if they would 'tally'. This tally for £3. 13s. 4d. is dated 1361. The largest notches represent pounds (3½), the next shillings (3), and the smallest pence (4). *Exchequer, K.R., Accounts Various E. 101/678/4*

Institute of Chartered Accountants

ACCOUNTANTS AT WORK

Engraving from the title-page of Warringem's *The Right Practice of Italian Bookkeeping*, 1672. Beside the ledgers are inkpots, sandbox, quills, and knives for cutting them

such as raw materials, cash, plant and machinery, and what Jones owed the business, were all included in an account called Miscellaneous Assets. Another rule is that previous 'single-entry' records must be put into 'double-entry' form by totalling the assets and liabilities, subtracting the liabilities from the assets (assuming that the business is solvent), and including this difference on the liabilities side of the accounts, where it is usually called Capital in a one-man business or partnership. These opening entries are usually made through a Subsidiary Book called the Journal (which is one of the Books of Original Entry), from which the information is copied, or 'posted', into the main account-book, which is called the Ledger. If the book-keeping is done by pen and ink on old-fashioned lines, the Ledger is a bound volume with numbered pages, in which at the outset as many pages are allotted, in alphabetical order, to each separate account as may be foreseen in advance. Such Ledgers, however, soon become overcrowded, and accounts reaching the end of their allotment of pages have to be carried

forward or back to any blank pages that may be found. Nowadays, loose-leaf Ledgers are more used. It is a rule of good accountancy that no entry may be made in the Ledger except on the authority of one of the Subsidiary Books. Here is an example from the Journal of J. Smith, who decides on 1 January 1950 to count up his assets and liabilities and to keep accounts on the double-entry system:

1950		Dr. £	Cr. £
1 Jan.	Cash	500	
	Stock (*of goods traded in*) .	1,500	
	Sundry Debtors (*amounts owed by customers*) .	1,000	
	Furniture and Fittings . .	200	
	Freehold Premises . .	5,000	
	Sundry Creditors (*amounts owing to suppliers of goods*)		1,200
	Capital, J. Smith (*balancing item: what he is worth*) .		7,000
	Being assets and liabilities at date . . .	£8,200	£8,200

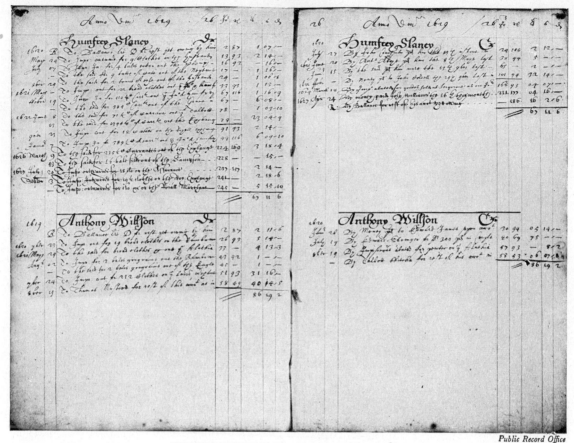

PERSONAL LEDGER OF THE LEVANT COMPANY, 1619
Debits to customers are on the left, and credits on the right. At the end of the year each account is balanced.
State Papers, Foreign, Archives S.P. 105/157

The details in brackets would not appear in the Journal; they are put in here to explain the meanings of certain conventional terms. 'Dr.' and 'Cr.' are used to signify the Assets and Liabilities sides of the Ledger respectively. To put an item on the left-hand, or Dr., side of an account is to 'debit' the item; to put it on the right-hand, or Cr. side, is to 'credit' it. The 'balance' of any account is the difference between the debit and credit sides. The accuracy of the double-entry posting of the ledger can be checked by listing all these balances, when the total of debit balances should equal the total of credit balances. This is called a Trial Balance.

It is found convenient, even in the smallest of businesses, to keep the record of cash and bank transactions in a separate book, called the Cash Book. This book then becomes both a part of the Ledger and also a Subsidiary Book, from whose evidence entries are made in the Ledger itself. Thus, if W. Jones paid by cheque to Smith some money owed to him, this would appear on the Dr. side of the Bank column of Smith's Cash Book, and on this evidence and authority the account of Jones in the Ledger would be credited.

Subsidiary Books called Day Books are kept in some businesses. They record Purchases and Sales of goods on CREDIT (q.v.), and Returns and Allowances made to or by customers. They save work, because only the monthly totals for Purchases, Sales, or Returns and Allowances need be posted to those accounts. Details affecting customers' accounts must, of course, be posted daily.

Accounts in the Ledger may be Real, Personal, or Nominal. (a) Real Accounts are records of physical assets, such as Cash, Furniture and Fittings, Plant and Machinery, Stock, Freehold Premises, and their balances are normally debit. (b) Personal Accounts are naturally the accounts of persons, principally customers, although, in a partnership, the partners also may have personal accounts. The Bank column of the Cash Book is a personal account, as the Banker is normally the debtor of a business. The balances of Personal Accounts may be debit or credit. (c) Nominal Accounts are those which record losses or gains, expenditure or income. It is from these that the profit or loss of a business is worked out. These Nominal Accounts are the crucial part of double-entry book-keeping, and must be explained in detail.

The debit, or assets, side of the accounts records the assets of the business, whether these are physical assets, such as goods, machinery, buildings, and cash, or assets in the form of debts owed to the business by other persons. The credit, or liabilities, side records who are the owners of these assets. If the business owes as much to outside creditors as it possesses in assets, then the liabilities side will record only the amounts owing to these outside creditors. If it owes less to outside creditors than it possesses in assets, then the proprietor of the business will himself own the balance of assets not owing to outside creditors, and the amount that he owns will be recorded in his Capital Account, as explained above. From this it follows that as assets increase, provided that liabilities to outside creditors do not correspondingly increase, the proprietor's Capital Account will also increase. If goods, standing on the assets side of the books at £1,000, are sold for £2,000 cash, then assets are increased by £1,000 and the proprietor's Capital Account is also increased by £1,000. If it is then found that the sale of these goods has necessitated a wages payment of £50 to the salespeople who sold them, cash assets will be diminished by £50 and the proprietor's Capital Account will also be decreased by £50. The Capital Account will therefore increase by the growth of assets through profitable trading, and will decrease through the shrinkage of assets caused by the payment of wages and similar expenses. As the Capital Account is a credit balance, it follows that all increases of it will be credits and that all decreases will be debits. It is found convenient in book-keeping to open separate accounts for the various ways in which these increases or decreases of the Capital Account may come about. It is

these separate accounts that are called the Nominal Accounts, and they must not be regarded as assets or liabilities. They are only detailed and temporary statements of how changes in the proprietor's Capital Account have come about, and they all eventually disappear when the financial results of the trading year are worked out.

To find the profit or loss for the trading year, the accuracy of the 'posting' must first be checked by taking out a Trial Balance. All the Nominal Account balances are then transferred to a Trading and Profit and Loss Account, in which they appear on the same side as they were on in the Ledger. The Trading Section shows gross trading profit; the Profit and Loss Section shows net profit, that is, the profit left after the expenses of distribution and administration have been deducted. Smith's Trading Account for the year 1950 might be as follows:

Dr.					Cr.
		£			£
Value of Stock at beginning of year	.	1,400	Sales . . .		9,000
Purchases of goods	.	4,500	Value of Stock at end of year	.	900
Warehouse wages	.	1,500			
„ expenses	.	150			
Gross Profit (to Profit and Loss Section)	.	2,350			
		£9,900			£9,900

His Profit and Loss Account for the same year might be as follows:

		£			£
Advertising	.	400	Gross Profit	.	2,350
Bad Debts	.	100	(from Trading		
Delivery charges	.	200	section)		
Salaries of office staff		1,000	Rent of premises		
Cash discounts allowed		50	sublet .	.	100
Depreciation on furniture and fittings	.	50	Cash discounts received	.	200
Net Profit (to Capital Account)	.	850			
		£2,650			£2,650

The items 'Bad Debts' and 'Depreciation' in the Profit and Loss section arise as follows. Not only is it necessary for all the Nominal Accounts to be transferred to the Trading and Profit and Loss Account, but there must be a survey of Real and Personal assets to make sure that they are really worth their book values. If, for example, the resale value of Furniture and

Fittings is less than their value as shown in the books, the difference between these values is really a loss, and must be debited to a Nominal Account called 'Depreciation', so as to state the book value accurately. Similarly, a debtor who can never be expected to pay must have his balance transferred from his Personal Account to a Nominal Account called Bad Debts, for it has ceased to be an asset and has become a loss.

The final stage is the drawing up of a Balance Sheet. The Nominal Accounts have all disappeared, and have become the single item of £850, this being net profit. This, which belongs to the proprietor, must be credited to his Capital Account. The Ledger will then contain only Real and Personal Accounts, and, if these balances are listed, the result will be:

Balance Sheet of J. Smith as at 31 December 1950

Liabilities			Assets	
	£	£		£
Sundry Creditors		500	Cash in hand .	40
J. Smith, Capital:			Cash at Bank .	760
on 1 Jan. 1950	7,000		Stock of goods .	900
Add net profit			Sundry Debtors .	1,500
for year 1950	850		Furniture and Fittings less Depreciation .	150
		7,850		
			Freehold Premises	5,000
		£8,350		£8,350

In Britain, but in very few other countries, Balance Sheets are usually presented with the liabilities on the left-hand side and the assets on the right. No reason except tradition seems to exist for this confusing convention, which reverses the normal order of the Ledger.

These are the essentials of accountancy. Naturally, there are many refinements. Mechanical methods may be used, as in banks; Ledgers may be loose cards instead of bound books; Day Books may be merely files of duplicated invoices. Day Books may be arranged in columns, so that the Purchases and Sales of different departments of a business may be shown separately, and departmental Profit and Loss Accounts be drawn up. Expenses may be expressed as percentages of TURNOVER (q.v.) or net sales, so that the progress of the business may be constantly watched and accounts be linked up with COSTING and STATISTICS (qq.v.). Provision for DEPRECIATION (q.v.) may be arranged by much less simple methods than those shown. The accounts of LIMITED COMPANIES (q.v.) must be presented in the form laid down by the Companies Act of 1948. Their capital being fixed, the 'balancing item' will be the undistributed profits remaining after payment of DIVIDENDS (q.v.), some of which remain undistributed for years and are called Reserves.

See also AUDITING; ACCOUNTING, MACHINE; BUDGETARY CONTROL.

BOOM, *see* TRADE CYCLE.

BOOT AND SHOE MAKING. 1. HISTORY. Boot and shoe making in Europe on modern lines dates from the 15th century when boots with heels were probably first revived in Spain. The general use of the heeled or 'European' shoe brought about great changes in the technique of boot and shoe making.

Since the introduction of the European type of shoe a device called a 'last' has been generally used. Lasts are wooden patterns of the type of foot the boots or shoes have to fit. In early days there were few lasts, and shoes were much the same shape from Elizabethan times to the early 19th century. The standard pattern, which had many small variations, was a shoe with a plain front, and a wide high tongue over the instep. The whole front was made in one piece. There was a back or 'counter', also in one piece, with two projecting portions overlapping the tongue on the instep and tied or buckled together.

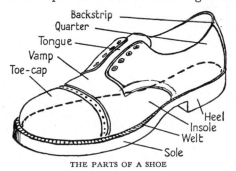

THE PARTS OF A SHOE

2. CUTTING. Even in primitive days shoemaking involved two main tasks, cutting the materials to shape, and shoe-making proper. Egyptian pictures show this plainly, even in the days of the Pharaohs, and modern illustrations of shoe-makers at work tell the same story. Shoe-making proper is subdivided into two main processes; stitching the uppers, and 'making' the shoes. The workers who form the uppers to the lasts, and attach the bottoms to the uppers, are now called 'making-room operatives'.

A piece of leather will stretch more in one direction than in another, and as some parts of a shoe must 'give' while others must not, the actual cutting of leather calls for much skill.

The cutting of sole leathers needs less varied skill than the cutting of upper leathers, as fewer kinds of hides are used. All the separate parts of the bottom of a shoe come from cattle hides only (although cowhide is not generally one of these). The amount of TANNING (q.v.) depends on the purpose for which the hide is to be used. Leather for the softer parts of the shoe is mildly tanned. Parts required for the sole itself are tanned so as to produce leather of maximum 'tightness', or minimum 'stretch' or 'give'. Cutters of sole leather must see that the lines of tightness in the hide run from heel to toe. The more mildly tanned portions of sole leather are not used as outsoles, but may be used as insoles, middle-soles, or stiffenings.

The upper leather cutter, or 'clicker', has to deal with the skins of most of the animals and reptiles in the world. His trade has always taken a long time to learn, and as newer materials come into use, his craft becomes still more complex. His real task is to select that direction of cut in his leathers which will make the resulting shoes most likely to wear well and keep their shape, having stretch where stretch is necessary, and tightness or resistance elsewhere. In this connexion it does not matter whether the clicker cuts his leathers with a hand-knife on a board (which is the old method) or whether he uses a modern machine. The means of making the cuts is secondary to where he makes them.

3. MAKING. In the old handcraft, or hand-sewn, system of working still used in the bespoke or made-to-measure trade, the makers usually carry the work personally through all processes, including finishing the bottoms of the shoes.

Shoe-making machines are, in the main, power-tools for doing the same work as was done by hand-tools in earlier days, but in machine-production there is more DIVISION OF LABOUR (q.v.). Making the uppers and making and fastening the soles are done by different workers. Stitching pieces to form the complete upper is called 'closing', and stitching by machine is a speedy job and relatively cheap in comparison with handwork. It has the advantage of allowing the uppers to be made in many separate pieces, and skins may thus be more fully utilized.

Soles are attached to boots and shoes by many

Behr-Hunot

CUTTING OUT SOLES BY MACHINE

The press descends on the knife which is shaped to cut the sole in one operation. When the press lifts, the knife is moved to a new position on the leather

means, chief of which are metal rivets, screws, or staples, wood pegs, and waxed threads. Each of these has its own particular application to different types of footwear.

Leather is, of course, not the only material used. Uppers are now made from many types of textile fabric; PLASTICS (q.v.) have recently been added, but their use is not yet extensive. Soles are often made of vulcanized rubber, and so are the wearing-parts of heels. Crêpe rubber soles are increasing in use.

Many complications arise from the use of these newer materials, particularly from the use of crêpe rubber. Usually the bottom of a crêpe-rubber-soled shoe has a thread-attached foundation, or 'carcase', to which the sole is fastened with cement. Vulcanized rubber soles are stitched, sewn, or nailed. There are modern synthetic cements which stick leather to leather, without any mechanical or structural fastening. The use of these will eventually have a great influence on the technique of shoe-making, and has already permitted the production of many unusual types which could not be made on the more traditional lines.

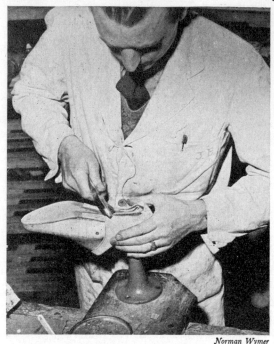

SHOE-MAKING BY HAND
Stretching the leather over the last

4. ORGANIZATION. The Worshipful Company of Cordwainers (*see* CITY COMPANIES) has always looked after and guarded the industry since it was granted a charter in 1439. 'Cordwainer' is probably an early corruption of 'cordovan', or 'cordovaner'; cordovan is an excellent soft leather originally made in the Spanish district of Cordova. Shoe-making guilds (*see* CRAFT GUILDS) were formed in various parts of Britain at different dates, and survived until the early 19th century. The Cordwainers' Company is still an active organization to-day, and runs the Cordwainers' Technical College in London.

The City and Guilds of London Institute has a long history, and has been a great help to the technical side of the shoe industry since the end of the guild and apprenticeship system. Most of the technical schools training shoe-makers to-day make the Institute's syllabus the basis of their instruction. The influence of the forgotten craftsmen of the past is therefore still felt within the trade.

Until about 100 years ago the industry was principally organized on the DOMESTIC SYSTEM (q.v.); except for cutting, the storage and classification of lasts, final dressing and packing, the work was done by out-workers in their own homes. The organization of the industry on a factory basis arose from economic rather than technical causes. Until shoe lengths and widths had been standardized throughout the country, it was impossible for a single maker to have an output large enough to justify the use of machinery in a big factory. When the standardization of sizes and fittings had been achieved, the industry began to swing over to the factory system (*see* STANDARDS, Vol. VIII).

The boot and shoe trade is one of the earliest examples in Britain of industrial organization on the 'vertical' system. A firm so organized controls the whole sequence of processes, from purchase of the raw materials to the selling of the finished article in the retail shop.

For centuries shoe-making has been the staple industry of many towns such as Northampton and Stafford. Northampton shod Cromwell's Ironsides in the 17th century. To-day Leicester, Bristol, Kettering, Wellingborough, Rushden, Leeds, and Norwich are the most important centres. Each centre specializes in certain qualities and types. Individual factories specialize very narrowly, and firms compelled to produce a wide variety of footwear tend to spread their production over several factories, often situated in widely separated towns. This is largely because the operatives themselves are also specialized, and naturally prefer to stick to the work for which they have been trained. Bespoke boot- and shoe-making, or the making of shoes to suit individual customers' measurements, still continues, and there is a growing overseas trade in this class of work.

See also TANNING; LEATHER; CLOTHING INDUSTRY.

BOTTLE-MAKING, *see* GLASS-MAKING.

BOTTLING (BEER). Although the fashion of bottling beer has arisen largely during the present century, it is known that beer was put into bottles as far back as Queen Elizabeth's days. With the invention of modern automatic filling machines, bottled beer has been steadily increasing its sales. Before the Second World War brought about a shortage of bottles and machinery, it is probable that at least a quarter, and possibly a third, of the total beer output was being bottled.

The modern beer-bottling depot is a large one-story building, whose bottling units are served by mechanical conveyor-belts. Unless

Ind Coope and Allsopp

BOTTLING BEER BY MACHINERY
Bottles are passed on a conveyor-belt in a continuous stream to be filled, crowned, and labelled

the bottling depot is part of an actual brewery, a battery of cold-storage tanks will hold the beer that arrives by pipe-line or tank-wagon. From these tanks the beer is run to the bottling units.

After crates of empty bottles are brought by lorry to the inward loading stage of a modern depot, and placed on the conveyor-belt, they are scarcely touched again by hand. Crates containing the four different sizes of bottle used are automatically sorted as they pass along the conveyors. Each crate arrives at the intake end of the bottling unit which is dealing with a particular size of bottle. The bottles are lifted from the crate and placed in the intake of a washing-machine, which cleanses them and passes them by conveyor to the filling-machine. A modern counter-pressure filling machine is an intricate piece of mechanism, capable of dealing with 600 dozen bottles an hour. A row of bottles is automatically placed in position, and down into their mouths comes a corresponding row of filling nozzles, adjustable to suit bottles of different heights and capacities—although, of course, only one size is used at one time. These nozzles first seal the bottles and fill them with compressed air, thus enabling the beer to flow in what is called a 'counter-pressure'. This is done to prevent any loss of beer during the filling process, which is called 'fobbing'. This

method has proved the most satisfactory way of ensuring that bottles are filled to a level height, which yet leaves a certain amount of air-space to allow for expansion. Dead accuracy has proved impossible, but every precaution is taken to guard against the imperfectly filled bottle. For instance, a girl watches the bottles that come out of the filling-machine on a conveyor, and as the bottles pass between her eye and a bright light arranged for the purpose, she pulls out any 'rogues' and puts them aside.

Next comes the stopping of each bottle by machine. For the smaller sizes of bottle a metal crown-cork is used. For the larger sizes, closed with screw stoppers, a machine may be used, but these are still often put in by hand. For beers which are to be pasteurized, the pasteurizing machine, which is the largest machine of all in the bottling unit, is next in the chain. Pasteurizing is a way of destroying any organisms in the beer by rapidly raising the temperature and then rapidly lowering it. A bottle sometimes bursts during this process.

Not all brewers pasteurize their beer. Some breweries prefer to chill, filter, and carbonate their beers—processes which are carried out before the beer reaches the filling machines.

The last machine in the bottling unit is the labeller, but paper labels are not universal.

Many breweries use bottles which, in their manufacture, have had a permanent label affixed. Obviously such labels must be limited to giving the name, address, and trade-mark of the brewery; at different fillings the bottle might contain different beers, so that the contents are indicated either by the colour of the metal crown or by words printed on the crown.

Last of all the conveyor takes the bottles to a point where the empty crates are again met, filled, and passed on to the bottled beer store, or direct to the off-loading stage for the outward-bound lorries.

While most breweries bottle exclusively their own beers, the well-known national brands—such as Guinness, Bass, and Worthington—are as a rule supplied in cask to local breweries or other firms who carry out the bottling; and the name of the particular bottler is to be found on the label in addition to the brand name of the beer or stout itself.

See also BEER BREWING; CASK-MAKING.

BREAD-MAKING, see BAKING INDUSTRY. *See also* VOL. XI: BREAD.

BREWERIES, see BEER BREWING.

BRICKS AND TILES. 1. Bricks and tiles, whatever their shape and colour, are made of burnt clay. The difference between them is in the way they are used. Bricks form part of a wall or arch, and must therefore be strong enough to carry the load of floors and roofs and to make a stable structure. They must be solid blocks, but small enough to be handled easily. They are made oblong so that they can be 'bonded' together, or interlocked with each other. By contrast roofing-tiles have no weight to carry; in fact, their own weight is carried by the roofing-timbers. They are therefore made as thin and as light as possible, but must be able to keep out the rain and snow.

2. HISTORY. The word 'brick' is only about 500 years old, but 'tile' is derived from the Latin *tegula*. Both bricks and tiles were used very early in architectural history. Well-burnt bricks were made in Mesopotamia at least 6,000 years ago, and there are still great heaps of them in the ruins of the city of Babylon. This was probably where the brick-making industry began. In Egypt bricks made of Nile mud mixed with sand and straw, and dried in the sun, were used from prehistoric times. In the Bible we are told how the captive Israelites had to make bricks for their Egyptian masters. To oppress them, the Egyptians made them collect their own straw and make the same number of bricks as if they had been given the straw to start with. Egyptian peasants still make bricks of mud mixed with chopped straw, and then laid out to dry in the blazing sun; and most of the houses of the villagers in the Nile valley are built of this primitive material. Ancient Egyptian mud bricks were far larger than modern bricks, and were heavy to handle, often needing two men to lift them. Many brick buildings were erected in the countries governed by the Romans. We find bricks and tiles in England in the ruins of the chief Roman cities. Roman burnt bricks were also large (about 2 feet square), but they were only about 2 inches thick.

The arts of brick-making and brick building were lost in Britain after the Romans left about A.D. 400, and it was not until the late Middle Ages that bricks were used again in Britain. Houses and some churches, such as that of St. Osyth in Essex, were then built of brick in many parts of East Anglia. Flemish weavers had settled there, and at first the bricks used were imported from Flanders and Holland. From Tudor times onwards brick buildings became common. In 1625 the present standard size of approximately 9 by $4\frac{1}{2}$ in. by 3 in. was enforced by law, although the thickness was often less than the standard 3 inches. Centuries of experience have proved this size of brick to be the most convenient for handling, and therefore the most economical of labour.

In medieval times most houses in London were built of timber and roofed with thatch (*see* HOUSES, HISTORY OF, Vol. XI). Serious fires occurred in 1135 and 1212, resulting in a mayoral order of 1245 that, in future, all houses in the principal streets should be roofed with tiles or slates. Nevertheless, timber houses (for example, Staple Inn, 1586) continued to be built up to the time of the Great Fire of 1666. Then wooden houses were forbidden, and this naturally gave a fillip to the brick-making trade and to the bricklayer's craft. Since then brick has been the standard material in England for walls and chimneys, except in certain districts where stone is easily obtainable; but even in those districts stone has been largely replaced by brick in modern times. Attempts have recently been

Norman Wymer

MAKING BRICKS BY HAND
The surplus clay is being removed from the mould

various ways it fosters technical education in the crafts of bricklaying and tiling.

3. BRICK-MAKING. Suitable clay or 'brick earth' for brick-making is found in most countries. It occurs in layers which were originally formed by the gradual disintegration of various rocks, then washed off by currents of water and deposited in the beds of rivers, lakes, or seas which have long since disappeared (*see* CLAYS AND SHALES, Vol. III). The clay contains a large proportion of the chemical compounds silica (about 60%) and alumina (about 20%), together with variable amounts of oxide of iron, carbonate of lime, and alkaline materials (*see* ALKALIS). The silica, which is really sand, makes the clay porous and prevents shrinkage. The alumina makes it soft so that it can be moulded. The oxide of iron and the alkalis affect its colour, and the lime has a binding action. Too much iron and lime may be harmful; and crystals or fossils consisting of carbonate of lime may actually shatter the brick while it is being burnt.

In England there are several well-known varieties of brick. Pink Flettons are made from the 'shaley' Oxford Clay, which is dug at Fletton near Peterborough, and elsewhere in the East Midlands. Yellow London Stocks come from deposits of limey clay found in Kent and Essex. White or pale yellow Suffolks come from mixtures of chalk and clay in Suffolk and adjoining areas, and the hard Staffordshire Blues used for heavy engineering work from clay rich in iron. Luton Greys are still made by hand from clay found in the Luton area.

The processes of brick-making are excavation, preparation, mixing, moulding, drying, and burning. Nowadays most of this work is done by machinery, and even when hand-moulding is done, mechanical excavators are generally employed to dig the clay. Before the clay-beds are reached, a layer of 'overburden', that is, of loamy vegetable soil, has to be removed. Sometimes this is as thick as 40 feet or more, but in England it is usually only a thin layer. For hand-made bricks the excavated clay is often exposed to the air for some months before the grinding process is begun. Grinding the clay, to ensure its fineness, is performed by mechanical crushers with rollers. The material is next 'screened' to remove any large particles that have survived the grinding process, and 'tempered' by adding water to give the clay its proper amount of moisture. This tempering is some-

made to find substitutes for brick, and many alternative systems of construction, mostly involving the use of concrete, have been evolved, but in several respects brick continues to hold its own. Brick should never be regarded as an inferior building material. If properly treated architecturally, it can be as beautiful in its way as stone, and it keeps its warmth of colour in all but the sootiest atmospheres. As the Roman work found at Verulamium (St. Albans) and elsewhere proves, brick is also extremely lasting, but this depends on the quality of the clay used and the efficiency of manufacture. All these remarks apply equally to tiles. One of the best examples of fine old brickwork in England is Hampton Court Palace. The earlier part, Wolsey's building (1515–23), is typical of Tudor work; the later part, Wren's building (1689–1702), shows English brickwork at its finest, and the bricks used have preserved their brilliant colour for nearly three centuries.

The Worshipful Company of Tylers and Bricklayers was founded in the City of London at some unknown date in the Middle Ages, and obtained its first charter in 1568. It is still in existence. It is one of the smaller CITY COMPANIES (q.v.) and has no hall of its own; but in

times called 'pugging', and is done by means of a 'pug mill'.

The clay is then moulded by hand or machinery. Hand-moulding consists in pressing a lump of pugged clay into a four-sided wooden or metal mould, rather larger than the finished size of the brick to allow for shrinkage. If it is desired to give the brick a 'sand face', which produces an attractive rough appearance on the exterior of a building, the moulder sprinkles sand inside the mould; otherwise water only is used, to prevent the clay from sticking to the mould. In mechanical moulding a continuous column or band of clay is forced through a mouth-piece of the desired size, and is cut off by wires into slices, each slice being the size of a finished brick when allowance has been made for shrinkage. In another process the clay may be fed into moulds, much as in the hand process.

The bricks are next dried, either out-of-doors for 3 to 6 weeks in long rows ('hacks'), or in heated brick tunnels in less than 48 hours; trucks of bricks are sometimes slowly moved mechanically through the tunnel. Drying is necessary because the bricks are too 'tender' immediately after moulding to be able to stand burning at once.

Burning, or firing, is a highly technical process, which may be carried out either in clamps or in kilns. A clamp is a primitive or temporary form of kiln, in which the 'green' (unburnt) bricks are stacked, with passages between them to admit air and fuel. The green bricks rest on a floor of burnt bricks, and the whole stack is enclosed in a temporary skin of two layers of burnt bricks and daubed over with clay. Fuel may be built into the stacks, or oil-firing may be used. Proper kilns are usually of either the continuous or the tunnel types. A continuous kiln contains a series of compartments in which all the successive stages of burning are carried on at the same time, the fire being regulated to travel round the various compartments at the right temperature and for the right period. In a tunnel kiln there are compartments or sections of tunnel for each stage of firing, and the green bricks are conveyed through them on trucks, the fire in each section remaining at a constant temperature.

4. TILE-MAKING. Clay roofing-tiles are made in much the same way, although their size is governed by British Standard Specifications (*see* STANDARDS, Vol. VIII). A plain tile is $10\frac{1}{2}$ in. long, $6\frac{1}{2}$ in. wide, and $\frac{3}{8}$ to $\frac{7}{8}$ in. thick. The tiles are made slightly convex on the outside so that each 'course' (or row) of tiles presses firmly

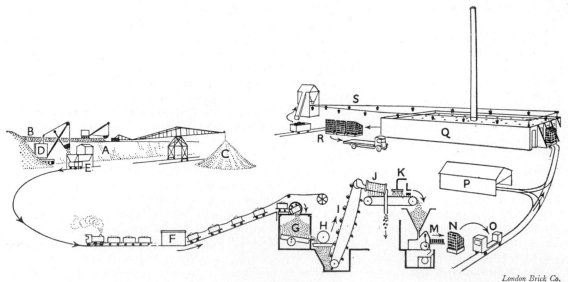

London Brick Co.

DIAGRAM OF A BRICKWORKS

A. Clay quarry. B. Spoil (topsoil, rock, &c.). C. Spoil dump. D. Clay excavator. E. Clay sorting machine with automatic loading into wagons. F. Chain loading station. G. Raw clay storage hoppers. H. Clay grinding pans. I. Ground clay elevator. J. Rotary screen. K. Water sprayer. L. Mixing plough. M. Brick pressing machine. N. 'Green' bricks loaded on car. O. Transfer car. P. Machines for sand facing 'green' bricks. Q. Kiln. R. Finished bricks. S. Endless ropeway delivering fuel to feeding holes in kiln top

'GREEN' BRICKS FROM THE PRESSES (M IN DIAGRAM) ARE LOADED ON TO ELECTRIC CARS WHICH TAKE THEM TO THE KILNS

down on to the course beneath, and thus keeps out rain. Each has two nail-holes near the top, and two projecting 'nibs', so that the tiles may be either nailed or hung to the wooden battens beneath. The specially-shaped tiles needed for the eaves, hips, valleys, and ridge of the roof are also made of the same materials. Tiles, as well as bricks, may be manufactured with glazed faces (*see* TILES, ORNAMENTAL).

See also BUILDING INDUSTRY, HISTORY OF.
See also Vol. XI: HOUSES, HISTORY OF.

BRISTLES, *see* BRUSHES.

BROKER. This is a person whose work, like that of an AGENT (q.v.), is to bring together a buyer and a seller. Legally there is no difference between a broker and an agent; both are regarded as the legal representatives of their 'principals' (the people employing them) and the principals are bound by any engagements into which their agents enter on their behalf. A broker, however, differs from an agent in the way in which he carries out his duties. This function is generally to introduce a buyer to a seller, leaving them to arrange and settle their business themselves. Payment may be transmitted through him, but he does not actually handle his principal's goods. An agent, on the other hand, acts practically as though he were part of his principal's organization; he may hold a stock of the goods; he signs contracts of sale for his principal, collects the money, and accounts for it to his principal.

In the commercial world, therefore, the word 'agent' is usually reserved for a person or firm dealing in a physical sense with actual goods, and 'broker' for one who deals with contracts on paper, such as transactions in foreign exchange, rates of freight on cargoes, insurance, and in STOCKS AND SHARES (q.v.). The word 'broker' is also applied to firms who arrange for the buying and selling of large quantities of commodities or produce, for this is done by means of a paper contract to accept or deliver goods at some future date. The actual physical delivery of the goods is handled by shipping and forwarding agents.

The words 'broker' and 'agent' are often loosely applied, and it is rather unsafe to suppose that all persons or firms using these names really merit them in the strict commercial sense.

See also AGENT.

BRUSHES can be classified as personal, household, trade, and industrial. Personal brushes include tooth-brushes, hair-brushes, shaving-brushes, nail-brushes, and brushes for cosmetics. Household brushes include scrubbing-brushes and brooms of various kinds, boot and shoe brushes, and clothes-brushes. Trade brushes are made for tradesmen or craftsmen, such as housepainters, artists, draughtsmen, and bill-posters. Some industrial processes involve the use of mechanical brushes, many of which are used in the textile industries.

The backs or handles of brushes are made of various materials: of metal, wood, bone, ivory, celluloid, rubber, vulcanized fibre, and different forms of plastic material. Metal backs or holders are usual for industrial brushes. Bone handles are usually made by machinery from the shinbones of cattle. Brush fibres must be stiff and resistant without being brittle, and they must also be reasonably flexible. There is much variety in the fibres used for brush-making, vegetable, animal, or synthetic. Of the synthetic fibres, NYLON (q.v.) is the one most frequently

used, not only for tooth-brushes, but also for personal, household, and industrial brushes. The most important vegetable fibres are coir and bass. Coir is the fibre that grows on the outside shell of the coconut. Most of the world's coir comes from Ceylon. It is a very popular brush material in Europe, although little of it is used in the U.S.A. Bass is a palm-leaf fibre, and the best comes from Brazil. It is used for making good-quality clothes-brushes. A coarser bass, called kittul, used for domestic scrubbing-brushes, comes principally from India, Malaya, and the East Indies (*see also* FIBRE CROPS, Section 8, Vol. VI).

Brush fibres of animal origin are either pigs' bristles or the hair of other animals. The pigs' bristles used in the trade come from the top middle part of the back and are removed after the animals have been slaughtered. Before the Second World War, China was the world's biggest exporter of pigs' bristles; Russia took second place. The southern provinces of China exported the stiff variety, and the northern provinces the soft.

Hair taken from the bodies of cattle is not used in brush-making, but the tufts of hair inside the ears are much used. This hair is known in the trade as 'ox hair'. Cheap cosmetic and shaving-brushes are often made from the face hair of goats. Real camel hair is not used for brush-making; the 'camel hair' brushes sold are generally made from the tail hair of squirrels. The hair of the badger is much prized in brush-making, and the best shaving-brushes are made from it. The finest quality of badger hair is known as 'silver top'; it is dark in colour, with a white tip (*see* HAIR TRADE).

In the brush-making trade the various fibres are called 'material'. Material is first subjected to various processes, such as grading, sizing, oiling, drying, combing, and bundling. The individual bundles of material that fit into the holes in the holders are called 'knots'.

Norman Wymer

MAKING BRUSHES BY HAND
Fixing the backs of dairy brushes

The first process in brush-making proper is to drill or bore the backs or handles to receive the material. The material is fixed into the handles by one of three different methods, 'drawn work', 'trepanning', and 'bone-setting'. In drawn work, which is used for most household and personal brushes such as tooth-brushes and nail-brushes, the material is passed through the hole in a loop of wire, which is then pulled tight. In the trepanning method, which is used for the best hairbrushes, channels are cut along the lines of the drilled holes, and wires are drawn tightly to connect the separate knots of material together. Bone-setting is the method used for household brooms and similar large articles. Each knot of material is dipped into heated tar or pitch, tied with cord dressed with tar, and twisted into its hole. All these three processes have now been fully mechanized. The brushes used by house-painters and artists have tin containers at the brush end of the handle and into these the material is inserted and cemented or vulcanized. The final or finishing processes in brush-making are glueing on the backs, to hide the fixing of the material, and, if the backs are decorative, covering them with such material as gold, silver, ivory, leather, or highly polished veneers.

Kleen-e-ze Brush Co.

BRUSH-MAKING BY MACHINERY

The machine fills the back with tufts at the rate of 80 tufts a minute

BUDGETARY CONTROL. This is the name given to a system of financial management in modern business, rather like the nation's annual Budget, or estimate of revenue and expenditure (*see* NATIONAL FINANCE, Vol. X). Before the adoption of budgetary control, financial management in business was not so precise. No exact estimates of income and expenditure were made in advance; money might run short at the most inconvenient times, and promising trading activities consequently have to be curtailed.

If a firm adopts budgetary control, its managing director and his chief accountant prepare a budgetary statement at the beginning of the trading year. The statement is based mainly on an estimate of the quantities and types of goods likely to be profitably manufactured or sold during the coming year. Past STATISTICS (q.v.), and the trends they show, play an important part in framing this estimate, which is the foundation on which the whole scheme rests. Influences that may cause during the year any changes in selling prices, in the prices of raw materials, and in wages and other costs, are taken into account. In businesses whose activities are organized into departments, the trading estimate is drawn up departmentally.

This forecast of future business is then expanded into detailed estimates of expenditure and income, month by month, for the firm's plans must not be checked at any point through lack of money. There may be special reasons why money may be likely to run short at different times of the year—seasonal buying programmes, for instance. Steps must be taken to guard against this by selling INVESTMENTS or obtaining bank LOANS (qq.v.). If the coming year's programme involves building extensions, replacing machinery, or buying new plant to expand the production of some particularly promising line, new CAPITAL (q.v.) may be necessary, and the budget should state its amount and the way in which it will be raised.

In a manufacturing business 'standard' costs and outputs, representing objectives to be attained by the various departments, are circulated to those in charge. In a merchanting or distributing business, weekly or monthly 'targets' are framed for each department. In department stores or big retail establishments the budgetary forecast takes account of periodical bargain sales or other 'events', and what these should produce in terms of actual money. Throughout the year the detailed budget enables the head of the business to keep a continuous check on the performance of the various departments.

See also BOOK-KEEPING; BUSINESS ORGANIZATION; STATISTICS.

BUILDING INDUSTRY, HISTORY OF.

The building industry still retains many traditional features and practices that have grown up through 60 centuries or more. Some of the processes of bricklaying, carpentry, plastering, and painting, known to the ancient Egyptians and Babylonians in the earliest times, are still in use to-day.

The history of the industry in Britain really begins with the Roman occupation. The excavated remains of Roman towns and villas (country houses) disclose brick or stone walls, tiled roofs, lead water-pipes, central heating by hot air carried up from furnaces through flues under the floors and up the walls, and beautiful mosaic pavements. Many examples of Roman craftsmanship in all the separate trades of the industry are also to be seen in the museums at York, Verulamium (St. Albans), and the London Guildhall. Methods of building in Rome itself are set out in a book written by the architect Vitruvius some 2,000 years ago. It tells of the ways of building, and the municipal by-laws, although all these practices would not have been followed exactly in the remote province of Britain.

After the Romans left in the 5th century, there was a long gap in the progress of building in Britain, which only revived after the Norman Conquest. Some building was certainly done during those 6 centuries, but it was rustic and rudimentary, and far inferior to the work of the Romans. The period from 1066 to the time of Elizabeth, a matter of 5 centuries, may be treated as a whole; for although architecture advanced from the stern castles and the massive round-arched cathedrals of Norman days to the graceful structures of late Gothic times, methods of building remained much the same.

During the 11th and 12th centuries the building of structures other than castles and parish churches and certain cathedrals was largely carried out by order of the numerous monasteries. It was long thought that the monks themselves designed and erected all such buildings, but it is now generally believed that the monasteries depended almost entirely upon hired laymen for all building work.

In any medieval building there were two leading people in charge of the work. One was financial and administrative; the other was the technically qualified 'master'. The first looked after estimates, wages, and bills for materials, and he sometimes provided transport. Sometimes he also furnished the materials. His title was usually *custos fabricae*, 'keeper of the works'. One official of this kind was William of Wykeham, the founder of Winchester College, who acted as 'Surveyor of the Works' at Windsor Castle in his early days. Another was Geoffrey CHAUCER (q.v. Vol. V). Although he was styled 'Clerk of the Works', or 'Devisor', he had no technical training, and was a civil servant in administrative charge of building operations at the Palace of Westminster.

Most of the materials used were obtained in Britain, but Caen stone from Normandy was imported in large quantities from very early times and was used for St. Albans Abbey and for St. Paul's Cathedral soon after the Norman Conquest. Brick was very little used in England before the 14th century, and then mainly in East Anglia. Many of the bricks used there were imported from Flanders, the craft of brick-work having been introduced by Flemish settlers. Belgian marble was also imported until it was largely replaced by native Purbeck marble (*see* MARBLE AND ALABASTER). Although most of the timber used was home-grown oak, the importation of softwoods from Scandinavia began in the 13th century, and Henry III ordered a chamber at Windsor Castle to be specially panelled in Norway pine.

All this imported material was shipped to the nearest harbour, or to a point on a navigable river nearest to the site of the building. No good roads then existed, the only alternative to water-carriage being packhorse transport, a slow and costly business. In some parts of England, notably the south-eastern and eastern counties, where no suitable stone was available locally, all English stone as well as foreign stone had to be water-borne; the stone for Eton College Chapel came from as far away as Huddleston in Yorkshire. The fine churches of Norfolk and Suffolk

Bibl. de la Ville, Geneva

BUILDING IN THE 15TH CENTURY

In the foreground a mason is carving a stone, and a carpenter is smoothing a joist with an adze. Men are laying
tiles on roofs and, behind, others are mixing and using mortar.

were mostly built of limestone from quarries in Lincolnshire, Northamptonshire, and Rutland; but many of them had walls and towers of local flint, with only the dressings, columns, and carved details in limestone. The expense of transport thus formed a substantial item in the cost of any medieval building, and for Vale Royal Abbey, in Cheshire, built by 1280 (where accurate accounts have been preserved) it amounted to three times the cost of the material, although the distance to be covered was only 4 or 5 miles. Roofs in medieval days were mostly covered with English lead. The use of tiles began in the 13th century, when kilns (furnaces for baking bricks) are known to have been in operation; and in 1212 the roofs of all London houses, which until then had been covered with thatch or wood 'shingles', were ordered to be tiled as a result of a disastrous fire. Slates, for roofing at Abingdon Abbey, are mentioned in 1404 (*see* SLATE INDUSTRY).

Building contracts in the Middle Ages were arranged between the employer and the various separate building trades. At that time, and indeed for centuries afterwards, there was no such person as the 'master builder' or 'building contractor', undertaking work in all the crafts. The important element in most medieval buildings was stone, and the most important craftsman on any building was the mason. Thus the person who carried out the functions of the modern architect, designing and superintending the erection of the building, was normally drawn from the ranks of the master-masons. The names of hundreds of such men are known, and the title most commonly applied to them was 'master' (*magister*, if in Latin documents), not 'master-mason'. They were mainly trained by a period of apprenticeship at the mason's bench; they used plans and models, and they were treated as professional men, sometimes taking on several commissions at the same time, just as a modern architect conducts his 'practice'. Their services were competed for by rival patrons.

Various medieval contracts with building trades have been preserved and published, as well as a large number of complete accounts for royal and church buildings. Sometimes the master-mason or master-carpenter would estimate for labour and plant only, the employer providing materials and transport; sometimes the contractor might include transport too, or even transport and materials. The number of

men employed on a single contract was often very large; for example, at Beaumaris Castle in the 14th century there were 1,630 men at work; and at Windsor Castle in 1361 no fewer than 1,360 masons were forcibly recruited from all over Britain.

The enormous amount and high quality of the building carried out in Britain during the Middle Ages, when the population was relatively small, suggests that a pious enthusiasm must have led to high output; but we now know that actual conditions of labour were not ideal. Hours of work were certainly long, usually from sunrise to sunset. Thus at York Minster, in the 14th century, 20 minutes was allowed for breakfast, an hour for dinner—followed by an extra hour for a rest in the summer—and a few minutes for a drink in the late afternoon. There were numerous saints' days which were observed as HOLIDAYS (q.v. Vol. IX), generally without pay. 'Wet-time', when the weather prevented certain building operations, was seldom paid for. In spite of research, it is almost impossible to estimate the real value of the WAGES (q.v.) paid in those remote times—only a few pence a day— or to compare them with modern rates, but it is fairly clear that modern wages are higher. There was a wide difference of pay between the grades of skilled and unskilled labour. Freedom for building workers was limited. There were fines for being late or drunk, for quarrelling, idling, losing tools, bad language, and obstruction of other workmen—usually 'foreigners', as workers from any other town were called. There were also frequent disputes between the members of the various craft guilds as to the precise tasks that each should do.

The CRAFT GUILDS with their elaborate system of APPRENTICESHIP (q.v.) and the guilds connected with building follow the same pattern. The Livery Companies of the City of London still exist to promote the interests of the various trades or crafts, and they include the building crafts of Carpenters, Glaziers, Masons, Joiners, Painter Stainers, Plasterers, Plumbers, Tylers and Bricklayers (*see* CITY COMPANIES). The elaborate organization of the FREEMASONS (q.v. Vol. X) began in the 17th century, with the admission of amateur members to the masons' guilds, on the ground of their special interest in the craft as antiquaries or patrons.

The sweeping social changes that followed the Renaissance and the Reformation affected the

BUILDING IN THE EARLY 19TH CENTURY
The methods had changed little since the Middle Ages

Towards the end of the 18th century the development of ROADS, CANALS, and BRIDGES (qq.v. Vol. IV), closely followed by the use of structural ironwork and the invention of the steam-engine, led to the rise of CIVIL ENGINEERING (q.v. Vol. VIII) as an industry allied to building. Possibly the appearance of the master-builder and general contractor about the same time may have been caused indirectly by these changes. Shortly afterwards the quantity-surveyor came into existence as an independent profession. TRADE UNIONS (q.v) in the various building crafts began with the foundation in 1800 of the Friendly Society of Carpenters and Joiners, and developed rapidly during the 19th century into the enormous federated unions of to-day. Yet, in spite of all these sweeping changes, the independent existence of the various crafts has still persisted in some parts of Britain, where the idea of the master-builder is still accepted with reluctance.

See also Vol. XI: HOUSES, HISTORY OF.

BUILDING INDUSTRY, ORGANIZATION.

The building industry plays a very important part in Britain's economy, not only by providing houses and public buildings of all kinds, but also because industry depends upon it for its factories. Every extension of demand for electrical power requires further power-stations, every effort to develop our production involves new factories, and even COAL-MINING (q.v.) needs pithead premises of modern type to replace out-of-date structures. But on the other hand the building industry depends indirectly upon coal in large quantities for three of its chief materials, bricks, cement, and steel, and the current cost of coal directly influences the cost of building.

The amount of building material imported from overseas is relatively slight, although timber and timber products, including certain building boards which are a BY-PRODUCT (q.v.) of the saw-mills, are important exceptions. Comparatively little building material is exported. In Britain the natural materials obtainable from the soil include stone, which is less used than formerly because skilled workmen are scarce; gravel and sand for making concrete; clay for making bricks, tiles, and cement; lime for cement and plaster; some of the components of glass; slates; some of the ironstone required for the iron and steel used; and a small amount of timber. Most of the timber needed is imported: SOFTWOODS

building industry in the 16th century. The Church lost its leading position as a patron of building. Wealthy merchants and noblemen built large mansions, and many colleges and schools were founded. Men called architects began to be employed, as learned persons who could apply the fashionable rules of Roman and Italian architecture (see ITALIAN ART, Vol. XII). But medieval conditions with regard to transport and the supply of materials persisted, with little change, except that more timber was imported. The various crafts continued to be separate.

The speculative builder first appeared in London towards the end of the 17th century. One famous speculator in building sites was a doctor, Nicholas Barbon, M.P., who died in 1698. He bought large mansions with their gardens, and then sold off small lots to builders who erected dwelling-houses on them. He was followed by many enterprising speculators who laid out the fine squares of Bloomsbury and the West End.

BRICKLAYERS BUILDING THE WALLS OF A SMALL HOUSE
Plumb rule and spirit level are used to keep the brickwork upright and level. (From *Building* by permission of the Controller of H.M. Stationery Office)

from Canada and the Baltic countries, HARD-WOODS from the Empire and Dominions (qq.v.). Efforts have been made in recent years to reduce Britain's demands for imported timber by using steel, concrete, and other home-produced materials. Much of the IRON ORE (q.v.) is imported. Lead comes from various countries abroad, including the Dominions. Asphalt is obtained partly from Trinidad, in the British West Indies, partly from the continent of Europe. ASBESTOS (q.v.) is another imported material. Marble for decorative wall-linings and paving is mainly imported, but a certain amount of real marble, and of limestone resembling marble, is found in Britain (*see* MARBLE AND ALABASTER). Between the First and Second World Wars there was an increasing tendency to import ready-made joinery, principally doors and windows, from Sweden, but difficulties in foreign trade have checked this.

Like agriculture, the building industry is distributed fairly evenly over the whole country. Also like agriculture, the industry tends to remain somewhat conservative, and unresponsive to new ideas. This is perhaps owing to its long history (*see* BUILDING INDUSTRY, HISTORY) and to its tradition of manual work carried out on the

site, or at benches in the master-builder's own workshops. Mechanization, however, is gradually changing the character of the industry, although not as quickly as in the United States; and PREFABRICATION (q.v. Vol. VIII), together with standardization, has certainly come to stay. The difference between building and CIVIL ENGINEERING (q.v. Vol. VIII) cannot be sharply drawn, for some very large firms operate as 'civil engineering and building contractors', and are equally prepared to erect the buildings of an aerodrome or to lay its giant runways; but most building firms confine themselves to building only.

A remarkable feature of the industry in Britain is the large number of very small firms. More than 40% of those registered in 1949 were 'one-man businesses', and nearly as many as this employed fewer than six operatives apiece. Only a small percentage of firms are large concerns with hundreds of workers. Inevitably there is a contrast between the organization of the normal, medium-sized building firm employing from 10 to 100 hands, and that of the normal engineering or manufacturing firm employing a much larger number.

The conditions of work, too, are entirely different. Most building takes place on sites miles away from the builder's premises, and is carried on out-of-doors with constant interruption by bad weather; while, without interruption, factory work can be carried on continuously. The larger staff employed in a normal factory also allows shift-working and holidays to be better organized, and permits apprentices to be released for day-training far more easily than is possible on the average builder's staff. In time, the spread of prefabrication will reduce work on the site to a minimum, but even then it will obviously be impossible to eliminate site-work altogether. Meanwhile, it is easier to recruit labour for a dry and warm factory than for work in the open in all weathers.

Builders in Britain may be roughly divided into three classes: the small 'jobbing builder', the speculative builder, and the building contractor. A single firm may carry out work under all three heads. A jobbing builder's business is often run by one man, and rarely employs as many as half a dozen men. A jobbing builder may himself practise all the crafts from bricklaying to plumbing, though he has probably been trained originally in only one of them.

Taylor Woodrow Const. L.d.

THE CONSTRUCTION OF GOVERNMENT OFFICES IN LONDON

The thirteen floors will be supported by a frame of steel girders. The walls are stone in the lower stories and brick above. Maximum height of the building is 135 feet.

Sometimes he practises a single craft, carpentry for example, and employs a bricklayer, a plumber, and a painter as his assistants, and is then very like the building contractor. Although he does not fit easily into the usual industrial division between employer and trained operative, he is a most useful member of the community. He is ready to help the householder in all emergencies, whereas a large and well-organized building firm is often too busy to risk slowing down carefully prepared time-tables on large contracts merely to adjust a flushing-cistern or replace a few roof-tiles.

The speculative builder erects buildings at his own risk in the hope of finding a purchaser. The work of speculative builders has sometimes been inartistic or structurally unsound, or both; but this need not be so, and sometimes it is above reproach. A house built by a speculative builder, to be sold to an unknown purchaser, may be as good in every way as a house erected by a contractor, to the designs of a competent architect, under strict conditions. The speculative builder himself may employ an architect to prepare the design, and for the sake of his own reputation and profit may observe as high standards of materials and workmanship as if he were bound by the terms of a strict contract. The speculative builder does not confine himself to dwelling-houses; he also erects factories, shops, and offices at his own risk, to sell or to let to prospective customers.

In the past the speculative builder has provided a high proportion of the houses in Britain. The State does not require any guarantee that a speculative builder is efficient, and anybody may set up in business as such. In 1937 an attempt was made to meet this defect by the formation of the National House-Builders' Registration Council, supported by a powerful group of architects, builders, and building societies. The Council produced a scheme by which houses would be offered to the public under a guarantee of materials and workmanship, and the scheme included model specifications. The various BUILDING SOCIETIES (q.v.) have served the needs of numerous people who could not afford to have their own houses built, or lacked the confidence to do so.

The general contractor, like the speculative builder, often begins in a very small way. The founders of many of the largest contracting firms in Britain have been ambitious and gifted craftsmen who have borrowed or saved sufficient CAPITAL (q.v.) to enable them to set up in business on their own. Before the building can begin, an architect has to draw up plans of the building. He often consults engineers about problems of heating and electricity. A 'quantity-surveyor' then draws up from the architect's plans a 'bill of quantities', which sets out the amount of labour and materials required to complete the job. The builder himself usually has to give the owner of the property an estimate of how much money the work will cost, and sometimes an owner will ask for estimates from several builders so that he can make a choice. When the building is actually going on, a 'clerk-of-the-works' watches the work to see that it is being done according to the architect's plan, and inspectors of the municipal authorities have to see that local by-laws are observed.

The type of labour employed on any contract varies with the type of building. According to a recent census it is about equally divided between the so-called 'skilled' and 'unskilled' grades of workmen. The former include craftsmen in the traditional crafts of CARPENTRY AND JOINERY (q.v.), masonry, bricklaying, slating and tiling, plastering, plumbing, and painting. Masonry, nowadays a much smaller trade than carpentry and joinery, has tended to decrease because of the expense of cutting stone by hand (see STONE DRESSING). Plastering, which involves delays in waiting for successive coats of wet plaster to dry, is being superseded to some extent by building boards. The technique of plumbing is also changing its character with the increasing use of copper, and with the introduction, especially into small houses, of completely prefabricated 'plumbing units', including the heating apparatus and sanitary fittings. The trades of slating, tiling, painting, and bricklaying retain most of their traditional character. The so-called 'unskilled' labour includes not only the labourers attached to the various traditional crafts, but also the increasingly high proportion of workers who handle prefabricated units and deal with concrete work, reinforced or otherwise. Some of this work demands a fair degree of skill. Electricians are not usually reckoned as belonging to the building trades.

Increasing efforts are now being made to manufacture in advance, inside a factory, every possible part of a building, so that work on the site will be reduced to a minimum. This may draw more workers to the industry. APPRENTICESHIP (q.v.) is sometimes difficult, partly because very small firms engaged on cheap buildings cannot easily train learners, and partly because so much building takes place on remote sites. Pre-apprenticeship training is provided in many Building Technical Schools. Training for apprentices is organized in part-time day-classes as well as in evening schools, and examinations for all the building crafts are conducted by the City and Guilds of London Institute for candidates from all over Britain.

See also STONE QUARRYING; TIMBER INDUSTRY; SLATE INDUSTRY; BRICKS AND TILES.

See also Vol. VIII: PREFABRICATION.
See also Vol. XII: ARCHITECTURE.
See also Vol. XI: HOUSES, HISTORY OF.

BUILDING SOCIETIES. Many people wishing to own houses cannot usually put up, in a lump sum, the rather large amount of money necessary. They aim to borrow the money, and to pay it back with interest over a long term of years, sometimes 20 or 25, at a yearly charge not much greater than the equivalent rent. British banks restrict themselves to lending money for comparatively short periods. It would therefore be outside banking business to lend money to people whose aim is ultimately to own a house. Building societies, therefore, have grown up in order to help people build or buy a house of their own.

The building society is essentially a British growth, because on the Continent, and in most overseas countries, houses and flats are either rented from owners who make property investment their business, or are bought and sold outright. Foreign banks, also, are less insistent than British banks on confining themselves to short-term transactions. Except in a few capital cities, therefore, there is no exact equivalent of the British building society.

When it receives an application for an advance, the society first proceeds to value the property which the applicant proposes to buy, or land on which he proposes to build a house. Having agreed on a valuation of the property, the building society will usually consent to advance up to four-fifths of the valuation, and sometimes up to nine-tenths of it. The prospective buyer then signs a mortgage deed (*see* PROPERTY LAW, section 4, Vol. X) in favour of the society, and the financial details are arranged between the buyer's solicitor and the society. The society then completes the purchase.

The current rate of interest on building society advances is about $5\frac{1}{2}\%$ per annum. Each successive payment consists of increasing portions of repayment of the capital sum borrowed, and decreasing portions of INTEREST (q.v.) on the remainder still unpaid. At the end of the 20 or 25 years of the contract, when the last instalment of capital and interest has been paid over, the society executes a conveyance or transfer of the property into the buyer's name, and he then becomes the owner of the property.

Building Societies are mostly registered under the FRIENDLY SOCIETIES Acts (q.v. Vol. X), and are not organized as ordinary limited companies under the Companies Acts: they therefore stand midway between public utilities and private enterprise. This means that their capital is not a fixed amount, and that fresh SHARES (q.v.) may be issued as business expands. In addition to raising CAPITAL (q.v.) by obtaining share subscriptions, the societies also accept large sums of money on deposit for fixed periods, and the funds they have to lend thus come from both sources. The societies have the duty of ensuring that their advances are regularly repaid and that they are not made against over-generous valuations of property. A borrower who fails to keep up his repayments will often receive consideration. Many societies arrange for a temporary cessation of instalments during sickness or unemployment; in certain circumstances, a new and extended contract is entered into.

Most of the houses financed by Building Societies in Britain are small houses in suburbs and the country. The same methods have been adopted elsewhere, but chiefly to help people to buy land for farming. 'Land and Mortgage Banks' have this use in America and the chief British Dominions.

BULK PURCHASE. This is the system by which the government of a country controls the import of food and raw materials and prevents the produce merchants importing as much as they could profitably sell. In modern times bulk purchase was first organized by Russia after the Revolution of 1917, although 2,000 years earlier the Roman government made similar arrangements for the import of breadstuffs for the population of the city. Bulk purchase was instituted in Britain as a war-time measure during the Second World War, for ships were scarce, and food rationing without such a system of control would have been impossible.

Bulk purchase involved the closing down of many of the produce and commodity markets open for free dealings before the war, such as the Liverpool Cotton Exchange, the London Metal Exchange, the London Corn Exchange, and other similar institutions in other cities. Government Departments, such as the Ministry of Supply and the Ministry of Food, decided beforehand the quantities of various goods that would be imported. These Departments then made direct arrangements for the supply of such goods with governments or central selling agencies abroad, and long-term agreements were signed covering requirements for a number of years in advance. The bulk purchase of some of these goods continued during the years of scarcity after the war. Trading questions of this kind now form an important part of the diplomatic relations between governments.

BUSINESS ORGANIZATION. 1. This means the detailed arrangements made in any business for taking decisions and converting them into action. There is little need for organization in a business where the owner is the only person employed in it—a small retail shop, for example. The owner of such a business both makes decisions and carries them into effect, and he can modify his policy as he carries it out. But in a large business there must be a division between the management who take decisions, and the staff who carry them out. Decisions reached by the heads of the firm must reach those who have to carry them out. Reports must also travel in the reverse direction, from the bottom to the

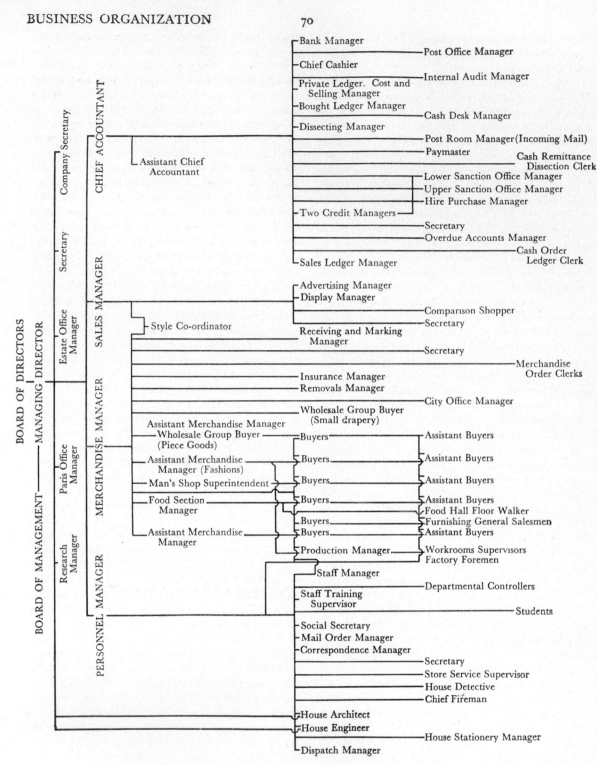

THE ORGANIZATION OF HARRODS, LTD., IN 1939
The chart shows how the various departments are controlled

top: for managerial policy, like tactics in a battle, must be continuously modified as circumstances change.

There is no standard pattern of organization for all firms, or even for firms engaged in the same line of trade. Much depends on how the business has grown up. Old forms of organization, adopted many years earlier when the business was young, may still work well, because everybody is accustomed to them, and they have become part of the tradition of the business. But there are two general principles of organization that should be followed by all concerns. The first is that the duties and responsibilities of everyone, down to the most junior employee, must be very carefully defined. Everybody should know precisely what his job is, and duties should neither be left undone because nobody has been made responsible for them, nor be overlapped by more than one person or department. Secondly, responsibility should descend from top to bottom in a straight line. Each individual should have a single superior only, from whom alone he receives his orders, and to whom alone he renders his reports.

2. POLICY AND MANAGEMENT. All businesses in Britain, with a few exceptions, are one-man firms, PARTNERSHIPS, or LIMITED COMPANIES (qq.v.). The exceptions are mostly of a large and important nature, including State-owned businesses, such as the POST OFFICE and British RAILWAYS; certain non-profit-making enterprises governed by Act of Parliament, such as the B.B.C. and the Port of London Authority (*see* PORTS, HISTORY OF, Vol. IV) and some municipal businesses run by BOROUGH COUNCILS (q.v. Vol. X), such as markets or bus services. Other special kinds of business organization are those of the CO-OPERATIVE SOCIETIES and certain PUBLIC UTILITY COMPANIES (qq.v.).

Many ordinary limited companies are no bigger than partnerships, and in their organization they follow the same pattern. Neither one-man firms nor partnerships can be of any great size, for their CAPITAL (q.v.) is limited to what the owner or partners can subscribe. In a one-man business of fair size the owner will decide policy and his subordinates will carry it out. Each department has a head who receives his instructions from the proprietor and makes his reports to him direct. In a partnership business the partners usually have different qualifications and interests. In such firms each partner is often

the active head of the department whose duties suit him best, and there are frequent meetings among the partners to compare notes and adjust policy. Such a form of organization comes very close to the ideal, as those who carry out policy are also those who decide what it is to be.

In large companies the problems of organization become complex. A company is owned by shareholders, but they do not decide on its policy or constitute its management; and they therefore entrust the management to a small body of directors, seldom more than a dozen and often not more than five or six, who are called the Board. The head of the Board is the Chairman, but in many companies his position is not strictly executive, and a managing director is appointed for the general day-to-day management of the firm. In some companies one or two of the directors may have specialized business knowledge, and may be able to put in full-time service. As in partnerships, such persons may be placed in executive charge of departments. It is important that the position of the managing director should not be weakened by such arrangements, and directors so appointed must not be allowed to take decisions on their own without reference to the managing director or to the Board as a whole.

3. ORGANIZATION OF DEPARTMENTS. There can be no set pattern. The departmental organization for a trading firm engaged solely in buying and selling goods must differ from that which would suit a manufacturing business. But there are certain general principles that most businesses follow. A strict division is usually made between finance and accounts (*see* BOOK-KEEPING), buying, selling, secretarial, and legal matters, ADVERTISING AND PUBLICITY (q.v.), and staff control and recruitment. The finance officer or accountant deals with the financial records and accounts, and with records of stocks and supplies of goods. Usually he also supervises the collection and assembly of STATISTICS (q.v.), and if the firm is run on scientific lines and adopts any form of BUDGETARY CONTROL (q.v.), it will be his business to see that the programme laid down in advance for each department is kept to as closely as possible. In a large business the responsibility for buying goods is usually given to a purchasing manager, merchandise manager, or chief buyer, although in a business dealing in several types of goods, as in a DEPARTMENT STORE (q.v.), a certain amount of discretion may be left to the departmental buyers themselves. The sales manager is responsible for sales, for the control of salesmen and travellers, and for testing the market in new lines of goods (*see* MARKET RESEARCH). The secretary's office keeps the registers of shareholders and attends to the transfer of shares from one person to another, and deals usually with legal matters and INSURANCE (q.v.), as well as the general routine administration and correspondence of the firm. The advertising or publicity manager is responsible for all sales literature in the form of booklets and pamphlets, window-dressing and other forms of display, the 'house magazine' of the firm, if it has one, and TRADE FAIRS and EXHIBITIONS (qq.v.). If the firm has a staff or personnel manager, he is usually responsible not only for engaging the staff throughout the business but also for watching their progress and transferring from one department to another people who are not in suitable positions. Unless there is a separate welfare officer, whose job it is to look after the general well-being of the workers, such duties generally fall to the staff manager. Staff managers, welfare officers, and others outside the main channels of organization work through the appropriate department head, with the permission and knowledge of the managing director.

See also FACTORY ORGANIZATION; DIVISION OF LABOUR; STATISTICS; LIMITED COMPANIES.

BUTCHERY, *see* MEAT TRADE.

BUTTER-MAKING, *see* DAIRY INDUSTRY.

BUYING DEPARTMENT, *see* FACTORY ORGANIZATION, Section 5.

BY-PRODUCTS. When a factory is engaged in making its main product, it sometimes cannot help producing other things as well. For instance, a furniture factory cannot help producing wood shavings, and a gas-works cannot help producing tar and ammonia when making gas. These minor products are known as by-products. Many of the most useful and profitable by-products of modern industry have been discovered accidentally. In the early days of industry, at any rate, it was not always known in advance what other things would be produced as sidelines to the main objective.

At first, by-products were often allowed to

L.N.A.

PIG FOOD, A BY-PRODUCT OF KITCHEN WASTE
Waste Food which has been treated in the Westminster City Council Food Utilization Plant. (Reproduced by permission)

run to waste, or were dumped as refuse. In the early stages of the development of modern industry competition was not particularly keen, but, as industry expanded, many firms were forced to discover ways of adding to the income they received from selling their main product. One obvious way was to consider the by-products of manufacture, and to see whether they also could be sold to the public. To find a market for them it might be necessary to advertise and thus to place their advantages before the public (*see* ADVERTISING AND PUBLICITY); or it might even be necessary to convert such by-products, by a separate manufacturing process, into something closer to what the public wanted.

Some by-products occur naturally, and are not manufactured. Many mineral ores such as lead and silver are often found together. Fire-clay is generally found under the coal seams. The main aim of the FISHING INDUSTRY (q.v.) is fish for cooking, but such products as cod-liver oil become available at the same time. In the TIMBER INDUSTRY (q.v.) various kinds of resins are produced. Whale oil is the main objective of whaling (*see* WHALING INDUSTRY, Vol. VI), but spermaceti, ambergris, and whalebone are also produced. COPRA (q.v.), the solidified white kernel of the coco-nut, and the fibre that covers the hard outer shell, are inseparable products of the coconut palm. In industry and commerce it is just as important to make full use of natural by-products as of those that have been manufactured.

The number of natural and manufactured by-products is very large indeed, and there are few manufacturing processes without at least one by-product. What we call the 'service' employments, which render services to the consuming public instead of making tangible goods for them, also have their by-products. Pig swill, for instance, is a by-product of the CATERING INDUSTRY (q.v.). Soot, a by-product of chimney-sweeping, is valuable not only as a manure but also in industry.

Some of the best examples of by-products come from our major industries. The history of the mineral oil industry is very largely the story of its development from a stage when all by-products were neglected to one in which a use is found for almost every one. Before the use of fuel-oil for raising steam, and before the invention of the INTERNAL COMBUSTION ENGINE (q.v. Vol. VIII), oil was mainly sought in order that it might be converted into paraffin or kerosene for lamps, and the residues were largely left to waste. But, nowadays, nearly all the by-products of mineral oil are utilized, and converted into various kinds of fuel oils such as crude oil and diesel oil, refined petrol products, solvent spirits, wax for candles, 'vaseline' or petroleum jelly, powdered carbon, and many other useful products.

There are many by-products of the IRON AND STEEL INDUSTRY (q.v. Vol. VIII). Carbon monoxide, an inflammable gas which is the main constituent of ordinary household gas, is a by-product of the smelting of the iron ore in the BLAST FURNACE (q.v. Vol. VIII). In the earlier days of the industry the hot gas was allowed to escape at the top of the furnace and to waste itself as a tall flame on coming into contact with the oxygen of the air. Later on, it was cleansed, and used for heating the steel furnaces and for firing the boilers in the power-house. The resultant saving in coal made it possible to sell pig iron or steel at a lower price than formerly. The Gilchrist-Thomas method of making steel, which was perfected just before

Tate & Lyle

BAGASSE, A BY-PRODUCT OF SUGAR MANUFACTURE WHICH IS USED AS FUEL AND TO MAKE PAPER

Bagasse is what remains of the cane when the sugar has been extracted.

1880, delivers as a by-product basic slag which is an ARTIFICIAL FERTILIZER (q.v. Vol. VI) for farm and gardens.

The work of the coal GAS INDUSTRY (q.v.) leads to many by-products, of which the most important are tar and AMMONIA (q.v.). Tar is a useful by-product itself, but if it is further treated, many additional by-products can be obtained, some of which are extremely valuable. Many synthetic DYES (q.v.) are by-products of coal tar and so are many drugs and medicines.

There are still many by-products that cannot yet be utilized. For example, no profitable use has yet been found for the vast slag heaps from the blast furnaces that disfigure so many of our large plants. At some plants this slag is ground into small pieces and tarred for road-making, but generally it has been found that this product could not compete with road-metal quarried in the usual way and tarred on the spot while it was being laid. In time the gradual exhaustion of our stone quarries may force a solution of the problem.

C

CABINET-MAKING. In early times furniture was regarded as a luxury that could be afforded only by the wealthy or the important, so much so that a great house would frequently contain only one chair, which would be used by the lord or master, lesser folk having to be content with a stool or even the lid of a chest. Not much of this early furniture remains. The 16th century is the earliest period from which much has survived, except for rare items and those which have been preserved in churches (*see* WOODWORK, HISTORY OF). This early furniture was usually of oak, a wood of which there was a plentiful supply in the forests, though other native timbers such as elm and chestnut were used for the less important pieces. Woodcarving was a favourite form of decoration even in earliest times. Conventional leafwork, geometrical tracery, pointed arches, and small repeat patterns were the chief subjects that delighted the carver in the days of GOTHIC ART (q.v. Vol. XII). INLAY (q.v.) was another form of decoration.

During the reign of Henry VIII there came a change in the design of furniture. The architecture of the RENAISSANCE (q.v. Vol. I), which in plan and decoration was based on the study of the classical buildings of ancient Rome, spread northwards from Italy, and the details of this new style were copied in furniture. It was not properly understood by northern craftsmen, however, and at first they produced a rather curious grafting-on of the new ideas to the older Gothic. Such details as rounded arches, pilasters, and scrolled carving were strangely mixed with traditional Gothic structure.

As time went on the Gothic forms were used less and less, until by the middle of the 17th century the Renaissance style had almost entirely replaced them. Furniture was still mainly made in oak, however, and the old methods of construction remained unchanged; and although furniture was more plentiful, it was still rather crude compared with what was to follow. Chairs had wooden seats and were as uncomfortable as ever, and bedsteads were of the four-poster kind with curtains to draw round.

Soon after the Restoration some very important changes took place, which had a great influence on design. Walnut began to be used for furniture in place of oak. Oak did not go completely out of use, but all fashionable furniture was made in the new style. Next came the new craft of veneering, which brought with it all

New College, Oxford

15TH-CENTURY OAK CHEST CARVED WITH BATTLE SCENES

sorts of changes in both construction and design (*see* PLYWOOD AND VENEERS).

A veneer is a very thin sheet of rare wood, with a handsome 'grain', which is glued down on to a groundwork of plain or common wood; apart from reducing the amount of expensive wood that needs to be used, it provides an ornamental surface. The full beauty of the wood can be displayed by cutting it in directions in which it would be too weak if used for the structure itself; and shield-like or oyster-like patterns can be produced by placing next to each other strongly marked pieces, one the reverse of the other (*see* picture). These early veneers had to be sawn by hand from big baulks or logs of timber, and to the craftsman of to-day it is a constant source of admiration that these old cabinet-makers could cut their veneers so thin. The probability is that they used a double-handed saw, with one man at each side of the log, so that the direction of cut could be closely controlled on both sides.

Finally, furniture-making became a special class of work on its own, and in many ways this was the most important development of all. In other words, the woodworker who specialized in furniture-making, that is the cabinet-maker, came into being. Hitherto the wood-worker had had to tackle all sorts of jobs in wood—he was the carpenter who worked in wood whatever the job might be—but now came the cabinet-maker who made furniture only.

As the cabinet-maker became more specialized and more skilful at his particular craft, furniture became finer and more delicate. At the same time life was becoming more refined and cultured: people needed not only chairs and tables, but also writing-desks, display cabinets, and upholstered chairs. The newly acquired skill of the cabinet-maker was able to meet this demand. In Great Britain the craftsmen never lost sight of the essential quality of the woods they used, and even the most delicate walnut chairs of the period of Queen Anne were sturdy, and as sound in design as they were in workmanship. On the Continent, and especially in France, first the BAROQUE and later the ROCOCO styles (qq.v. Vol. XII) of architecture were more strongly developed than in England, and they had a greater effect on furniture design. The exuberance of the Baroque is reflected in the richly ornamental gilt-and-marquetry furniture of the reign of Louis XIV; the more delicate and

Frank Partridge & Sons, Ltd.

WILLIAM AND MARY WALNUT BUREAU CABINET
The veneer is arranged to make a symmetrical pattern of the grain of the wood.

intimate style of the Rococo can be seen in the carved fronts of escritoires or writing-desks, and in the exquisite inlays of bronze, marble, and tortoise-shell with which the wood was embellished (*see* INLAY AND MARQUETRY).

The walnut fashion did not last long in England. Yet another new wood, mahogany, began to be used. This was brought over from the West Indies, and its great value for furniture-making was soon recognized. Its quality was reliable, it took a fine polish, and it could easily be worked once a craftsman got used to it. By about 1730 it had almost replaced walnut, at any rate for fashionable furniture. Towards the middle of the 18th century certain cabinet-makers had become famous. The first was CHIPPENDALE (q.v. Vol. V), who made some of the finest furniture for the wealthy classes.

Victoria and Albert Museum

ARMCHAIR OF CARVED MAHOGANY, ABOUT 1755

The back corresponds with an illustration in Chippendale's *Director*, a book of furniture designs which was used by cabinet-makers in his day

He should be regarded as a fine cabinet-maker who turned out fine furniture in the prevailing style, rather than as a designer. His furniture was invariably in mahogany, decorated with carving and frets (*see* FRETWORK); inlay was never used.

Chippendale had a wide influence on other cabinet-makers, and his name was applied to many kinds of work. At that time fashionable people had a romantic interest in distant places and distant ages. Therefore workmen produced Chinese Chippendale, in which Chinese objects such as pagodas and bells were used as decoration, and Gothic Chippendale, with its pointed arches and tracery. Many Chinese works of art were being brought to Britain and imitated by craftsmen, particularly in pottery and porcelain, though the results were often unlike the originals.

Towards the end of the 18th century Hepplewhite, Robert and James ADAM (q.v. Vol. V), and Sheraton became well known. There was a revival of inlay for decoration; and satinwood, a new wood from the Indies, began to be widely used, although mahogany continued in use as

well. Generally, designs became lighter. As the wealth of the middle classes increased, the demand for furniture grew. Hepplewhite and Sheraton, as well as Chippendale, published books on furniture, and cabinet-makers all over the country took their designs from these books.

Like Chippendale, Hepplewhite was a practical man with a flourishing cabinet-making business. Perhaps the most characteristic of Hepplewhite pieces is the chair, the 'shield-back' being the most famous. He used both inlay and painting, in addition to a refined and delicate form of carving, which usually took the form of vases, festoons, draped cloth, swags of husks, ears of wheat, and small classical subjects.

Adam was essentially an architect; but he designed a great deal of furniture for the houses he built, and some of it was made by Chippendale in his workshops in St. Martin's Lane. In furniture design, as in architecture, Adam drew almost entirely from classical and Italian forms, though he followed the French fashion of his day in preferring painted decoration to carving. He employed famous artists to ornament his furniture with exquisite paintings, and made constant use of such objects as fans, wreaths, urns, and honeysuckle for decoration.

Sheraton's designs were delicate and refined, with inlay, painting, and a small form of carving as a decoration. Sheraton chairs generally had comparatively low backs, and both arms and backs were mostly straight as viewed from the front or top, being shaped only to a side view.

In the 19th century furniture began to be less gracefully designed, and after a time came the heavy style of the Victorian period: although, from the point of view of strength of structure, most of it was splendidly made. A small band of craftsmen and designers, who included Ernest Gimson (1864–1919), tried to improve design, and their work gave rise to what is known as the Cotswold tradition, but had little effect on furniture as a whole.

In the early years of the 20th century 'period' style furniture became fashionable and popular. This took details from old period furniture, adapting the whole to modern requirements, so that the decoration was often purely superficial and unrelated to the structural design. It was in the later 1920's that the modern movement of design began. The introduction of reliable PLYWOOD (q.v.) and laminated board enabled large, unbroken surfaces to be produced without danger of shrinkage; the growing shortage of certain fine timbers led to the increased use of veneering; and such decoration as carving became too expensive for most people. Features of 'modern' furniture are, therefore, the use of veneers, wide unbroken surfaces, and the elimination of framed and panelled construction (*see* CARPENTRY AND JOINERY). As a change from the 'period' style, much decoration is avoided. The bulk of modern furniture is made by machines in factories. The cabinet-maker has no part to play in this manufacture by machinery, and the tradition of good design has grown feeble. But there still remain some cabinet-makers who carry on the old practice, making furniture which is traditional in its understanding of the right use of wood.

See also TIMBER INDUSTRY; FURNITURE TRADE.

CAMEL HAIR, *see* HAIR TRADE.

CANNING INDUSTRY. The preserving of foodstuffs, by heating or chilling or sealing, or a combination of two of these methods, now makes it possible for people to have a great choice of foods, without regard to the season of the year or the distance over which the food has been carried. If foods are kept for a few days in the air, they decay through attack by YEASTS, MOULDS, BACTERIA, and other types of microorganism (q.v. Vol. II). By the canning process, however, the product is enclosed in a sealed container so that no infection can reach it, and the contents of the container are then sterilized by heat. This heat-sterilization destroys any initial infection which may have been present on the food or on the interior of the can. The process avoids the necessity of using chemical preservatives, and products thus treated may be stored for many months or years without serious deterioration.

SIDEBOARD IN AFRICAN MAHOGANY WITH ROSE-WOOD HANDLES AND MOULDED DOORS
Made by Gordon Russell Ltd., designed by Messrs. Booth and Ledeboer,
F.R.I.B.A., F.S.I.A.

In the present century the canning of beef has become an important industry in many countries; farmers depend on canning to help them sell their products, while the metal industries supply a great deal of steel and tin for canning. Canning fish, such as salmon, herrings, and sardines, is another important industry. In Canada and the U.S.A., for example, there are canning factories near the rivers where the salmon are actually caught (*see* SALMON FISHING, Volume VI).

Meat, fish, beer, fruit, and vegetables are all suitable for canning on an industrial scale. Most foods are prepared in roughly the same way, but there are slight differences in the temperatures used. The foods are sorted for size or quality, and then softened for easy filling. After filling, which is usually automatic, air is exhausted from the cans, which are then closed and sterilized. The canning process was invented in 1810 by François Appert, a Frenchman. Napoleon and his Quartermaster-General, who had to solve the problem of feeding far-flung armies, are said to have been keenly interested in the process (*see* SUPPLIES IN WAR, Vol. X). The early

Batchelors' Peas, Ltd.

CANS OF VEGETABLES BEING PUT INTO RETORTS IN WHICH THEY ARE STERILIZED

attempts at canning were not a success, largely because the cans used were not coated with a layer of tin inside, and were corroded by the acids in the foods. The later use of tinplate, which was mild steel coated with tin, made canning a commercial success. The tin coating on the inside of the can is not proof against food acids, which react chemically with it, but in such minute quantities that there is no danger to health. Lacquering is now used for the inside of cans that are to contain the more acid foods. Modern can-making plants can turn out 300 cans a minute.

In Britain the canning of fruit and vegetables is particularly important. The various processes, which apply in general to other foods, are as follows.

1. PREPARATION. The first stage in the process consists of preparing the raw material by removing diseased fruit, and throwing away the waste portions such as stalks from plums, cherries, or blackcurrants, or plugs (hulls) from strawberries. Vegetables, carrots, potatoes, and other root vegetables are peeled, washed, and trimmed, and only the clean edible parts are used. Fresh peas are removed from the pods, and freed from stalks and leaves. Most of this work is done

mechanically; but in all cases a final inspection of the material is carried out, and the last traces of waste are removed by hand. Delicate fruits, such as strawberries and raspberries, cannot be treated mechanically without serious damage to their tissues. These are, therefore, prepared entirely by hand, and filled directly into the cans. In the packing of a high-quality product it is also customary to select fruits or vegetables which are all of the same size. This size-grading improves the appearance of the product, and assists in obtaining uniform colour and texture.

2. BLANCHING. This consists of a preliminary heat-treatment. Vegetables are heated for a short time in boiling water before being packed into the cans. This process acts as a final cleansing, and also removes gases which might otherwise cause abnormal pressure in the cans during the sterilization process. Blanching softens vegetables and so allows more uniform filling of the cans. Fruits are not blanched, owing to their soft texture, and it is therefore necessary to give them a somewhat longer exhaust treatment (*see* Section 4).

3. FILLING. Most fruits, and any vegetables that are large or irregular in shape, are filled into the cans by hand. Small vegetables, such as peas or dried beans, are filled mechanically by machines with an output of about 100 cans a minute. Immediately after filling, brine is added to the cans of vegetables, or syrup to those of fruit, leaving an empty space (head-space) of about ⅜ in. in depth to allow for expansion of the contents on heating. The syrup is made by dissolving cane-sugar in water, and sometimes a small amount of colouring matter is added, as the natural colour of the fruit tends to fade on sterilization or during its period of storage.

4. EXHAUSTING. The filled cans now pass through a pre-heating process known as ex-hausting, which removes any gases from the tissues of the fruit or vegetables, and reduces the amount of air in the headspace of the can. This is done by passing the cans through a steam tunnel, or a shallow box containing water at 170 to 180° F., for 5 to 12 minutes. The general practice is to give such heat-treatment as will enable the can to be closed at a temperature of 160 to 170° F., and if it is correctly carried out the closed cans will have a partial vacuum equivalent to a pressure of 12 to 16 inches of mercury—that is, the pressure inside them will be only about half the pressure of the outside air.

5. CLOSING AND STERILIZING. As they emerge from the exhaust box, the cans are supplied with lids and hermetically sealed by a closing-machine. They are then ready for sterilizing. Fruits, because of their high acidity, are easily sterilized by immersing the cans in boiling water for 8 to 15 minutes. This may be done in open tanks, in retorts, or by means of automatic cookers. Vegetables, which have little acidity, cannot be sterilized at boiling-point, and are heated for about 30 minutes under steam pressure at a temperature of 240° F. The steri-lization process is usually carried out in steel vessels, each holding about 1,000 cans. As soon as the cans have received the correct heat-treatment, cold water is admitted and the cans are cooled down to a temperature of about 90° F. They may then be transferred directly to the labelling department, or may be held in store until they are required for dispatch.

6. LABELLING. Cans of fruits and vegetables are usually labelled by automatic machines which handle 150 cans a minute. They are then packed into fibre-board cases, either by hand or by automatic machinery. The cases are sten-cilled with a description of the contents, and are then sealed and loaded for distribution to the wholesaler or retailer.

See also COLD STORAGE.

CANTEENS, *see* CATERING INDUSTRY.

CAPITAL. In finance and business this word has many meanings. To the economist it means tools and machines which make it possible for a workman to increase his output. The expression 'national capital' means the total quantity of buildings, railways, docks, factories, plant and machinery, and tools existing in a country at any given time. There is also the political definition of capital as industrial pro-perty or INVESTMENTS, a capitalist being an owner of such property and earning PROFITS (qq.v.) from his control of industrial enterprises.

The more usual meanings, however, are the industrial and financial ones. The capital of a commercial or industrial firm is, in a broad sense, the total of shares issued by it (*see* STOCKS AND SHARES). But businesses may often use capital which is more than the total shares or stock issued: for example, they may issue DEBEN-TURES, or may obtain LOANS (qq.v.) from their banks or extended credit from the merchants who supply them: all these methods will increase the amount of capital which the business actually uses.

In the financial sense capital is practically the same thing as savings. A firm engaged in 'company finance' is principally concerned with obtaining the savings of private investors, in order that they may be put at the disposal of firms needing capital.

The expressions 'fixed' and 'circulating' capital are used by directors of companies, financiers, and accountants. By 'fixed' capital they mean the amount of capital which has been more or less permanently turned into land, buildings, plant, and machinery, and so cannot easily be turned again into money. By 'circulating' capital they mean that part of capital which is continu-ously changing the form in which it is invested, being sometimes invested in one way and some-times in another. For example, in times of poor trade the circulating capital of a merchant may consist of money only, or possibly of investments on which he draws INTEREST (q.v.), because he cannot employ his capital more profitably in actual trade; but when trade is good his capital may become transformed into stocks of goods, into debts owed to him by his customers, and so on.

That part of circulating capital which is available for the day-by-day working purposes of a business is called 'working' capital. The accountant usually defines working capital as the difference between current assets (such as cash, bank balance, stock-in-trade, and book debts) and current liabilities to creditors.

Fixed capital for the larger concerns is usually arranged through ISSUING HOUSES (q.v.). Fixed capital, being savings locked up in the buildings and equipment of a particular concern, cannot be withdrawn at will; and so bankers, whose investments must always be easily convertible into cash, are clearly not the proper persons to provide such capital. Continental banks often do this, but it is generally against the traditions of British banks. In times of really brisk trade British banks will temporarily increase a firm's circulating or working capital by granting loans and overdrafts, or will lend money to manufacturers and merchants so that they may grant increased credit to their own customers; but they look upon the permanent provision of such capital as outside their own province, and as the business of the issuing houses.

A firm is 'under-capitalized', or short of capital, if the total amount of capital raised is not enough to prevent its continually asking banks and similar institutions for loans. A concern is 'over-capitalized' when it has received, from shareholders or partners, so much money capital that it cannot profitably use all of it in trading or manufacturing, with the result that much of it has to be left idle in the bank, or invested in securities giving a lower rate of interest than the profits of merchanting or manufacturing.

A slight measure of over-capitalization is necessary to a growing business. Wisely run businesses provide for extension and development by what is called 'ploughing back profits'. This means that the whole of the profits are never distributed to shareholders, but a considerable amount is kept back and put into reserve. This practice has exactly the same effect on a firm's finances as a regular annual increase of capital.

In a national sense, a community's real capital, such as factories, railways, ships, plant, and machinery, must be continuously growing, to enable it to keep its place among the nations of the world, and to secure a steady rise in the STANDARD OF LIVING (q.v.). During a war its stock of real capital will not only be damaged and destroyed, but will also have suffered from lack of maintenance and repair. This was the state of affairs in Britain after the Second World War.

See also EXCHANGE AND TRADE; LIMITED COMPANIES; INVESTMENT; INTEREST; PROFITS.

See also Vol. X: CAPITALISM.

CARAT, *see* ASSAYING.

CARDING, *see* WOOL-SPINNING, Section 2.

CARPENTRY AND JOINERY. 1. HISTORY. Little woodwork has survived that is older than 1,000 years, but a few examples of doors and furniture from ancient Egypt, at least 3,000 years old, are preserved in the British Museum. These show that many of the joints used to-day for framing woodwork were known at that early date, and that some of the tools still used have an equally distant ancestry (*see* WOODWORK, HISTORY OF). Hardly any specimens of Greek and Roman woodwork remain to us. But they have been written about, and many specimens of Roman tools are exhibited in a number of museums (for example at Reading), which show the originals from which modern saws, chisels, and other tools were derived (*see* Fig. 1). During the Middle Ages in England, primitive wooden huts gave way to framed houses of timber, the spaces between the framing being filled with brick, stone, or wattle and daub. These were commonly called half-timber houses. Thousands of them still survive, especially in those parts of England where timber was the most plentiful building material, and where stone was scarce—as in the west midlands and the southeastern counties (*see* HOUSES, HISTORY OF, Vol. XI).

In the early Middle Ages, the man who carried out the structural timber work for buildings was called a 'wright', and was a maker of carts before he began to erect framed houses. The Latin word for cart or wain was *carpentum*, and the man who made it was a *carpentarius*, a carpenter. Cartwright and Wainwright are still common English surnames. The joiners seem to have appeared much later on the scene in England, as upholsterers and makers of the

GULLIVER AND THE LILLIPUTIANS

Late 19th-century poster for display in shop windows

CARPENTERS REBUILDING THE ROOF OF GRAY'S INN HALL, LONDON

The trusses are raised into position by a derrick. This roof reproduces the medieval hammer-beam roof which was destroyed in an air-raid in 1941

few articles of wooden furniture used in Gothic times. In the late 17th century Joseph Moxon, in a book on the building crafts, wrote that 'Joinery is an Art Manual whereby several Pieces of Wood are so fitted and joined together . . . that they shall seem one intire Piece'.

From 1666, the date of the Great Fire of London, structural carpentry in England was mainly confined to floors and roofs. It continued to be used for these purposes in public buildings, factories, and churches for nearly two centuries more. It was then gradually replaced by iron, steel, and reinforced CONCRETE (q.v. Vol. VIII). A surprising number of the industrial and commercial premises in London that were destroyed by incendiary bombs during the Second World War had timber floors, roofs, and partitions dating from Victorian and Georgian days. To-day structural carpentry is chiefly used for

dwelling houses, although even there it is giving way to other materials.

When timber-framed houses became fewer, and less carpentry was needed, more work was given to joiners. They began to line the homes of the wealthy with wood panelling in Tudor times, and this attractive type of woodwork continued to be made up to the end of the 18th century. Staircases, too, became elaborate and often beautiful. The import of timber into Britain from abroad grew steadily from the Middle Ages onwards, and by the outbreak of the Second World War had become very great. After that war, owing to Britain's comparative poverty far less foreign timber could be bought. Its use in building was reduced, and this affected the crafts of carpentry and joinery. The fall in the incomes of the wealthier classes makes it unlikely that Britain will go back to the elaborate

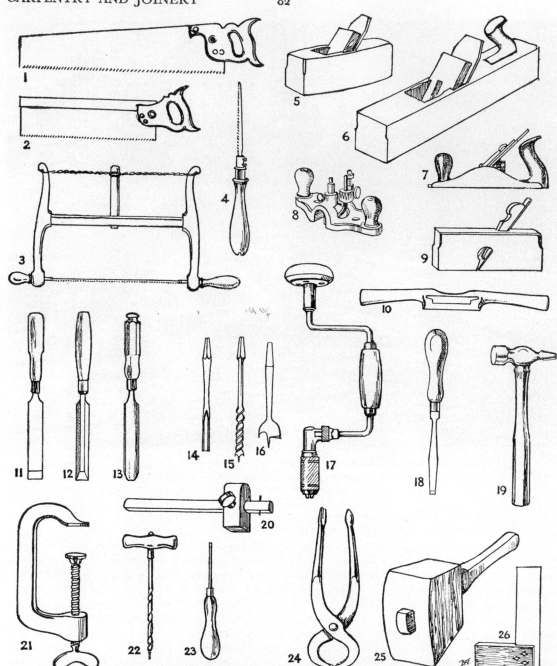

FIG. I. CARPENTRY TOOLS

1. Hand saw. 2. Tenon saw. 3. Bow saw. 4. Pad saw. 5. Smooth plane (wood). 6. Jack plane. 7. Smooth plane (steel). 8. Router. 9. Rabbet plane. 10. Spokeshave. 11. Firmer chisel. 12. Bevel edge chisel. 13. Gouge. 14. Shell bit. 15. Twist bit. 16. Centre bit. 17. Brace. 18. Screwdriver. 19. Warrington Hammer. 20. Marking gauge. 21. G Cramp. 22. Gimlet. 23. Bradawl. 24. Pincers. 25. Mallet. 26. Try square

panelling and the lavishly planned and decorated staircases of bygone days—except, possibly, in public buildings.

2. MODERN PRACTICE. In modern practice carpentry means roofs, floors, timber partitions, and other portions of the structural woodwork of a building. Joinery includes windows, doors, staircases, cupboards, and other fixed woodwork details which are not structural because they do not support the weight of the building. Generally speaking, carpentry includes all the structural woodwork carried out at the building itself, while joinery consists of the lighter woodwork prepared beforehand in the joiner's workshops. The making of movable furniture is an entirely separate trade, which is called Cabinet-making. Although woodworkers employed by large firms of contractors usually specialize in one craft or the other, the majority of craftsmen are competent to undertake both carpentry and joinery, and in small building firms are expected to do so.

Among the numerous old Livery Companies of the City of London there are two separate companies: the large Carpenters' Company, founded in 1333, and the much smaller Joiners' Company (*see* CITY COMPANIES). They both had bitter squabbles in the 17th century about the dividing line between their two crafts. To-day the Carpenters' Company takes the lead in organizing the training for all the various building trades, including joinery, at its Trades Training School. Examinations in carpentry and joinery, as a combined subject, are conducted annually by the City and Guilds of London Institute. During the present century the rapid development of machine-made joinery has led to the appearance of another trade: that of the woodworking machinist. His training differs greatly from that of the carpenter-joiner, who is concerned principally with hand-work; but woodworking machinists can hardly do without some knowledge of carpentry and joinery, and modern carpenters and joiners should understand WOODWORKING MACHINERY (q.v. Vol. VIII).

Other changes have come from the use of PLYWOODS AND VENEERS (q.v.), and of steel and other materials for casement windows and other fitments previously made of wood. Mass production and prefabricated joinery have also grown. Doors, windows, and even staircases are now factory-made, and replace work formerly done

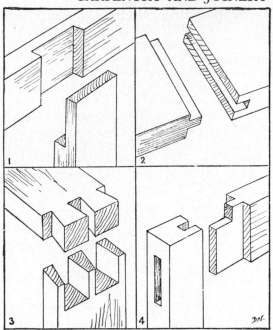

FIG. 2. WOOD JOINTS

1. Halved joint. 2. Housed joint. 3. Dovetail joint.
4. Mortise and tenon joint

in the building contractor's workshops. A large number of fitments, which used to be made by joiners direct from the architect's drawings for the building, are now ordered from manufacturers' price-lists. The selection is made from standard patterns, and of these there is a fairly wide choice. Specifications have now been drawn up by the British Standards Institution for wooden doors, casement and sash windows, cupboards, staircases, gates, picture rails, skirtings, mouldings, and many other items. All these fitments are matters for the joiner. The carpenter is still left with roofs and floors to construct, provided that timber is used, but steel and reinforced concrete increasingly tend to replace it. The traditional joints in woodwork, mortise and tenon, and dovetail, for instance, the joiner's pride from time immemorial (*see* Fig. 2), have had to be modified to suit woodworking machines, and are often replaced by other methods of joining. The development of well-made plywood and veneers, held together by very strong glue, has led to the use of flush doors which have a single flat surface instead of panels. They are made of a light frame of cheap timber, without mortises or tenons, which is covered and strengthened by a very thin layer of some more ornamental and expensive type of wood.

In most of the municipal houses, schools, and factories, that form the main bulk of the building permitted since the Second World War, the only work left for the carpenter-joiner is the roof and the floors. Sometimes it is not even as much as that. Other parts are prefabricated, and his own task is merely to fix them in position. Yet one new branch of carpentry has been introduced in the present century: the making of wooden 'form work', or shuttering, to serve as moulds for reinforced concrete. Meanwhile, apprentices continue to be trained in all branches of their craft, and are rigorously examined by the Carpenters' Company, the City and Guilds of London Institute, and other educational bodies.

See also WOODWORK, HISTORY OF; TIMBER INDUSTRY; FURNITURE INDUSTRY.

CARPET MAKING

CARPET MAKING Like many other TEXTILES (q.v.) carpets are woven; but they need to be thicker and stronger than most textiles to stand up to the hard wear they receive. The best carpets can last for hundreds of years (see CARPETS AND RUGS, Vol. XI).

There are two main types of woven carpets and rugs: pile and smooth-faced. The foundation of a pile carpet is two sets of threads, the warp and the weft, which are interwoven just as in other textiles (see WOOL WEAVING). But this foundation is hidden from the surface of the carpet, which is composed of extra threads with cut or looped ends which are woven into the foundation in such a way that the ends stand up perpendicular to it. It is these which form the pile, taking nearly all the wear and making the carpet soft and warm; and it is in these that the pattern is made.

There are two methods of making the pile. In the first, short threads are knotted by hand on to the warp, between the rows of the weft. Most hand-woven carpets and rugs are made in this way. In the second, extra warp threads, several times longer than the foundation warp, are woven into the fabric so that they form little loops standing up between each weft thread. These are left as loops (as in hair-cord carpets), or are cut (as in Wilton carpets). The foundation is usually undyed, and the pattern is made by using threads of different colours for the pile. This is the method generally used for machine weaving.

Smooth-faced or tapestry-woven carpets and rugs have no pile and are woven simply with a warp and weft. But, to give extra strength and thickness, the weft is put in loosely, and is then beaten down to cover the warp. Patterns are woven in the same way as in TAPESTRY (q.v.); coloured weft threads form the design, and the warp is usually undyed. Some primitive peoples, such as the AMERICAN INDIANS (q.v. Vol. I), make rugs in this way, and they are made also at Aubusson in France (see Fig. 1.)

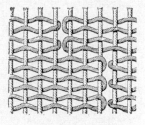

FIG. I. TAPESTRY WEAVE
The pattern is made by different coloured weft threads

Carpets are made of wool, silk, cotton, linen, hemp, jute, and occasionally of gold and silver thread. Wool is the most important material, although cotton is often used for the foundation. Until recently the yarns used were dyed with vegetable dyes: madder or cochineal for red, indigo for blue, Persian berries or turmeric for yellow. For the secondary colours the wool would be double-dyed: green, for example, being made by dyeing the wool first blue and then yellow. Nowadays synthetic dyes are used for most machine-made carpets and for many hand-made ones (see DYES).

2. MANUFACTURE. The loom, the wooden frame on which a carpet is woven, may be a very crude structure. Among the nomadic tribes of Asia in the desert lands it is often taken to pieces and carried about during the summer wanderings, and re-erected when quarters are taken up for the winter, when most of the carpet and rug-making is done. Most looms consist mainly of a framework, usually

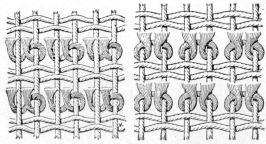

FIG. 2. PERSIAN AND TURKISH KNOTS
(Figs. 1 and 2 from A. F. Kendrick and C. E. C. Tattersall, *Handwoven Carpets*, Benn Bros.)

vertical, to which the warp threads are attached (sometimes to rollers) at the top and bottom. One or more rows of the foundation weft threads are woven alternately with each row of loops or pile knotted across the warp. One way of knotting is to thread a ball of wool through the warp, tie a knot, and then cut the wool to leave the length of pile required; another is to make the knot, and at the same time to take the wool round a short iron rod, making a loop which is then cut to length by drawing the knife-like edge of the rod through it. Two kinds of knot are used: the Persian, in which each of the two ends protrudes between separate weft threads, and the Turkish, in which two outstanding ends alternate with two weft threads. The Persian knot produces a closer and finer surface; but it takes more time, and has been largely replaced, even in Persia, by the Turkish knot (*see* Fig. 2).

After knotting and cutting, the work is beaten close together with a weighted wooden or metal comb, to make a firm structure. Finally, the projecting tufts are carefully clipped to an even surface. The fineness of the carpet depends on how much care is taken over these various processes, and also on the original closeness of the warp threads. Cheap carpets may have no more than 12 tufts of pile to the square inch, while in carpets of the finest quality there may be as many as 400. The weaver usually follows the design by placing it behind the loom, so that he can see it through the warp. Machine weaving largely copies these various processes, reducing handwork to a minimum.

3. PERSIAN CARPETS. The earliest Persian carpets still in existence date from the 16th century. They are as fine as anything that has been made since; travellers to Persia in the 17th century told of the royal workshops where the carpets were made. They were used not only in palaces and houses but in the mosques or temples as well. The designs of the early carpets were usually floral, with curving lines (as in the Chinese carpets) rather than angular lines, although the Persians are famous also for their hunting, vase, and garden designs. The colours used are very rich. In the 17th century Persian designs were woven in India, and it is difficult to distinguish the Indian from the Persian. For the most sumptuous carpets—probably woven as royal gifts to foreign courts—silk was used.

4. CHINESE CARPETS. These are difficult to

Victoria and Albert Museum

A PERSIAN CARPET LOOM WITH A PARTLY FINISHED
RUG ON IT

date, because the same designs have been used for long periods. They have certainly been woven from early times. Silk is often used, and the weaving and finishing are comparatively coarse. The designs, though partly floral, also include human figures and animals, and much symbolism in lines and curves. Yellow is the favourite colour, and the other colours used are rather delicate in tone.

5. TURKEY CARPETS. Very few old examples of these remain; but it is known that Turkey exported carpets to Europe, especially to Italy, in the 15th century, because they appear in pictures of the period. The designs of the Turks are much more conventional and angular than the Persian, and geometrical motifs and arabesques are chiefly used, red being the favourite predominating colour. Ushak, near Smyrna, in Asia Minor, is the centre of manufacture to-day.

6. CENTRAL ASIAN CARPETS. In this region rugs have been woven for many hundreds of years. The people are chiefly nomadic, a whole tribe moving from one pasture to another, and the rugs were used for decorating their tents and for covering the entrances. They are usually woven in the tapestry manner, with rather bold geometrical designs. The rugs from the Turkestan regions show marked Chinese influence.

7. FRENCH CARPETS. The French imported carpets from the East for some time before they began their manufacture themselves. The Savonnerie and Aubusson carpets are the most famous, the former being very fine pile carpets, the latter tapestry-woven. Both were made from the 16th century onwards, and in design they reflect the French art of the time.

8. ENGLISH CARPETS. The craft was not established in England much before the early 17th century, as floors were then generally strewn with rushes—even in palaces (*see* FLOOR COVERINGS, Vol. XI). At first Turkey carpets were imported, and the early English carpets were influenced either by Turkish design or by the English embroideries of the period. By the middle of the 18th century important carpet weaving centres were established at Wilton, near Salisbury, and at Axminster, in Devon; these survived until their place was taken by power-loom weaving, whose present-day headquarters are Kidderminster, in Worcestershire.

See also WOOL WEAVING.
See also Vol. XI: CARPETS AND RUGS.

CARTEL, *see* COMBINES.

CASHMERE (HAIR), *see* HAIR TRADE.

CASH REGISTER, *see* ACCOUNTING, MACHINE; *see also* Vol. VIII: CALCULATING MACHINES.

CASK-MAKING. The making and repairing of casks is called 'coopering', and is a craft that can be traced back to the 13th century, although it is probably much older than that. Oak 'staves', some 4 inches wide and $1\frac{1}{4}$ inches or more thick, are the traditional materials, rather wider pieces of oak being used for the ends or 'headings'. Oak from around Memel, on the Baltic, has long been considered best for the purpose, but since the Second World War difficulties of trade with eastern Europe have cut off this source of supply. American oak has been widely used, but has been found to give an unpleasant taste to beer, and casks made of it have therefore to be given a lining of brewer's pitch after they are made. Oak from various other countries has been tried, and Persian oak among others has been found satisfactory. Only selected 'butts', or trunks, of oak can be used; knots must at all costs be avoided. The timber must also be cleft, that is, split, and not sawn, otherwise it will not stand up to the strains imposed by bending it to shape, although sawn boards will do for heading the ends of casks. 'Cask' is the word used by brewers and coopers; the more popular word 'barrel' is really a unit of measurement. The term 'barrel' means to a brewer a cask holding 36 gallons, just as a 'hogshead' holds 54, a 'kilderkin' 18, a 'firkin' 9, and a 'pin' $4\frac{1}{2}$ gallons.

Nowadays most casks are made for the BEER-BREWING trade, although they are much used also in the WINE TRADE and in the CIDER industry (qq.v.). The methods used by the cooper prevail wherever wooden casks are made.

To make a cask by hand, the cooper takes some twenty straight staves. He shapes them to a curving taper from the centre towards each end; and in the middle, where most of the bending is to take place, he hollows them out on the inner side, and makes the groove at either end which is to take the edge of the heading. To make them pliable, the staves are stood on end in a circle, with a hoop around to hold them, and a fire of shavings is kindled inside. A great wooden hoop is now drawn round the top of the staves. This is driven down with heavy hammers until the staves are sufficiently drawn together to enable a smaller hoop to be slipped over. So the process continues, until six hoops are on; then they are slackened back in order that the two headings may be fitted.

In these days casks are generally made by machine. In the cooperage will be found

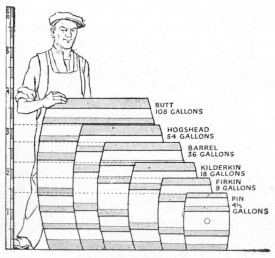

THE SIZES OF BREWERS' CASKS

Whitbread and Co.

MAKING A CASK

The heading is being shaped to fit the cask which has two of its hoops in place

machines to shape the staves, cut the grooves, 'chamfer' or trim the ends of the staves to form the characteristic shape of the 'chime' or rim at the end of the cask, and shape up the headings. There are even machines that make the staves pliable by heating them in steam, and others that drive on the hoops. But the craftsman cooper is still to be found in almost every brewery, where he is indispensable for the constant repair of casks—fitting a new stave, or re-shaping a joint, for there are more than 70 feet of joints in a cask, and none must leak. Rushes are placed between the edges of one stave and its neighbour to assist in making a good joint, but in the main the cask relies on perfect fitting and the enormous pressure applied by the hoops to make it quite tight.

Casks made of layers of timber, made on the principle of PLYWOOD (q.v.), have been used as well with some success, the advantage being that only the inner and outer faces need necessarily be of oak. Containers of stainless steel have also been used for beer.

To fill the cask, a bung-hole is provided midway down one of the staves, which is often made a bit wider than the rest to make up for the strength lost through boring the hole. In one of the headings, near the rim, will be found the tap-hole. This is a smaller aperture which takes the draw-off tap to which, with beer casks, the piping is connected in the public-house cellar. The tap-hole is closed at the brewery with a plug. After the cask has been filled, the bung-hole is closed by driving into it a wooden disk with tapered edge known as a 'shive', in the centre of which a small hole is bored partly through. When the cask has been set up in the public-house cellar, this hole receives a 'spile', or small peg of porous wood, which affords an adjustable means of letting air into the cask as the level of beer goes down.

See also BEER BREWING; WINE TRADE.

CATALOGUES, *see* WHOLESALE TRADING; AUCTION.

CATERING INDUSTRY. This includes all enterprises providing food outside people's homes. Those that provide accommodation as well as meals belong properly to the HOTEL

THE RAMPONAUX TAVERN
A popular 18th-century tavern in the suburbs of Paris

INDUSTRY (q.v.). The catering industry in any country is specially interesting, for the way in which it reflects social and economic changes. In fact, it is almost possible to write a social history of a country by studying changes in its cafés and restaurants.

Until the 18th century eating outside the home was not practised nearly so widely as it is to-day. In the country the traveller had to rely largely upon the coaching INNS (q.v. Vol. IV), highly efficient places which were ready to serve some sort of meal at any time of the day or night. In the towns light refreshments, such as cakes, pastries, and sweet or savoury jellies, were served in the back parlour or upper rooms of the pastry-cook's shop, but, apart from this, the taverns were the only public eating-houses. These were quite distinct from the ale-houses, which did not serve meals, and they catered for all classes. From the 16th century the custom of eating out became more popular when the 'ordinary' was established: a meal served at a fixed price and a fixed time, like the modern *table d'hôte*. The hour of serving it varied from century to century as the fashionable dinner hour varied. One of the most popular 16th-century 'ordinaries' was at the tavern opened by Richard Tarleton, the comedian of Shakespeare's day, off Newgate Street, and many other London taverns, such as the Mermaid, the Devil, and the Mitre, adopted the same practice. During Stuart times many French taverns were opened in London,

serving elaborate and expensive meals, but still following the practice of the ordinary. One of the most famous of these was Pontac's in Abchurch Lane, where the fixed price was a guinea. It was frequented by Pepys, the diarist, and, in the 18th century, by Swift, the author of *Gulliver's Travels*.

The smaller and humbler taverns were sometimes known as 'dives', because the diners ate in a room below the ground floor, often actually in the kitchen. The meals in such places were extremely cheap. Smollett, in *Roderick Random* (1748), describes a meal in a dive: 'We sat down at a board, and dined upon shin of beef most deliciously; our reckoning amounting to two-pence halfpenny each, bread and small beer included.'

From the 17th century onwards, the introduction into Europe of the new beverages, coffee, cocoa, and later tea, caused a new type of catering establishment to become popular, the coffee-house. This idea came to Europe from Turkey: the first in London was established by a Turk in 1652, the first in France at Marseilles in 1671. During the remainder of the 17th century coffee-houses were opened all over Europe. They were frequented by the literary men of the 18th century, such as Addison, Steele, Swift, and Dr. Johnson, and many of these houses became celebrated CLUBS (q.v. Vol. IX).

The ordinary restaurant, as we know it to-day, is directly descended from the tavern. The word

Cadbury Bros.

YOUTHS' DINING-ROOM AT BOURNVILLE, BIRMINGHAM
A modern factory canteen

is French, and meant originally a special kind of restorative soup, being applied to a French tavern where this was served. It later came to mean an eating-house with separate tables for the diners. The first place of this kind was opened in France in 1780, and as France then led the world of fashion, eating-houses on the same model were opened shortly afterwards in other continental countries, and also in the West End of London. During the first years of the 19th century the restaurant had almost replaced the tavern as the most favoured type of eating-house. In some places, such as the City of London, the traditions of the tavern remained to some extent, notably in the 'chop-houses', with their high-backed wooden pews, where the customer picked out his own chop or steak for the grill. For many years these were the typical eating-houses for professional and business men, and a few still survive.

With the coming of the railway in the 19th century the coaching inns lost a good deal of trade, but the demand for the town restaurant increased. French, Austrian, and Italian immigrants, escaping from political repression in their own countries after the revolutions of 1848, set up in British cities the many restaurants which still bear their name. Numbers of the refugees settled in the Soho district of London and the cheap, yet good, restaurants opened for them also became popular with British people. The restaurant habit in London dates from this

time, although it never became as widespread as on the Continent. From the 1870's it became correct for women of fashion, if properly escorted, to dine in restaurants, as they had not done previously. About this time, too, as part of the laws passed to put down the widespread drunkenness, restaurants were obliged by law to close shortly after midnight; they had formerly remained open much longer.

The early railway companies found that travellers on long journeys needed meals. At important junctions there were station restaurants before the restaurant-car was invented (*see* RAILWAY COACHES, Section 5, Vol. IV). At stations such as Swindon even the express trains used to stop long enough for the travellers to get out and have a hearty meal. At Wolverton, in Buckinghamshire, a royal dining-room was built at a wayside-station so that Queen Victoria, when travelling to the north, could alight from the royal train and enjoy her lunch in comfort. Refreshment rooms were provided at smaller stations; the northern lines generally ran their own, but the southern companies preferred outside contractors.

One of the results of the INDUSTRIAL REVOLUTION (q.v.) was that young men began to come to the towns and cities, particularly to London, in growing numbers, as shop assistants, clerks, and apprentices, and to enter the professions. From the end of the 19th century, when the use of the typewriter became more widespread, many young women followed their example. There were not enough restaurants for all these people until multiple-branch cafés began to open. The pioneer firm opened its first London branch in 1884, and its competitor and successor 10 years later. As London grew, new branches were opened, and the movement spread to the larger provincial towns.

Both firms opened large 'popular' restaurants, on many floors, in the West End and other parts of London, and had factory premises fairly close to the centre of London, where food supplies for their branches were prepared and distributed. Other and smaller firms followed their example.

Contracting for meals has always been a function of the catering industry. The multiple-branch firms have special departments which will supply furniture, crockery, meals, and staff for any social occasions, such as weddings, and even for large-scale shows or exhibitions, where they may have to cater for tens of thousands of people in a day.

Until the Second World War began in 1939, service in these new popular restaurants was by waiters or waitresses at the larger restaurants, and by waitresses alone at the smaller cafés. In the U.S.A. popular restaurants had grown up in another way, for habits were different and wages higher, so that restaurant-owners found it cheaper to run snack-bars, and cafeterias or self-service restaurants. Between the First and Second World Wars the snack-bar spread to Britain, and chains of milk-bars were opened by milk and dairy firms. Owing to a shortage of waitresses in Britain during the Second World War, when women were needed for war work, many of the popular cafés adopted the American cafeteria system, which continued when peace came.

There are two other important aspects of the catering industry—factory canteens and the British Restaurants. The first had been started a long time ago by progressive firms, and to-day many firms provide canteens in which their employees can buy their meals. These canteens are sometimes run by an outside firm of caterers, or they may be organized by the employers themselves, or by a committee of employees. British Restaurants were started during the war to supplement the shortage of other restaurants due to damage from bombing. They are run by the local authorities.

See also HOTEL INDUSTRY.
See also Vol. IV: INNS.
See also Vol. XI: COOKING, HISTORY OF.

CELANESE, see RAYON.

CEMENT. Strictly speaking, any powdered substance is cement if, when mixed with water, it is able to be moulded, and then to set hard as it dries. It is used in building, either as a mortar to bind together bricks, stones, or concrete blocks in walls and other structures, or as one of the components of CONCRETE (q.v. Vol. VIII). No other material, except perhaps steel, has had such an influence on modern architecture and modern civil engineering. The Romans called this material *caementum* or *cementum*. Nearly 2,000 years ago Vitruvius, a Roman architect, wrote a famous manual of architecture and building construction. In it he mentioned that 'there is a kind of powder which, by nature, produces wonderful results. It is found . . . round

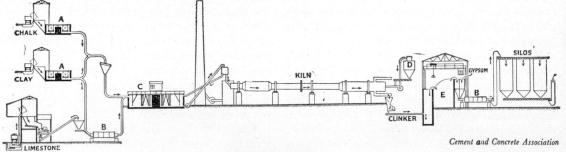

Cement and Concrete Association

THE MAKING OF CEMENT

Cement slurry is made of chalk or limestone and clay. The chalk is broken up with water in a wash mill (A), clay is also mixed with water in another wash mill and limestone is crushed in a ball mill (B) with clay slurry. The slurry is stored in tanks (C) and fed from them to the kiln which is heated with powdered coal from (D). Clinker is formed which is stored in E. This is ground in a ball mill with gypsum to form Portland cement which is stored in silos until it is bagged and dispatched

Mount Vesuvius. This, being mixed with lime and rubble, not only furnishes strength in other buildings, but also, when piers are built in the sea, they set under water.' By 'setting' he means hardening under water, which is one of the most valuable properties of cement; but the same property of 'setting' is useful in all forms of building.

The Romans discovered that certain substances could be ground and mixed with lime and water so that they combined slowly to form a 'hydraulic' cement, that is, one which resisted water. Their secret was lost for centuries, but when the English engineer, Smeaton, was commissioned in 1756 to build the first Eddystone lighthouse, he succeeded in finding in South Wales a natural cement which served his purpose, because it set hard under water. For some time afterwards, 'natural cement' was used, and the term 'Roman' was applied to one variety obtained from Sheppey. Modern cement, however, is an entirely artificial product. It was invented by a Leeds bricklayer, Joseph Aspdin, who patented it in 1824, although he is said to have made the discovery in 1811. He added suitable clay to finely ground limestone, burned the mixture, and ground the resulting product. He named it 'Portland cement' because of its supposed resemblance to Portland stone, although there is little real resemblance between the two. When we speak of 'cement' to-day, we generally mean Portland cement, which is far stronger and more lasting than any of its 'natural' predecessors, particularly as the basis of reinforced concrete.

Like brick, cement is especially valuable in British building because all its ingredients are found within the country (*see* BRICKS AND TILES). Its preparation also involves the use of large quantities of coal. Cement can become a component of concrete by mixing it with bulky material known as 'aggregate', such as gravel, broken bricks, or clinker. Although cement works are found in many parts of Britain where limestone or chalk is available, the chief concentration of the industry is in north Kent, along the banks of the Thames estuary and the Medway. Here suitable alluvial clay from the rivers, and chalk for burning and mixing with it, are found close together, and coal can be shipped right up to the quays beside the various works. As a result, the landscape is studded with tall, grey factory chimneys. Enormous quarries, or

Cement and Concrete Association

CEMENT SLURRY IN STORAGE TANKS (C IN DIAGRAM)

The slurry is stirred by a revolving barrow and agitated by compressed air. The pipe on the right takes the slurry to the kiln

excavations, have been dug into the chalk hills, and all the houses and vegetation are covered with the grey-white dust that comes from the works.

The two essential constituents of cement are calcareous (chalky) substances containing lime, and argillaceous (clayey) substances containing silica and alumina. About two-thirds of the finished product consists of lime. After the ingredients have been mixed in the right proportions, and water has been added, the mixture is ground wet in a 'wash-mill'. This produces a liquid mass known as 'slurry', with the consistency of thick cream. The slurry is then burned at a very high temperature—1,400° to 1,450° C. Formerly the burning was done in a brick or stone kiln shaped like an ordinary lime-kiln. To-day cement is burned in a rotary kiln, a huge steel cylinder 10–12 feet in diameter and 150 to 500 feet long, which revolves very slowly on its axis. The wet slurry is fed into the top end, and slides down gradually to the lower end where the fire is injected. During this process, the powdered limestone or chalk is decomposed into

Cement and Concrete Association

ROTARY CEMENT KILN SEEN FROM THE FIRING END

Kilns may be 10–14 ft. in diameter and 300–500 ft. long, producing up to 500 tons of cement in 24 hours. In the foreground are coolers to cool the clinker

lime and carbon dioxide, the lime combining with the clay to form white-hot clinker. After cooling, the clinker is ground to an extreme fineness in 'ball-mills' containing steel balls. The powder that comes out of the mill is cement, ready for packing and dispatch.

For use in building, whether as an ingredient of mortar or of concrete, the cement must be kept dry until it is actually needed. Cement for mortar is mixed with sand and with a carefully graded amount of water. Cement for concrete has an 'aggregate' added as well. It then 'sets'— that is, dries and hardens—slowly or quickly according to the proportions of the ingredients in it, to suit the purpose for which the concrete is intended. It eventually becomes as hard as rock; indeed, if it is used as mortar, it often becomes harder than the bricks or stone blocks that it joins together.

There are sundry varieties of Portland cement, some bearing the names of firms who make them, and including rapid-hardening, quick-setting, white, and waterproofed cements.

See also BUILDING INDUSTRY, HISTORY OF.
See also Vol. VIII: CONCRETE; CIVIL ENGINEERING.

CERTIFICATE OF ORIGIN, *see* OVERSEAS TRADE.

CHAIN STORE, *see* MULTIPLE SHOPS.

CHALK MINING. Chalk has many industrial uses. It is a limestone of rather loose texture occurring in many parts of eastern, south-eastern, and southern England. Most chalk contains flints, which have been formed from the fossils of tiny organisms living in the sea in remote ages (*see* LIMESTONE, Vol. III).

In the New Stone Age, which began about 2500 to 2000 B.C., men wanted flints to make axes to cut down trees. Forests had to be cleared so that the early farmers could have fields for flocks and herds to graze in as well as land for corn-growing. To get the flints, New Stone Age man began mining in the chalk. This developed into a regular industry in south-eastern and southern England, as for instance at Grimes Graves in Norfolk, at Brandon on the borders of Norfolk and Suffolk, and on the Sussex Downs, as well as in the chalk regions of France and Belgium across the Channel. The mines were dug down as circular shafts, 10 or 15 feet across and up to 20 feet deep; and, when the best flint layer was reached, galleries were dug sideways into the chalk to get out the flint lumps. A mine, therefore, had a central shaft leading from the surface of the ground, with galleries at the bottom, radiating out like the roots of a tree.

When the galleries had been dug as far as was safe, other shafts were dug near one another and the excavated chalk would be thrown back into a disused shaft. In time, therefore, there would be a group of shafts, some filled in, some open, and all with galleries underground branching out and sometimes connecting with one another. The tipping back of excavated chalk from new shafts into the old ones meant, however, that the galleries did not get filled up, except at their mouths, so that when modern archaeologists came to dig out the filling from the shafts of these flint-mines, they found the galleries just as they were left 4,000 years ago, and they could crawl along in the tracks of the original miners. All the digging in New Stone Age times was done by wedging out chalk blocks with deer-antlers and shovelling them up with the shoulder-blades of oxen, so the task must have been enormous. In the open galleries these antler picks have been found as they were dropped by the last miners out of the

A.C.L. Brussels

PREHISTORIC FLINT MINE AT SPIENNES, BELGIUM
Galleries have been tunnelled into the chalk leaving columns to support the roof

shaft, and some even show the imprint of the fingers and thumbs on the chalk coating on the handles. On the roofs of the galleries stains of smoke from torches or primitive lamps (a wick in a dish of fat) can also still be seen.

All around the mines have been found the waste flakes and bits of flint left over from the manufacture of axes. There is evidence of much specialization, or DIVISION OF LABOUR (q.v.); in fact, the industry seems to have been organized almost like a modern factory, on continuous-production lines. The different types of flint waste show that one worker did the first rough-ing-out, and passed it on to another near by who did the finer flaking, and so on (*see* PREHISTORIC TOOLS AND WEAPONS, Vol. I).

In modern days British chalk deposits are still mined for their flints. These are greatly used in the POTTERY industry (q.v.) and in road-making; from the Middle Ages onwards they have also been a favourite building material, although this use is slowly dying out.

But the main purpose in chalk mining nowa-days is to get the chalk itself. Chemically, chalk is calcium carbonate; when burned it becomes lime, which is calcium oxide—sometimes called quicklime to distinguish it from the slaked lime or calcium hydrate formed when quicklime is mixed with water. Chalk in its natural form is also used as a fertilizer, and it is one of the raw materials of the CEMENT industry (q.v.). It is used in the manufacture of rubber articles and in the preparation of wallpaper, and some of the harder and more rocky kinds are used as building-stone. In the mineral-water industry chalk is the material from which the carbon dioxide is made which produces the gassiness in the drinks. Whiting, which is an important constituent of putty and is also much used for polishing jewel-lery and plate, is made out of ground chalk mixed with water and later evaporated.

See also Vol. I: PREHISTORIC MAN.
See also Vol. III: LIMESTONE.
See also Vol. VI: LIME.

CHAMBERS OF COMMERCE. These are voluntary associations of business men, mer-chants, and financiers. Their aim is to look after local industrial and commercial interests, collect and distribute information and STATISTICS (q.v.), uphold standards of business honesty, and main-tain the quality of products and so safeguard the reputation of the town or district. Some-times they supervise certain types of commercial education.

The Guild Merchant of the Middle Ages,

which was an association of all merchants in a city or town, was the forerunner of the modern Chamber of Commerce (*see* CRAFT GUILDS). Our modern term is a literal translation from the French, and it was the French who took the lead in the modern revival of the old medieval Guild. In Britain, Chambers of Commerce appeared at the end of the 18th century and became more numerous during the 19th, the London Chamber of Commerce being founded in 1881. The members of these Chambers were commercial and industrial firms. Later they formed the Association of British Chambers of Commerce, to act as a general clearing-house for their activities.

In 1911 Joseph Chamberlain inspired the Federation of Chambers of Commerce of the British Empire; and in 1920 Belgium, France, Great Britain, Italy, and the United States formed the International Chamber of Commerce. The membership of these two bodies was restricted to local and national Chambers of Commerce, and to associated bodies such as the Federation of British Industries.

CHARCOAL is wood that has undergone the same treatment as coal receives when it is made into coke. This treatment is technically called 'destructive DISTILLATION' (q.v.), and nowadays takes place in closed vessels from which air is excluded; these are heated, and the gassy constituents of the wood are driven off, leaving a black, brittle, and porous substance behind. This is the charcoal. In earlier times it was made by piling pieces of wood in the form of a rough pyramid, with plenty of room between the pieces for air to circulate, and covering the pile with earth and setting fire to it.

Charcoal has had many uses, though for some it has now been replaced by the powdery carbon or lampblack obtained as a by-product of certain processes in oil refining. One of its important properties is its capacity to absorb odours and colours; some chemicals that are not colourless in their manufactured state may be made so by being agitated in water containing powdered charcoal, or by being filtered through granulated charcoal: this is also the material used in filters for drinking-water.

As charcoal is a very pure form of carbon (although not as pure as the diamond, which is the purest form known to science), it is often used by metallurgists for SMELTING (q.v. Vol.

VIII) small quantities of metallic ores into metal that is required in its purest form. The British iron industry, before the discovery and use of coke, smelted its ores with the aid of charcoal. It is one of the constituents of GUNPOWDER (q.v. Vol. VIII). It used to be the basis of black paints and printing inks before it was replaced by the modern products of the oil refineries. It is still used for the preparation of the finest types of Indian INK (q.v. Vol. IV). Animal charcoal, made from calcined bones, is used in SUGAR REFINING (q.v.).

CHARTERED ACCOUNTANT, *see* AUDITING.

CHARTERED COMPANIES are formed by Royal Charter or by Act of Parliament. Many trading companies have been formed in this way, among them the Bank of England, the Gas Light and Coke Company, the P. & O. Steam Navigation Company, and the Royal Mail Steam Packet Company (*see* COMPANIES). In modern times this method has often been used by professional associations, such as the Institute of Chartered Accountants, the Chartered Institute of Secretaries, and the Royal Institute of British Architects.

The most famous of the chartered companies have been those formed to explore and colonize new lands, and to develop trade between them and the home country. The earliest of these was the Company of MERCHANT ADVENTURERS (q.v.). This was formed at the end of the 13th century, to develop the cloth trade in that part of north-west Europe then known as Flanders, and now including north-east France, Belgium, and the Netherlands.

The next big chartered company was the Russia Company, formed in 1555. Sebastian CABOT (q.v. Vol. V), the famous navigator and explorer, was its first governor. Queen Elizabeth encouraged further companies. The Eastland Company was given a charter in 1579, to trade in the Baltic lands and Scandinavia and to challenge the influence of the HANSEATIC LEAGUE (q.v.). In 1581 the Levant Company was formed to capture from the Venetians and the Genoese some of the trade of the Near East. In 1588 the first of a series of African Companies was founded, and in 1600 the most famous of all the chartered companies, the EAST INDIA COMPANY (q.v.).

The Stuart kings continued the Elizabethan

Fox Photos

CHARCOAL BURNING IN KENT

In the foreground a pile of wood is being prepared for burning, and behind are burning piles

CHARTER OF THE INCORPORATION OF THE LEVANT COMPANY

Granted in 1661 by Charles II, confirming letters patent giving trading rights to the Company by James I. The company was first chartered in 1581. *State Papers, Foreign Archives (S.P. 105) 108 (M.P.M. 1)*

tradition. Another company operating on the west coast of Africa was given a charter in 1618. The two earlier African Companies were merged in a new Company of Royal Adventurers into Africa in 1663. This was a more ambitious project than the others, and took in the whole of Africa as far as the Cape of Good Hope. The Royal African Company of England, founded in 1672, became its successor. In 1670 Charles II gave the HUDSON'S BAY COMPANY (q.v.) its first charter. The 18th century was not noteworthy for the formation of new companies. The South Sea Company was, however, founded in 1711, but did not conduct any serious business of exploration or colonization. Its activities were almost brought to an end by the financial disaster known as the SOUTH SEA BUBBLE (q.v.), although it lingered on for many years before it was finally liquidated.

The chartered companies were very prominent in the earlier years of Britain's overseas development, and at that time served a useful purpose. They gave to associations of traders the prestige and power that came from operating under Royal Charter. Most of the enterprises meant adventuring into more or less unknown lands. War was then very frequent, and British lines of communication lay mainly across the seas; trading and exploring adventures were almost bound to lead to the use of troops and warships, and a single unfortunate encounter on the high seas or abroad might, for the sake of prestige, drag the country into war. Yet the Government could hardly manage such trading enterprises direct, however much it might have been interested in their success. To make it easy, therefore, for the Government to control what went on in one part of the world, a single trading company would be given exclusive rights there. Control could be exercised in other ways. The charters were not granted for indefinite periods, but were subject to periodical renewal. When the time for renewal came, the Government could change the original conditions, if it thought fit. The right of appointment of the governors of these companies, and in many cases of their directors, was also reserved by the Government. Many governors were either members of the royal family itself, like Prince Rupert, cousin of Charles II, who was the first governor of the Hudson's Bay Company, or they were leading statesmen. Moreover, at a time when taxes were few, and hard to collect, and the Treasury was always short of money, the Government could arrange for a share in profits as part of the price to be paid for renewing a charter. Apart from all these reasons, the chartered company was an obvious form of organization in an age when strict Government control of overseas trade was regarded as the normal thing (*see* MERCANTILE SYSTEM).

The 16th and 17th centuries were the heyday of the chartered companies. During the 18th century opinion began to harden against trading privileges in any part of the world being reserved for a single concern. Agitation against the companies increased, and the competition of free-traders, whom the companies called interlopers, was allowed to grow. Although some of the companies remained in being longer than others, by the beginning of the 19th century nearly all of them had ceased to exist in their original form.

The free-trade temper of most of the 19th century did not encourage chartered companies (*see* INTERNATIONAL TRADE, Section 4), but towards the end of the century the leading European powers began to compete for colonies in Africa (the 'scramble for Africa' as it was called) and elsewhere overseas. The chartered companies were then revived. The British North Borneo Company was formed in 1882, and, like the East India Company, not only traded in its territory but governed it. After the Second World War its administration was taken over by the British Government.

One of the most famous of the late-19th-century companies was the British South Africa Company, formed in 1889 to develop Bechuanaland and the lands north of it. It owed its existence to the enterprise of Cecil RHODES (q.v. Vol. V), and it ruled Rhodesia from 1905 until 1923, when it was deprived of its administrative

powers. This company and the Hudson's Bay Company still survive as commercial corporations, the British South Africa Company now being mainly interested in mining and prospecting.

See also COMPANIES; TRADE, HISTORY OF.

CHEESE-MAKING, *see* DAIRY INDUSTRY, Section 4.

CHEMICAL INDUSTRY, *see* CHEMISTRY, INDUSTRIAL.

CHEMISTRY, HISTORY OF. The study of the nature and composition of the different forms of matter, and of the interactions which can take place between them, is the science of CHEMISTRY (q.v. Vol. III). In early ages, primitive man had found out by trial and error how to carry out a number of chemical processes. By the time of the ancient EGYPTIAN CIVILIZATION (q.v. Vol. I) the more civilized men knew how to extract and work copper, tin, iron, and the precious metals, how to make pottery, glass, soap, and pigments, and how to bleach and dye textile fabrics. These arts were the beginnings of the chemical industries.

The early scientific study of chemistry, known as alchemy, grew up in the first few centuries A.D. at Alexandria in Egypt. There two important things came together: one was the practical knowledge of the men who worked in metals, pottery, and dyes; the other was the learning of the earlier Greek philosophers. These included Heraclitus, Empedocles, Hippocratus, and Aristotle, who had long debated the nature of MATTER (q.v. Vol. III). At the same time alchemy was much influenced by ideas from the East about MAGIC and ASTROLOGY, or foretelling the future from the stars (qq.v. Vol. I).

The Greek philosophers held that all matter was made up of the same four 'elements'—earth, fire, air, and water. Many people, therefore, thought that, if those elements could be rearranged, one substance could be changed into another. For instance, a base metal such as lead could perhaps be turned into gold. The chief aim of the alchemists was to find a way of doing this.

Alchemy came under Arab influence when the armies of ISLAM (q.v. Vol. I) conquered Egypt during the 7th century. They carried its study into western Europe when they advanced into Spain. Many Arabic words are still used in chemistry, for example, 'alkali', 'alcohol', 'borax', and even 'alchemy' itself, which means 'the art of Egypt'.

The greatest of the Arabic alchemists was Jabir ibn Hayyan, possibly the same person as Geber, the author of two important books on alchemy known from Latin translations dating from the 13th century. Jabir claimed that mercury and sulphur should be reckoned as 'elements', like the air, fire, earth, and water of the Greeks. He said that all metals were composed of mercury and sulphur in different proportions. To transmute a base metal to gold would require a change in these proportions, and this change was to be brought about by the action of some mysterious substance which came to be called 'the philosopher's stone'. Alchemists searched in vain for this substance for several hundred years.

Alchemy was studied widely in Europe during the 12th and following centuries and attracted the attention of many learned men, including the 13th-century alchemist, Roger BACON (q.v. Vol. V). Bacon's writings show that he was familiar with the work of the early Arabic alchemists, and he also describes the manufacture of gunpowder.

Though the alchemists were doomed to failure in their efforts to make gold, they were none the less learned men engaged in a perfectly serious study. Their work led to the growth of a great deal of new chemical knowledge and of methods of making experiments. Many of the later European alchemists, however, were complete frauds who preyed upon trusting people by all sorts of tricks, and the subject fell into disrepute. By the time of Paracelsus (1493–1541) the aim of the alchemists had changed from the making of gold to the making of medicines. In particular they sought a fanciful substance called the 'elixir of life', which was to cure all ills, and which some people thought would turn out to be the same as the philosopher's stone (see MEDICINE, HISTORY OF, Vol. XI). This phase of chemistry lasted till about 1700.

In this period an increasing number of workers made and recorded chemical experiments in what we should regard as a scientific way. Agricola (1495–1555) studied and wrote of metallic ores and the methods of making pure metals and metallic compounds from them. He also laid the foundations of chemical analysis. The transition from alchemy to chemistry was further advanced by van Helmont (1577–1644) who studied carbon dioxide and other gases.

It was the 17th-century Irishman, Robert BOYLE (q.v. Vol. V), who finally overthrew the traditions of alchemy and began the era of modern science. In his book *The Sceptical Chymist* (1661) he insisted on the use of the scientific method of experiment, observation, and deduction. He gravely questioned the old theories of the composition of matter based on the Greek and Arabic 'elements'. He defined an element—as we still do to-day—as a substance that cannot be split up into simpler substances. Boyle made many careful experiments on the properties of gases, and established the law relating to pressure and volume which bears his name (see PRESSURE, Vol. III).

During the next 100 years chemical investigations were mainly directed towards the preparation of gases and the study of the composition of the air and of the process of 'combustion' or burning. Almost all men of learning at that time accepted a theory of combustion which is now known to be false—the theory of 'phlogiston'. It was thought that everything which would burn, such as coal, paper, wood, and so on, was composed of its own ash together with phlogiston; the phlogiston was believed to be lost during burning, leaving only the ash. Later came the preparation of oxygen by Scheele and Joseph PRIESTLEY in 1774, and this was followed by the brilliant researches of the French scientist LAVOISIER (qq.v. Vol. V), which finally overthrew the phlogiston theory. The fact was proved that burning is the interaction of oxygen (which forms one-fifth of the air) with whatever substance is being burnt.

The atomic theory of John Dalton (1766–1844) was the foundation-stone on which the rapidly growing science of chemistry in the 19th century was built. Of the 90 elements of which the earth is composed (see MATTER, Vol. III) only about 28 had been truly identified in 1800. By 1850 this number had risen to 54, and by the end of the century to 80. The elements were arranged in a 'periodic table', according to their atomic weight, by Mendeleev in 1869 (see table, pages 278–9, Vol. III). The discovery of radioactivity by Becquerel in 1896 was followed by the discovery of radium by Madame Marie CURIE (q.v. Vol. V). This led to the structure of the atom being made clear by Lord RUTHERFORD (q.v. Vol. V) at Cambridge in 1920. Later came

Alinari

THE ALCHEMIST
Painted by Giovanni Stradano in 1570. Now in the Palazzo Vecchio, Florence

AN EARLY 19TH-CENTURY CHEMIST'S LABORATORY

the splitting of the atom and the using of ATOMIC ENERGY (q.v. Vol. VIII).

Since the middle of the 19th century two new and very important branches of chemistry have grown up: these are organic chemistry and physical chemistry. Organic chemistry is the study of compounds of the element carbon. Originally these compounds were all natural products such as sugar, starch, the colouring matters of plants, and so on. Hundreds of thousands of other carbon compounds which do not occur in nature have now been made in the laboratory; in fact more compounds of carbon are known than of all the other elements put together. They include the majority of the chemical substances that we meet in our daily life— DYES, PLASTICS, MEDICAL SUPPLIES, and artificial textile fibres such as RAYON and NYLON (qq.v.).

Physical chemistry studies the composition of chemical substances, in particular the character of molecules and the ways in which they interact with or influence each other.

See also Vol. III: CHEMISTRY; MATTER; ATOM.

CHEMISTRY, INDUSTRIAL.

From the earliest days of civilization man has been carrying out chemical processes for the ordinary needs of his life.

As long ago as 4000 B.C. the Egyptians and Sumerians had discovered how to dye clothes, and to smelt ores from which they made the metals for their weapons and implements. They had learned how to convert herbs and various animal and mineral substances into medicines; they knew how to make glass from sand and soda, and how to colour it; they mined copper, silver, and gold; they tanned their leather to prevent it from decomposing.

To do all these things, the people of these early civilizations needed many natural substances. The ALKALI (q.v.) that they used for glass, for example, came from dried-up salt beds in Egypt. Dye-stuffs came from the roots and berries of plants, or from lichens and fungi; the famous Tyrian purple that dyed the garments of the Roman Emperors was obtained from a shell-fish found in the Mediterranean (see DYES).

As the centuries passed, man learned more and more about these changes from one sort of matter into another. Scientists began to study the changes in order to explain and control them (see CHEMISTRY, HISTORY OF).

By the 18th century a vast store of chemical knowledge had been built up throughout the world. As the INDUSTRIAL REVOLUTION (q.v.) developed during the next hundred years, a demand arose from the new, expanding industries for many different substances. The same alkali that the Egyptians had used was wanted for glass, textiles, leather, paper, and soap; more and more dyes were needed for the cloth that was coming from the mills in Lancashire and Yorkshire; limestone was now a raw material greatly needed by many industries from agriculture to steel; and salt was in demand for innumerable industrial processes. All these raw materials were now required, not only for direct use but also for indirect. Chemistry had shown how they could be changed into all sorts of new materials which in their turn were needed by industry.

Salt, for example, obtained from the brine wells of Cheshire, was used for making glass and pottery. But it was also converted into other chemicals. It provided chlorine for making into the bleaching powder that the textile mills required; it yielded hydrochloric acid, which became a vital raw material for the iron and steel and similar industries. Combined with lime, it was turned into the alkali that had until then been provided by natural deposits in other countries. Sulphur, and sulphur-bearing ores like pyrites, were used for making sulphuric acid —needed by almost every branch of industry in one way or another (*see* ACIDS).

the alkali, chlorine, hydrochloric acid, sulphuric acid, and other industrial chemicals to feed the 'workshop of the world', as Britain was then known.

The discovery in 1856 of mauveine, the first synthetic dye-stuff, by a British research chemist, William Henry Perkin (*see* DYES), was the beginning of an entirely new branch of industrial chemistry, and within a few years synthetic

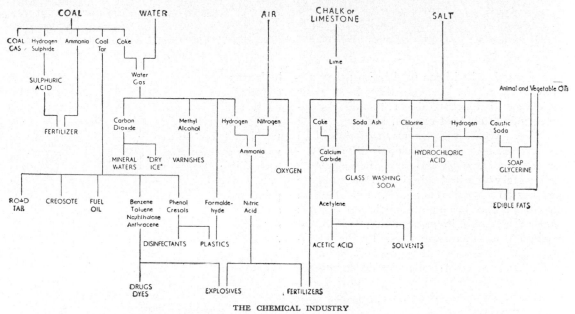

THE CHEMICAL INDUSTRY

Chart showing the main products of the chemical industry and how they are derived

So, by the early 19th century, there had grown up in Britain an industry to provide these raw materials that were needed by the developing industries. This was what we now describe as the heavy chemical industry. It used simple raw materials provided by nature, such as salt, lime, and sulphur, and turned them into a range of new materials that industries required. The materials that were made are what we call industrial chemicals.

Naturally, industrial chemical production became centred in localities near the sources of raw materials. Salt-works grew up in Cheshire, to evaporate the brine that was pumped from the wells. Nearby the alkali industry developed, using salt from Cheshire and lime from the quarries in Buxton. Sulphuric acid was made in the same region, using sulphur brought from Sicily, or sulphur-bearing ores shipped from overseas. From these chemical factories came

dye-stuffs had become a most important industry. The raw materials used by this industry were the chemicals obtained by the DISTILLATION of coal-tar (q.v.): for instance, aniline, benzene, toluene, and anthracene. The coal-tar industry itself was, at this time, not very old. At the beginning of the 19th century William Murdoch had begun the development of coal-gas lighting. As the coal-gas flame began to flicker in the streets and larger buildings of Victorian England, gasworks sprang up all over the country to supply the gas that was needed. The gas was made by heating coal in closed containers called 'retorts' until the gas was given off, and with it came a variety of liquid materials, including the sticky black mixture which we describe as coal-tar.

Coal-tar was found to contain many different chemicals which had originated from the decomposed vegetable material that we call COAL (q.v. Vol. III). These chemicals were different

A GENERAL VIEW OF THE IMPERIAL CHEMICAL

from those that had been used before; they are organic chemicals, because they have their origin in organic materials. They are all derivatives of the element carbon, and since those days they have become the raw materials of an entirely new branch of the chemical industry— the organic chemical industry. Perkin's dye-stuffs factory was its beginning. Dye-stuffs are complicated organic chemicals, and research into their nature became the nucleus of organic chemical research in general and led to the production of other substances. By the beginning of the present century industry began to make PLASTICS (q.v.) from organic chemicals. Since then many other things have been made: fibres such as nylon, drugs, insecticides, vitamins, and paints.

During the last few years another source of organic chemicals, petroleum, has become important. Petroleum is thought to be the remains of tiny marine animals that lived in prehistoric times. Until the 1930's petroleum was used largely as a source of heat or energy; it was a convenient thing to use in ships' engines and cars. Later, chemists found in it a source of new types of organic chemicals, and hundreds of different chemicals are now being produced by the distillation of petroleum.

The third great source of industrial organic chemicals is vegetable matter. Corn and other agricultural products can be turned into alcohol, which has become an industrial chemical of first-rate importance. It is used for making all sorts of things, from synthetic rubber to perfumes, and it is produced in hundreds of thousands of tons every year.

Instead of distilling coal to get coal-tar, the scientist learned to make organic chemicals direct from coal—for example, by treatment with hydrogen gas. This converts the coal into chemicals of the petroleum type. Similarly, the coke, which remains in the retort after coal distillation, is turned into organic chemicals by treating it, red hot, with steam and air. In this way we get materials that are used for making such things as waxes and synthetic fats.

In Great Britain to-day industry is using the primary raw materials, such as coal, lime, salt, and the air itself, for a tremendous variety of secondary, or made-up, chemical materials needed by many industries. The present century has seen Britain established as one of the chief laboratories of the world.

See also ACIDS; ALKALIS; DYES; MEDICAL SUPPLIES; PAPER-MAKING; RAYON; CHEMISTRY, HISTORY OF.

See also Vol. III: CHEMISTRY.

CHEMIST'S SHOP, see MEDICAL SUPPLIES.

CHEQUE, see BANKING.

CHINA, see PORCELAIN.

CHINA CLAY. This is a fine, soft, white clay used in the making of pottery, paper, and other articles, and formed by the natural decomposition of feldspar, one of the chief components of granite. In the U.S.A. and other countries it is known as 'kaolin', from the place in China where it was first used.

Feldspar turns into clay by a slow geological process, either by the weathering effect of surface water on the granite (see DENUDATION, Section 1, Vol. III) or by the action of hot solutions coming up from deep down in the earth. The first leads to shallow deposits, and the second to deep ones; the deeper the clay, the greater the quantity and the better the quality and colour.

INDUSTRIES WORKS AT BILLINGHAM-ON-TEES   *I.C.I.*

The most easily developed of the world's important deposits of china clay are in Britain, in the granite areas of Cornwall and Devon, such as St. Austell, Bodmin Moor, and Dartmoor. At St. Austell there are about 100 pits, and some of the most famous have a working depth of over 340 feet. These still have great untapped reserves, which it is estimated will last for at least 100 years, on the basis of a production of 1 million tons a year. Large reserves of this good clay in Cornwall and Devon are on high ground, from 700 to 1,000 feet above sea level, where there is also plenty of clear water. These two natural conditions, height of ground and abundant water, are important to the extraction of the clay, and largely determine the cost of mining.

Although the term 'mining' is used, in this industry the clay is actually washed down from the open sides of the pit by means of a high-pressure hose called a 'monitor', mounted on a movable stand and handled much as a fireman directs water on a burning building. There may be as many as four or five monitors in a large pit.

The clay-laden water, called 'slurry', flows into special pits, where the coarse grains of sand (quartz) and other impurities settle. The clay-water is then pumped to the surface of the pit, and the process of refining is repeated through a series of channels until the smallest particles of sand have gone. The liquid clay, now free of grit, is allowed to settle in tanks, to the consistency of cream; it then flows through pipelines to other tanks, where it remains for about 8 weeks so that the solid particles may settle to the bottom and the surplus water evaporate. In some pits this process is shortened by the use of filter-presses.

The clay, when dry enough to be handled, is taken to the drying-kiln, a long, low shed with a floor of fire-brick slabs covering flues which conduct heated air under the clay. The same shed provides storage room, called a 'linhay', where the clay is kept until shipment.

From the linhays, which are usually near a railway siding or a deep-sea port such as Plymouth and Falmouth, the clay is distributed by lorry, rail, or coastwise shipping and canal to various destinations in Britain, such as the Potteries in Staffordshire. During the present century nearly three-quarters of the output has been exported by sea direct to the U.S.A. and Canada, the largest consumers, and to many European countries.

When the industry was first set up in the 18th century, after William Cookworthy found clay near Porthleven (Cornwall) in 1755, the main use of china clay was for making POTTERY (q.v.). Since then the clay has been increasingly used as a filling and coating substance which greatly improves the quality of paper. Mixed with a pulp consisting of rags, wood, or esparto grass, the clay gives paper a finer texture for printing ink, and also makes photographic paper glossy. Good printing paper has about 16% of clay, and paper with a high gloss has 25% (*see* PAPER-MAKING).

Although china clay is still mainly used for pottery and paper, it also plays an important part in the making of rubber, paint, asbestos products, fire-bricks, cement, linoleum, oilcloth, insecticides, leather, chemicals, and medicinal preparations. It is used to stiffen textiles, and is used in cosmetics as a basis for face-powder. During the First World War a number of new uses were discovered for china clay as a substitute for certain chemicals that

CHINA CLAY PITS AT ST. AUSTELL, CORNWALL
Tanks filled with slurry in which impurities settle to the bottom. In the background are white waste tips

come from abroad and could no longer be obtained.

Even the waste from the clay-pits provides valuable BY-PRODUCTS (q.v.). The spectacular white pyramids, which are so conspicuous a feature of the Devon and Cornwall landscape, yield the sand from which concrete blocks for housing have been made for over 50 years. These dumps, sometimes containing a million tons of waste, provide a special quartz sand useful for making cement, and also flake-mica, used as a substitute for glass in furnaces and stoves because of its great resistance to heat.

Before the Second World War the china-clay industry ranked second only to coal in tonnage and value of raw materials exported from the United Kingdom. Since the beginning of the century the annual British output has varied from 500,000 to 800,000 tons. The output of the industry is not due solely to the favourable natural conditions in which the clay is found, nor to mechanical power, which has progressed from the famous Cornish beam steam-engine of the 18th century to gas, to oil, and finally to electricity. It is due just as much to the skill and judgement of the individual clay-worker, using age-old methods of refining and drying, in pits

where the post of 'pit-captain' is often passed from father to son.

See also CLAY; PAPER-MAKING; POTTERY.
See also Vol. III: ROCKS.

CHOCOLATE, *see* COCOA AND CHOCOLATE.

CIDER-MAKING. Cider is the fermented juice of apples, and is an apple wine of the same kind as wine made from grapes, although it contains less alcohol. Spain was the first country in Europe to make cider, and it has been for a long time a popular drink in France, particularly in Normandy. In the Middle Ages it was popular in many parts of England, and especially in East Anglia, but there is no record of its having been made before the 17th century in the west of England, which is now a great cider country. The drink went out of favour in England at the end of the 18th century, and the taste for it revived very slowly. During the First World War the EXCISE duties (q.v. Vol. X) on cider, as well as on whisky and beer, were greatly increased, and this prevented the revival of the popularity of cider. After the war the tax was reduced and since then there has been some revival of the English cider industry.

As happens with wine, fruit grown in certain districts and on certain soils makes better cider than other fruit, and it is in Devon, Hereford, and Somerset that the best cider apples are grown in England. English cider has hitherto been made from pressed and pulped apples by a process of natural FERMENTATION (q.v. Vol. II)—the same process as that by which wine is made. Fermentation must not be allowed to advance too far, or the wine will have too much acidity. Cider, like grape wine, can be either still or sparkling (*see* WINE TRADE). The best sparkling ciders are made, like champagne, by being put into bottles before fermentation is fully complete, but the sparkle is given to the cheaper ciders by the artificial introduction of carbon dioxide gas.

There is an annual cider-sampling ceremony in Somerset in May; at this ceremony a modern cider artificially fermented from a champagne yeast was first introduced.

Perry, made from pears instead of apples, is made by the same methods as cider.

CIGARETTES, *see* TOBACCO INDUSTRY.

CINEMA, *see* ENTERTAINMENT INDUSTRY; *see also* Vol. IX: CINEMA, HISTORY OF.

CINQUE PORTS, *see* Vol. X, CINQUE PORTS.

CITY COMPANIES. The Livery Companies of the City of London are the successors of the earlier CRAFT GUILDS (q.v.). There are twelve principal companies: the Clothworkers, Drapers, Fishmongers, Goldsmiths, Grocers, Haberdashers, Ironmongers, Mercers, Merchant Taylors, Salters, Skinners, and Vintners. There are also about sixty minor companies. Some of these, the Carpenters and Leathersellers for instance, are wealthy and important.

The City Companies began as craft guilds in the late Middle Ages. Many of the craft guilds in time split up because the interests of the master members came into conflict with the interests of the worker or apprentice members. Such guilds became guilds of masters only, or 'liverymen', entitled to wear the 'livery' or the ceremonial uniform of the guild. Some of the more influential of these masters' guilds obtained Royal Charters forming them into corporations or companies; and so they developed into the City Companies of London.

Until the 16th century the companies retained a direct connexion with their trades, training

H. P. Bulmer and Co.

A CIDER PRESS
The apples, wrapped in sacks, are pressed beneath a large hydraulic press

apprentices and newcomers, regulating wages and other payments, watching over the standard and quality of work done, and controlling conditions of entrance to the trade or craft. But by the 18th century most of the companies had given up these duties, for guild control over industry and commerce had disappeared in favour of the small, independent master or the big company. They still carried on their charitable and benevolent work, looking after their old or infirm members and often pensioning their widows; they remained interested, as always, in education; and, as their charters had often conferred such privileges on them, they played an important and influential part in the civic government of the City of London, and in nominations for the office of Lord Mayor.

They also retained their wealth, and had even added to it in spite of various attempts to take it from them. Their riches had often made them the targets of jealous or moneyless kings, or of their finance ministers. After the Reformation and the dissolution of the monasteries, ministers such as Thomas Cromwell turned to the City Companies for money, and they lost a lot of their wealth and property during this period of plundering. Charles I and Charles II, who were always short of money, also took money from the companies, sometimes openly and blatantly as forced levies or loans, sometimes more politely in the guise of subscriptions to various objects. They had just begun to recover from these losses when the Great Fire raged across the City of London in 1666, and their magnificent halls and treasures and many of their records were largely swept away. Their recovery from this blow was a very slow and painful process.

By that time their functional position in English trade and industry had disappeared. They had become close corporations of influential City merchants and manufacturers, and many of their members followed trades very different from those which their companies had once so carefully supervised and controlled. For there had always been two ways in which would-be entrants to the companies could qualify as members. The practice of the trade concerned was, of course, one way. The other was to be the son of an existing member, even though he followed a different trade. Thus, the son of a Vintner was eligible to become a Vintner too, even though he practised as a lawyer, for instance. By the 18th century a City Company had therefore become a kind of club, where members of varied interests could dine and discuss business together, and where influential strangers could be hospitably entertained. As London became a larger and more populated city, and property owned by the companies in it rose in value, their wealth accumulated, until at the beginning of the 20th century it had become very considerable indeed.

There, are however, a few companies that are still occupied with details of their original trades. Of these the most noteworthy is the Goldsmiths Company. The annual 'trial of the pyx', or approval of new coins turned out by the Royal Mint, is still their responsibility; and it is at Goldsmiths' Hall that the Assay office is located, where the hall-marking of gold and silver is carried out (*see* ASSAYING). The Apothecaries Company still looks after the soundness and purity of medicines.

Many of their names now mean something different from what they meant hundreds of years ago. 'Grocer' nowadays means someone who keeps a retail shop and deals in provisions; the name originally came from the French word for 'wholesaler', and meant a merchant on a large scale. The first whale-oil from Greenland was handled by the Grocers Company. They founded Oundle, the public school in Northamptonshire.

'Mercer' now means a merchant in silks and satins. The word originally came from the Latin *mercator*, meaning merchant. The early Mercers dealt not only in silk, woollen, and cotton textiles, but also in oils, wines, spirits, and some metals. Richard (Dick) Whittington and Sir Thomas Gresham, the great financier of Queen Elizabeth's reign, were both Mercers. Dean Colet, the founder of St. Paul's School, was a great benefactor of the Company, and his portrait hangs in their hall. The Company runs a school in London.

The Drapers got their name from the French word for cloth—*drap*—and made and dealt in woollen cloth.

S I R,

BY Virtue of a Precept from the Right Honourable the LORD MAYOR, you are deſired by the MASTER and WARDENS of the Worſhipful Company of STATIONERS, to meet at *Guildhall*, on *Monday* the 29th Day of *September*, 1777, at Nine of the Clock in the Morning, in your Livery Gown and Hood: From thence to attend the preſent LORD MAYOR to St. *Laurence*'s Church to hear a Sermon: And then to return to *Guildhall* to elect a LORD MAYOR for the Year enſuing.

Marſhall Sheepey, Beadle.

INVITATION TO MEMBERS OF THE LIVERY COMPANIES TO ELECT A LORD MAYOR OF LONDON
The invitation bears the arms of the Stationers Company

GOLDSMITHS HALL IN THE 19TH CENTURY
Coloured engraving after T. H. Shepherd

Their records mention their having fitted out a ship for John Cabot's voyage to explore Newfoundland at the end of the 15th century. The Merchant Taylors originally made armour and camp equipment as well as clothes, in what is now Threadneedle Street. Their Company founded the public school of that name. The Skinners also founded one: Tonbridge, in Kent. As their name suggests, they dealt with skins and furs. The Haberdashers, who also run a school in London, absorbed several minor guilds, including the hatmakers or Milliners, so called because their craftsmen came originally from Milan, in northern Italy. The work of the Ironmongers was formerly much closer to that of the wholesale iron and steel merchant than to the retail dealings in hardware of the ironmongers of to-day. To the Vintners Company, who dealt in wines, belonged not only the importers of wine but the keepers of inns and taverns where wine was sold. The Clothworkers Company included members of the guilds of the shearmen, fullers, dyers, and weavers. The Fishmongers' records contain two names of interest: Sir John Gresham, who founded Gresham's School, at Holt in Norfolk; and Doggett, the original promoter of the annual race by the Thames watermen for Doggett's Coat and Badge (*see* BOAT RACES, Vol. IX).

Many of the trades carried on by some of the lesser companies are now things of the past. This is particularly true of the companies dealing with the making of bows and arrows: the Bowyers, Stringers, and Fletchers—this last from the French *flèche*. The Barber Chirurgeons originally did the work of doctors and dentists, as well as shaving and trimming hair. The Cordwainers dealt with leather, including the tanning process and the making of boots and shoes; the French word for one who keeps a boot and shoe shop is still *cordonnier*. The Founders cast vessels out of metals other than iron, principally brass and pewter. The Horners made drinking vessels and musical instruments out of horn. The Loriners, or Lorimers, made the metal parts of horse equipment, such as bits and spurs, both now forgotten trades. The craft of the Patten-makers goes back to the days when it was impossible to walk the foul, slushy streets of London without the rough wooden clogs, or pattens, which the members of this Company turned out. The Plaisterers Company still survives, and was originally known as the Pargetters. The Scriveners used once to carry out the duties now performed by solicitors. They had a great deal of trouble with illiterate apprentices, who lacked the perfection of grammar and style that their masters thought necessary; a bad apprentice was ordered to a grammar school until he should be 'erudited in the books'. The Turners made parts of household furniture; and the Upholders —who were the forerunners of our modern upholsterers—assembled them. One of the most famous of the minor City Companies was the Woolmen's Company; this has now lost the important place it held in the great days of the English wool trade (*see* WOOL TRADE, MEDIEVAL).

It seems to be the fate of the companies that they should become prosperous after disasters. The Second World War did not injure the Companies as much as the Great Fire, although several halls were damaged and some entirely destroyed; the gaunt ruins of Salters Hall, for instance, were for many years visible from St. Swithin's Lane. But the economic consequences of the war have to some extent hampered their ancient tradition of hospitality, and compelled them to adopt an austerity very different from the days before the war, when it was a memorable experience to dine in one of their magnificent halls, and to be served from their beautiful plate and silver. They still live on, however, as a picturesque part of the traditional greatness of the City of London. Their names survive throughout the Commonwealth and the United States as the surnames of countless families of English stock, some of whom do not know, perhaps, that their names are those of the trades followed by their forefathers.

CLAY PRODUCTS, *see* BRICKS AND TILES; POTTERY; CHINA CLAY.

CLEARING HOUSES. These are organizations which economize time and labour in settling what business men owe to each other. If each of six business firms, for example, had one buying and one selling deal with each other in a day, the daily total of transactions would be thirty. If all these transactions were settled separately, thirty separate cheques would have to be made out, paid into the various banks, and dealt with by the bankers (*see* BANK ACCOUNTS); and a good deal of clerical labour would be wasted on all these details. But if the six firms formed a Clearing House for the 'clearance', or settlement, of what they owed each other, all transactions during the day would be reported to the clearing house, which would strike a balance at the close of business. Some firms would owe money and others would be owed money; the total owed would equal the total to be received. It would then only be necessary for each firm owing money to draw a cheque in favour of the clearing house, and for the clearing house to draw cheques in favour of the firms that were

Committee of London Clearing Bankers

THE CENTRAL CLEARING HOUSE DURING THE SECOND WORLD WAR

An average of a million cheques pass through the Clearing House every day

owed. All firms belonging to the clearing house could, in turn, provide the necessary clerical labour, or each firm could pay a subscription that would cover expenses: a subscription that would be much less than the expenses if no clearing house existed.

The first clearing house in Britain was the London Bankers' Clearing House, started at the end of the 18th century. By the turn of the 19th century it occupied a large building in Post Office Court, off Lombard Street, in the City of London. It was started originally by the London private bankers, to do away with an excessive number of inter-bank journeys, or 'walks', by an army of walk-clerks. The joint-stock banks were admitted in 1854.

Since the First World War bank amalgamations have greatly reduced the number of member-banks, and the present members are: Bank of England, Barclays, Coutts, District, Glyns, Lloyds, Martins, Midland, National, National Provincial, Westminster, and Williams Deacons. The BANK OF ENGLAND (q.v.) acts as banker to the others, and adjusts their accounts at the end of the day for what they are due to pay or to receive. This settlement is, of course, in respect of the large number of cheques that are paid in daily to each member bank, and which represent claims against the banks on which they are drawn.

The Railway Clearing House was another institution of this kind, although it has now lost its former importance. It was started in a very small way in 1842, with less than half a dozen clerks, but grew later into a large concern. It used to share out among the various railway companies the money received for passengers or goods booked on 'through' journeys over several different lines. In the earlier days of railways the booking office at, say, King's Cross might sell a ticket to Edinburgh, involving journeys over the Great Northern, the North Eastern, and the North British Railways, then separate lines. Each line would have to receive its share of the fare, and these shares were calculated by the Railway Clearing House.

Since nationalization (*see* RAILWAYS, HISTORY OF, Vol. IV), the clearing-house staff deals with accountancy and other work for British Railways. The clearing-house system is much used by other concerns, although there is often no special building, and the arrangement is then called a clearing department. The Exchanges, dealing mostly in produce or commodities, are the principal users of this system. Among the most important clearing departments is that of the London Stock Exchange.

See also BANKING; BANK ACCOUNTS; STOCK EXCHANGES.

CLOTHING INDUSTRY. Until the middle of the 19th century men's outer clothes were hand-made to order, by the same methods which are still used in the (hand) 'bespoke' tailoring trade. The Americans were the real pioneers of the ready-made clothing industry. It was an American, Singer, who invented the first practical sewing-machine, which led to the large-scale production of clothes in the U.S.A. Singer's machine was introduced into Britain in 1851, and a ready-made clothing industry became established in the West Riding of Yorkshire, principally in Leeds, and in London. To start with, each piece of cloth in a garment had to be cut out singly by hand; but in a few years a Leeds

Wallis and Linnell

CUTTING OUT SUITS
The mechanical knife cuts through a number of thicknesses of cloth

firm invented a mechanical cloth-cutting knife, which worked on much the same principle as a band-saw. This made it possible to cut several thicknesses of cloth at a time, to the same original pattern.

The early manufacturers, both British and American, turned out garments in a few stock sizes only, and the market for ready-made clothes was therefore only of use to the few men who were themselves of stock size. The real foundation of the wholesale ready-made clothing industry, as we now know it, was a scientific study of human measurements made by an American firm in the second half of the 19th century. It was found that the measurements and proportions of any hundred men chosen at random would differ only very slightly from those of any other hundred men similarly chosen. It became possible to plan such a range of sizes and fittings that nearly every man in the country would find a garment to fit him without the need of any alterations. For a long time British social traditions prejudiced many people against ready-made clothes. Britain, therefore, lagged behind the U.S.A. in adopting a large range of sizes and fittings.

The British industry was greatly helped by the big demand for uniforms in the First World War. The war also broke down many old conventions, and increased the demand for ready-made clothes. After the Second World War there was still less formality in dress; the tight and accurate fit of former days no longer interested the average man so much as the colour and design. The British section of the industry is now very efficient, and has even successfully invaded the American market. It is still located principally in Leeds and London. Mechanical knives have been improved, and can deal rapidly with as many as fifty thicknesses of cloth at a time. Portable electrical knives have also been invented, for use where the industry is not organized on factory lines. There are no operations still done by hand in the tailoring trade that cannot be done mechanically in the ready-made industry. Even the making and stitching of buttonholes, and the stitching on of buttons, are done mechanically at great speed. In Leeds, ready-made clothing manufacture is a factory industry on continuous production lines, the cloth passing from machine to machine until the finished garment is ready. In London the industry is mainly organized on the 'outworker' system,

and garments in various stages of manufacture travel from one small workroom to another. There are, however, a few clothing factories in London on the Leeds model, although not on the same large scale.

See also WOOL INDUSTRY, MEDIEVAL, SECTION 2.
See also Vol. XI: CLOTHES, HISTORY OF.

COAL-GAS, *see* GAS INDUSTRY.

COAL-MINING. 1. Most British coals belong to the Carboniferous age (*see* EARTH, HISTORY OF, Vol. III). The commonest types, known as bituminous, are used in domestic grates, and for gas-making, coke manufacture, and general manufacturing processes. The highest class of coal is the type known as anthracite. Between the two come the semi-smokeless steam coals. Bituminous coals are characterized by their banded structure, dull hard layers of 'durain' alternating with bright shiny layers of 'clarain'. They ignite easily, usually contain a good deal of gas and tarry matter, and burn with a smoky flame. Steam coals burn less easily, almost without smoke, and give out great heat; they were in great demand for steam shipping until OIL (q.v.) came into wide use as a fuel. Anthracites are smokeless and hard to ignite; they will not burn without a strong draught, but they contain little ash. Anthracite and steam coals are found chiefly in South Wales and Scotland.

Coal occurs in seams varying in thickness from an inch or less to as much as 30 feet, but the seams generally worked are from 18 inches to 8 feet. If the seams 'crop out' at the surface they can be worked by opencast methods (*see* MINING). Mechanical shovels are then used to remove the overlying soil and to dig out the coal. Other seams may be hundreds of yards underground, and it is then necessary to sink shafts to reach them. There are a number of collieries to-day whose deepest workings are over 1,000 yards below the surface. The seams may lie horizontally in the earth's crust, but often they are folded and tilted, and also 'faulted' or broken (*see* ROCK FORMATION, Vol. III). No two collieries will therefore have the same natural conditions to contend with.

2. COAL GETTING. Coal was originally 'hand-got' by the miner with his pick, aided at a later stage by gunpowder; but to-day most of the output is obtained from 'faces' where the seam is first undermined by a COAL-CUTTER driven by

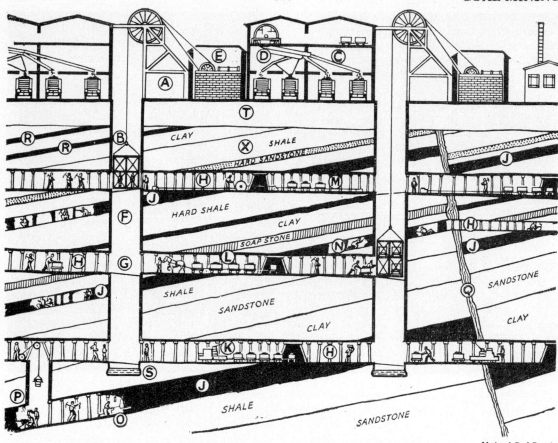

National Coal Board

FIG. I. THE INTERIOR OF A WORKING COAL MINE

A. Winding machinery for cages. B. Cages. C. Shoots for filling railway trucks. D. Screens for sorting coal into sizes. E. Power plants for winding cages, pumping, &c. F. Pit shafts. G. 'Keeps' for stopping cages. H. Galleries leading to coal seams. J. Seams of workable coal. K. Electric traction. L. Horse-drawn trucks. M. Endless ropeways for truck traction. N. Miners at work in narrow seams. O. Miners using mechanical coal cutters. P. Miners using pneumatic drill preparatory to blasting. Q. Fault or break in the stratification. R. Thin seams of coal, not worth working. S. Reservoir where water collects and is pumped out.

electricity or compressed air, then broken down by special safety Explosives, and loaded by shovel on to a Conveyor-belt running along the length of the coal face, which may be 100 or 200 yards long (qq.v. Vol. VIII). On many faces, instead of a rubber conveyor-belt, an endless scraper-chain is used to drag the coal along to the main trackway or 'road'. Here it is loaded on to another belt, or direct into the small trucks called 'tubs' or 'trams', which hold from 10 to 15 cwt. each. The tubs are then drawn by steel ropes along the roads to the pit bottom, where they are hoisted to the surface in 'cages' carrying about six tubs at a time.

This way of coal-mining is known as the 'longwall' system, the faces being in effect long walls of coal which are stripped or loaded out daily. Thus each face advances from 4 to 5 feet a day, usually in a direction away from the shafts. To protect himself, the miner sets steel or wood props to hold up the roof as he removes the coal. Fig. 2 shows a typical machine-cut face, equipped with coal-cutter, conveyor, and steel roof supports. After the cut coal has been loaded out and these props set, the conveyor is moved forward, and the coal cutter travels the length of the face, cutting the coal ready for the next day. The back row of roof supports is also withdrawn, allowing the roof to collapse; and from the broken fragments 'packs' or walls are built to protect the roads and prevent the roofs from breaking down too near the coal face. Meanwhile other men are engaged in 'ripping', which is the operation of blowing down the roof in the

FIG. 2. A CUTTER-LOADER AT WORK UNDERGROUND
The cutter loads the coal on to the conveyor-belt (seen at left)

roads to make them high enough. This is particularly necessary where the seam is thin. The rock thus blown down is also put in the packs, so far as is possible. Where there is more rock than can be dealt with in this way, it has to be loaded and sent out of the pit, forming the 'tip' that is a conspicuous feature at most collieries. In some collieries machines are used not only to cut the coal, but also to load it on to the conveyor. With them six men can fill out a face that would need eighteen or twenty men filling by shovel.

Another system is known as the 'bord-and-pillar', or 'stoop-and-room' system. It is best adapted to seams lying at shallow or moderate depths. The plan is to drive a large number of roads in the seam in two directions, roughly at right angles. These are the 'bords', and thus the seam is split up into a large number of 'pillars', each from forty to a hundred yards square. These pillars of coal are afterwards extracted, starting often from the colliery boundary and working back towards the shafts. In mechanized bord-and-pillar working, each bord

is cut by machine; the coal is blasted down, and then loaded by a mechanical shovel—which can pick up over a ton a minute—into rubber-tired 'shuttle' cars which transport it to the main conveyor. Similar methods are employed to extract the pillars.

3. HAULAGE. In most British mines the filled coal is taken from the seams to the pit bottom by small tubs and wire ropes. This system is costly, and wasteful in manpower. Some collieries use belt conveyors to transport the coal right to the shaft, but rails still have to be laid along the underground roads to take in to the face the supplies of props and other materials needed. Many new mines are now being laid out for locomotive haulage. The locomotives transport the coal in large mine cars holding 3 or 4 tons apiece, from a main loading-point in the seam to the shaft. They are powered by diesel engines, or less commonly by electric motors and batteries. Trolley-wire locomotives, used extensively in American and Continental mines, are not permitted in Britain, the risk of a spark causing an explosion being considered too great. Locomotive haulage, besides being economical in manpower, is useful in taking the colliers to their work. The system requires large straight roads to be maintained, and is most easily adopted where the seams are flat. Fig. 3 shows a typical installation.

Haulage by pit ponies is still a common practice in the collieries of South Wales, Northumberland, and Durham, but the practice is fast dying out.

4. VENTILATION. Ventilation is one of the most important problems in coal-mining. Every colliery to-day has at least one fan at work, night and day, sending fresh air round the underground workings. It is rather a surprising fact that for every ton of coal wound up the shafts as much as 5 tons of air may have to be circulated. Nearly all coal seams contain poisonous or inflammable gases which, if allowed to accumulate, would make the air unfit to breathe, or dangerous because of the risk of explosion. The chief poisonous gas is carbon dioxide, which together with nitrogen forms the miners' 'blackdamp'. This is not a breathable gas, owing to the lack of oxygen in it (see RESPIRATION, Vol. II). The chief inflammable gas is 'firedamp' or methane, which forms with air an explosive mixture when there is between 5% and 15% present. It is because of this risk of explosion that naked lights are forbidden underground, and only SAFETY LAMPS (q.v. Vol. VIII) are used, either developed from the original Davy lamp or of the modern electric pattern. Electricity for power purposes is also strictly controlled, and so is blasting to bring down the coal or rip the roof. These restrictions remove the possible causes of ignition of firedamp, but the first line of defence is ventilation, which sweeps away the gas as it is given off, and prevents it from ever accumulating sufficiently to form an explosive mixture.

In deep mines a second reason for circulating large quantities of air is to keep the working-places cool. The temperature of the rocks of the earth's crust may increase by roughly 1° F. for every 60 feet we descend, and at a depth of 800 yards may approach blood heat (see EARTH, Vol. III). Men could not work efficiently under these conditions, unless the air current kept working faces relatively cool. An elaborate system of roads has to be maintained underground to convey to the faces the fresh air descending the 'downcast' shaft, and to bring

National Coal Board

FIG. 3. A DIESEL LOCOMOTIVE HAULING TUBS OF COAL

back the return air by a different route to the 'upcast'.

5. SHAFT-SINKING. Most collieries to-day are served by two or more shafts; it is rarely the case that the seams can be reached by adits (see MINING) or tunnels driven from the surface. The choice of site for these shafts calls for great care and judgement on the part of the mining engineer. They must be convenient to railways, so that the coal raised may easily be sent away. They should also be near the centre of the area of coal to be extracted, to prevent the underground haulage roads becoming too long. The shafts are sunk by boring a large number of blasting holes or 'shot holes' in concentric circles, charging them with explosive, firing them, and then loading out the broken rock (see BLASTING, Vol. VIII). As the shaft deepens, it is lined with brickwork or concrete to support the sides and keep out water. When the seam is reached, roads are driven out in the coal for some distance before the faces are opened out, leaving a pillar of coal to protect the shafts from possible damage from subsidence caused by extracting the coal around them. This is necessary not only for the safety of the men underground but also for reasons of cost, since a pair of deep shafts may cost half a million pounds to sink and equip, and they have to last the full life of the colliery—perhaps 100 years.

6. SCREENING. The winding-engines are generally steam-driven. Steam is generated at the colliery from the small coal, mixed with washery refuse that cannot be sold. A number of pits in Britain, however, are equipped with electric winders. Usually the tubs are raised in cages (or large lifts) and emptied at the surface, but 'skip' winding is a system now being increasingly practised: the tubs or mine cars are emptied in the pit bottom into bunkers, which feed the coal into large steel boxes or skips each holding 7 to 10 tons. The skips are drawn up the shaft, and at the top they are emptied automatically on to a belt which takes the coal to the screens or the washery (*see* Fig. 4).

Originally coal was sold unscreened, just as it came from the pit. To-day it is not only separated into different sizes—best house lumps, cobbles, nuts, beans, peas, and so on—but the larger sizes may be also picked over by hand to remove 'dirt' or rock that may have become mixed with the coal. Small coal cannot be hand picked, but is treated in a washery. It is immersed in a liquid with a density greater than

that of coal, but less than that of the dirt. The coal, therefore, floats, and is skimmed off, dried, and sold; dirt sinks, and is removed from the bottom of the wash-box and sent to the tip. There are various other ingenious ways of separating clean coal from dirt.

The British coal-mining industry to-day employs about 700,000 men. It produces over 200 million tons of coal a year, three-quarters of which is cut and conveyed by machinery. The known reserves of coal underground are estimated to be sufficient for at least 400 years at the present rate of extraction.

See also MINING; COAL-MINING, HISTORY OF; TRANSPORT.

See also Vol. III: COAL.

See also Vol. VIII: FUELS; MINING MACHINERY.

COAL-MINING, HISTORY OF. 1. EARLY

HISTORY. Coal has been used by man for many more years than is generally believed, but written records of its use in earlier times are scanty. The hard coal called anthracite, which is almost pure carbon, is named after a Greek word; coal was mentioned in the 4th century B.C. as being used by blacksmiths. Coal was used during the Roman occupation of Britain, for unburnt coal and cinders have been found in excavations made by archaeologists on the sites of the old Roman settlements. Most of these discoveries were made in Northumberland, which is still a famous English coalfield. But it is not until A.D. 852, long after the Romans had left, that we find any written record of its use in Britain. The Saxon Chronicle of the time states that the Abbot of Peterborough let the lands of Sempringham to Wulfred, one of the conditions of the lease being that Wulfred was to send to the Abbey every year a quantity of fuel, to include '12 loads of coal'. In the early 13th century Henry III granted a licence to dig for coal at Newcastle-on-Tyne. The Rolls of Parliament refer to shipments of coal from Newcastle to London in 1306. Scotland, particularly Fifeshire, was also a coal-producing area in those early days. It is recorded that, in the 13th century, the monks of Newbattle were working the 'sulphurous stone that burns', but it was not much used except in the local salt-making industry.

'Carrying coals to Newcastle' has long been an English saying, meaning the doing of some quite unnecessary task. In early days, although coal was being mined in other parts of the

National Coal Board

FIG. 4. SCREENING COAL

Coal below 7 inches in size passes through the screen in the background. Larger pieces pass along the belt to an automatic pick which breaks them down

AN 18TH-CENTURY COAL PIT IN SHROPSHIRE
Horses turn the wheel which works the hoists and pack-mules carry the coal. Engraving after G. Robertson, 1788

country, the Newcastle coalfield had the largest output, and local mining and trading were under the control of the Hostmen, a CRAFT GUILD (q.v.) or trade brotherhood which received a charter from Queen Elizabeth in 1601. Later, in the 17th and 18th centuries, the output of Newcastle and north-east England increased. This was mentioned by Daniel Defoe, the author of *Robinson Crusoe*. In his *Tour thro' the Whole Island of Great Britain*, published between 1724 and 1726, he wrote of the growing shipments of 'sea-cole' into London: the name was given because the coal was carried by sea. The trade was growing because, at that time, wood was becoming scarce all over the country, and Londoners were being forced to use coal instead of wood, although they did not take very readily to the new fuel at first. Newcastle and Whitby were the main ports for the shipment of coal to London, and a well-known riverside tavern at Wapping in East London—'The Prospect of Whitby'—was so named because the Whitby sailing colliers used to anchor in a reach of the river just offshore.

By the end of the 17th century the coal-mining industry had become well established in various parts of Britain. Between 1700 and 1750 the British output of coal rose from 2,612,000 tons to 4,774,000 tons, and by the end of the 18th century it was over 6,000,000 tons. Mining was done by very primitive methods, most of the workings being reached by cutting through hillsides, to avoid deep mining for which there was neither engineering knowledge nor equipment. No coal-mine was more than 1,000 ft. below the surface. By the end of the 18th century steam power was being used for winding engines and for pumps to suck water out of the pits (*see* COAL-MINING). Apart from other obstacles, deep mining in most districts was impossible until steam-driven pumps could be used.

2. THE MINEWORKER. The lives of the early mining population were full of hardship. Miners' families to-day often talk about 'the bad old days'. Women, and boys and girls sometimes as young as 7 years, were employed underground in Britain during a working day of anything from 10 to 12 hours; women were harnessed to 'tubs' or 'trams' filled with coal, and did the work done later by the pit ponies. Their menfolk, although stronger physically, were in many parts of the country little better than slaves; in the North, and in Scotland, they were often fettered with chains, working in gangs. They were tied to a particular colliery, in much the same way as the villeins were tied to their manors in the time of the FEUDAL SYSTEM (q.v. Vol. X). If a colliery owner sold his interest in a colliery to someone else, his workers were also transferred to the new owner. It was not until 1775 that the bondmen colliers of the North were freed by Act of Parliament, and another 3 years passed before another Act brought to an end the life-slavery of the Scottish colliers. But even this freedom was not complete, and it was not until 1799 that these mineworkers became as free as workers in other industries.

When the 19th century opened, the British coal-miner was no longer a slave in the eyes of the law, but women and children were still employed underground. Hours were long, and the work was very dangerous, for few safety precautions were taken. Falls of rock caused many accidents, but the greatest danger was from 'fiery' coal, which gave off a gas that formed an explosive mixture with air. This was chiefly 'firedamp' (carburetted hydrogen). The only lights then used underground were naked candles or oil lamps, both of which were dangerous. The miners themselves became concerned over the frequency of accidents and explosions, and in 1813 the local miners formed at Sunderland a Society for the Prevention of Accidents in Coal Mines. The Society employed Sir Humphry Davy to make suggestions for lowering the

number of accidents, and in 1815 he invented a successful safety lamp. It was based on the principle that wire gauze will not allow a flame to pass through it, and the safety lamp originally devised by Davy was an ordinary oil lamp with the burner and flame completely encased in wire gauze. The first of Davy's new lamps was used at Hetton Colliery in 1816.

Meanwhile Parliament became interested in the problems of work and welfare in British coal-mines, and from 1800 onwards many Committees were set up to make inquiries. But changes in the law came slowly. Until the middle of the 19th century conditions remained extremely bad, and women and children still hauled trucks. It was not until 1842 that Lord Shaftesbury got a Bill through Parliament which forbade the underground employment of women and girls, and of boys less than 10 years old. The Coal Mines Regulation Act of 1850 made rules for the safer running of coal-mines, and appointed Government inspectors to visit them and see that the law was being carried out. Shaftesbury's Act of 1842 had also brought to an end the 'tied' labour that still survived in the Staffordshire coalfield, much on the lines of the old Scottish bondman system.

Further laws were passed, and by the opening of the 20th century coal-mining in Britain had become safer. But the miner's life remained hard. In 1908 an Act was passed restricting the working day to 8 hours only, but during and after the First World War British coal-miners became increasingly restive over wages and conditions. The work of coal-mining has always had a great influence on the character of those who carry it on, and this is true of other countries as well as of Britain. Usually they live in ugly and gloomy surroundings, and they work either alone or in small groups, and not in large groups like factory workers. Their loneliness at work breeds great independence of character, and has sometimes tended to make them broody and ruminative in times of trouble. The records of the past history of their industry, and of the ways in which the early

GIRL PULLING A COAL CART IN A THIN SEAM
From the Report of the Royal Commission, 1842

miners were treated, make them suspicious of those in control over them; by contrast, their trusted leaders have often fought hard on their behalf against employers and governments, and the miners have developed a tremendous sense of loyalty to such leaders. In fact, in many parts of Britain, some of these leaders have become almost a religious legend; this is particularly true of William Abraham, still affectionately remembered as 'Mabon', the Welsh leader of the early 20th century.

By the end of the First World War it was obvious to the Government that there

Topical Press

A MINER AT WORK ON THE COAL FACE IN A NARROW SEAM

was grave discontent in the British coal industry, and a Royal Commission of Inquiry was set up under the chairmanship of Mr. Justice Sankey. The Commission's Report was not unanimous, but all recommended that the State should buy out the surface landowners who were paid ROYALTIES (q.v.) on every ton of coal raised. No important legislation followed this Report. In 1925 the price of coal fell seriously, through foreign competition and a world-wide depression in coal-mining; the depression was probably brought on by the increasing use of oil fuel afloat and ashore. The colliery owners wished to reduce costs by cutting wages, but the miners resisted and threatened to strike. The Government then promised to pay out a SUBSIDY (q.v.) that would make a cut in wages unnecessary. This subsidy was to end on 30th April 1926. Another Commission of Inquiry was also appointed, under the chairmanship of Sir Herbert (later Lord) Samuel, which issued its Report on 6th March 1926. Its recommendations did not please either the Government or the miners; and, as the Government would not renew the subsidy, a nation-wide strike began on 29th April. All the other important British TRADE UNIONS (q.v.) came out in a General Strike in support of the miners. The actual General Strike was only (in the phrase of the time) 'a nine-days' wonder', but the strike in the coalfields lingered on for many months. It was not until the Second

World War that statesmen generally agreed on the desirability of NATIONALIZATION (q.v. Vol. X) as soon as the war ended. So, on 1st January 1947, the mines were transferred to national ownership, and the National Coal Board became the controllers and managers of the entire British coal-mining industry.

3. WORLD GROWTH. During the second half of the 19th century coal production increased in several countries, but chiefly in the United States and in Germany. After the American Civil War and the successful war of the Germans against the French (1870–1), America and Germany began to expand their industries, and soon became important rivals of Britain. As their coal-mining grew, so did their steel works which depended on coal. So, by the end of the century, America, Britain, and Germany were three gigantic industrial powers. One consequence of this was the building of a large German Navy to compete with the British Navy.

America has greater reserves of coal, lying unmined in the earth, than any other country. The U.S.S.R. comes second, Germany third, and Britain fourth. America is also the chief producer of coal, Germany coming second. In 1946 America produced 534 million metric tons, Germany 226 million, and Britain 190 million. This shows that there is a close link with steel, for America makes 48% of the world's steel,

Britain 17%, and Germany 6% (*see* Iron and Steel, Vol. VIII).

The chief U.S. mines are in the Appalachian mountains, stretching southwards from Pennsylvania. Three-quarters of her coal comes from these regions.

Germany's chief coal-mines are in the valley of the Ruhr River, a part of the highly industrial Rhine region, but much coal also comes from the Saar. After the Second World War the German mining region of Silesia was transferred to Poland. Owing to the war the Ruhr, which before the war produced more than two-thirds of all German coal, became the most intensely industrialized region of Europe, and is notable for coke ovens, blast furnaces, iron and steel works, rolling mills, chemicals, and heavy engineering.

There is also an important coalfield in northern France and Belgium.

See also Coal-mining.
See also Vol. X: Industrial Welfare.

COAL-TAR DYES, *see* Dyes.

COCOA AND CHOCOLATE.
These are made from the beans or kernels of the Cacao tree (q.v. Vol. VI) which is grown in the tropics. The cacao bean originally came to Europe from Mexico, where it had been found by Cortes, the conqueror of that country (q.v. Vol. V), to be a valued article, not only of diet but also of trade. The beans were used as Currency (q.v.) as well

Cadbury Bros.

A 'MELANGEUR' IN WHICH THE CACAO BEANS ARE
GROUND WITH SUGAR

as the foundation of a beverage known as *chocolatl*, from which the word 'chocolate' is derived. Chocolate in the early days was always prepared as a drink, and the secret of making it was held by the Spanish Court for nearly 100 years. It then spread to England through Italy, Germany, and France, and in the 17th century a Frenchman opened a 'chocolate house' in Queen's Head Alley, Bishopsgate, in the City of London, for the sale of the drink. The new beverage became fashionable, although at that time chocolate was most unpalatable by comparison with the modern product. No sugar was used in its preparation, and the drink frequently included maize and spices. Sugar was introduced into chocolate in the later part of the 18th century, by Joseph Fry of Bristol. He was the first person in this country to make chocolate more or less in the modern way, and he founded the famous Bristol firm of J. S. Fry and Sons.

The cacao beans are obtained from the pods of the plant. The ripened pods are split open by hand on the plantations, and the beans are extracted, with the pulp in which they are embedded. The beans are left to ferment, and are then dried in the sun. When dried they are packed into bags and dispatched to the countries of manufacture. The heat of the tropics prevents chocolate from being manufactured there, as the liquid chocolate would not set hard.

Four operations are necessary before the final product is ready. The beans are first roasted, a process which develops the peculiar chocolate flavour, and also loosens the husk, which has an unpleasant taste. When the beans have been broken in a special machine, the shell or husk can be easily separated from the pieces of bean by an air blast. After roasting, most manufacturers blend the beans by mixing together different varieties, each of which has its own individual aroma. Then the beans are ground in a machine known as a 'melangeur'; sugar is added, together with vanilla, or whatever special flavouring is desired. The mixture now becomes a paste. The third operation is to refine this paste by a machine called a 'refiner', which has three or more rollers which not only grind but tear the fibres which constitute about half the volume of the bean. This combination of movements is achieved by varying the speeds of the rollers.

The final operation is to add more 'cocoa butter', a vegetable fat already present to some

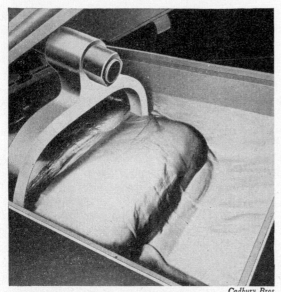

Cadbury Bros.

'CONCHING' MILK CHOCOLATE TO MAKE IT SMOOTH

degree in the mixture. Cocoa butter as a separate ingredient can be extracted from fresh cacao beans under pressure. The chocolate mixture is then worked in a conche—a machine consisting of a series of granite troughs, in each of which a heavy roller is turning. For the best qualities of chocolate the mixture is worked in this machine for several days and nights, a process which makes the chocolate so smooth that no separate particles are perceptible to the palate, and which

Cadbury Bros.

CENTRES FOR CHOCOLATES PASSING THROUGH THE 'ENROBER' TO BE COATED

helps to develop the full chocolate flavour. The chocolate is now ready to be filled into metal moulds and allowed to set. After setting, the moulds are emptied, and the familiar bars and other shapes are ready to be packed and dispatched.

Nut and fruit fillings are sometimes used, and these are added to the chocolate just before it is poured into the moulds. Milk chocolate is made by using mild flavoured cacao beans, and adding milk, in dried powder form, to the mixture before refining. In making chocolate confectionery, which consists of other sweetmeats covered with chocolate, the 'centres', as the sweets in the chocolate are called, are dipped in heated liquid chocolate; a certain amount adheres to the 'centre', which is then placed on a flat tray to set again. In large-scale production the centres are fed on to a conveyor-belt, which carries them through a curtain of liquid chocolate and deposits them on another belt (often imprinted with the name of the maker), where they set until they are ready for packing. The machine responsible for this process is called an 'enrober'.

Cocoa as a product distinct from chocolate came into use in the mid-19th century. The discovery of how to extract the fat, or cocoa butter, from the beans was important to the development of both chocolate and cocoa. After part of the butter has been pressed out, the residue is in the form of a hard cake. This is ground to a powder, sieved through very close-meshed screens, and it is then what is known familiarly as 'cocoa'. Cadbury Bros. first made a 'cocoa essence' in England in 1866, and they were followed by Fry's in 1868. The heads of both these firms were Quakers; in fact, all the oldest chocolate manufacturing houses in England were started by Quakers, who are also notable as having been among the first to introduce social welfare schemes for their workers.

Chocolate is affected by heat and damp, and must be carefully packed. If it is exported to hot countries, a wrapping of tinfoil or aluminium-foil usually protects each piece. If the temperature rises above 80° F., the chocolate softens and becomes liquid, and would soon ooze away. Even if the chocolate becomes soft, the foil retains it in one piece until it can cool off and harden again.

See also SUGAR CONFECTIONERY.
See also Vol. VI: CACAO.

COINING. This is one of the earliest national-ized industries, for since 1850 the making of our coinage has been a State monopoly. There is now only one State coining plant in Britain, at the Royal Mint in London, not far from the Tower Bridge. There is still, however, a com-pany in Birmingham which turns out coins and medals for foreign governments and public bodies. It is a very serious offence for an indi-vidual to make 'coin of the realm' or to colour metal to make it pass for a genuine coin.

The first process in coining is the melting of the metal in small furnaces heated by gas. This is done in open containers called crucibles about 2 feet high. These are lifted in and out of the furnaces by men wearing fireproof clothing, with loose ASBESTOS gauntlets (q.v.), coming well up the arm, which enable them to handle the red-hot crucibles without injury. The molten metal is then run into moulds and allowed to cool. When cooled, it comes out of the moulds in long thick slabs, which then go into the ANNEALING furnaces (q.v. Vol. VIII) to be reheated to a temperature high enough to soften them for the rolling process.

Rolls of different sizes then squeeze the hot, soft metal into long thin strips of the thickness of the particular coins to be made. The width

Keystone

IN THE CUTTING ROOM AT THE ROYAL MINT
As they are cut the blanks pass over a sieve through which imperfect ones drop

of the strips varies with the coin. To obtain the benefits of a rapid run of production of coins made from the same sized strip, the Mint makes the same type of coin for several days on end. Thus not all coins can be seen in process of manu-facture at the same time.

From the rolls the strips are passed through machines which punch out from them circular pieces of the size and weight of the coins that they will eventually become. As yet, these pieces have no impress of a coin on them, and are called 'blanks'. A good deal of oil has been used to lubricate the strips in their series of journeys through the rolls, and when they come out they are oily and greasy, and must be thoroughly cleaned before they go to the coining presses. They are therefore washed in a weak sulphuric acid solution and dried in revolving automatic driers. After the blanks have been punched out of the strips, the scrap metal goes back to the melting crucibles.

The blanks are then sent to the coining presses. Each press is fitted with hard steel dies above and below, one bearing the head design and the other the tail. The dies used for making gold, silver, and cupro-nickel coins are designed to give such coins a 'milled' edge. Until the invention of the reducing machine in the time of Charles I, all coins were produced from dies cut by hand. As no two dies were alike, there was considerable variation in any issue of coin-age. The reducing machine, however, accu-rately reduces to any desired size the model made by the artist. This model, an electrotype, is usually four or more times the size of the coin. The steel reduction, to the size of the coin, is called a punch. After hardening, a steel impres-sion is made from it, known as a die. From this a number of impressions are made: these are the working punches. From these working punches are made the working dies. This method en-sures that a tremendous number of pieces can be struck, all identical.

The working dies are put in every press, and cold blanks fed into the machine at the rate of about 100 a minute. The striking pressure is about 120 tons. Mass production on this scale became possible only with the invention of special steels. Automatic counting mechanism is incorporated in these presses, and the number of blanks that have passed through any machine and have become coins can easily be checked.

From the coining presses the completed coins

THE PRESS-ROOM AT THE ROYAL MINT, 1809

The blanks are put in the press by the kneeling man and stamped on both sides by turning the lever above. Coloured aquatint by Rowlandson and Pugin from Ackermann's *Microcosm of London*

go through some very careful processes of inspection. The first is by eye, to see that every coin has received the impress of the die on both sides, and, where necessary, a milled edge. Rejections are few, but they do sometimes occur. The coins then pass from the inspection room into the testing and weighing-room. Here the coins are carried on conveyor-belts through extremely sensitive machines which automatically reject any coin that is imperfectly shaped or weighs much less than the standard. Afterwards they are put into canvas bags, which are stencilled in black ink with the names and addresses of the banks, governments, or institutions to which the coins are to be sent.

See also COINS.
See also Vol. X: MINT.

COINS. From the study of the coins of different nations we can learn not only about the religion and mythology of ancient civilizations, but also about the places where they traded and the routes they took (*see* TRADE ROUTES, Vol. IV). Metals, such as gold and silver, were used as CURRENCY (q.v.) in very early times; we read in the Bible that Abraham was 'very rich in cattle, in silver, and in gold'. The value of these metals was judged by their weight. They were not coins in the sense that they were 'struck' or engraved with a device which guaranteed their weight and purity.

Coins were first struck on the coast of Asia Minor in the 8th century B.C. The first coins were of *electrum* or pale gold, and were a mixture of gold and silver. Croesus, the King of Lydia, famed for his wealth, was the first to introduce pure gold coins. The Persian coins, known as *darics* (so called after the Persian King Darius), were also made of gold. The right of making coins belonged to the king alone, though the

The early coinage of Rome was a cumbrous coinage of bronze only (we read of farmers taking their money to the market in their carts). This was replaced in the 2nd century B.C. by the silver *denarius*, a coin rather smaller than a shilling. When Julius Caesar was at the height of his power, the Senate granted him the right to put his head on the coins. The claimants to power on his death usurped this right, so that by the time Augustus had consolidated the empire, portraits were common on Roman coins. Augustus put his head on one side, and some aspect of his sovereignty was depicted on the other. The Roman imperial coinage was extensive in gold, silver, and copper, and the general type remained unchanged till the end of the empire. The various invaders, Franks, Vandals, and others, who destroyed the Western Empire, issued rough copies of Roman coins, and it was not until Charlemagne's reforms about A.D. 800 that the west had a good currency again. A predecessor of Charlemagne introduced the silver penny, which was the only silver coin of Europe till the end of the 13th century. It was copied everywhere in the West.

The first important coin of European com-

Ashmolean Museum

GREEK AND ROMAN COINS, HEADS AND TAILS

1. Aegina. Silver didrachm. 2. Athens. Silver tetradrachm. 3. Macedon. Philip II gold stater. 4. Rome. Julius Caesar silver denarius. 5. Rome. Augustus silver denarius

Ashmolean Museum

EARLY EUROPEAN COINS, HEADS AND TAILS

1. Gold bezant of the late Byzantine Empire. 2. Florin of Florence. 3. Sequin (ducat) of Venice

governors of his provinces were sometimes allowed to strike silver coins of their own for special reasons.

The earliest coins of the Greek cities carried the device of the city that issued them. The coins of Aegina had a sea-tortoise, and those of Phocoea a seal. The famous coins of Athens had on one side the head of Athena, the patron goddess of the city, and on the other an owl, which was the bird sacred to the goddess. After their victory over the Persians at Marathon, the Athenians added an olive branch. Athenian 'owls' were made of silver which was mined in large quantities in the silver mines at Laurium. When Alexander the Great conquered many lands, his gold and silver coins replaced most of the local currencies. When he died, his successors put a portrait of his head on his coins.

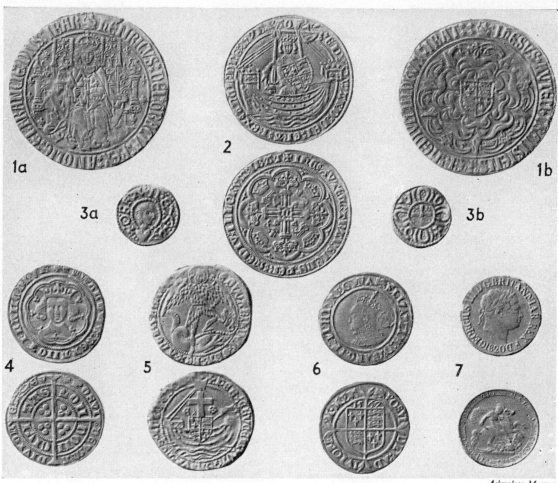

Ashmolean Museum

BRITISH COINS, HEADS AND TAILS

1. Henry VII gold sovereign. 2. Edward III gold noble. 3. Offa of Mercia silver penny. 4. Edward III silver groat.
5. Edward IV gold angel. 6. Elizabeth silver sixpence. 7. George III gold sovereign

merce was the *bezant*, which was the successor of a gold coin called the *solidus* struck by the Emperor Constantine. The *bezant* got its name from Byzantium (later Constantinople, now Istanbul), and remained the standard gold coin of Europe until the florin and ducat were coined in the 13th century. The word 'florin' is derived from Florence, where the first was struck in 1252. The Venetian *ducat*, later known as the *sequin*, remained an important international coin until the beginning of the 19th century.

The British gold sovereign and half-sovereign were coins of international importance in the 19th and early 20th centuries, but many centuries of coinage history passed before they appeared. During most of this time silver was

the metal generally used. There were a few native British coins before the Roman occupation, but they were not of original design, being mostly imitations of the 'stater', a coin struck by Philip II of Macedon, the successor of Alexander the Great. During the occupation of Britain the Romans introduced their own coins, many of which have been dug up and are now in the museums. After the Romans left, it was some time before native-made coins reappeared. Offa, King of Mercia, who lived in the second half of the 8th century A.D., introduced the silver penny, which was the standard English coin for many centuries. It was often cut into halves and quarters for convenience in business. To avoid this necessity Edward I coined silver halfpennies and farthings. He also tried to introduce the 'groat' or silver fourpenny piece, but it was unpopular and was dropped. Edward III successfully reissued the groat, and in 1344 he coined the gold 'noble'. Edward IV introduced the gold 'angel', and Henry VII the first 'sovereign'.

The foundations of modern British coinage were really laid in the 16th and 17th centuries. Edward VI introduced silver shillings and Elizabeth introduced silver sixpenny and threepenny pieces. They proved to be much more popular coins than the groat and the half-groat (or twopenny piece), which were gradually withdrawn. The first 'guinea' was coined by Charles II in 1662. It was really a sovereign, worth 20s., and was called a guinea because it was made of gold from the Guinea Coast. Charles II also introduced the crown, the half-crown, and the shilling, all beautifully made by new machinery at the MINT (q.v. Vol. X). In 1717 the value of the guinea was altered from 20s. to 21s. There was no great change in the British coinage until 1816, when the sovereigns and half-sovereigns which continued to circulate until 1914 were made with St. George and the Dragon on the 'tail'. The British florin or two-shilling piece was not issued until 1848, and the double florin or four-shilling piece not until 1887. This and the crown or five-shilling piece were unwieldy and unpopular, and their coining was dropped. The only newcomer to the British coinage is the brass threepenny piece, introduced shortly before the Second World War.

See also CURRENCY; MONEY; PRIMITIVE MONEY; COINING.

COKE, see Vol. VIII: COKE OVEN; FUELS.

COLD STORAGE. The cooling of food and wine receptacles, even during long journeys, by snow, ice, or freezing mixtures has been known to man for thousands of years, but REFRIGERATION (q.v. Vol. VIII) by mechanical means was not invented until 1861. Many years passed before the mechanism was sufficiently reliable to be trusted. The first cargo of frozen meat came to Britain from South America in 1878, and in 1879 another frozen cargo was brought over from Australia. By the following year all steamship lines across the Atlantic were equipped with cold-storage plants, and now there

Fox Photos

STACKING MEAT IN A COLD STORAGE PLANT AT THE LONDON DOCKS

The frost-covered cooling pipes are attached to the roof

is hardly a large ship on the world's deep-sea routes that is not so equipped.

Refrigeration, both afloat and ashore, has changed the trade in perishable food-stuffs. The development of refrigeration at sea has been accompanied by the erection of cold-storage WAREHOUSES (q.v.) at the docks and in large cities. Refrigeration has revolutionized the MEAT TRADE, the fruit trade, and the EGG and GROCERY trades. It has greatly helped the HOTEL and CATERING industries (qq.v.). It has made it possible for all kinds of new services to be offered to people: for example, many department stores have large underground refrigerated chambers for the mothproof storage of customers' furs.

Of late years few improvements have been made in large-scale refrigeration, with the exception of temperature regulation and more efficient ventilation. Fruit, for example, presents considerable problems in refrigeration, for fruit, as it ripens, gives off carbon dioxide gas, and air circulation is an absolute necessity. In the early days of refrigeration control of temperature was rather uncertain; for safety, foods had to be held at lower temperatures than might otherwise have been necessary, and this was rather damaging to some kinds of food-stuffs. Most modern cold-storage plants now maintain steady coolness within a range of 3 degrees. Small-scale refrigeration for shops and homes has increased. Most shops selling perishables now have refrigerated counters whose temperature is automatically controlled, with plate-glass fronts that give shoppers a clear view of the goods displayed inside. Removable wire trays are fitted to promote the air circulation necessary if unsealed food is displayed, and condensation—which would prevent the plate-glass fronts from being transparent—is avoided by making fronts of three separate glass panels with air spaces between each pair. Refrigeration for ice-cream vendors and for vans delivering food-stuffs is now usually arranged by insulated containers filled with 'dry ice', which is solid carbon-dioxide-gas snow produced mechanically. Quick-freezing is the most recent development of all. In this the U.S.A. was a pioneer. Quick-freezing involves the formation of minute instead of large ice crystals in the material frozen. This is less damaging to the flavour and texture of most food-stuffs than slower freezing.

See also Vol. IV: SHIP.

COLLOTYPE, *see* PROCESS REPRODUCTION.

COMBINATION ACTS, *see* TRADE UNIONS, HISTORY OF.

COMBINES. Competition in industry or commerce may sometimes develop into 'cut-throat' competition. This means that the various firms engaged may repeatedly cut their prices lower and lower, in order to increase their individual sales and make more PROFITS (q.v.). A healthy amount of normal competition keeps a business on the alert; but cut-throat competition may upset a long-term plan, and even cause such disturbance that in the end a whole industry becomes inefficient or unprofitable.

To avoid this all the firms in an industry may decide to act in combination instead of individually. When they do this they are said to form a 'combine'. There are many ways of doing this. One method is to form a Trade Association, which maintains an office and a small staff out of subscriptions by individual firms belonging to it, and from time to time sends out instructions concerning the minimum prices at which their goods may be sold, maximum discounts allowed to customers, conditions of delivery, and so on.

A form of combine which interferes much more with individual freedom of action is that known as a 'cartel'. This word is of German origin, and the idea is German. The cartel is a more highly developed type of trade association. The firms belonging to it are given instructions, not only in regard to selling-prices, but also as to what they may manufacture, and the territories or countries in which they may sell.

The most fully developed type of combine is the 'trust'. This is an amalgamation of several smaller subsidiary companies into one master company, sometimes called the 'holding company'. This company either takes over all the share CAPITAL of the subsidiary LIMITED COMPANIES, or else it acquires enough SHARES (qq.v.) which carry powers to vote at meetings to enable it to control their policy. Sometimes the management of affairs is entrusted to the holding company's own board of directors; but sometimes the smaller companies are allowed to carry on their own management without more interference from the holding company than would be expected in a cartel.

See also MONOPOLY.

COMMERCE. The finance of production and the movement and marketing of goods are the concern of commerce. The normal practice of commerce is to help industry with the supply of capital and credit and to arrange the shifting of both raw materials and goods in process of manufacture from stage to stage until the completed goods are in the hands of the consumer.

Most writers consider that commerce includes finance; but some separate the two, saying that commerce is concerned with the movement of goods, and finance with providing the money necessary for such movement. On the whole commerce is concerned with movement: the movement of products from the mines and fields, from one country to another, from one merchant or manufacturer to another, and from stage to stage until the completed goods are finally in the hands of the consumer. But each movement requires money. Primary producers have to be paid; shipping and other transport services have to be paid for; goods have to be stored and warehoused—very often they have to be stocked for long periods, until the industries using them are ready to take them. A large amount of money is also necessary to finance the business of distributing the completed goods from factory to wholesale house, from wholesale house to shop, and from the shopkeeper to the consumer. So it is really much simpler to consider commerce as including finance.

Commercial activities might therefore be summarized as follows: the organization of MONEY and BANKING, and of CREDIT for short and long periods; TRANSPORT in all its forms; WHOLESALING, WAREHOUSES, and distribution by RETAIL TRADING; the provision of CAPITAL by investors and its collection by finance and ISSUING HOUSES; the organization of STOCK EXCHANGES (qq.v.), through which capital in commercial and industrial enterprises may change hands; the organization of the various produce and commodity markets where goods are bought and sold; and finally, the organization of ADVERTISING AND PUBLICITY (q.v.), and all the methods that exist to tell the consumer what there is for him to buy and where he can buy it.

Even this is not quite a complete list of all the specialized branches of the commercial world, and the student of commerce is always coming up against something new. There are company lawyers and chartered secretaries, skilled in company law and procedure; accountants and auditors; all kinds of agents and brokers; and specialists in more limited subjects, such as average adjusters in marine insurance, assessors in fire and accident insurance, chartered agents for PATENTS (q.v.) and status inquiry agents. These all exist because it pays other members of the commercial world to employ them for their own particular jobs.

See also TRADE, HISTORY OF.

COMMERCIAL TRAVELLERS, see REPRE-SENTATIVES.

COMMISSION. This is the usual form in which AGENTS and BROKERS (qq.v.) are paid by the firms and individuals who employ them to buy and sell goods on their behalf. It consists of a percentage on the value of goods sold or bought.

Usually commission on sales is quite easily arranged. Obviously the selling merchant wishes to obtain the highest possible price, and, if he pays his agent or broker a straight percentage on that price, the total commission will rise as the selling-price of the article rises, and both parties will be satisfied. It is not quite so easy to fix commission arrangements for brokers and agents who act as buyers. In some trades the buying services are paid for by a straightforward percentage commission; but it may sometimes be necessary for the firms employing the agents or brokers to arrange a sliding scale commission, which will go up as the price at which goods are bought goes down.

Commission, in addition to being paid to agents and brokers, is often paid to sales assistants, and to travelling REPRESENTATIVES (q.v.). Formerly many such people were paid almost entirely by commission; but nowadays the tendency is to pay more in the form of fixed salary and less in commission.

COMMODITY MARKETS, see MARKETS.

COMPANIES. These are associations of many people, formed to carry on business with a CAPITAL (q.v.) subscribed by all of them. The old word for 'capital' in English was 'stock', and the money put up by those subscribing the capital of a company was called the 'joint stock'; from this came the name 'joint-stock company', although nowadays this name is only used in Great Britain for LIMITED COMPANIES (q.v.).

Companies existed in ancient Rome; but we know little about how they were formed, or how they were controlled by the State. Our first definite knowledge dates from the late 14th century, when large companies began to be formed to take part in INTERNATIONAL TRADE (q.v.), and later in the exploration and development of foreign lands. In those days the State kept a firm control over business of all kinds, and companies could only be formed if their members obtained a charter from the king or ruling prince, laying down strict regulations as to what they could and could not do. Hence such companies were called 'CHARTERED' COMPANIES (q.v.). The first of these chartered companies in Great Britain was the Company of MERCHANT ADVENTURERS. Others were formed later, among them being the EAST INDIA COMPANY, and the HUDSON'S BAY COMPANY (qq.v.).

When the English Revolution of 1688 gave Parliament more control over financial and

ONE OF THE FIRST SHARE CERTIFICATES OF THE GAS LIGHT AND COKE COMPANY, ISSUED IN 1812
The company was incorporated by charter

commercial matters than it had possessed in the days of kings ruling by 'divine right', companies could only be formed (or 'incorporated') by Act of Parliament. The first important company to be formed in this way was the BANK OF ENGLAND (q.v.) in 1694. This way of forming companies still exists to-day, although it is only used when the proposed companies seek special privileges for themselves which Parliament must carefully consider beforehand. The majority of modern companies are formed in the much simpler way described in the article on Limited Companies.

See also PUBLIC UTILITY COMPANIES; STOCKS AND SHARES.

COMPETITION, *see* MONOPOLY.

CONCRETE, *see* CEMENT; *see also* Vol. VIII: CONCRETE.

CONDENSED MILK, *see* DAIRY INDUSTRY.

CONFECTIONERY, *see* SUGAR CONFECTIONERY; BAKING INDUSTRY, Section 3.

CO-OPERATIVE SOCIETIES. 1. The Co-operative movement began in the first half of the 19th century. In Britain the INDUSTRIAL REVOLUTION (q.v.) had by then enormously affected the lives and conditions of the ordinary working people. The old DOMESTIC SYSTEM (q.v.), by which goods were manufactured by the workers in their own homes, had almost been replaced by the factory system. Profits were rising and the workers felt that wages were not rising correspondingly, and that their interests were being neglected. In such conditions reformers such as Robert OWEN (q.v. Vol. V) felt that the best course for the workers would be to produce and distribute goods for themselves, and among themselves. If this was to be done, the necessary money would have to be put up by the working classes themselves. It was suggested that the CAPITAL (q.v.) for manufacturing enterprises should be subscribed by those who were going to work in them, and that the capital for marketing and retailing the goods made should come from the consumers who would buy them. The movement therefore aimed at encouraging 'producers' societies', which would provide goods and services, and 'consumers' societies', which would look after their distribution.

2. PRODUCERS' SOCIETIES. These were not at first very successful, but by 1939 there were nearly fifty of them in the Co-operative Federation, and their sales totalled almost £5 million a year. Their main difficulty was to find enough capital for any individual concern. Industry had become highly mechanized. In the early days it was sufficient to allow for spending, say, £10 on machinery for each worker; but as time went on perhaps even £100 would not be enough. This meant that the amount which a worker in a co-operative factory would have to subscribe would be far beyond his modest means. Producers' co-operation was, however, extremely successful in agriculture, where such heavy capital expenditure was not necessary—particularly in Denmark and north-west Germany (*see* CO-OPERATION IN FARMING, Vol. VI). It was also successful in industry in Russia before the Revolution, when the stage of using a great deal of machinery had not been reached. The Russian *artel*, or co-operative producers' society, is still a feature of modern Russia.

3. CONSUMERS' SOCIETIES. These have been very successful, and compete strongly with privately owned firms. The first retail shop on the modern model was opened in 1844 in Toad Lane, Rochdale, by a body of weavers called the Rochdale Pioneers. The method of finance they adopted has lasted to the present day. It had the advantage that, as business developed and increased, the amount of capital available for development and expansion increased also. To form a consumers' society, a sufficient number of persons were asked to promise support, and were then asked to take SHARES in it (q.v.). The minimum holding was generally only £1, and an absolute maximum of £200 was fixed by law in 1878, to prevent wealthy people from obtaining control. Shares could be paid for by small regular instalments, or out of the dividend or rebate on purchases. General policy was in the hands of a committee elected by the members; but day-to-day work was carried on by managers and staff, appointed on the same conditions as in private firms. The trading policy was to sell goods at about the prices charged by private firms, and then, at the end of the trading year, to calculate what profits had been earned. These, after enough had been kept back for reserves and expansion, were shared out among all the members. This share-out was not in proportion to the number of shares held, as it is in an ordinary LIMITED COMPANY (q.v.), but in proportion to the amount of money spent on his purchases during the year by each member of the Society. This rebate, or dividend, on goods bought is generally called the 'divy'.

The consumers' co-operative movement met with great opposition from ordinary private firms, and after a very promising start it seemed in danger of declining and even dying out. The great difficulty was the buying of wholesale supplies in markets controlled by merchants hostile to the movement. For this reason the Co-operative Wholesale Society was formed in 1862. Its object was to buy goods in large quantities for the local retail societies to sell, and also to buy raw materials overseas and distribute them to the retail societies. The C.W.S., as the English Wholesale Society is called, was successful from the very start, and a Scottish Society was founded a few years later. The capital of the wholesale societies is provided by the retail societies, who receive the same kind of dividend on their purchases as their own customers receive from them. The wholesale societies do not set out to make profits, but to balance incomings and outgoings and to leave a small surplus for reserves and emergencies. They now have a vast business. They control tea and coffee plantations overseas, their own fleet of ships, and operate processing and canning factories. To finance all these operations there is also a C.W.S. Bank.

Of recent years great improvements have been made in the methods of the co-operative movement. The range of products dealt in by the retail societies, and bought or produced by the wholesale societies, has widened. Beginning originally as grocery stores, some of the shops of the big retail societies are now more like DEPARTMENT STORES (q.v.), handling men's and women's clothing, furniture, household hardware and ironmongery, china and glass, boots and shoes, cigarettes and tobacco, and practically all the

A POTTER'S WHEEL

The seated man is turning the wheel while the potter moulds the clay

Co-operative Society

THE ORIGINAL STORE OF THE ROCHDALE PIONEERS OPENED IN 1844 IN TOAD LANE, ROCHDALE

lines catered for by an ordinary department store owned by a private firm.

The movement has always paid considerable attention to education and political activities, and a recent development has been the taking over of a large hotel in the Bloomsbury district of London. There are nearly 1,200 retail societies in Great Britain, with a membership exceeding 8 million and an annual TURNOVER (q.v.) of more than £250 million.

See also CO-PARTNERSHIP.

COOPERING, *see* CASK-MAKING.

CO-PARTNERSHIP. This means sharing the ownership, and to some extent the management, of industry between owners or shareholders, on the one hand, and workers on the other. The idea behind co-partnership is that it is likely to increase the loyalty of workers to their firm and to increase efficiency by removing to some degree the causes of industrial discontent. Many so-called partnership schemes have been launched at different times, but most of them have been closer to profit-sharing than to true co-partnership, and profit-sharing does not differ essentially from the system of paying bonuses in addition to WAGES (q.v.).

Like many other aspects of the workers' movement, co-partnership was first preached as a useful industrial doctrine just before the middle of the 19th century. Among its early advocates were the economist, John Stuart MILL, and the philosopher Herbert SPENCER (qq.v. Vol. V). Co-operation (*see* CO-OPERATIVE SOCIETIES) was a parallel movement, and came to the fore at the same time. Robert OWEN (q.v. Vol. V) was prominent in all the movements for the betterment of workers' conditions; he was a pioneer of co-operation, and was also an enthusiast for co-partnership. He is reported to have told a business acquaintance, who was rather uncertain about adopting such a scheme, that it was well worth paying one's workers £5,000 a year to prevent them from wasting £10,000. It was a long time, however, before the idea took practical shape. The first important move towards its adoption in Britain was made in London in 1889, when the South Metropolitan Gas Company instituted a profit-sharing system. This was at first merely a system of bonuses in addition to wages; but in 1894 it was converted into a co-partnership by arranging that workers' shares of PROFIT (q.v.) should be invested in the company's capital, and that worker-shareholders should have the right of nominating directors to the board. Other gas companies followed suit, and in 1908 the largest gas concern in the country, the Gas Light and Coke Company of Beckton, London, adopted the scheme. Several industrial firms in the Midlands and the North did the same, and one of the most successful schemes was that adopted by a great Yorkshire wool firm at Batley in the 1890's.

True co-partnership really means giving workers a stake in the business; for this they do not, like shareholders, pay any money, although any money profits later distributed to workers may be invested in the firm's SHARES (q.v.). Many schemes, by which workers may subscribe on preferential terms for shares in the companies they serve, are co-partnership schemes to a limited extent only. This last is the only form in which the co-partnership movement has made any headway in the U.S.A. A big American soap firm launched such a scheme in 1912. To be eligible for membership of it, an employee had to own capital stock in the company to the amount of a year's wage or salary. The company were prepared to advance, at an interest rate of 3% per annum, 97½% of the money required for such purchases, so that employees had to put up an actual cash deposit of only 2½%. This scheme included a provision by which worker-investors were guaranteed against loss through any fall on the STOCK EXCHANGE (q.v.) in the market-price of the stock they had bought. This forestalled a frequent objection to co-partnership schemes of this sort—that they mean a financial risk to workers in speculative industries whose shares fluctuate in value (*see* STOCK EXCHANGE). Most workers think that the money risks of running a business should be borne only by shareholders, and should not be shared by the workers themselves.

An important Bill was introduced in the French Parliament in 1913, but failed to pass. If it had, a nation-wide scheme of co-partnership might have prevented much of the labour trouble that developed in France later on. The Bill proposed that every commercial and industrial company should be compelled to endow its workers with one-fifth of its total share capital, on which they would receive the same rate of dividend as other shareholders and also exercise the same voting rights for the appointment of directors (*see* BUSINESS ORGANIZATION). A rather similar idea formed part of the election programme of the British Liberal Party in February 1950. A scheme rather on the French model was adopted in 1929 in the large London store now known as the John Lewis Partnership, when a director, Mr. John Spedan Lewis, handed over a large portion of his own shareholding to a trust for the benefit of the employees of the firm.

COPPER-MINING. Copper was probably the first metal used by man. When copper is alloyed with tin it forms bronze, and during the Bronze Age about 4,000 years ago (*see* PREHISTORIC MAN, Section 5, Vol. I) the countries that possessed copper were the leading communities. Copper is principally found in the form of ores or compounds of the metal, although there are in the world considerable deposits of more or less pure metallic copper. Sometimes more valuable metals, such as silver, are found with the copper, and their presence makes low-yielding copper ores profitable to mine. There are extensive deposits of metallic copper in the Lake Superior

U.S. Information Service

COPPER ORE AWAITING FINAL GRINDING IN BALL MILLS WHERE IT IS GROUND TO THE CONSISTENCY OF FLOUR

district of the U.S.A. and at Monte Catini in Italy. The bulk of the world's production comes from the ores called malachite and copper pyrites. World production is about 1½ million tons a year, and the principal modern producing countries are the U.S.A., Chile, and the Katanga district of the Belgian Congo with the adjacent territory of Northern Rhodesia. Two big financial groups, one British and one American, are responsible for most of the copper production of Northern Rhodesia.

Copper has wide uses in modern industry. It is used alone or alloyed with tin or zinc to form bronze or brass, or with other metals. It resists rust and corrosion extremely well, and is much used for the vessels and plant of the BEER BREWING and CHEMICAL INDUSTRIES (qq.v.). It is used in the building industry for hot-water boilers, water piping, and sometimes as a roofing material. A recent use of copper in the building industry is for damp-courses, to prevent damp travelling upwards through walls. In modern industry the most important chemical compound of copper is the sulphate. This has a wide range of uses: dyeing, textile printing, and electro-plating are some of them. It is very effective as an antiseptic, both for human beings and for animals; and it is used as an INSECTICIDE and FUNGICIDE in gardening (q.v. Vol. VI).

It is also considerably used for the prevention of rot and decay in timber.

See also MINING.
See also Vol. III: METAL ORES.

COPRA. This is the dried kernel or 'meat' of the COCO-NUT (q.v. Vol. VI), the principal producing countries being Indonesia, the Philippine Islands, Malaya, and Ceylon. As the shells of coco-nuts have no commercial value, it is more economical to ship the dried kernels only. The fibre covering of the shell, which is called 'coir' (*see* TEXTILE FIBRES), is then removed and the nuts are split open for drying, which is necessary to prevent the nuts from decaying. There are several methods of drying and a simple and primitive method, which has been used since the trade began, is to expose the split kernels to sun and air, after which the 'meat' comes easily away from the shell. This method is still used in many of the coco-nut-growing districts of the world, and a white copra of quite good quality is produced which goes by the name of 'sun-dried' in the trade. A copra of better quality fetching a higher price is produced by drying the split shells artificially in 'kilns', or in long tunnels through which hot air is passed. The tunnel system is operated in Samoa, and the West Indies make much use of mechanical rotary driers. In all the artificial drying processes the shells provide a cheap and convenient fuel for the furnaces.

Well-dried copra contains about 60% of coco-nut oil. In some of the producing countries the oil is extracted locally, and coco-nut oil then becomes the commodity of export. But copra

Lever Brothers

COPRA, THE DRIED FLESH OF THE COCO-NUT

itself is still exported in considerable quantities, the oil being then extracted abroad. The extraction is carried out either by mechanical pressure, or by the use of petroleum solvents (*see* OILS, VEGETABLE).

Coco-nut oil has many uses in modern industry. It is an important ingredient in one of the main processes of SOAP manufacture (q.v.), especially of 'marine' soap, which lathers fairly well in sea-water. The unrefined oil has a characteristic smell and taste but both of these can be eradicated by refining. The refined oil is used for making MARGARINE, vegetable fats, shortenings for use in the BAKING INDUSTRY (qq.v.), salad oil, and cooking oils. In the making of cheap chocolate, coco-nut oil is often used as a substitute for cocoa butter.

CORK is the bark of two species of evergreen oak which grow principally around the shores of the western Mediterranean. The chief sources of modern cork are Spain and Portugal, which at some periods have produced together nearly four-fifths of the total world output. Small quantities also come from southern France and French North Africa, and from Italy and Sardinia.

The first stripping of bark, the 'virgin cork', is cut when the trees are 15 to 20 years old. It is of poor quality and cannot be used for bottle corks, and until fairly recently was looked upon as practically useless. The second cut, made after about another 10 years, is also of poor quality, but the third and later strippings produce good cork fit for use as bottle corks. The bark is cut from the trees in strips, which are flattened under weights and soaked for a few minutes in boiling water. They are then compressed in a HYDRAULIC PRESS (q.v. Vol. VIII), baled, and sent down to the coast for export.

Cork was well known to the ancient Romans. They used it for the soles of shoes, and to support people and fishing-nets in water. There is no record of its use for bottles until the 15th century. It is now used for mats, hat-linings, and in the making of artificial limbs. Before the First World War a firm in the City of London made men's top-hats and bowler-hats out of cork, and it was widely used for making tropical helmets. Ground into fine dust and mixed with linseed oil, cork has been used for many years in the making of LINOLEUM (q.v.). A use has now been found for 'virgin cork'. It is ground and used for second quality linoleum and also for the manufacture of corkboard for insulating purposes, particularly in refrigerating machinery.

See also Vol. II: Stems, Section 1 (*d*).

CORNISH MINING. There are many references in Greek and Roman classical literature to the Cassiterides or Tin Islands, but there is no proof that these were the Isles of Scilly or even the mainland of Cornwall. Traces of old smelting-pits, whose date can be fixed between 300 and 200 B.C., have been found during excavations on the Cornish moors, and many ancient writers mention a trade in tin as having taken place between south-west Britain and the Mediterranean about the beginning of the Christian era. All this, however, is vague, and our earliest piece of written evidence regarding Cornish tin-mining is the Tinners' Charter of 1201. There were then four Stannaries, or mining districts, Launceston, Lostwithiel, Truro, and Helston, and each was administered by a warden. 'Stannary' comes from the Latin for tin, *stannum*. Under the Charter, the 'tinner' was granted many privileges, the greatest being that of 'bounding': that is, entering and enclosing any land to search and dig for tin; for this he had to pay the lord of the manor a toll, usually about a fifteenth part, called the 'lord's dish'. The tinner's work was regarded as of national importance; he was free of taxes and Tithes (q.v. Vol. VI) and, unless summoned by his warden, he was exempt from military service. He also had the right to divert and use any stream to help his work. He was subject to no court of law but the Stannaries Court, and this privilege freed him from serfdom to the lord of the manor and gave him the sturdy independence of character which is the heritage of the Cornish miner.

In return for these freedoms the tinner had to obey 'coinage' laws. He had to carry his smelted metal by packhorse or mule—their tracks can still be seen across the lonely Cornish moors—to one of the coinage towns: Liskeard, Lostwithiel, Truro, Helston, and Penzance. In the Coinage Hall the tin was assayed and weighed, and stamped or 'coined' with the arms of the Duchy of Cornwall (*see* Assaying). Before the tin could be sold, the tinner had to pay a toll of about 4*s*. a hundredweight. As coinage took place only four times a year, the tinner was often

R. F. Gibson

ST. JUST UNITED TIN MINE WHICH WAS WORKED FOR SOME DISTANCE UNDER THE SEA IN THE 19TH CENTURY
Land's End can be seen in the background

in great straits for money, and frequently fell into the hands of moneylenders. The Cornish men of those days were regular SMUGGLERS (q.v. Vol. X), with a boat in every creek, and some of the tin neither saw the Coinage Hall nor paid a toll. What passed the coinage in the usual way was shipped to London. The London pewterers, whose skill was world-famous, used much of it for pewter ware for rich men's tables, but a great part found its way to the Continent and the Far East. Among other uses, it was mixed with the metal from which cannon and church bells were made, and it was used for plating or lining copper pots. Coinage was not abolished until 1838. The Stannaries, of which Sir Walter Raleigh was at one time Lord Warden, lasted until the end of the 19th century.

Before the 17th century tin was mainly 'streamed' in rivers and on the moors, and the tinner lived a solitary, outdoor, independent life, often far from villages. When the rich deposits of rock, long ago washed down by rivers, were worked out, a search began for underground veins or 'lodes', which, according to some old miners, could be located by the flickering of marsh gas, called 'Jack o' Lantern'. Underground mining involved the joint production of tin and copper, as the tin lay beneath the copper. The great problem of underground mining was drainage. Waterwheels, worked by men or horses, were replaced in the early 18th century by steam pumps, such as those invented by Newcomen, Boulton and Watt, and later by Hornblower and Trevithick. The introduction of gunpowder for blasting increased the output, but added to the many dangers of the miner's life, which was much less healthy than that of the tinner or streamer. Cornish mines became very prosperous in the 19th century, after the highly efficient Cornish beam pumping-engine had been invented by Richard Trevithick. This was the great copper period, when mines such as Dolcoath—between Camborne and Redruth—employed 1,600 men, women, and children, and Cornwall produced three-quarters of the world's annual output.

In earlier days the mines were worked under a rather curious system. The initial cost of installing machinery was borne by shareholders called 'adventurers'. The miners, called 'tributers', worked independently in parties, consisting usually of two men with one or two boys. Instead of a settled wage, the miners received

W. J. Bennetts & Sons

A 'GUNNIES' OR WORKED-OUT PORTION OF THE LODE (VEIN) 2,160 FEET FROM THE SURFACE AT THE DOLCOATH TIN MINE, CORNWALL

a 'tribute' or percentage of the total ore they brought to the surface. They provided their own tools, candles, ventilation, and transport, and as their livelihood depended on their skill and judgement, they became good working geologists rather than mere labourers. General underground management was in the hands of a bal-captain ('bal' is the Cornish word for mine).

Tin-dressing was done on the surface, or 'grass' as it was called. This was a trade in itself, needing much skill and experience, and was carried out on contract. The tin ore was first broken down with hammers and then washed in flowing water in a sloping, square stone trough called a 'buddle'. 'Buddling' was usually done by women or girls called 'bal-maidens'. When the fine, black tin sand came out, it was made into piles, assayed, and divided into three shares: for the 'lord's dish'—land-owner's ROYALTIES (q.v.)—the 'adventurers', and the 'tributers'. It was then smelted down into pure tin. Much of the desolate countryside of North Cornwall is the result of the poisonous fumes of arsenic and sulphur which killed all the plant life in the neighbourhood. Now, the arsenic and sulphur are conserved as BY-PRODUCTS (q.v.).

Conditions in the mines, though very bad by modern standards, were much better than in the Midland collieries, with their abuse of child labour (*see* COAL MINING, HISTORY OF, Section 2). In Cornish mines children were kindly treated, did light jobs only, often made their own contracts, and in the early 19th century were not employed under 10 or 12 years old. Even the depression of the 1840's, the 'hungry forties', as they were called, led to no riots in Cornwall like those in the north, although the starving miners protested very forcibly about the export of Cornish wheat. The relationship of lord, adventurer, and tributer was usually friendly, although London adventurers were not popular. But as mines grew deeper, the health of the miner was impaired by the heat and dust, and many fell victims to tuberculosis.

In the 20th century the introduction of electric power and pneumatic drills brought a renewal of prosperity, and the First World War called forth all Cornwall's resources in tin, tungsten, and arsenic for industry. The history of Cornish mining, with its great hazards has always been one of alternating periods of prosperity and depression. The depressions were due either to outside events, such as the replacement of pewter by earthenware, the discovery of copper on the shores of Lake Superior, and tin in Malaya, or to the shortsightedness of the 'adventurers', who abandoned mines when copper gave out because they did not see that tin lay beneath. The depression of 1894–8 drained Cornwall of its mining population. A great exodus began to the gold mines of South Africa, California, and Australia (*see* GOLD-MINING), and to the silver mines of Mexico and South America. Many Cornish mines became derelict at this time, but a considerable number survived until the great post-war slump in 1921. But mines from the Arctic Circle to the Equator reaped the benefit of the age-old skill of the 'Cousin Jacks'—as the Cornish miners were called—and people who had hardly heard of Cornwall came to use Cornish mining terms.

There was another brief period of activity in the Second World War, when tin could not be obtained from Malaya. The Cornish School of Mines at Camborne, the home of Trevithick, still trains mining engineers in the old tradition; and both at Camborne and at Redruth Cornishmen manufacture mining tools and equipment that are exported all over the world. It is said that uranium (*see* ATOMIC ENERGY, Vol. VIII) exists in Cornwall in small quantities.

See also MINING; TIN.

COSMETICS INDUSTRY.

The making of cosmetics (from the Greek word meaning 'to adorn') has been an important industry for thousands of years. The Pharaohs of ancient Egypt, for example, were always buried with the toilet articles they would need in the next world, and among these were small alabaster jars or vases filled with various kinds of perfumed unguents (*see also* COSMETICS, HISTORY OF, Vol. XI).

The British trade in cosmetics dates from the Crusades, when many eastern products were introduced into Britain and foreign habits were acquired, but the preparation and sale of cosmetics did not become an important industry until the late 19th century. Since then, their use has increased considerably, particularly in western Europe and America, mainly because women began to have much more freedom than they had before. The demand for cosmetics increased greatly after the First World War. In recent years the U.S.A. has led the world in the quantity and variety of cosmetics used. There are several reasons for this. The climate is drier, and the sunlight more intense and damaging to the complexion than in Britain. The American STANDARD OF LIVING (q.v.) is higher in the cities, and the earnings of women higher than in Europe. The use of cosmetics is greatly influenced by fashion, and, although American production is on an immense scale, the U.S.A. still imports many varieties from Paris, the fashion capital of the world, and from London.

1866 was an important landmark in the industry; in that year Henry Tetlow investigated the properties of zinc oxide and discovered its usefulness in the preparation of rouges and face powders. The ingredients used in the modern cosmetics industry are generally simple and quite cheap: borax and carbonate of soda for bath salts, celluloid and petroleum solvents for nail varnish, zinc oxide and CHINA CLAY (q.v.) for rouges and face powders, oils and waxes for cold cream, stearic acid for brushless shaving-creams and vanishing cream, chalk and powdered pumice for tooth-powders and pastes, lanolin and cocoa butter for lipsticks, and oils and gums for brilliantine and men's hair-dressings. The high cost of some cosmetics is due largely to the heavy expense of ADVERTISING (q.v.), for the industry is highly competitive. Attractive packing is also expensive, and high-quality natural PERFUMES (q.v.) add to the cost of making the more select preparations.

Goya Ltd.

THE BASE FOR LIPSTICK BEING GROUND IN A MILL

COSTING. 1. This is the art of finding out how much it really costs to produce certain goods or services. Cost accountants are not just ordinary accountants, but belong to a special professional body of their own, the Institute of Cost and Works Accountants. The difficulty of working out the cost of production of any goods or service arises mainly because costs of production consist of two parts: 'prime cost' and 'overhead charges'. The first are fairly easy to ascertain; the second are easy enough to ascertain as a total, but difficult to distribute accurately among the various lines of production carried on. Thus, in firms making a standard article by mass production, costing is fairly simple; but in firms producing a variety of different articles it becomes much more complicated.

2. PRIME COST is the cost of the labour, the materials, and the expenses directly involved in the production of one particular article or service. To find out the labour charges for various jobs in a factory, forms called 'time sheets' are prepared for each separate job, or for each batch or 'run' of product made, and on these are filled in the hours worked by the various employees. Similar 'job' or 'batch sheets' are used for the raw materials or stores issued and used, and also for those expenses that are directly incurred on any particular job or batch. Machines called 'time-recorders', for noting the times at which workers begin and finish a particular job, are a great help in finding out

exactly how much of the prime cost is taken up by labour charges.

3. OVERHEAD CHARGES are all the indirect expenses of running a factory which cannot be directly related to any particular batch of goods turned out. Overhead charges can be subdivided further into 'factory overhead' and 'general overhead'. Factory overhead includes such items as the rent, rates, taxes, and insurance of the factory; motive power, fuel, lighting, and heating; wages of storekeepers, timekeepers, clerks, superintendents, and managers; freight and carriage on raw materials, and repairs, renewals, and DEPRECIATION (q.v.) of plant and machinery (the lessening of value owing to age or wear and tear).

There are several ways in which factory overhead may be added on to prime cost in order to arrive at factory cost or production cost, and the method adopted must depend on the type of business. In small firms rule-of-thumb methods are used: the average weekly or monthly production is known, and the past year's total factory overhead can be divided by 52 or 12 and the necessary amount added on to prime cost. In larger firms more scientific methods are attempted; each separate item of factory overhead may be apportioned to prime cost in a different way. Thus any motive power expenses can be divided out between various machines according to how many hours each has run;

other expenses may be split up according to the number of articles made, or according to their different values. Lighting and heating expenses can be divided up according to the sizes of the various 'shops' that are being lighted or heated, and so on.

General overhead is made up for the most part of the following items: rent and maintenance of the administrative offices; travellers' expenses and COMMISSIONS (q.v.); salaries of clerks, accountants, and managerial staff; expenses of delivering goods to customers; discounts; bad debts; and INTEREST on bank loans and DEBEN-TURES (qq.v.). When the total has been found, the same problems of dividing it out arise as with factory overheads, and must be solved on the same lines.

When general overhead and factory overhead are added to prime cost, the result is 'total cost'. It is to this that the profit percentage or margin

must be added in order that the selling price may be fixed.

See also BOOK-KEEPING; BUSINESS ORGANIZATION; FAC-TORY ORGANIZATION.

COST OF LIVING. This is the relationship between the money which people receive as WAGES (q.v.), salaries, and other incomes, and the prices of the goods and services on which the money is spent. One might work out the cost of living at any particular date by selecting a representative family, who receive a certain income, and calculating the total cost of all the things on which they normally spent their money. But such a calculation would apply only to people in the same circumstances and with the same money income. To give a more general picture, what is usually done is to calculate the cost of living for a representative family at a chosen date, and then by a statistical device

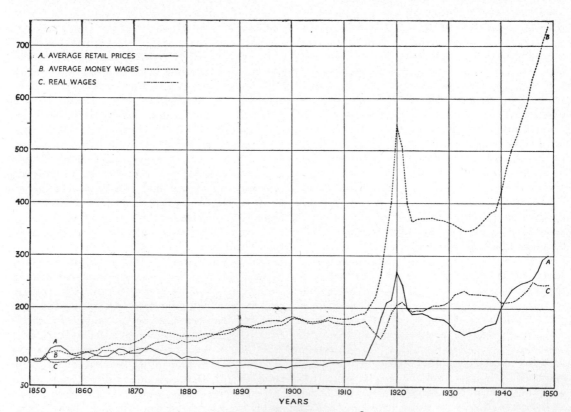

THE STANDARD OF LIVING IN BRITAIN FROM 1850 TO 1949

The curve A shows the average prices of goods, B the average money wages for each year, both starting in 1850, with the index number 100. A does not show money actually spent but the price at which goods could be bought. Money wages are not actual earnings, for these would be affected by overtime and unemployment. C shows the real value in goods of the money wage rate, allowing for the changes in money wages and in the prices of goods. It indicates, therefore, the standard of living. (Layton and Crowther, *An Introduction to the Study of Prices*, London and Cambridge Economic Service)

called an Index Number (*see* STATISTICS) to express subsequent changes as so much per cent. of the original calculation.

To do this, representative working-class families are interviewed, and a list is made of the things on which they normally spend money: different kinds of food, rail and road transport, clothing, fuel, rent, and so on. The answers given by the different families are then averaged. All the things they would normally buy are then priced on the date chosen as the standard or base for the index-number. A rough index-number could be then made by totalling up the prices of the different goods and services, but this would have the disadvantage that the price of a loaf of bread would be added, say, to the price of a hundredweight of coal, and more loaves than hundredweights of coal are usually bought by most people. So the various prices are therefore 'weighted', or multiplied by the number of times those particular things are bought in an average week or month. The money total thus arrived at is added up, and the total at the date taken as base called 100. If at the base date the goods priced cost £5, and at a later date the same bundle of things cost £6, then the index number would be $100 \times \frac{6}{5}$ or 120. It is, of course, true that not all classes of the population spend their money in the same way, but this device provides a reasonably sound basis for measuring changes in the cost of living.

Before the First World War the base used was the average for the year 1900. Prices moved up considerably during the First World War, and, until July 1947, the average of July 1914 was used as the base. During the Second World War there was a further considerable rise in prices, and social habits had changed greatly since 1914. So from 17 July 1947 a new index of retail prices was made by the Ministry of Labour and National Service, the prices prevailing on that date being considered equal to 100.

Some examples may be given of movements in the cost of living between 1914 and the present day. The July 1914 index of 100 had moved up to 269 by December 1920, but by July 1923 the index had declined to around 170, where it remained for several years until December 1927. Since the construction of the new Ministry of Labour index in July 1947, the index had moved to 113 by the early part of 1950.

Some industries pay wages on a sliding scale, which moves upwards and downwards to correspond with movements of the cost of living index. TRADE UNIONS (q.v.) and other interested bodies watch the index very carefully, as the welfare of their worker members depends not so much upon their money wages as upon what economists call their 'real' wages, that is, the quantities of things that money wages can buy.

See also STATISTICS; STANDARD OF LIVING.

COTTAGE INDUSTRY, *see* DOMESTIC SYSTEM.

COTTON INDUSTRY. 1. HISTORY. Cotton is a textile fibre of great antiquity, although it was not used in England for manufacturing purposes until the middle of the 17th century. India used cotton long before it was mentioned in written records, and India was the first country to grow it on a large scale. Indeed, from about 1500 B.C. until the end of the 15th century A.D. she was the world's leading maker and exporter of cotton fabrics, and these were extremely fine and of very high quality. This was remarkable, as the cotton then grown in India was, as now, rather short in staple, that is, in the length of the fibres, and of comparatively poor quality. The fineness and quality of these fabrics owed more to painstaking craftsmanship than to the quality of the raw material, and the equipment used for their manufacture was extremely primitive.

The secrets of cotton manufacture were introduced into Europe by the Mohammedan invaders who swept westwards from the 7th century onwards. In the 14th century, when part of Spain was under Moorish rule, Granada and Barcelona were manufacturing centres.

Long before cotton manufacture started in Britain, Englishmen had known of Indian cotton goods, and had bought them from the Venetian galleys that visited the south coast every year (*see* SHIPPING). Continental Europeans, mainly Protestant refugees from Flanders, introduced the industry into England in the middle of the 17th century. East Anglia and south Lancashire, being already engaged in the wool textile industry, were the districts in which most of the refugees settled. Cloths made of cotton alone were not at first manufactured in Britain. Wool, which suited the climate of the country, was widely used for outer garments and coverings and for the undergarments of men and women, while women's dresses were chiefly made of linen or wool. There was no large overseas market for

THE CARDING MACHINE

The short fibres or 'waste' are removed. The cotton fibres come from the machine as a filmy web, which is passed through rollers to become 'silvers'

Cotton Board

century Lancashire had become the centre of the industry, with Liverpool as the port to which the raw material was brought, and Manchester as commercial and financial head-quarters. The new cotton materials were cheaper than linen, and began to displace it. Districts such as Paisley and Glasgow, which had previously specialized in linen manufacture, changed to cotton spinning and weaving.

The industry made great progress during part of the 19th century, but there were occasional setbacks. During the American Civil War of 1861–5 the Union (northern) states had command of the seas, and successfully blockaded the ports of the Confederate (southern) States. And so Britain was unable to obtain imports of American cotton, and Lancashire was very hard hit for some years. There was a revival after the end of the war, but between 1873 and the end of the century there was a prolonged depression in industry, and the cotton industry was affected as much as any. There was a severe fall in the value of silver, which was then used as money by some of the countries of the East, notably India and China. The purchasing power of these countries dwindled, and they were no longer able to buy from Lancashire as many cheap cotton 'piece-goods' (cotton woven to standard length, for sale as a piece). Increased foreign competition in the cheaper varieties also hurt Lancashire, and bad trade and shortage of money on the continent of Europe led many European countries to expand their own cotton industries and to depend less on imports from Britain. Another difficulty was caused by the raising of the American TARIFF (q.v.), or customs duty, on yarns and fabrics from abroad. But by the beginning of the 20th century the British cotton industry had greatly revived; the East had once again become a fairly big buyer, and markets in the Dominions and Colonies were expanding. Foreign competition was mainly in the cheaper lines, and Lancashire began to turn out more of the finer yarns and fabrics.

This prosperity did not last, and the industry was advancing towards a crisis, which was postponed by the outbreak of the First World War. After that war there was a shortage of goods in general—cotton goods among them, and the mills were kept going feverishly until this shortage had been overcome. But in 1920 there was a world collapse of trade and of prices, and it was then generally realized that Britain was no longer

cotton goods, and until quite late in the 18th century the spinning machinery available could only spin cotton yarn strong enough to be used as weft in the weaving processes, because the warp strained the yarn more than the cotton could stand. Cotton was therefore used for weaving cloths of mixed yarns. Fustian, a mixture of cotton and linen, was one of the mixed fabrics made; and bombazine, a favourite material for the women's dresses of the 17th century, was a mixture of real silk and cotton.

There were great changes in the industry in the 18th century. This was a period of great colonial expansion, during which Britain gained political control of overseas settlements, mostly with a tropical or sub-tropical climate, where cotton goods could be sold in increasing quantities. Improvements in textile machinery made possible the spinning of stronger cotton yarns which would serve for use as warp. The southern states of America began to grow raw cotton on a big scale. Between 1780 and 1800, raw cotton imports from abroad increased ten times, and the southern states of America became Britain's greatest single supplier. By the end of the 18th

THE DRAW FRAME
Slivers on the right are drawn through rollers to make the fibres lie parallel

supreme in the cotton industry. There were many reasons for this. Japan, taking little active part in the war, seized the opportunity to expand her own cotton industry and to develop an immense export trade. In India the political nationalist movement, seeking independence from British rule, was becoming influential and the Government encouraged the growth of an Indian cotton industry. The war had prevented many other countries from getting supplies from Britain, and these countries also started cotton industries of their own. The final blow was the increase of the import duties on British cotton goods by certain countries, particularly the U.S.A. and South America. The effect of all these influences was catastrophic for the British industry, and fell particularly hard on Lancashire, its main centre. The export of cotton piece-goods dropped from nearly 7,000 million linear yards in 1912 to under a quarter of that figure in 1938. Between 1912 and 1938 the number of people employed in the industry was nearly halved. Cotton had become one of Britain's 'depressed' industries. By 1945 not much more than one-

third of those who were working in the industry in 1924 were still engaged in it. Although methods of making synthetic fabrics, such as RAYON (q.v.), had been perfected since the First World War, Lancashire did not take them up fast enough to restore her lost export trade. Out of total world exports of 700 million square yards of rayon piece-goods in 1937, Japan exported 500 million, and fairly large quantities were exported by Germany and Italy.

During the Second World War it was impossible to put any remedies into effect. But soon after it ended a Working Party (or Commission of Inquiry) was set up by the Government to examine various schemes and suggestions, and to state what should be done 'to strengthen the industry and render it more stable and more capable of meeting competition in the home and foreign markets'. The main recommendations of the Working Party were that the mechanical equipment of the mills, much of which was old-fashioned and inefficient, should be modernized and increased; that to pay for this existing firms should put up sums of money; that the new machinery when received should be more efficiently used by the general adoption of a double-shift system instead of the single-shift system then in vogue (*see* FACTORY ORGANIZATION, Section 3); and that collaboration with the rayon and other synthetic fabric industries should be increased as much as possible. After 1946, STATISTICS (q.v.) showed that the output of the industry had improved considerably.

See also Vol. VI: COTTON.

COTTON MANUFACTURE. 1. MANUFACTURING PROCESSES. The main processes of manufacture in the cotton industry are much the same as those in the WOOL INDUSTRY (q.v.), and the machines operate on the same general principles. The raw cotton, as it comes away from the plant in the cotton fields (*see* COTTON, Vol. VI), contains a large proportion of seeds, which are removed by the process of 'ginning'. In earlier days this separation of the seeds was a lengthy process that had to be done by hand; but in 1793 Eli Whitney, an American, invented the 'gin', an apparatus with saw-like teeth that extracted the seeds mechanically. Whitney's original invention has since been considerably improved, and modified 'saw-tooth' gins are still largely used, as well as the more complicated roller-gins. The ginning process is usually performed in the actual cotton-fields, for normally two-thirds of the weight of the harvested cotton is seed, and the cost of sending away the raw cotton is reduced if the seed is removed on the spot.

The ginned cotton is closely packed in bales under great pressure, to be shipped. At this stage it looks very much like raw wool, except that it is creamy white, and does not feel greasy to the touch. It can be 'teasled' into separate fibres, which vary in length from about ½ in. to just over 2 in., according to quality. The longer the 'staple' or length of the fibre, the higher the grade of cotton, and the finer the yarn that can be spun from it. After unbaling at the port of entry, the cotton is cleaned, and is then subjected to the 'carding' process (*see* WOOL SPINNING, Section 2); this removes the shorter fibres, which would not make good yarn. What is removed by the carding machines is called 'waste', and has many uses. Sometimes it is spun into coarse yarn, either by itself, or mixed with short-stapled Indian cotton; sometimes it is mixed with wool and used for weaving the

cheaper clothing fabrics of wool and cotton mixture; it also has other uses, such as the making of dusters and the wicks for oil-lamps. The cotton comes out from the carding machines as long 'slivers' or ropes, in which the individual cotton fibres lie roughly parallel to each other. For short-stapled cottons carding is the last process before actual spinning. Long-stapled cottons usually pass through a further 'combing' process, much as wool does in the making of worsted yarns. It is this combed cotton which is used for spinning the finer 'counts'. The 'count' of any particular quality of yarn is the number of 'hanks' or lengths of yarn that will turn the scale at a pound, each hank being 840 yards long. The finer the yarn, the less it will weigh, and the higher the count. Counts vary from about 300's (called 'three hundreds') for yarn made from the best Sea Island cotton, to about 20's ('twenties') for yarn made from ordinary Upland American.

After being combed, the slivers are passed through the 'drawing frame', which combines several slivers together, and at the same time draws them out into a single sliver in which the straight and parallel arrangement of the fibres is made more definite. When they come out of the drawing-frame, the slivers are passed through a succession of machines called 'fly-frames', which gradually reduce their thickness and prepare them for the spinning process. In this the slivers are still further drawn out, and given the 'twist', which converts them into actual yarn.

Two principal types of spinning-machine are used in the Lancashire cotton industry. One is the ring-frame, which spins continuously and does not need very close and constant watching. The other is the self-acting 'mule', which combines in an improved form the original ideas of Hargreaves's spinning 'jenny' and Arkwright's roller-spinning frame. The mule needs more attention than the ring-frame, for its operation is intermittent and not continuous. Until recently the mule was regarded as the better machine; it was believed to produce a softer and better yarn, and was used for spinning the finer counts. The ring-frame, on the other hand, has hitherto been used mainly for the spinning of the coarser yarns. There are roughly five mule-spindles in Lancashire to every ring-spindle. Lancashire is rather backward in its spinning equipment (*see* COTTON INDUSTRY). The mule-spindle is a type which no other country uses on anything like this scale and, except for special orders and replacements, the leading textile machinery makers have ceased to make mule-spindles. Early in the present century mule-spindles were generally considered essential for spinning any yarns finer than 60's. Ring-spindles have now been greatly improved, and are regularly used abroad for the spinning of yarns finer than 100's.

The final process in cotton spinning is 'doubling' which means the twisting together of two or more yarns to make 2-ply, 3-ply, or multi-ply yarns. Not all yarns are 'doubled'; much depends on the purpose for which they are going to be used. Sometimes single yarn is put through the doubling process merely to put an extra twist in it. Sometimes doubling is done in order to make a yarn of mixed cotton and wool, or of mixed cotton and silk, or of other textile mixtures. The doubling process gives a more even count, and also confers more strength on yarns that are to be used as warp in the weaving process (*see* WOOL WEAVING), and therefore have to stand extra strain. All yarn destined for use as sewing-thread, or for the lace and hosiery trades, is doubled as a general practice. Some of the coarser counts of yarn are also doubled, and are used for making heavy canvas. The doubling process more than doubles the strength of the combined yarn, as compared with the strength of the individual yarns that go to make it—in much the same way as a rope of three strands is more than three times as strong as any individual strand.

Cotton weaving does not differ in essentials from the methods used for the weaving of wool and other textile fabrics. In weaving equipment also Lancashire is very much behind the rest of the world, and particularly behind the United States. A Government committee's report in 1946 stated that only about 4% of the total of looms used for weaving in Lancashire were automatic, while in the United States 95% were automatic. The cloths woven are mainly for making up as clothes, and for household and furnishing uses, although many cotton cloths are used for industrial purposes. Most of the industrial cloths are made by the weaving mills, and are bought from them by the industrial users; for example, shoe-linings are mainly made in Lancashire and sold to merchants in Leicester or Nottingham, who pass them on to the BOOT AND SHOE INDUSTRY (q.v.). Sometimes the

Cotton Board

MULE SPINNING

Rovings (thin slivers) from the bobbins are drawn out and twisted into yarn by the forward movement of the carriage in front of the operator. When the carriage runs back the yarn is wound on to spindles below

Cotton Board

RING SPINNING

Rovings from the bobbins are drawn out still finer by rollers and then twisted into yarn. There is no movable carriage and the process is continuous

industrial users buy yarn and weave their own cloths. For example, many makers of tires own mills for the weaving of their tire fabrics, and many of the surgical-dressing fabrics are woven in mills owned or controlled by the firms that deal in them.

After weaving, most cotton cloths pass through various finishing processes, unless they are to be sold unfinished as 'greycloth'. The main finishing processes are bleaching, sizing, dyeing, calendering, mercerizing, and printing (*see* TEXTILE PRINTING). Chlorine BLEACHING (q.v.) is most usual in Britain, but bleaching by hydrogen peroxide is increasing, particularly in the United States. Calendering is a mechanical process to give lustre and 'feel' to cotton fabrics; mercerizing gives a silky sheen or lustre, and is a combination of mechanical and chemical processes—the fabric is held under tension, and not allowed to shrink, during immersion in a bath of caustic soda.

2. ORGANIZATION. The British cotton industry is composed of many separate kinds of firms. There are the merchants in raw cotton, including the Liverpool merchants and brokers, whose business was suspended when the Government Cotton Control took over the wartime BULK PURCHASE (q.v.) of raw cotton in 1941; the yarn merchants; and the piece-goods merchants who deal in woven fabrics. The producing side of the industry includes the spinners, the doublers, the weavers, and the finishers. Both merchants and producing firms tend to specialize. A spinning firm usually spins either fine or coarse yarns, but not both. Weaving firms usually weave a restricted selection of fabrics. Many yarns have to pass through intermediate processes before they are woven; sometimes these processes are undertaken by spinners, sometimes by weavers, and occasionally by specialist firms who do nothing else.

Usually spinning firms are larger than weaving firms, and more than one-third of all spindles are owned by large combines. The waste spinners and the doublers are usually small firms. The finishing section of the industry consists principally of small firms, who work mainly on COMMISSION (q.v.), but there is a small number of large concerns. Finishers normally specialize in one of the finishing processes only. In the industry there are some very large combines, which are organized 'vertically', that is, they include many firms which between them cover all the processes in the industry. But on the whole the industry is organized 'horizontally'— the various firms of specialists work separately. The producing firms work mainly to the orders of 'merchant converters'. The converters have to keep in touch with the changing taste and fashion of the market. They are mostly small firms; in fact, about 500 firms account together for about nine-tenths of all the orders placed.

3. LOCATION. The cotton industry is mainly centred in Lancashire, because the damp climate was originally an advantage to this industry. A damp climate is no longer so important, as mechanical 'humidifiers' have been invented, which can increase the moisture in the air. The chemical industry of Lancashire and Cheshire has been an important influence in preventing the cotton industry from moving elsewhere.

Outside Lancashire, and the neighbouring parts of Cheshire, Yorkshire, and Derbyshire, the only big centres of the cotton industry are Glasgow, Paisley, and Belfast, although the north-west Midlands—close to the headquarters of the lace and hosiery trades—have some importance.

Towns and districts tend to specialize. On the spinning side, Oldham and Rochdale are the main centres for the coarser counts, and Bolton for the finer counts. Waste spinning is done principally in Rochdale, Heywood, Stockport, and Stalybridge. Paisley was once the home of the famous Paisley shawls, made either from cotton alone or from cotton and silk. This trade collapsed between 1870 and 1880 through fashion changes, and Paisley has now become an important centre for spinning sewing-thread. A few mills in Belfast spin cotton yarns, mainly for mixture with the flax yarns that are the chief product of the district.

On the weaving side, the Blackburn and Burnley districts specialize mainly in plain cloths. Nelson and Colne make plain and coloured fabrics for clothes, including brocades, poplins, and sateens. The Preston area makes fine plain cloths and sheetings. Poorer quality sheetings are made from waste yarns in the Rossendale district. Oldham makes fustian, and Bolton quilts; Scotland still makes decorated cloths, ginghams, muslins, and poplins. The trade in dhotis—loose lengths of thin fabric used as garments in India—was centred in Accrington and Blackburn, but has fallen since manufacture has increased in India itself.

Finishing firms are less concentrated together. Finishing processes often depend upon plenty of fresh, soft, and running water, and finishing works are often widely scattered, many being in remote valleys. Most finishing firms are in the Lancashire area, but the Vale of Leven, in Scotland, is an important centre for calico-printing.

See also COTTON INDUSTRY.
See also Vol. VI: COTTON.

COTTON-SEED OIL, *see* OILS, VEGETABLE.

CRAFT GUILDS. These were perhaps the most important economic organizations of the later Middle Ages. A craft guild consisted of all the skilled workers of a single trade, or 'craft', working together within a town. It was the offshoot of an earlier form of guild, the Merchant Guild, then known as 'Guild Merchant', which was a mixed association of all the qualified traders of a town, with special rights for its members to engage in WHOLESALE TRADING and RETAIL TRADING within the town (qq.v.) on market days and at other times, without having to pay either tolls or customs. There were a hundred towns in England with merchant guilds, of which the first was set up at Burford in Oxfordshire, as early as 1087.

Craft guilds were first introduced in the reign of Henry I. These guilds grew rapidly as little groups of skilled craftsmen formed organizations of their own in all the important towns of England. Eventually, in town after town, the single Merchant Guild gave way to a whole series of these new organizations.

The craft guild had three classes of members: masters, journeymen, and apprentices. The apprentices were the learners. 'Till a man grow unto the age of 23 years, he is not grown to the full knowledge of his craft.' Apprenticeship was the means of acquiring a technical education. It was based on a contract between the two parties. The master promised to keep his pupil 'as a prentice should be, that is to say meat and drink, hose and shoes, linen, wool, and his craft to be taught him, and nothing hid from him thereto'. In return the apprentice promised to be obedient, to protect his master's property, not to steal—'not even by 6*d.* in the year'—not to frequent inns or gaming-houses, nor to marry without permission. The favourite dream of the medieval apprentice was to marry his master's

British Museum

MASTERS OF STONE AND WOOD GIVING EVIDENCE OF SKILL IN THEIR CRAFTS BEFORE THE CONSUL OF THE GUILD AT FLORENCE

Illumination from the Flemish manuscript *Des Proprietez des Choses*, 1482 (Roy. MS. 15, E. II, f. 265)

daughter. The length of apprenticeship varied. At first it lasted until the master declared his pupil able and well instructed. Gradually the London custom of 7 years' apprenticeship was imitated, until by the Statute of Apprentices in 1563 it became the law of the land.

When the APPRENTICE (q.v.) had completed his term, and was qualified in his craft, he could seek employment as a journeyman—a word of French origin, meaning working and paid by the day. He was usually expected to stay on for a year with his own master; and, before he himself could be admitted as a master, he was called upon to prove that 'he was full perfect in his craft' and 'of good conversation and living'. He was also at times required to provide a sample of his work, or 'masterpiece', as it was then sometimes called. These careful regulations were made to encourage a sense of responsibility, and to protect the public and the craft from unskilled workers who would discredit the trade.

Some years would pass before a journeyman

gathered enough capital to set up as a master; but, during the golden age of the craft guilds, tools, skill, and a little money to buy raw materials were all that were required, and the step from workman to master could be quite easily taken. Later on, when the artisan or skilled worker found it difficult to rise to be an employer, the system of craft guilds had broken down. By the 15th century journeymen were beginning to form their own guilds to protect their special interests, and by the 16th and 17th centuries they had their own officers and regulations.

The craft guilds comprised only skilled workmen. In this way they were unlike our modern TRADE UNIONS (q.v.), for they consisted only of the qualified men of their trades, and at no time did they include the whole body of workers within a town.

Inside the guilds there was supposed to be no competition; but, as will appear, this ideal broke down. Members of the same guild were 'brothers', pledged to help each other. Any guildsman, for example, was entitled to share in a purchase another guildsman had made, at the price that had originally been paid. Men were supposed to work 'for the honour of the guild' and for the good of the community. It was thus the object of the guild to protect the consumer against bad workmanship: shoddy goods, for instance, or under-weight parcels. A craftsman who produced inferior or fraudulent wares was not only bringing disgrace upon the craft as a whole, but was also in danger of bringing down the price of the article, and therefore he was fined for his offence. Not all medieval workmen were reliable. 'A medieval craftsman', it has been said, 'was not called a man of craft for nothing'. We can still examine many of the rules that the guilds made to deal with this sort of problem. The rules at Bristol, for example, were very strict, and 'Bristol-fashion' became a phrase applied to any job well done. Bad workers were fined, and consumers had the right to complain to guild officers.

Another useful purpose of the guild was to bring together all the workers of a particular trade, so that they could fix wages and prices. The medieval idea was that fair wages and prices could be fixed in the best interests of both producers and consumers (see USURY). It was easier to fix them in the Middle Ages, because craftsmen in a particular industry then usually lived together in a single quarter of the town. Some of these quarters still survive: Butchers' Row in York sees the same trade carried on, in the same buildings, as it was centuries ago.

Not all the time of the wardens or governors and craftsmen was taken up with work, and regulations concerning work. The guilds emphasized the religious and social side of life. They also acted as FRIENDLY SOCIETIES (q.v. Vol. X). They had craft guild pageants, and on holy days they performed mystery plays: the word 'mystery' meant mastery, or craftsmanship. Each guild would make itself responsible for one scene from a MIRACLE PLAY (q.v. Vol. XII). The visit of the Three Kings to the cradle of the Infant Jesus was taken by the goldsmiths, for the making of crowns and jewels was their special care. The story of the Flood was taken by the shipwrights, whose skill and traditions went back to the builders of the ark. Many of these miracle plays were in the spoken English of the day, and some have survived to this day—among them the pageant of the guild of shearmen and tailors at Coventry.

The ideals of the guilds look so attractive that it is sometimes difficult to understand why the system broke down. Some of the causes of their final decay lay within the guilds themselves; others outside them.

The first sign of the breakdown of the craft guild system was the growth of separate journeymen's guilds, which were associations of wage-earners formed inside the craft guilds, but maintaining a distinctive and independent existence. The success of the craft guilds had depended on good relations between masters and journeymen and the possibilities of journeymen becoming masters. In the 15th and 16th centuries many of the journeymen were sinking into the position of permanent wage-earners. This period of social change-over was accompanied by disputes between masters and journeymen about wages and hours. In 1441, for example, the London bakers were complaining that their servants had a brotherhood and livery, that is, a ceremonial uniform, and were demanding higher wages 'than they were wont to have of old time'; while in Coventry, in 1526, there were fierce disputes between master cappers (capmakers)—the main craft of the town—and their journeymen about an extension of working-hours. These and similar conflicts led to a clash between masters and journeymen, and to

GUILDHALL, LONDON, 1808
Coloured aquatint by Rowlandson and Pugin from Ackermann's *Microcosm of London*

frequent attempts by the masters to crush the new journeymen's guilds.

In Elizabethan England the journeymen's guilds had completely established themselves in many crafts, and had secured recognition from the State. They were composed mainly of small masters dependent on large masters for their livelihood, and no longer dealing direct with consumers. In London, which was far ahead of the rest of the country, the rich masters were tending more and more to drop out of manufacturing. They were no longer real craftsmen, but rather dealers and merchants.

Out of the new wealthy merchant traders emerged the great London Livery Companies, such as the Mercers, Merchant Taylors, and Haberdashers; and a clear-cut distinction could be drawn between the Livery—those merchants who could afford to buy the uniforms and pay for the feasts and pageants—and the Yeomanry —consisting of small masters, who did not sell

to the public or manufacture directly for them, but for the Livery. When Henry VII became king, and entered London in triumph in 1485, he was met by over 400 guildsmen riding on horseback and wearing bright mulberry-coloured gowns. The London guilds had by then become rich closed companies, with wealth and authority (*see* CITY COMPANIES).

Over the country as a whole, the older craft guild organizations were breaking down. In 1438, at Bristol, the cordwainers (shoemakers) were confessing that they had ceased to appoint wardens, and that no one took any more notice of the fines they imposed. As they declined— and the decline can be traced in the smaller number of miracle plays and pageants performed —the guilds began to be more and more exclusive in their organization, keeping new members out, and restricting their privileges to certain select families. This crippled their life, and compelled less wealthy craftsmen to leave the over-controlled industry in the towns, and to move towards the freedom of the countryside. This movement of industry away from the towns was quickened in Tudor England, and played a big part in the extension of the DOMESTIC SYSTEM of production (q.v.).

Some of the gaps left by the decline of the guilds were filled in by the Government. As early as 1437, an Act of Parliament claimed that 'the masters, wardens, and people of the guilds . . . make themselves many unlawful and unreasonable ordinances . . . for their singular profit and common damage to the people', and went on to order that all guild rules should be submitted to the local authorities or justices of the peace for approval. In 1504 national supervision became law, and guild rules had to be approved by the judges. In 1547, during the Reformation, the property of all religious guilds was taken over and vested in the Crown. These changes all reflected a period of guild decline. In 1563 the Government tried to preserve some of the most important features of the old system, and it drew up an elaborate code for industry, called the Statute of Apprentices. This laid down that wages were to be fixed annually by JUSTICES OF THE PEACE (q.v. Vol. X), that 7 years' apprenticeship for all trades and handicrafts was to be made compulsory all over the country—this had been the custom of London before—and that labour was not to be hired for periods of less than a year. There were many good intentions behind this famous statute, but the policy that it suggested was already out of tune with many of the new forces of the times. In the 17th century Charles I tried to encourage the setting-up of new craft guilds in London, but it was an impossible task; the guild system had been well suited to small towns and to local markets, and to restricted trade; but it did not fit the conditions of a new age.

See also TRADE UNIONS; DIVISION OF LABOUR; DOMESTIC SYSTEM; CITY COMPANIES.

CRAFTSMANSHIP. As the word is generally used, this means knowledge of a trade in which some form of skill with the hands is necessary. The opposite of the craftsman in modern industry is the 'machine-minder', one who merely sees that the machine he is in charge of is running properly, and perhaps performs at intervals some purely routine job, the success of which is not affected by his own judgement or skill of eye or hand. Some crafts can be assisted by machines, and do not cease to be crafts merely for that reason; other crafts or trades are handicrafts, and machines cannot assist them in any way, although, of course, tools are used. The tools, however, have to be guided by hand, and without the skill of the hand that guides them they can perform no useful services. A bricklayer or mason is a handicraftsman of this kind; he uses no machines. But many true craftsmen make much use of machines. A potter, for example, who uses the mechanical contrivance called the potter's wheel (see POTTERY), is truly entitled to be called a craftsman because, although it is the wheel that whirls round his lump of clay, it is the skill of his hand that fashions it. Similarly, in trades that make more use of machinery than the pottery trade, skill with the hands is necessary for many purposes.

The welfare of a country depends largely on the number and skill of its craftsmen. Countries possessing few craftsmen remain economically backward. There is a tendency in highly industrialized countries for the number of craftsmen to diminish as industrial processes become more and more mechanized, until in certain trades they practically disappear. This is a fact well known to governments and to organizations such as TRADE UNIONS (q.v.) which have the welfare of workers at heart, and the institution of APPRENTICESHIP (q.v.) is encouraged both by unions and governments so that the supply of craftsmen may be maintained. This is illustrated by certain measures that have been taken in Britain since the end of the Second World War. There has been a great decline in the number of trained craftsmen who are stonemasons, and at one period over 100 Italian stonemasons were imported to help build a waterworks dam in South Wales (see STONE DRESSING). In the boat and yacht building trades craftsmanship was safeguarded—even during the worst period of timber shortage—by the Admiralty 'hardship' scheme, under which yacht builders were allowed a licence for timber if they could prove that without it they would have to dismiss their craftsmen. The Royal MINT (q.v. Vol. X) still occasionally strikes gold sovereigns, although they are not needed for currency purposes, the sole motive being to preserve among the Mint's craftsmen a knowledge of the craft of coining in gold.

To some extent the passing of the craftsman,

A HIGHLY SKILLED CRAFTSMAN BLOWING GLASS

He is blowing 'coquilles' of curved smoke-coloured glass from which sun-glasses and goggles are made

or his transformation into a different kind of craftsman, is inevitable. A few examples may illustrate this. In earlier days no wood or stone could be carved unless each individual piece of carving was done from start to finish by a skilled worker. Nowadays a skilled worker is needed only to make the mould or 'masterpiece', from which a machine can make hundreds of copies of the original. Similarly, in the machine industry of earlier days, the independent skill of every worker at his bench was necessary for good performance. Nowadays the skill necessary has shifted from the worker at the bench to the machine-tool or jig-designing office; and, once the necessary machines have been designed, arranged, and set, the rest is automatic.

See also APPRENTICESHIP; CRAFT GUILDS; TRADE UNION HISTORY.

CREDIT. The word 'credit' comes from a Latin word meaning belief or trust. In com-merce a person is said to receive credit when he receives goods or money on the understanding that he will pay for the goods, or repay the money, in due course. The simplest form of credit is 'personal credit', which many of us receive from time to time when we buy goods in a shop and suddenly discover that we have left our money at home. If the shopkeeper knows and trusts us sufficiently, he will allow us to take the goods at once and make payment later. When a shop allows a customer to have a regular monthly account, it is still personal credit, although of a more definite kind.

Between merchants and manufacturers this form of mutual trust is known as 'trade credit'. The terms on which it is given vary greatly. The usual credit arrangement among merchants is that payment must be made by the end of the month following the date of invoice: thus, goods dispatched on 15 January should be paid for on or before 28 February. Most firms which allow credit have their terms of business printed on their invoices or monthly statements. Merchants often find that it pays them to encourage an even quicker settlement of debts by offering a cash discount, often of $2\frac{1}{2}\%$ (or 6d. in the £), on all goods paid for within 7 to 10 days of the date of invoice.

A more special type of credit is 'bank credit'. The simplest form of bank credit is the 'overdraft': when the banker gives permission for a customer to draw out money in excess of the balance he has at the bank (*see* BANK ACCOUNTS). Overdrafts are occasionally granted against purely personal security: that is, against the customer's promise to repay by some pre-arranged date. More often some sort of SECURITY is insisted on, such as government bonds, STOCKS AND SHARES (qq.v.), or guarantees entered into by the customer's partners or by other responsible people. The advantage of an overdraft is that the borrower has to pay INTEREST (q.v.) only on the amount actually overdrawn.

The other way of borrowing money from a bank is by a 'loan account'. This is opened for the customer at an agreed rate of interest. The full amount of the loan is charged against the customer's account, and placed to his current account for him to draw against. He pays interest on the total amount of the loan, however much or little of it he spends.

Among other forms of credit issued by bankers are circular or travellers' 'letters of credit' for use when the customer is travelling abroad. The letter of credit states the limit up to which he may draw money; it is accompanied by a booklet containing the names of the bank's agents in various towns all over the world. It is signed by the customer. The holder of a letter of credit draws as much foreign money as he needs abroad by writing ordinary cheques on his account, which are cashed up to the limit of his credit. The cheques eventually reach his own bank, and are charged to his account. Travellers' cheques are really letters of credit for round sums of money, printed on detachable forms like cheques. Another method is the 'open credit', by which a banker advises one of his own branches, or a particular banking office abroad, that it may safely cash his customer's cheques up to an arranged limit.

Some firms specialize in providing a service called 'credit rating'. They find out from the trade-connexions of the firms whose rating they are assessing, and also from their bankers and other sources of information, how reliable the firms are, and up to what sums of money they can safely be trusted in the ordinary way of business. The firms are rated A, B, or C, or on a similar basis, according to their credit-worthiness. The ratings are then printed in book form and are made available to subscribers to the service. Firms providing this kind of service also act as general commercial inquiry agents.

It is also possible to insure against losses caused by granting credit to firms or individuals who turn out to be so unworthy of it that those granting the credit lose their money (*see* INSURANCE). 'Credit insurance' is one of those branches of insurance in which the insurer himself is always asked to bear a considerable portion of the risk insured against. If this were not done, firms might be tempted to increase their business by granting credit too recklessly.

'Hire purchase' and 'payment by instalments' are special forms of credit, by which a person who buys something need not pay the whole price at once but can spread out the payment over a period of time. For these transactions a written agreement is drawn up between the seller and the buyer. Under a hire-purchase agreement the goods are delivered to the 'hirer' on payment of a small deposit of money, but they remain the legal property of the seller until the last of a series of weekly or monthly instalments has been paid. Until 1938 the law in Britain worked very much to the advantage of the seller, so that, if the hirer failed to meet even the last few instalments, the seller was entitled to take back the goods and also to keep the instalments that had already been paid. This might, and often did, cause great hardship to buyers. The Hire Purchase Act was, therefore, passed by Parliament in 1938, and this laid down (*a*) that if the hirer had already paid at least one-third of the purchase price, the seller could not obtain possession of the goods without an order from a court of law; and (*b*) that a court could order the remaining instalments to be spread over a longer period than that of the original contract. The Act applied, in general, only to transactions not exceeding £100.

The other system of instalment selling is called 'deferred payments'. A written agreement is drawn up, as for a hire-purchase transaction, but the goods become the property of the buyer after payment of the first deposit.

Both these systems may be used not only when an ordinary customer buys something in a shop (in which case the credit is called 'consumer credit'), but also when manufacturers and merchants want to buy goods. Manufacturers may obtain new plant or machinery by paying instalments spread over a number of years; a merchant may, for example, equip himself with a new fleet of motor-vans in the same way. It is thus possible for a business firm to bring its equipment up to date by payments out of profits, without increasing its capital. There are firms that specialize in financing transactions of this kind; one of the largest is the United Dominions Trust, which works in close association with the Bank of England.

In modern days governments watch very closely the total amount of instalment credit. If it grows too large, it may lead to an increase in the demand for goods when goods are scarce, and this causes inflation (*see* NATIONAL FINANCE, Vol. X). By altering from time to time the law concerning instalment selling, governments may do much to control its total amount. Consumer credit of this kind was legally forbidden during the Second World War, and was only very gradually restored afterwards.

See also BANKING.

CREDIT NOTE, *see* INVOICE.

CURRENCY. Currency is not quite the same thing as coinage. A country's coinage is the actual metallic coins that it uses; but other kinds of money may be 'current'—or passed from hand to hand as money. All money that is current, and is reckoned by counting and not by weight, is currency. Thus guineas, sovereigns, half-sovereigns, half-crowns, shillings, pennies, and so on, are currency because they are coins, and because they pass from hand to hand without being weighed. Bank-notes are currency for the same reason, although they are not part of the coinage.

Pitt Rivers Museum

NOTE ISSUED IN FRANCE DURING THE FIRST WORLD WAR

Notes were issued by local Chambers of Commerce for use in their district to make up for a shortage of small coin

MONEY (q.v.) need not necessarily be currency. Throughout the world various things have been used as money at different times, ranging from cattle to the small shells called 'cowries', and including the precious metals, uncoined, and passing from hand to hand by weight (*see* PRIMITIVE MONEY). Primitive communities have money of this sort, but a precious metal is not usually made into coins until a later stage of development. By making it up into coins a properly organized government guarantees the weight and 'fineness' of metal used. (Fineness is the proportion of precious metal in an 'alloy' or mixture which contains also base metal for hardening purposes.)

Coinage is nearly always a State responsibility (*see* MINT, Vol. X); but currency other than coinage need not necessarily be so—although in modern times it usually is. From the 17th century onwards, in England and Wales, paper currency in the form of bank-notes was issued by private bankers on their own responsibility, and according to their own individual designs (*see* BANKING). But by 1921 the Treasury and the BANK OF ENGLAND (q.v.) had become jointly responsible for all such issues. In Scotland and Ireland, however, the issue of paper currency is still left to commercial banking firms.

'Legal tender' means any form of currency which may legally be 'tendered', or offered, to merchants and individuals in payment for goods or debts, and in payment of taxes and other

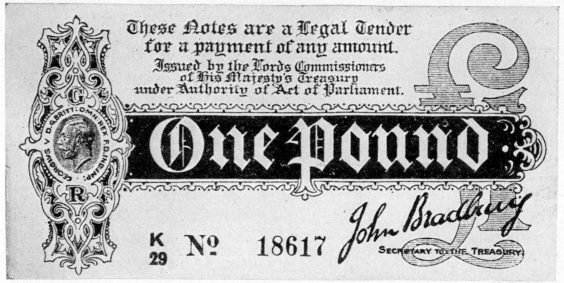

THE FIRST BRITISH TREASURY NOTE ISSUED IN 1914
Because the signature of the Secretary to the Treasury is so legible these were often called 'Bradburys'

debts to the Government itself. When any coins or notes are made 'legal tender', people to whom money is due are obliged by law to accept those coins or notes. In England and Wales at the present time the £1 and 10s. notes of the Bank of England are legal tender without any limit; silver coins (including the copper-nickel alloy which looks like silver) are legal tender up to a limit of £2; and copper coins (which are really made of bronze) and threepenny bits are legal tender only up to a limit of 1s. for any one transaction. In Northern Ireland and Scotland the bank-notes of certain local commercial banks are legal tender as well as the moneys just mentioned. Bank of England notes over £1 are not legal tender in Northern Ireland or Scotland.

Between 1821 and 1844 the only kinds of currency in England and Wales which were legal tender without limit were the gold sovereign and the half-sovereign. The Bank Charter Act of 1844 added Bank of England notes as legal tender in England and Wales. This situation lasted until August 1914 when, owing to war difficulties, Treasury notes were printed as additional legal tender without limit throughout Great Britain. These ceased to be issued in 1928.

Between 1821 and 1914 the coinage of Great Britain consisted of golden sovereigns and half-sovereigns, and silver and copper coins. The gold coins were literally 'worth their weight in gold': that is, they could have been sold by weight for their face value. But if a half-crown of those days had been sold by weight, it might have fetched only a shilling, while a penny might have fetched less than a farthing. These silver and bronze coins were called 'token coins', to distinguish them from the full-value gold coins. Bank-notes are worth nothing in themselves. They are not token coins, but token currency.

Nowadays the difference between the token and non-token currency of Great Britain is of historical interest only. The gold sovereign is no longer in circulation, and no unit of our modern currency, whether bank-note or coin, could be sold as paper or as metal for anything but a mere fraction of its face value. As the result of two world wars we have reached a stage where all our currency is token currency.

See also MONEY; COINS; BANKING.

CURRENT ACCOUNT, *see* BANK ACCOUNTS.

CURRYING is one of the finishing processes of the leather trade. In the days of the CRAFT GUILDS (q.v.) there were two different sets of craftsmen engaged in leather manufacture: the tanners who prepared and tanned the hides, drying them out into 'crust' leather; and the curriers who 'dressed' and finished the crust leather. This separation of the two trades lasted for centuries, and in 1604 James I checked a tendency towards amalgamation by making a law that no one should be permitted to practise both crafts. This law is no longer in force, but the historical division of the leather trades still persists, and many firms to-day buy crust leather from tanners and specialize in currying or dressing only.

If the leather that emerges from the vegetable TANNING process (q.v.) is merely dried out, it is harsh, of uneven thickness, and lacking in water-proof qualities. The currying process corrects these defects, its main purpose being to put grease into the leather to make the leather strong, supple, and waterproof. In the past the process was needed for boot and shoe uppers, harness, straps, saddlery, coach hoods and tops, and leather jerkins. Currying is carried out to-day on leather for footballs, driving-belts, harness and bridles, straps, hoses, cases and bags, and the uppers of heavy-duty footwear worn by farm-workers, miners, seamen, and soldiers. The process differs in detail according to the nature of the tanning and the purpose for which the leather will be used. A typical example is the treatment applied to vegetable-tanned ox-hide that is to be used as driving belting for machinery. The 'backs' of the hides, which will be used for this purpose, will have been separated from the 'bellies' by the tanner. The currier buys the backs and first soaks them in warm water or weak tan liquor to soften them. He then thoroughly cleans them, either by working over the surface of the grain with a brush and a 'slicker'—a hand tool with a broad, blunt blade—or by machinery. When the hide has been partly dried, its thickness which varies from place to place, is evened up. This used to be done by slicing off thin films of leather with a special knife that had a sharp cutting edge at right angles to the blade. To-day this very skilled operation is done either by a machine in which the hide is pressed against a rapidly revolving cylinder fitted with spiral knife blades; or by splitting off a thin layer with a machine in which the hide is pressed, edge on, against the edge of a band knife travelling at a high speed. Next comes the greasing. An old process, still much used for the best quality leathers, is called 'hand-stuffing'. The damp leather is coated on both sides with a layer of dubbin: the original dubbin was of equal parts of tallow and crude cod-liver oil, but other mixtures are now sometimes used. The leather is then hung to dry slowly in a warm room, where the water evaporates, the leather absorbs the liquid portion of the dubbin, and the more solid portions of the dubbin are left on the surface to be scraped off later.

Gandy Ltd.

SCOURING LEATHER AFTER IT HAS BEEN TANNED

The hide is soaked in water and cleaned by this machine which, fitted with scouring stones and brushes, moves rapidly over the table on which the hide is laid

For many purposes hand-stuffing has been replaced either by 'drum-stuffing' or 'dipping'. In drum-stuffing, the leather, when still damp, is put into a drum containing molten grease. This is absorbed into the leather. In dipping, the leather is first dried and then dipped into the grease. After greasing, there may be further treatments.

One old hand process was to soften the leather by folding it over on itself, grain to grain, and working it backwards and forwards with a wooden tool, called a 'pommel'. In the olden days this particular operation was the true currying process, although the term is applied to-day rather to the greasing process.

See also HIDES AND SKINS; TANNING; LEATHER; BOOT- AND SHOE-MAKING.

CUSTOMS DUTIES, *see* OVERSEAS TRADE; TARIFF.

CUTLERY INDUSTRY. Cutlery includes table and carving knives, the knives used by such tradesmen as butchers and boot and shoe-makers, artists' palette knives, pocket-knives and penknives, pruning-knives, barbers' razors, scissors, carving-forks, and steels for sharpening. The industry is one of the oldest in England. It is practically confined to the Sheffield district, where the trade was already well established in the time of the 14th-century poet, Chaucer. There are some firms operating in Birmingham and other provincial towns, and a few firms specialize in tradesmen's cutlery in London.

Perhaps there is no industry in the country in which ancient traditions die harder than in cutlery. In Sheffield some of the old CRAFT GUILD (q.v.) conditions still prevail, and this is apparent in the division of the industry into three branches, forging or 'goffing', grinding, and finishing. Before the First World War methods of producing cutlery had not greatly altered from the Middle Ages, although power was used to drive grinding-wheels and to operate heavy hammers for some of the forging processes. But many types of knives and cutting-blades were still being hand-forged under the craftsman's hammer, and finished and polished by hand. Since 1918 there has been more mechanization, particularly for forging and grinding, but the production of high-class cutlery is unlikely ever to be completely mechanized.

There are three main divisions of the industry:

shaping and forging the pieces of steel from which the articles will be made; tempering, grinding, and polishing; and assembling and finishing. There are very few firms in the trade engaged in each of these divisions and carrying out every process from the raw steel to the finished article. The main division of labour in the trade is between firms that forge or 'goff' the blades, and firms that grind, polish, assemble, and finish. Quite a number of small firms carry out only a single process, and much work in the industry is done on the 'outworker' system. Grinding is a branch of the trade in which outworkers are still very numerous. In the days before steam, when water was the motive power for working heavy forging hammers and driving grinding-wheels, land speculators built factories along the banks of the streams. They then let space or rooms in these 'tenement' factories to small craftsmen working on their own account, and provided them with the necessary heat, light, and power. In and around Sheffield this system still prevails to some extent, although it is on the decline since the motive power provided is now steam or electricity. Many outworkers still work in these tenement factories. Others work at piece-rates for an employer who provides them with space, light, and power, for which he charges a rent, and pays according to the amount of work done. In the cutlery industry the small craftsman is not at a disadvantage compared with the large-scale manufacturer, for many of the processes can be carried out either with quite simple machinery or entirely by hand.

Machinery is being increasingly used for the cheaper articles, but much handwork by skilled craftsmen is still necessary for those of higher quality. The blades of the best table-knives are machine-forged from short bars of good steel. Machines may be used to shape the shoulder or 'bolster' at the handle end of the blade, and the 'tang' or extension for fitting the handle. The cheaper table-knives are made from strip steel, rolled and shaped mechanically. After being shaped, the blades are hardened, and then tempered by being re-heated to a low temperature and rapidly quenched in water. The blades of pocket-knives and penknives are tempered slightly harder than table-knives. The word 'penknife' is a title handed down from the days when the smaller blade of a pocket-knife was used for sharpening quill pens. Grinding is the next process. It is now largely mechanized, but

Joseph Rodgers & Sons

MAKING A TABLE-KNIFE BLADE

The blade is forged from a ¾ ft. bar of stainless steel about ½ in. square. First the metal is drawn out in a heavy press (top left), then it is hammered to make the bolster or shoulder (top right). The tang which fits into the handle is drawn out and the blade is spread out. Next the blade is cut out (lower left). It undergoes finishing and hardening processes and is finally ground (lower right) and polished

there are still many hand-grinders in Sheffield and also in Solingen, which is the centre of the German cutlery industry. Barbers' razors are 'hollow ground': apart from the actual edge itself, the thinnest part of the blade is in the centre. Safety-razor blades, being straight, are produced and ground mechanically. Each blade of a pair of scissors is forged separately from slightly milder steel than is used for knives. High-class pocket-knives are hand-forged, and fitting the springs of such knives is a highly skilled branch of the trade.

D

DAIRY INDUSTRY. 1. This is one of the most important industries in many countries. Australia, New Zealand, Denmark, Canada, and parts of the U.S.A. are all notable for dairy produce. In Britain the main activities of the dairy industry are the production of milk, its collection from the farms, its processing, and its sale either as a liquid or as a manufactured product.

Milk may be sold direct to the public by the farmer, or it may be produced by the wholesale supplier from whose farms it is collected (*see* WHOLESALE TRADING) and first taken to a country depot. There the lids of the churns are lifted, and the milk is tested by a checker. Should any milk have a taint, the churn is placed on one side and the milk is given a laboratory test; if it fails to pass this, it may be returned to the producer. On the Continent, though not in Britain, unsatisfactory milk of this kind is manufactured into other products.

The sound milk is then weighed and measured and tipped into a stainless-steel tank and the milk is cooled to about 38° F. It is then pumped into a rail or road tanker, which consists of a stainless-steel shell, lined with glass-enamel or aluminium, and insulated against changes of temperature by a 2- or 4-in. layer of cork. A tanker may hold up to 3,000 gallons of milk, and in this large bulk the milk retains its low temperature for long periods. The tanker is dispatched during the afternoon and night to the town processing depot. There the milk is thoroughly mixed, and a sample is taken for chemical and bacteriological examination. If these are satisfactory, the milk is transferred, either by a pump or by compressed air, into a storage tank in the dairy. It is then drawn off for PASTEURIZATION (q.v.) and the pasteurized milk then passes into a 'finished' milk tank. From this tank it is drawn off as required, and goes to the filling machine or filler, where it is filled into bottles.

Milk bottles must be thoroughly cleaned and sterilized before they are filled. At large dairies these operations are carried out by a bottle-washing machine, in which the bottles receive a series of rinses at different temperatures. On being discharged from the bottle-washing machine, the bottles are first inspected for any imperfections and then passed along a CONVEYOR (q.v. Vol. VIII) to a machine in which the bottles are filled, sometimes by air suction. The filled bottles are capped, usually with an aluminium foil, which is placed over the mouth of the bottle, and fixed firmly by pressure. The bottles are then placed in a crate and taken by motor lorry to the dairyman, or to the retail branches of a big dairy firm, where the milk is held overnight in a cold store, and then delivered to the public the following morning.

Homogenized milk is ordinary milk which has been forced through small holes under very high pressure to break up the fat globules into much smaller ones. These tiny fat globules do not rise to the surface to form a cream layer, as the fat globules in ordinary milk do. Instead, the fat remains evenly mixed throughout the milk, which appears almost twice as creamy in tea and coffee.

Sterilized milk is homogenized milk which has been heated in a sealed bottle, under pressure, to temperatures well above boiling-point. Such milk is virtually sterile (free from living organisms), and keeps for a long time.

2. CREAM is separated by passing milk at a temperature of about 100° F. through a separator, in which a layer of conical plates revolves at high speed. The fat globules, being lighter than the rest of the liquid, collect in the central part of the separator and form the cream, which flows out through a pipe. The separated milk, being heavier, is discharged by another pipe. The cream must be separated before butter is made.

3. BUTTER is essentially the fat of milk, and should not contain more than 16% of water. There are two main types of butter: sweet cream butter for which the cream is not soured before churning, and ripened or soured cream butter. Sweet cream butter has a much fuller flavour than sour but keeps for less time. Milk is first

Express Dairy Co.

A DAIRY WHICH BOTTLES 100,000 GALLONS OF MILK A DAY

The machines in front are filling bottles; at the back bottles are being washed, and on the balcony there are pasteurization plants and milk storage tanks

passed through a separator to give a cream of about 38% fat. If ripened cream butter is to be made, lactic streptococci are added, and the cream is held at a temperature of about 60° F. until the required degree of souring has been obtained. When ready for churning, the cream is cooled to a temperature of about 58° F. and cold water is added.

The butter churn is a wooden barrel that is rotated to give the cream a series of violent shocks. This causes the fat globules, which are in the cream, to come together, and separate from the water. The newly made butter must be thoroughly washed with cold water, to remove from the fat as much protein as possible. The butter is finally 'worked', or squeezed and punched, by rollers or other devices, until it has acquired the right consistency and contains the

required amount of water, that is, just below 16%. The butter may be salted, and is finally packed into 56-lb. boxes. Butter must be kept away from metal, otherwise it will have a stale or rancid taste.

4. CHEESE is probably the most interesting milk product from the scientific point of view, as it involves physical, chemical, and bacteriological changes in the milk. Most cheese was once made only in farm-houses, but most of it is now made in factories. The most important variety made in England is Cheddar. The milk is put into a vat, and is first 'ripened' or soured by allowing lactic streptococci to grow in it at a temperature of about 70° F. When a certain acidity has been reached, the temperature is then raised to about 84° F., and a small proportion of rennet (a milk-curdling substance)

is added. After about half an hour a fairly firm junket or curd is formed by the action of the rennet on the soured milk. This is then cut into small cubes, and the temperature is gradually raised to just over 100° F. The particles of curdled matter, or curd, must be stirred continuously, and, when the curd has contracted and hardened, a greenish-yellow liquid, called whey, is run off and the particles of curd are allowed to sink to the bottom where they come together to form a sort of mattress. This is then cut into pieces, which are piled on the sides of the vat to help the drainage of the whey. During this time the acidity is continually increasing, and this helps to separate the whey from the curd. Finally, when the curd has reached the right condition, it is 'milled' or torn into small particles, mixed with salt, and packed into a hoop or mould. The moulded curd is then placed in a press for 2 or 3 days, by which time it has become a 'green' cheese. Cheddar cheese is usually graded after about a month, and is considered ripe or fit for eating in about 9 or 12 months, though the right age for eating it is entirely a matter of taste. The cheese retains practically all the fat and casein, or chief protein, in the milk, and a certain proportion of the other constituents, and is a very rich food.

5. MILK POWDER OR DRIED MILK. Milk is dried by two main methods, the roller and the spray process. By the roller method hot milk is fed in between two special rollers which are practically touching each other, and which revolve about 5 times a minute. The rollers are hollow, and are heated by steam. The milk quickly dries and forms a film on the surface of the roller; this is carried round until it meets a knife which scrapes it off. The film then drops into a box, or into a trough, from which a screw-conveyor passes it along to the sifting, grinding, and packing departments. In the spray process hot concentrated milk is sprayed into a drying-chamber; various devices are used to produce a very fine spray, in which the tiny globules rapidly lose their moisture in a current of hot air. The finely divided powder is then collected at the bottom and packed into tins. Spray-dried milk is a fine white powder, easily reconstituted in water to form a product very like the original milk; but spray powder does not possess as good keeping qualities as roller powder, unless special care is taken. Roller powder is not easily reconstituted, and has an 'oxidized' flavour resulting from chemical changes in the fat.

6. CONDENSED MILK. Whole or skimmed milk is first heated to about 173° F. It is held at this temperature for some time, and then drawn into a large copper vessel with steam-heated coils at the bottom. Cane-sugar is added to the milk and the mixture is condensed at a temperature of just over 122° F. until it has reached a concentration of about 2¼ times that of the original milk. The condensed milk is then drawn off, pumped through coolers, and filled into tins or barrels. It owes its good keeping quality to its high concentration of cane-sugar, which acts as a preservative.

7. EVAPORATED MILK differs from condensed milk in not containing any added sugar, and is sterilized in the tin under pressure. Milk is first pre-heated, clarified, and homogenized, and then concentrated up to about twice its original content in solids. It is then filled into tins, and the tins are passed into a special pressure-heating apparatus in which the concentrated milk, under pressure, is raised to a temperature well above boiling-point. This kills all bacteria.

See also Vol. VI: CATTLE, CARE OF.
See also Vol. XI: MILK; BUTTER; CHEESE.

DEBENTURES are loans to LIMITED COMPANIES, usually at a fixed rate of INTEREST (qq.v.). The 'debenture holders', or persons lending the money, accept the assets of the company as security for their money.

There is a great difference between debentures and STOCKS AND SHARES (q.v.). A share is what its name implies: it is a share in the fortune or misfortune of the company in which it is held. If the company earns profits, the shareholders will receive a dividend; if no profits are made they will receive nothing. But the position of a debenture-holder is safer. The borrowing company must sign a trust deed, a legal contract pledging the company's land, buildings, machinery, plant, and other assets as security for the loan. The Trust deed names a body of TRUSTEES (q.v. Vol. X) to act for the debenture-holders, and promises that the arranged rate of interest shall be regularly paid, whether profits are earned or not; it also lays down that, if the interest is not regularly paid, the trustees may be given certain rights over the business and may control its management, until either regular payment of interest can be made again, or the company's assets have been turned into cash so that the debenture-holders may be repaid.

Debentures may be 'redeemable', that is, the whole loan may be repayable to the lenders at a fixed future date; or 'irredeemable', which means that they are a permanent loan to the company. A 'participating debenture' has all the advantages of a debenture and also one of the advantages of a share: it brings in a small dividend, payable out of the company's profits, as well as its own interest.

In spite of the severe penalties in case of default, it is rather an advantage for a company whose business is profitable to borrow money on debenture. It has to pay only low rates of interest for capital on which extra profits can be earned for its 'ordinary' shareholders.

See also DIVIDEND; LOAN.

DEMAND, *see* SUPPLY AND DEMAND.

DEPARTMENT STORES. There are conflicting views concerning the origin of the department store, or big retail shop which sells several different kinds of goods. It has been suggested that the department-store movement in Britain was started in the second half of the 19th century by a small group of Civil Service clerks, who bought a chest of tea at wholesale price at the London AUCTION sales (q.v.) and divided it among themselves. This group later expanded into the Civil Service Supply Association, a large department store with premises in the Strand and in the City. A more likely explanation is that Aristide Boucicaut, a Frenchman, originated the movement in 1852 by founding the Paris Bon Marché. The first department store outside Paris was opened in the U.S.A. in the late 1850's, very soon after Boucicaut opened up in Paris. In 1860 William Whiteley opened his big London store in Bayswater, and claimed to be 'the universal provider'. Other London merchants soon followed William Whiteley's example.

The provincial department store—at least on a small scale—goes back very much farther in the history of British RETAIL TRADING (q.v.). The local 'emporium', or big shop specializing mainly in drapery and household furnishing but often selling also women's wear, millinery, household hardware and ironmongery, and sometimes grocery, was a feature of Regency and Victorian England, mentioned frequently

AN 'EMPORIUM' IN A PROVINCIAL TOWN

in the contemporary novel. In Mrs. Gaskell's *Cranford*, for example, Miss Matty goes into one such shop 'to buy the tea, select the silk, and then clamber up the iron corkscrew stairs that led into what was once a loft, though now a fashion showroom'. Smith, the Nottingham draper, who afterwards included a banking department in his manifold activities and became more famous as a banker than as a draper, ran an emporium of this kind. The only difference between an emporium (from the Latin word for the Greek *emporion*, a shop) and the department store of the late 19th century and the present day is in scale and scope. The giant department stores of modern cities not only sell more kinds of goods, but provide more comfort for those who shop in them. The drapery, clothing, and household-furnishing trades have, however, supplied the foundations for the later development of the department-store movement. In the London suburbs, and in the larger provincial towns, there are many small-scale department stores which from small beginnings have become large stores. Those in the Brixton, Balham, Clapham, Peckham, Holloway, and Stratford districts of London are examples of this.

The arguments in favour of the department store are that customers are likely to spend more if they can buy all they want in one shop, and that, as they walk through the store, they may be tempted to buy other goods besides those they have specifically come to buy. To attract the customer and display goods to advantage, department stores must have an atmosphere of spaciousness and even luxury. A great deal of what might be selling-space is devoted to passage-ways, corridors, and staircases, and to restaurants, cafés, lifts, escalators, and very often banking halls. These things cost much money, and the bill for lighting and heating is a large item. Prices in department stores are usually no lower than those of ordinary shops, and certain goods are often even more expensive. The internal organization of a department store is highly complex, and buying is usually centralized under the control of a merchandise manager. It is their immense buying power which enables them to compete successfully against firms that have lower overhead charges (see Costing), because manufacturers and whole-salers are always prepared to make price concessions for large quantities. Of recent years a number of previously independent department stores have come under a single ownership and management. Many of the companies control establishments both in London and in the big provincial cities. The 'chain' department store, such as Woolworth's and Marks and Spencer's, with a series of branches throughout the country, is a special development of the department-store movement.

See also Self-service Stores; Multiple Shop.

DEPOSIT ACCOUNT, see Bank Accounts.

DEPRECIATION. This means the decrease in the value of a business firm's property as compared with its value when first bought or constructed. The plant and machinery of a factory are particularly liable to depreciation. Wear and tear is the main reason, for even with good maintenance and repair no machine will last for ever, or work as well after years of use as it did when first bought. Machines may also lose value because they are superseded by better or more up-to-date machines; the reason for their depreciation is then called 'obsolescence'. Freehold property may depreciate as time goes on, in spite of careful maintenance and repairs; Leasehold property depreciates so far as to possess no value at all when the term of the lease expires, for the owner will then lose his right to occupy and use the property, (see Property, Vol. X).

When a business firm makes up its accounts at the end of its trading year, to find out its profit or loss for the period (see Book-keeping), the amount of depreciation that various items of property have suffered must be allowed for in the accounts. There are several ways in which these depreciation allowances may be calculated. Some are simple and some are rather complicated, and much depends on the nature of the property concerned. It is easy to work out the amount that must be allowed for every year as the depreciation on leasehold property, for it is definitely known in advance that on a certain date such property will be of no value at all, and the problem is merely one of simple arithmetic. But many depreciation calculations must to a large extent be guesswork, although the more polite word 'estimate' is used by accountants. The total amount of depreciation for the year is one of the losses or expenses of the business, and must be subtracted from the trading profit earned in order to arrive at the true net profit.

The Companies Act of 1948 compelled Limited Companies (q.v.) to state clearly in their balance sheets the original cost of various items of property, and the cumulative total of depreciation allowed year by year up to the date of the accounts, so that shareholders and others studying the balance sheets could make sure that depreciation had been reasonably allowed for, and that the value of the various items of property had not been overstated.

Depreciation is not allowed by the Income Tax authorities as a loss or expense in running a business. Instead of depreciation they allow a deduction from trading profits of what is called a 'wear and tear allowance'. This is often less than the amount of depreciation estimated by firms.

See also Book-keeping.

DEPRESSION, see Trade Cycle.

DESIGN, see Vol. XII: Design; Industrial Art.

DIAMOND INDUSTRY. The earliest diamonds came from India. In the 18th century they were found in Brazil, and in 1867 deposits were found near Kimberley, in South Africa. Since then South Africa has been the world's leading producer.

1. Diamond-mining. Diamonds are found below the surface in various formations of rocks and in the gravels of river-beds (see Diamonds, Vol. III). They used to be mined or washed by

the methods used in early GOLD-MINING (q.v.). The diamonds of the Kimberley area are mined by more modern methods. Below the surface layer of rock there lies a deep diamond-bearing layer, bluish-green in colour. This is known as 'blue ground' and goes down to unknown depths. The diamond-bearing rock or 'dirt' is mined and brought to the surface, and then spread out and exposed to the weather on extensive 'distributing floors' on the outskirts of the mining area. As it lies it is then pounded by road-rollers, until it crumbles and disintegrates. It is next washed and stirred in pans, which have a spinning device to sweep the diamonds and other heavy mineral matter to the outside edges. This material is then passed through a stream of water, which washes away

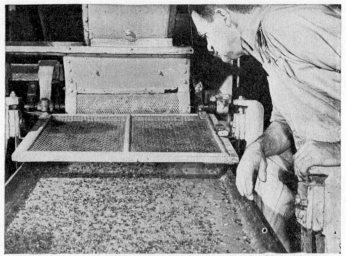

Diamond Trading Co.

SEPARATING DIAMONDS FROM OTHER MINERALS

As the rocky material slides down a greased and sloping table, any diamonds stick to its surface while the rest runs off

further dirt, and then the actual diamonds are separated from the other minerals. Until the early 20th century this was done by hand-picking, but it was then found that a vibrating greased surface would catch up any diamonds in material passed over it and would allow other mineral matter to pass away; so this method is now generally used. The world's biggest diamond mining company is De Beers Consolidated Mines, whose headquarters are at Kimberley. De Beers is an amalgamation of several small mining concerns and workings which was brought about in 1889 by Cecil RHODES (q.v. Vol. V) and Alfred Beit.

2. CUTTING AND POLISHING. The most valuable diamonds are large, individual crystals of pure carbon. Less perfect forms, known as 'bort' and 'carbonado', are clusters of tiny crystals. Until diamonds are cut and polished they do not sparkle like those seen in jewellers' shops. The jewellers' polished stones are called 'brilliants'. In a rather crude form the cutting and polishing of gems was known to the ancient Egyptians, and in the Middle Ages there were gem-cutters' guilds in north-west Europe. A revolutionary change in methods of cutting and polishing was made in 1476 when Ludwig van Berquen, of Bruges, invented the use of a swiftly-revolving wheel with its edge faced with diamond powder. The name 'bort' is given to such powder, as well as to the natural crystalline material mentioned;

it is also given to badly flawed or broken diamond crystals, useless as jewels, that are broken into powder for working purposes. Diamond itself is the only mineral hard enough to cut and polish diamonds. Some diamonds are naturally harder than others; for example, Australian diamonds are harder than South African, and cannot be cut or polished with South African bort. It may be necessary to split or cleave the larger stones before they are cut or polished; every diamond has a natural line of cleavage, along which it may be split by a sharp blow with a cutting edge. A fully-cut diamond has 58 facets symmetrically arranged; van Berquen himself devised this arrangement. For cutting or faceting, the stones are fixed into copper holders and held against a wheel, edged with a mixture of oil and fine diamond dust, which is revolved at about 2,500 revolutions a minute. The final polishing is done with fast-revolving leather or felt disks treated with diamond powder. Amsterdam and Antwerp have been the centre of the diamond cutting and polishing industry from the Middle Ages onwards.

The jewel value of brilliants depends greatly upon their colour or 'water'. The usual colours of diamonds are white, yellow, or blue-white, and the blue-white brilliants are the stones of the finest water and command the highest prices. During their formation some diamonds absorb metallic oxides from the surrounding rocks and

ROUNDING THE DIAMOND BEFORE THE FACETS ARE CUT

The diamond is fixed in a lathe and revolved against another diamond on a stick. The dust ground away is used in other parts of the process for grinding

take on their colour. Thus black, green, and pink diamonds have occasionally been found.

3. THE TRADE IN DIAMONDS. Gem diamonds are a luxury, and the demand for luxuries changes much more than for necessities. If supply were not controlled in some way, changes in demand would lead to wide and disturbing movements in the price of diamonds. For these reasons the trade in diamonds has been closely controlled since the formation of De Beers: so much so that illicit diamond-buying (I.D.B.) was made a punishable offence by the Government of what was then Cape Colony. Practically the whole world trade in diamonds is controlled by the Diamond Corporation of Kimberley, a company owned by De Beers, which has buying contracts not only with South African producers but also with the producers of other countries. The Diamond Corporation has a London office close to Hatton Garden, which is the centre of the diamond trade of Britain and conducts a large share of the diamond trade of the world.

The trade in diamonds is not only in uncut gem-stones and polished brilliants, but also in bort and carbonado. Carbonado comes from Brazil, and in appearance is not unlike small pieces of coke. Diamonds are much used in industry for cutting and grinding. Most industrial diamonds are either carbonado or natural bort, carbonado being usually preferred. Such diamonds are fixed into the rock-drills used in mining and civil engineering, for driving holes into rock before blasting, and for tunnelling and sinking bore-holes (*see* MINING ENGINEERING, Vol. VIII). They are also used for edging cutting blades and tools, and band, circular, or wire saws for sawing stone. Diamond-faced tools are used for cutting and drilling glass and porcelain, for engraving delicate mathematical and scientific scales, and for dentists' drills. Diamond has also been found to be the best material for use in fine wire drawing: a tapering hole is made in a piece of diamond, through which is pulled the rod being drawn into wire. Industrial diamonds are also used as bearings or jewels in watches and electric-meters. During the year 1949 the Diamond Corporation disposed of just under £20 million of gem diamonds and over £8 million of industrial diamonds.

Diamonds are dealt in by weight. The unit used is the carat, and there are 5 million carats to a ton. Before 1939 the world production of all kinds of diamonds was about 8 million carats yearly. Of this, South Africa produced 4 millions, the Belgian Congo nearly 2 millions, and other parts of the world the remainder.

See also JEWELLERY TRADE.
See also Vol. III: DIAMONDS.

DISCOUNT, *see* BANK-RATE; BILLS OF EXCHANGE.

DISPENSING, *see* MEDICAL SUPPLIES.

DISTILLATION. Many industries use the process of distillation. The making of perfume, cosmetics, whisky, brandy and other spirits, and of industrial alcohol depends on distillation. It is an essential process in oil refining. It is also used at sea, and in countries without fresh water, for making drinkable water out of salt or brackish water.

Distillation involves heating a substance, usually a liquid, until it turns into vapour, and then condensing the vapour back into liquid by rapidly lowering its temperature. Liquids with solids dissolved in them can be distilled to obtain either the pure liquid or the solid: pure water or salt from sea-water, for instance. Other liquids, that are really mixtures of two or more different liquids, are distilled in order to separate one liquid from another. For example, wine is distilled so as to produce brandy, which is, broadly speaking, wine-flavoured alcohol. Solids such as tar, which vaporize at a comparatively low temperature, can be distilled in the same way as liquids.

The temperature at which any liquid boils depends upon the PRESSURE of the atmosphere (q.v. Vol. III). If the pressure on its surface is lessened, the boiling-point decreases; and high-boiling substances are often conveniently distilled by combining a moderately high temperature with reduced pressure. When it is not practicable to vary the pressure, liquids not dissolvable in water can often be distilled by allowing steam to mix with their vapour. Many liquids such as crude oil consist of a mixture of several chemical compounds, each having a different boiling-point. Such liquids can be distilled in stages. The compounds with the lowest boiling-point are distilled off first; then, as the temperature is raised, those with a higher boiling-point are distilled; and so on. The different distillates from this multiple distillation process are called 'fractions', and the process is called 'fractionation'.

'Destructive distillation' is the technical name given by chemists to the process of breaking down the chemical structure of a material by heating it without access of air. CHARCOAL (q.v.), for example, is made by the destructive distillation of wood or bones, and COKE (q.v. Vol. VIII) by the destructive distillation of coal. The process was originally worked to obtain the residue left in the 'retort', but now important uses have been found for the other substances (such as tar) which are formed and which vaporize, and are then condensed.

For the simplest distillations in a laboratory the liquid to be distilled is placed in a glass retort with a long tapering neck, and heat is applied (Fig. A). If the cooling effect of the air on the long glass neck is insufficient to condense the vapours, the retort is replaced by a flask to which is connected a condenser—a long central tube of glass, surrounded by a glass 'jacket' with an inlet connected to a running cold-water tap, and an outlet to a tube discharging into a sink (Fig. B). As the vapour comes away from the flask, it is condensed to liquid in the colder temperature of the central tube, and is then drawn off. Industrial and the more elaborate labora-

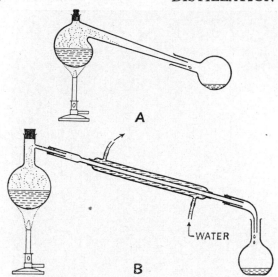

A. SIMPLE DISTILLATION. B. USING A CONDENSER

tory condensers are made on the same principle, but a spiral coil or 'worm' takes the place of the straight central tube, and condensation takes place more quickly and efficiently because a greater surface is constantly exposed to the cooling influence of the surrounding running water. The complete apparatus, consisting of retort, condenser, and receiver, is called a 'still'. In industry the still and its connexions, including the 'worm', are generally made of metal, often copper, but sometimes stainless steel or even silver is chosen, so that it is not corroded by the vapours and liquids used. The copper 'pot' still, used for the first stage in the distillation of WHISKY (q.v.), is of this type.

The disadvantage of the simple laboratory still

W. A. Green

MAKING POTEEN (WHISKY) IN IRELAND IN A PRIMITIVE STILL

Scotch Whisky Association

THE UPPER PART OF A COFFEY STILL

The nearer column is the analyser and the other the rectifier. The columns are 30 ft. high, continuing below the floor

and the pot still of the type described is that they can only operate intermittently, and the retort must be freshly charged for each distillation. Another disadvantage is that they do not lend themselves to the separation of mixtures of several liquids, each with a different boiling or condensing point. About 100 years ago a practical apparatus that would do this was invented, and this is still often called by the name of its inventor, Aeneas Coffey. In the whisky industry it is more usually called a 'patent' still. Coffey's still has since been improved, but its principle remains unchanged.

A modern Coffey still consists essentially of two vertical fractionating columns, called the 'analyser' and the 'rectifier'. Each is subdivided horizontally into a series of separate chambers, by means of perforated copper plates. Steam is allowed to pass into the bottom of the analyser, and to rise, at considerable pressure, through the holes in the plates. The liquid mixture to be distilled is introduced through the top of the analyser, and is prevented by the pressure of the ascending steam from falling through the holes in the plates. The hot steam, bubbling through the liquid mixture on the plates, vaporizes much of it, and carries off the vapours to the next column, the rectifier; liquid that has escaped vaporization collects on the plates, is carried away in a pipe, and pumped again to the top of the analyser. In the rectifier, liquid with the highest boiling-point tends to condense nearest to the vapour inlet; and, by using a suitable number of perforated plates, the vapour mixture can be caused to condense into the required number of liquid 'fractions', each drawn off at an appropriate level in the column.

This method of steam distillation does not suit all liquids: in the distillation of oil, for example (*see* OIL REFINING), steam is only used for a final cleansing or 'stripping' process. The liquid mixture is first vaporized, and then condensed into 'fractions' in a 'fractionating tower' subdivided into chambers and working on the same general principles as the rectifier of a patent still.

DIVIDEND. This usually means payments made to people who own STOCKS AND SHARES in LIMITED COMPANIES (qq.v.). Under British law dividends may only be paid out of earned profits, although they do not have to be paid out of the profits of the current year: they may be paid out of the accumulated profits of past years.

Dividends on CAPITAL (q.v.) may be expressed as a percentage of the capital or otherwise. Dividends on stocks are always expressed at so much per cent. For example, if a company with a capital of £100,000 in ordinary stock earns a profit of £11,000, it may decide to distribute £10,000 of this in dividend, putting £1,000 to reserve. It would then declare a dividend of 10% on the ordinary stock of the company, which means that every holder of ordinary stock would be paid a dividend at the rate of £10 for every £100 of stock he held. Dividends on shares are usually expressed at a rate per share: a company with a capital of £100,000 in £1 shares would distribute a 10% dividend by declaring a dividend of 2s. per share.

The word 'dividend' is also used to describe instalments paid out of the estate of a bankrupt to his creditors (*see* BANKRUPTCY, Vol. X), and also (often in its shortened form, 'divy') for the rebate on the value of purchases given by CO-OPERATIVE SOCIETIES (q.v.) to their members.

See also INTEREST; PROFITS.

DIVISION OF LABOUR. This means that workers specialize in one form of employment, instead of spending their working-day on a series of different tasks. Strength, skill, and intelligence differ very much from man to man, and those who are good at some things may be bad at others. Trying to do everything for oneself can lead to everything being done inefficiently; a jack-of-all-trades is often master of none.

The history of man's economic life, that is, of his efforts to supply himself with his material wants, such as food, clothing, and shelter, is therefore a history of increasing division of labour, or specialization at one particular job. Primitive man looked after himself; he hunted animals for food, clothed himself in their skins or furs, and either lived in caves that nature had already provided or made rough huts out of branches and animal skins. But even in the life of primitive man there was an elementary division of labour between man and woman; and at a very early stage in man's development, the man hunted and fished while the woman cooked, made pots and clothes, and looked after the children. Our modern and highly complex system of division of labour has developed, step by step, from this early and primitive specialization. Each step has been taken because it has led to greater efficiency in the production of goods: either to better quality, or to a larger quantity turned out in a given time, or to both.

Division of labour may be either simple or complex. The division is simple when groups of people specialize in different trades or crafts: some people are farmers, some are blacksmiths, some are builders, some are clothworkers, some are priests, and so on. The STANDARD OF LIVING (q.v.) of the people living in a social group where simple division of labour is practised will be higher than it would be if no division of labour existed. The farmer's annual output of farm produce, the clothworker's weekly output of cloth, and so on, will be greater if each person is allowed to concentrate on the job for which he is best fitted. Skill of this kind is often handed down from father to son.

Complex division of labour exists when crafts or trades become split up into sub-crafts or sub-trades, or into a series of consecutive processes.

Under simple division of labour there might be the separate trade of builder, but at different times during the day or week a builder might be a mason, a bricklayer, a carpenter or joiner, a plumber, a slater or tiler, and a labourer carrying about stone, bricks, mortar, sand, and cement. This would lead to inefficiency, as the skill of an able craftsman at one particular job would be wasted on attempts to do other jobs, or on mere unskilled labour. A system of complex division of labour, in which each general trade, such as building, has specialists in its various sub-branches, makes for greater efficiency, greater cheapness, and better quality of workmanship.

A more advanced stage is reached when labour is divided not by sub-trades but by processes. This happens in modern machine-production, when a machinist is not a general machinist, passing from one process to another, but is occupied with only one process in a series. This more advanced division of labour has generally been found to make for greater output and better work, although there is a danger that it may lead to boredom and monotony: in which case a personnel or staff manager must specialize in overcoming these tendencies, assisted perhaps by the technique of the psychologist (*see* INDUSTRIAL PSYCHOLOGY).

Differences between one country and another, or between areas of the same country; differences

Monotype Corporation

A MACHINIST OPERATING A VERTICAL MILLING MACHINE WHICH IS SHAPING A PIECE OF METAL TO FORM PART OF A PRINTING MACHINE

of soil, of climate, of mineral deposits, of physical contour, of human development lead to geographical or territorial division of labour. The damp climate of Lancashire, for instance, may make it easier to spin in that county the delicate and brittle fibres of the cotton plant. The soil and climate of Canada may be ideal for the growing of wheat. The Union of South Africa may possess deposits of diamonds or of gold-bearing quartz. The *meseta*, or high, dry table-land of Spain, may suit admirably the merino sheep.

All these forms of division of labour not only make for a great diversity between the various persons of a country, and between the populations of different countries, but they lead also to a cheaper and more bountiful production of wealth, as the economist calls the goods and services that men consume in order to satisfy their material and spiritual wants. But they also have other consequences. They create great human and social problems. These arise because there is a division of labour between the governors and the governed, the managers and the technical workers, the professions and the trades, the brain-workers and the manual workers, the economically rich nations and the economically poor ones. Such division nearly always leads to differences in the rewards and WAGES (q.v.) received by the various groups, and to the separation of people into different social classes.

Complicated division of labour of this kind usually leads to still further division. As soon as the division of labour has got beyond the family and has affected small mixed groups of workers in a village, town, or district, it is certain that the specialists in different trades or processes of manufacture will be producing a surplus of goods or services beyond their own personal or family requirements. The builder, for example, will have a house of his own already, and will not wish to live in the others he builds; the cloth-worker's family can perhaps consume what he makes in a tenth of his working time, but he is faced with the task of disposing of what he makes in the other nine-tenths. All these surpluses of goods must be disposed of, or sold, in some way. So must men's services, for the village school-master, or doctor, for instance, does not wish to consume his whole output of education or medical knowledge. All sorts of problems therefore arise connected with EXCHANGE AND TRADE, SUPPLY AND DEMAND, as with VALUE AND PRICE,

UNEMPLOYMENT, and—if the surpluses have to be disposed of outside the country where they have been produced—RATES OF EXCHANGE (qq.v.). Finally, the amount of division of labour already existing will have to be expanded by people who specialize not in producing goods but in finding a market for them and distributing them, and in matters connected with MONEY and BANKING (qq.v.).

So in a modern community division of labour is not only extensive but complex. Not only is each separate trade or industry a part of this division, but in each of these there is a further subdivision. There arises also a vast and varied army of specialists, such as advertising agents, auctioneers, shopkeepers, agents, travellers and representatives, bankers and their clerks, financiers, stockbrokers and stockjobbers, pawn-brokers, accountants, brokers, managers, and transport workers of all kinds. These people do not directly produce goods, but the services of most are essential to our complex modern scheme of production and distribution. Those who pay for their services could not perform their specialized tasks as cheaply themselves.

See also LABOUR; UNEMPLOYMENT; SUPPLY AND DEMAND; INDUSTRIAL REVOLUTION; DOMESTIC SYSTEM.

DOCKS, *see* WAREHOUSES; *see also* Vol. IV: PORTS AND HARBOURS.

DOMESTIC SYSTEM. This means production by workers in their own houses, with comparatively simple tools or machinery. The system covered many different sorts of manufacture, and took two principal forms. In one, the small family producers would sell their wares direct to a merchant or middleman, who would then offer them on the market. In the other, the system was more complicated. A big merchant would supply the workman with materials, and then collect the manufactured goods back from him. He would pay the workman piece-rate WAGES (q.v.), so much per piece of work accomplished. In this second form, the so-called 'putting-out system', there was often considerable specialization of processes, or DIVISION OF LABOUR (q.v.). In making wool, combers, carders, and spinners would carry out only one process in their houses, and the putter-out would then pass on the unfinished articles to a second set of domestic workers to improve them or finish them off.

The putting-out system was an old one, and

Parker Gallery

A FAMILY PREPARING FLAX FOR SPINNING

Linen fibre is extracted from the stem of the flax by beetling and scutching (beating with a mallet and knife) and hackling (drawing it through wires). Coloured engraving by N. Hincks, 1791

many putters-out grew very wealthy by it. Caxton writes that the mother of St. Edmund Rich, Mabel the Rich of Abingdon, who lived in the 13th century, 'put out wool for to spin'. The system became far more important in Tudor times. The wealthy clothiers, finding their enterprise cramped by the restrictions of the guild system which laid down standards of work and rates of pay (*see* CRAFT GUILDS), moved from the towns to find workers in the peasants' cottages throughout the country villages. In such isolated surroundings, where there was no tradition of industrial employment, they could pay smaller wages and expect bigger production. The system lowered costs and prices, and increased the profits of the new leaders of industrial enterprise. Although the system was most general in the textile industries, it was to be found also in the hardware districts of the Midlands.

In the West Riding of Yorkshire the cottage manufacturer always bought his own wool, spun it for himself, and sold it to the merchants. He was no mere wage-earner, but an independent producer. In the West of England, where the woollen industry was still very important, the workman never owned the material or the goods, and was simply paid a piece-rate or 'making-wage' by the clothier who employed him. When the factory system began to spread at the beginning of the 19th century, rich clothiers, even in the West Riding of Yorkshire, began to undermine the independence of the small domestic producer. Power was becoming concentrated in the hands of the big producers.

From the worker's point of view the chief feature of the system was that he worked at home. The family, not the factory, was the working unit. The weaver sat at his loom, the wife at her spinning wheel, and the children helped as much as they could, which was often a great deal. Conditions were often extremely difficult for the workers. They had to work long hours, either for small wages or low profits, and in either case they bore the whole burden of bad trade and unemployment. A ballad of the late 17th century tells of a merchant putter-out saying of himself and his workers:

If trade goes dead, we will presently show it,
But if it grows good, they never shall know it . . .
Our workmen do work hard, but we live at ease;
We go when we will and we come as we please.

Insecurity of livelihood was coupled with the necessity for hard work. Children were expected to do a good share of this. Defoe, the author of *Robinson Crusoe*, who sang the praises of the domestic system at Halifax in Yorkshire, boasted that there was 'hardly any thing above 4 years old but its hands are sufficient to itself': that is to say, busily at work. Another writer on the Halifax of those days claimed that this employment 'not only keeps their little minds from vice but . . . takes a heavy burden from their poor parents'. At Norwich, it was claimed that 'the very children, after 4 or 5 years, could everyone earn their own bread'. Far from the factory system being the start of child-labour—as it is often accused of being—it merely threw the spotlight on it, and quickened the public conscience.

Yet the domestic system had compensations. The worker could often combine industry and agriculture. There were many small clothiers' properties in Yorkshire, for example, from 3 to 15 acres of land on which the owners kept a cow or two, a pony or donkey, and perhaps a few chickens and ducks.

The workman also could take rather more holidays in his own time than he was able to do after the INDUSTRIAL REVOLUTION (q.v.) had established a new factory discipline. Indeed, this kind of worker was often taken to task for idleness. It was said that if he could earn enough to live on in 3 days' work, he would enjoy himself for the rest of the week, usually in the ale-house. This was partly a reaction against the extreme monotony of his work: for throwing a shuttle backwards and forwards was a tiring task, which only came to an end with the development of a machine—in this case the flying shuttle, invented by Kay in 1733. A London writer, Francis Place, described the lot of these workers: 'I know not how to describe the sickening aversion which at times steals over the working man and utterly disables him . . . from following his usual occupation, and compels him to indulge in idleness. I have felt it, resisted it to the utmost of my power, but have been obliged to submit and turn away from my work. This is the case with every workman I have ever known.'

The domestic system was destroyed, or reduced to very small areas of industry, by the factory system. This change-over took a long time, mainly in the 19th century. The domestic system had obvious disadvantages from the employer's point of view. Carrying and fetching raw materials and finished goods took up far too much valuable time. It left the worker with so much freedom that he could never be relied upon. The factory was a more convenient working unit, where workers could be disciplined, and extra profits secured from large-scale working.

While the new factories were being built and extended, workers on the old system were the victims of the change-over. The plight of the handloom weavers was a serious one in the early 19th century, and their complaints played a large part in such movements of social unrest as Chartism (see TRADE UNIONS, HISTORY OF). Their wages went steadily down. In 1799 they were earning on an average 26s. 8d. a week; during 1825–32 wages were down to 6s. 4d.; and in the 1840's, the 'hungry forties' as they were called, many workers died of starvation. The weaving of cotton cloth, like the spinning of cotton yarn, was turned into a factory industry. The transformation of the woollen industry was less quick, and that of the knitting trades even slower. But the new forces of economic expansion and concentration eventually blotted out the old method of production.

See also LABOUR; CRAFT GUILDS; FACTORY ORGANIZATION; TRADE UNIONS, HISTORY OF; DIVISION OF LABOUR.

DOUBLE ENTRY, *see* BOOK-KEEPING.

DRUGS, *see* MEDICAL SUPPLIES.

DRY-CLEANING. 1. HISTORY. The modern practice that we know as dry-cleaning originated in France, where as early as 1850 a cleaning process without moisture—*nettoyage à sec*—was carried out with 'camphene', an oil of turpentine distilled for burning in lamps. Dirt is mainly held in a fabric by a thin film of grease, and the advantage of using a spirit is that it removes the grease and dirt without disturbing the finish, colour, or texture, as cleaning with water often does. Dry cleaning was unknown in the United Kingdom until 1866, when a Scottish firm in Perth brought a number of men from a Paris dyeing and cleaning works to use the French method. The new industry spread to England, mainly in centralized factories, which got their work through branch offices in various towns.

Until the First World War dry-cleaning was looked upon largely as a luxury. The need to clean thousands of uniforms during the war and the high prices of clothes after the war made dry-cleaning popular, and steam-pressing machinery shortened the time taken over press- ing garments. In the 1920's 'valet' pressing shops sprang up. These did not undertake their own dry-cleaning but sent the garments to the cleaning factories, which returned them un- pressed to the 'valet' shops. Later, small local dry-cleaning plants were opened, using non- inflammable solvents.

Many dry-cleaning firms also dye and moth- proof garments and household fabrics. Some firms do fireproofing and waterproofing as well. After the Second World War dyers and cleaners were twice as much in demand as before it. More than £16 million is estimated to have been spent on this work in 1949.

2. TECHNIQUE. Two main cleaning solvents are in use to-day: white spirit and trichlorethyl- ene. Each has its particular merits. A third solvent, perchlorethylene, is also finding favour among some cleaners, but is more used in tropical climates because of its comparatively low evaporation rate. A solvent must be chemi- cally stable both in storage and under repeated distillation.

Each article sent to be cleaned is first exam- ined for tears and for oddments left in the pockets. Then it is given an identification number, and sorted into the proper bin according to the colour, weight, and nature of the material. Silks and woollens, and light colours and dark, are separated from each other, as also heavy and light garments. Articles next go to the dry- cleaning machine, in which they are stirred and dipped in the cleaning-spirit. The cleaning liquid is kept clear by 'clarification', the dirty liquid being passed through a filter which keeps

back the particles of dirt. After the dirt has been extracted the clean solvent is returned to the machine.

When all possible dirt has been removed by the action of the solvent, articles are placed in an extractor, a spinning device which draws off most of the excess solvent by centrifugal force; the final traces are then dispersed by evapora- tion in a dryer through which air passes. The article goes next to the 'spotter', whose task is to take out any stains which may have resisted the cleaning solvent; this delicate work is usually done by trained girls. These marks are removed by chemicals which loosen and then dissolve the staining substances. A spotter must be familiar with all types of fabrics—wool, silk, linen, rayon, nylon, crêpe, satin, taffeta, and so on—and must know which chemical will remove a stain with- out damage to the fabric and its colouring. Much of the art of spotting lies in 'shading out' gradually from the centre of the mark, so that no unsightly ring will remain. Then the articles pass, often by overhead conveyor, to the finish- ing department. Here they are 'reshaped', and pressed by steam and hot-air machines. Each article is inspected before being sent to the customer.

The trade maintains a staff of scientists, work- ing with the University of Leeds, who test new fabrics and carry out research.

See also DYES.
See also Vol. XI: CLOTHES, CARE OF.

DYES. 1. EARLY HISTORY. Dyed fabrics dating back to 2000 B.C. or earlier have been found in Egyptian tombs, and the Roman historian Pliny refers to a well-established dyeing industry in ancient Egypt. Both Plutarch and Virgil men- tion the rich purple now often referred to as 'Tyrian purple', and in the Bible there are several references to dyed hangings and gar- ments, as in the story of Joseph's coat of many colours. In early British history Queen Boadicea is said to have worn a multi-coloured tunic, and the Romans are known to have had a dyeing industry at Silchester.

The dyes used in those days were not the chemical substances which we know to-day as 'synthetic', or more often as 'coal tar', dye-stuffs. The ancients had to rely for their dyes upon natural materials. They used plants, wood, shellfish, or sometimes simple metal salts such as ALUM (q.v.) and some of the coloured iron

INDIAN DYERS AT WORK

Hanks of cotton yarn are being dyed in a 'direct dye' bath containing a solution of dye-stuff in water

I.C.I

compounds. Even to-day some places still use natural, as opposed to synthetic, dye-stuffs; in the Western Isles of Scotland the crofters dye their wool by using lichens and sea grasses and weed, boiling them in water to extract the colouring matters.

Many distinct colours were produced by the ancients, yet the range of actual dyes was small. The variety was probably due to the skilful use of 'mordants'. A mordant is a chemical, generally a salt of chromium, aluminium, tin, copper, or iron. Mordants, themselves, are not dye-stuffs, and do not necessarily colour materials at all; but when they are applied before a dye-stuff, they 'key' the dye-stuff on to the fabric, and jointly produce a coloured effect. One mordant can be used with a number of different dye-stuffs, or one dye can be used with a whole series of mordants, to give a range of different final colours.

In early days only the wealthy could afford the rarest dye-stuffs. Tyrian purple was reserved for royalty and noblemen. The ordinary people wore dull, drab shades, such as browns, buffs, and blues.

The bulk of European cloth was dyed with extracts of plants such as safflower, woad, weld, madder, and similar wild growths. In the East, where indigo grew in profusion, its characteristic blue shade was the colour most widely seen in hangings, clothes, and decorations.

One method of decoration by dyeing, that of *batik*, is still practised in the East Indian island of Java. There the cloth, before it is dyed, is painted with wax in a decorative pattern. The part of the cloth that is covered with wax does not absorb the coloured dye, and the result is a pattern of light lines or spaces on a coloured background. More colours can be added by waxing the dyed portions and then dipping the cloth in other dyes.

2. MODERN HISTORY. The story of the modern dye industry begins in England in 1856, when a young chemistry student, W. H. Perkin, was trying to manufacture quinine. This valuable medicine could be got only from the bark of the cinchona tree. He failed to make quinine, and produced merely a red powder. He tried again, and produced a black substance. This, on extraction with alcohol, gave a rich, violet-coloured product which, to his amazement, coloured cotton. His failure was actually one of the most brilliant failures in the history of industrial chemistry, for his violet-coloured compound was the tiny seed from which has grown one of the world's greatest chemical industries—the manufacture of synthetic dye-stuffs.

This new dye-stuff was called 'mauveine'. Perkin discovered it at a most favourable time, for organic chemistry was then beginning to attract research workers. Meanwhile other scientists in France, Germany, and Britain became inspired by his pioneer work and soon began their own exploration of the new field of colour chemistry.

Within 12 years a number of new synthetic dye-stuffs had been manufactured. Within 25 years great progress had been made, both in pure scientific research and in dyeing practice in industry itself. The initiative had by this time passed into the hands of German chemists. Their discoveries in theoretical chemistry, and their skill in adapting them industrially, made it possible to manufacture alizarine and indigo artificially, and to develop the azo dye-stuffs.

Old methods were given up, and the discovery of a synthetic indigo dye ruined the indigo-planters of Bihar, in India.

The azo dyes, even to-day, still provide the largest class of synthetic dye-stuffs in common use. Their production was due to the work of Griess (1864), a chemist employed by a brewer in Burton, who discovered the reaction between nitrous acid and primary amines. (Amines are chemical derivatives of AMMONIA (q.v.).) Perkin's work had resulted in a dye-stuff of the type known as 'basic'. Dyes of this class are extremely brilliant in shade, but on exposure to light they are not very 'fast', that is, they do not retain their colour well. The azo dye-stuffs can be applied to a wide range of fibres and fabrics; they are moderately 'fast', provide a very wide range of shades, and include the groups known as 'direct cotton', 'acid wool' and 'mordant' dye-stuffs. The first group dye cotton directly, that is, im-mersion of cotton in a solution of the dye-stuff in water gives dyed cotton. The acid-wool group dye wool from an acidulated dye bath, whilst the mordant dye-stuffs colour materials only when applied after, or along with, a suitable mordant.

In 1880 a British chemist called Holliday found a method of producing insoluble azo dye-stuffs actually on the fibre itself. It is now the generally accepted means of producing reds, wines, maroons, and a large number of associ-ated shades, which remain 'fast' in spite of washing, bleaching, and exposure to light. Practically the whole of the typical red yarn used in the manufacture of towels is dyed with the present-day successors of Holliday's discovery.

At the beginning of the 20th century a Ger-man chemist, Bohn, prepared the first of a most famous series of dye-stuffs which later became known as 'vat dyes'. A series of chemical treat-ments in a vat caused the fibre itself to be dyed. These vat dye-stuffs were fast.

Until then, the colour chemists had had to deal only with natural fibres, such as cotton, wool, and linen. But now synthetic fibres began to be made which had totally unexpected properties. Acetate RAYON (q.v.) caused many troubles at the outset, for it could not be dyed by any of the dye-stuffs existing on the market

I.C.I.

COTTON YARN BEING LOWERED INTO A DYEING MACHINE
The dye is circulated through the vessel by a pump so that it penetrates thoroughly the yarn on the bobbins

at the time, but in 1922 the first special dye-stuffs for colouring acetate rayon were developed.

Dye-stuffs are used in a large number of industries, as well as for textile colouring. Leather, fur, rubber, paint, distemper, wood stains, buttons, wallpaper, and even some food-stuffs are coloured.

Since most synthetic dye-stuffs come from coal-tar derivatives, dye-making must always be important to a country that has coal deposits. Britain, which first discovered the possibilities of synthetic dye-stuffs, has recovered her place as a leading producer, after having temporarily lost it to Germany. Although the different synthetic dye-stuffs in current production in this country number thousands, and the capital invested in their manufacture amounts to many millions of pounds, the search for new and better dye-stuffs continues. Research, both in the laboratory and in the works where dye-stuffs are used, is the corner-stone upon which the industry is built.

See also CHEMISTRY, INDUSTRIAL.

E

EARTHENWARE. This is the term used for all kinds of soft POTTERY (q.v.). By 'soft' the potter means that the ware has been 'fired' at the comparatively low temperature of not more than 1100° Centigrade. Before earthenware receives a glaze it is porous, can be scratched with a knife, and is granular or earthy in texture; in all these matters it is distinct from STONEWARE (q.v.). Earthenware includes many apparently different types of pottery, from primitive ware to modern plates and dishes.

The secret of glazing earthenware successfully was brought in the 12th century to Spain by the Moors who had conquered that country. From the 16th century onwards the knowledge of the process gradually spread through the rest of Europe, and the wares made received various local names: the French, for example, called them 'faïence' after Faenza, a pottery town in Italy, and the Dutch called them after their pottery town of Delft. When the ware began to be made in England, early in the 17th century, it was called Lambeth delft or Bristol delft according to where it was made.

The early English delft ware was rather heavy and easily chipped. But by using a new mixture of clay and other materials, Josiah WEDGWOOD, the English pottery maker (q.v. Vol. V), produced a very successful cream earthenware, suitable for general table purposes. The discovery of kaolin or CHINA CLAY (q.v.) and china stone in Cornwall about 1768 led to further improvements, and the composition of earthenware has changed very little since that time.

Vessels of unglazed earthenware, being porous, allow the slow evaporation through their pores of liquids put into them. Since a liquid which is giving off vapour is also losing heat, porous vessels have always been popular as coolers. The butter-coolers and butter-dishes of the present day, usually of a reddish-brown colour, are made of unglazed earthenware.

The general methods of shaping, firing, glazing, and decorating earthenware are described in the article on POTTERY (q.v.).

See also STONEWARE; PORCELAIN.

Victoria and Albert Museum

FAIENCE DISH MADE IN ITALY ABOUT 1540
It is made of tin-glazed earthenware, painted in blue with the story of Hercules and Antaeus

EAST INDIA COMPANY. The Honourable East India Company was the greatest of the CHARTERED COMPANIES (q.v.) formed between the 14th and the 19th centuries to develop overseas trade. It was founded on 31 December 1600 by a Royal Charter granted by Queen Elizabeth to the 'Governor and Company of Merchants of London trading into the East Indies'. The first convoy, consisting of four ships under the general command of James Lancaster, left Torbay in April 1601. It reached Achin, in Sumatra, in June 1602, and returned to England with a large cargo of spices.

At the date of the first charter the world outside Europe was still not fully explored, and ideas of the exact whereabouts of the East Indies were rather vague. The term 'East Indies' in the title was originally meant to include all countries east of the Cape of Good Hope, or west of the Straits of Magellan at the southern end of South America. These extensive ideas of the lands in which the Company was to operate were soon curtailed, for the trading companies of other countries had already got a foothold in many lands.

In those days the custom was to grant exclusive rights of trading to a single company of merchants in any area. The first charter was for 15 years. The Company had, to start with, no permanent CAPITAL (q.v.), so it bought or built ships with money lent by its members, who then used the ships to carry their own cargoes. The cargoes were sold on arrival in the East, and other cargoes were shipped home and sold in their turn; a 'voyage account' was then made out, and the proceeds were shared among the subscribers in proportion to their individual subscriptions. From the first, PROFITS (q.v.) were large, and on some voyages were as high as 100%.

The Company's charter was renewed in 1609 by James I. The earlier financial plan was altered, and subscribers were invited to put up money for voyages conducted by the Company as a whole, instead of voyages for their own account and profit. This decision was influenced by the disturbed state of the world. Independent ventures meant small convoys, which were much exposed to attack by PIRATES (q.v. Vol. IV) or by the ships of enemy countries; a large convoy of the Company's entire fleet was stronger.

Although the main objects of the merchants founding the Company were trade and commerce, the foundation of the Company was to some extent a political move against the Dutch, who had reached the East Indies first and whom the English wished to drive out. The Dutch had been there for many years; they looked upon the East Indies, and particularly the remoter islands such as Java and Sumatra, as their own; they resented the English Company's arrival, and soon trouble began between them. The most serious incident was the Amboyna massacre of 1623, when some British settlers were tortured and killed by order of the Dutch Governor. This convinced the Company that it was hardly strong enough to claim the farther East Indies from the Dutch. It therefore confined its trading to India, Burma, and Ceylon.

This penetration into India was extremely successful, and was favoured by the attitude of the Mogul Emperors, who then ruled over the greater part of that country (see INDIAN CIVILIZATION, Vol. I). In 1608 Captain Hawkins obtained permission to build a 'factory', or trading depot, at Surat, north of Bombay. In the south,

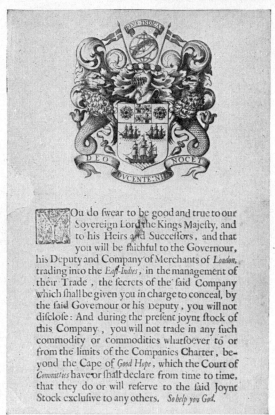

AN OATH OF FIDELITY TO THE EAST INDIA COMPANY

near Madras, a factory was established at Masulipatam. In 1635 the Company was granted trading rights in Bengal and a factory was established at Hooghly, on the river of that name, north of Calcutta. In 1640 southern India headquarters were set up at Fort St. George, Madras. The charter was renewed by Oliver Cromwell in 1657. The Company now obtained the subscription of a permanent capital fund, and traded as a company, instead of merely controlling the independent trading activities of its members.

The Company had not confined its activities solely to trade and commerce. It had been forced to set up a civil administration in and around its factories; and to maintain and preserve its influence it had raised and used troops. Following the custom of the time, its ships were armed. When its charter was renewed by Charles II, the Company was given powers which gradually transformed it from a trading company into an apparatus of government. It could acquire and administer territory, fortify its possessions, issue and regulate its own coinage, engage in military and naval operations, conclude peace treaties and trading agreements with rulers of States, and generally pass the laws necessary to carry out all these duties and responsibilities. In 1662 Catherine of Braganza, the daughter of the Portuguese Royal House, married Charles II. She brought as part of her dowry some of the Portuguese possessions in western India, including the island of Bombay, with its magnificent natural harbour. In 1668 Charles II gave this prize to the East India Company.

To simplify and decentralize administration, the three 'presidencies', or provinces, of Bengal, Bombay, and Madras were formed. The cities of Bombay and Madras were already the Company's commercial headquarters, and they now became the administrative capitals of their respective presidencies. In 1690, after a series of local battles, Job Charnock, once an obscure clerk in the Company's Bengal service, secured Calcutta as the Company's Bengal headquarters. Calcutta became the capital of the Bengal Presidency, and later the capital of British India. From this time onwards the political history of the Company really becomes the history of British India itself. One of the greatest British statesmen in India was Robert CLIVE (q.v. Vol. V), who began as a clerk in the Company.

Neither in its political nor in its commercial career did the Company have an entirely smooth passage. From the late 17th century onwards its commercial interests were increasingly damaged by 'interlopers', or private traders, who voyaged in their own ships and were neither members of the Company nor bound in any way by its rules. These interlopers objected strongly to the Company's privileged position, and were determined to secure the legal right to trade on their own account. Resistance to the Company's MONO-POLY (q.v.) increased as the years went on. In the late 18th and early 19th centuries the disadvantages and dangers of monopoly, and the advantages of free and unrestricted trade, were pointed out by Adam SMITH (q.v. Vol. V) and other economists. Their views were seized upon by the interlopers—or 'free traders'—and many statesmen and politicians became converted to their point of view. Resistance to the Company's privileges was now organized in Parliament. This movement was successful in 1813, when the Company's privileged position in Indian trade

and commerce was abolished. Foreseeing that this was bound to happen, the Company had in the meantime extended its trading activities to China, and had acquired a monopoly of the China tea trade. But opposition to the Company's special position in the trade of the East as a whole was now general, and this last monopoly was taken away in 1833. The Company then gradually ceased to be a trading concern; for a time it confined itself to political and administrative matters, and did much to extend the frontiers of British India and to consolidate the British hold on that country. In 1858 its organization and functions were taken over by the government of Queen Victoria as a result of the Indian Mutiny.

The Company's main line of communication was naturally by sea. As early as 1609 the Company constructed its own dockyard at Deptford on the south bank of the Thames, and here and elsewhere were built the famous East Indiamen. Excepting only, perhaps, the ships of the British and foreign navies, the East Indiamen were the finest and best-found ships afloat. The training and discipline of their crews were second only to those of the Royal Navy; their manning was in many respects superior, as the Company could afford good pay and conditions at a time when the NAVY (q.v. Vol. X) still had to rely largely on the press-gang for recruiting. These magnificent ships were fully armed, nominally to fight pirates and rivals in self-defence, although many actions were provoked by the Company's ships. The post of master of an East Indiaman was a most profitable one, for masters were allotted a certain amount of cargo space for themselves and received also a bonus on the profits of their voyages; some masters of East Indiamen were able to retire as wealthy men after only 5 years' command.

When the trading of the Company dwindled, its administrative work grew. Addiscombe College was founded in 1809, on the same lines as Sandhurst, to train officers for the Company's army. Of the Addiscombe-trained officers, Lord Roberts, the distinguished general, was perhaps the most famous. A training college for civil administration was also needed: Haileybury, the public school just south of Hertford, began as the Honourable East India Company's College.

'Trade follows the flag' was a slogan of the 19th century. Those who used it believed that the political occupation of a country, and the

Parker Gallery

THE EAST INDIA HOUSE, LEADENHALL STREET, LONDON
Coloured engraving, 1833

setting-up of orderly government, must come before trade and commerce. The East India Company is a great example of the contrary, for in India the flag followed trade. At the summit of its power the Company touched great heights. It set out to develop trade and commerce with the East Indies. It was forced by the pressure of events gradually to drop its trading activities, to concentrate on those that were political, to administer an immense and growing territory, and finally to cede all it had built up to its parent Government.

See also CHARTERED COMPANIES; TRADE, HISTORY OF.
See also Vol. I: INDIAN CIVILIZATIONS.
See also Vol. III: INDIA.

ECONOMICS.

The famous Cambridge economist, Alfred Marshall, defined economics as the study of mankind in the ordinary business of life: that is, in getting a living or in helping to satisfy the material wants of others. The word 'economics' comes from a Greek word meaning the prudent management of one's family business affairs, and has come to mean the study of business affairs in general. A study of economics must begin with a study of COMMERCE and INDUSTRY (qq.v.). One must know a great deal

about the organization of business in one's own country and abroad before going on to study the underlying forces that control business. It is with these forces, and with what causes them to change, that the economist principally deals.

The average business man who makes or sells goods is interested in the same things as the economist; but he solves his problems very often by rough rule-of-thumb methods rather than by scientific ones, and he is more concerned with the working of his own business and less with the working of the country's or the world's business as a whole. The task of the economist is much wider than that of the business man, although many business men make use of the economist's technique without knowing it, and the best of them do this deliberately. When the business man tries to work out future changes in the market-price of his goods, or in the quantity he can profitably sell, he is doing for his own firm what the economist is continuously trying to do for the wider community. Economics is to business what MECHANICS is to ENGINEERING (qq.v. Vol. VIII). It is the theory behind the practice.

Economics is now an important science, as important as Mechanics, and quite as wide.

Like other sciences, it has developed from modest and rather slow beginnings. It first began to be important in the 17th century. The early economists tried to understand the working of commerce and industry so as to advise statesmen how the general welfare of the people might be improved. The economists were able to tell the statesmen about the results likely to follow changes in the laws or customs governing trade, hours and conditions of labour, the currency, the banking system, and so on. Because of its usefulness to politicians, what is now called economics was first called Political Economy, and this title is still used at some of the universities.

'Economics' became a more popular title than 'Political Economy' towards the end of the 19th century, when most people in Britain believed that commerce and industry would flourish best without any supervision by the Government. The subject then became much more scientific. Scientists spend much of their time in trying to work out statements that are generally or universally true under all conditions, and these statements are called scientific 'laws'. Most scientific laws are also statements of cause and effect: they state that if certain circumstances change, the conditions resulting will change also. Economists try to work out the 'laws' of the business world, and on the whole they are fairly successful. Like other scientists, they have to start from certain working assumptions, and their main assumption is that everybody tries to get the greatest material satisfaction for the least cost in labour or effort or money. Economists try to work out what kinds and quantities of goods are likely to be produced and sold, and at what prices; what proportions of people's incomes will be saved and spent; how WAGES, INTEREST, rent, and PROFITS (qq.v.) will be fixed; what the value of MONEY (q.v.) will be, at home and abroad; what will be the trend of SUPPLY AND DEMAND, or the relation of VALUE AND PRICE (qq.v.); and how changes in TAXATION (q.v. Vol. X) will affect all these things. In brief, the economist tries to study what will be produced, and how this will become distributed among the various classes of the population. One of the main aids to study is the use of STATISTICS (q.v.).

As in most other sciences, there are two branches of economics: pure and applied. Pure economics is the study of a rather imaginary business world, or of a portion of it, in which people's economic behaviour is assumed to be much simpler than it actually is in the real world of everyday affairs. The applied economist tries to look at problems as they really are, with all the complications of the real world included. He applies the findings of pure economists to real situations; and his purpose is to guide the decisions of business men and politicians. Put in another way, the pure economist constructs the intellectual tools and the applied economist makes use of them. It is reasonably easy, particularly for those with a mathematical turn of mind, to master pure economics; to master applied economics is far more difficult. Very often the problem that an applied economist has to solve is so full of unknown quantities, which cannot be given precise values, that it is amazingly difficult for him to work out a definite answer. The applied economist must have not only a deep knowledge of his subject, but also a broad and general knowledge of human nature, combined with a flair for seizing instinctively on the real essentials of a problem. Lord KEYNES (q.v. Vol. V), one of the world's greatest economists, defined economics as a technique of thinking which assists one to the correct rather than the false conclusion. More than this cannot be claimed for economics, and the good economist is merely one less often wrong in his prophecies and conclusions than the bad one.

Economists are being increasingly used in the business world. Business men have come to realize, more and more, the necessity for planning production ahead, for only by careful planning can goods be produced cheaply, and money will be lost if a plan is carelessly embarked on and then interrupted. Business men can work out the technical details of their plans; but they want to know in what kind of business world they will have to market their goods when ready. They must try to look into the economic future, so as to find out in advance what scheme of prices, what amount of consumer demand, what opportunities of overseas sales, and so on will be in existence months, perhaps years, ahead when their plans have matured into actual production. Business men alone can hardly hope to solve these problems, and for their solution they are increasingly relying on the economist. The larger the typical business firm grows—and NATIONALIZATION (q.v. Vol. X) is making some firms really immense—the more need there will be in commerce and industry for the trained economist. Modern business is extremely scientific; and the more scientific it becomes the more its planning and managerial offices resemble a laboratory of applied economics.

See also MONEY; INTERNATIONAL FINANCE.
See also Vol. X: NATIONAL FINANCE.

EGG TRADE. Although there was an international trade in eggs before scientific methods of preserving them were discovered, it did not reach its present importance until the invention of COLD STORAGE (q.v.). Before then eggs were shipped to London in a new-laid condition from Denmark and Holland and the Baltic ports of eastern Europe. On arrival in London they were sold by AUCTION (q.v.), by the 'long hundred' of 120, on the Provision Exchange in Tooley Street, on the south side of the Thames, not far from London Bridge. In the modern trade several methods are used for transporting eggs over long distances. The highest-quality eggs are shipped abroad in a new-laid condition and carried at low temperatures in the refrigerated holds of the steamers. Other eggs, coming from farther inland, are cold-stored at the points

of collection and travel under refrigerated conditions throughout—both on the trains abroad and in the steamers that bring them to this country. The housewife's method of preserving eggs in waterglass is also used on a commercial scale: the eggs are pickled in a limy solution and carried in large tanks, packed sufficiently tightly to prevent breakages. Another modern method of transporting eggs is in large cylindrical containers from which all oxygen has been withdrawn, as decomposition by bacteria or otherwise is only possible in the presence of oxygen.

Before shipment eggs are carefully graded and packed. 'Candling'—holding each egg in turn up against a strong light, which allows its inside to be examined by eye—is an important process in grading. Infertile eggs travel best, and in overseas countries egg producers for the export trade are encouraged by merchants and distributing organizations to produce infertile rather than fertile eggs. Farm eggs, when the infertility cannot be assured, seldom enter into the international egg trade, which is mainly supplied by specialist egg producers. There are fashions in the egg trade, as in all others. For the Jewish market, for instance—as in Johannesburg, New York, and some English cities—white eggs are preferred to brown, and producers for

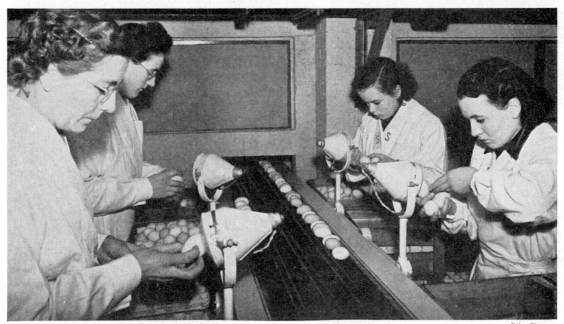

John Topham

CANDLING EGGS AT A PACKING STATION
The graded eggs travel to the packing room on a conveyor-belt

this market must select their breeds of hens accordingly.

Egg production on a commercial scale is a difficult branch of industry, in which the producer is additionally handicapped by the fact that his output is high when prices are low, and low when prices are high. This suits the egg merchant, who can buy eggs in the plentiful season and store them until they can be marketed in the scarce season. In many parts of the British Commonwealth, and in Denmark and similar countries, the producer's defence against seasonal rises and falls in price has been co-operative marketing. A good example of co-operative marketing is the co-operative egg-circle, a favourite form of organization in the Union of South Africa. A member of such a circle receives throughout the whole year an average price for his eggs, which is roughly midway between the low price of the plentiful season and the high price of the shortage season. A penny or so per dozen is retained by the head office of the egg circle to cover its expenses.

See also Vol. VI: POULTRY.

ENAMEL. 1. TECHNIQUE. Enamel is a glassy or vitreous substance, very similar to flint GLASS (q.v.), which is melted under great heat and then spread as a thin layer over metal objects as a decoration. The craft of enamelling must not be confused with the painting or spraying of baths, basins, and other vessels, with a glossy paint called 'enamel'.

Enamelling is done on gold, silver, platinum, copper, or iron. It is at its best when pure metals are used, but alloys such as brass, gold of 22 carat or less, and standard silver are also suitable.

Before the enamel is melted it has the appearance of coarse powder or tiny chips of hard material. This material, called 'flux', consists of natural stone (flint or silica) mixed with red lead, borax, and other salts. To give the enamel the colour which the artist wishes, oxides of metals are mixed with the flux. The chief oxides and the colours which result are: iron for red; lead for yellow; copper for blue or red; tin for milky white.

The flux is fused at a high temperature (700–900° C.) for a long time, until a clear, transparent glass is produced. This is ground down to a fine powder, which is laid on the metal and heated again. The temperature is such that not only will the enamel melt, but the surface of the metal

Ashmolean Museum

CHAMPLEVÉ ENAMEL MOUNT FROM A CROSS

The figure is metal with the head in relief and the background is filled with coloured enamels. Made at Limoges. 13th century

will be softened enough to unite with it permanently. After this firing, the enamel can be rubbed down to make it smooth and polished. Different colours must be kept separate from each other, otherwise the colours would mix when heated. To ensure this there is a band of metal between each colour. This band is made in one of two ways, either by the *champlevé* or the *cloisonné* method. In *champlevé*, the enamel is laid in hollows sunk into the surface of the metal. The metal is usually cast with these hollows ready. *Cloisonné* means 'in cells'; strips of metal are soldered to the surface of the object, thus producing small enclosures, which are filled with enamel. Finer designs can be produced by this method.

Another method is to cover the whole ground with translucent enamel of one colour through which are seen the metal patterns beneath. These patterns may be engine-turned (mechanically cut) or chased (*see* GOLD AND SILVERWORK).

17TH-CENTURY CHINESE CLOISONNÉ ENAMEL DISH

Bands of metal separate the colours and form the wave pattern in the centre of the dish
(Diameter 26 in.)

Coloured enamels which have no bands separating the colours are made by painting on uncoloured enamel in oxide pigments similar to those used in making coloured enamel. When heated the colours fuse with the enamel.

2. History. Enamelling has been done in Europe certainly from the time of the ancient Greeks. The craft probably came with the Romans to northern Europe, and in the East *cloisonné* enamel has a long history. The Celts, Romano-British, and Saxons decorated bowls, swords, shields, and jewellery with *cloisonné* enamel. The early enamel was thick and opaque, being only partially turned into glass, but the colours and designs were very rich.

Limoges in France was the great centre of enamel making from the 12th to the 17th centuries. The early work produced then was *champlevé* on brass, and was used to decorate such articles as caskets, crosses, and candlesticks. The enamel was opaque, and sometimes the figures, or their heads alone, were modelled in relief. The craft suffered severely when Limoges was sacked by the Black Prince in 1370, and the enamellers only recovered their fame in the 15th

Ashmolean Museum

THE BEHEADING OF JOHN THE BAPTIST

Plaque enamelled in colours, heightened with gold, on a black background. Made at Limoges, mid-16th century

century. In the 16th century they produced enamel pictures and miniatures. The subjects were painted on an enamel ground laid on copper, which was then fired. Often only black and white were used, with pale tints for the flesh. Sometimes gold or silver leaf was laid under the enamel to heighten its brilliance.

In the 18th century the method of enamelling over a chased ground was used for snuff-boxes, watch-cases, and other small objects. Enamelling over an engine-turned pattern was also introduced in the 18th century.

The craft of enamelling has changed little from its earliest days. Labour-saving machines can be used for some parts of the process, but the principles underlying the craft are the same as they were.

See also Jewellery Trade; Pottery.
See also Vol. XII: Romanesque Art.
See also Vol. XI: Jewellery.

ENGRAVING. This is a method of making a design on metal, either for decorative purposes or else to take prints from it on paper. For making prints the writing or design is first engraved on a metal plate, usually of copper or steel. Copper is softer to work, but the hardness of steel makes it possible to produce finer lines than would be possible on copper. A copper plate, being of soft metal, will not stand up to more than about 5,000 prints; a steel plate or steel-faced copper plate will produce many more copies. The engraver carves his design on to the metal with a short steel tool called a 'burin', with a specially sharpened cutting end. Plates for printing are engraved with the design in reverse, so that they will print the right way round when paper is brought into contact with them. To take a print, the plate is inked and all surplus ink carefully wiped off. The ink settles into the engraved portions of the plate, more ink remaining in the deeper than in the shallower cuts. The printing-press (*see* Printing) is then used for taking the actual copies.

Engraving was used in the ancient civilizations for writing or designs on precious stones and metals (*see* Gold and Silver Work), and it is still used for such purposes to-day. Prints from engraved plates or surfaces were not made in Europe before the introduction of paper in the 15th century. Some of the earliest prints on paper were taken by goldsmiths and armourers, who wished to preserve a record of the designs

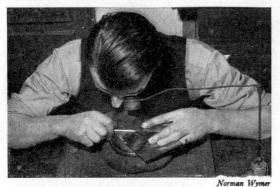

Norman Wymer

ENGRAVING ON COPPER

engraved on the plate and armour. In the 15th century playing-cards were printed from engraved plates, as well as maps and, later, book illustrations. The Bank of England used to engrave its banknotes, but no longer does so. The notes or 'bills' of the U.S. Treasury, which are the paper money of the United States, have always been engraved. All British postage stamps were once engraved, and some still are. High-class visiting cards and invitation cards are engraved and so are some letterheads for business and professional stationery. For illustrating books the method of engraving is expensive, and is used only for high-class work and limited editions.

The illustration of most books is done by transferring the picture or drawings to the plate by photography, and etching the design with acid (*see* PROCESS REPRODUCTION).

See also Vol. XII: ETCHING AND ENGRAVING; WOOD-ENGRAVING.

ENTERTAINMENT INDUSTRY. Entertainment is now an organized industry with many branches, and some of the firms in it are very large and control many smaller subsidiaries. The industry may be said to include all indoor, and occasionally a few outdoor, entertainments other than purely sporting events such as horse and dog race-meetings, athletic meetings, games matches, and boxing tournaments. Opera, concerts, ballet, plays, musical comedies, revues, variety entertainments, cinema shows, circuses, and fairs are all included in the industry, as well as 'sponsored' broadcasting by ordinary commercial firms in countries where this is permitted (*see* BROADCASTING CORPORATIONS, Vol. IV), and semi-military entertainments such as the Royal Tournament and the Aldershot Tattoo.

In some form or other the characteristic feature of the operatic and theatrical section of the industry has always been the promoter, the person who finances and bears the risk of production, meeting the losses if it is a failure, or taking the profits if it is a success. In earlier days the promoter was almost always one single person, although he might bring in non-working partners who were prepared to back him with money. More recently this work has generally been done by groups or syndicates, but at the head of them there is usually a single dominant personality with great knowledge and experience and, which is often more important, a real flair for gauging public taste. The late Sir Charles Cochran, who backed and promoted many productions in the world of entertainment and sport, was a typical personality of this kind. A still more recent development has been the merging of promoter and theatre-owner in a large company owning a chain of London and provincial theatres. There have always been, however, a few famous actor-managers who have kept clear of financial syndicates and have run their own productions. Arthur Bourchier was one of these, and he used to claim that he was the only London actor-manager of his day who had his own theatre and was not subservient to any financial backer.

The MUSIC-HALL (q.v. Vol. IX) began to become commercialized at the turn of the century. Moss Empires Ltd. was formed in 1899, Variety Theatres Consolidated in 1904, and the Stoll Theatres Corporation in 1907. The music-hall was then in a stage of transition from the 'saloon' or smoking-concert to its more modern form, and the formation of big companies hastened the change. These companies acquired chains of variety theatres in London and the provinces, mostly putting on two duplicate shows a night, and making direct contracts with artists for whom they found engagements at their various 'houses'. In London, artists would be 'billed' at two or more theatres in the same evening.

In recent years some of these companies entered the screen section of the entertainment industry; for example, Moss Empires became associated with the Gaumont-British Picture Corporation. But, in comparison with the U.S.A., this section of the British industry is still undeveloped.

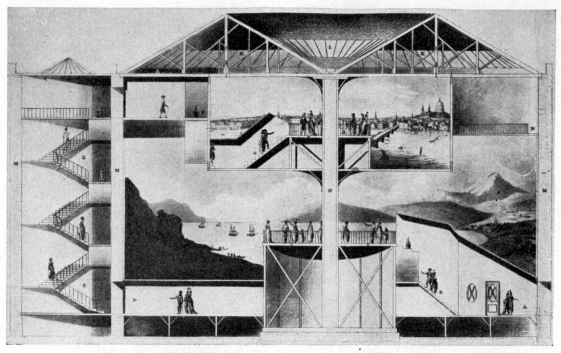

SECTION OF THE ROTUNDA, LEICESTER SQUARE, IN 1801, WITH PANORAMAS PAINTED ROUND THE WALLS
Looking at panoramas was a popular entertainment in the 19th century

Before 1913 the cinema in Britain was dominated by American and French interests. An early American pioneer in London was George C. Hale, who in the early years of the present century opened in Regent Street a cinema show called Hale's Tours. The audience sat in seats arranged like those of an American open rail-coach; the films were of landscape subjects and gave the illusion that the spectators were seated in the observation car at the rear of a moving train. Later the Biograph and Vitagraph Companies of America opened theatres in central and suburban London, where screenplays were shown (*see* CINEMA, HISTORY OF, Vol. IX). Pathé's of Paris were at that time the leaders in the French section of the industry, and they also soon opened cinema theatres in Britain. Naturally, the films shown in these theatres were American or French. After the First World War a native British industry began to develop, particularly when the silent films were replaced by talking films. Development has been slow and American influence is still strong; for example, in 1950 Warner Brothers, an American organization, owned nearly 40% of the CAPITAL (q.v.) of Associated British Pictures Corporation.

'Block booking' has become an important feature of the commercial organization of the cinema industry: the exhibitor contracts in advance with the big film-producing firms to show a stated number of their films over a pre-arranged period, and usually advances a certain amount of money on account, which assists the producer towards the cost of production. In return, the producing firm promises that the films to be delivered will be of a high standard of attractiveness. Block booking, which was started in the U.S.A. and spread to Britain, made it desirable for film producers to own their own theatres, for if they did not they might get the worst of any bargain if the exhibitors banded together against them. The most notable feature of the commercial organization of the industry to-day is this widespread ownership of cinema theatres by the producing firms. This gives the industry stability, for the production of a spectacular modern film is a very expensive matter. Many American films cost a million dollars each to produce, and the cost of some British films comes very close to this. Of the total cost, the actors receive about a quarter, the director about one-tenth, the scenario writer and his assistants about one-eighth, and the art director about one-eighth for his own services and for the provision of scenery and scenic effects.

The entertainment business is one of the first to suffer in times of poor trade, for most people naturally economize on entertainment before they cut down expenditure in other directions. Poor times affect the theatre section particularly; rents and costs of production are high, and are sometimes only just covered when the house is fairly full. It is out of the difference between a fairly full house and a packed house, particularly when the 'run' of the production is a long one, that the profit of a production really comes. Agencies have, therefore, grown up to help to fill theatres and other places of entertainment by making booking easier and more convenient, and to earn their own profits or commissions at the same time. The larger agencies book blocks of seats for the run of the production, and sell them to the public at a small premium on the price charged by the theatre box-office. Such agencies are really wholesale dealers in seats (*see* WHOLESALE TRADING). Besides the large agencies there are many small firms or even individuals, all of whom are mere AGENTS (q.v.). They obtain their seats from the larger agencies, or from the box-offices direct, and charge a small booking fee. The agencies do not restrict their activities to the stage and screen, but book seats also for all kinds of sporting events, such as Henley Royal Regatta and the Tennis Championships at Wimbledon. In fact, there is little in the world of entertainment, in its widest sense, with which they do not concern themselves, and their dealings include vantage-points from which to view the Oxford and Cambridge Boat Race or royal processions.

See also Vol. IX: THEATRE, HISTORY OF; BALLET; OPERA; CINEMA, HISTORY OF.

ESTATE AGENT, *see* AGENT.

EVAPORATED MILK, *see* DAIRY INDUSTRY.

EXCHANGE AND TRADE are part of the economic life of most modern communities. Without them we should lack the variety of goods and services that most of us can now share, and in so far as this variety contributes to a higher STANDARD OF LIVING (q.v.) we should not be as well off as we are. It has taken centuries for exchange and trade to grow up to their present size, and, if we could draw a curve to represent this development, it would not be a smooth one but a series of ups and downs. For the process of development has often been interrupted by wars and invasions, and by other happenings that have caused powerful nations to decline. The history of Britain provides an example. Britain reached a high level of economic development during the Roman occupation. The departure of the legions caused the country's economic life to return to a much more primitive stage, and it is probable that 6 or 7 centuries passed before the loss was made up. Some 1,500 years have passed since the Roman legions left; during this long period the economic life of Britain has sometimes been prosperous and sometimes less so; but on the whole the record is one of continuously expanding exchange and trade.

The economic life of any community is that part of its life that is spent in satisfying material wants: for food, clothing, shelter, and so on. If these wants are satisfied within the family—as they still are in some backward or primitive communities—there are then no surplus goods to dispose of; all that is produced is needed to keep the family alive. The technical name for this type of economic system is a 'subsistence economy'.

This name would also be given to an economic system that has developed one stage further, such as a small village community of several families. In fact, this is what economists really mean when they talk or write of a subsistence economy, for human families have seldom, if ever, lived in complete isolation and been dependent solely on the labour and effort of their own members. The family subsistence economy is therefore difficult to track down in the records of history, and the best examples we have of it are among such primitive races as still survive, or in works of fiction such as *The Swiss Family Robinson*. Of the other and more general kind of subsistence economy, the village group, historical records are very full indeed. The English Manor of the Middle Ages is a typical example. The manor was a self-contained and self-sufficient village community, having little intercourse with towns or with other communities like itself. The fields and woods produced the material for bread and meat, fuel, and beer, and the wool and skins for rough clothing and footwear. There was

THE LONDON CORN EXCHANGE, 1809
Merchants are inspecting samples of grain in small bags. Coloured aquatint by Rowlandson and Pugin from Ackermann's
Microcosm of London

little left for the people of the manor to exchange for what they could not produce themselves. Some trade existed in the towns; and those towns that were ports traded not only with inland towns but with ports overseas. When we talk of the economic system of the early Middle Ages as being based on subsistence, we do not mean that there was no exchange or trade at all; we mean only that those who exchanged or traded were rather unimportant exceptions to the general rule.

When the exchanging or trading of surplus goods with other people becomes more important than the production of goods for direct consumption by the community itself, the system by which economic life is then carried on is called an 'exchange economy'. In England the change from a subsistence to an exchange economy can be said to have become fairly general by the middle of the 14th century. In

1348–9 an epidemic plague which was known as the Black Death reached England from the Continent and affected most parts of the country. Many manors lost half their population, and their land became more than was needed for the subsistence of those left alive. The lords of the manors, who had depended on the labour of their villeins, or serfs, for the farming of their own land, now found themselves short of labour; and the serfs or peasants began to realize that being fewer in number, they had therefore become more valuable. At the same time there was a demand for wool by the cloth-making towns of Flanders, and many manors turned their arable land into sheep pasture and began to grow more wool. This needed fewer workers than agriculture. The peasants were also able to influence their lords to accept rent in money, or in a share of the produce raised, instead of in labour services rendered, as had been the system formerly. By the time all these influences had worked themselves out, England had become an exchange economy, the surplus goods of the towns going to the surrounding country and villages, and these disposing of their produce to the towns. Much of the wool went abroad in the end.

This mutual exchanging benefited both town and country. Each could reap the advantages of DIVISION OF LABOUR (q.v.), or specialization in one particular branch of economic activity. The farmer was a more efficient farmer by being a farmer only; the craftsman in the town became more efficient by working at his particular craft. Both parties gained by exchanging their un-wanted surplus for what they wanted more urgently. A further gain arose from the increasing use of MONEY (q.v.). If all business had been done by 'barter', or exchanging one article for another, it would have been much less satisfactory. The trouble about barter is that both parties to a transaction are obliged to take what is going instead of what they really want; such transactions are only satisfactory when there is what economists call a 'double coincidence of wants', and this happens very rarely. Money is generally acceptable to everybody; a sale for money confers on the seller the power of choosing from among many goods the particular one that he most wants, and it gives him also the chance of postponing his spending, or saving for the future, if he prefers to do so. It is therefore almost certain that a community that has developed into an exchange economy will go a stage further and become a money economy. England had reached this stage by the end of the 15th century.

The economic system of a single nation is called a 'national economy'. But this is not necessarily a final stage of development. There is the further stage of a 'world economy', in which many nations are, in an economic sense, 'members one of another'. In a world economy, exchange and trade have passed beyond the borders of a single nation, and involve the whole world. Additional advantages come from this further development. Division of labour can become extended geographically or territorially; each country that is a member of the world economy is able to exchange its surplus either for goods that it cannot produce at all or for those that it cannot produce cheaply enough.

Building up a world economy took many centuries, and was obstructed and delayed by the jealousies and rivalries of nations. It had to wait, first, for the small world of the later Middle Ages to expand into something larger. Trade at the end of the 15th century, when Cabot sailed for Newfoundland, was mainly confined to Europe, although a little trade took place on its eastern borders, particularly with Asia Minor, Central Asia, and China, and to a small extent with the East Indies. The TRADE ROUTES (q.v. Vol. IV) followed by the incense caravans of Arabia, and the Great Silk Road from China carried traffic even in medieval times. But the enlargement of the world, from an economic point of view, really dates from the period known as the Discoveries, when Vasco da Gama, Columbus, Cabot, and others sailed southwards and eastwards and westwards and discovered lands till then merely dreamed about. The period of the Discoveries was followed by the exploration and occupation of the new lands, and by the development of trade. Individual merchants were neither strong enough nor wealthy enough for these tasks, and the work was undertaken by large companies of merchants, operating under exclusive charters granted by their governments (see CHARTERED COMPANIES).

There followed three centuries—the 16th, the 17th, and the 18th—of international rivalry, economic struggle, and intermittent war. But, in spite of these complications, it was a period in which trade was expanded and enlarged; and when the series of struggles ended temporarily with the long peace after Waterloo a world economy was not far off. For many years before that time the economic benefits of a widespread division of labour and unrestricted exchange and trade had been preached by the famous economist Adam SMITH (q.v. Vol. V) and his disciples. Smith's views gained general acceptance; although some countries, for political reasons, put up trade barriers, all were broadly agreed that a general extension of trade was in itself desirable. This extension was fostered by a great development of BANKING (q.v.), which now became an international rather than a purely national business, and these new international bankers helped merchants to spend money freely beyond their own national frontiers.

The economic history of the 19th century is really a record of the growth of a world economy; the farthest point was reached, perhaps, in 1914, just before the First World War upset the world's trading habits.

Since then two world wars have been fought. The expansion of the world economy has been checked, and there has been a tendency for world trade to contract. The state in which the world now finds itself is not unlike the period of the MERCANTILE SYSTEM (q.v.) in the 17th and 18th centuries, when nations were struggling among themselves for economic and political supremacy. Some of the old restrictions of that time have come back again. Barter—in the form of bilateral, or two-sided, trade agreements between pairs of nations—has reappeared as an occasional feature of international trade, and the free spending of money anywhere and everywhere has ceased to be possible.

See also COMMERCE; MERCANTILE SYSTEM; MONEY; TRADE, HISTORY OF; TRADE CYCLE; FINANCE.

EXCHANGE, RATES OF, *see* RATES OF EX-CHANGE.

EXCISE, *see* TARIFFS; *see also* Vol. X: CUSTOMS AND EXCISE.

EXHIBITIONS. In industry and commerce the word 'exhibition' means a special kind of TRADE FAIR (q.v.), usually sponsored by the Government of a country and organized on a national scale. The true exhibition covers all a country's industrial activities, and aims to attract universal attention. Unlike an ordinary trade fair, it has a definite political purpose, and is held at some specially significant time. The first exhibition of all, for instance, the British Great Exhibition of 1851, was held a few years after the outbreak in 1848 of revolutions all over the Continent, and its aim was to show the economic strength of Britain in a disordered world. The Festival of Britain of 1951 was timed not only to be a centenary celebration of its predecessor but also to advertise to the world Britain's recovery from the economic strain of

Parker Gallery

THE CRYSTAL PALACE, HYDE PARK, 1851
Coloured engraving by Augustus Butler

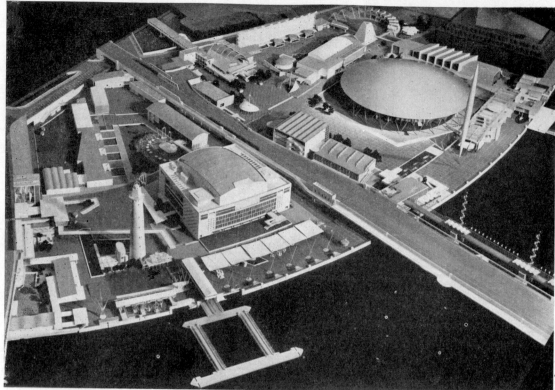

Festival of Britain

MODEL OF THE FESTIVAL OF BRITAIN EXHIBITION, 1951
In the centre is the Concert Hall and on the right the Dome of Discovery

the Second World War. In the same way the Paris Exhibition of 1878 advertised the recovery of France from the Franco-Prussian War of 1870–1. Other important exhibitions have been the British Empire Exhibition held at Wembley in 1924 and 1925, shortly after the end of the First World War, to advertise the variety of Commonwealth products, and the important exhibition held in Philadelphia, U.S.A., in 1926, to celebrate the 150th anniversary of American Independence.

In most exhibitions the architectural design of the buildings is usually well ahead of contemporary fashion. Many famous buildings have been associated with exhibitions. A great feature of the British Exhibition of 1851 was the Crystal Palace, then erected in Hyde Park and later removed to a site near Sydenham; it was destroyed by fire in 1936. A great new concert hall and outer buildings were erected on the south bank of the Thames for the 1951 Festival of Britain.

At the Paris Exhibition in 1878 the Palace of the Trocadero was specially built to house the exhibits. The steel-built Eiffel Tower, a landmark of Paris, was built for the Paris exhibition of 1889. For the Paris Exhibition of 1937 the Palais de Chaillot, which in 1948 became the meeting-place of the General Assembly of the United Nations, was built to replace the Palace of the Trocadero.

The word 'exhibition' is also used in Britain for such annual events as the Schoolboys' and Schoolgirls' Exhibitions, which are national and in a sense universal, although they are held only for a limited section of the population. Such events as the Model Engineering Exhibition and the Ideal Home Exhibition are really trade fairs, being concerned with the products of one group of industries only.

See also TRADE FAIRS.

EXPORTS, *see* INTERNATIONAL TRADE; OVERSEAS TRADE.

F

FABRICS, *see* Cotton Industry; Linen Industry; Wool Industry, Modern; Textile Fibres and Fabrics; Wool Weaving; Rayon; Hosiery and Knitwear.

FACTORY ORGANIZATION. 1. The aim of any manufacturing business is to produce goods as efficiently and cheaply as possible. To do this, there must be a careful arrangement of the various tasks that have to be carried out, and of the factory buildings, machines, and equipment. The main channels of command and of responsibility do not differ very much from those of any other business (*see* Business Organization); but manufacture introduces problems that would not have to be solved in a business engaged merely in buying and selling.

Certain general principles apply to all kinds of industries. The main problems of factory organization may be classed under four headings: the siting and layout of the factory; the type and extent of the machinery and equipment to be used; the control of employees or 'personnel', and the arrangement of their various duties; the planning and control of production, including the accurate calculation of the costs incurred in the various stages or processes of manufacture (*see* Costing).

2. Siting and Layout. The choice of a location for the factory depends on the industry itself (*see* Localization of Industry), and the size and arrangement of the factory buildings themselves should be suited to the work that will be carried on in them. They must be as light and airy as possible. Fluorescent lighting is now widely used in factories for providing a light without glare, and approaches most nearly to daylight. Special shadow-proof lighting can also be installed where close or delicate work is being done. Good ventilation must be provided, and its extent will depend on the work carried on; some industrial processes give rise to poisonous gases, and the workers must not be allowed to breathe them. General working conditions must comply with the rules laid down in the Factories Act, 1937, which includes special provisions for dangerous industries or processes.

The 'ground-level' type of factory suits the small, specialized manufacturing business well, but it would not suit a brewery or a biscuit factory, or a similar large enterprise involving a sequence of many processes. Beyond a certain size, a one-floor factory becomes difficult to supervise and control. If the ground-level type suits the business, it is ideal; it has no upper storeys, and is usually constructed with 'saw-

Monotype Corporation

GROUND LEVEL FACTORY WITH 'SAW-TOOTH' ROOFS AND NORTH LIGHTS

McDougalls

INSIDE A 'GRAVITY' TYPE FACTORY

This view of a flour mill shows how the grain is fed by
gravity from hoppers in the floor above

tooth' roofs, which make it possible to fit large
skylights and reduce artificial lighting. Such
buildings are very suitable for heavy machinery,
whose foundations can be sunk into the ground.
The other type of building is the 'gravity' type,
which has several storeys. The top floor is
generally used for the early stages of manufacture, and lower floors for later stages; the final
stages, such as packing, storage, and distribution, are organized at ground-level. Modern
steel and concrete building construction now
makes it possible to carry out most kinds of
heavy work on upper floors (*see* BUILDING CON-
STRUCTION, Vol. VIII).

3. MACHINERY AND EQUIPMENT. The amount
of machinery to be installed in any factory is, in
the main, a question of the comparative costs of
labour and machinery (*see* PRODUCTION). But
there are some industrial processes for which
machines are essential, as hand-labour without
machinery could only turn out an inferior
article (*see* CRAFTSMANSHIP). Machinery can be
very expensive to buy and to keep in good
repair. Its value may fall quickly, not only
through age but also because it becomes out-of-
date and has to be replaced by more efficient
models (*see* DEPRECIATION). If there is not enough

work in a factory to keep machines running, the
machines become expensive to run, and the
manufacturing cost of each article will rise. On
the other hand, if machines are worked too
much, they wear out more quickly, and the bills
for repairs and maintenance become larger.
It often pays best to arrange work on a double-
shift system, so that the extra expense of maintaining and replacing the machines is spread
over a larger volume of production. Machines
and machinists must not be left idle for lack of
materials. If a continuous flow of production is
aimed at, it is usual to install endless-belt CON-
VEYORS (q.v. Vol. VIII), which move over
rollers at a set speed, so that the work moves
from worker to worker without interruption.
The conveyor system does not suit all forms of
production, and other devices have frequently
to be used, such as overhead cranes or grabs,
gravity chutes, or hand-operated trucks or
trolleys.

Machines must, of course, be kept in motion.
The motive power used naturally varies with the
industry; the processes of some industries make
some forms of motive power more economical
than others; for example, coke-oven and blast-
furnace gas, which are by-products, are the main
sources of power in the manufacture of iron and
steel. The use of electrical power has now made
possible great changes in factory motive power.
Before electricity was introduced, motive power
was usually provided by steam, gas, or oil engines, which were connected by belting with
a series of overhead shafts and pulleys, from
which further belts were connected to the actual
machines. This had two disadvantages: a
failure of the power-plant would throw all the
machines out of use at the same time; and the
main shafts and pulleys would have to be constantly revolving, even if only a few machines
were actually operating. Electricity avoids the
second of these disadvantages if each machine
is provided with its own motor. The chance of
a general breakdown cannot be avoided, even
with electricity, although the modern 'grid'
system of POWER TRANSMISSION (q.v. Vol. VIII)
reduces this risk. Some factories have generating
plants of their own, either for regular use with
the main supply as a stand-by, or for emergency
use during a failure of the main supply.

4. PERSONNEL. Since the WAGES of labour
(q.v.) are generally the largest single item in
manufacturing costs, workers in a factory must

be carefully selected for their suitability for the work they have to do. In a large factory there is often a Personnel Manager, trained in modern methods of staff supervision and selection (*see* INDUSTRIAL PSYCHOLOGY). Sometimes there is also an Education or Staff Training Officer, who conducts a works school for the specialized training of employees. The manager or personnel manager will keep a record card for each employee in the works, which shows the dates of his original appointment and of any promotion; the various grades through which he has passed, with their wage-rates; his holidays, other absences, and similar information. All but the senior executive staff are normally required to get a time-card stamped when they 'clock in' and 'clock out' of the works. Except in the smallest factories, this is done by an automatic printing device attached to a clock, as only by some such method can strict time-keeping be secured. The recruitment of the 'key' workers in a factory— such as shop foremen, section managers, the designing and drawing-office staff, 'progress chasers', and inspectors—requires special care. Close contact must exist, with periodical meetings, between these employees and the higher supervisory staff and the management. Pleasant working conditions, and such things as works canteens, welfare schemes, and bonuses paid on WAGES (q.v.), all encourage good working relations, and reduce an undue amount of absence from work ('absenteeism'). The management of human beings at work, however, is a difficult art, although it is nowadays much assisted by science (*see* SCIENTIFIC MANAGEMENT).

5. PLANNING. In all businesses of any size, manufacturing or other, policy is the concern of the Board of Directors. Usually a Managing Director is appointed to take day-to-day control, and to supervise the activities of the rest of the staff including the Works Manager, who is responsible for actual production (*see* BUSINESS ORGANIZATION). The output of any factory naturally depends on the orders received, and these are the concern of the Sales Manager and his outside REPRESENTATIVES (q.v.) and staff. Contact between the managing director and sales manager is close and constant, for on it depend the decisions as to what shall be produced, and in what quantity. These decisions are passed on to the Planning Department.

The job of the planning department is to arrange and combine machines, materials, and men so as to turn out the product as cheaply and efficiently as possible. It is assisted by two other specialized departments: the Drawing and Design Office, and the Buying Department. In the first of these, designs are elaborated, both for the articles to be produced and for the machines and other tools to make them with; and detailed drawings are made, from which photographic copies or 'blueprints' are taken for use in the shops where actual production will take place. It is the job of the buying department to estimate and buy the quantities of various materials that will be needed—raw materials or semi-finished goods. Assisting the buying department is the Stores Department, responsible for the actual storage of the various materials and components, and for records of their value. In a small concern the stores department reports direct to the works manager, and there is no separate buying department; in a very large factory, which may be one of a group, the buying department is usually at the head office of the whole concern.

In a large factory, turning out goods to customers' special orders, there is usually a Progress Department. This watches the progress of work through the factory; a 'chasing schedule' is drawn up, showing the various dates and times at which successive stages of manufacture should have been completed; and the 'progress chaser' makes a daily check. Priority orders are specially watched to make sure that there is no departure from the time-table originally laid down for them. A large factory would also have an Inspection or Process Control Department to ensure that manufactured articles reach the required standard. Finally, the Dispatch or Distribution Department undertakes the packing and forwarding of articles to customers.

Throughout the whole process of manufacture costs are carefully calculated and watched (*see* COSTING). Economies may be found possible by studying the comparative costs of doing the same job in different ways. A well-organized factory is not static; it is always seeking more perfected forms of organization and more efficient methods of production, so that its ability to trade in a competitive world may be increased.

See also BUSINESS ORGANIZATION; PRODUCTION; LOCALIZATION OF INDUSTRY.

FACTORY OVERHEADS, *see* COSTING, Section 3.

FACTORY SYSTEM, see INDUSTRIAL REVOLUTION.

FAIRS, see TRADE FAIRS.

FELLMONGERING. In a commercial sense the skins of sheep differ from those of other animals, as the wool is worth considerably more than the skin itself. Hence the special trade of fellmongering has developed. The fellmonger buys sheepskins carrying wool and separates the wool from the pelt, selling the wool to the wool merchant and the pelt to the tanner. The way in which the wool has been loosened since quite ancient days is by hanging the skins for a few days in a warm, moist atmosphere; bacteria then grow in the wool and destroy the roots, so that the wool can be easily pulled out. This method produces the best wool, uncontaminated by chemicals, and is still much used, although the pelts are liable to be damaged. A quicker and more modern method is to paint the inner surfaces of the wet skins with a strong solution of sodium sulphide, thickened with lime. The sulphide spreads through to the wool roots and destroys them, and after a few hours of treatment the wool can be pulled off. This modern process has now largely replaced the older one; it is safer

for the pelt, but not so good for the wool. Fellmongered pelts can be preserved by treating or 'pickling' them with a solution of salt and sulphuric acid (see ACIDS). Millions of sheep skins are imported into Britain in the pickled state.

See also WOOL INDUSTRY, MODERN; TANNING.

FELT. 1. Most people have used felt, but few people know what it is. It is a fabric in which the individual fibres are closely entangled—higgledy-piggledy, like a bundle of hay—until they form a compact, substantial layer. The random arrangement of fibres is quite different from the orderly way in which the yarns or threads are arranged in woven and knitted fabrics.

Wool felts have been made from very early times. MONGOLS (q.v. Vol. I), for instance, will put layers of wool on to a large mat, sprinkle them with water, grease, and oil, and then roll up the mat. This process is repeated until the wool fibres have matted together to make a firm felt. Such felt has been used for the Gilgit boots much worn by soldiers serving on the North-West Frontier of India. The same type of primitive felt, spread over a framework and tied down with ropes, makes the *yurta*, or tent, in which the nomadic Mongols live.

Nobody really knows just what causes wool to felt. The simplest, and perhaps the most likely, theory is that felting is connected with the tiny scales, visible only under the microscope, with which the surface of each wool fibre is covered. If a pile of wool fibres is lubricated by oil or moisture, and is subjected to friction and pressure, the outer fibres work their way inwards into the pile, dragging other fibres with them. As a result, the whole pile tightens up and becomes more compact. In time, a firm sheet of matted fibres is made in this way, and this is what we call felt.

Two kinds of felt are made in this way: non-woven felt and woven felt. There is also needle felt, an imitation made mechanically.

Non-woven or piece-felts consist of the higgledy-piggledy arrangement of wool fibres just described. To-day these non-woven felts are usually made from wool fibres about $1\frac{1}{2}$ inches long, and from 'noil'—the short fibres of wool about $\frac{3}{4}$ to 1 inch long that are separated from the long ones in the combing process (see WOOL SPINNING). The wool used is obtained from merino SHEEP (q.v. Vol. VI) which are famous

Norman Wymer

REMOVING THE WOOL FROM A SHEEPSKIN WHICH HAS BEEN TREATED WITH CHEMICALS for felting wools of fine quality. Non-wool fibres, such as asbestos, cotton, rayon, jute, fur, and hair, may be added for cheapness or for technical reasons, according to the use for which the felt is intended.

The raw wool is first scoured to remove grease; vegetable matter such as burrs and seeds is also removed. The selected lots of wool are spread on the floor in layers, one on top of another. Vertical slices of the pile are then fed into a mixing machine, and finally agitated by a blower. This causes a very thorough blending of the wools used.

The blend is then carded (*see* WOOL SPINNING) by passing it over revolving cylinders covered with fine pins, which open out the fibres and make them roughly parallel. The web of wool which results is called a 'batt'. The batts are laid crosswise alternately, one on top of the other, sometimes to a height of 3 feet, in appearance like a pile of sheets of cotton-wool. The batts are then 'soaked' in steam, and hardened under pressure. In a later 'fulling' process the batts are rolled, lifted, pounded, and compressed by mechanical hammers; in the old days this was done by hitting the felt with wooden mallets.

2. WOVEN FELT. A woven felt is produced by 'milling' a woven wool fabric. The wool is specially selected for its felting qualities and spun and woven in the usual way. Milling is a shrinking process, in which the cloth is compressed in soapy water or acid solution to render it firmer and more compact, while the weave structure of the fabric becomes hidden by the felting of the surface fibres, giving the fabric so treated a blanket-like appearance. In fact, a blanket is merely a woven felt, with the surface fibres brushed up again to make it warm and fluffy.

Compared with other felts, woven felts have great strength and resistance to fraying, and stand up well to hard wear. They are also very efficient insulators of heat.

3. NEEDLE FELTS. Needle felts are not necessarily made of wool, the felting being imitated mechanically. A layer of fibres, which may be animal (wool and hair) or vegetable (jute), is fed into a 'needling' machine with a piece of hessian which serves as a backcloth. The needles then push the fibres through the backcloth, leaving them fast between the threads. This is repeated on the other side of the cloth, and the result is called a needle felt. Needle felts can be produced relatively cheaply, and so they are used

Paul Popper

KIRGHIZ PEASANTS OF CENTRAL ASIA MAKING FELT

when appearance does not matter: amongst other purposes for carpet underlays, and heat, sound, and vibration insulators.

3. FINISHING FELTS. After being dyed, the felt is 'tentered', or dried under tension, by hooks attached to its edges. (This is the origin of the expression 'on tenterhooks'.) If very dense, 'rock hard' felts are required, the batts are pressed as well. Such felts are used for grinding and polishing precious stones (*see* DIAMOND INDUSTRY).

Some felts are left rough, as in felt bases for typewriters, but others may be cropped to remove surface fibres—a process like mowing a lawn—and then smoothed with sandpaper: as in the making of hats, from the trilby to the 'ten gallon' hat of the Western cowboy. An ordinary wool felt hat begins as a loose cone-shaped jumble of fibres 18 inches high, 48 inches round the base, and 1½ inches thick.

Felts may be stiffened with size, or treated with resins, to make them keep any shape to which they may be moulded. This is how bowler hats are made. The other uses of felt include footwear, washers and gaskets for machinery, and the self-sealing petrol tanks for aircraft that increase safety in flying.

The 'art and mystery of felt-making', as it used to be called, was once under the control of the Feltmakers Company. The Worshipful Company of Feltmakers—one of the ancient guilds or Livery Companies of the City of London (*see* CITY COMPANIES)—was granted a

MAKING FELT HATS IN THE 19TH CENTURY

Royal Charter by James I in 1604, but it was probably in existence in the 15th century. Even in this scientific age felt-making is still very much an 'art and mystery'.

See also Textile Fabrics.

FERMENTATION, *see* Beer Brewing; Wine Trade; Industrial Alcohol; Cider.

See also Vol. II: Fermentation.

FIBRE, *see* Wool Industry, Modern; Cotton Manufacture; Linen Industry; Silk; Rayon; Copra; Hair Trade; Jute; Felt; Rope-making; Brushes; Textile Fibres and Fabrics; Nylon.

See also Vol. VI: Fibre Crops.

FINANCE. This branch of commerce is concerned with providing Capital (q.v.) for business enterprises, and with dealings in the ownership of this capital after it has been raised. The financial world, therefore, includes Banks, Building Societies, Issuing Houses, the various institutions forming the Money Market, and the Stock Exchanges (qq.v.). The ordinary investing public, whether they are private persons or commercial firms and institutions, are also part of the financial world, although some of them seldom realize it.

In Great Britain the banks are the main collectors of the money and savings of the general public. They use these funds for making 'short-term advances' (or lending money for short periods), principally to merchants and manufacturers who want to borrow money until their goods have been sold. The building societies finance the long-term loans required by those wishing to build or buy houses. The issuing houses arrange for the collection of long-term capital for commercial and industrial firms. As a result of all these activities, various interest-bearing or dividend-earning securities come into existence. The Money Market deals in bills of exchange and in short-dated securities; the Stock Exchanges deal in securities of longer date.

Finance can be subdivided into private or commercial finance and public finance. The methods above described belong to commercial finance. Public finance is considered in detail in Vol. X, under the heading of National Finance. It deals with the management of Government expenditure, and with the collection of the necessary money by taxation and other means. Expenditure which cannot be covered by taxation has to be financed by borrowing. When the Government wishes to borrow, it makes use of the financial organizations in the City of London and other parts of the country, just as private individuals and business men do. Government Treasury Bills are handled on the Money Market, and Government Loans on the Stock Exchange.

See also International Finance.

FINANCE, INTERNATIONAL, *see* International Finance.

FIRECLAY, *see* Vol. VIII: Refractories.

FIRING, *see* Bricks and Tiles; Pottery; Earthenware.

FISH TRADE. Fish is one of the staple foods all over the world, and the fish industry is one of the most ancient and widespread (*see* Fishing Industry, Vol. VI). The industry includes the catching, marketing, and distribution of fish caught by trawlers, drifters, and smaller craft.

A FISHMONGER'S SHOP
19th-century Aquatint

Over 1 million tons of fish are landed at the fishing ports of Britain every year, and for this the fishing-boat owners and the fishermen receive about £40 million. To provide the fish that can be seen each day on the slabs of the fishmongers' shops, or which appear on the tables of hotels and restaurants, or are cooked in fried-fish shops, the industry works day and night all the year round. The fishermen do a hard job, and theirs is one of the most hazardous of callings, requiring great endurance.

The fish industry falls into two divisions: the catching of white fish, or 'demersal' (a Latin word for 'under-water', applied to fish that live near the beds of shallow seas), and the catching of herrings, or 'pelagic' fish (a Greek word for the sea, applied to surface-swimming fish). Total landings of both classes into Britain are enough to provide a pound of fish a week for everyone in the population. White-fish catching is done by deep-sea trawlers (see TRAWLING, Vol. VI), by smaller vessels of Scandinavian origin using

seine nets, and by small inshore motor-boats which fish with long baited lines (see HERRING FISHERIES, Vol. VI).

The fish, which are bedded in broken ice in the hold, are first unloaded into huge baskets, then swung ashore and dumped on the floors of the quay sheds, where they are sorted into piles.

The big trawlers start landing at midnight. By eight o'clock each morning hundreds of fish merchants and their workers start buying and packing fish. Ice is specially manufactured in large factories, and in it the fish is packed, ready for dispatch by special express fish trains to the inland fish-markets. Billingsgate in London was actually established as a market in 1699, although fish have been sold there since Roman times. It is now the largest inland fish-market in the world, distributing about 500 tons of fish each working day—enough to provide a fish meal for 3 million people. The fish are sold by AUCTION (q.v.); sometimes by Dutch auction, when the auctioneer offers his fish at a high

Graphic Photo Union

SCOTTISH FISH GIRLS GUTTING HERRINGS AT YARMOUTH

The herring season starts in Scotland and moves south with
the shoals of fish, finishing at Yarmouth and Lowestoft

figure and reduces it until a buyer is tempted to begin the bidding. The unit in the sale of herrings is the 'last'—nominally 100,000 fish, but actually 132,000, since herrings are counted in units of 132 ('long hundred') instead of 100. From the ports themselves, or from the inland markets, the fishmongers and fish-friers are supplied, and 24 hours after the fish are caught they are on sale all over the kingdom. It is surprising, but true, that often fish from the ports reaches its destination faster than a railway passenger could travel the same distance. A great deal of fish is now quick-frozen and placed in COLD STORAGE (q.v.). There is therefore plenty of fish in the winter, when stormy weather makes it difficult to catch fish—especially in the far north, where there is total darkness for many weeks on end.

Britain also imports a large quantity of fish, particularly scarce kinds, such as plaice, sole, and haddock. These come from Norway, Denmark, and Belgium. Foreign vessels also land fish in British ports, and there is a considerable shellfish industry: Scotland is the second largest producer of lobsters in the world, Canada holding first place.

See also COLD STORAGE.
See also Vol. II: FISHES.
See also Vol. VI: FISHING INDUSTRY.

FLAX, *see* LINEN INDUSTRY; *see also* Vol. VI.: FIBRE CROPS.

FLINTS, *see* CHALK.

FLOUR MILLING. Grinding or milling is the process of breaking down the hard grains or cereals into a powder or a meal. 'Flour' is the term commonly used for the fine powder into which the wheat grain is milled for making bread and confectionery.

Primitive man, when he had threshed and winnowed his grain, ground it to produce a form of flour. He generally used two stones, grinding the corn on a flat stone with a 'muller', a ball-shaped stone which was held in the hand. This method of grinding is still in use; not long ago modern mullers were still on sale in East Africa. In the same way, the primitive technique of 'hulling' rice with some form of pestle and mortar is still seen in India and elsewhere. A later development was the quern or hand-mill, with two circular millstones, the upper one of which was made to revolve by a handle. Millstones were also sometimes driven by animals, generally oxen, which were harnessed to a baulk of timber fastened to them. They then walked round the millstones in a large circle. Water-mills are known to have been in use shortly before the birth of Christ. By this means the current of a stream turned a wheel which made the millstones revolve. In the 12th century it was discovered that the wind would turn a wheel if large sails were attached to it, and for the next 600 years windmills were seen in most landscapes. Steam power began to take the place of the windmill at the end of the 18th century, although the change was slow. Steam power had replaced the windmill in grinding wheat flour for human use while the windmill still continued to be used for grinding other cereals into feeding-stuffs for farmers' livestock. Until 1881, when the roller mill was invented, even steam-power milling was done by revolving grindstones. The technique of roller-milling was not perfected until 1914.

After threshing, the wheat grain consists of about 85% starchy material, 2% embryo or germ, and 13% husk. The technical name for the starchy constituent of the wheat grain is 'endosperm'. Qualities of flour differ with what is called the 'extraction' rate, that is, the percentage of the whole grain that is actually used

W. A. Green

GRINDING FLOUR IN A QUERN

Querns are still sometimes used in the western islands of Ireland

W. A. Green

GRINDSTONES IN A WATER-MILL

The corn is fed from the shute into the hopper and thence between the grindstones

McDougalls

SPIRAL SEPARATORS (8 IN DIAGRAM) IN A MODERN MILL

As the grain runs down, round seeds such as peas are thrown to the outside

Hovis

ROLLER MILLS (15 IN DIAGRAM) FOR GRINDING FLOUR

The semolina falls from the floor above into the roller mills. Windows in the casing allow the process to be watched

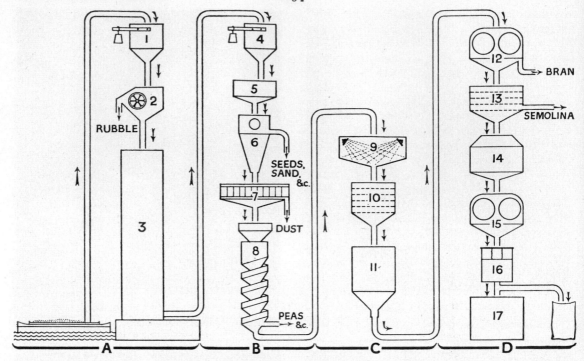

DIAGRAM OF FLOUR MILLING

A. The wheat is taken from barges by suction and weighed (1), coarse stones and rubbish are removed (2), and it is stored in silos (3)
B. Dry-cleaning plant where wheat is weighed (4), scoured (5), seeds and sand removed by rotary separator (6), dust sucked out (7), and peas, &c., spun off in spiral separators (8)
C. Washing with water (9), conditioning (10), and storing (11). It is now ready for milling
D. Rollers remove the bran (12), making semolina which is sieved (13) and purified (14). Roller mills grind the semolina into flour (15) which is sieved (16) and stored in bins (17) or sacks

for milling into flour. In Britain during the Second World War the extraction rate went up as high as 85%, but it was later reduced to 80%. The portion left, which is not milled into flour, is used for feeding livestock, and is given different names according to its composition. Bran is essentially the husk of the wheat grain, with a small quantity of endosperm (which cannot be fully extracted in milling) mixed with it. Other offals (as these residues used to be called) contain less husk and more endosperm than bran contains. The old word 'offal' has now been taken over by the meat trade, and is no longer used in milling circles. Wheat products other than flour are now called by the general term 'wheat food'.

Britain imports her wheat from Canada, U.S.A., Australia, India, and Russia. The nature of the wheat grain varies considerably in different parts of the world, and different wheats produce different flours. Some wheats produce flours which have what millers and bakers call 'strength', and others produce 'weak'

flours. Strong flours absorb plenty of water when the flour is mixed into dough, and also produce a dough from which well-shaped loaves, which will not crumble, may be baked. 'Weak' flours are unsuitable for modern bread-making, but may be used for biscuit-making.

Before the milling process begins, the wheat must be cleaned and conditioned. It is first roughly sieved to remove straw, dirt, sand, and other impurities. It is then given a conditioning process, which varies with the quality of the wheat itself. If the grain of the wheat is particularly hard or flinty—and this is true of most North American wheats—it must be dampened before being milled. Home-grown English and many European wheats are too damp and have to be dried. After conditioning, the husk is separated from the kernel by modern roller machinery. The grain goes through several series of rollers revolving at different speeds, the difference in speed varying with the stage of milling reached. The number of stages may be anything from three to five, but occasionally is as many as six. In the early stages the husk is almost entirely separated from the kernel, but a certain amount of husk still remains. In the later stages the amount of husk is gradually reduced, according to the extraction rate aimed at. The old millstone process was not as successful as the roller process in separating the husk from the kernel; the stones bruised the husk and caused some of it to be reduced to powder, which could not be removed. But there is still a considerable demand, particularly by country women who bake their own bread, for stone-ground whole-meal flour. Many country mills produce also stone-ground feeding-stuffs, poultry meals and other meals.

Between the various stages of grinding in a roller mill, and also after the final rolling, the flour is 'bolted' or sieved. It is then bleached, for in its natural state wheat flour tends to be yellowish in colour and unattractive in appearance.

See also BAKING INDUSTRY.
See also Vol. VI: WHEAT.

FLOWER TRADE. The flower trade of Britain is conducted principally by specialist shops and by street hawkers and barrowmen, although many greengrocers run a flower department. The variety of flowers and foliage dealt in by an up-to-date florist is considerable, and there are nearly 200 different kinds in many florists' catalogues. There is much scope for original artistry in many branches of the trade, particularly in the making of wreaths and bouquets. The windows of many florists' shops are often beautifully designed. Cornwall and the Scilly Islands, particularly the latter, are the most important districts of the British Isles for flower growing, although other districts contribute, and Lincolnshire is famous for tulips. Marketing is done mostly through the fruit-markets and merchants, and Covent Garden is the main market for London.

Many people like to give flowers to mark birthdays, anniversaries, and other social occasions. After the First World War an organization was set up by which orders for supplies of flowers could be telegraphed from any part of the world to another; it took as a motto 'Say it with flowers'. This organization, which was started in the U.S.A., was called the Florists' Telegraph Delivery Association. It has been

Fox Photos

WIRING FLOWERS AT THE MODERN SCHOOL OF FLOWER-WORK, LONDON

succeeded by Interflora, whose members are the leading florists of every town in the English-speaking world. Its essential feature is a financial clearing system (*see* CLEARING HOUSES) through which money handed in by the sender in one currency may eventually be paid to the actual supplier of the flowers, often in a different currency. There are also several smaller schemes of the same nature, with a more local application. That launched in 1923 by the Liverpool Fruiterers' Association has members in the six counties of North Wales, and in Shropshire, Cheshire, Lancashire, Cumberland, Westmorland, and the Isle of Man.

See also Vol. VI: MARKET GARDENING.

FOREIGN EXCHANGE, *see* RATES OF EXCHANGE.

FOREIGN INVESTMENT, *see* INTERNATIONAL FINANCE.

FREE TRADE, *see* INTERNATIONAL TRADE.

FRETWORK is a form of ornamentation, done by sawing out a number of holes, of more or less

Frank Partridge and Sons
MAHOGANY TABLE WITH FRETWORK DECORATION
18th century, in the style of Chippendale

intricate shapes, from a thin sheet of rigid material, usually wood. It differs from marquetry (*see* INLAY AND MARQUETRY) in that the holes are not later filled in with contrasting material, though they may on occasion be backed with it. Thomas CHIPPENDALE (q.v. Vol. V) made effective use of fretted brackets and other parts on his furniture. In the Victorian age, fretwork, like so many other forms of ornamentation, became over-elaborate, with little regard to general effect. Wood of various kinds, including plywood, is most generally used, and fretworkers can get the wood in ready-planed sheets of different sizes and thicknesses. Fretwork can also be done in the softer metals, such as aluminium, brass, or silver, and in such materials as ebonite, celluloid, ivorine, or perspex.

Patterns are transferred to the work by tracing, pricking through, or by pasting on the wood, the paper on which they have been drawn. The waste part is then sawn away, the blade of the saw being kept at right-angles to the surface of the wood. Interior pieces are started with a drill. A fine saw-blade, no thicker than a piece of wire, is then passed through. When the pattern has been completed, any imperfections are removed with a file, and the work is finished by rubbing with sandpaper. For putting the work together, glue, fine screws, or panel-pins may be used, or close-fitting joints may be cut in the wood. Finally, the work is stained and polished, or painted.

Hand fretwork is still occasionally used by cabinet-makers for certain forms of decoration, although it is mainly popular at the present day as a domestic hobby. Where fretwork has to be used on a commercial scale, it is produced by special machinery.

See also CABINET-MAKING; WOODWORK, HISTORY OF.

FRUIT AND VEGETABLE TRADE, *see* GREENGROCERY; CANNING INDUSTRY.

FURNITURE INDUSTRY. 1. WOOD FURNITURE.

The furniture industry is one of the smaller of the major industries of Britain. At times it has employed as many as 90,000 people —half the number employed in the COTTON INDUSTRY or in BOOT- AND SHOE-MAKING (qq.v.). But, although small, the industry is very important, as its products enter more directly into the lives of the people than those of many larger industries.

The industry is not only small in itself, but the proportion of small factories is greater than in any other trade. The amount of machinery used is less, and more of the work has to be done by hand. In fact, in the Shoreditch district of London one still sees hand-barrow loads of half-completed furniture being trundled from workroom to workroom. Only in the largest factories is it possible to make any use of the mass production methods used generally in modern industry to speed production and reduce costs. Woodworking machines are expensive to buy and to keep in repair, and they can only be made to pay if they are continuously used. The output of the average small factory does not justify the purchase of more than a few of the simpler wood-working machines, such as a saw-bench, a planer, and possibly a moulding machine.

The craft of furniture-making has tended to grow up in or near large towns, where the demand for its products is greatest. Furniture has always been heavy and bulky to transport, and since its raw material, wood, can be found all over the country, the industry has never been tied down, like steel or shipbuilding, to a few parts of the country. Furniture-making has remained a local, and almost a cottage, industry (*see* RURAL CRAFTS, Vol. VI).

London and High Wycombe in Buckinghamshire are exceptions to this general rule. High Wycombe is almost exclusively a furniture town, where the growth of the industry was encouraged by the abundant timber from the local beech forests, and the nearness of a huge consumers'

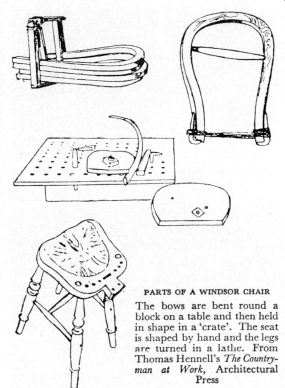

PARTS OF A WINDSOR CHAIR

The bows are bent round a block on a table and then held in shape in a 'crate'. The seat is shaped by hand and the legs are turned in a lathe. From Thomas Hennell's *The Countryman at Work*, Architectural Press

market in London. High Wycombe was the original birthplace of the 'Windsor' chair, and has always been prominent in chair-making. The London industry was at first carried on inside the city itself, and when London grew too big for its city walls the industry moved gradually northwards. It has continued this movement ever since; and even to-day the more enterprising makers are still tending to move farther north, towards the new industrial estates where there is sufficient space for their modern factories.

Until recently the commonest furniture timbers have been the HARDWOODS (q.v.), such as oak, beech, and mahogany. The technique of making wood furniture in a modern factory— even in a large one—does not differ greatly from the methods of the early cabinet-makers, such as Hepplewhite, Sheraton, and CHIPPENDALE (q.v. Vol. V). All wood furniture is made from separate pieces joined, screwed, or glued together. The difference between a modern furniture factory and the workshops of the 18th century lies mainly in the mechanical aids now used to fashion the individual pieces, and to perform the processes of joining, glueing, and polishing. These modern methods are cheaper,

but their results do not surpass in artistic beauty those produced by the laborious care of the earlier handcraftsmen.

Economic and social changes, and the big increase in population, have broadened the demand for furniture in general, and have caused the masses of the people to desire styles and designs that were once beyond their reach. During the present century there has therefore been a great expansion in the production of 'period' or 'reproduction' furniture: that is, simplifications of the earlier craftsmen's designs, but factory-designed and factory-made. A large market has also grown up in antique or second-hand furniture, as big houses have been given up by owners or tenants now too heavily taxed to live in them.

The most modern movement of all in wood-furniture making has been the production of the so-called 'utility' furniture. In the later years of the Second World War, and in the years following it, designs were simplified by Government order, and ornament, finish, and polish were reduced to a minimum. This furniture is made not only of wood, but also of newer materials.

2. MODERN MATERIALS. Outside the home, materials other than wood were used for furniture quite early in the 19th century. Steel sheeting was one of the earliest materials to be used, at first for park chairs and other outdoor furniture, and later for office and factory furniture. Its strength and ability to stand hard knocks gradually made it more popular than wood.

Steel furniture is built up from a number of flat sheets trimmed to shape, bent in huge presses, and then welded together. Paint is sprayed on by a paint-sprayer and dried by heating the furniture in special drying-ovens.

Steel tubes are also used; most people have sat on a tubular steel chair at a lecture or a concert. This kind of chair was invented in Germany in 1925. Since then, steel tubes have been used for all kinds of furniture—chairs, tables, couches, stools, and hospital beds. Many such pieces, particularly chairs, are made to 'nest' or fit together, so that they can be stacked compactly when not in use. Steel-tube furniture is made by first bending the tubes in a machine; and then welding them together and spray-painting or electro-plating them. Aluminium tubes and sheets are also used, for aluminium, which is lighter than steel, has a pleasant natural surface that does not need painting or plating.

Parker Knoll

A CHAIR BEING CLAMPED TOGETHER IN A FRAME WORKED BY COMPRESSED AIR

It has been widely used for bus-seats because of its lightness. In Switzerland the latest coaches on the mountain railways are built largely of aluminium, which gives them a beautifully light and clean effect.

Plywood is another successful new material which is likely to be more widely used, as it has many advantages over ordinary woods. It is lighter and stronger; it neither splits nor warps; and it can be obtained in wider pieces than ordinary wood, so that the whole of one side of a wardrobe or chest-of-drawers may be made out of a single piece. Plywood furniture can be made with simple flat surfaces, which are easier to keep clean than solid wooden furniture with its moulded framings and decorations. A further advantage comes from the large number of wood veneers, many of them very beautiful, that can be used for facing the plywood (*see* PLYWOODS AND VENEERS).

Useful as flat plywood is to the furniture-maker, the most attractive use of the material has

been in its curved or moulded forms. Some years before the Second World War a Finnish plywood manufacturer began a series of experiments in making furniture entirely out of bent plywood. He and his designer, the Finnish architect Alvar Aalto, were very successful in their efforts, and their 'Finmar' furniture became widely known in the late 1930's. The chair illustrated is a typical example of their work. The seat and back are made of one thin sheet of bent plywood, while the arms and legs are made from strips of birch laminated together. Laminated plywood shapes are made by coating the separate sheets of wood with glue, and then pressing them in moulds of the required shape until the glue has set.

Moulded plywood is a special form of plywood which is curved both ways. The fuselage of the famous Mosquito aeroplane of the Second World War was built entirely of moulded plywood. Two thin skins of three-ply are used on a core of balsa wood, which is one of the lightest woods known. The resulting 'Scotch plywood', as it is called, is only just over half an inch thick, and is enormously strong in relation to its weight. The use of plywood in wartime aircraft construction led furniture manufacturers to experiment with it. Moulded plywood is made as bent plywood is, except that the veneers have to be laid on in narrow-shaped strips—rather like the segments of leather on a football—so as to get the double-curved shape.

PLASTICS (q.v.) are also likely to be widely used for the furniture of the future. Moulded plastics have already been used for the cases of radio sets. Laminated plastics are being used for table tops; these are plastics reinforced during manufacture by sheets of paper or fabric. They are immensely strong and tough, and are ideal for any pieces of furniture that have to stand hard wear (*see* PLASTICS IN INDUSTRY).

Wrought iron is an ancient material that was revived during the acute timber shortage at the end of the Second World War. In olden days it was not greatly used for chairs, chests, or tables, although some tables were supported on frames of wrought iron, and the hinges and handles of chests and cabinets were made from it. But it had a great vogue for gates, for the handles, hinges, and decoration of doors, for standing- and table-lamps, and for the balustrading of staircases. In modern times it has been used once more for standing- and table-lamps, for bedside and other tables, and for

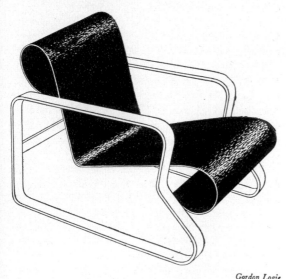

Gordon Logie

A 'FINMAR' CHAIR WITH BENT PLYWOOD SEAT AND BACK AND ARMS OF LAMINATED WOOD

trolleys and electric fires. In earlier days it was usually burnished black; nowadays it is usually painted. It is heavy, but of course practically indestructible, and in certain settings it has grace and attractiveness.

See also CABINET-MAKING; WOODWORK, HISTORY OF.

FUR TRADE. 1. HISTORY. The trade in furs is a very ancient one, but throughout the centuries it has changed its character. It began by being a purely local trade in articles of necessity for people living in northern climates: it still is to-day in such countries. Only where ROMAN CIVILIZATION (q.v. Vol. I) had spread were furs traded outside northern regions with the peoples living in more temperate climates. The trade then ceased to be local and became international, but at the same time it became a trade in luxuries instead of in necessities. As trade in general expanded in Europe during the Middle Ages (*see* TRADE, HISTORY OF), the fur trade expanded also. But it still remained a luxury trade, and this was emphasized by the sumptuary laws allowing only people of high rank to wear furs and rich clothing materials. In the Middle Ages England's sources of supply were north and central Europe, and in the fur trade the HANSEATIC LEAGUE (q.v.) was very prominent: in fact one of its most important depots, or 'factories' as they were called, was at Nijni Novgorod in Russia, which has been a big fur market for centuries. Once North America was colonized, the sources of supply of furs became more varied. The early French settlers were very keen fur-trappers. In the 17th century the HUDSON'S BAY COMPANY (q.v.) was founded to exploit the resources of northern Canada, and it still occupies a leading position in the fur trade of the world.

Since the middle of the 19th century the fur trade, except for the rarest and choicest skins, has ceased to be a luxury trade. There have been several reasons for this change. In the U.S.A. the introduction of centrally heated houses and flats led to a fashion for light indoor clothing, and this made it necessary to put on fairly heavy furs when people went outside. Increased outdoor activities, as well as the invention of the motor-car (which was an open vehicle in early days) made furs popular. The more even distribution of wealth, and the advancing STANDARD OF LIVING (q.v.) in the U.S.A., also helped the trade to increase. Although in Britain central-heating in homes has been comparatively rare, the British market for furs has increased so that furs of the cheaper varieties enter more into the modern trade than previously.

2. SUPPLIES OF FURS. Many furs are trapped and used locally, and are not exported. Those that are exported are usually consigned to AGENTS or BROKERS, and sold by AUCTION (qq.v.) at fixed times every year. Before the Second World War, London, Leipzig, and New York were the most important market centres. Leipzig was the big world market for furs of Russian origin, but its trade was interrupted by the war. London is the chief world market. Public auctions on the London market consist of a small number of furs consigned to outside fur brokers and a larger number imported and sold by the Hudson's Bay Company at their own auction-rooms. The Hudson's Bay Company holds four large sales a year at Beaver Hall in the City of London, and many small special sales. Furs are sold by catalogue and the actual skins are not displayed in the auction rooms. They are stored in various London WAREHOUSES (q.v.), where they can be seen by prospective buyers. The same general methods are used in New York and Leipzig. There is a special London market in Australasian rabbit skins. These skins are becoming increasingly important for the cheaper fur trade. Auctions of rabbit skins are held in London six times a year, where skins are sold not only to manufacturing furriers but also to the Hat Trade.

3. THE FURRIER. A manufacturer of fur is called a furrier. Furs are animal skins with the fur or hair still in place, and before manufacture they need much the same treatment as HIDES AND SKINS (q.v.). The first process is called 'dressing'. This consists of making the skin into soft, pliable leather; thinning down the leathery part of the skin itself, cleaning the whole pelt, and removing foreign bodies and dirt; and preserving and increasing the natural shine or lustre of the fur. The processes for furs are like those described under TANNING (q.v.). After dressing, the next process is dyeing. Of recent years many improvements have been made in the dyes used, and in dyeing methods. Clever dyeing can make many furs attractive that would otherwise look cheap. The fur going under the trade name of 'coney' is actually dyed rabbit. Dyed marmot is a cheap substitute for mink, and dyed musquash for seal. After dyeing, the final process is the actual manufacture of the garments. Formerly this meant sewing together, by hand methods, small skins to make a larger area or garment, but nowadays machines are used. Handicraft, however, is still necessary; one of the most important tradesmen in fur manufacture is the cutter, who still works by hand and on whose skill depend the economical use of the skins and the avoidance of waste.

4. PRINCIPAL FURS. The following are some of the principal furs hunted or farmed. The values, where quoted, were current in 1950. The trade name is used, followed by the correct English name when this is different.

Beaver. This was the most important fur during the early colonization of North America. At one time beavers nearly died out in many states, but they are now protected and give a large annual crop.

Chinchilla is a very soft fur which does not wear well and is not in great demand.

Ermine (Stoat) is the white winter coat of the stoat. It is used particularly for trimming ceremonial robes.

Fox. The two main types are the red fox and the white arctic fox.

(*a*) White (Arctic) Fox. This is found in Arctic regions. The fur is brown in summer and white in winter, the white pelts often being dyed (£10 to £12). The blue arctic is slaty-blue in winter, and from it blue fox fur, which is highly valued, is obtained. Blue fox is now successfully farmed (£5 to £8).

(*b*) Red Fox. This is found in America, Europe, and Russia. The furs are used in great numbers, many being dyed. (32s. to 38s.)

The Silver Fox is a rare variety of the red fox. It used to be an extremely expensive fur, but the silver fox is now successfully farmed in America and Europe. It is a black fur with long silver guard hairs (£8 to £9). Varieties called platinum and white face are now being bred, valued up to £8.

Lamb. Enormous numbers of lamb-skins come from Central Asia, Afghanistan, Persia, India, and South-west Africa under different names —astrakhan, broadtail, caracul, Persian, and Indian. Some are curly coated, others have silk patterns. Nearly all are dyed black or dark brown and are used for less expensive coats and collars. The best Persian lamb skins are very silky, and fetch the highest prices.

Mink. This is one of the most valued and hard

wearing of small furs. Natural mink is a glossy, rich, seal brown; but many new types have been bred on fur farms.

Mole. Large numbers, mostly British and European, are now used mainly for linings and trimmings. The skin is commonly imitated by shorn, dyed, and cut rabbit fur. (80s. per 100.)

Musk-rat or Musquash. The most important fur bearer of North America, several million pelts reaching the market annually. Many skins are plucked or sheared and dyed to represent more valuable fur. It is known also as Hudson seal or seal musquash.

Opossum. The American Opossum has a rather coarse, long and grey fur, with very long lighter coloured guard hairs, which are not removed. It is distinctive in appearance, but low in value (7s. 6d.). The Australian Opossum has very short, close, woolly, smoky-grey fur. It is the chief fur-bearing animal of Australia.

Otter. Several species, mostly from Canada and Russia, are used in the fur trade. The fur is always short, sleek, and durable and usually unhaired.

The Sea Otter, also known in trade as Kamchatka Seal, is probably the most valuable of all furs to-day. It is found only on North Pacific coasts, and recently nearly died out; but under strict protection it is again increasing. It has a rich glossy silver-brown fur. In recent years the largest and darkest skins have fetched as much as £500 and £600. In 1933, out of seven furs on the London market, five averaged over £110 each, and the best sold for £160.

Rabbit. Generally called Coney in the fur trade, rabbit is usually treated by shearing and dyeing to imitate other furs. Some domestic fur rabbits have fur of good quality and colour. (Wild, average 1s. each; domestic varieties 6s. to 7s. each.)

Sable. This is a small brown northern carnivorous animal allied to the martens. The true sable is only found in Siberia, but the Hudson Bay or American Sable (Canadian Marten) is considered by many to produce as fine a fur. It is one of the most important furs from North America (£11 to £13). The Russian or true sable has been hunted until its numbers are seriously reduced; but it is now protected by the Russians, and attempts are being made to farm it. Its beautifully soft fur is a rich yellowish brown, sometimes almost black (£110 to £120.)

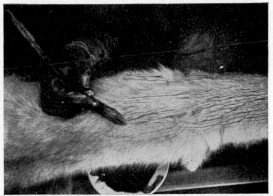

'TIPPING' A FUR WITH A GOOSE FEATHER
After dyeing, colour is added to the tips of the fur

C. W. Martin and Sons

IRONING A FUR WITH A ROTARY IRON
This gives a gloss to the fur

Seal (Alaskan Fur Seal). By far the most important fur seal is this North Pacific species, breeding in great numbers on Primilov and Commander Islands. It used to be killed by the hundred thousand, but is now protected, and limited numbers are taken annually under strict United States Government control. It is the most hard wearing of all fur, and of good appearance. It is nearly always unhaired and dyed. Cape seals are also used.

Squirrel. Great quantities of the Russian and Siberian skins in the thick silver-grey winter coat are used for coats, either natural or dyed. It is a very pretty soft fur, but not very hard wearing. Canadian squirrels are also much used.

Wallaby (Kangaroo). Several species of the smaller kangaroos and wallabies are exported from Australia in large numbers. The fur is short, sandy or brown, and rather poor.

Most of these animals are described in Vol. II. See also Vol. VI: FUR FARMING; FUR HUNTING.

G

GAME, *see* POULTRY AND GAME.

GAS INDUSTRY. The Gas Light and Coke Company, formed by Act of Parliament in 1810, was the first concern in Britain to manufacture gas for street and domestic lighting on a commercial scale. When the gas industry was nationalized in 1949, the company owned the largest gasworks in the world. This is Beckton on the north bank of the Thames, which is supplied with coal by its own fleet of colliers and serves a large part of Greater London.

In 1659 Thomas Shirley had discovered in Lancashire an escape of inflammable gas from the ground. This came very probably from a seam of 'fiery' coal very close to the surface. His discovery greatly interested an Irish clergyman named Clayton, and led him to experiment with the DISTILLATION of coal (q.v.). He successfully produced an inflammable gas, which he collected in bladders. He would then prick a hole in a bladder and ignite the gas to amuse his guests. Like many a leisured gentleman of his time, Clayton was more interested in pure than in applied science, and did not appreciate the industrial possibilities of his experiment. It was not until the end of the following century that the commercial possibilities of gas were proved.

The technical founder of the modern gas industry was William Murdoch, a Scotsman, who was in the service of the famous pioneer steam engineering firm of Boulton and Watt, of Birmingham. He was commissioned by his firm to go to Redruth, in Cornwall, to erect some of their pumping-engines for the local mining industry. Here he experimented with the distillation of gas from coal as Clayton had done, and in 1792 he succeeded in lighting his office with the new gas. In 1807 the first street in London

was lighted and the Gas Light and Coke Company came into being three years later. The plant first used was manufactured for the company by Boulton and Watt. The company's early career was difficult and unprofitable. There was a general prejudice against the new kind of lighting because of its supposed dangers: fire, explosion, and poisonous fumes. The new industry also roused the opposition of the whale fisheries, and the oil and tallow trade hitherto responsible for means of artificial lighting. For the first 5 years of its existence the company paid no DIVIDEND (q.v.), but it managed to pay one in 1817. From that time onwards steady progress was made. Within 10 years from the foundation of the London company many provincial gasworks had been established, and by 1829 there were 200 companies throughout the country.

In these early years there was a good deal of ruinous competition between the different gas companies. Rival companies often ran their mains down the same roads, and sought business from the householders living in them. Shortly after 1850 many rival companies began to amalgamate in self-defence, and to enter into 'zoning' arrangements by which a single company would be alone responsible for supplies in its own allotted district. By the Metropolis Gas Act of 1860 Parliament confirmed these zoning arrangements for London.

To start with, the industry aimed only to supply gas for street lighting and the lighting of factories, warehouses, shops, and public buildings. The early burners were crude, providing a naked jet of flame in the shape of a 'fishtail'. Incandescent lighting, using a 'mantle' of ramie thread, was perfected towards the end of the 19th century. But the companies were greatly interested in other possible uses for gas. James Sharp of Southampton was a pioneer in the use of gas for cookery, and in 1850 he gave a demonstration lecture in Southampton at the Polytechnic Institution. He cooked a meal by gas on the platform, and it was eaten with enjoyment by the audience without any of the ill effects that had been prophesied. The supply of gas for cooking in private houses was soon organized by the companies, and they gradually succeeded in persuading the CATERING INDUSTRY (q.v.) of the advantages of the new system. To-day gas is used for cooking in a very large number of the homes in Britain and equally extensively in catering establishments. Gas fires

Gas Council

GASWORKS AT BECKTON, LONDON, THE LARGEST IN THE WORLD

In the foreground and background are gas holders, one full and the other empty, and in the centre is the carbonizing plant containing the retorts where the coal is distilled in order to produce gas

for the heating of rooms next came into use, but more slowly. They were followed by gas water-heaters, of which the first made its appearance in 1863. The domestic gas refrigerator and the gas clothes airing and drying cabinet were not introduced until the present century.

The modern industrial uses of gas are very widespread. Most industries whose processes depend on heat treatment make some use of it. The bakery, biscuit, and confectionery industries make very considerable use of it. Gas itself, or the coke which is a BY-PRODUCT (q.v.) of gas manufacture, is the fuel principally used for the heating of GLASSHOUSES (q.v. Vol. VI). Modern steel-making would be impossible without gas. It is greatly used in the glass industry. Many of its by-products are important raw materials of the chemical and allied industries. AMMONIA (q.v.) is one; tar is another. Tar is not only indispensable for modern roadmaking, but is also the basis of a long and growing list of useful products. From it come disinfectants, PLASTICS, a number of synthetic DYES and drugs (qq.v.), EXPLOSIVES (q.v. Vol. VIII), food flavourings, insecticides, and many other things. CREOSOTE, which is used for preserving wood,

particularly railway sleepers, comes from tar, and so does benzole, a fuel for INTERNAL COMBUSTION ENGINES (q.v. Vol. VIII).

For a good many years it was thought that gas was not a product which could be transmitted easily over long distances as can electricity. But in fact a 'grid' system, for making the surplus supply of one district available elsewhere, was applied to gas long before it was arranged for the distribution of electricity. In west Yorkshire particularly, where there are large numbers of industrial COKE OVENS (q.v. Vol. VIII) which manufacture coke for ironworks, the large surplus of by-product gas has been put to domestic uses over a wide area by means of lengthy pipe-mains.

For some years the underground production of gas from coal below the surface of the earth has been successfully undertaken in the U.S.A., and in 1950 experiments were made in Britain. The system involves the sinking of two boreholes. Down one of these the air supply will travel to the coal seam, which has been ignited previously by an incendiary cartridge, and up the other borehole the gas will travel to the surface. An advantage of this method is that coal below normal household and industrial quality can be turned into useful fuel instead of being left unmined.

The gas industry was one of the pioneers of CO-PARTNERSHIP (q.v.) and profit-sharing in Britain. The first company to adopt this system in 1889 was the South Metropolitan Gas Company. By 1949, when the industry was nationalized and co-partnership arrangements were ended, more than half the gas undertakings in the Kingdom had followed the example of the South Metropolitan Company.

See also Vol. VIII: GAS MANUFACTURE.
See also Vol. X: STREET SERVICES.

GLASS-MAKING.

1. Glass was long believed to have been the chance discovery of some Phoenician merchants camping on a sandy shore in Syria thousands of years ago. They took some large lumps of carbonate of soda from their cargo and used them to support their cooking-pots over the fire. Next morning in the cold ashes they found lumps of glass, made by the melting of the sand in the presence of the ALKALI (q.v.). This story, related by Pliny the Elder in his *Natural History*, is now discredited, and according to the great archaeologist, Sir Flinders Petrie, glass was being regularly made in ancient Babylonia much earlier than this. Glass is still made to-day by heating together in a furnace some form of silica (sand, flint, or quartz: *see* MINERALS, Vol. III) with an alkaline 'flux' (usually potash or soda) which helps it to melt. In the great heat obtainable in some modern furnaces no flux is needed, and glass is occasionally made from silica alone.

The earliest glass that has come down to us is in the form of stone beads coated with blue glass, much in the same way as metals are covered with ENAMEL (q.v.). These beads were found in Egypt, and may date from as early as 4000 B.C. For at least 2,000 years after this glass was used only for ornament, in imitation of precious stones. It was coloured, just as it is to-day, by the addition of various metallic oxides (*see* METAL ORES, Vol. III), such as chromium for green, cobalt for blue, and manganese for pinkish-purple. This very early glass let the light through, but was not transparent; and its natural tint, if not artificially coloured, was greenish. In time it was discovered that greater transparency and crystal whiteness could be given by adding an oxide of manganese, which came to be known as 'glassmakers' soap'.

2. HAND-MADE GLASS. The first glass vessels were made by winding threads of hot molten glass round and round cores of clay, which were then withdrawn. But the great landmark in the history of glass-making was the discovery in Syria, just before the Christian era, that glass could be 'blown'. Hand-blowing, as it is rather wrongly called, is a method still used to-day. One end of a long iron tube is dipped into a fireclay pot or crucible of red-hot molten glass. When enough of the sticky 'metal' (the word used by glass-blowers) has been gathered on the end of the tube, it is swung clear of the furnace and given a round shape by being rolled on an

1. MOULDED CHAMPAGNE GLASS WITH TWIST STEM, ENGLISH, 1750–80

2. CUT GLASS TUMBLER WITH ENGRAVED DECORATION, ENGLISH, 1791

Ashmolean Museum

3. WINE GLASS, VENETIAN, 19TH CENTURY

MAKING LEAD CRYSTAL GLASS AT STOURBRIDGE, WORCS.
The man in the centre is 'gathering' molten glass in the furnace; on the right it is being 'marvered', and on the left
a workman is shaping the blown glass in a 'chair'

iron table called a 'marver'. Seated in a 'chair' with long flat parallel arms, the craftsman blows down the other end of the tube, producing a bubble in the glass. With wonderful skill he gives this the final shape he wants, periodically returning it to the mouth of the crucible to keep it soft enough for working. He may make the bubble longer by swinging the rod around him, or shorter by spinning or rolling it along the arms of his chair; he may pinch or shape it with tools or cut it with shears; when he has finished blowing he may transfer it to an iron rod called a 'punty' (or 'pontil'). All the time he keeps revolving it, so that it retains its round shape and stays in a central position on the tube or rod instead of sagging downwards.

A method of glass-blowing that needs less skill, and so may actually be older than the system just described, is for the bubble to be blown inside a mould of baked clay or stone, whose shape the finished glass vessel then retains. A mechanical form of this process is widely used to-day for making in metal moulds such articles as bottles and electric bulbs by automatic machinery (*see* Section 3).

Window-glass called for special methods in order to produce flat panes. Although the Romans in their later days had made small panes of window-glass by casting them on a flat bed, window-glass was made by blowing in the Middle Ages and until the invention of glass-making machinery in the 19th century. Very few dwellings had glass in their windows before the end of the Middle Ages; windows were closed with a leather curtain or a wooden shutter (*see* WINDOWS, Vol. XI); glass was, however, used for churches in those days. In making window-glass two methods were used. For 'crown' glass a bubble was blown, transferred to a punty, and then alternately heated and spun until it finally opened out to a flat disk, which might be as much as 4 feet across. It was then cut free from the punty with shears, and into the required size. As glass in those days was very expensive to make, the central piece with the 'bullion' or blob left by the punty was generally used as well as the flat sheets, and this is often seen in ancient windows. By the other method, used for making what was called 'broad' glass, a bubble was blown and then swung round until it lengthened out to a cylinder. The ends of this were cut off, and it was then cut with shears along its length, and flattened. This method is still used to make the old-style glass used for stained-glass windows.

In the course of the centuries the peoples of many lands had carried on and improved the craft of glass-making. During the Dark Ages the craft was kept alive by the Franks and the Gauls, to whom it had been introduced by the Romans. Documents of the 7th and 8th centuries tell of requests from Britain for the sending over of continental glass-makers, and in the 13th century the glass industry had become well established in the south-eastern counties of England. The glass-makers had to move about from place to place in search of fresh timber, owing to the great amount of wood burned in melting the glass; and because of this the glass of this time was known as *waldglas*, or 'forest glass'. It had a beautiful greenish tinge.

By the 13th century also the famous glass-makers of the city of Venice had brought to a high state of perfection a glass very different from the *waldglas* of the north. Venetian glass was almost colourless, like ROCK-CRYSTAL (q.v. Vol. III), from which it got its local name of *cristallo*. Venetian glass vessels of this period were very beautiful. The stems of the goblets and glasses were swelled out into 'knops' or bulges, possibly containing an air bubble, or into graceful baluster shapes, and ended in wide firm bases. The glass was often engraved by means of a diamond point. Venetian glass-makers were brought to England, and for over 100 years Venetian glass was made in London.

England contributed the next great advance in glass-making. In 1674 George Ravenscroft invented 'flint glass', sometimes called 'glass of lead' because it used lead oxide as a flux. The new glass was heavier than Venetian and even closer in appearance to natural rock-crystal. Although it melted at a lower temperature than Venetian glass, it never flowed as easily, and so it was not as well suited for blowing thin. By the end of the 17th century nearly 100 glass-makers were making flint glass in Britain, and within the next 50 years English glass reached its highest level of artistic design.

The 18th century saw the introduction into England of an entirely different method of decorating glass, by 'cutting' or grinding it away by pressing it against a revolving copper or iron disk fed with emery and water or else corundum and oil. This method worked particularly well with flint glass, but was checked by a heavy tax levied by the Government between 1745 and 1845, which made it more profitable to make glassware of a lighter design and less suitable for deep cutting. Glass-makers evaded the duty by setting up works in Ireland, and some famous glassware was produced at such places as Waterford, Cork, and Dublin.

3. MACHINE-MADE GLASS. Meanwhile mechanical methods and new processes were being invented. The first large factory for casting plate-glass was opened in England in 1773. In 1810 England was also responsible for the invention of a mechanical method of pressing glass vessels in moulds of the shape of the outside of the vessel. In 1886 the first automatic bottle-making machine was patented.

To-day the highest quality glass vessels are still hand-blown, but most modern glass is produced mechanically. Hollow vessels are made either in pressing or blowing machines, according to their shape. Such articles as dishes, jars, plates, lenses, bowls, and thick tumblers are fashioned by an automatic pressure plunger which descends on to molten glass poured into a mould. Blowing machines are of several types, and are worked by compressed air. What are called 'press and blow'

Chance Bros.

AUTOMATIC MACHINE FOR PRESSING AND MOULDING GLASS
Tumblers are being removed from the moulds

machines make wide-mouthed ware such as jam-jars and milk-bottles. Other blowing-machines, called 'blow and blow' machines, make hollow ware with narrower necks in two stages. The first machine makes what is called a 'parison', which is a glass shape with a neck of the proper size but with the body of the vessel smaller and thicker than is finally desired. The parison is then transferred to a mould, where it is given a second blowing and is finally shaped. Electric bulbs have long been made in Britain on a type of machine which can produce nearly 100,000 bulbs a day, but machinery of American design has now increased output, and one kind of machine has an output of nearly one million bulbs a day.

Sheet glass for windows is drawn out through rollers. Plate glass is poured in a molten state over a casting table of iron. As it pours out it is rolled by a massive iron roller into a sheet, and after being re-heated in an ANNEALING furnace (q.v. Vol. VIII) is cut, ground by water and sand, and polished with rouge by felt rubbers. Thin plate glass is made at less expense by squeezing out a continuous ribbon of glass between two rollers, instead of using a casting table. Wired safety glass is made by unrolling wire netting over sheets of glass during manufacture, while a fresh layer of glass is rolled on top so as to 'sandwich' the netting within. Laminated safety glass of patented types is made from sheet or sometimes from well-polished plate glass. A layer of transparent cellulose material (see PLASTICS) is sandwiched between two layers of glass and is then subjected to high pressure in a hydraulic press (see Vol. VIII, p. 213). Such glass is reasonably safe when fractured, because the splinters stick to the internal layer of cellulose.

Pyrex or fireproof glass is made, by all the methods above described, from a mixture of silica and boric oxide. Optical glass also is made by the same methods as ordinary glass, but as it must be of the same consistency and transparency in every part it is necessary to stir the mixture constantly during melting and manufacture. The secret of successful stirring was discovered by a Swiss in 1790. The raw materials for optical glass must be extremely pure, and great care must be taken in mixing and refining them.

See also Vol. XI: GLASS WARE.
See also Vol. XII: STAINED GLASS.

GOLD AND SILVER WORK. 1. HISTORY.

Gold and silver were found and worked almost as soon as man began to use metals at all. Both metals are found in a nearly pure state, often together, and objects were made of the natural alloy as well as of the pure metals.

At first gold and silver were used chiefly for jewellery and small objects (see JEWELLERY TRADE), though the Egyptians covered with gold plates the mummy cases and wooden objects placed in tombs. The Cretans (see MINOAN CIVILIZATION, Vol. I) made gold drinking-cups decorated with scenes in relief. The Greeks made statues with a wooden core covered with gold and set with precious stones. Nearly pure gold was used in early times. This is soft, and was worked principally by beating with a hammer. It was also pulled into wire. Weapons were decorated with gold inlay on bronze, or with gold plates; silver bowls were engraved or embossed.

Few early examples of the goldsmith's work have escaped destruction, but some treasures, buried for safety, have been found. Torques—twisted gold neck-bands—show the characteristic richness of Celtic ornaments. Silver bowls, probably brought from Rome or Byzantium, have been found in Saxon graves.

In the Middle Ages the work of goldsmiths reached a high technical level. Most of the work which survived was made for churches: chalices, crosses, and, richest of all, the shrines of saints. These were often covered with gold and inlaid with precious stones and decorated with ENAMEL (q.v.).

In the 16th century goldsmiths and silversmiths generally worked for customers who commissioned objects such as salt-cellars and plates to decorate their houses and especially their tables. Hans HOLBEIN and other eminent artists made designs for silverware, and the Italian goldsmith Benvenuto CELLINI (qq.v. Vol. V) made very many beautiful pieces, including a large golden salt-cellar for the Pope.

The heavy and ornate gold and silver plate of the 17th century gave place to a lighter style in the 18th century. On the Continent objects were decorated in the Rococo style of the period (q.v. Vol. XII), but in England a simpler and more classical style was preferred. Robert ADAM (q.v. Vol. V) designed silver teapots and candlesticks of a style in keeping with his houses and furniture.

Norman Wymer

'PLANISHING' THE BODY OF A SILVER CUP

The body has been beaten into shape from a flat piece of silver

Norman Wymer

SOLDERING THE SPOUT TO A TEAPOT

The body of the pot, the spout, and the handle are moulded separately

The taste for heavy ornament in the 19th century is seen in the gold and silver work of the period, but in the 20th century there has been a return to simpler designs. The same methods of working the metals have been used continuously since the earliest times, although handwork is now much more assisted by machinery. And the same methods of decoration, chasing, engraving, repoussé, and inlay, are still used.

In the year 1327 the Goldsmiths Company (*see* CITY COMPANIES) was incorporated. It was responsible for the quality of the work of craftsmen, both in material and in design, and for the ASSAYING (q.v.) and hall-marking of gold and silver ware. It still seeks to promote good design and watch the interests of its craftsmen.

2. METHOD. Gold and silver are easily worked; in their pure state they are highly malleable (that is, they can be bent and flattened by hammering), and can be cut with a knife. The raw material is supplied by the bullion and assaying firms, who smelt the ores (*see* SMELTING, Vol. VIII) and make the gold and silver sheet and wire for the craftsmen. Pure gold and silver

are so soft that another metal must be added to make an ALLOY (q.v. Vol. VIII) strong enough for modern manufacture; pure copper is generally used. For instance, 18-carat gold is 18 parts of gold and 6 parts of copper; 24 carat is pure gold. What is called 'sterling' silver is 925 parts silver to 75 parts copper, though our silver coins of to-day have much less silver in them than this. Modern silver which bears the 'hall-mark' (*see* ASSAYING) is of this guaranteed quality. Silver is also made in other proportions for other uses.

Silver is generally used for articles for the table and for household use, and for ceremonial occasions (*see* TABLE SILVER, Vol. XI). Gold is used for more personal things such as JEWELLERY (q.v. Vol. XI), or serves to enrich silver objects. The working of the two metals is much alike. Whichever metal is used, it is first cleaned by 'pickling' or 'annealing'. To pickle, the metal is placed in a bath of warm sulphuric acid diluted with water. A few moments of immersion clean and dissolve any dirt which may be on the surface of the metal, which is then ready to be worked upon. ANNEALING (q.v. Vol. VIII) is the process of bringing the metal to a dull red heat (not more than 670–740° C.) on the forge with the aid of a blow-pipe. This burns off any dirt and evens out any stresses and strains in the metal, making it soft enough to work.

To make a beaker or vase, a sheet of metal of the required thickness is marked out, and cut to a circle of the correct size. It is then 'domed' into a cup-like shape by being beaten with a doming-hammer into a hollowed block of wood. Before the next process, it must be annealed again. It is next 'raised', by being placed on a steel stake the shape of the finished vase, and beaten with a raising-hammer. In this process the metal is hammered in upon the stake in concentric circles, until the rim is reached. The repeated hammering hardens the metal, and so occasional annealings, to soften it, will be necessary before the shape is perfect. The metal will be covered with the marks from the blows of the raising hammer, and these have to be removed with the planishing hammer. This hammer has an almost flat, polished steel face which leaves flat marks on the metal. These are made to overlap each other in concentric rings, so that in time the raising marks are smoothed out.

The foot of the vase is made in a similar way— only, of course, from a smaller piece of metal. A ring of stout wire is generally soldered to it to give it strength and stability. To ensure a proper union between the solder and the metal surfaces to be joined, a chemical substance known as a 'flux' is needed; this dissolves the oxides in the metal and solder, and prevents oxides from forming during the heating process. In gold- and silver-work the flux used is borax, ground up and mixed with water into a creamy paste. This is painted on those parts of the work where the solder is required to run. The foot is then heated in a forge until the solder melts—which it does at a temperature only just below the melt-ing-point of the metal. By this action the foot becomes soldered to the body, and the work is ready to be decorated. The vase can be chased or repoussèd, engraved and carved, inlaid, enamelled, nielloed or colour-treated, gilded or silvered, or embellished by being encrusted with filigree (metallic lacework) and precious stones.

3. CHASING AND REPOUSSÉ are applied either to beaten objects or to castings. Repoussé work is modelled in relief (from the back) by means of punches and a special hammer. In chasing, which gives a much sharper, clearer effect than repoussé, the design is cut in the face of the metal

Ashmolean Museum

JAMES II GOLD DOUBLE WATCHCASE

Repoussé and pierced work with the bust of the king be-tween the figure of Fame and cherubs; below, a ship and a fortress. (Actual size)

Ashmolean Museum

SILVER EWER, 1727–8

The decoration around the top and foot is chased and engraved, the coat of arms engraved. The applied straps are cast and the handle is cast and chased with chisels or gravers. The term 'chasing' is also used for the 'finishing' of cast surfaces, when blemishes and rough projections are removed, and the surface and ornamentation are cleaned up and sharpened.

4. ENGRAVING is much like chasing. It is usually applied to flat surfaces, the designs being carried out with gravers and scorpers. The designs are first 'pointed' on to the object with a steel point, either freehand or by tracing, and are then followed all over with the graver, which is a very sharp-pointed tool of hardened steel. This removes a thin shaving, or 'sliver' of metal, and leaves in the surface of the metal a thin furrow or trough; this is V-shaped, and has a brilliant, glittering look from the sharpness of the cutting tool. The scorper is used rather like a wood chisel, paring away a broad shaving of metal; in this way designs can easily be cut in low relief. For objects afterwards decorated with ENAMEL (q.v.), particularly rich effects can be got with the graver and scorper, since the flash of the cut metal shows through the transparent enamel.

5. INLAYS are made by piercing and cutting out shapes of different metals, and fitting them into one another to make a design, the whole forming a band or motive which can then be applied to a larger article. 'Damascening' is an inlay of gold and silver wire on iron or steel. The name comes from Damascus, where this art was used at the time of the Crusades for the decoration of weapons.

6. NIELLO is a process of great antiquity, which has for centuries been used in the East. It has even been found on objects taken from very ancient

Ashmolean Museum

SILVER WATCHCASE, EARLY 17TH CENTURY

With design in niello

Egyptian tombs (*see* EGYPTIAN CIVILIZATION Vol. I). Niello is a black alloy of silver, lead, copper, and sulphur, which melts easily. When melted into the channels left by an engraved design, it shows the decoration as black upon a silver or gold background.

7. SILVER GILT is a way of covering silver with a thin film of gold. The oldest and best method is to apply an amalgam (or mixture) of gold and mercury to the surface. The modern commercial way of gilding is by ELECTRO-PLATING (q.v. Vol. VIII).

8. POLISHING. This process needs great care. After any work in silver has been cleaned in a pickling bath, its surface is 'stoned' carefully all over: that is, it is rubbed with a substance called 'water-of-Ayre stone'. This removes the film of oxide formed on the work during annealing, and all file-marks and scratches. It is then polished with charcoal and oil to which a little crocus powder is added, then by rouge and paraffin. After being washed in hot soapy water and dried, an application of dry rouge on a chamois leather gives it the most brilliant finish. Gold is polished in the same way, except that, after the charcoal and oil process, all plain surfaces are burnished over with steel or agate burnishers and finished with rouge and water. Silver is sometimes oxidized to tone down its glaring whiteness. This can be done by exposing it to the fumes of sulphuretted ammonia or other chemical compounds of sulphur. Ammonium sulphide, the material most generally used, gives a range of colour from purplish-black to a pale golden straw, the depth of colour depending on the strength of the solution and the length of time the article is exposed to it. Gold can be coloured in the same way, if it is first warmed until almost too hot to handle.

See also GOLD-MINING; SILVER-MINING; ASSAYING; JEWELLERY TRADE.

GOLD-MINING. Gold is one of the few metals to be found in the earth's crust in actual metallic form (*see* METAL ORES, Vol. III). Gold neither rusts nor tarnishes, being the most 'noble' of all metals, and it is found in many widely scattered regions throughout the world as 'native gold'.

In ancient times gold possibly first caught the eye of man as bright yellow particles or small nuggets. These would have been found in pockets in the dried-out beds of rivers flowing through regions of gold-bearing rocks. Such rivers, through the centuries, caused the rocks to disintegrate and washed away the resulting sand and mud, leaving the heavy metallic gold concentrated in crevices, particularly in the slower-running reaches of the rivers.

The earliest important sources of gold were

probably the river-washed (alluvial) deposits of Abyssinia and various parts of central Africa. Here, and later in India, China, and in many regions of which we have no record, gold was collected through the centuries by simply washing the light sand from the heavy gold. Very infrequently large nuggets of gold occur in river gravels. The Blanche Barkley nugget found in Australia weighed 146 lb. The largest recorded nugget was the Welcome Stranger, found in 1869 in a cartwheel rut in Victoria. This weighed 183 lb.

Most alluvial or 'placer' deposits are soon worked out. In the days when they were the only source of gold, production was scanty and spasmodic. In many countries, therefore, efforts were made to extract the gold from the various hard rocks, in which it existed as 'veins' or 'reefs'. The first operation was to crush the rock. Hollowed-out stones, in which the gold-bearing quartz could be crushed by stone hammers, or by large rocks worked by levers, have been found in Wales, central America, the Pyrenees, and Transylvania in south-east Europe; and the methods used in the mines of Upper Egypt 1,900 years ago have been described by Diodorus Siculus, the Greek historian.

In these early gold-mines the ore was first crushed to a fine powder, and then washed with water. The heavy particles of gold settled to the bottom of the hollow stone-container or mortar, and the worthless lighter material was washed away. It was, however, always difficult to prevent the smaller and finer particles of gold from being carried away with the water and powdered rock and lost. To prevent this, the water and sand were allowed to trickle over raw sheepskins or goatskins, in which the flakes of gold became entangled, and this probably gave rise to the legend of the Golden Fleece.

A big step was taken over 2,000 years ago when mercury was first used as a collector of gold. If a pulp of crushed ore and water is ground with mercury, the gold forms a stiff amalgam with the mercury. The amalgam is easily collected and washed free from the rocky material, and is then heated in simple retorts. The mercury is vaporized and distilled over, ready to be used again, and the gold is left as a residue, which can later be melted and refined.

Until the middle of the 19th century gold was mined on a small scale by these simple methods. In the Middle Ages Hungary and Transylvania

Canadian National Film Board

PANNING FOR GOLD IN YUKON TERRITORY, N.W. CANADA

were the most important centres of gold-mining in Europe. Later, from about 1750 to 1850, gold was discovered in the Ural Mountains, Brazil, Mexico, Peru, and Chile. But none of the new deposits was worked energetically, and until about 1830 the world's output of new gold appears to have remained steady at about 12 tons a year, or 400,000 troy ounces by the goldsmiths' measure. From 1830 to 1850 output started to rise slowly, mainly because gold was found in Siberia, where it lay in alluvial deposits of ancient rivers (see ROCKS, Section 3, Vol. III).

In 1849 gold was discovered by Colonel Suter in California, and then began the first of a series of 'gold-rushes' which were to recur at intervals for the rest of the century. The inhabitants of San Francisco rushed to the diggings as soon as they heard the news, and were later joined by emigrants from all over the world; ships were diverted from their ordinary routes to bring them from as far away as China or Australia. By the end of 1849 nearly 100,000 emigrants had poured into 'the Golden State', as California was called. People flocked in from the towns in the eastern states, travelling by sea, or over land in trains of covered wagons. The overcrowding caused the most appalling conditions: many, far from making their fortunes, died of starvation or disease before they even reached the diggings. The miners of this period, like the one in the song *Clementine*, were called 'forty-niners'. Two years later, rich deposits of gold were found in Australia by the Californian gold-digger Hargreaves, and in 1884 gold was found in South Africa, in the Transvaal. The Klondike region of the Yukon, in north-west Canada, was first exploited in 1896, and the last of the great gold-rushes took place in 1900, to the Nome area in Alaska, the United States territory beyond north-west Canada.

In all these areas the metal was found in rich but comparatively shallow deposits near the surface, so that gold-mining was an individual operation, and at first a sheet-iron pan was all the equipment needed. This was filled to about one-third of its capacity with 'pay-dirt', and water was added. After the contents had been mixed, the pan was shaken so that the mud slipped over the edges of the pan, leaving the yellow specks of gold at the centre.

Soon after the first gold-rush to California in 1849, a more specialized piece of apparatus, the 'cradle' or 'rocker', was introduced. This was a wooden box, 3 to 6 feet long and about 18 inches wide, fitted in a sloping position on rockers like those then used for children's cradles, and provided with crosswise slats nailed to the bottom. One man shovelled in the sand and gravel through a screen or sieve at one end, and the cradle was rocked by a second man who poured on water from a dipper filled from a nearby water-hole. The sand was thus well mixed with the water, the lighter material was washed away, and the gold particles were trapped in the pockets at the base. Sometimes a little mercury was added to help to catch the gold.

Cradles were soon replaced by 'sluice boxes', wherever water was available in quantities. These often consisted of hundreds of boxes, with slats or 'riffles' nailed in various patterns to the bottom which trapped the gold from the sand, as this was washed through them by water from a diverted stream. The boxes were 'cleaned-up' at regular intervals, and on these occasions it was often necessary to station a man with a shot-gun to guard against raiders.

As a result of the gold-rushes the world production of gold during the years 1850 to 1890 jumped to an average of 150 tons a year. Nearly all of this was collected by simple means. By 1905, however, the cream of the rich alluvial deposits had been skimmed off, and the Witwatersrand or Rand in South Africa had become the world's chief producer of gold. Here, and in other major gold-producing regions of the world at the present time, it has become necessary to quarry and mine for the gold-bearing rock. Gold-mining is no longer a one-man adventure, but has become a highly organized industry. The first step is, as before, to crush the ore finely and to set free the gold particles; for this purpose heavy mechanically operated stamps are still widely used. Each stamp weighs from half a ton to a ton; it is raised by a cam to a height of about 10 inches and then dropped so as to pound the ore in a steel 'mortar box' at 60 to 90 strokes a minute. The steady roar of hundreds of stamps in action is heard in gold-mines day and night in South Africa, Australia, and California. Water is usually fed into the mortar boxes with the ore, and the resulting pulp is then led away in channels for further treatment.

When stamps are used, the larger particles of gold are usually recovered by amalgamation. Sometimes mercury is added to the mortar boxes during stamping; more usually, nowadays, the pulp coming from the mortar boxes is made to flow over copper plates covered with a film of mercury. The stiff amalgam of gold and mercury which is formed is treated for the recovery of the gold. Even under the best conditions, however, it is not possible to recover all the finer particles of gold by amalgamation; and if the gold in the ore is contaminated with other metals only a very small proportion of actual gold may be recovered.

By far the most important process for treating gold ores is the cyanide process, which was first used in 1890 at a mine in Johannesburg. It rapidly replaced all other methods of treating gold ores, and in a few years cyanide plants were to be found in all gold areas of the world. A very weak solution of sodium or potassium cyanide (usually containing only 0·02 to 0·05% of the cyanide) will dissolve gold (and silver). Oxygen must be present, and the solutions must therefore be well aerated. To operate the process, the gold-bearing ore is crushed finely, either by stamps or rollers, or in various kinds of ball or

South African Railways

POURING REFINED MOLTEN GOLD INTO MOULDS

tube mills—rotating horizontal cylinders in which hard steel balls or rods reduce the charge of rock to powder. The method of crushing depends on the nature of the rock. The crushed ore is then transferred to large circular steel vats, where it is treated with the weak cyanide solution.

After all the gold has been dissolved, the cyanide solution is decanted from the ore and powdered zinc is stirred into the liquid. The zinc is attacked and dissolved by the cyanide, and the gold and silver are rejected and thrown out of the solution as a fine mud. The precious metals thus 'precipitated' are recovered by filtering the solutions through cloth, and are cleaned with acids and melted in clay crucibles or open pots.

The gold obtained in this way, as well as the gold obtained by amalgamation or by panning, is never pure, and may contain up to 50% of silver, as well as appreciable quantities of copper, lead, iron, and other base metals. It is usually melted in small clay crucibles placed in a coke fire, and cast into bars of 'crude bullion'. This crude mixture of many metals needs to be refined. The modern method of refining is the chlorine process. The bullion is simply melted again in a clay crucible, and a stream of gaseous chlorine, from a cylinder of the compressed gas, is passed through the melt from a clay pipe

which dips below the surface. In these conditions the chlorine combines with the silver and with any of the base metals present, and forms chlorides which collect as a crust on the surface. When all the impurities have been removed, the gold is cast into bars, ready for use.

The chlorine process rapidly and cheaply refines gold to a fineness of 99·6%, but it does not remove platinum itself or any of the platinum group of metals. If platinum metals are present, or if gold of the highest possible purity is needed, the gold may be refined electrolytically by the Wohwill process, a modified electro-plating operation (*see* ELECTRO-PLATING and ELECTRO-LYSIS, Vol. VIII).

See also MINING; ASSAYING.
See also Vol. III: METAL ORES.
See also Vol. XI: JEWELLERY.

GOLDSMITH BANKERS, *see* BANKING.

GOODWILL. In the business world this word means the money value of a firm's reputation and connexion among its customers. This value may have been built up for years by the special qualities of the owner, partners, or directors of a business; or the business may possess secret or patent processes of its own, or have specially valuable connexions, or be situated in some exceptionally favourable place. Notices are often seen to the effect that a firm has acquired the goodwill and assets of another firm: in other words, it has taken over not only its buildings, plant, and other assets, but also this extra earning power built up in the past.

Goodwill may therefore be an extremely valuable asset; but it is seldom entered in the account-books as one, unless new partners are being taken in, or if the firm is being taken over by another firm, or is being 'wound up' for any reason such as BANKRUPTCY (q.v. Vol. X), and so ceases to exist. Partners or directors selling a valuable business can often get the purchaser to pay a large sum for goodwill. This will vary, and will depend on whether the business is steady and solid or merely speculative. Goodwill is usually calculated on the basis of so many years' 'purchase' of average PROFITS (q.v.). Thus, a firm in a steady line of business whose profits have averaged £2,000 a year might reasonably ask £6,000 for goodwill—or '3 years' purchase' of average profits. But no hard and fast rule for calculating the value of goodwill can be laid down: it depends very much on the state of trade, and on business confidence in general, at the particular time when it is being estimated.

See also LIMITED COMPANIES.

GOVERNMENT LOANS, see INTERNATIONAL FINANCE.

GRANITE, see STONE QUARRYING.

GRAPHITE is of the same chemical composition as DIAMOND (q.v. Vol. III); both are forms of carbon. The great difference between the two is that the diamond is the hardest mineral known and graphite is one of the softest. Graphite occurs in nature in the free state, as veins in igneous or volcanic rocks and limestones (see ROCKS, Section 2, Vol. III). 'Plumbago' and 'blacklead', the common names for graphite, are apt to mislead. Plumbago suggests the Latin word for lead, which is *plumbum*, and blacklead actually includes the word lead, but graphite has nothing to do with lead.

Graphite is not very widely distributed. The principal deposits are in Ontario in Canada, and in Siberia, Mexico, and Ceylon. There were important English graphite mines at Borrowdale in Cumberland, but they are now

Royal Sovereign Pencil Co

MAKING PENCILS

The lead slips (made of graphite) have been pressed into shape and are ready for their wooden cases

almost exhausted. Until recently the world relied on natural sources for its supplies, but graphite can now be made artificially from other forms of carbon. Powdered carbon or powdered anthracite can be hardened into graphite by ELECTROLYSIS (q.v. Vol. VIII). Graphite can also be made artificially from carbon in the high temperatures of the electric furnace.

Graphite has many uses in modern industry. It is used to make crucibles, or heat-resisting containers, for treating metals and other substances in furnaces. Lubricants of a semi-solid nature are made from it, particularly those used for the chain-drives of bicycles and motor-cycles. It is one of the principal ingredients of grate-polish and some of the metal-polishes. It is used for electrodes in arc lamps, and in dynamos and magnetos for the carbon brushes which pick up the electric current. The most widely known use of graphite is for making pencils, and for this purpose Cumberland graphite was renowned.

GREENGROCERY. This trade deals with fruit and vegetables, which pass through various channels to be sold mainly in shops, municipal markets, street markets, and by hawkers or barrowmen. A small amount of trade is done direct with householders by Bretons and other Frenchmen who travel round the country selling onions brought from Brittany. Greengrocers themselves are not the only people to sell green-groceries, for nowadays many grocers handle them. In country districts wholesale green-grocery firms distribute to village grocers' shops; they can cover a wide area with lorries driven by travelling salesmen.

More fruit is imported than is produced in Britain, and many overseas countries contribute to British supplies. Bananas were introduced in the 1890's. In the early days they arrived rather irregularly and spasmodically from the Canary Islands—some hard and green, which no amount of nursing was ever likely to get into an edible condition, and some ripening so fast that they went black and rotten before they could be sold. In 1901 bananas were first brought from the West Indies, and since then the trade has been very highly organized, and a special fleet of banana steamers runs regularly between the West Indies and Avonmouth docks, near Bristol. Early ripening methods were rather haphazard, and on arrival the bananas were hung in the sun,

COVENT GARDEN MARKET IN THE 19TH CENTURY
Covent Garden became a fruit and vegetable market in the middle of the 17th century

or smothered in damp straw or sacks, in order to make them ripen. Heated rooms have now been installed, where the bunches can be kept for some time in a humid atmosphere; this results in quicker, more thorough, and more even ripening, and in clean, well-coloured, and mellow fruits. Grapes—hot-house, cold-house, and outdoor— are grown in Britain and the Channel Islands, and come also from many countries abroad. Among Commonwealth countries, Australia and the Union of South Africa are prominent; and Spain, Portugal, France, and Italy are important suppliers. Imported apples come principally from Canada, Australia, and New Zealand. The trade in citrus fruits (oranges, lemons, and grapefruit) is of modern growth. In the early days Spanish and Jaffa oranges were the only ones seen in the British market, but nowadays North and South Africa, Brazil, and Australia send in large quantities. The producing countries have their own marketing and packing organizations, and these maintain a high standard of quality and grading. The Citrus Fruit Exchange of South Africa controls the marketing and advertising of citrus fruits in that country, and there are similar organizations in other countries. London, Liverpool, Hull, and Manchester are the principal import ports. Grapefruit come from the orange-producing countries. Spain and Italy are the chief sources of supply of lemons, but they come also from Cyprus,

Palestine, Syria, Brazil, and the Union of South Africa.

Refrigerated ships were first used for fruit about the beginning of this century. All fruit that travels for more than 10 days has to come

Fox Photos

COVENT GARDEN TO-DAY
A porter carrying fruit baskets

in one of them, and their use has made it possible for us to eat oranges, apples, grapes, and other fruit all the year round. A refrigerated fruit ship has a carrying capacity of between 250,000 and 500,000 cubic feet of cargo.

Britain imports a smaller share of vegetables than of fruit, for most vegetables are highly perishable and cannot be transported very far. Tomatoes are imported in large quantities. They first came on the British market in the 1890's, Their introduction was difficult at first as people were not quite certain whether they were vegetables or fruit; some people thought they were a queer kind of plum, to be eaten with sugar. Glasshouse tomatoes are grown in parts of Britain on almost industrial lines, particularly in the Lea Valley, between Enfield and Brox-bourne, north of London. The glasshouse industry is also highly organized in Guernsey and Holland. Valencia, Italy, the Canary Islands, and North Africa add to these supplies with large quantities grown in the open.

See also CANNING INDUSTRY; GROCERY AND PROVISIONS.
See also Vol. VI: GLASSHOUSES; VEGETABLE GARDEN; FRUIT GROWING; CITRUS FRUITS.

GROCERY AND PROVISIONS.

The trade of grocer is a very ancient one, although the goods in which the grocer deals have changed much throughout the years. The early grocers in England were called 'pepperers', and the current French word for grocer is *épicier*, which literally means 'spicer'. The early English pepperers dealt mainly in peppers and spices from the East, which were brought over every year by the fleets of Venetian sailing galleys which then did the carrying trade between northern Europe and the East.

Our modern word 'grocer' comes from the French *grossier*, which means 'wholesale dealer'. The first Grocers Guild or Company was founded in 1345 by a score or more of pepperers of the City of London. Like other guilds it soon developed into a Livery Company of wealthy merchants, who were wholesale and not retail dealers. Later the word 'grocer' was used by retail dealers in what we now call 'groceries', and the older title of pepperer or spicer has been given up.

After the Middle Ages wholesale and retail grocers began to deal in far more goods than before. In the middle of the 17th century tea, coffee, and cocoa were imported from abroad,

and became popular new beverages. At that time grocers dealt principally in those three articles; also in spices; in certain cereals, particu-larly rice; in currants, raisins, prunes, and similar dried fruits, and nuts; and in delicacies such as olives and anchovies, which came from nearby countries and could be sold quickly in the days before it was known how to preserve food. Most grocers were also provision dealers, and dealt in bacon, butter, and cheese.

At the end of the 19th century many more foods were being dealt in by the grocer. Bottling, canning, and other methods of preserving foods had been invented, and certain things that had hitherto been prepared only in the home, such as jam, cakes, biscuits, sauces, chutneys, and pickles, were made in factories. Improvements in the manufacture of MARGARINE, and in the methods of COLD STORAGE (qq.v.) in the ware-house and the shop, have in the present century enlarged the range of groceries and provisions still further.

The grocer and provision-merchant of to-day deals in the widest range of goods of any retailer, and they come to him from all parts of the world. He handles oats and barley from England and Scotland; semolina and macaroni, which are wheat products; maize and cornflour, which is made from maize starch; the wide variety of manufactured breakfast cereals; biscuits, rusks, and cracknels; and beans, peas, lentils, tapioca, and sago. He deals in a wide variety of fruits from many parts of the world. In the grocery trade the term 'dried fruits' is used for grapes, figs, and dates, whilst dried plums, peaches, apricots, apples, and pears are usually called 'evaporated fruits'. Currants, which are small black seedless sun-dried grapes, take their name from the city of Corinth, and Greece is still a big producer, although Victoria and other states of Australia export large quantities. Sultanas are white seedless grapes whose original home was the shores of the Caspian Sea in western Asia; Australia is now the biggest supplier to the British market, but Smyrna (in Turkey), Greece, and South Africa also contribute. Raisins come from Australia and the Cape Province of South Africa. Dried figs come mainly from Smyrna. Pressed dates come from the Euphrates Valley in Iraq, but Tunis and Algerian dates, processed and packed in Marseilles, are imported into Britain in greater quantity. Evaporated fruits such as apples,

Cadbury Bros.

A 19TH-CENTURY GROCER'S SHOP

pears, and apricots come from the mainland of Australia and from Tasmania.

The grocer's ancient trade in spices and flavourings is still carried on. Pepper and ginger come to him from the East, together with nutmegs and mace. Cloves are imported from Singapore and Madagascar, cinnamon from Ceylon, and bamboo shoots from China. Turmeric, an ingredient of curry powder, comes from the East Indies, and apart from entering into the grocery trade is often used in the textile industries as a dye. By contrast with these products of distant countries, all mustard comes from East Anglia in England, where Norwich is the main centre of manufacture.

The modern grocer deals also in a bewildering variety of canned goods, many of which are imported. Salmon comes mostly from the northern Pacific, lobster from the Maritime Provinces of Canada, and crayfish from South Africa. Canned herrings are a British product. Since the Second World War Australia has become Britain's principal supplier of canned fruits, although some come from the West Indies and the Union of South Africa. California, in the U.S.A., was once the most important source of dried, evaporated, and canned fruits, but

when Britain found it necessary to economize in dollars, she greatly reduced her American imports.

The small one-man business is still the typical and most numerous unit in the grocery trade, although the work the grocer has to do has greatly changed. In earlier days, and in certain districts well into the present century, the grocer bought and blended his own tea to suit the local water and the taste of his customers. Very few retail grocers do this to-day, although many still buy, roast, and grind their own coffee, and some grocers who specialize in coffee put their roasting-machines in the window. The changes that have affected most branches of RETAIL TRADE (q.v.) in Britain and abroad have had more influence on the grocery trade than on any other. Ready-packed goods, selling under a trade name or 'brand', are now much more numerous than goods bought in bulk and personally selected by the grocer himself. Moreover, although the one-man grocer's shop outnumbers the other types, yet in no branch of trade has the MULTIPLE SHOP (q.v.) made such inroads into individual proprietorship. Many of these multiple grocery concerns started as wholesale dealers, with the distribution of package teas as their main objective, as some of the titles of the older multiple chains suggest: for example, the International Tea Company's Stores, and the United Kingdom Tea Company. Tea-tasting is a highly skilled job, and tea blending is easier if done on a large scale. But such firms soon began to deal in other groceries, and to-day most of the big multiple grocery firms are manufacturers and wholesalers to the trade in general as well as suppliers to their own chains of retail stores.

The widespread use of ready-packed branded goods has lessened the amount of skill and knowledge the individual grocer needs, so that groceries and canned or bottled provisions are now handled by all sorts of other retailers, such as dairies, butchers, and greengrocers. The retail side is not the only branch of the grocery trade that has changed; the system of BULK PURCHASE (q.v.) by the Government has now made the MINISTRY OF FOOD (q.v. Vol. X) the biggest wholesale grocery organization in Britain.

Many grocers who began life in a small way have risen to wealth and importance. Lord Devonport, Food Controller in the First World War, founded the International Stores. James Lever, the father of the first Lord Leverhulme, was a retail grocer, and Lord Leverhulme began his career in his father's business. Sir Thomas Lipton was perhaps the most successful grocer in Britain; as a boy assistant he slept under the counter of a Scottish shop, and later he became the head of the immense firm that still bears his name, and a leading figure in international yacht-racing.

See also GREENGROCERY.
See also Vol. XI: FOOD, HISTORY OF.

GUILD SYSTEM, *see* CRAFT GUILDS.

GUMS AND RESINS. Gums are organic substances formed in various plants. A gum may trickle through the skin or bark, or it may be reached by making a cut in the bark. Gums are vegetable matter, but resins are either of a vegetable origin or produced artificially. The main difference between gums and resins is that gums will dissolve in water and not in organic liquids (such as alcohol), while resins will dissolve in organic liquids but not in water.

1. GUMS. The best-known gum is Gum Arabic, so named because in ancient times it used to be collected at Arabian ports for shipment to Europe, though it has sometimes been called Turkey Gum, because in the Middle Ages the trade shifted to Turkey. To-day the Sudan supplies most of it. Gum Arabic comes from various species of acacia plant, and is chiefly used as an adhesive, and in the making of cold-water emulsion paints and of show-card colours.

Gum Tragacanth is obtained from wild shrubs which grow in the mountainous districts of Persia and Asia Minor. It is partly gum and partly resin, consisting of a small quantity of gum which will dissolve in water, a little starch and cellulose, and a large proportion of a substance which swells in water. It is chiefly used as a binding material in the manufacture of pastel crayons, and sometimes as a 'medium' for painting on linen.

Dextrin (British Gum) is a synthetic product derived from starch, and is largely used as a substitute for Gum Arabic. Farina, which is prepared from potato starch, is rather similar.

2. NATURAL RESINS. There are two main types of natural resin. 'Recent resins' have come from living trees, and are obtained by 'tapping' the trees; fossil resins come from trees that have died and decomposed. Fossil resins are usually found buried beneath the ground; they are very hard, and are mainly used in the preparation of oil varnishes (*see* PAINTS AND VARNISHES).

The Copal resins are obtained from tropical and sub-tropical regions, and are mostly of the fossil type. Of this type Congo Copal is the most important as a constituent of varnish. It is among the hardest of the natural resins. East Indian Copals range from varieties as hard as Congo to very soft types. They form a link between the oil varnish resins and the soft resins that will dissolve in spirit. In South America there are varieties of Copal whose full uses are not yet known.

New Zealand provides the fossil Kauri resin, derived from the largest forest trees in the North Island. The bulk comes from the peat swamps, but Bush Kauri is obtained from the living trees. These Kauri gums were at first used in furniture varnishes, particularly for pianos and carriages, for they gave a very high gloss; but they take some time to dry, and Congo Copal is now more used.

The hardest resin of all is AMBER (q.v. Vol. III), which is of great antiquity. Most of it comes from the coast of Prussia, where it is collected by dredging. Some is also obtained inland by mining.

The most important of the recent resins is Damar, obtained from trees in east Indian forests. This variety is soft, and melts readily at low temperatures; it will dissolve in the cold in turpentine and petroleum spirit, but not in alcohols. It is principally used in spirit varnishes.

A Mediterranean shrub yields the resin known as Mastic, which is rather brittle and smells like balsam. It is used in high-class paper varnishes and for varnishing pictures. It is put on mixed with a spirit to render it liquid; when the spirit or 'solvent' has evaporated, the film of hard resin which is left behind is waterproof. Its disadvantage is that it darkens in the course of time, but the film can easily be removed by exposing the picture to alcohol vapour. This resin, in the form of alcoholic solutions, can be sprayed as a fixative for pencil and crayon drawings.

Sandarac, known by the other names of pine gum, white pine resin, and gum juniper, comes from North Africa. It is very useful for coating metals, as a thin coat gives a brilliant lustre. Accroides and Dragon's Blood are varieties of the Sandarac species, used for colouring spirit varnishes and metal lacquers.

The Oleo-resins are soft and easily moulded because, unlike 'recent' resins, they contain a large proportion of what are called 'essential oils' (*see* OILS, VEGETABLE). Typical Oleo-resins are Elemi, Copaiba, and Canada Balsam. When the material taken from pine trees is distilled to make turpentine (*see* DISTILLATION) the residue left behind is called Rosin or Colophony. Because of its method of manufacture, it is a semi-artificial resin. Rosin is a product which finds its way into a wide variety of finishing materials.

Oriental lacquer is a natural resin which, after being applied as a varnish, hardens to a tough dark film, taking a fine polish and being very lasting. It comes from a native Chinese tree, and is the basis of the famous lacquer-ware developed by the Chinese over 3,000 years ago (*see* LACQUER, Vol. XII). Burmese and Indian lacquers are slightly inferior varieties.

'Paint Manufacture'

SORTING FOSSILIZED KAURI GUM IN NEW ZEALAND

Shellac, a substance extracted from trees by insects, is described in the article SHELLAC.

3. SYNTHETIC RESINS. Synthetic or artificial resins are products built up by the chemical reaction of comparatively simple compounds. The most commonly used types are alkyds, phenolics, maleics, melamines, and urea-formaldehydes.

Alkyds are used in producing a type of varnish which is useful in the preparation of stoving finishes (*see* PAINTS AND VARNISHES).

Phenolics are used in the preparation of moulding, varnish, casting, laminating, and PLYWOOD (q.v.) resins.

Maleic resins are used for full gloss paints and white stoving finishes. Melamine resins are normally mixed with others for stoving finishes. Urea-formaldehyde resins are used as adhesives, for treating paper and textiles, and in the manufacture of baking-enamels.

See also CHEMISTRY, INDUSTRIAL.

GUNNY, *see* JUTE INDUSTRY.

H

HAIR TRADE. Hair is much used in modern commerce both for spinning into yarn and weaving into fabrics. Human hair has been used for such purposes in the past, and in the East in earlier days the curtains and hangings of Buddhist temples were often made from hair contributed by devout worshippers. The hairs most used nowadays are animal hairs, such as mohair, cashmere, horsehair, and camel-hair. There is also a small use for rabbit-hair.

Mohair is the hair of the Angora goat, and is sheared from the coat of the animal once a year, like the fleece of a sheep. As its name suggests, this animal was originally bred in Turkey, one of the most important countries exporting mohair; Angora is another form of the name Ankara, the capital of modern Turkey. The animal has been acclimatized very successfully in the Union of South Africa, and that country now ranks next to Turkey as an exporter of mohair. The U.S.A. is the largest grower in the world, but is also the largest consumer, and has little surplus to export. Turkey still leads other producing countries in quality, but the Union of South Africa now comes very close. Mohair is chiefly used for making carpets and rugs, and upholstery with a 'pile', or rather thick woolly surface. Fabrics made from it are exceptionally hard-wearing, and are much used for upholstering the seats of railway carriages and motor-cars, which are subject to hard and constant wear. Mohair takes dyes very easily, and makes beautiful rugs and carpets with a very long pile. It is the principal material from which theatrical costumiers make actors' Wigs (q.v. Vol. XI).

Cashmere is the name given to the fine, soft hair of the Kashmir goat. It is not sheared or cut from the body of the animal, but is collected during the moulting season. Some of it is plucked by hand from the animal, and the rest is picked up on their grazing grounds or from the twigs of bushes and shrubs that they have rubbed against. The animal is a native of Kashmir in northern India, and Srinagar, the capital of the country, is an important centre of the spinning, weaving, and embroidery trades. Cashmere shawls are famous, and very attractive bedspreads and other fabrics are produced. Little raw hair is exported from Kashmir. When it can be obtained, the hair is much used by British and American manufacturers for underwear and dress materials of the highest quality. China was formerly the biggest supplier to the world market.

Camel-hair is obtained during the moulting season, in the same way as the hair of the Kashmir goat. Camels must work during the moulting season as well as any other, and hair shed on the march or in camp is carefully collected. China was the biggest exporter of camel-hair before the Second World War, but the trade diminished during the political disturbances that followed it. The principal industrial use of camel-hair is in the weaving of cloth for men's overcoats.

Horsehair, which is coarse and tough, has many uses. The manes and tails were spun into yarn and made into upholstery cloth in Victorian days. Horsehair fabric is still used in some countries, particularly in the U.S.A., for upholstering railway carriage seats. Unspun horsehair is used in Britain for stuffing mattresses and upholstery, and for stuffing and padding garments in the men's tailoring trade.

Rabbit-hair, which is imported mainly from Australia, is sometimes spun into yarn, from which many of the cheaper articles of clothing are made. Sometimes this yarn is mixed with superior yarn to make composite fabrics.

See also CARPET MAKING ; FELT ; WOOL WEAVING ; UPHOLSTERY; CLOTHING INDUSTRY.

HAIRDRESSING PREPARATIONS, see COSMETICS; *see also* Vol. XI: HAIRDRESSING.

HALL-MARK, *see* ASSAYING, Section 2.

HAND-WEAVING, *see* WOOL WEAVING.

HANSEATIC LEAGUE. This was a confederacy of several seaports and trading towns in northern Europe, formed in the 13th century. When the League was founded, trade was exposed to many difficulties and dangers. The sea swarmed with Pirates (q.v. Vol. IV) and the land with robbers. For some years before the League was formed, princes and other rulers of small states and cities had furnished armed escorts for merchants and their goods. But these armed escorts were so costly to provide that they were eventually withdrawn, and the merchants were left to organize their own protection as best they could. This system of local protection became inefficient and extortionate, and provided no real security. The merchants, therefore, sought a remedy in unity, and the League was formed. The name adopted was *Hansa*, an old Baltic word meaning a league. The title used by Englishmen was either Hanse or Hanseatic League, and its members—all foreigners, of course—were called Hansards.

The League began in rather a small way as a commercial alliance of the two important German seaport and trading towns of Hamburg and Lübeck. This move was so successful that other towns began to join. During the height of its influence it included about ninety towns on the coast and inland, scattered over the length and breadth of Germany, and including towns in what is now Holland. Its area ran roughly from what is now the Russian province of Latvia in the Baltic, southwards to Cracow, westwards to Breslau and Cologne, and then northwards to Amsterdam. Lübeck was its headquarters, and outside its own area it had important trading centres in Novgorod in Russia, in Bergen in Norway, in Bruges in what is now Belgium, and in London. Its London depot was called the

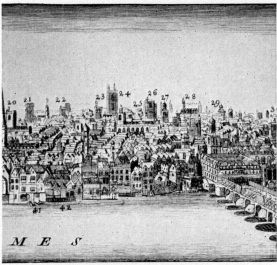

PART OF THE CITY OF LONDON SHOWING THE STEELYARD (NO. 41)

From a 17th-century engraving of London before the Fire

'Steelyard', on the site of what is now Cannon Street Station in the City of London. One of the City Corporation's plaques commemorates this to-day.

By the 14th century the League had become well established. It had also attained most of its objects, which were to protect its member towns and their merchants from pillage and robbery; to develop overseas trade; to bargain with foreign rulers for trading privileges and concessions; and to organize an administrative machine to control and run its affairs generally.

It opened up in England at a time when the economic development of the country was backward. English merchants then lacked either the organization or the capital for conducting overseas trade on their own. So the League had little difficulty in obtaining privileges from English kings. The trading centres of the League in each country, the London Steelyard for instance, were called 'factories': a name used later by the East India Company (q.v.) for its own trading centres in many parts of India.

During the height of their influence in England the Hansards had the same privileged status as the officers of the East India Company later obtained in India, and kept themselves completely aloof from the ordinary life of native Englishmen. They were a kind of alien commercial aristocracy. The League imposed a discipline almost like that of a monastery on the

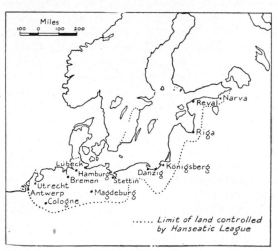

THE HANSE TOWNS

Staatsarchiv, Hamburg

A HANSEATIC PORT

A town crane was provided for loading and unloading ships. 15th-century painting

staff of its foreign 'factories', and insisted that certain grades should remain unmarried, like the Roman Catholic clergy.

Such a system was possibly necessary at the time, when English kings were keen to develop overseas trade, and could not turn to any efficient body of English merchants. Yet it was bound to cause much jealousy and friction, and these did not take long to appear. Earlier kings encouraged the League because it represented an easy way of collecting taxes on goods. Later kings encouraged an independent organization of English merchants—the Company of MERCHANT ADVENTURERS (q.v.). The struggle between the Adventurers and the League was long and bitter, and did not end until in 1587 Queen Elizabeth abolished the privileges of the Hansards in London. The League kept the ownership of the Steelyard, but this ceased to be a trading head-quarters. On the Continent its organization remained in being, although as the years passed the League gradually lost its commercial privileges in various countries. When the Steelyard in London was finally sold in 1853, the League then existed on the Continent in little more than

name, binding together for political and com-mercial purposes various cities of northern Ger-many. But before the Franco-Prussian War of 1870 was fought, the German Chancellor, BIS-MARCK (q.v. Vol. V) formed his North German Confederation, and the League's independent history came to an end.

See also CHARTERED COMPANIES; TRADE, HISTORY OF.

HARD CURRENCY. This term came into use after the Second World War. Any country's money that is scarce abroad is a 'hard currency'; the hard currencies of 1950 were principally the United States dollar, the Spanish peseta, the Swiss franc, and the Portuguese escudo. The normal way of obtaining a foreign country's money is by the export of goods; the foreign buyer gets the goods, and the bankers of the exporter's country obtain the price of them in foreign money. A country's imports must be paid for in foreign money, and what a country can import is normally limited by what it can export. But it is not necessary for import and export transactions to be done direct between the two countries concerned; for instance, Britain can obtain dollars not only by selling goods to the U.S.A. direct, but also by selling manufactured goods to, say, Malaya, using the Malayan money so obtained to buy Malayan rubber, and then selling the rubber for dollars to the U.S.A.

Before the First World War, and in a lesser degree between the First and Second, this normal way of obtaining foreign money could be supplemented by borrowing from the bankers and investors, and sometimes from the govern-ments, of the countries whose money was scarce (*see* INTERNATIONAL FINANCE). Some currencies became 'hard' in the period following the Second World War because the volume of international lending and borrowing and the pattern of INTER-NATIONAL TRADE (q.v.) had changed. The 'hardest' currency in the post-war period was the United States dollar, mainly because the U.S.A., a very wealthy nation, needed to import com-paratively little.

During that period Britain adopted a policy of strictly limiting imports such as tobacco from areas of hard currency, and of trying to sell in-creasing quantities of exports to those areas, such as the products of the MOTOR INDUSTRY (q.v.). Holiday-makers could no longer choose freely what countries they would visit, as the small amount of hard currency available was reserved by the Government for business travellers.

See also CURRENCY; INTERNATIONAL TRADE; RATES OF EXCHANGE.

HARDWOODS. 1. In the timber trade the classification into hardwoods and softwoods is a purely botanical one, and there are timbers in the hardwood class that are really quite soft to work. Hardwoods come from the so-called broad-leaf trees such as ash, beech, teak, oak, rosewood, and mahogany (*see* TREES, BROAD-LEAVED, Vol. VI).

A vast number of different hardwoods is found in the world. Many are used only locally, and never come to Europe; but it is reckoned that of the 30,000 or so kinds of tree that have been given individual botanical names, at least 2,000 to 3,000 are being used every day in one part of the world or another.

Timbers produced in a temperate climate are generally of a more even type than tropical woods, and they do not normally show the same extremes of colour, grain, and hardness. Timbers from the tropics are often either very hard and heavy like teak and mahogany, or very light and soft like balsa; many are beautifully coloured and figured.

The British Commonwealth has much fine timber. In Africa, for instance, Nigeria, the Gold Coast, Sierra Leone, Uganda, Rhodesia, and Tanganyika produce a wide range, including mahoganies, beautiful cabinet-woods such as Guarea, Muninga, and Avodire, and strong constructional woods like Iroko, Afzelia, and Ekki. British Honduras, in Central America, produces some of the finest mahogany in the world, and from British Guiana comes greenheart. About one-third of the world's forest resources are in South America, which has the biggest reserve of tropical timber. Burma grows the best teak.

2. PRINCIPAL HARDWOODS. The following are some of the more important hardwoods used in industry:—

(*a*) Ash. It is usually considered that the quality of British ash is superior to that of ash grown in other parts of Europe. From the U.S.A. comes 'Tough White Ash', while an ash with a rather more decorative grain grows in Japan. Ash is very strong and elastic, and is used for many purposes, including tool handles of all kinds and hockey-sticks and other sports goods.

(*b*) Balsa is only half the weight of cork, and is the lightest and softest of commercial woods. Our main supplies come from Ecuador, where the trees grow almost incredibly fast, reaching in 7 years a height of 70 feet and a diameter of 2 feet. Balsa is not strong, but it is an excellent heat insulator, and is used in refrigerators and for making sun-helmets. Its most popular use is for MODEL AEROPLANES (q.v. Vol. IX), but it has also been used in building real aircraft, including the famous 'Mosquito' aircraft of the Second World War.

(*c*) Beech is a strong hardwood which is easily turned on a lathe and bends well. It is a good all-round timber and much used for domestic articles, such as brush-backs, wooden spoons, and chairs. Supplies come either from British woodlands or from Central Europe.

(*d*) Birch is one of the most important woods in the manufacture of PLYWOOD (q.v.). Finnish birch plywood is made from the silver and common birches, and Canadian yellow birch is also used as a plywood timber. Small quantities of birch are used for 'turned' articles, such as bobbins, spools, and domestic woodware.

(*e*) Chestnut. The wood of the sweet chestnut is very like oak in appearance, although it lacks the silver grain so characteristic of oak, and it is not as strong. It is often used as a general substitute for oak, and also for fencing and walking-sticks. The wood of the horse chestnut is white, soft, and woolly, and is little used.

(*f*) Elm. The common elm of the countryside provides a useful, tough timber, but it needs careful seasoning. Its principal use is for coffins, but it deserves a better and wider use. Wych elm is straighter grained and more elastic, and is used, like ash, for tool handles and sports goods. Rock elm from Canada has many uses in the shipbuilding industry.

(*g*) Greenheart is an extremely hard and heavy timber. It is very durable, and is so elastic that it is the best wood for fishing-rods. It is also used for canal lock gates and the timbering of wharves and jetties, as it resists the SHIP-WORM (q.v. Vol. II). Our main supplies come from British Guiana.

(*h*) Hickory is a hard, white, very elastic timber from North America. Like ash and wych elm, it is used for the handles of pickaxes, shovels, and other tools, and for sports goods.

(*i*) Jarrah is an Australian hardwood, dark red in colour, strong, hard, and heavy. It strongly resists fire, and is much used for sleepers on the tracks of the London tube railways. It also makes good flooring, and is an excellent wood for heavy construction such as wharves and bridges. The tree is one of the hundreds of Eucalyptus species found in Australia.

(*j*) Lime is a whitish, soft, fine-textured wood that can be worked easily in all directions of the grain. For this reason it is a favourite among wood-carvers. Most of the famous wood carving of Grinling Gibbons, who worked for Sir Christopher Wren, was done in lime. British supplies are either home-grown or come from European countries. A special lime is imported from the U.S.A. under the name of Basswood.

(*k*) Mahogany is of many varieties. The earlier importations were of Spanish mahogany and came from the West Indies, mainly Cuba and San Domingo. Small quantities still come from Cuba and provide the finest quality wood, rich in colour, fine in texture, stable and often richly figured (grained). From Central America comes Honduras mahogany, a close relative of the Spanish but softer and lighter in colour; this also is a fine timber. Most of our mahogany supplies now come from a different (though related) genus in Africa; this wood is coarser textured, and less stable than those previously mentioned, but it is quite suitable for furniture and interior woodwork. In the period of scarcity following the Second World War it was used occasionally for 'strip' flooring.

(*l*) Maple. The most important kind is the Rock, Hard, or Sugar Maple of Canada. It provides a white, hard, strong timber. It is very popular for dance-hall and other floors that have to stand hard wear.

(*m*) Oak is probably the most widely used hardwood in Britain, and its uses range from furniture to beer-barrels. For some purposes English oak is the finest in the world. It is strong and well-figured, but needs careful seasoning. Oak from central Europe (Austrian, Volhynian, and Slavonian Oak) is milder, and so is often preferred by joiners and cabinetmakers. Other oaks used are Japanese, which is milder still and not so durable, and the White and Red Oaks from North America.

(*n*) Teak is one of the most useful hardwoods in the world. It is extremely durable, very stable, has little corrosive effect on metals, and resists fire. It is the best timber for ships' decks, and is also excellent for joinery, floors, and constructional work. It is greatly used in the yacht-building and boatbuilding industry. The main supplies come from Burma, and we get teak also from Siam, Java, and India.

(*o*) Walnut. There are two true walnuts: the European and the American Black walnuts. The first is found in many European countries, mainly in France, Italy, Russia, and Britain. France is the largest present source of supply. Walnut is used mainly for decorative purposes.

A number of unrelated timbers are also called walnut, because of a superficial resemblance: for instance, Australian or Queensland walnut. This is greatly used for veneers in interior decoration (*see* PLYWOODS AND VENEERS); but it lacks the typical grey colour of true walnut and tends to have a rather striped appearance. African walnut is pale brown, with widely spaced, thin, black stripes; it is closely related to the mahoganies, with which it grows in West Africa.

(*p*) Other hardwoods. Some rather interesting hardwoods were once largely used, but have lost their early importance. Rosewood is a dark, richly figured wood which has been used for over 300 years in the FURNITURE and CABINET-MAKING trades (qq.v.), especially as a veneer for pianos. It is still occasionally used for knife-handles and billiard-tables. Satinwood is a beautiful golden-yellow wood, with a high lustre, which was once very popular as a veneer for furniture. It is now little used, except for decorative brush-backs and similar small articles. Sandalwood is now almost unknown in Britain; at one time it was a favourite wood for lining ornamental boxes, because of its fragrant and persistent scent. The sawdust is used for the manufacture of joss-sticks and incense.

See also TIMBER INDUSTRY; SOFTWOODS; CABINET-MAKING; FURNITURE INDUSTRY.

See also Vol. VI: FORESTRY; TREES, BROADLEAVED.

HEMP, *see* ROPE-MAKING.

HESSIAN, *see* JUTE INDUSTRY.

HIDES AND SKINS are the raw material of the leather manufacturer or tanner. When man first used animal skins is not known. Skins, even when preserved by TANNING (q.v.), do not last as long as stone, pottery, metals, and bone, and our knowledge about the early use of skins is vague. The numerous flint scrapers and bone and ivory bodkins in our museums show that

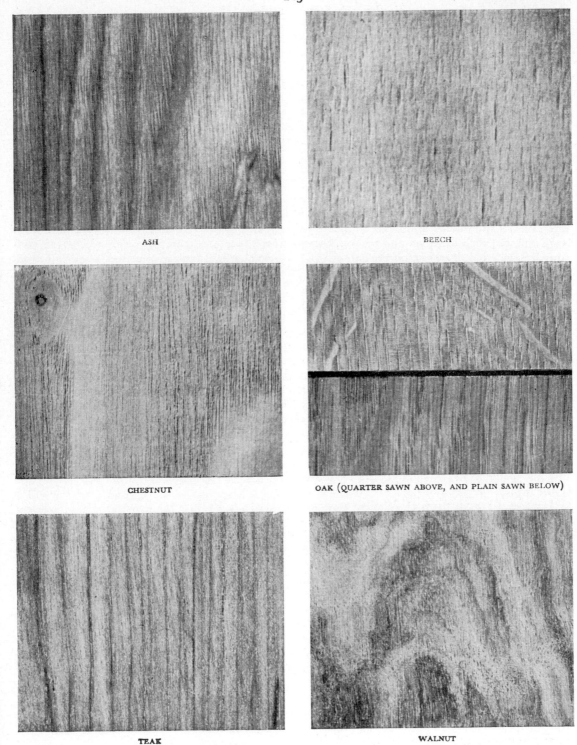

ASH

BEECH

CHESTNUT

OAK (QUARTER SAWN ABOVE, AND PLAIN SAWN BELOW)

TEAK

WALNUT

Timber Development Association

HARDWOODS

Quarter sawn means sawn through the centre of the trunk; plain sawn is any other cut

tens of thousands of years ago, in the early Stone Age, skins were being prepared and used long before textiles. To-day hides and skins are essential raw materials and important articles of commerce.

Any animal skin can be made into leather, but the skins chiefly used come from cattle, sheep, goats, pigs, and horses. To a lesser extent the skins from dogs, deer, kangaroos, reptiles, marine animals, fishes, and birds are also used. Snakes, alligators, crocodiles, lizards, seals, whales, walruses, sharks, plaice, dogfish, and ostriches all contribute to leather manufacture. 'Hide' is the trade word for the skins of the larger animals, such as full-grown cattle and horses; and 'skin' for the smaller animals and immature large animals, such as calves and ponies. Some skins are made into leather after the hair or wool has been removed; but the skins of the fur-bearing animals, and sometimes of sheep, lambs, and ponies, are dressed with the hair or wool still in place (*see* FUR TRADE).

Surprisingly large numbers of hides and skins are used in leather manufacture. Each day a fair-sized sole-leather tannery will tan 1,000 hides, and a large 'glazed goat' tannery may deal with 10,000 skins. Britain obtains large supplies from her own cattle, sheep, and horses, but enormous quantities of skins must come from abroad. Most hides and skins are by-products of the well-organized MEAT TRADE (q.v.), but many—especially those from the less common animals—come from remote and primitive parts of the world. Expeditions go to polar waters to hunt seals; and tropical jungles, swamps, and rivers are searched for lizards, snakes, and crocodiles. Cattle hides come mainly from the meat-packing works of the U.S.A., from the *frigorificos* or meat-freezing establishments of South America, and from Australia. Smaller quantities come from East and West Africa, Central America, and the Sudan. Sheepskins are imported from Australia, New Zealand, Argentina, and South Africa. Goatskins come from India, Pakistan, Ethiopia, Arabia, and Nigeria; lizard skins from East and West Africa, India, South America, Indonesia, and Malaya; crocodile skins from South America, India, Malaya, and Madagascar; and python skins from India and Malaya. Veterinary surgeons, flaying instructors, and hide-and-skin inspectors are sent out from Britain to the less advanced countries of the Commonwealth, to supervise the raising, killing, and flaying of animals, and to ensure the production of good-quality hides and skins that will suit the purposes of the leather trades.

There is usually a long interval between flaying the skin off the animal and putting it into work at the tannery. If the flayed skins were left wet they would go bad, like meat; and they must therefore be preserved in some way. The commonest method is salting. This involves sprinkling the skins with salt on their inner side; or immersing the skins in strong salt solution or brine, after which they are drained and sprinkled with solid salt. The salting method leaves the skins slightly moist and heavy, and sometimes the salted skins are dried out. This avoids the transport of useless weight—a consideration in primitive countries, where hundreds of miles of carriage by mule, camel, or even human transport may be involved. A method found convenient in primitive or tropical countries is to stretch the skins out on the ground or on frames, and to dry them in the sun, or preferably in the shade. Sheepskins are often freed from their wool, and then 'pickled' in a solution of salt and sulphuric acid (*see* FELLMONGERING). Beetles and other insects eat skins, and must be kept away by sprinkling the skins with such chemicals as white arsenic, naphthalene, or

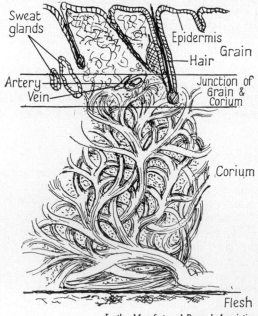

Leather Manufacturers' Research Association

SECTION OF HIDE (MUCH ENLARGED)

D.D.T. Large numbers of hides and skins come to England from India and Pakistan in a roughly tanned condition. This 'crust' leather, as it is called, is dressed in England into lining, gloving, shoe-upper, and fancy leathers.

Hides are sold by weight, the trade unit being the pound. The best English ox-hides cost about 1s. 10d. a pound, and a single hide may cost about £5. Sheepskins are sold by the dozen; a pelt without the wool is worth about 5s. Python skins are sold by length, the price being about 15s. a metre. Crocodile skins are sold by width, at about 8s. an inch. (These were 1950 prices.)

Not every part of an animal skin is used in leather manufacture. An animal skin is really a structure of three separate layers of tissue. The outermost layer is the 'epidermal' system, consisting of the epidermis proper, the hair or wool, and the sweat or fat glands. The whole of the epidermal system is removed from the skin before tanning, unless it is to be made into a furskin or woolskin for rugs or clothing. The innermost layer is the flesh, which connects the skin loosely to the underlying meat or muscle. This layer is also cut away before tanning. The third, or intermediate, layer is the 'corium' or 'derma' or true skin. It is a fibrous structure, and in its surface layer—just beneath the epidermis—the fibres are very fine, forming the tough grain of the leather which we see. It is this corium layer which the tanner makes into leather. It is to the closely interwoven and inter-knit fibre structure of the corium that leather owes its virtues: its flexibility, strength, and elasticity; its resistance to abrasion and its non-fraying edges; and its unique power of allowing water vapour and air to pass through it while resisting penetration by liquid water itself.

See also CURRYING; TANNING; LEATHER.

HIRE PURCHASE, *see* CREDIT.

HORSEHAIR, *see* HAIR TRADE.

HOSIERY AND KNITWEAR are both knitted fabrics. They differ from woven fabrics in that they are made from one continuous yarn by the formation of a series of loops, in contrast to the interwoven warp and weft threads of woven fabrics (*see* WOOL WEAVING). The industry began in Britain in the 15th century, when hand-knitting was introduced from the continent of Europe. By the 16th century hand-knitting had spread throughout Britain, and it still survives in parts of Scotland and Ireland as an organized branch of the industry.

Hosiery was the first textile industry in the country to become mechanized, although at first progress was slow. In 1589 the Rev.

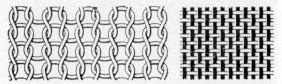

DIAGRAM TO COMPARE KNITTED AND WOVEN FABRICS

William Lee, a country parson who had no mechanical training or experience, invented the stocking-frame. His first invention was fitted with rather coarse needles and could deal only with woollen yarn, but some years later he produced an improved frame with finer needles upon which silk stockings could be made. At this period of British industrial history machinery was very unpopular, and those who invented it met with hostility and often actual violence. Lee and his brother James, together with some workmen, therefore emigrated with their machinery to Rouen, in France. The Lees were no more popular in France than in England, and William died in Paris in 1610. James, however, brought back to England nearly all his brother's stocking-frames, and after setting them up temporarily in London, he transferred them to Nottinghamshire, which has since been the great centre of the industry in Britain. The stocking-machine was at first used only for high-quality hosiery, chiefly of silk.

Lee's original machine was improved as years went on, but there was no important improvement until 1869. In that year a patent was granted to William Cotton, a native of Leicestershire, for a machine that has since become known as Cotton's Patent. This machine automatically increased or decreased the number of stitches required to produce a fashioned garment. It is still in regular use in the industry.

It was many years before the industry became fully organized on a factory basis, and even as late as 1870 the bulk of it was organized on the 'outworker' or DOMESTIC SYSTEM (q.v.). From Nottingham, its original home, the industry spread to the surrounding country and to Leicester, and later to Scotland, notably to Hawick, Kilmarnock, Stewarton, Greenock,

A CIRCULAR KNITTING-MACHINE

The fabric emerges from the centre of the machine in tubular form

British Celanese

and the higher earnings of most women increased the demand for stockings that were 'fully-fashioned' (shaped all the way up), so that the factories could not make enough. For every 100 women who lived in Britain in 1930, about 150 pairs of fully-fashioned stockings were sold in the shops in the year; only 15% of these were made in Britain, the rest being imported. But by 1939, for every 100 women in the population, nearly 500 pairs were sold in the year, and home production had increased to nearly half of the total. The main raw materials of the industry are worsted, wool, cotton, rayon, and pure silk yarn, and some Shetland wool, cashmere, angora, and alpaca. NYLON (q.v.) is an important new material growing in popularity.

Glasgow, Lanark, and Airdrie. In recent years other districts have entered the industry, and the greater London area is now important. With the growing demand for silk and rayon goods Leek and Macclesfield—where the yarns are spun— have become prominent towns in the industry. Several seaside towns (particularly Yarmouth, Blackpool, Southport, Bournemouth, and New- quay) have set up knitwear manufacture as a profitable regular alternative to the holiday industry, which is only seasonal.

Fashion changes have had much to do with the expansion of the industry in recent years. Silk and cotton blouses have been largely replaced by jumpers, pullovers, and cardigans, and knitted fabrics or jersey cloth are much used for women's suits and dresses. Increased output has enabled prices to be lowered, and people who used to patch and repair their garments now more often replace them with new ones. More people now send their washing to laundries; the garments are, therefore, out of use longer than if they were washed at home, so that it is necessary to own more garments. Moreover, children's clothes, which used to be home-made, are now more often bought ready-made. Fashion has also affected the hosiery section of the industry. The wearing of short skirts increased the demand for stockings of silk, rayon, or nylon,

Although all branches of the industry make use of the knitting process, different machines are used for different products. Large stocking machines of the modern type are capable of knitting sets of thirty or more pieces of shaped fabric at the same time, each piece being later seamed on other machines to form a fully-fashioned stocking. Small hand-operated 'flat-bar' machines produce single pieces of shaped or unshaped fabric for the making of outer garments. Cotton's Patent knitting-frame, which automatically varies the number of stitches, is used for the making of high-quality fully fashioned underwear and outer wear. The cheaper type of product is made on circular machines, which knit the stocking or garment in its final circular form. The separate seaming used for fully-fashioned wear is therefore unnecessary, although the various circular sections such as the arms and body of a man's vest, need to be finally seamed together.

See also WOOL INDUSTRY, MODERN; COTTON INDUSTRY; SILK; RAYON; NYLON.
See also Vol. XI: KNITTING.

HOTEL INDUSTRY. There are very many grades between what the industry calls the 'palace hotel' at the top of the scale, and the small temperance hotel, little better than a tiny boarding-house, of a small country town or village. The number of hotels of each kind varies with every change in social life and in the distribution of money income among the people who use hotels, whether they come from home or from abroad.

Hotels and travelling have always been closely linked, and the modern hotel industry is really the product of the transport revolution that began with the railway age (*see* RAILWAYS, HISTORY OF, Vol. IV). Inns and taverns have existed for centuries, and the records of all the ancient civilizations mention them (*see* INNS, Vol. IV). The hotel industry, however, dates from the early 1870's. By that time the habit of railway travel had become general, and for various reasons the railways and their stations had often been built far from the main roads and the old coaching inns. Most of this railway travel was on business, but pleasure travellers began to be attracted by the beautiful inland and coastal scenery through which the railways passed. At the same time many more people from other countries were coming to Britain to buy British manufactures. Social changes also created a need for hotels. In the early part of the 19th century, as in much earlier times, travellers from abroad were usually put up and entertained in the private houses of their friends and acquaintances. As industry expanded, and wealth became more widely distributed, people who could not previously afford to travel now found themselves able to do so, and not all of them could arrange for private hospitality. All these factors led to the building up of the hotel industry as we know it in Britain to-day.

The railway companies took a leading part in developing hotels in the earlier days; they realized that there would be a direct profit in providing hotels, and they also counted on an increase of passenger traffic when new hotels had made travelling more comfortable.

The earlier railway hotels were planned to be comfortable and convenient for the travelling population, but they did not aim at any very high standard of luxury. Hotels of this sort were the Queen's Hotel, Birmingham, built in 1852, and the North Western Hotel, Liverpool, opened in 1871. It was the Midland Railway (now merged in the London Midland Region of British Railways) which pioneered the 'luxury'

railway hotel. The first great hotel of this kind opened in England was the Midland Grand Hotel at St. Pancras Station, London. It was opened in 1873, when the Midland Railway had extended southward and acquired a London terminus. Its architect was Sir Gilbert Scott. He had originally drawn up plans for a new Foreign Office in Whitehall, and when this project was dropped by the Government, the Midland Railway Company bought Sir Gilbert's plans and built their new hotel to his designs. From about this time onwards the railways took the leading part in building hotels in the main British industrial centres, and their station hotels became the backbone of the industry outside London itself. The last of the big provincial railway hotels to be built was the Midland at Manchester, opened in 1903, and for many years the leading provincial hotel in the country. The rebuilding of the Queen's Hotel in Leeds was completed in 1938, to the designs of the architect who had built the Dorchester Hotel in Park Lane, London. The increasing amount of pleasure travelling from the late 19th century onwards led many of the railway companies to open hotels outside the industrial centres, in coastal or inland holiday districts, including Wales, Cornwall, Scotland, and Ireland. After the First World War the increasing use of the roads checked fresh building by the railways.

The example of the railways was soon copied by private interests. Hotel building on a big scale required a good deal of CAPITAL (q.v.), which was one reason why the railway companies were prominent. In those days large sums of money were easy to find for any business promising profit. The Grand Hotel in Trafalgar Square and the Langham Hotel in Portland Place were two of the earliest 'luxury' hotels built in London by non-railway syndicates. They set the pattern for a great improvement in London and provincial hotels. The 1880's saw the opening of the Savoy and the Metropole in London, and the Metropole in Brighton. The Hotel Cecil in London, later pulled down, also belonged to this period, and was one of the largest hotels ever built in Britain. In the early 1890's the Carlton, another hotel of the highest class, was opened at the corner of Pall Mall and the Haymarket. The Ritz in London was opened in 1905; the Ritz in Paris (named after a Swiss hotel-manager) had been built just before the close of the 19th century. Between the First and Second

Canadian Pacific Railways

CHÂTEAU FRONTENAC, QUEBEC, ONE OF THE WORLD'S 'LUXURY' HOTELS
It was built in 1898 and contains 700 rooms

World Wars such hotels as the May Fair, the Park Lane, Grosvenor House, and the Dorchester were built.

More modest hotels also began to be built. The wealth of the country was becoming more widely distributed among its people. The motor-car and the motor-cycle were becoming cheaper and more numerous. Improvements in road surfaces increased the range and speed of the ordinary pedal bicycle. New opportunities, therefore, presented themselves to the hotel trade. In London J. Lyons and Company, who already ran an extensive chain of popular restaurants and cafés (*see* CATERING INDUSTRY), opened the Strand Palace and Regent Palace Hotels shortly before the First World War, and the Cumberland Hotel just before the Second World War. These hotels aimed at comfort and a modest standard of luxury for the traveller of moderate income. In the larger provincial towns the railway hotels

were already established, but smaller towns sometimes had only the old coaching inns (many of which then required repair and modernizing), the better class of public-house, and the small boarding-house. Two firms, Trust Houses Limited and The People's Refreshment House Association, set about modernizing and improving hotels in the smaller towns and villages. Business men using motor-cars could now avoid the out-of-date and unattractive provincial hotel by driving on elsewhere, and economical management could be helped if week-end holiday-makers could be attracted. Capital needed for improvements of this kind could not be raised by each hotel singly, and from this time the 'chain' system, or the ownership of branch-hotels by a central organization, became a feature of the medium-class hotel industry.

An efficient hotel industry is of economic importance to any country. The TOURIST INDUS-

TRY (q.v.) (that part of the travel industry which caters for visitors from overseas) was already earning much foreign currency before the Second World War; since then, because of Britain's difficult economic position, the tourist industry has become a vitally important 'invisible' export (*see* INTERNATIONAL TRADE). The interests of the British hotel industry are looked after by the Hotels and Restaurants Association of Great Britain. About 1870 the first of a series of attempts was made to organize the industry internationally. In 1946 the International Hotel Association was formed; 3 years after its foundation twenty-nine nations were represented on its council, and 2,300 individual hotel managements were members.

See also CATERING INDUSTRY; TOURIST INDUSTRY.

HOTEL MANAGEMENT. 1. ORGANIZATION.

The organization of the smaller hotels is naturally not very elaborate, but that of the leading hotels follows a general pattern. Many of these hotels are grouped into a single large directing company, whose managing director is responsible for policy and for co-ordinating the management of the members of the group. For each separate hotel there is a manager who is its chief executive officer. He often has an assistant manager to act in his absence and assist him generally, but usually without any special functions of his own. Under the manager and reporting direct to him are the accountant and his staff, the engineer and the maintenance staff, and, in larger hotels, the staff manager and the 'house detective', who looks after the property of the hotel and of its guests.

The day-to-day working of the hotel is usually subdivided into three main departments: house, food, and drinks. The house department includes the reception office, the hall-porter and his staff, and the housekeeper and her staff. The reception office is responsible for the booking and letting of rooms, the presentation and payment of accounts, keys, letters, telephone, records, inquiries, and safe-deposit arrangements for guests' valuables. The housekeeper is in charge of the cleaning and maintenance of all the public rooms, including staircases and corridors. She is also responsible for the linen and other furnishings of bedrooms, and for ordering and maintaining stocks of linen, furnishings, and cleaning materials. The housekeeper is also responsible for the service and cleaning of bedrooms, and supervises the staff of chambermaids and valets. The hall-porter is in general charge of all the uniformed staff, including footmen, page-boys, liftmen, luggage porters, and cloakroom attendants.

The food department is usually in two subdivisions, the kitchen and the restaurant. The chef (*chef de cuisine*) is in charge of the kitchen, supervising the ordering, cooking, and dressing of all food and the preparation of the menus. The restaurant manager is in charge of the restaurant and grill-room, and manages the staff of waiters. He is responsible, also, for the stocks of table linen, cutlery, china, and glass.

The drink department is in charge of the

British Transport

GLENEAGLES HOTEL, PERTHSHIRE, SCOTLAND

THE KITCHEN OF A COUNTRY HOTEL

Whitbread & Co.

staff must be engaged and maintained, even if bedrooms remain vacant and the restaurants and other public rooms have few customers. A hotel has therefore to meet very heavy standing or overhead charges (*see* COSTING), and its rate of TURNOVER (q.v.) is low. Other trades, such as greengrocery, may sell during the year goods valued at twenty or thirty times their actual capital; a hotel will be fortunate if its total receipts add up in any year to half the capital sunk in the enterprise.

The successful financial management of a large hotel depends principally on its having a sufficiently large number of bedrooms for letting. There are hotels in London and the provinces that have never been profitable since they were built, largely because their bedroom accommodation is too small. Even if there are enough bedrooms, a high percentage must be kept constantly occupied, and in this respect Britain is less well situated than other countries, notably the U.S.A. Local conditions have helped the American hotel industry. The United States is a country of long distances, where 'out-and-home' business journeys can rarely be completed in a single day. American business travellers are forced to spend at least one night away from home, and for most of them it is more economical to organize a longer absence and to visit a series of cities in turn. By contrast, the London business man can often do business in a provincial city and return to London the same evening. A British provincial hotel is also under a handicap compared with a London one. London has its attractions, even during the week-end, and the departure of business guests from hotels on Friday afternoons is counterbalanced to a limited extent by an influx of country visitors to London. Provincial hotels, except at holiday resorts, have few week-end visitors.

The more favourable financial situation of American hotels has made it easier for them to raise capital. The result has been, not any superior standard of comfort and service in the American first-class hotel as compared with its

cellar manager, who is responsible for ordering and maintaining an adequate and varied stock of wines and spirits, and for controlling their issue to the restaurant, the other public rooms, and the bars.

2. MANAGEMENT. Until the First World War the managers and the staffs of leading British hotels were foreigners, mainly French, Swiss, Italians, and Germans. At that time Germans were most numerous. The war made it necessary for the hotel trade to do without many of these, and during and after the Second World War an even smaller proportion of foreigners has been employed. It has not always been easy to find British managers and staffs. In many European countries hotel management is a profession whose secrets are handed down in a family from generation to generation, and apprenticeship is begun at an early age. There is now in Britain a Council for Hotel and Catering Education, which has planned a full scheme of training for the trade, including a period spent in Switzerland, a country that has produced many famous hotel keepers, and where the family tradition of hotel management is strongest.

The financial management of hotels is not a simple matter. Most large firms have to borrow money for building and equipping their hotels by mortgaging their property on security (*see* DEBENTURES). High rates have to be paid to local authorities, and the furnishings and equipment have to be kept in good condition and periodically renewed and modernized. A large

British counterpart, but a higher proportion of hotels of the first or second class in the United States than there is in Britain.

The 'seasonal' type of hotel, such as the Highland hotels in Scotland, and similar hotels at summer coastal resorts, has its own management problems. These are sometimes solved by the hotel closing down during the 'off' season; sometimes by a scale of different charges at different seasons; the charges are increased during busy times, when the demand for rooms is rather heavier.

In Britain a hotel which serves alcoholic drinks has to have a full public-house licence, although the selling of drinks is only part of its business; in this respect British law differs from that of other countries. Attempts have been made to change this situation, but have not so far resulted in any changes in law. The financial arrangements of smaller hotels were affected by the Catering Wages Act passed by Parliament in 1943, which set up a Catering Wages Commission to regulate wages and conditions of work in the hotel and catering industries.

See also HOTEL INDUSTRY; CATERING INDUSTRY.

HUDSON'S BAY COMPANY. After the EAST INDIA COMPANY (q.v.), the Hudson's Bay Company is possibly the most famous of the great CHARTERED COMPANIES (q.v.) founded from the 15th century onwards. It was set up after two Frenchmen had made perilous journeys into the great northern forests of Canada, where the Cree tribe of Red Indians lived, and brought back a valuable collection of furs in 1660. In the French Canadian city of Montreal the Frenchmen could not get the terms they wanted for future trading, so they came to England. Prince Rupert, cousin of Charles II, saw chances of a profitable trade in furs, and in 1668 he organized a voyage from England to test the truth of the Frenchmen's reports. As a result, in 1670 the King granted a charter to Prince Rupert and seventeen others to form the Company of Adventurers of England trading into Hudson Bay. The charter gave the Company exclusive rights of colonization, government, and trade in what are now the northern and western portions of Ontario and Quebec, the whole of Manitoba and Saskatchewan, the southern half of Alberta, and the south-east corner of the North-west Territories. The Company's territory was given the name of Rupert's Land; and the first settlements were made on the shores of James Bay, and on the banks of the Churchill and Hayes rivers on the western shores of Hudson Bay.

As far as trading went, the venture was successful from the beginning. Increasing numbers of Indian traders journeyed to the Company's posts with valuable loads of furs and bartered them for other goods offered by the Company. But it was not found so easy to push into the interior and to carry on with exploration and settlement. There were many difficulties: the severe climate, lack of knowledge of the country, the vast distances to be covered, and, later, the rivalry of French traders from the south. For many years the Company could do little more than hold on to a few isolated posts on the coast; their posts were sometimes attacked and destroyed by French expeditions, for during the Company's early years there was almost continuous war between England and France. The Company was near ruin when England and France signed the Peace of Ryswick.

Later the French adopted a new system of trading which threatened the Company's interests. The Company had hitherto established fortified posts on or near the shores of the Bay, to which the Indian tribes had to bring the furs. But in 1731 the French fitted out in Montreal the first of a series of strong expeditions, which penetrated through the prairie provinces to the foothills of the Rocky Mountains and established trading posts in the actual hunting grounds in which the Indians trapped the animals. The Indians often preferred to deal with the French traders, as they were thus saved the long, troublesome, and often dangerous journey to the distant northern posts of the Hudson's Bay Company.

The Company also faced difficulties in England, for in 1749 a hostile group in Parliament tried, but without success, to deprive the Company of its charter. Urgent instructions were sent to the trading posts in Rupert's Land. The Company's men were ordered to push their posts farther inland, to explore the interior with energy, and by living amongst the Indians to increase the Company's influence over them.

In 1759 General WOLFE (q.v. Vol. V) captured Quebec, and the next year Montreal surrendered. The military power of the French in Canada had been broken. But the Company still had to face the competition of independent traders. As British immigration increased, this competition grew.

Royal Geographical Society

THE HUDSON'S BAY COMPANY'S POST AT RIGOLET, LABRADOR

The Hudson Bay route was not the only way into the great forests of the north: another route lay by the tributaries of the St. Lawrence river and across the Great Lakes and the prairies. Rival companies were formed which made use of this southern route. In 1784 nine companies, operating from Montreal, amalgamated into a single concern called the North West Company, largely controlled by men of Scots ancestry who had settled permanently in Canada.

The struggle between the two companies became very bitter. At some of the more important centres, trading posts and forts were built by each company side by side; for nearly 40 years there was fierce economic rivalry between them, and often violence and bloodshed. As a result the Indians increased their trapping of animals to a point where normal replacement by breeding could not keep pace with the numbers killed. Competition had become ruinous; and the only remedy was the amalgamation of the two rival companies, which took place in 1821.

The Hudson's Bay Company now entered upon a great period of its history. Exploration, settlement, and administration went ahead peacefully and purposefully. The Company's posts were extended north and west, and as far as the Pacific Ocean.

In 1867 the Canadian Provinces were formed into the Dominion of Canada; so in 1869 Rupert's Land and other settled districts were taken over from the Company. In compensation the Company received £300,000 in cash and the right to one-twentieth of the land, in any township settled by the Company, outside the northern forests and within the 'fertile belt' between Lake Winnipeg and the Rocky Mountains. The Company thus acquired 7 million acres of land.

Unlike the East India Company, which had ceased both to trade and govern by 1858, the Hudson's Bay Company still lives on to-day as a commercial corporation, with various interests in Canada and outside it.

See also FUR TRADE; CHARTERED COMPANIES.

I

IMPORTS, *see* INTERNATIONAL TRADE; OVERSEAS TRADE.

INDENTURES, *see* APPRENTICESHIP.

INDUSTRIAL ALCOHOL is a liquid known to scientists as 'ethyl alcohol'. This is not only the active constituent in alcoholic drinks (wines, beer, cider, whisky, gin, brandy, and rum), but is also very important to industry. In 1948

Britain used some 50 million proof gallons of spirit, equal to 100,000 tons of pure ethyl alcohol. The pure alcohol has a specific gravity of 0·794 and boils at 78° C.

The substances made from it, or with its aid, include acetic acid (used for PLASTICS, such as cellulose acetate); polishes, varnishes, lacquers, stains, paints, and enamels; embrocations, tinctures, liniments, and lotions for medical use; soap, perfumes, and COSMETICS (qq.v.); insecticides, plant washes, sheep-dips, and veterinary medicines; the liquid for compasses, spirit-levels, and thermometers; de-icing and anti-freeze solutions; many lubricating and other industrial oils; anaesthetics such as ether and chloroform; drugs such as insulin, and DYES (q.v.).

The growth of the organic chemical industry during the 19th century created a need for large quantities of alcohol; the need increased after 1929, when Britain began the large-scale making of acetic acid for plastics, and of alcoholic solvents. Until recently industrial alcohol was made by FERMENTATION (q.v. Vol. II) of the sugars either in or producible from starches.

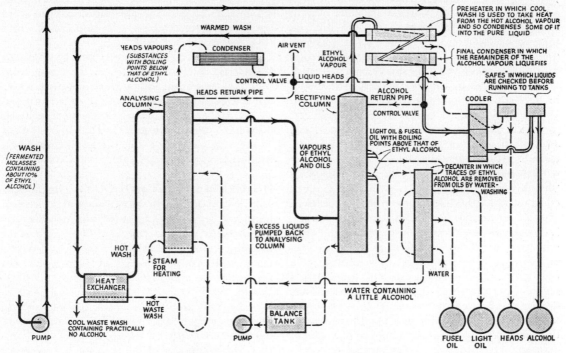

Distillers Co.

DIAGRAM TO SHOW HOW INDUSTRIAL ALCOHOL IS MADE FROM FERMENTED MOLASSES ('WASH')

Starting from the bottom left-hand corner, the thick lines show the route of the 'wash'. The dotted lines show how other substances are recovered (fusel oil is the basis of amyl acetate and various drugs), how heat is used over again, and as much pure alcohol as possible obtained

These starches were found in cereals (wheat, barley, oats, rye, maize, and rice); in tubers (potatoes, cassava, artichokes, sweet potatoes, and yams); in roots (sugar beet, mangolds, and sugar mangolds); and in molasses. Since cereals, tubers, and roots are needed for food, molasses has become the only material used for industrial alcohol in Britain. It is a syrup (uncrystallizable) which remains after the manufacture and refining of cane- and beet-sugar. Molasses is dense and sticky, varying in colour from light yellow to almost black, and contains about 50% of sugars which can be converted into alcohol. Cane molasses is imported in tankers from the West Indies and Cuba, but molasses is also available from the beet sugar industry in Britain.

The fermentation is caused by the enzyme action of special strains of YEAST (q.v. Vol. II). This is grown in laboratories, in test-tubes and small flasks, and then transferred first to small tanks, and then to large fermenting-vessels with a capacity of up to 100,000 gallons. These vessels have been filled with molasses diluted with water to reduce the sugar concentration to 10% or 12%, and with the correct amounts of acid and nutrients for the yeast. The fermentation takes at least 50 hours to complete, at a temperature of 85° to 95° F. During the process carbon dioxide gas is evolved; this is collected, purified, and compressed to a liquid, which is either sold in steel cylinders or turned into the solid form known as 'dry ice'. Dry ice has many industrial uses: it is used as a safe explosive in mines, and as the refrigerating material in ice-cream containers. It is often employed in engineering works when steel tires are fitted on to wheels by 'shrink fitting': the wheel is chilled to make it contract until the tire has been slipped on to it.

After fermentation, the liquid, called 'wash', is distilled in large copper stills, which may deal with 10,000 gallons of wash in an hour (see DISTILLATION). The wash is fed into the top of a tank called the 'analysing column', fitted with a series of perforated plates; as the liquid trickles down, it is heated by steam which is blown in at the bottom. The alcoholic vapours, which are thus driven off, pass into the bottom of a second column. Here they are concentrated or 'rectified', pure alcohol vapour being taken off at the top of the column, condensed, and run into large storage tanks, from which it is distributed to the users in drums and tank wagons by road and rail.

About 6 proof gallons of spirit are produced from 1 cwt. of molasses (see diagram).

Most of the 'Plain British Spirit' thus produced is sold as such for industrial purposes. It is colourless, with a slight, rather pleasant 'spirituous' smell and a sharp taste, but it has little real flavour; the various tastes of alcoholic drinks come from other substances. It is, of course, drinkable, and consequently the excise authorities keep very close watch on its use, to ensure that the tax or 'duty' is paid on any spirit which is not used for an approved purpose. The spirit can be 'denatured' and rendered undrinkable, by the addition of wood naphtha (crude methyl alcohol), mineral naphtha, pyridine, diethyl phthalate, and other substances with an unpleasant taste, thus producing the various grades of 'methylated spirits'.

Scientists have sought other and cheaper ways of making industrial alcohol. One method arises from the 'cracking' process applied to crude petroleum oil, and first used for making petrol. In this process, ethylene (C_2H_4) is formed among the BY-PRODUCT gases (q.v.), and this can be converted to ethyl alcohol by a chemical reaction, which adds on to each molecule an oxygen atom and two hydrogen atoms—the elements of water (see CHEMISTRY, Vol. III).

In countries where there is plenty of cheap electricity, calcium carbide can be made from limestone and coke, and on treatment with water this yields acetylene (C_2H_2); if two hydrogen atoms are added to each acetylene molecule, ethylene is again produced, and can be converted to ethyl alcohol as before. Ethyl alcohol has a molecular formula C_2H_5OH.

INDUSTRIAL PSYCHOLOGY. The modern science that deals with the workings of the human mind and with man's impulses and behaviour is PSYCHOLOGY (q.v. Vol. XI). The important branch, called industrial psychology, which deals with human beings at work, was not recognized as a separate study until the First World War. During that war Britain had to increase her production of munitions, and to maintain a high rate of production, and a high degree of contentment among workers was essential. In the middle of the war the Government appointed a committee to study these matters, and their discoveries, which are now everyday knowledge, seemed revolutionary at that time. One of the things the committee discovered was

Distillers Co.

AN INDUSTRIAL ALCOHOL DISTILLERY

In the foreground are spent wash tanks, and carbon dioxide storage cylinders are beyond them

Nat. Inst. of Industrial Psychology

A MAN BEING TESTED FOR HAND AND EYE CO-ORDINATION

The man controls the pencil with two handles and has to make it follow a pattern printed on the paper

that the relationship between a man's working hours and his output was not simply a question of arithmetic. For instance, if men worked a 12-hour day instead of a 10-hour day there was not necessarily an increase of one-fifth in the output of goods turned out. In fact it was discovered that, if the working day were shortened, the output of a worker was more likely to go up than to go down. If hours were made longer, the output might even fall. Also, if the working day were shortened, absenteeism through sickness or other reasons would be less. Another interesting discovery was the nature of the 'work curve'. If output were measured at various intervals throughout the working day, and the results plotted on a graph and joined up into a smooth curve, the curve would show a rise at the beginning, then a period of little change, and then a fall towards the end. Short rests of about 10 to 15 minutes were found to have a good effect on output; they not only raised the general average position of the work curve but also shortened the period during which output fell. Further, these rest periods increased output not only during the periods that followed them but

also in the periods before them. It looked as if the prospect of prolonged and uninterrupted work made workers slack off, whereas the prospect of a rest acted as a spur.

These original discoveries have been improved and enlarged since 1917. Great strides have been made in this new science, although many people have doubted its value, and some are hostile to it. Industrial psychologists are often criticized because they seem to lay undue emphasis on output. But they use output only because it is a convenient way of measuring contentment: one cannot directly measure a human being's contentment at work; but, if the assumptions of industrial psychologists are true, output provides a reasonably good measuring-rod for contentment. In any event, the industrial psychologist's approach to output is not the same as that of the engineering specialists who originated TIME AND MOTION STUDY (q.v. Vol. VIII), which is concerned with the study of workers at various tasks, so as to eliminate unnecessary movements and reduce the time taken on a job. The engineer is concerned with output as a measure of efficiency; the industrial psychologist uses it as a measure not only of efficiency but also of the human contentment he is trying to promote and increase.

In 1921, shortly after the First World War, the National Institute of Industrial Psychology was founded in London to organize and improve the study of the science, and to give advice to industrialists. One of its purposes was vocational guidance, that is, advising men and women entering industry or commerce about the jobs which are most likely to suit them. Vocational selection is another of its subjects, that is to fit those already working in a factory or business into those jobs that will suit them best, and where they will not be 'square pegs in round holes'. Vocational selection is easier than vocational guidance. To move somebody from a job for which he is obviously unfitted, to one where he is likely to do better, is simpler than to probe deeply into his general mental make-up and advise him what job he should look for. The Institute also works out schemes for the vocational training of workers in the work they will have to do.

Another important branch of the work of the Institute is factory management. Good management, to the industrial psychologist, means more than mere efficiency; it means a happy relationship between workers and managers. The well-managed factory should possess loyal workers, with a sense of unity and a common purpose. Industrial psychologists have made much progress in investigating the reasons why some managements are good and some bad. Some of their most interesting inquiries have concerned the influence on workers of monotonous jobs, and of the conditions in which they work. Different people react differently to monotonous work: tasks that would be monotonous to one man are welcomed by another, and some workers actually prefer monotonous tasks. In regard to working conditions, perhaps the most interesting experiments were those conducted at Hawthorne, New Jersey, U.S.A., before the Second World War. These experiments included changes in lighting, in the layout of factories and workrooms, in the organization of rest periods, and in the introduction of music while at work. But it was found that improvements in working conditions were not entirely the cause of the increased output and the much greater contentment; an important factor was that the workers appreciated the interest in them that was being shown by the management.

See also FACTORY ORGANIZATION.

INDUSTRIAL REVOLUTION. This is the term used to describe a whole series of changes in the methods of work and in the organizing of industry that have taken place since the 18th century. These changes, which were accompanied by a great increase in the population of England and other European countries, were revolutionary in their effects upon the daily lives of all kinds of people. The steam-engine, which provided a new source of industrial power, has had as striking an influence on human history as any great political upheaval, and inventors such as James WATT and Richard ARKWRIGHT can be compared in historical importance with poets like WORDSWORTH and statesmen like NAPOLEON (qq.v. Vol. V). It was indeed the French Revolution which first suggested another use of the word 'revolution'; a French economist said that while France had had a political revolution, England had had an economic one. But the phrase did not come into general use until it was chosen as the title of some lectures given by the historian Toynbee in 1881.

It is impossible to describe this enormous series of industrial changes as being the result of any single cause. At the beginning of the 18th century, however, two important factors were at work. In the first place, trade at home and abroad increased very rapidly; this increased saving and investment and encouraged business adventure, particularly among British industrialists. In the second place, at the beginning of the 18th century the forests of England were gradually being wiped out, and it became increasingly difficult to find suitable fuel. The shortage of trees, and difficulties in the way of importing foreign timber, led to an increased demand for an alternative fuel. This created a need for technical improvements in the COAL INDUSTRY (q.v.), and for the increased use of coal instead of charcoal for iron smelting.

Coal and iron were the two most important raw materials of the early Industrial Revolution. Without their joint use it would have been impossible to develop either the stationary steam-engine or the locomotive. The result was that the iron and coal areas of the country gained tremendously in importance. Great new industrial regions, such as the Black Country in Staffordshire, developed an entirely new sort of environment for men to live in. The landscape became dominated by industry. A town like Sheffield, which grew up in one of England's beauty spots, became a nest of small workshops and furnaces, which removed the last traces of the earlier natural setting.

Coal and iron took the place of wood, water, and wind, which had provided the industrial power of earlier periods of history. They in turn have been supplanted by electricity, light-alloy metals, and PLASTICS (q.v.); during the course of the so-called Second Industrial Revolution which followed on the invention in 1867 of ELECTRIC MOTORS and GENERATORS (qq.v. Vol. VIII). The widespread use of electric power has affected industry quite as much as steam once did, and we ourselves are living in a period of continued industrial revolution at least as striking as that of the late 18th century. Once technical change had accelerated, it proved impossible to check its pace.

The inventors of this period were backed by the business men who put their inventions to general use. The great technical genius of James Watt was allied with the business initiative of Matthew Boulton, a Birmingham business man, who went into partnership with Watt to make the Soho engine works in Birmingham the most

AN EARLY 19TH-CENTURY FACTORY AT TEWKESBURY

The men are making stockings by machine, and children are employed for spinning and unskilled work. The supervisor wears a top hat

important industrial enterprise of the 18th century.

An inventor was often a very unpopular person. He was frequently accused of taking bread from out of the mouths of the poor. Hargreaves, for instance, the inventor of the spinning-jenny (see below), had his cottage at Blackburn attacked by an angry mob, intent on destroying his machine. The early manufacturers also had to keep a close watch on their factories, to prevent their being attacked. There is a vivid description of such an incident in *Shirley*, by Charlotte Brontë (*see also* LUDDITES).

Changes in the production of coal and iron were followed by others. During the 18th century there was a rapid growth in other industries, such as POTTERY and TEXTILES (qq.v.) The most important maker of pottery was Josiah WEDGWOOD (q.v. Vol. V), who in 1754 invented a 'new green earthenware, having the smoothness and brilliant appearance of glass'. The work of Wedgwood led to a great change in the everyday habits of the people, and began that

narrowing of the gap between rich and poor that is still going on. At the beginning of the 18th century ordinary people ate from wooden trenchers or platters, while the well-to-do laid their tables with pewter ware. In this, and in other ways, the Industrial Revolution provided new materials for the consumer, just as it provided new machines and techniques for the industrialist.

The story of textiles is even more spectacular. COTTON (q.v.) was the industry which changed most. There had been big improvements in weaving after the invention of the flying shuttle by Kay in 1733; weavers could now work much more quickly and produce cloth of greater width. But the spinners could now no longer keep pace with the weavers, and the weavers began to complain of being short of material. As early as the 1730's a spinning-machine was invented, and in 1764 Hargreaves patented his new 'spinning-jenny', which he called after his wife. Other inventions followed, one leading to another. The most important were Arkwright's water-frame and Crompton's 'mule'. Inventions for spinning now led to further inventions for weaving. Cartwright invented a loom which was driven by water-power, and eventually steam-power was harnessed first to the cotton and then to the wool industries. There was a widespread demand for cotton cloths, which the new machines helped to meet. There were also opportunities for making good profits; and Richard Arkwright, who had begun as a travelling dealer in hair, realized when wigs went out of fashion that cotton was a far more profitable business. Arkwright was the first big factory organizer, and did much to introduce new machines.

The rise of the factory system produced some of the most important social consequences of the Industrial Revolution. Factories have a relentless discipline of their own; workers must arrive to time, and work side by side for definite hours and for wage-payments. The factories produced a new sort of industrial worker who owned none of his working tools or machines, and was employed for long hours to increase the profits of the factory-owner. There were many good masters, but—as one of the advocates of factory reform stated—'a steam engine in the hands of an interested or avaricious master is a relentless power to which old and young are equally bound to submit'.

The factory system developed most rapidly in the 30 years after the end of the war with Napoleon (1815), and the speed of development and urgency of its expansion led to many abuses, which were only abolished with the making of a national factory code of regulations. This code was extended and improved throughout the 19th and 20th centuries, and reached its climax in the Factories Act of 1937 (*see* INDUSTRIAL WELFARE, Vol. X).

But it was a long time before factories were to be found in every part of the country. At first they were mainly situated in the textile districts of the north; by contrast, Birmingham and the midlands were districts of small workshops.

The factory gathered workers together in one place; the new transport system, based first upon roads and canals and then upon railways and steamships, helped first to unify England and then to make the world as a whole a much smaller place. Just as the invention of the steam-engine gave men an increased control over the forces of nature, so the changes in transport enabled them to gain an increased control over the obstacles of distance and time. Long journeys were made easier; oceans and continents were crossed. The world was opened up to industry and trade.

Improvements on the roads were made by such men as John Metcalfe, better known as Blind Jack of Knaresborough, and Telford, and Macadam (*see* ROADS, HISTORY OF, Vol. IV). Some of the improvements can be measured by the shortened times of journeys by stage-coach; even before the beginning of the railway age it had become possible to travel long distances in a single day. Road improvements were preceded

AN EARLY 19TH-CENTURY STEEL WORKS AT SHEFFIELD

by river improvements, and by the building of CANALS (q.v. Vol. IV). Business men played a large part, for the building of canals greatly reduced transport costs. Wedgwood, for example, was largely instrumental in having the Grand Trunk Canal built. Brindley's 7-mile canal from the collieries at Worsley to Manchester halved the price of coal in the city. What had been done by improved road and water transport was magnified many times by the introduction of railways (*see* RAILWAYS, HISTORY OF, Vol. IV). The Stockton and Darlington line was opened in 1825, and the line from Manchester to Liverpool five years later. The great 'railway mania'—the craze for building as many railways as possible—came between 1844 and 1848. By the end of that burst of building there were 5,000 miles of railway in operation in Britain. STEAMSHIPS (q.v. Vol. IV) did for the world what railways had done for England. The first transatlantic steam voyage was made in 1819, and the first steam voyage from London to Calcutta 6 years later. Goods and raw materials could now be transported freely and cheaply to and from all parts of the world, which was fast becoming a single, vast market.

This change-over from a local to a world market has caused some of the most important long-range effects of the Industrial Revolution. Through the extension of markets, countries and peoples have come to know more of each other, and have become more dependent on each other for foodstuffs, raw materials, and manufactures. The building of a world economy has only come about at the price of disputes and anxieties. UNEMPLOYMENT (q.v.) and depression have tended to become international instead of merely national or local, and there is a great deal of quarrelling between governments over such things as trade agreements.

The Industrial Revolution is a challenge as well as an achievement. It provided challenging problems that have appealed to men's hearts and enlisted their energy. It threw a spotlight on many evils and even horrors—smoky, dirty, and overcrowded towns, for instance, and the overworking of women and children. Its abuses were firmly attacked, but not all its problems have been solved, nor all its abuses remedied.

As to its achievement, opinions will always differ, for each generation looks on history with different eyes. If we try to measure the achievement, we must balance the tremendous increase in the goods and services that we can now enjoy —everything from cotton shirts to motor-cars— against a loss of many things that can never be replaced—the green fields of Sheffield, or the pride and skill of the individual hand craftsman.

See also DIVISION OF LABOUR; EXCHANGE AND TRADE; DOMESTIC SYSTEM.

See also Vol. X: INDUSTRIAL WELFARE; POOR LAW.

INDUSTRY. Most human occupations are either industrial or commercial. Those engaged in industry produce or make things. Those engaged in COMMERCE buy and sell them, or TRANSPORT them from place to place, or provide services such as BANKING and INSURANCE (qq.v.) that assist industry.

Industries can broadly be classified as either extractive or manufacturing. The first, as their name suggests, extract materials from the land or water. MINING (q.v.) is an extractive industry, so also are fishing, whaling, agriculture, horticulture, and forestry, which are dealt with in Vol. VI. Some of these, such as the mining of coal and iron, extract materials whose quantity is limited, and which are not replaced by nature when they are removed. Other extractive industries, such as agriculture or forestry, if they are well managed, do not take more out of the soil than can be restored.

Manufacturing industries are concerned with transforming one type of material into another,

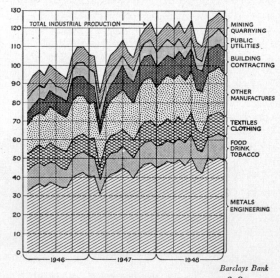

Barclays Bank

INDUSTRIAL PRODUCTION IN BRITAIN, 1946–8

The width of the bands indicates the contribution of each main industry

or converting a raw material into useful goods. For example, manufacture transforms iron ore, coal, and limestone, which are products of the extractive industries, into iron and steel, which are manufactured products. Similarly, forestry is an extractive industry, but the making of WOOD PULP, and the making of NEWSPRINT (qq.v.) from the pulp, are manufacturing industries.

People often talk of the HOTEL INDUSTRY, the CATERING INDUSTRY, and the TOURIST INDUSTRY (qq.v.). The word 'industry' in this sense has now passed into general usage, but it is better to put such activities into a class of their own and call them direct personal services.

INDUSTRY, LOCALIZATION OF, *see* LOCALIZATION OF INDUSTRY.

INLAY AND MARQUETRY. Both these crafts are used for the decoration of furniture and wood panels. Inlay consists of glueing in small pieces of different or contrasting material, flush with the surface of the wood. Oak chests or cupboards of the 16th century, for example, often have simple geometrical designs inlaid in holly or poplar (which are much whiter woods than oak) and bog-oak (which, until ebony came to be imported, was about the blackest wood available). In marquetry the whole surface of the wood is covered with a sheet of veneer into which the pattern or ornament, cut from a contrasting veneer, has already been fitted and glued. Veneer, which has been used in British CABINET-MAKING (q.v.) for some 300 years, is a sheet of very thin wood, perhaps no thicker than a postcard, which can be glued over a carcass or panel of less ornamental wood, and then polished. Both inlay and marquetry are flat forms of decoration; they rely for their effect on the colour of the wood, the direction of the grain, and the outline of the inlays. Carving, on the other hand, gets its effect from the shadows thrown by the varying surfaces of the wood (*see* WOODWORK, HISTORY OF).

The design for inlay must be simple in outline, so that the wood can be cut without too much difficulty. The individual pieces must also be fairly small or they would become unmanageable. To inlay a piece of furniture, a piece of paper is first glued to the wood to be inlaid, and each piece is sawn out with a fine saw. Ornamental lines can be made by saw cuts which show up dark when filled with glue. The places

Victoria and Albert Museum

ARMCHAIR INLAID WITH HOLLY, CHERRY, AND BOG OAK, ABOUT 1600

in the piece of furniture into which the inlay is to fit are 'chopped down' with gouges and chisels, the recess being made perfectly level with a router (a special kind of plane). The inlay is glued into place; as the glue sets, it shrinks, tending to pull the inlay downwards and to make a perfect join. A final levelling and polishing of the piece of furniture completes the work.

In marquetry the design can be much more elaborate and delicate than in inlay. There are two methods of cutting the veneers for marquetry. In the first the veneer for the background and that for the inlay are fixed together, and the design is sawn through both in one operation. They are then separated, and the pieces of veneer are interchanged; the two make a perfect fit, since a marquetry saw is very fine. A piece of paper is glued over the surface to hold the inlay in place, and the whole is then glued down on to the groundwork. Finally, the surface is cleaned up and polished. In the second method, several different veneers can be used for the background veneer, and those for the inlay

Victoria and Albert Museum
WALNUT AND MARQUETRY CABINET ON STAND,
LATE 17TH CENTURY

Victoria and Albert Museum
WARDROBE MADE BY BOULLE FOR LOUIS XIV,
LATE 17TH CENTURY
Made of ebony with marquetry of white metal and brass
on tortoise-shell, with ormolu mounts

are cut separately. The design is first drawn on paper, and then pricked out with a series of fine holes. By placing this master pattern on a second sheet of paper and dusting a dark powder over it, the design can be transferred, as many duplicates being made as there are to be different kinds of veneer. These are then glued to the veneers, and the design is cut out, assembled, and fixed as in the first method.

In the early days the cutting of the design was done entirely by hand. Later, the marquetry-cutter used a 'donkey', a device by which the veneer could be gripped in upright jaws and turned as the sawing required, the saw being held taut in a frame which was free to move on guides. It was thus always at right angles to the veneer. If the same design is to be used for a number of articles, several thicknesses of veneer can be cut at the same time. For every two veneers two complete designs are produced, both alike in outline but with the veneers reversed.

Marquetry was introduced into England by William III, and by the time of Queen Anne it had developed into a craft of great delicacy and beauty. In France, towards the end of the 17th century, the Italian style of marquetry, with tortoiseshell and metal inlays, had been developed by Boulle, and reached a high standard; it is now known as Buhl-work. French furniture became increasingly elaborate during the 18th century, and was decorated with inlay, marquetry, and gilt bronze carving; but in England the fashion for marquetry did not last long. It was revived in a different form towards the close of the 18th century, and continued until the opening years of the present century, when a tremendous amount of marquetry was used. It then fell into disuse except for reproductions of old furniture. In recent years there has been a revival in the large landscape panels sometimes used to decorate walls in public buildings. In many liners the rooms are decorated with pictorial marquetry panels.

Many substances other than wood have been used for inlay work. In ancient Egypt and Rome, ivory, mother-of-pearl, and even precious or semi-precious stones were used. From the 15th century the craft was widely practised in Italy, where great use was also made of coloured marbles (*see* MOSAICS, Vol. XII). The inlaying of metal into metal is described in GOLD AND SILVER WORK.

See also WOODWORK, HISTORY OF.

INNS, *see* HOTEL INDUSTRY; *see also* Vol. IV: INNS.

INSURANCE. This is a method by which firms and private individuals may 'insure' or make sure that, if certain unwanted events happen to themselves or their property, compensation up to an agreed sum will be paid. Not all risks lend themselves to being covered by insurance. Broadly speaking, the ordinary risks of business and speculation cannot be covered. The risk that buyers will not buy goods at the prices offered is not of a kind that can be statistically estimated—and risks can only be insured against if they can be so estimated. All risks lie in the future, and the only hope of knowing what the future will bring is to study what the past has brought. Figures of past experience can serve as a guide to the future. For example, if we know how many outbreaks of fire there have been in one part of a city over a number of years, and the type of building most usually affected, we can work out with surprising accuracy how many fires each year there will be in the future. With few exceptions, insurance can only be used to cover risks about which figures of the past are available.

The legal basis of all insurance is the 'policy'. This is a printed form of contract on stout paper of the best quality. It states that in return for the regular payment by the insured of a named sum of money, called the 'premium', which is usually paid every year, the firm or person

A 19TH-CENTURY FIREMAN, ROYAL EXCHANGE ASSURANCE

accepting the risk will pay a sum of money or compensation for loss, if the risk or event insured against actually happens. The wording of policies, particularly in marine insurance, often seems very old-fashioned; but there is a sound reason for this. Over a large number of years many law cases have been brought to clear up the meanings of doubtful phrases in policies. The law courts, in their judgements, have given these phrases a definite and indisputable meaning, and to avoid future disputes the phrases have continued to be used in policies even when they have passed out of normal use in speech.

The premium for an insurance naturally depends upon how likely the risk is to happen, as suggested by past experience. If companies fix their premiums too high, there will be more competition in their branch of insurance and they may lose business. On the other hand, if they make the premiums too low, they will lose money and may even have to drop out of business. So the ordinary forces of supply and demand keep premiums at a level satisfactory to both insurer and insured.

Working out the chances of events happening in the future depends to a great extent on what STATISTICS (q.v.) are available to show how frequently the same events have occurred in the past. Some of the information needed comes from the past experience of the insurance firms themselves; other information comes from pub-

FIRE MARK OF THE ROYAL EXCHANGE ASSURANCE

Assurance Companies owned their own fire engines in the 18th and early 19th centuries and attended only those houses which were insured by them. Such houses had fire marks nailed to their walls to identify them. (Reproduced by permission)

E. W. Tattersall

THE LUTINE BELL AT LLOYD'S

The bell is rung when important announcements—such
as the loss of a ship—are made

lished statistics. The skilled statisticians employed
by life insurance firms are called actuaries.

All risks about which there are past statistics
lend themselves to insurance. As there are many
ways in which these risks can be classified,
there are many specialized branches of insurance, the principal ones being: Life, Fire and
Accident, Marine, Burglary, Motor-car, Employers' Liability, Fidelity Guarantee, and Credit
insurances.

Fire and Accident Insurance deals not only
with ordinary fire risks, but with damage to
property by gales, floods, frost, lightning, and
similar natural occurrences. This branch also
writes policies insuring individuals against personal accident. As its name suggests, Marine insurance is concerned with the insurance of ships
and cargoes, and in this branch LLOYD's (q.v.
Vol. IV) in London mainly specializes.

Those who run motor vehicles are obliged by
law to insure themselves against claims brought
by 'third parties' (that is, people other than the
insurance company and the insured person), but

are not legally obliged to cover themselves
against the risk of total or partial loss to the
actual vehicle. The law also makes employers,
whether in business or at home, liable to pay
compensation if someone who works for them
is injured or killed while at work. Employers'
Liability policies are written to cover such risks.

A Fidelity Guarantee policy compensates
business firms for losses through fraud, theft, or
embezzlement by dishonest employees.

Credit insurance covers merchants and manufacturers against risk of loss through debtors
going bankrupt and failing to pay their debts.
Credit insurance was once entirely in the hands
of private firms, and the companies so engaged
covered credit risks in the export as well as the
home trade; but in 1926 the British Government,
through the Department of Overseas Trade, set
up the Exports Credits Guarantee Scheme, and
it is now difficult for private companies to
compete in credit insurance in the export trade.

There is one insurance company which also
issues an unusual kind of policy—the 'pluvius'
policy (from the Latin word meaning 'rainy'),
which insures against the risk that an outdoor
entertainment or sports event might be spoiled
by bad weather. One would think that a risk of
this sort could hardly be covered, but the weather
statistics of past years allow it to be done.
Another type of insurance policy is that taken
out by political parties to cover lost deposits
at an election. This was done by the Liberal
Party in 1950.

Life Insurance is a very specialized branch of
insurance, and while many companies do not
touch it, certain others handle nothing else.
The earlier policies were written to provide for
a man's widow or dependants after his death;
but in recent years life insurance has become
much wider. Companies now issue endowment
policies, by which the insured person is paid a
lump sum, or else an income for life, on reaching
a specified age. Endowment policies are taken
out by many large firms in order to organize
pension and superannuation funds for their
staffs. Survivorship policies are often taken out
by business partnerships, to cover the risk of the
death of a partner: partnerships are normally
dissolved by death, and it would be a hardship
to have a prosperous business compulsorily
wound up.

Of the institutions that carry on insurance,
some specialize in only one branch of insurance,

while some of them 'write policies' in many branches. In Great Britain they consist principally of Lloyd's and several important limited companies, some of which have a very large capital. Lloyd's is not a company; it is, in fact, a professional association.

Lloyd's at work is an impressive sight. Hundreds of 'underwriters' and their clerks sit in straight-backed and rather uncomfortable-looking pews, while brokers, acting on behalf of would-be insurers, crowd the entrance and pass messages to the uniformed porter standing in a rostrum in the centre of 'the Room'. As he shouts out the names of the firms called, an underwriter comes out, and the broker goes to his table to transact his business. All business is verbal, done by word of mouth without any formal signing of documents: the underwriters merely initial slips of paper stating the risks covered and the premiums charged.

The words 'underwriter and 'underwriting' are particularly associated with Lloyd's, although these terms are also used among the companies and in the capital market (*see* Issuing Houses). The word 'underwriter' came into use because Lloyd's policies were originally initialed at the foot by the various members who joined together to insure the larger risks.

An underwriter may be offered a risk too large for him to accept alone, though he is reluctant to refuse it. He then accepts the whole risk, but passes on portions of it to other underwriters. The passing-on is called reinsurance, in which some companies specialize. A risk may be passed on when the proposal is received, or later. Sometimes, as when accidents happen to ships at sea, the chance of successful salvage is so small that rates for reinsurance are extremely high. If one reads that a ship aground off the Cornish coast in February is being reinsured at Lloyd's at a premium of 95 guineas per cent., it is safe to conclude that her chances are slender.

Social Insurance (q.v. Vol. X) is a national, and not a commercial matter; it covers the death, sickness, disablement, old age, and unemployment of almost all citizens. To a limited extent the national scheme uses the methods of the commercial world: the benefits received bear a reasonable relationship to the contributions paid; but if the contributions fail to meet the cost of the scheme as a whole, the difference is paid for by the general body of taxpayers.

INTEREST. In the business world no person with capital to spare would lend it to anyone else unless he were paid for doing so, because he would naturally consider the money as safe with himself as elsewhere. Capital (q.v.) is, therefore, comparatively scarce. Like everything else that is scarce in economic life, it commands its own price; and this price is known as 'interest'.

The rate of interest which has to be paid will vary with the period for which capital is borrowed and also with the nature of the Security offered (q.v.). To lend money at all involves some risk. The longer the loan, the greater is the risk of its not being repaid, and so rates for short-term loans are lower than those for long periods.

Interest is not the same thing as Dividends (q.v.), which are paid out of the profits made by a business. Interest is arranged in advance, and has to be paid at the rate then fixed. If a business can earn profit at a higher rate than that of the interest at which it can borrow capital, its total profits may rise, and the dividend it can pay to its ordinary shareholders may be higher than it could otherwise be.

No simple rule can be laid down for fixing rates of interest. Broadly speaking, these vary according to how much capital is being offered for investment and how great the commercial and industrial demand for it is at any particular moment. In times of prosperity or boom, the rates of interest may rise; in times of depression they may fall very low. If there is an alteration in the amount of capital that is being saved by people generally, interest-rates may alter as a result. During and after the Second World War, incomes were high and there was little in the shops to spend money on. Savings were therefore considerable; and, although the demand for capital was high, the rate of interest remained low. When saving decreased in 1949 and 1950, interest-rates rose. But government control, by limiting the number of industrial and commercial borrowers, can make interest-rates lower than they would be in an absolutely free market.

See also Dividend; Profits.

INTERNATIONAL FINANCE is the system by which the surplus savings of a more highly developed country are used to assist the economic life of a less advanced country. Within a single country an industry or area short of CAPITAL (q.v.) can borrow from the wealthier parts of the country. For example, in Britain the surplus wealth of London investors and financiers can be placed at the disposal of Birmingham and Glasgow manufacturers. But in the past it often happened that a country's own savings were insufficient to enable it to develop as fast as it wished, and such a country had then either to get the necessary capital from abroad, or remain economically backward. This lending and borrowing between nations is called international finance.

Until 1914, when the First World War broke out, nearly all the lending was done by private investors, and the borrowers were sometimes industries and sometimes governments. International finance first developed on a large scale in the middle of the 19th century, when railways were being built in the U.S.A. In spite of their growing wealth, insufficient capital could be obtained from such cities as New York, and the railways therefore sold their BONDS (q.v.) to private investors in London and other wealthy centres. Later, for the construction of the Canadian Pacific Railway, money was borrowed in New York and many European cities, as the necessary capital could never have been found in Canada itself. The governments of countries where railways were being constructed and operated by the State borrowed in London, Paris, and other wealthy cities, and in this way the money was found to build railways in Russia, India, and Australia. Later in the 19th century London provided an immense amount of capital for the railways of Argentina and Brazil. This assistance helped to develop Argentina, and to make that country wealthy; so that many years later the Argentine Government was able to buy back the railways from the British investors who owned them.

During the First World War governments began to lend direct to each other. The Government of the U.S.A. made loans to Britain so that she could buy American munitions of war for herself and her allies, and Britain made similar loans to her allies. Most of these loans were not repaid, and were eventually 'written off' or cancelled. In 1946, after the Second World War, the U.S.A. made a large loan to Britain for the restarting of British industry after so many years of war. These big loans from one government to another are for sums much larger than could be obtained from private investors, and are now the most prominent form of international finance. All the same, international lending by private individuals still continues; in 1950, for example, British investors were invited to subscribe for bonds issued by the City of Johannesburg in the Union of South Africa.

In the past some of these international transactions have led to friction between governments, usually because interest or capital has not been paid out punctually. But the system of international finance helps the less wealthy or more backward countries to develop their resources and to make them available for the rest of the world, and both the lending and the borrowing countries reap a benefit. For example, by helping to build railways in the Dominions and elsewhere, which opened up new lands for producing wheat and meat and other products, Britain was herself helped to feed her increasing population.

The Lend-Lease system of the Second World War, when the U.S.A. made large gifts of foodstuffs and munitions to Britain, and the Marshall Plan, by which similar gifts were made for the reconstruction of Western Europe, differ from international finance of the type described above. Such gifts are really military subsidies to allies or future allies, although they do assist economically the countries receiving the gifts.

See also FINANCE; MONEY MARKET; RATES OF EXCHANGE.

INTERNATIONAL TRADE. 1. Trade between nations is necessary in modern life because most countries are either unable to produce certain things as cheaply or as well as certain other countries, or cannot produce them at all. Climate, raw materials, and the skill and the character of the inhabitants all play their parts in this connexion. For instance, before the invention of the 'humidifier', a machine which provided artificially moistened air, the moist climate of Lancashire was particularly suited to COTTON MANUFACTURE (q.v.), for cotton fibre, which Britain imports in large quantities, is brittle and tends to break if it is spun in a dry atmosphere. Wheat is best grown where a heavy winter snow-fall soaks well into the soil and a short dry summer ripens the plant quickly: so Canada and south-west Russia are specially good for WHEAT growing (q.v. Vol. VI). When different countries specialize in the production of different commodities, so that they have more than enough for their own needs, international trade is the result.

Great Britain is particularly dependent upon overseas trade. Corn crops are grown in Great Britain, but some cereals cannot be grown as well or as cheaply as in other countries. Britain, however, was the first country in the world to develop manufacturing industry on a large scale, and so there are many skilled workers and managers whose knowledge has been passed on from generation to generation. This allowed Britain to increase greatly the output of manufactured goods from the late 18th and early 19th centuries onwards. As the overseas production of food-stuffs increased in about the same proportion, Britain was able to get enough food to provide for a rapidly growing population by selling her manufactured goods to countries overseas and spending the money on buying agricultural products.

2. BALANCE OF TRADE. In 1949 the value of Britain's total overseas trade was over £4,000 million. Of this just under £2,300 million were imports, and just over £1,800 million exports. Imports of food, drink, and tobacco account for about half the total imports in a normal year, and the raw materials of manufacturing industries for about a third. Most British exports are in the form of manufactured goods, the proportion varying between 70% and 85% in a normal year. The difference between a country's 'physical' exports (or exports in actual goods) and physical imports is called its balance of trade. Physical exports and imports are often called 'visible', because they can be seen and handled. So these figures show that in 1949 the visible imports were much bigger than the visible exports, and therefore the balance of trade was said to be 'unfavourable'.

3. INVISIBLE EXPORTS AND IMPORTS. All export transactions are not physical, or visible. For example, if foreigners use British ships to move their goods, her shipping industry earns foreign money just as much as if she exported motor-cars. Or, again, if the underwriters of Lloyd's are asked by foreigners to insure them against fire and marine risks (*see* INSURANCE), they too earn foreign money. All such transactions, which do not involve payments for actual goods, yet which give bankers increased balances in foreign currencies, are called 'invisible' exports; transactions in the opposite direction, giving foreign

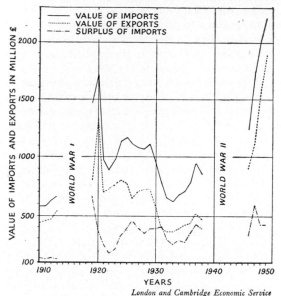

BRITISH IMPORTS AND EXPORTS, 1910–49

banks the command of credits in British banks, are called 'invisible' imports. Thus, if people travel abroad, the money they spend in other countries really represents an invisible import. It is for this reason that the amount of money which many governments allow their citizens to spend on foreign travel is strictly limited; for even if invisible exports are added to visible ones, there may still be a gap between a country's total exports and its total imports, and this has to be filled by borrowing foreign money. The American loan granted to Britain in 1946 was arranged to give the British people time to reconstruct their industry after the war and so to bring total exports and total imports more into line with each other (*see* INTERNATIONAL FINANCE).

When all invisible items have been added in, the difference between total exports and total imports of all kinds, visible and invisible, is called a country's balance of payments.

4. FREE TRADE. From the 16th to the 18th centuries, most economists and other writers on overseas trade believed that a country should always try to have a favourable balance of trade, which would be paid for by other countries in gold or silver. They argued that those countries with the biggest stocks of precious metals would be the richest and also the best prepared for war (*see* MERCANTILE SYSTEM). But from the end of the 18th century economists began to realize that one could not eat, wear, or live on the precious metals, and that a country's wealth was more likely to be increased, and its STANDARD OF LIVING raised (q.v.), if obstructions to free international trading were removed.

The economists used two main arguments to prove their case. They argued, firstly, that it would pay any country, where a particular commodity cost more to produce than abroad, to give up producing it and to import it instead. From this it followed that all attempts to restrict international trade by import duties (see TARIFFS), which made cheap goods from abroad artificially dearer in the home country importing them, were entirely wrong. This took for granted that one country might have an absolute advantage over another in the production of certain goods, and so it was called the doctrine of Absolute Advantage. For instance, in the early 19th century, soon after these ideas had been published, Britain had an absolute advantage over the rest of the world in manufacturing cotton and woollen textiles; whereas Virginia in the growing of tobacco, and the Carolinas in the growing of raw cotton, had an absolute advantage over Britain.

The second argument was called the doctrine of Comparative Advantage. This held that it would be beneficial in the long run if a country —even if it possessed an absolute advantage over the other countries in the production of everything—concentrated on the production of those goods in which its comparative advantage over other countries was greatest, so that other countries would be able to concentrate their productive efforts in those directions where their inefficiency was comparatively least.

By the middle of the 19th century these doctrines had led to the political policy of Free Trade. This aimed at removing all taxes and other regulations which restricted both imports and exports. For nearly a hundred years Great Britain practised Free Trade, but very few overseas countries followed her example.

5. PROTECTION. The opposite policy to Free Trade was called Protection. The Protectionist argued that foreign producers, who could undersell home manufacturers, might upset or even ruin whole industries; and so the home manufacturer should be shielded against foreign competition in various ways (see QUOTAS; SUBSIDIES; TARIFFS) Early in the present century these arguments became more convincing, because

certain foreign industries adopted the habit of 'dumping' or selling their goods abroad more cheaply than at home. In this way they could keep up a high output, which cut down costs and increased profits; and on balance they gained, because what they lost by selling cheaply abroad they made up for by raising their prices at home.

Dumping gradually won more converts to Protection, and so did the growing need to prepare for war. Between the First and Second World Wars Great Britain gradually swung over from Free Trade to a policy of Protection, but not nearly as far as other countries did. Britain still had to import large quantities of food-stuffs and raw materials, and therefore did not tax these, but as British industry needed to sell the goods it manufactured, protective steps were taken against the manufactured goods of other countries.

Britain was so seriously weakened economically by the Second World War that she could afford only a limited quantity of imports, and the State regulation of imports was therefore adopted. Before the war Britain was able to pay for many imports out of the large sums paid by foreigners as interest and dividends on British money invested in their countries. These investments shrank severely through war, and exports were encouraged so as to keep imports at a satisfactory level.

See also OVERSEAS TRADE; STANDARD OF LIVING; TRADE, HISTORY OF.

INVESTMENTS, see STOCKS AND SHARES; DEBENTURES; LOANS; BOND; BANKING.

INVISIBLE IMPORTS AND EXPORTS, see INTERNATIONAL TRADE.

INVOICES. Business men use the word invoice for what ordinary people call 'bills'. In modern business invoices are usually forms printed in duplicate or triplicate, with serial numbers, and bound into books. The firm's name and address are printed boldly in the middle of the form, and above it are lines on which the name and address of the buyer of the goods may be written of typed. The rest of the form is ruled in columns so that the quantities of different goods ordered, their price, the value of each separate purchase, and the total amount, can be clearly seen.

Invoices used in the wholesale trade usually state when payment is expected, and what cash

AN 18TH-CENTURY RECEIPTED INVOICE

It records the sale in 1781 of Milk of Roses, Essence of Musk, and Oil of Jasmine, by Richard Warren, Perfumer, to Sir Ralph Payne

discount will be allowed if payment is made earlier than the stipulated date.

When we buy goods for cash in a shop, the invoice, or bill, is receipted at the time of purchase. If payment is not made at the time of purchase, an account is opened for the buyer, and most of the entries in the seller's account-books are made from the invoices. At the end of the month the purchaser receives what is called a 'statement'. This is a copy of the buyer's account in the firm's books; it includes the total of all invoices issued during the month, together with any balance already owing; from this total payments made during the month and the amounts of any credit notes issued are subtracted.

Credit notes are forms like invoices, generally bound in books with serial numbers and usually printed in red ink, whereas invoices are printed in black. Credit notes are used when a purchaser returns unsatisfactory or damaged articles, or if he complains about the quality of goods and arranges with the seller a reduction in the price. Invoice totals are debited to customers in a firm's books; credit notes and cash payments are credited (see BOOK-KEEPING).

If payment is made for the total of the monthly statement, it is usual for buyers to attach their statements to their cheques; the statements then come back receipted by the seller. Receipts for sums of £2 and over must bear a two-penny stamp. Payments of less than the total of a statement are called payments 'on account'. Receipts are usually written on special receipt forms, also often bound up in book form and serially numbered.

See also PAYMENT; CREDIT.

IRON AND STEEL, see Vol. VIII: IRON AND STEEL INDUSTRY.

IRON ORE, or ironstone, is mineral rock containing compounds of iron. Iron has been used by man since quite early times, but records suggest that it was used in ancient Assyria and Egypt long before it was worked in Europe. Its use in Europe dates from about 1000 B.C. Very little iron is available in pure metallic form save for meteorites (see METEORS, Vol. III), and as meteorites are rare and very small, meteoric iron is of no commercial importance. The iron that is used in modern industry is in the form of METAL ORES (q.v. Vol. III), which are chemical compounds of iron and other elements. The ores principally found are the ferric and ferrous oxides and carbonates, and the oxides known as haematite and magnetite are the most used. Both these ores are widely distributed in the earth's crust, but many of the deposits are of no industrial value. Sometimes they are situated in remote and economically backward countries. Sometimes they are inaccessible, not because they are distant, but because there are no transport communications to make their use profitable. Sometimes they are too far away from the coal and limestone needed for the extraction of the metal from the ore by iron SMELTING (q.v. Vol. VIII). Sometimes the metallic content of the deposits is poor, and it does not pay to work them, for it will naturally be more profitable to transport rich ores than poor ores over long distances. A great deal depends on the means of transport available. In many parts of the world ironstone deposits are a very long way from industrial areas and from coal, but water transport makes it profitable to mine them and take the ores to the

QUARRYING IRON ORE AT LONG HARRY MINE, GREETWELL, LINCS.

The principal British ironstone deposits are in Lincolnshire, Lancashire, and Northamptonshire. In the Cleveland district of Yorkshire there is still some good quality haematite of very low phosphorus content, but mining operations are becoming deeper and more expensive every year. Over the rest of the country ironstone deposits are mostly phosphoric, and those principally worked to-day are around Frodingham and Scunthorpe in Lincolnshire, and Corby in Northamptonshire. Before the First World War, Britain imported considerable quantities of low-phosphorus ores from northern Spain. Later the making of steel from phosphoric ores became technically more efficient, and imports from Spain decreased. After the Second World War imports of Spanish ore fell still further, not only for technical reasons but also because Spain had become a HARD CURRENCY area (q.v.). Sweden has always been a big exporter of haematite ores to Britain.

See also MINING.

See also Vol. VIII: IRON AND STEEL INDUSTRY.

furnaces. This is particularly true of the Lake Superior ores of the U.S.A., and of the Spanish ores that are exported through the port of Bilbao. The Lake Superior ores are a very long way from coal, but they are easily mined by open-cast methods with modern digging and excavating machines (*see* COAL-MINING). The ore is mechanically loaded into large lake steamers—a 10,000-ton ship can be loaded completely in half-an-hour—and carried to the iron and steel plants on the shores of Lake Erie, hundreds of miles away. Northern Spain also is not an industrial area, but the ore deposits are so close to the sea that they can be easily transported to industrial countries where they can be profitably used.

Whether an ore can be profitably mined or not depends not only upon its yield of metallic iron, but also upon other chemical elements that may be in it. Iron smelted from phosphoric ores is brittle and, until the late 19th century, was useless for steel-making; many large deposits of ironstone in Europe, particularly in Lorraine, Belgium, and Luxembourg, had no commercial value because of their high content of phosphorus. But in 1879 a way was found of making steel from phosphoric iron. Since then the world's phosphoric ores have been greatly used, although ores low in phosphorus always command a higher price in the market.

ISSUING HOUSES. This is the name given to certain firms in the financial world which make a practice of finding CAPITAL (q.v.) for business firms, public corporations, and governments. No one is obliged by law to make use of the services of issuing houses: any organization is free to decide for itself whether the profits it can earn, or the taxes it can collect (if it is a government), will pay a dividend or rate of interest high enough to attract capital from private investors. It can then put advertisements in the newspapers and invite the public to subscribe the capital needed. But there is always a chance that the investing public may not think the offer tempting enough, in which case those who are seeking capital may find that they have spent a lot of money on publicity and yet have failed to raise the capital they need.

Issuing houses are able to guarantee that the

capital wanted will be found. In London such firms are either specialized companies with considerable capital of their own and long experience of this work, or old-established MERCHANT BANKERS (q.v.). An issuing house must know, or be able to get in touch with, a wide circle of firms having plenty of free capital. Its directors or managers must be in close contact with commerce and industry, and quick to sum up the possibilities of a venture. They must study the financial markets very closely, to know the prices at which shares can be successfully marketed or placed, or the rates of interest at which money can be borrowed successfully.

An issuing house works in this way. Suppose a limited-liability company has already collected subscriptions of £50,000 from its own directors, and now wants to raise an extra £500,000 from the public. It approaches an issuing house, taking with it estimates of the profits it expects to make. These will be studied by the issuing house and, if necessary, corrected. Now the issuing house has to make up its mind whether or not the issue is worth making. If it decides to go on with it, the next step is, with the help of the directors of the company, to draft a 'prospectus'. This is a legal document, giving particulars of the company's directors, the nature of the proposed business, and estimates of profits to be earned. Copies of this will be handed by the issuing house to persons who are asked to 'underwrite', or guarantee, part of the capital required. If they agree, they will sign underwriting agreements.

These underwriting agreements are not definite promises by the underwriters that they will 'subscribe firm', or provide capital up to the number of shares underwritten: if they were, there would be no point in trying to get public subscriptions at all. The underwriting agreements are simply a form of insurance against the risk that the public may not subscribe. What the underwriters actually promise to do is to subscribe for any shares which are not taken up by the public. As compensation for undertaking this risk, each underwriter is paid an agreed commission, usually about 2%. Underwriters themselves often 'reinsure' their underwriting risks with sub-underwriters, giving them part of their own commission.

When all the underwriting contracts have been signed, the prospectuses are published in the Press, are put on the counters of all the impor-

tant branches of the company's bankers, and get more publicity through being recommended by stockbrokers and others. A stated date and time are advertised for the opening of the public subscription list.

If the proposition is a good one the public response is often overwhelming, and more money is subscribed than is asked for; but sometimes this apparent success is deceptive. One kind of City speculator, called a 'stag', makes it his business to fill up applications for newly issued shares that he thinks will go well. As most new shares are paid for by a small initial deposit, and the balance by instalments, a relatively small sum of money can give a 'stag' control of quite a number of shares. These he hopes to sell at a profit, as soon as dealings in the shares commence on the Stock Exchange.

Whether the issue has been 'stagged' or not, everything has gone well for the issuing house and the underwriters so long as public applications have been received for at least as many shares as were offered for subscription. In this event the underwriters would get commission without having to subscribe for any shares at all. But suppose the public did not like the issue, and put up subscriptions for, say, only 50,000 £1 shares instead of the 500,000 offered. In this case each underwriter would have to subscribe for nine-tenths of the shares he had underwritten. If he underwrote 10,000, he would have to subscribe for 9,000; but he would receive commission on the full 10,000 originally underwritten.

Of course, the issuing house must be paid for its trouble and risk. Usually a contract is arranged by which the company gives the issuing house a fixed fee—which might be about £25,000 in the example given. Out of this the issuing house is expected to pay all printing and advertising expenses, the underwriting commission, and all other incidental expenses of the issue.

Because of the difficult financial conditions which followed the Second World War, capital issues are now rigidly controlled by the Government, through a Capital Issues Committee. For many years there has been an Issuing Houses Committee, to which all properly established issuing houses belong. It is through these two bodies that commerce and industry now obtain such finance as the restrictions permit.

See also CAPITAL; FINANCE; BANKING; INSURANCE.

J K

JEWELLERY TRADE. Jewellery has been found in the tombs of ancient civilizations such as those of the Egyptians 4,000 years ago. The principal tool of the ancient jeweller was the hammer. With this he reached a remarkable level of skill in beating out gold and silver into plates and ware of even thicknesses, to be embossed, plated, or twisted later into various objects of beautiful design. By the 14th century B.C. jewellers in Egypt were masters of all the more important processes used to-day—chasing, ENGRAVING (q.v.), soldering, and enamelling (*see* GOLD AND SILVER WORK). Some 800 years later Etruscan jewellers in Italy had perfected a technique that no one has since imitated with any success; they were able to produce on the surface of their gold-work a rich grained appearance as though fine gold powder had been evenly sprinkled all over it. There was a decline in jewellery making in the early Middle Ages; but later the art of the jeweller revived, and perhaps reached its peak in the 16th century with the work of Benvenuto CELLINI (q.v. Vol. V).

The jeweller's art has always been closely related to the taste and fashion of the period. In the 19th century, for example, jewellery, like architecture, was often heavy and over-elaborate. Our own times have seen a revival in taste, and the work of the best craftsmen to-day can stand comparison with the past. This work has been helped by the introduction of platinum as a jeweller's material, in addition to the silver and gold used from time immemorial (*see* METAL ORES, Vol. III). The use of platinum, a more accurate knowledge of the various precious-metal alloys and their strengths, and better standards of design in general, have led to lighter and more graceful work. In modern jewellery-work, particularly when making use of fine stones, the jeweller strives to reveal the beauty of the stones themselves, and to make their setting unobtrusive rather than to smother and dwarf them by elaborate surrounds or settings.

The craft of the jeweller is different from that of the goldsmith and silversmith (*see* GOLD AND SILVER WORK). Broadly speaking, the goldsmith and silversmith make larger articles for household and personal use, while the jeweller confines himself to ornaments that will be worn actually on the person. The jeweller is therefore responsible for such articles as rings, brooches, bracelets, ear-rings, necklaces, lockets, pendants, hair ornaments, buttons, studs, links, badges, medallions, buckles and clasps, charms, tie-pins, hatpins, and similar articles. He also decorates, although less frequently, such articles as watches, clocks, pocket-knives, pens, and pencils. In or on these may be mounted precious or semi-precious stones and other decorative objects in wide variety—plastics, beans and seeds, small shells, birds' feathers, and beetles' and butterflies' wings. Mountings are made from many metals, the precious metals not being the only ones used. Copper, nickel, brass, pewter, and many other alloys, hard enough to be worked upon and suitable for personal wear, are used.

Articles of jewellery are made in many ways. They may be built up into intricate patterns and designs from pieces of plate-metal combined with wire. They can be made up in sheet-metal that has already been chased or ornamented with repoussé work (*see* GOLD AND SILVER WORK). They may be cast by various methods which give the effect of carving, chasing, or piercing; and they may be stamped or pressed out of sheet-metal. Any article of jewellery may be further enriched by ENAMEL work (q.v.), or by the addition of the precious stones and other decorative objects just mentioned.

The jeweller's most important tool is the blowpipe, with which he solders the various parts of the finished article together. Soldering is not unlike bricklaying on a miniature scale, solder being the mortar that is used to build up the whole piece of jewellery. The jeweller's other tools are those used by other metal-workers; in some workshops hand-tools are used, and in others power-tools. A piece of equipment used by the jeweller, and not much used by other metal-workers, is the draw-plate— a hardened steel plate containing a series of holes through which wire can be drawn by means of tongs. Wedding-rings, for example, are made

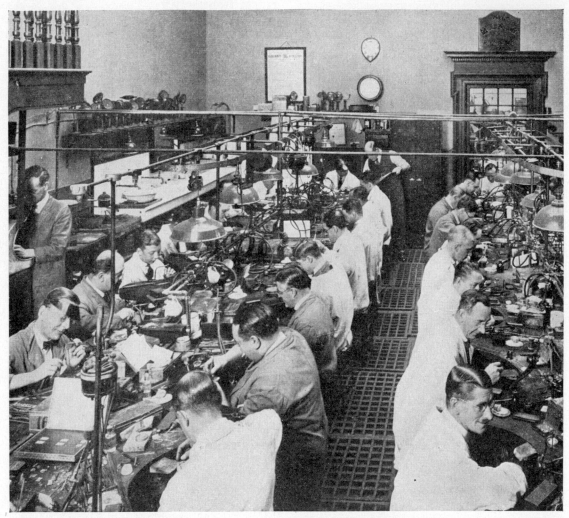

DIAMOND MOUNTERS MAKING PLATINUM MOUNTS FOR JEWELLERY
The workshop is Cartier Ltd.'s subsidiary company, The English Art Works, London

by drawing a strip of wire through a draw-plate having a hole of the required section and thickness, cutting the strip into the required lengths, bending each cut piece into a circle, and then soldering the ends together. Casting is the method usually employed when a number of identical articles are required. The master-model is first made in metal, plaster, or wax. From this master-model impressions are made in damp sand, forming a mould. Molten metal is then poured in and allowed to cool and set. The type of metal casting that gives the most faithful copy of the original but involves a good deal of time and expense is what is called the *cire perdu* process (French for 'lost wax'). A wax model is packed round with clay or other moulding material; the wax is then melted out and the hole filled by pouring molten metal into it. A new wax model is of course required for each subsequent casting. Stamping produces objects by pressing the metal between two shaped steel surfaces called 'dies'. As the making of these dies is very expensive, stamping is used only for the large-scale production of jewellery of the same pattern, and not by the jeweller-craftsman. Stamping differs from casting in that it usually produces the object in two halves, which have then to be joined together.

In the high-class trade a piece of jewellery is usually made from start to finish by a single

'Watchmaker, Jeweller, and Silversmith'
MOUNTING STONES FOR A GEM-SET NECKLACE

craftsman, who is a master of his art. In that portion of the trade which produces the cheaper and more popular jewellery, repetition work is the rule, and the article being fashioned passes from worker to worker and process to process until it is completed. Jewellery-making is not generally organized on factory lines like other industries, although some of the firms in the cheaper-class trade are thus organized. This is particularly true of some of the firms in Birmingham, which is the centre of the mass-produced trade in both real and imitation jewellery. The Clerkenwell district of London is the centre of the high-class trade in Britain.

See also GOLD AND SILVER WORK; DIAMOND INDUSTRY. See also Vol. XI: JEWELLERY, HISTORY OF.

JOINER, *see* CARPENTRY AND JOINERY.

JOINT STOCK COMPANY, *see* COMPANIES.

JOURNEYMEN, *see* CRAFT GUILDS; APPRENTICESHIP; TRADE UNION HISTORY.

JUTE INDUSTRY. This makes use of the coarse fibres of the jute plant, which is grown almost exclusively in India and Pakistan (*see* FIBRE CROPS, Section 2, Vol. VI). Cloth from jute has been hand-made in India for several hundred years, but it is only since the early 19th century that jute has been commercialized and that jute fabrics have become the world's most popular packing materials. To those outside the industry jute is usually associated with the material from which sacks and bags are made, but its various uses are more extensive and cover practically every industry. It is used, for instance, in the manufacture of most types of floor-coverings and upholstery, for bags and pockets for carrying food-stuffs and grains, and in the steel-components industry for bags for nuts, bolts, and nails; flower-growers use it for shielding plants; and plumbers carry it about for 'lagging' the outsides of pipes and water tanks to resist sharp changes of temperature, and for making watertight gaskets at pipe-joints.

British industry first handled jute in the early 19th century, when the EAST INDIA COMPANY (q.v.) sent samples to Britain to be tested. The coarse fibre had to be softened before it could be spun into a usable yarn. The obvious place to choose for manufacture was Dundee, then the centre of the British flax and whaling industries; for it was found that by soaking or 'batching' jute in an emulsion of whale-oil and water the fibre became soft and could be spun with ease on the existing flax machinery of the LINEN INDUSTRY (q.v.). By slow steps, and after much trial and error, the jute-weaving industry became firmly established in Dundee by 1838, and for many years that city was the only jute-manufacturing centre in the world. Later, the industry was opened up in many towns in Europe and America, and many mills were established by British firms in India.

Jute is mainly manufactured into cloth known as 'gunny' or 'hessian'. 'Gunny' is a word of doubtful origin which includes all types of sacking materials woven from jute. 'Hessian' is the word used for the more loosely woven forms of sacking. The term 'hessian' is said to have been first used by the Americans, when during the War of Independence they fought against the Hessians, the troops brought by George III from the German district of Hesse. These troops followed the old custom of protecting themselves from the rain by placing sacks over their heads.

Jute Industries Ltd.

SACKING CLOTH BEING PUT THROUGH A CROPPING MACHINE AT A JUTE FACTORY IN DUNDEE
The surface must be cropped because of the hairiness of the jute.

Both kinds of material are now known in India by the name of 'gunny'.

The Crimean War (1854–6) helped the British jute industry. Russia's Baltic provinces were then, as now, the main sources of flax. The war stopped these supplies, but increased the demand for sacks and canvas. Dundee stepped in to fill the gap, with jute as a substitute for flax, and from 1854 to 1857 experienced its first boom. Shortly afterwards, during the American Civil War, supplies from the Southern States were cut off by the Northern blockade, and Dundee again did well. As the industry grew, specialization began. The Indian mills made most of the gunny fabrics, while Dundee concentrated on the finer fabrics used for canvas, tailors' interlinings, and the backing of linoleums. Soon the superiority of Dundee jute goods became accepted all over the world, and Dundee prospered reasonably well until the world-wide depression of the 1930's (see TRADE CYCLE). Plant had been expanded and methods improved, in both Dundee and India, until more jute goods were being produced than people were prepared to buy. But by 1937–8, when the world production of jute reached its peak, all that was produced could be sold.

During the Second World War the Indian mills prospered through the large orders placed by the British and other governments for sandbags and similar goods. By contrast, the Dundee section of the industry suffered severe setbacks. Many thousands of workers left the industry during the war, and manufacture was restricted to essential war materials. When peace came, workers were unwilling to return to the industry, and supplies of raw jute were scanty and shipping space was short. To prevent British stocks of raw jute from falling too low, manufacturers were allowed to have only 80% of their pre-war supplies.

Because of a serious shortage of food in 1946 in India and Pakistan, former jute areas were used for growing urgently needed food crops. Jute fibre grew scarce and costly all over the world, consequently British manufacturing costs also increased considerably. Thus jute, which at one time was known as the cheapest and best of all packing materials, became both scarce and expensive.

In 1947 the separation of British India into two self-governing States made further problems for the jute industry, for four-fifths of the raw jute crop is grown in Pakistan, whilst most of the mills are in India.

See also Wool Weaving; Textile Fibres and Fabrics. See also Vol. VI: Fibre Crops.

KAOLIN, *see* China Clay.

KAPOK. This is a vegetable substance, one of the lightest materials known. It is a kind of floss that can be torn or teasled out from the seeds of a tree that grows in India and farther East. It is used as an upholstery material for stuffing light chairs and cheap mattresses, particularly mattresses used for camp-beds. Kapok is an exceptionally buoyant material in water, and it is much used as a stuffing for ships' life-belts, and as a lining for life-saving waistcoats and similar garments. Seats and cushions for sailing dinghies and small yachts are often stuffed with kapok, and can thus be used as emergency lifebuoys as well as cushions. Cork (q.v.) was formerly used for these purposes, but kapok has been found more efficient. It is much more buoyant than cork: if tightly compressed, kapok can support more than thirty times its own weight in water. Another great advantage that kapok possesses over cork is that after being thoroughly soaked in water it dries much more quickly. For use at sea, where articles may be frequently wetted, Java kapok from Indonesia is generally considered superior to the Indian variety. Kapok is sometimes used for surgical dressings, in place of absorbent cotton-wool and similar materials.

See also Vol. VI: Fibre Crops.

KNITWEAR, *see* Hosiery and Knitwear.

KNIVES, *see* Cutlery Industry.

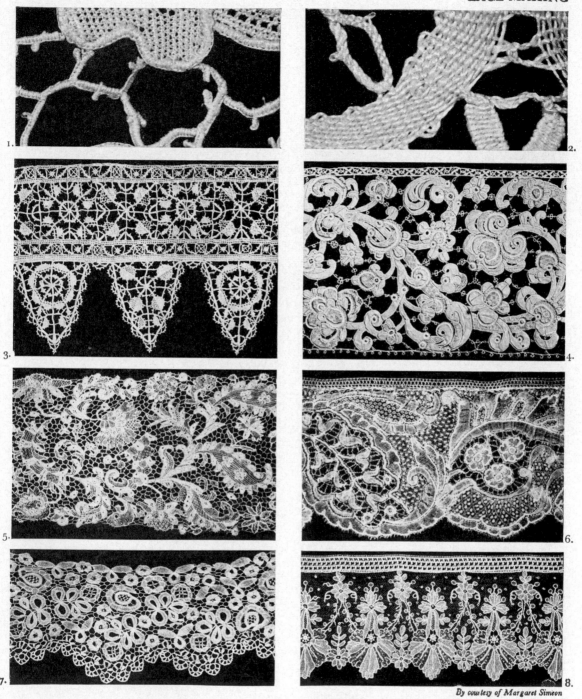

By courtesy of Margaret Simeon

EXAMPLES OF HAND-MADE LACE

1. ENLARGED DETAIL OF NEEDLE-POINT LACE. 2. ENLARGED DETAIL OF PILLOW LACE. 3. RETICELLA WITH PUNTO IN ARIA EDGE, needle-point, late 16th century (7 in.). 4. VENETIAN ROSE-POINT, needle-point, mid 17th century (6 in.). 5. POINT DE FRANCE, needle-point, late 17th century (3¼ in.). 6. POINT D'ANGLETERRE, pillow, early 18th century (2½ in.). 7. HONITON LACE, pillow, mid 19th century (3¾ in.). 8. BRUSSELS POINT DE GAZE, needle-point, late 19th century. (3½ in.) The measurements are of the actual widths of the specimens

John Jardine

VERTICAL LOOM FOR MAKING CURTAIN LACE
The warp threads can be seen descending from above

examples of this lace were produced at Valenciennes, Binche, Brussels, and Mechlin (Malines) in the early 18th century.

In England lace was made from the 16th century onwards in styles very like those of Italy, France, and Flanders, but usually less delicate. During the 16th and 17th centuries lace-makers came to England as refugees from religious persecution in France and Flanders. To help the English workers who were taught by these refugees, Charles I and Charles II forbade the import of foreign lace, but there was extensive smuggling. Fine Brussels pillow lace came to be known as *point d'Angleterre* (English stitch)—probably to disguise its foreign origin. Honiton, in Devon, was an important centre, and hand-made lace is still made there. Buckinghamshire and Bedfordshire were also centres of the craft in England.

After the invention of machine lace, the handicraft lost a great deal of its importance. The 19th-century styles were often imitations of old types, such as rose-point. Brussels was the most important centre in Europe, making a fine needle-point lace called *point de gaze* and a pillow lace known as *point duchesse*. A lot of silk lace, both black and white, was made and exported from Malta. In Ireland the craft was established as a relief measure in the famine periods of the early 19th century, and the Limerick lace of

that period is famous. Similarly, in Venice lace-making was re-established to relieve great poverty and unemployment. The fashion for wearing lace died almost completely in the early years of the 20th century, and very little hand-made lace is now produced.

2. MACHINE-MADE LACE. In 1768 net was first made by machinery. It came to be used very frequently by hand-workers, to replace their own hand-made 'ground'. Needle-point and pillow-lace patterns were sewn on to the ground —a much quicker procedure than making the whole piece by hand. The net was also embroidered with 'tambour' stitch, which looks like chain-stitch but is made with a crochet hook.

Between 1770 and 1790 many attempts were made to adapt the stocking frame used in the HOSIERY industry (q.v.) for the production of machine-made lace. It was John Heathcoat's invention of the bobbin-net machine in 1809 that really laid a firm foundation for the machine-made lace industry. Heathcoat set up his first machines in Loughborough in Leicestershire. His original invention was much improved in 1813 by John Leavers (or Levers), and the lace produced was a very good imitation of hand-made Brussels. The first Leavers looms were set up in Tiverton, in Devon, in 1815, and in the following year Heathcoat himself decided to move there when his Loughborough factory, with all its plant, was wrecked by the LUDDITES (q.v.). The Nottingham district, which had been the centre of the hand-made section of the industry since the 16th century, remained the leading locality of machine-made lace. Modified Leavers looms are still used in Nottingham. In 1834 Leavers succeeded in applying the Jacquard machine or harness loom (*see* WOOL WEAVING) to the lace-making loom; it became possible for quite intricate patterns to be produced mechanically. In the early days of these inventions the machine section of the industry was organized on the 'outworker' or DOMESTIC SYSTEM (q.v.); firms owning machines hired them out to workers who made net and lace for their own account. About the middle of the 19th century the industry began to be fully organized on factory lines.

The modern machine-made lace industry of Britain is now organized in six sections, of which the first three are the most important. The Leavers section makes fancy lace, hair-nets, and veilings, and is chiefly located in the Nottingham area. The Leavers loom has been little changed, and only an expert can distinguish between the lace made on it and the hand-made product itself. The section of the industry next in importance makes lace-furnishing fabrics and curtain nets; its main centre is now the Irvine Valley in Ayrshire, although Nottingham is still important. The first patent for a machine to make lace curtains was taken out in 1846, and by the middle of the century the Nottingham area alone was operating 100 machines. The machines now used have changed little, although those that use the Jacquard fitment are rather large and complicated. The modern curtain machine can make simultaneously eight curtains up to 5 feet wide, and has been adapted to make cellular or open-texture woollen blankets. A third important section of the industry makes plain net or bobbin net; Tiverton and Barnstaple in Devon, and Chard in Somerset, are the main centres. Bobbin net is a machine-made imitation of plain hand-made pillow lace, and on the bobbin-net machine is produced *point d'esprit*—a plain net with small decorative spots at regular intervals. The other sections of the industry make warp lace, braid lace, and embroidery. The embroidery section, using a continental process and continental machines, produces machine-made embroidery, either on plain net or on a temporary fabric base of acetate material

(*see* PLASTICS), which can be dissolved away, leaving only the embroidery. Lace trimmings of narrow width are made either by the braid-lace section, or on ordinary Leavers looms. If made on the Leavers loom, the separate narrow widths of lace are connected together during manufacture by draw-threads, which are afterwards withdrawn.

The British machine-made lace industry is much affected by fashion changes. Between 1880 and the outbreak of the First World War, it had to meet very serious competition from French manufacturers, and foreign competition continued after 1918 until foreign imports were taxed in 1925 and the industry was to some extent stabilized. During the Second World War the Government kept certain sections busy with orders for mosquito and sandfly nets for use in tropical and sub-tropical theatres of war.

See also Vol. XI: NEEDLEWORK; EMBROIDERY.

LACQUER, *see* GUMS AND RESINS, Section 2.

LADING, BILL OF, *see* BILL OF LADING.

LATEX, *see* RUBBER MANUFACTURE; *see also* Vol. VI: RUBBER.

LEAD occurs as a mineral ore in Derbyshire in England, and in Germany, Spain, America, and Australia. The ore most generally found is lead sulphide, which is called galena. Lead is one of the few metals in which Britain was once self-supporting; and at the beginning of the 19th century British production was almost two-thirds of the world's output. Spain was then a large producer, and still is. In the late 19th century the famous Broken Hill lead and silver mines of New South Wales were opened up, and in 1888 Australia headed the list of producing countries with an output of 18,000 tons. At present the U.S.A. is the largest producer, but uses nearly all her output herself. The principal exporting countries are Australia, Mexico, and Spain. The Derbyshire mines are still being worked.

Lead has many uses in industry. Printing types are made from an alloy of lead and antimony; the stereotype plates used in printing are made from a similar alloy, with the addition of bismuth. Lead, hardened with arsenic, is used to make shot for sporting guns. PEWTER (q.v.) is an alloy of lead and tin. Alloys of lead and other metals—tin, copper, and antimony—

Ministry of Works

13TH-CENTURY LEAD WINDOW 'QUARRY' FROM RIEVAULX
ABBEY

method. From the 13th century onwards lead 'quarries' were often used for ventilation in windows: these were rectangular or diamond-shaped panels, pierced to allow a free passage of air. Lead fonts, beautifully modelled and skilfully cast and moulded, are often found in medieval churches. Decorative tops or 'heads' of rainwater-pipes are also quite common. But it was not until the 17th century that lead was used on a large scale for pure decoration. Gardens, then often planned on formal lines, were decorated with lead vases, flower-pots, cisterns, and statues. The well-known statue in Edinburgh of Charles II riding a horse is cast in lead. At the end of the 18th century lead figures and designs were used to decorate wrought-iron gates and balustrades. Lead is not much used for ornamental work to-day.

See also MINING.

See also Vol. III: METAL ORES.

are used to line bearings in engineering work. In its pure form lead is widely used for many purposes in building, as piping for plumbing work, and to make vessels which resist corrosion for the chemical industries. The oxides and similar compounds of lead have wide uses as pigments in paint manufacture, and in GLASS-MAKING and the glazing of POTTERY (qq.v.).

Although the softness of lead limits its use, and makes it impossible to decorate it with very fine designs, it has been much used for ornamental work in the past. For this it can be beaten or cast in a mould, casting being the more common

LEADENHALL MARKET, *see* MEAT TRADE.

LEATHER is made from HIDES AND SKINS that have been subjected to various treatments, of which TANNING is the most important (qq.v.). Some materials that are often thought to be leather are not really leather at all. This is true of parchment and vellum, once used for writing, which have not gone through any process of tanning. It is also true of rawhide, a material from which high-class luggage is often made; the hides used for rawhide are not tanned but 'limed', that is soaked in lime and water.

Leather was one of the first materials used by man for clothes, coverings, and vessels. From the earliest times, until well after the Middle Ages, bottles and drinking-cups were made of leather. 'Black Jacks' were leather drinking-vessels, their insides being covered with pitch to make them watertight. Leather buckets were in regular use until the 19th century; they may still sometimes be seen in churches, where they are kept full of water as a precaution against fire. In early times leather was used for armour; to-day in MOTOR-CYCLE RACING (q.v. Vol. IX) it is still used for crash-helmets. The leather jerkin or loose long waistcoat was the standard outer wear of the English worker and peasant for centuries, and it became a general military garment in the Second World War.

Modern uses of leather still cover a wide range. The footwear industry is perhaps the largest

By gracious permission of H.M. the King

LEAD CISTERN AT KENSINGTON PALACE, 1746

individual consumer (*see* Boot- and Shoe-making). Leather, as well as the untanned rawhide, is used for travelling-luggage, for women's hand-bags, and for document and note-cases. It is the best material for the permanent binding of books. The most suitable leather for this purpose is Russia leather, which is calf or cowhide tanned by a special process, and with a characteristic grain stamped on the wet leather after tanning. Harness and saddlery, made in England from English leather, have a reputation higher than that of any other country; a modern use of saddle leather is for bicycles and motor-cycles. The glove industry requires soft fancy leathers. Leather has many uses in the Clothing Industry (q.v.). The 'wind-cheater' or golf blouse is a modern variant of the leather jerkin. Leather waistcoats, and leather underclothing for sports purposes, are much worn. Many belts and dress trimmings are made of leather. It is also much used for upholstering furniture and for de-corative wall panelling. It is used to make many kinds of fancy goods, such as cigar and spectacle cases and watch-guards. The balls used in cricket, hockey, football, and baseball are made of leather, and many sports bags and accessories are either made from it or finished with it. Its purely industrial uses are also very varied. It is much used for pump washers and gaskets, for belting to drive machinery, for lining the friction clutches of motor engines, and for hoses and for industrial protective gloves. Among its miscel-laneous uses are the making of surgical ap-pliances and artificial limbs, bellows, carriage spring attachments, military equipment, and razor strops.

The British leather industry has two sections, heavy and light. As the bulk of their raw materials come by sea from abroad, the heavy sections are located mainly in seaport towns and cities such as London, Birkenhead, Liverpool, Bristol, Glasgow, and Hull. Some inland Lan-cashire towns are also important. In the light section the Midland districts are the busiest cen-tres, although London itself is also prominent. Walsall, in Staffordshire, has been for centuries the centre of the saddlery and harness trades, and, with the decline of horse transport, has successfully switched over to other forms of light leather goods. Northampton, Leicester, Ketter-ing, Nottingham, and Leeds are also important towns in the light section. Glove-making in leather is principally concentrated in the Yeovil

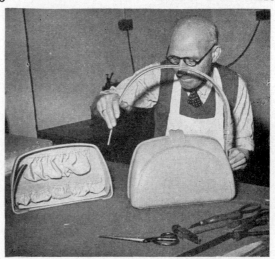

Norman Wymer

FIXING THE HANDLE TO A LEATHER BAG

district of Somerset and in Worcestershire, although it has of recent years extended into other parts of the country.

Leather can be dyed, moulded, and worked with tools. The *cuir bouilli* process is sometimes used for moulding leather into shape. It is not quite certain how this process was originally worked, but it was probably done, as it is to-day, by soaking the leather thoroughly in water until it can be hammered or pressed into shape and decorated. It is then heated until it is dry, when it will always retain its shape. Leather

Dorondo Mills

ASSEMBLING LEATHER BELTING FOR USE ON MACHINES

bottles, 'Black Jacks', and bags were made in this way, and to-day the process is used for such things as cigar-cases and the corners of suit-cases.

Leather may be decorated by being modelled, tooled, or incised. For modelling, the leather is damped and the design is pressed into it with a rounded steel tool. To give higher relief portions can be pressed up from beneath. Designs may also be drawn in line or hammered on with a hot tool. The design can also be cut or 'incised'. All these methods can be combined. When the leather is dry, the design can be painted or dyed and then polished. It is then made up by hand, or by machine stitching, or by thonging with thin strips of leather.

See also HIDES AND SKINS; TANNING.

LEATHER-CLOTH. The coating of woven fabric with paint, varnish, oils, and similar substances has been known since the Middle Ages. At first, coating was done for decoration. Later, it was found that fabrics were protected from wear and weather by coating, and materials such as oil-cloth and floor-cloth were introduced. Leather-cloth is one of these materials, coloured and shaped into a grainy surface to look like natural leather.

The making of leather-cloth has enormously increased because there is not enough real leather in the world to meet the demand. There has been a big increase in the demand for leather upholstered furniture, and leather upholstery for cars, aeroplanes, and railway carriages; and as mass-production methods have made it necessary for upholstery to be made in standard widths, in roll form and of known quality, in place of the odd-shaped skins previously used, leather-cloth has proved more practical than real leather for some purposes.

The coating materials are based on drying-oils (*see* OILS, VEGETABLE, Section 4), nitrocellulose, or PLASTICS (q.v.). If drying-oils such as linseed are used, they are usually thickened by heating, then coloured by the addition of pigments or dye-stuffs, and thinned with spirit to make them spreadable. Lacquer-type coatings are prepared from a mixture of nitrocellulose dissolved in a solvent (*see* PAINTS AND VARNISHES) and mixed with a substance such as castor-oil to make it more yielding. Plastic materials consist of rubber-substitutes which are built up from acetylene gas.

The material chosen as the basis of a leather-cloth is usually a woven cotton fabric. Sateen and twill are both popular. There are many ways of applying the coating to the fabric, but usually the material is passed over a long table, and the coating is poured on to its surface, and spread by a metal strip, which extends across the width of the material and nearly down to its surface. The gap between the blade and the material roughly determines the thickness of the film. Then the fabric is passed through a short, heated tunnel for drying. The number of coats varies from three to thirty, and a decorative pattern may then be pressed on to the surface of the coating. A coating of contrasting colour is sometimes put on, to fill the pattern marks.

Materials and fabrics used for leather-cloth are so chosen that the coating lies only on the surface of the fabric: unlike those used for making oil-skin or proofed fabrics, in which the varnish penetrates into the actual fibres of the material. Leather-cloth is a comparatively cheap, hard-wearing, and easily cleaned material. It is free from sweating or tackiness in warmth or heat, and from brittleness under conditions of extreme cold.

See also WATERPROOFING.

LEGAL TENDER, *see* CURRENCY.

LETTERS OF CREDIT, *see* CREDIT.

LIABILITIES, *see* BOOK-KEEPING.

LIMESTONE, *see* CHALK MINING; STONE QUARRYING; *see also* Vol. III: LIMESTONE.

LIMITED COMPANIES obtain their CAPITAL (q.v.) from many members, or shareholders; if a limited company does not prosper, the loss of each shareholder is limited by law to what he originally invested.

Companies without 'limited liability', as it is called, are rather dangerous concerns for the man of small means to put his money in. A hard-working man who has saved a few thousands of pounds might put only £100 or so into a company with unlimited liability, but if it went wrong and owed more than it possessed, he might be forced to turn the rest of his property into money to help pay the company's debts. He might even have his house seized and sold. The novels of Dickens and other writers about life in England before 1850 mention several hard cases of this kind. There is an example in *David Copperfield*.

Before 1855 limited liability could be granted by the Charter or Act of Parliament which brought a company into being, if the Government thought this right. The liability of the shareholders of the Bank of England, which was founded in 1694 by an Act of Parliament, was limited by a later Act. In the early 19th century the Royal Mail Steam Packet Company and the Peninsular and Oriental Steam Navigation Company were formed by Act of Parliament, and the liability of their shareholders was limited to the amounts they subscribed. This method, however, was expensive, as it meant paying for a Private Act of Parliament, and small concerns could not afford it. The result was that the expansion of commerce and industry, at the end of the 18th century and the beginning of the 19th, was carried out mainly by unlimited liability companies, and many families were ruined by these failures.

This situation led to a good deal of political agitation. In 1855, therefore, the first important Companies Act was passed, and this was amended and improved in 1862. These Acts allowed the formation, or 'incorporation', of companies through an official in London called the Registrar of Joint Stock Companies, and liability was limited to the amount of money each person or 'subscriber' invested in shares. These changes greatly helped Britain's industrial development, as capital was less difficult to get when subscribers could judge the limit of their risks. At that time shares of unlimited liability companies were often difficult to buy or sell on the Stock Exchange; this held up enterprise, for people do not like putting up money unless they can get it back in an emergency by selling their shares.

Under the new rules the persons who wished to form themselves into a company first drew up and signed a Memorandum of Association. This stated the company's title and purpose, its 'authorized' capital (or maximum capital considered necessary), and into how many and what classes of SHARES (q.v.) this capital was divided. As well as the memorandum, there was a small booklet, called the company's Articles of Association, giving detailed rules for the management of the company; and also a 'prospectus', stating how the company proposed to carry on its business, and what profits were likely to be.

All these documents were then 'filed' or deposited with the Registrar, together with a payment for stamp-duty on the authorized capital, as well as certain registration fees. All companies incorporated under the Companies Acts had to end up their titles with the word 'Limited', so that traders dealing with them would know that it might be unsafe to give them CREDIT (q.v.) beyond the amount of their capital. The details of registration could be arranged if only a very small amount of capital were subscribed to start with, but it was naturally necessary to obtain larger investments of money (or 'subscriptions') before actual business could be started. This might be arranged privately by the original shareholders, or with the help of one of the ISSUING HOUSES (q.v.). The prospectus had to be published before subscriptions were invited. At the end of each trading year the directors and secretary of the company were legally obliged to send a copy of the accounts to the Registrar. The register of shareholders also had to be filed with him, and kept up to date as changes took place.

Early in the present century the business world pressed to be allowed to form companies more easily. So in 1910 a new Act allowed the incorporation of 'private' limited companies, the earlier ones being called 'public' companies. At least seven persons were necessary to form a public company, but private companies could now be formed by a minimum of two persons. Private companies did not have to file a prospectus, or their annual accounts, with the Registrar, and they could thus keep the details of their business private.

A Board of Directors is responsible for the policy and management of every company formed under the Companies Acts, and the head of the Board is called the Chairman. The necessary decisions are taken at regular Board Meetings, whose proceedings are recorded in a Minute Book. The details of management are usually entrusted to a Managing Director. Every company must have a Secretary, and must register his name, and the address of the company's office, with the Registrar of Joint Stock Companies. The Secretary is the official channel of communication between the company and the Registrar, and he is responsible for seeing that all legal requirements are satisfied. These are now wider than they were, as a new Companies Act was passed in 1948, which made it necessary for companies to give much more information than before to their shareholders, or to persons who might become shareholders. The stamp-duty on the capital of newly formed companies is now 10/- for each £100.

Britain was the pioneer of the modern limited company, and her example was soon copied by other countries. Although the British pattern is generally followed in the U.S.A., American limited companies are called 'corporations', and the contraction 'Inc.' (meaning 'incorporated') is used at the end of their titles instead of the contraction 'Ltd.' (meaning 'limited') used in Britain. An interesting difference between North American and British limited companies is the 'no-par-value' share. In Britain a share always has a nominal value, which is the figure printed on the share certificate: it may be £1 or 5s., or whatever sum was originally paid for the share. This is said to be its value 'at par'. Its real value, or market value, is often quite different. This depends on how much another person is willing to pay a shareholder for his shares. If, for any reason, it is thought that a company is likely to make large profits, then people will pay high prices for its shares, no matter what their nominal or 'par' value. Their market value can change several times in one day (*see* STOCKS AND SHARES). In the U.S.A. and Canada the 'no-par-value' share is really a much more logical idea. The fixed nominal value given to British shares tends to make the original shareholder think that his shares should always be worth at least the money he first paid for them, but he is often disappointed. In Britain, no reduction of the nominal value of a share is allowed without the permission of the Law Courts.

See also COMPANIES; STOCKS AND SHARES; DEBENTURES; CREDIT; PARTNERSHIP.

LINEN INDUSTRY. 1. Linen is probably the first textile to have been used by man. In ancient civilizations many people were kept busy growing FLAX (q.v. Vol. VI), which is the fibre from which linen is made, and spinning and weaving that fibre into linen yarn and linen cloth. The antiquity of linen can be judged from the many references to it in the early books of the Bible, for example, in Exodus, in Isaiah, and the first Book of the Kings, where it is said 'And Solomon had horses brought out of Egypt, and linen yarn: the king's merchants received the linen yarn at a price'.

It is believed that the original home of linen was ancient Egypt, and that it was distributed throughout the known world by the great trading race of Phoenicians (*see* TRADE, HISTORY OF). As a result, some countries of Europe, including ancient Greece and imperial Rome, gradually took to making linen. The Roman Emperors spread the knowledge of linen manufacture throughout the Roman Empire, and when the barbarians overthrew the western part of the Roman Empire, in the 5th century A.D., this knowledge survived in various parts of the Empire, including Britain.

Records of linen-making in Ireland can be traced back to the 13th century, though linen was made before then; the modern industry was founded in the 17th century by the Earl of Strafford, then Lord Deputy of Ireland. The linen industry began to grow when the Irish woollen trade was declining. Although the wool industry was discouraged by taxation, Ireland was given practically a MONOPOLY (q.v.) of the linen trade, which consequently expanded and flourished.

When the French king revoked the Edict of Nantes in 1685, during the French religious strife, tens of thousands of Protestant refugees from France, skilled in the making of fine linens and other textiles, fled to England and other

Drapers' Record

A LINEN HACKLING MACHINE

The fibres of flax are drawn between steel-toothed comb belts to straighten them and remove the 'tow' (short fibres)

countries. Thousands of them settled in Ireland, where their industry and skill greatly helped the linen industry. The present headquarters of the industry is what used to be known as the province of Ulster, but is now called Northern Ireland.

2. Unlike wheat and corn, which are reaped by machines, the flax crop is pulled by hand. The stalks of the plant contain the fibre which is to become linen. This fibre, being of the type known as bast fibre, is concealed in the stem, and must be carefully separated from the outer covering and the inner core of the stalk, both of which are useless. The flax must first be steeped for several days in dams full of water. These dams, with their heaps of large stones, which weigh down the flax while steeping, are a distinctive sight in flax-growing areas. This steeping process is known as 'retting'.

After about 7 days' retting in the water, during which the gummy substance binding the fibre to the stem has become loosened, the flax is removed from the dams and is carted away to the 'spread fields'. There the cart is driven up and down while the driver drops wet bundles of flax at intervals. Other workers come after him, loosening the bundles and spreading the flax out on the grass to dry, shaking it at the same time to make sure that the drying and colouring of the flax take place evenly.

The fibre has been loosened from the stem, but still remains hidden within it, and must be released. When the flax stalks are passed between fluted rollers in a 'scutch' mill, the useless woody portions of the stems are broken up; these are then whipped, or 'scutched', with flat, wooden blades, revolving like miniature windmills. This frees the flax fibre from the woody portions of the stem, making it look rather like tresses of human hair.

3. SPINNING. The scutched flax fibre reaches the spinning-mill in the form of strands, about 3 feet long. The spinner must transform these into a continuous and even yarn. The first process is the natural one of combing the fibre by hand to straighten it. A man called a 'rougher' divides the mass of fibre into convenient handfuls; then, catching a handful by one end, he gives it a skilful flick to open out the fibre at the other end like a fan, and draws the fibre over a series of pins. The fibre then receives a more scientific combing by a series of pins in a 'hackling' machine.

The separate pieces of fibre are laid length-

Irish Linen Guild

WEAVING LINEN DAMASK ON A JACQUARD LOOM

The pattern is made by the crossing of the warp threads. Cloths with patterned weaves are made on Jacquard looms

wise, with the ends of the pieces overlapping, on slowly moving leather belts, which carry the fibre between rollers and over sets of pins. This movement combs the separate lengths into one continuous ribbon of fibre, which is gradually drawn out finer and finer, until at last the spinning-frame gives the scientific twist which transforms the ribbon of fibre into strong and compact linen yarn. In the spinning-frames the yarn is drawn through troughs of warm water, to soften the natural gum of the flax and thus help the fibres of the yarn to bind firmly together.

4. WEAVING. The basic principle of weaving, by interlacing two sets of yarns or threads, is described in the article WOOL WEAVING.

5. BLEACHING. This means giving the linen a white colour instead of its natural brown. Linen is bleached to-day on the same principles as in the days when it was spun and woven by hand, and bleached at home. The old home methods consisted of boiling the fabric, spreading it out on the grass, and exposing it for weeks or months to the bleaching action of the weather. Then followed steeping in buttermilk, scouring thoroughly with soap and water, and finally rinsing in pure soft water (*see* BLEACHING).

Fundamentally, the same procedure is followed to-day, although science has added to and controlled the processes more exactly. A familiar sight in Northern Ireland is the 'bleach green', with acres of grass covered with linen.

After bleaching, the cloth is 'beetled', which gives the linen a smooth shining surface. The cloth is wrapped around large rollers; these revolve slowly, while wooden blocks or 'beetles' fall on the linen in regular succession. The rattle of the beetling machines is a familiar sound in the quiet of the Ulster countryside.

See also Vol. VI: FIBRE CROPS.

LINER, *see* SHIPPING; *see also* Vol. IV: LINER; STEAMSHIPS, HISTORY OF.

LINOLEUM. This is not the same as floor-cloth, a floor covering that was in use for a very long time and only fell into disuse about the beginning of the Second World War. Floor-cloth was made by applying many coats of linseed-oil paint to a sheet of hessian or sack-cloth—a coarsely woven fabric made from jute. Each coat of paint took several days to dry, and the whole process would, therefore, take many weeks to complete. By contrast, linoleum is the result of building up one very thick coat of linseed base. Linoleum has been made since the 19th century and was invented by an Englishman called Frederick Walton. A material based on rubber had been invented earlier as an alternative to floor-cloth; but, as the price of rubber increased, efforts were made to find a cheap substitute. Walton noticed that thick films of linseed-oil paint on the outside of paint cans or on the top of open cans of paint were rubbery in nature; and he conceived the idea of making a rubber substitute by drying large quantities of linseed-oil, which in those days was an exceedingly cheap and abundant raw material. There are now two methods of doing this, each using a treated oil made by dissolving small quantities of lead compounds in hot lin-seed-oil. The lead makes the oil dry more quickly, so such a treated oil is called a 'driered' oil.

In one of these two processes sheets of thin cotton fabric are hung 6 inches apart in a tall, heated building, and the oil is flooded over the cotton at intervals of 24 hours, which gives sufficient time for each film to dry. In this way, over a period of 6 months, layers of dried oil from 1 to 2 inches thick are built up, and, when

LINOLEUM CEMENT BEING POURED OUT OF A MIXER AT THE YORKSHIRE DYEWORK & CHEMICAL COMPANY'S WORKS
(From an article by M. R. Mills in *Paint Technology*)

a shed is emptied, from 100 to 200 tons of dried oil are taken out to be made into linoleum. The second of the two processes is mechanical. Batches of about 1 ton of oil at a time are heated in vessels fitted with agitators, which whisk the oil into a fine mist through which air is blown. When the oil solidifies, it is quickly emptied out of the vessels. At this stage it is rubbery. To give it a leathery hardness, it is next heated in a pot with about a quarter of its weight of rosin or gum. The product is called 'linoleum cement'.

To make a plain linoleum a composition is made up. This consists of about 40 parts of linoleum cement, 40 parts of a mixture of ground cork and woodflour (thin sawdust), and 20 parts of colouring material or 'pigment'. Ochres, siennas, and whiting are typical examples of pigments (*see* PAINTS AND VARNISHES). The mixing of all these materials is done in a series of heavy steam-heated mixers, and the final product is broken down into small particles. At this stage the various coloured materials are called 'linoleum mixes'.

The next process is to sheet the linoleum mix on to a base of hessian. This is carried out on a machine called a 'calender', which is like a gigantic mangle with four rolls, all steam-heated and each about 7 feet long and 2 to 3 feet in diameter. The granulated linoleum mix is sprinkled uniformly on to the hessian, just before it is fed to the first two rolls. In passing through the calender, the heat and pressure make the material plastic, and it fuses together and binds itself to the backing. Different coloured effects can be obtained by mingling the various coloured linoleum mixes before calendering. Other effects, such as marble, granite, parquet, and inlaid linoleums, are obtained by varying the way the material is handled.

The next stage is maturing. As it comes from the calender, the linoleum is soft and crumbly. It is placed in tall, heated buildings called 'stoves' where it hangs in the heat for several days, often as long as a fortnight, until it hardens. It is then taken out, the edges are trimmed, and the linoleum is rolled and packed for dispatch.

Printed linoleum is plain unmatured linoleum, on which a pattern is printed by a rotary print-ing-press using a particular type of paint called 'print paint'. After being printed, the material is fed to the 'stove', where the linoleum matures and the paint dries.

Linoleum can be made in thicknesses of up to $\frac{1}{4}$ inch and with care it can wear for 20 years. The industry is not a big one. There are about a dozen British firms, of which four are large. Most of the factories are in Fifeshire in Scotland. There are two in Lancaster and one at Staines near London, where Walton carried out his first experiments.

LINSEED OIL, *see* Vol. VI: LINSEED.

LITHOGRAPHIC PRINTING, *see* PROCESS REPRODUCTION, Section 5; *see also* Vol. XII: LITHOGRAPHY.

LIVERY COMPANIES, *see* CITY COMPANIES.

LLOYD'S, *see* INSURANCE; *see also* Vol. IV: LLOYD'S.

LOANS. A loan may mean anything lent by a lender to a borrower. In banking and com-mercial practice 'loan' generally refers to a fixed sum of money, lent to a borrower for a definite period of time; the word distinguishes this kind of lending from a credit or overdraft (*see* BANK ACCOUNTS) which may fluctuate in amount and be repayable at some indefinite date. In Stock Exchange business, however, the word is used for the securities (sometimes called 'obligations') of governments or local authorities. These Government or municipal loans always carry a fixed rate of INTEREST (q.v.).

The reasons for Government borrowing are explained in the articles LOCAL FINANCE and NATIONAL FINANCE in Volume X. In the past, when the Government's control of municipal finance was weaker than it is now, municipali-ties or city councils often made loan arrange-ments on their own responsibility, through private ISSUING HOUSES (q.v.). But nowadays most of these transactions are arranged through the BANK OF ENGLAND (q.v.). The rate of in-terest to be offered is decided beforehand, and depends on market conditions. In that case a notice is inserted in the newspapers by the Bank of England, on behalf of the Government or municipality concerned, stating that the Bank will be prepared to receive money (called 'sub-scriptions') up to a stated limit; each subscrip-tion is payable in instalments spread over a period of months.

A register of holders of such loans is usually kept at the Bank of England. Before the Second World War, Government and municipal loans could be transferred only if the sellers, or their authorized agents, went in person to the Bank of England. Nowadays transfers of ownership are usually arranged by a document called a Transfer Deed, which is signed by buyer and seller. This is used for practically all Stock Exchange securities.

Interest warrants on State and municipal loans are posted by the Bank of England to the registered holders, either quarterly or half-yearly.

See also BOND; BANKING; SECURITY; INTERNATIONAL FINANCE.

LOCALIZATION OF INDUSTRY. This term, or the term 'location of industry', describes how certain industries are confined to particular parts of the world, or to particular parts of a country.

Many influences may cause an industry to settle down in a particular place. The presence of raw materials is one of the most important influences. This is especially true of what are called the primary or 'extractive' industries, such as mining, agriculture, forestry, and fishing.

For instance, gold-mining must be done where the gold exists; crops must be grown where the climate and soil are best suited to them; fish must be sought in those parts of the sea in which they happen to live. Sometimes Nature herself alters the location of an industry; the departure of herring shoals from the Baltic to the North Sea some centuries ago is an example of this.

The secondary or manufacturing industries are localized for much more complex reasons; there have been several changes in the general pattern over the past few hundred years. At first the tendency was for manufacturing industries, as well as the primary or extractive industries, to settle near the sources of their raw materials. For example, the cloth industry of the late Middle Ages grew up mainly in the towns and villages of the Cotswolds and of East Anglia, where sheep grazed and provided the wool. Location of this kind can continue as long as an industry uses only hand-machinery and local raw materials. But, as soon as power is used, an industry must move towards the sources of power, and as soon as imported raw materials are mainly used the industry may have to move nearer to a port. For example, as soon as water-power began to be used for the various processes of the wool industry, the worsted industry of East Anglia moved to the West Riding of Yorkshire where there were streams to turn water-mills (see WOOL INDUSTRY, MODERN). The cotton industry settled near Liverpool, the port to which the raw material was shipped.

A change in the kind of power used often leads to a change in the location of an industry. It was possible that when steam, raised from coal, replaced water as a motive power for heavy machinery, the cotton and wool textile industries might have had to leave Lancashire and Yorkshire, and move towards the coal-fields. Luckily for these industries, seams of excellent coal existed on the spot, and so a change was avoided. For many years the position of the British coal-fields more or less controlled the location not only of the 'heavy' industries (those handling metals and chemicals in great bulk), but of others also (see COAL-MINING, HISTORY OF). This is still true of the heavy industries, but new forms of power, such as electricity, or oil-fired boilers, have made it possible for the light industries (those which make or assemble most of the ordinary everyday articles) to move elsewhere. This change took place slowly. At first it was cheaper to generate electricity near the coal-fields, where there were already many industries that would want the current. Moreover, until the development of the electricity 'grid' (see GRID SYSTEM, Vol. VIII) between the First and the Second World Wars, it was not easy to transmit electricity over long distances, or to transfer the surplus current of one district to one where current was short. But even before the grid was ready, light industries began to move away from the coal-fields and the older industrial districts, and towards London and other southern towns. Here there were two advantages—nearness to a good market and plenty of labour.

These two factors have always influenced location, but their importance has increased. In the 19th century labour was more 'mobile' than to-day, that is to say, workpeople were more willing to move from district to district in search of work. Also, housing difficulties were much less serious than they are to-day. Manufacturers have always liked to have a large market 'on their doorstep', for it is easier to distribute and sell goods in a compact and highly populated area like London, with millions of inhabitants, than elsewhere. Between the First and Second World Wars, the attractiveness of London's large market, and its abundant supply of many kinds of labour, caused many industries to migrate towards it. This movement led to some unfortunate results. The building of new factories and housing estates caused much congestion, and slowed down transport. The efficiency of workpeople suffered through long and overcrowded daily journeys. When the Second World War broke out in 1939, many industries had left the older centres, such as South Wales and the Tyne, which had therefore become 'depressed areas', while London had become overcrowded. A Royal Commission was set up to consider difficulties that had arisen and to suggest remedies. Of the remedies actually adopted after the war, the most important were the formation of 'satellite' towns outside London, and the encouragement of manufacturers to move back to South Wales and the North (see TOWN AND COUNTRY PLANNING, Vol. X).

All these, however, are not the only things which affect industrial location. Important influences are tradition and the fact that people do not always like to change their ways. Apart from the fact that an industry that has always been in a certain place will tend to remain there,

MAP OF GREAT BRITAIN SHOWING THE POSITION OF THE CHIEF INDUSTRIES, EXCLUDING AGRICULTURE

the longer it stays the more it will build up around it a supply of labour that thoroughly understands its work and its problems. Birmingham, for instance, has been the centre of the manufacturing JEWELLERY TRADE (q.v.) for over 100 years. Yet there are no particular reasons for this, other than local skill and tradition. This is also true of the clock and watch industry in the Clerkenwell district of London, the TANNING industry of Bermondsey in London, the BOOT AND SHOE industries of Norwich and Northampton, and the CUTLERY trade of Sheffield (qq.v.).

In a general sense the strongest influences are, in order of importance, (*a*) natural or geographical advantages, (*b*) nearness to raw materials, (*c*) the presence of the right kinds of labour and skill, (*d*) good facilities for dispatch or for selling. The SHIPBUILDING INDUSTRY (q.v.) has become concentrated on the Clyde, on Belfast Lough, on Tees-side and Tyneside, for natural and geographical reasons. The COTTON INDUSTRY (q.v.) settled in Lancashire originally for other reasons, but has continued there because Lancashire has a damp climate, well suited to the brittle fibres of the cotton-plant. Northampton continues to be the headquarters of boot and shoe making, not because hides are more easily obtained there, or tanning more easily done, but because the local labour has been schooled for many years in the techniques of the industry. Various secondary industries choose ports such as London or Glasgow as their headquarters, some because they are dependent on imported raw materials, others because the large populations of such cities make selling and distribution easier.

No really simple explanation of industrial location is possible. One must consider each industry separately, and weigh up the various influences and counter-influences in its history, before one can work out the precise reasons why it is where it is to-day.

LOCK-OUT, *see* TRADE UNIONS.

LOOM, *see* WOOL WEAVING.

LUDDITES. In the early 19th century a movement of workers was formed whose object was the wrecking of factory machinery. These men were called Luddites. Little definite is known about this movement. Some historians believe it to have been a widespread national secret society with many branches throughout Britain. Others think that there was no national movement, but only a series of disconnected local movements. There is also no general agreement as to why those in the movement took this particular name. A half-witted worker named Ned Ludd was prosecuted in 1779, more than 30 years before the Luddite riots began, for the wilful destruction of a machine, and the movement may have adopted his name. Although its leader was never identified, he was known as General Ludd or sometimes King Ludd, and he may have taken his name from the earlier Ned.

The first outbreaks occurred in and around Nottingham at the end of 1811. Masked men visited factories in the dead of night, and broke in and smashed up machinery. The members of the movement were all hand-workers, who had either been dismissed because mechanical methods needed fewer men, or were suffering because, on piece-work (*see* WAGES), they could earn very little in competition with factory workers. Their view was that the new machines were taking away their livelihood.

In the Nottingham riots many stocking- and lace-frames were destroyed, and other riots broke out in the spring of 1812 in Yorkshire, Lancashire, Derbyshire, and Leicestershire. The Government put down the movement very severely, and in 1813 many Luddites were brought to trial at York Assizes. In this mass-trial numbers of the accused were sentenced to death, and others were transported to overseas penal settlements for long periods (*see* TRANSPORTATION, Vol. X). After the York trial the movement temporarily collapsed, possibly because General Ludd himself was one of those tried and sentenced. But it was revived in 1816 during the depression that followed the end of the war with France. Nottingham was again the first city to be affected, and, as in 1812, the riots spread over the whole kingdom. The return of prosperity and rising prices brought the Luddite movement to an end.

See also INDUSTRIAL REVOLUTION; TRADE CYCLE; TRADE UNION HISTORY.

LUMBER, *see* WOOD PULP; *see also* Vol. VI LUMBER CAMPS.

M

MACHINE ACCOUNTING, *see* ACCOUNTING, MACHINE.

MAGNESIUM, EXTRACTION OF. Ores or compounds of the metal magnesium are found in many parts of the earth's crust, magnesium compounds accounting for over 2 per cent. of the earth's solid volume (*see* METAL ORES, Vol. III). The commercial ores of magnesium are usually magnesite or dolomite, and the metal is obtained not only by the ordinary SMELTING and refining processes, but also by ELECTROLYSIS (qq.v. Vol. VIII). The bulk of the magnesium now used is obtained by electrolysis. In Britain an important method of producing magnesium was formerly the electrolytic treatment of sea-water, which contains 0·125% of the metal. Other methods are now more profitable, though in war-time the electrolysis of sea-water is still important.

In appearance magnesium is a brilliant white metal rather like silver, although if exposed to the air its surface soon becomes dulled by OXIDA-TION (q.v.), as it forms an oxide with the oxygen of the air. For this reason magnesium for laboratory purposes is usually kept in sealed containers. Magnesium burns with an intense white light, very rich in chemically active violet rays, and in ribbon or powder form it is much used in photography, particularly for interiors or for photographs taken at night time. It also plays a part in the making of fireworks. Its military uses include the making of incendiary bombs, and of 'tracer' bullets which show the path of their flight. Magnesium light alloys are being increasingly used in AERONAUTICAL ENGINEERING (q.v. Vol. VIII). Many of the magnesium minerals are of economic impor-tance. Chrysotile ASBESTOS (q.v.) is one; meer-schaum is another, this having once been a popular material, particularly in Germany, for the bowls of tobacco pipes.

Some compounds of magnesium are used in medicine. Magnesium oxide, or magnesia, is one of these. Epsom Salts is the common name for magnesium sulphate, whose medicinal value was first discovered nearly 400 years ago in the reign of Queen Elizabeth.

MAIL-ORDER TRADING. This means the sale of goods direct to the customer through the post instead of the more usual system of selling them through shops. There are two kinds of mail-order trading. The first is that done by firms which do not specialize in mail-order alone. Most large city shops, particularly DEPART-MENT STORES (q.v.), have mail-order depart-ments. Goods are advertised in newspapers and periodicals, and catalogues or price-lists are handed or posted to customers. The customers then post their orders to the store, and the goods are sent off. Payment is made by several methods, varying with the type of store and the customer's standing. If the customer has an account with the store, the goods will be charged against it; if he is not known to them, or cannot be safely given CREDIT (q.v.), he may be asked to send 'cash with order', or the goods may be sent to him by the Post Office C.O.D. (cash on delivery) service. The customer can often safe-guard himself against an unsatisfactory purchase by asking for goods to be sent 'on approval'. Mail-order trading of this kind does not differ essentially from ordinary trading. The main difference is that the customer does not inspect and select from a range of goods at the time of purchase.

The other form of mail-order trading is done by the specialist firm that sells in this way only. A firm of this kind has no shop, and its goods are not open to inspection, although they may be sent on approval. It works from a central ware-house or depot in a convenient town or district, and finds its customers by advertising for them. Some specialist mail-order traders deal in one or two limited lines of goods; others deal in a wide range. A feature of specialist mail-order houses dealing in a wide range of goods is their printed catalogues, which are often very elaborate.

Some of the department stores with mail-order departments do not differ greatly from the specialist mail-order traders. Their mail-order departments account for a very large part of their total TURNOVER of sales (q.v.) and, like the specialist houses, they send an elaborate and profusely illustrated catalogue to actual or prospective customers. Gamage's in London have run an important and profitable mail-order department of this kind since the close of the 19th century. Specialist mail-order houses are more prominent in the U.S.A., owing to the vast distances of the country, and the isolation in which most of the farming population live. The largest American firm is Sears-Roebuck, whose catalogue is an enormous volume, covering practically everything that the American consumer needs.

See also RETAIL TRADING; DEPARTMENT STORES; SELF-SERVICE STORES.

MALTING. Barley malt is the basic material in BEER BREWING (q.v.), and the great bulk of the malt is used for that purpose. But malt has other uses: whisky, malt foods, vinegar, bread, and so on; and the art of the maltster is to produce the right kind of malt for each purpose. Distinct types of malt are used for the various kinds of beers; some very light in colour for the pale ales, others so dark that they are called black malt. The colour of the malt affects the colour of the beer.

Malt is barley or other grain which has just begun to sprout. To the eye, a grain of barley and a grain of malt appear to be alike; but, if each is bitten, it will be found that, while the barley is hard, the malt can be crunched easily with the teeth, and tastes rather like a sweet biscuit. This change in texture is brought about by starting the grain of barley into growth, just as it would begin to grow if sown in the earth.

The first step in malting is to steep the barley in water, and then to spread it out evenly, some 6 inches deep, on one of the floors of the maltings or malthouses. Here it germinates, and is allowed to lie for about 5 days. During this time it is frequently turned over, by men using wooden shovels. By this time tiny rootlets have appeared on the grain. The skill of the maltster consists in judging just the right stage to which this growth should be allowed to go, and in deciding when growth should be slowed up by spreading the grain more thinly, or when it should be stopped altogether. The malt is dried and slightly 'cooked' by spreading it on the floor of a kiln, where the heat from the fire beneath can pass up through it; in more modern practice, hot air is passed over the malt. Sieving then removes the tiny rootlets from the grains of malt. These rootlets, known as 'malt culms', are a valuable food for poultry and cattle.

There are variations on these methods. In the more modern maltings pneumatic chutes and conveyor-belts are used to lessen human labour. In the 'drum' maltings germination takes place on what is, in effect, a slowly revolving floor, thus

TURNING THE GRAIN ON A MALTING-FLOOR

Whitbread and Co.

The Brewers' Society

A MODERN MALTING DRUM

The drum is slowly revolved, giving the same effect as hand
turning on the malting-floor

eliminating the need for turning the malt over
by hand. In the older maltings work has to be
shut down entirely from May to September,
because the weather is too warm for the process;
but modern science has provided suitable means
of AIR-CONDITIONING (q.v. Vol. VIII), which
enable the right degree of warmth and humidity
to be maintained throughout the year.

    See also BEER BREWING.
    See also Vol. VI: BARLEY.

MANAGEMENT, see BUSINESS ORGANIZATION;
SCIENTIFIC MANAGEMENT.

MANILA, see ROPE-MAKING.

MARBLE AND ALABASTER. The word
'marble' is derived from the Greek *marmaros*,
which means sparkling stone. Ever since the
times of the Greeks and Romans, it has been
recognized as one of the most decorative and
beautiful building materials. In a technical
sense marble is any kind of limestone which has
a crystalline or granular structure and is capable
of taking a high polish. It may be snow-white,
or it may be brightly coloured. If a piece of
white statuary marble is broken, the sparkling
facets of the grains that compose it are easily
seen. Marble is a form of limestone which is
metamorphic, that is, it has changed its original
form as a result of pressure and heat within the
earth's crust (*see* ROCKS, Section 4, Vol. III).
The streaks and veins of colour, which give
diversity to all varieties except pure white
statuary marble and black marble, come from
metallic compounds and impurities in the stone.
The colours chiefly found are yellow, orange,
red, grey, green, and, more rarely, purple and
blue. For building in Britain marble is hardly
ever used in the form of large structural blocks,
but generally in thin panels or slabs, which are
often used as a decorative lining for solid walls
of brick. The slabs are usually about ¾ inch thick,
and secured to the backing by brass cramps let
into the marble and the backing. Damp harms
marble, destroying the polish on which the
brilliance of its colour depends. Marble is therefore seldom used for the outside of buildings in
the comparatively damp atmosphere of England.

    Most of the marble used in Britain is imported.
It usually arrives by sea in large blocks, which
are nowadays sawn and polished by machinery.
The machines can saw as many as twenty slabs
at the same time (*see* STONE-DRESSING). Grinding
and polishing are done by revolving 'rubbers',
first with iron and then with felt. Machines
have been invented for turning and polishing
columns and balusters, and others for making
mouldings.

    The most famous buildings of Athens, and
notably the temple of the Parthenon (dedicated
in 438 B.C.) on the ACROPOLIS (q.v. Vol. XII),
were made of solid marble from Mount Pentelicus, cut and polished by hand. The colour was
originally white, but in time it weathers to a
beautiful golden yellow. Parian marble, which
is also white, and was much used by the Athenians, came from the Greek Island of Paros. The
Romans used both these varieties chiefly as thin
wall-linings, but also favoured *verde antica* (old
green); its name indicates its colour, and many
people consider it to be the most beautiful of all.
Many famous buildings of the Middle Ages in
Italy, such as the Campanile at Florence, and the
Cathedral and the Baptistery at Pisa, are entirely
faced with marble, as are many of the finest
mosques in Cairo, and the TAJ MAHAL at Agra
(q.v. Vol. XII). The Taj is made of local Indian
marble, which in that country is very plentiful,
and is often used for flooring offices, public buildings, and private houses. Some of the ancient
marble quarries, including Mount Pentelicus in
Greece, are still working; but the chief source of
white marble to-day is Carrara, near Pisa, in

Italy. Here enormous quarries continue to produce large quantities, for building as well as for statuary.

Black marble, much used for floors, is chiefly obtained from Belgium and Ireland. Fine green marble comes from Sweden, Switzerland, and Connemara in Ireland. Several so-called English marbles are, strictly speaking, merely limestones capable of taking a high polish; examples are Purbeck and Hopton Wood (Derbyshire) marbles, both greyish in colour, and several Devonshire marbles, mainly red.

Alabaster is another form of limestone, pink or red and white, and often beautifully clouded or veined. It is used for decoration in building. The hard Oriental alabaster, used by the ancients, is sometimes incorrectly called onyx marble, but is a stalagmite or stalactite. English alabaster is largely composed of gypsum (a sulphate of lime), obtained especially in Derbyshire and Nottinghamshire. It is very soft when first quarried and can therefore be carved with great detail. It hardens on exposure to the air. In the 14th and 15th centuries it was much used for tombs and statues, which were carved in workshops near the quarries and exported all over England and the Continent. To-day English alabaster is popular for electric light bowls and other fittings, and also for memorial tablets.

MARGARINE. The modern margarine industry owes a great deal to the enterprise of the Dutch, who were the first to manufacture margarine on a commercial scale. The product was originally invented by a Frenchman during the difficult time of food shortage in the Franco-Prussian war of 1870–1. This first margarine was a mixture of milk and oleo oil, an animal fat produced from suet. Some Dutch business men took up the new invention, and the first factories of any size were set up in the village of Oss in Holland soon after the Franco-Prussian war. The animal fats used at first came from France and Austria, but later from the meat-packing industry of Chicago, which was rapidly developing manufactured oleo oil as a BY-PRODUCT (q.v.). Rotterdam, a convenient port of entry, has been closely associated with the Dutch margarine industry ever since.

The Dutch had few sources of animal fats in their own colonial territories, and research on the possibilities of vegetable oils went on for many years. In 1883 a way was found to utilize for margarine the increasing production of oil from

E.N.A.

A BULLOCK CART TAKING MARBLE FROM THE QUARRIES AT CARRARA, ITALY

GROUNDNUTS and other TROPICAL OIL-SEEDS (qq.v. Vol. VI) grown in Indonesia, and this discovery greatly helped the Dutch industry. Early in the present century Sabatier found that vegetable and animal oils could be hardened by the 'hydrogenation' process, that is, by treating them with pure hydrogen gas under pressure. Later it was found that whale oil, as well as many of the vegetable oils, responded particularly well to this hydrogenation process. The Dutch firm of van den Berghs then opened up in Britain, but it was not until after the First World War, when butter was in short supply, that the margarine produced reached its present high quality. The firm of van den Berghs was bought up by the big combine, Lever Brothers, and for many years the two main margarine firms were Levers in Britain and Anton Jurgens in Holland. In 1937 Levers in Britain, and the Dutch Margarine Unie, which had incorporated Jurgens, were amalgamated as Lever Brothers and Unilever. This firm now practically controls the margarine production of the world.

Whale oil is still an important constituent of margarine, and the principal vegetable oils used come from groundnuts (or peanuts), cottonseed, coco-nuts, soya beans, palm kernels, sunflower seeds, and other oil-bearing plants. Sometimes these oils are imported in a refined state, but usually they have to be refined during manufacture (*see* REFINING). The oils used must also be bleached or decolourized, and have all smell removed by a process of deodorizing. Fuller's earth is a common decolorizing agent, and deodorizing is usually done by blowing steam through the oils under high pressure. Flavour is given to the mixture by adding skimmed or separated milk.

The law takes care that margarine, which is only a substitute, is not passed off on the public as butter itself. The Food and Drugs (Adulteration) Act of 1928 defines margarine as 'any article of food, whether mixed with butter or not, which resembles butter and is not milk-blended butter', and directs that every package containing margarine must have the word 'margarine' marked upon it.

See also OILS, VEGETABLE.
See also Vol. VI: OIL-BEARING PLANTS

MARKET. A market exists whenever there are buyers and sellers of anything for a money price. A market need not be an actual building,

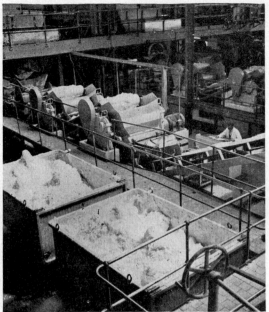

Van den Berghs and Jurgens

MARGARINE BEING ROLLED IN MULTIPLEX MACHINES TO MAKE IT SMOOTH AND PLIABLE

It travels from the hopper (top left) through three sets of rollers to the conveyor-belt (right)

although it is often convenient that there should be one. The estate market, for example, in which landed property changes hands, has no single building in Britain set aside for such dealings. The MONEY-MARKET (q.v.) is another market which does not possess a building of its own. All that a market needs is willing buyers and sellers able to get in touch with each other. The foreign exchange market consists simply of the governments and bankers of the world, linked together by a system of cables and telephones.

An exchange is, of course, a market in the general sense of that word; but the term is nearly always used to describe a building in which dealings take place in goods not actually on view there. Buyers and sellers are usually dealing in contracts on paper, entitling them to receive, or binding them to deliver, certain quantities of something at a certain date. On the Liverpool Cotton Exchange, for example, there is no actual cotton displayed for sale; instead dealers contract to buy or sell certain recognized grades for immediate or future delivery (*see* COTTON INDUSTRY).

The word 'exchange' is also used to describe buildings in which purely financial dealings are carried on. Thus the London Stock Exchange deals in documents entitling their possessor to receive a rate of INTEREST, or a rate of DIVIDEND, on an INVESTMENT (qq.v.). The Foreign Exchange Market deals only in bank balances in various countries, but it is called a market rather than an exchange because it has no building of its own.

Exchanges can be further classified into financial exchanges and produce exchanges. The Stock Exchange is a financial exchange. The Baltic Mercantile and Shipping Exchange, in St. Mary Axe, London, is both a financial and produce exchange. On its financial side members are dealing in the 'chartering' or hiring of ships, usually tramp steamers, to carry bulk cargoes. In such transactions no actual goods or contracts concerning any goods are changing hands. But before 1940 the Baltic also dealt in the grain cargoes loaded into those ships, and this side of its business makes it a produce exchange. The Liverpool Cotton Exchange is, of course, a produce exchange pure and simple.

A feature of all exchanges, whether they are financial or produce exchanges, is that business may be done on them in contracts for future as well as for immediate settlement. Freedom to deal for future settlement is at present greatly restricted by Government controls. Before the First World War dealers could arrange to buy on the Liverpool Cotton Exchange for delivery a year or more ahead, and similarly could arrange to sell for future delivery. On the Corn Exchange in Mark Lane, London, dealers could do the same sort of thing—and likewise on the Metal Exchange, the Iron and Steel Exchange, and the Coal Exchange. On these produce exchanges, contracts to buy and sell were either 'spot' or 'forward'. A spot contract was one to buy or sell for immediate delivery; a forward contract was to buy or sell for future delivery, the date being named. Spot transactions were usually given that name; forward transactions on some exchanges were called by that name and on others were called 'futures'.

As dealings on produce exchanges take place without the buyer ever seeing the goods, business has to be confined to the sort of commodity whose quality can be described beyond all argument—either in words, or by reference to a named grade or quality which all dealers would interpret as meaning the same thing. Obviously, then, it would never do for produce

exchanges to deal in such things as meat, vegetables, or fish, which have to be looked at before their quality and value can be known. The places where such commodities are dealt in are therefore generally called 'markets'. Well-known examples in London are the Smithfield Meat Market, the Spitalfields and Covent Garden Fruit and Vegetable Markets, and the London Commodity Exchange in Mincing Lane, dealing in tea, coffee, spices, and other Eastern products. But all rules seem to have their exceptions, and one of the most important markets of this kind is called the Wool Exchange; it is near the Guildhall in the City of London.

On some of these markets the dealers do their business after they have already inspected the commodity—either in WAREHOUSES (q.v.) at the docks, or elsewhere—and they fix a price by mutual bargaining. But on most of the commodity markets an AUCTION (q.v.) is the normal way of buying and selling: an auctioneer mounts a raised platform, called a 'rostrum', in the centre of the room, and sells to the highest bidders the various consignments or 'parcels' of commodities offered for sale that day. These are sometimes on show in another part of the market building; or they may be temporarily warehoused elsewhere; sometimes, as at Spitalfields, they are left outside in carts and lorries, and samples are brought into the auction room. As in an ordinary auction of furniture at a sale held in a house, the goods are 'knocked down' by a tap of the auctioneer's hammer on his desk, the last and highest bidder getting the goods.

As well as the permanent markets housed in buildings, and handling their own limited range of products, there are many auction rooms which are not given the name of market. At the Mart in Queen Victoria Street, London, for instance, there is an auction room for landed property; but naturally only a very small part of the property dealings in the country takes place in it, and it is not called the British Estate Market. Likewise there are the famous auction rooms called Christie's, in London, at which antique furniture, pictures, jewellery, and various other objects of art are auctioned from time to time; but this, too, is by no means the only market of its kind. Throughout the country there are also various fairs and markets, and regular sales of horses and livestock.

This big network of markets is of great service to the commercial world. Business would be far

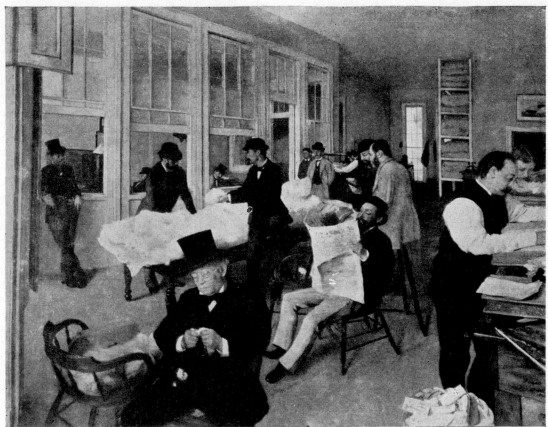

Pau Museum

THE NEW ORLEANS COTTON EXCHANGE
Painting by E. Degas, 1834–1917

too difficult and expensive if manufacturers, importers, and merchants had to track down individual buyers and get them to buy their goods. In the days before the Second World War the exchanges and markets were centres that attracted all the important buyers in the kingdom. The main markets were in the larger ports, such as London and Liverpool, where many of the imported commodities came direct. Later the system of BULK PURCHASE (q.v.) by the Government largely took the place of these various markets. Purely financial transactions are still centred in London, the principal city for the country's banking, foreign exchange, investment, and shipping dealings. By market organization the seller gets a higher price than otherwise; the consumer benefits because the expense is lessened of transporting goods to the small buyers all over the country; perishable products also reach the customer in better condition. By

doing 'forward' business a manufacturer or merchant can cover his future wants for a long time ahead, without having to put down any noney until the actual date of his contract. In these big, centralized markets the dealers can detect even small changes in the conditions of SUPPLY AND DEMAND (q.v); changes in price warn producers of possible over or under-production, so that they are able to cut down on unprofitable lines, or to open up lines where there is a temporary shortage.

Most market dealings are done through BROKERS (q.v.), who are members of the exchanges or markets in which they specialize. Brokers are told by the manufacturers, merchants, importers, or shippers what goods to buy or sell, and so on; the prices may be either limited or left to their discretion. On the financial and produce exchanges they arrange the necessary contracts with other brokers. If a broker happens to get orders from different customers to buy and sell the same grades and quantities at the same time, he can arrange the whole business inside his own office by drawing up a contract between buyer and seller, and can charge commission to both parties. This practice is called 'marrying' buying and selling orders. Most exchanges, however, have rules limiting the extent to which this may be done.

See also Vol. VI: MARKET TOWNS.

MARKET RESEARCH. This is a scientific way of obtaining information about the taste and preferences of the buying public. The Americans, who have always been more ready than any other nation to use scientific methods as an aid to business, were the first to start market research.

Market research has become almost indispensable for successful business. In the Middle Ages, and until even the early years of the INDUSTRIAL REVOLUTION (q.v.) before the growth of railway communications, most goods were hand-made for a purely local market. The task of finding out what the consumer thought of the goods offered to him was therefore very easy. As the Industrial Revolution went on, factories grew larger and firms made goods for a wider market. By the end of the 19th century a single manufacturer might be selling his goods not only in his own country but over the whole world. It was therefore essential that manufacturers should find out scientifically whether the goods they were turning out were what the consumer really wanted. Research was also necessary to find out many other kinds of information. For example, the consumer might like the article, but not the way it was packed, or the size and design of the package. Moreover, it might be sold on terms which did not suit the shopkeeper, so he might refuse to stock it. A very good instance of what could happen without market research was the experience of the exporter of egg-cups to India, who assumed that hens all over the world laid the same sized eggs. Another manufacturer took care to make inquiries and, finding that Indian eggs were smaller than British, made egg-cups slightly smaller than the standard British size, and thereby captured the Indian market from his competitor.

The marketing problems of all manufacturers are not the same. Some manufacturers are already selling a particular product, and they make use of market research to increase their sales of it. Others are not yet making a particular product, but are thinking of doing so; they wish to learn beforehand what consumers think about existing products, so that if possible they may improve on them. Then there are manufacturers who wish to launch some newly invented product, such as a safety razor instead of the old-style razor. All these three problems are different, and the methods of market research must vary in each case.

Market research for the first two types of product involves first of all office-work and then 'field' work. The office-work is based on such figures or STATISTICS (q.v.) as happen to be available. A manufacturer of a commodity already on the market will have figures of his total sales in any particular country. These figures must be analysed or 'broken down' in various ways. A useful break-down might be into districts, in some of which the average shopper would be wealthy, in others poor. The trend of these sales figures over several years should then be studied to discover where sales of the product are increasing and where they are falling off. This preliminary office-work will provide ideas to go upon before the 'field' part of the research is started, which involves asking the consumers and shopkeepers to give their opinion. It is impossible to question all customers, even in one district, so the people who carry out the research must rely on a statistical law: if a large enough sample of consumers is chosen at random, the results will differ only slightly from the results obtained if every single consumer had been approached. For field work in market research at least 1,000 persons are often interviewed; if the research is to cover the whole country, 100 persons might perhaps be chosen from each of ten different representative districts. Each person on the list is then asked to give answers to a form or questionnaire containing not more than seven or eight questions, each easily understood and capable of being very simply answered. The questions chosen will naturally depend on the product itself, and on the information the manufacturer wants. A research conducted by one of the big film-producing companies to attempt to gauge the public taste in films would naturally involve totally different questions from those asked in a questionnaire dealing with toothpaste. Answers to the questionnaire can be obtained either by calls on the persons interviewed, or through the post. Interviewers need to be carefully trained and experienced, otherwise they may 'lead' the persons interviewed, that is, they may suggest answers instead of letting the persons speak for themselves. Skill is needed to interpret the replies, as many consumers give different replies to a questionnaire from those they would give in ordinary conversation. So what is called 'interview bias' must be allowed for. If forms are sent out by post, usually it happens that only a small proportion of replies is received—generally from people who are interested, or from those who always like to make themselves prominent —and this bias must be corrected also.

Research investigators may also get permission to sit unobserved in retail shops in various parts of the country, so as to study at first hand what brands or products are being bought by customers, and what they say when they cannot get the brand they ask for. The great difficulty in personal research is to get people to give an honest opinion. It is a help if the personal investigation can be checked in some other way. For instance, many manufacturers open what are called 'laboratory' or experimental shops, merely to get information on the demand for their products in a particular district.

When the product is a new and untried one, there must first be preliminary office-work to discover whether it has any chance at all. Although many new products are unknown and untried, they are nearly always substitutes for something else that is already being sold: for example, the first vacuum-cleaner was a substitute for the handbroom. Much of the preliminary office-work naturally deals with the price at which the article could be profitably produced. More information may be got by distributing samples to people who might be likely to buy the goods. For expensive fitments, such as vacuum-cleaners, local demonstrations are given instead, and the people who attend them are questioned. These preliminary lines of inquiry are usually followed by an experimental sales and advertising campaign in a small area. This area should contain a large mixed population of all classes. Some Midland towns, such as Leicester, are favourite choices for this kind of campaign.

Market research is now mainly carried on by special firms that have made a long study of the most successful methods. Some large manufacturers organize their own market research, but these are few. Problems become more difficult when overseas markets are explored. The British Export Trade Research Organization (generally known as B.E.T.R.O.) aimed at making a specialized study of market conditions in all countries where British exports are sold. Its work was helped by the commercial branch of the British Foreign Service.

See also STATISTICS; BUSINESS ORGANIZATION; ADVERTISING AND PUBLICITY.

MARKETS, STREET, see STREET MARKETS.

MARQUETRY, see INLAY AND MARQUETRY.

MASONRY, see STONE DRESSING.

MASS PRODUCTION, see PRODUCTION.

MEAT TRADE. Before the days of railways and refrigerated ships, the towns of Britain depended for their meat supplies upon the live cattle, sheep, and pigs that could be driven along the roads to the markets. Butchers who bought animals in the markets took them to their own slaughter-houses for killing and preliminary cutting up. Salting and curing were then the only known ways of preserving meat, and, as far as the poor communications permitted, there was a fairly extensive trade throughout the country in bacon and hams. In many of the large seaport towns the salting of beef and pork, for provisioning merchant ships and the ships of the Royal Navy, was an important activity. The supplies of live animals came only from within the kingdom itself.

By the middle of the 19th century the population had grown so large that Britain was unable any longer to provide all the meat for her people, and live cattle began to be imported from abroad. North America was at first the principal supplier, and later South America. The North American trade in live cattle for slaughter became so important that one line of steamers— the Atlantic Transport Line—specialized in this trade only. Meanwhile the railways had made it possible for British butchers to draw on more distant and isolated parts of the country for their supplies of live cattle, which could now travel in cattle-trucks instead of losing condition on a long walk to market.

During the 19th century public opinion caused

NEWGATE MEAT MARKET, LONDON, IN THE 19TH CENTURY
Engraving from the *Illustrated London News*

many laws to be made in Britain to prevent dirty and unhealthy practices. Local authorities were given power to inspect and license private slaughter-houses, or abattoirs as they were called, and to insist on clean conditions. Towards the end of the century public slaughter-houses began to be set up.

It was not until the invention of COLD STORAGE (q.v.) that there was any important change in the meat trade. The first experimental cargo of frozen beef and mutton arrived in London from Australia in 1880, and 2 years later New Zealand began to export mutton and lamb. From then onwards the import of frozen or chilled meat began gradually to replace the transport of live animals, but many years passed before the amount of refrigerated cargo-space in ships was sufficient to bring the trade in live cattle to an end, and imports still came in from North America until the outbreak of the First World War. South America, Australia, and New Zealand, particularly the first and last, took up refrigeration on an important scale. Vast abattoirs and freezing-plants—called in South America *frigorificos*—were established at such ports as Buenos Aires in the Argentine, Monte-

video in Uruguay, and Christchurch in New Zealand. The famous Canterbury lamb, which has nothing to do with the English city in Kent but comes from the Canterbury plains of the South Island of New Zealand, found a popular and growing market in Britain (*see* NEW ZEALAND, Vol. III).

In these overseas abattoirs the carcasses of cattle were quartered into weights that could be more conveniently handled, while those of sheep and lambs were left whole. The carcasses were then loaded into the steamers. Before the Second World War two distinct methods of refrigeration were used. Mutton and lamb can stand a temperature below freezing-point without losing their flavour and tenderness; but, although beef can be frozen during the voyage, it loses quality and flavour much less if it is conveyed at a temperature just above freezing-point. Beef so transported is called 'chilled'. This difference affected the type of refrigerated ship used in the different branches of the trade, and also the method of stowing the cargo. Carcasses of frozen lamb and mutton could be piled up in the hold like any other solid cargo, except that the pile had to be rather shallow or the bottom layers might be spoiled by heat generated through the weight and pressure on top of them; but each quarter of chilled beef had to hang individually by a separate hook from the deck above. Moreover, as chilled beef was not fully proof against decomposition in a temperature above freezing-point, the refrigerated holds had to be filled with carbon dioxide gas to kill the tiny organisms of decay. The gas needed space in which to circulate, and therefore a given weight of chilled beef required more cargo space than frozen meat.

There was an efficient marketing organization to distribute the meat. In the distant countries from which Britain's supplies came, the monthly 'fat stock' sale was not only an opportunity for seller and buyer, but also an important social event. In all the big seaport towns to which the steamers came, and also in large inland provincial cities such as Birmingham, there were meat-markets where the carcasses were sold, and cold stores where meat not needed for immediate sale could be kept. Smithfield in London, and the market of the same name in Birmingham, were typical examples. To these markets came not only imported meat, but also home-killed meat from animals sold at the weekly 'marts' throughout the country (*see* MARKETS, Vol. VI). Over 40,000 butchers' shops, more than half of them small one-man businesses, distributed the meat to the consumers. Some of these shops were owned and controlled by the big South American companies, who were engaged in every branch of the trade. The British and Argentine Meat Company operated *frigorificos* in Argentina and Uruguay, controlled the Union Cold Storage Company (which had branches on the Continent), and owned thousands of retail shops through which their own meat was distributed.

When the Second World War broke out in 1939, many changes took place in the trade. Meat was imported direct by the Ministry of Food (*see* BULK PURCHASE), which also bought all animals for slaughter bred within Great Britain; the meat was allotted to butchers according to the number of their registered customers, and prices were laid down by the Ministry. Moreover, through difficulties in obtaining foreign currency, the amount of meat that can be imported from foreign countries is limited by what Britain can afford. And so she has turned to the Commonwealth for supplies.

See also Vol. VI: CATTLE, CARE OF, section 7.

MECHANICAL ACCOUNTING, *see* AC-COUNTING, MACHINE.

MEDICAL SUPPLIES. These include drugs, dispensed and packed medicines, surgical dressings, and simple surgical appliances such as bandages and plaster. The main channel by which they reach the public is the chemist's shop or pharmacy. During the 18th century chemists and druggists emerged as a distinct professional body, and in 1841 founded the Pharmaceutical Society of Great Britain, an organization distinct from the older Society of Apothecaries, and also an examining body. Only qualified pharmacists are allowed by law to be in charge of chemists' shops.

1. MEDICINES. The supply of medicines is closely controlled by the Pharmacy and Poisons Act of 1933. The Act does not insist that all medicines shall be sold only at chemists' shops, but it provides that medicines containing poisons must be sold in such shops only. Each sale has to be made under the supervision of a qualified pharmacist, who must also be a member of the Society, and still on its register. The Society has a Law Committee, which helps it to carry out its part in administering the 1933 Act. The Committee's inspectors and agents make periodical visits to pharmacies, drug stores, and other places where medicines are sold, to ensure that the provisions of the Act are being carried out. Other authorities, including borough and county bodies, have power to make test purchases under the Food and Drugs Act, and to submit any test prescription for dispensing under the NATIONAL HEALTH SERVICE Act of 1948 (q.v. Vol. X). The Home Office carries out inspections under the Dangerous Drugs Acts, to ensure obedience to the law controlling dealings in dangerous and habit-forming drugs, such as morphine and cocaine.

The British Pharmacopoeia is a book published by the General Medical Council, and contains a list of current medical preparations with notes on methods of testing, and standard doses. It is kept regularly up to date, and lays down the standard to which many drugs must legally conform. Drugs prepared by individual pharmacists are now being largely supplanted by factory-made products. The growth of advertising has also caused a great increase in the sale of branded and proprietary goods (*see* RETAIL TRADING), instead of those prepared and packed by the

Boots Pure Drug Co.

A LABORATORY WHERE DRUGS ARE ANALYSED AND TESTED

individual pharmacist. Advertised medicines fall into two main classes: those advertised to the general public, and intended for direct use by the people themselves; and those advertised to doctors, chemists, and hospital staffs, for use mainly under medical supervision. Manufacturers tend to specialize in one of these two classes only.

As knowledge increases, numbers of new drugs that have a specific action are being discovered and prescribed. Because of their complexity, these preparations are usually made in manufacturers' laboratories, and the dispensing work of pharmacists is consequently being simplified. Many of these substances are prepared as compressed tablets, which are convenient to use and handle; the dose to be taken can be arranged with absolute accuracy. Tablets have very good keeping qualities, and they are easy to manufacture. Certain preparations on doctors' prescriptions—for example, bottles of medicine or special injections—still have to be made up on the spot, and cannot be obtained directly from the manufacturer (*see* MEDICINE, HISTORY OF, Vol. XI).

2. CHEMISTS' SHOPS. The total number of chemists' shops in Britain is about 14,700. Of these about 8,000 are in private ownership;

2,000 are MULTIPLE SHOPS (q.v.) owned by such firms as Boots, Timothy White's and Taylor's, and their associated companies; about 900 are owned by the CO-OPERATIVE SOCIETIES (q.v.), and there are about 3,600 operated by small limited companies. The old difference between the multiple shop and the other types has recently become less marked. The privately owned chemist's shop can give a highly personal service, but the large-scale multiple shop has the advantages that arise from large financial resources, greater buying power, and the ownership of its own manufacturing and wholesale departments. A number of the smaller companies conduct wholesale business and have their own manufacturing departments, and some of them have grown up from smaller concerns with a laboratory at the back of the original shop. Many specialized retail pharmacies are equipped with a 'sterile' room for making up prescriptions which involve precautions against contamination by bacteria (*see* BACTERIAL DISEASES, Vol. XI). A few specialist pharmacies concentrate principally on the supply of surgical instruments and appliances. There are some of these in and around Wigmore Street, close to the Harley Street district, which is the main London centre of the consulting branch of the medical profession.

Certain medicines not containing poisons, and other medical supplies, are sold to the public through drug stores, grocers, and other channels. A drug store can be opened and managed by an unqualified person, but the use of the names 'chemist', 'chemist and druggist', 'pharmacy', and 'pharmacist' is restricted by law to registered pharmacists.

The National Health Insurance Act of 1911 introduced on a large scale the State-aided supply of medicines. It also restricted the dispensing of Insurance Act prescriptions to pharmacists, or persons under their direct supervision. At that time the majority of private prescriptions in England and Wales were dispensed by doctors themselves, or by their dispensing assistants. Since the National Health Service Act became law in 1948, however, dispensing by doctors has decreased, and dispensing by chemists has increased. During the first year of the service 187 millions of its prescriptions were dispensed.

3. SOURCES OF SUPPLY. The sources of supply of finished medical preparations are varied, but can be classified under four headings: vegetable, synthetic (artificially made), animal, and miscellaneous. The principal substances, and the ailments for which they are used, are described in the article DRUGS AND MEDICINES in Vol. XI.

Drug research is continuously adding to the number of these preparations. This form of research is mainly carried out in the laboratories of firms specializing in the manufacture of drugs to be used under medical supervision. Its success rests largely upon the progress made by postgraduate research workers in universities, particularly in the fields of chemistry and biology.

See also CHEMISTRY, INDUSTRIAL.

MEDIUM OF EXCHANGE, *see* MONEY.

MERCANTILE SYSTEM. This was a name given to a body of economic ideas held by certain British statesmen and economists during the 17th and 18th centuries. These ideas concerned the regulation of trade and industry within Britain itself, and the management and control of overseas trade, to make the nation economically powerful and self-sufficient: that is, only dependent on foreign countries for such goods as Britain was unable to produce herself. The title of 'mercantile system' was given much later, and not by those who conceived the ideas, but by those who thought them wrong. The famous economist Adam SMITH (q.v. Vol. V), although he did not invent the phrase, made great use of it, usually in a hostile and rather reproachful sense. It was Adam Smith's criticisms, in the main, that caused the mercantile system to be replaced by a set of ideas utterly different, namely the Free Trade theories of the 19th century.

The practices were based, to start with, on the idea that it was the business of the Government itself to take control of overseas trade. It was argued that certain kinds of trade, if left uncontrolled and unregulated, allowed imports to come into the country without enough exports going out. This kind of trade meant a drain of money out of the country; the money went out in a very real sense, for in those days money was made of gold and silver, and consequently one country's money could be melted down and recoined by any other nation. The statesmen of the mercantilist period therefore aimed at what we call a favourable balance of trade: a total of exports greater than the total of imports. This would cause precious metals to flow into Britain from the countries that were buying from her more than they sold to her. Everything that would compel the foreigner to pay her in coin, everything that would diminish what she bought abroad, would therefore tend to increase this favourable balance of trade, and would lead to an increasing inflow of the precious metals. So, with this object in view, imports and exports were strictly controlled and regulated. This control did not stop short at goods alone. Any business that meant paying money to foreigners was carefully watched. Payment of this kind, for instance, took place when foreign ships were allowed to carry goods into and out of Britain. Money was not only paid for the goods, but, of course, for the use of the ship to carry them in as well. So various NAVIGATION ACTS (q.v.) were passed by Parliament; these forbade the shipment of goods between Britain and certain other countries in any vessels that were not British.

There are other mercantilist practices which

COVER OF AN 18TH-CENTURY OFFICE FILE
Justice and Britannia are seated one each side of the Custom House. Above is a British merchant ship

go back to earlier periods. As far back as the reign of Henry VII the law compelled French exporters of wine to England to use English ships when they were available. Although England under Edward VI was no longer Catholic, the fishing trade was encouraged by an Act passed in 1548, which enforced fish-eating on the old Catholic days of fasting. The growing of corn in Britain was encouraged by import duties or TARIFFS (q.v.) against foreign corn, so that the country might be independent of foreign supplies and in a position to feed itself from its own production, especially in time of war. Later, to make sure of materials for shipbuilding, Queen Elizabeth ordered the home growing of hemp for rope and cordage, and of flax for sails, and the increased planting of oak trees.

In its later years the mercantile system was seriously criticized, on the ground that it was a policy which made the nation powerful as a whole, instead of making its individual citizens prosperous. Yet serious problems faced British statesmen. Each of the leading nations was struggling to become supreme in the world of that time, and wars were frequent. A Free Trade policy—to which Britain did not become converted until the second half of the 19th century—would have meant that Britain in those earlier days would have depended on foreign nations for food and essential war stores, and this would have been dangerous in war time because of the risks of blockade or attack. The mercantile system was one which kept the nation independent for strategic or military reasons.

The statesmen and writers who were keenest to increase the store of gold and silver in Britain were called 'bullionists' by their critics: for these metals, before they are coined into money, are known as 'bullion'. Precious metals had then one great advantage, which they have not fully lost. Men all over the world will accept them, so that in time of war, or of threats of war, a nation that has plenty of these metals can buy from other lands all kinds of necessary and useful stores.

The mercantile system is being revived, and at the end of the Second World War British statesmen were as much concerned with a favourable balance of trade as were their 17th-century predecessors. Many of the old mercantilist practices have returned, and imports and exports are rigidly controlled by the issue of licences, so as to prevent an excessive shrinkage of Britain's

stock of dollars and other 'scarce' foreign currencies (*see* HARD CURRENCY).

Economists no longer claim Free Trade as the only sensible economic policy. They realize that Free Trade is an ideal that can only come true in a peaceful world, and they marvel at the hundred years of freedom from major wars, from Waterloo to the First World War, which made this ideal workable for a time. It is because the world politics of the mid-20th century are so very like those of the 17th and 18th centuries that the world is returning again to something very like the old mercantile system.

See also OVERSEAS TRADE; CURRENCY; RATES OF EXCHANGE; INTERNATIONAL TRADE; SHIPPING; TARIFFS.
See also Vol. X: NATIONAL FINANCE.

MERCHANT ADVENTURERS. This was a powerful organization originally built up in the 13th century round a body of English merchants who traded in the Netherlands, mainly in cloth, at their own risk. To secure greater protection they looked out for special privileges. As early as 1296 they received a charter from the Duke of Brabant, and by 1360 they were an organized company with their own set of rules. They made great strides in the reign of Henry VII, when they were granted a private coat of arms and a new charter, and by that time they had extended the scope of their operations from the Netherlands 'to all the Townes and Portes lying between the river Somme in France and the German Sea'.

The expansion of their trading activities in the 15th and 16th centuries brought them face to face with two serious rivals: the MERCHANTS OF THE STAPLE and the HANSEATIC LEAGUE

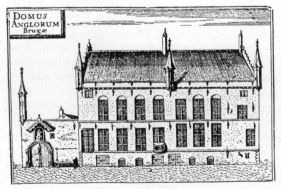

THE HOUSE OF THE ENGLISH MERCHANTS AT BRUGES, BUILT IN 1468

From A. Sanders, *Flandria Illustrata*, 1641–4

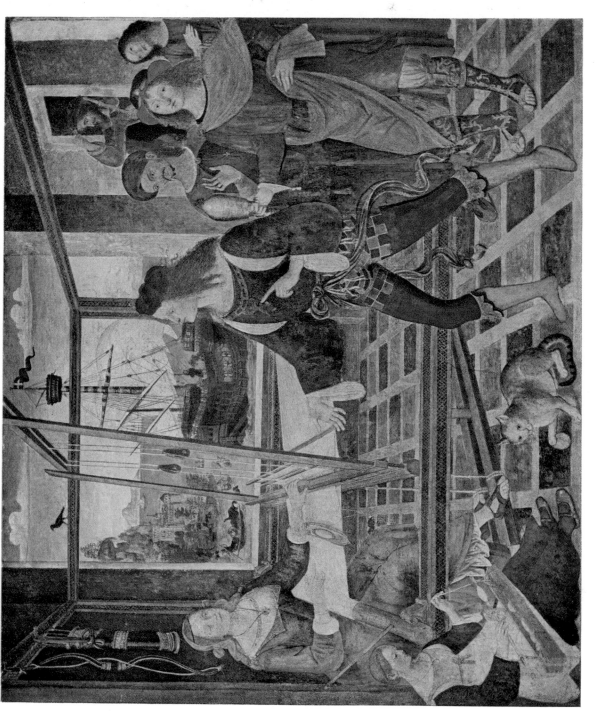

THE RETURN OF ULYSSES

Painting by Pinturicchio (1454–1513) showing a 15th-century loom and spindle

(qq.v.). They had no difficulty in overcoming the first. The Staplers dealt in wool, the Adventurers mainly in cloth, which was beginning to be far more important than wool in English foreign trade. While the Staplers lost ground, the Adventurers gained it. Furthermore, there was a contrast in the trading methods of the two bodies. The Staplers were content to bring back home the money earned in overseas trade, or to lend it abroad—even to the Adventurers. The Adventurers used their gains to buy foreign goods, such as timber and canvas, pitch and tar, which they then imported into England and resold to increase their profits.

The Hanseatic League was a more serious competitor, and rivalry lasted for many years between the two groups. The League had long enjoyed special privileges in London, and owned their own depot, the Steelyard. During the 15th century, in the early stage of the rivalry between the League and the Merchant Adventurers, the League succeeded in securing most of the trade in the Baltic and Scandinavian markets. They even secured from Edward IV a confirmation of their privileges in London. Later, the Merchant Adventurers lost all their trade first in Antwerp, and afterwards in Hamburg. But they never altogether lost their continental foothold. They made vigorous efforts to get trade in German markets, and were finally successful. In 1578 the Germans withdrew all the trading privileges of the Adventurers in Hamburg, but Queen Elizabeth retaliated by revoking the rights of the Hanseatic League in London. The rivalry continued bitterly, and it was not until 1611 that Hamburg finally gave way, and the triumph of the Merchant Adventurers was complete.

Although the Merchant Adventurers were vigorous in their trading activities, much of their energy went into the attempt to secure a complete monopoly in cloth dealing.

Their organization was that of a regulated company, with very strict rules of admittance (see CHARTERED COMPANIES). They made a close scrutiny of would-be members, and there were sometimes complaints that their entrance fees were too high. Their restrictions did not end here. Their officers—the Governor and his Court—had great authority over all members, and could levy heavy fines for offences, with no chance of the defendants appealing to civil courts. At times the officers even checked the

A 16TH-CENTURY CLOTH MERCHANT'S SHOP

enterprise of their members by limiting their transactions to a fixed number of cloths. They were allowed to trade in foreign towns only on certain days—Mondays, Wednesdays, and Fridays—and rules were laid down as to the length of time for which they could give CREDIT on their sales (q.v.). They had their eyes wide open for trading opportunities, but their charters were self-protective, providing against too much individual initiative. We find little in their charters about expansion, but a great deal about restrictions and controls.

Because of their wealth and importance the Merchant Adventurers became involved in politics. Kings used the Company to collect export duties and to provide loans. Both Henry VII and Queen Elizabeth were well aware of the uses to which the Company could be put. In the 17th century the Company supported Parliament against the King in the Civil Wars, and contributed heavily towards Puritan expenses. Despite this, in 1661, after considerable financial losses, their rights were restored by Charles II.

With the coming of William and Mary the Company was deprived of its monopoly of the export of woollen manufactures, and its trade was thrown open to all English merchants. This was not, however, the end of the Company. Most of the cloth trade was still in its hands in the 18th century, when its extensive privileges and organization gave it a decided advantage over its rivals. But the continental wars of that period, and the consequent insecurity of trade, drove English merchants to seek new markets in India and America, and allowed much European commerce to fall into other hands.

In the 19th century free competition created a new kind of commercial world. Commerce freed itself of restrictions, and economic expansion was no longer confined within the limits of a single trading organization. There was no place for a body like the Merchant Adventurers.

See also CHARTERED COMPANIES.

MERCHANT BANKER

MERCHANT BANKER is a name used for certain influential banking firms which began as merchants and which do a business different from that of an ordinary banker. They finance international trade by allowing exporters to draw BILLS OF EXCHANGE (q.v.) on them, and they find large sums of money for governments and important industries.

The merchant bankers of southern and central Europe in the late Middle Ages and Renaissance periods (between A.D. 1100 and 1500) made big profits, and some made vast fortunes. The most successful and well-known firms were the Medici of Florence, and the Fuggers of Augsburg in southern Germany. In those days most wealth was in the hands of very few people, so, instead of borrowing the savings of the general public, as modern governments can do, the kings and princes got their money by arranging loans with the big merchant bankers. The bankers naturally insisted upon knowing what the money was for, and it was necessary to let them into many State secrets. They therefore became extremely well-informed on politics and statecraft, and they soon became 'powers behind the throne'. They were shrewd enough not to lend money for war unless they were fairly certain that their borrowers were going to win; and their influence behind the scenes of European politics was sometimes great. *The Fugger News-Letters* is a book that illustrates the knowledge and influence possessed by this Augsburg banking-house in the

THE SIGN OF THE MERCHANT BANKING HOUSE OF N. M. ROTH-SCHILD AND SONS, ST. SWITHIN'S LANE, LONDON, E.C.

14th and 15th centuries. The novel *Romola*, by George Eliot, throws light on the merchant princes of Florence.

From northern Italy and southern Germany merchant banking extended eastwards, westwards, and northwards, particularly during and after the 17th century. In the 18th century the first office of the house of Rothschild was opened in Frankfurt. Branches were opened later in Vienna, Paris, and London. As trade expanded, London became not only a great international centre but also the headquarters of the merchant banking world. In the 19th century the growing importance of the United States led to the opening of merchant banking houses in New York, some of which were branches of European houses. Others, like the famous firm of J. P. Morgan and Cø., were American firms.

These later merchant bankers continued to keep in close touch with governments, and they were usually as well informed on political matters as statesmen themselves. In fact they often received information long before the statesmen got it: a member of the firm of Rothschild reached London with the first news of the result of the Battle of Waterloo, and his firm greatly profited by it. Each merchant banking house was in close relationship with one or more foreign countries: Hambro's Bank with the Norwegian Government, Baring's with the Argentine

Government, Rothschild's with Brazil, Schröder's with Germany, Lazard's with France, and Morgan, Grenfell and Co. (the London house of J. P. Morgan and Co. of New York) with the United States. In fact, before the United States created a State banking system like our own Bank of England, the firm of J. P. Morgan and Co. was the American Government's financial agent. Morgans were also the New York agents of the British Government during and after the First World War.

The profits of merchant bankers from the finance of international trade are possibly less than they used to be, and less government borrowing comes the way of the merchant bankers. They are, however, still extremely wealthy and influential. Those in London are now largely occupied as ISSUING HOUSES (q.v.); and in 1947 the British Government employed a syndicate of seven of them to guarantee a big issue of capital for the South Wales steel industry.

See also BANKING.

MERCHANTS OF THE STAPLE. From the
11th to the 13th centuries England's overseas trade was largely in the hands of foreigners. The most important commodity produced—wool—was handled by foreign merchants: Flemings, Italians, and Germans. But gradually there grew up English wool merchants in competition with the foreigners. This group, later called the Merchants of the Staple, were anxious to gain a foothold on the Continent, where they could fight foreign competition and corner the English wool trade.

A 'staple' was a depot, where wool was deposited so that customs duties and tolls on it could be collected. It was obviously useful for the king to have one regular channel through which England's leading exports normally passed, so that he could collect his taxes more easily. It was this royal interest in the staple which turned it from a voluntary body of merchants into an important official organization. Edward I played a leading part in this story. In 1275 Parliament granted him the right to levy a duty on sacks of wool and sheepskins. In order to ensure efficient collection the king encouraged the setting up of staples at fixed points, through which all wool exports were sent.

There were two big problems, however. Where should the staples be, in England or abroad? And how many staples should there be,

British Museum

CALAIS, THE STAPLE TOWN FROM 1363 TO 1558
Drawing, about 1525 (*Cotton MS. Aug. I, ii, 70*)

one or several? The English wool-growers, and many of the small merchants who dealt in wool as a sideline, would have preferred to have had no staple at all. This opinion was shared by many of the foreign merchants, who did not want to see Englishmen gain a privileged control of the trade. On the other hand, the wealthy English merchants wanted one single staple, preferably abroad, where they had powerful connexions. The English country wool-dealers and clothiers would have preferred an English staple, where they could gain complete control of the market.

Different groups used their influence to suit themselves, and so, from the end of the 13th century down to 1363, the staple town was frequently changed from one place to another. In particular Edward III, who fought complicated continental wars, switched it about to suit his political programme. At one time it was in St. Omer, at another in Bruges, then in Antwerp, and then in Middelburg. Between 1326 and 1327, and between 1332 and 1334, it was in England, in a set of different scattered staple towns. In 1363 it was moved to Calais—a French port which then belonged to England—and, with a few intervals, it remained there until Calais ceased to be English in 1558. By that time cloth and not wool had become England's most important export, and the Merchants of the Staple had given way in importance and influence to the Company of MERCHANT ADVENTURERS (q.v.).

The Staplers were organized from the start as a company of merchants with their own Mayor and Council. Originally they comprised the whole body of English merchants engaged in foreign trade. The wool merchants who made up the organization were the wealthiest merchants in England, drawn from all over the country. In 1313 they were officially recognized as the central wool-trading body. Fifty years later, when the staple was set up in Calais, it secured a virtual monopoly of the export of wool and leather, and as time went by the Staplers in Calais became not only traders but also effective rulers. Although they did not live in Calais, they paid the Calais garrison and controlled the government of the town, and remained a body of great importance until they were challenged by the new cloth-manufacturers. The change from wool to cloth as England's chief export was the most important factor that destroyed

their position. There is a pathetic note in their records 7 years before the fall of Calais. 'At thys day the hoole fellowshippe be so discomforted that they are mynded to forsake the staple for to seke theire poore livynge some other way.' They could only comfort themselves with the thought that, in face of such trials, 'there is no fellowship of merchants under any Christian prince that could have so sustained like burden and damage'.

The Merchants of the Staple, before their importance dwindled, competed strongly with the Merchant Adventurers, and contended that the latter should pay admission fees for the right to trade in cloth. The Merchant Adventurers were too successful for the Staplers, however, and in the end got complete control of the cloth trade.

See also CHARTERED COMPANIES.

MERCURY, or quicksilver, is one of the most interesting metals, as it remains liquid at any temperature likely to be met with in most parts of the world except the very coldest. It only becomes a solid when it has been cooled down to below the temperature of 38° below zero Fahrenheit, that is, 70 degrees of frost. It was first mentioned about 300 B.C. in Greek literature, and was then prepared from the ore called cinnabar, or the red sulphide of mercury (see METAL ORES, Vol. III). Later it was much used by the alchemists in their experiments with metals (see CHEMISTRY, HISTORY OF). Most of our modern mercury still comes from the red sulphide, which is found principally in Spain and Italy, and in California, Oregon, Nevada, and Arkansas in the U.S.A. Very often small quantities of metallic mercury are found in these deposits in a free state (that is, not chemically combined with other substances). There is the famous Almaden mine in Spain, 140 miles south-west of Madrid, which has been producing mercury for 2,000 years and is still the biggest individual mercury mine in the world (the name Almaden comes from Arabic words meaning 'the mine'). For many years Spain was the world's leading producer of mercury, but Italy has now overtaken Spain. The U.S.A. is the world's third producer, and Canada is now the fourth. Until 1938, when the Pinchi Lake mine in British Columbia was first worked, no mercury was mined in Canada at all. Mercury fumes are dangerous to health, and the air in mines, and also in refining and manufacturing plants, is

explosives. The metal itself is also used for THERMOSTATS (q.v. Vol. VIII) or automatic heat controllers, and for many forms of electrical contacts and switches: in fact, these uses account for just under one-fifth of the total world output of mercury. Mercury compounds, such as calomel, are much used in medicine, both for internal use and in preparing ointments.

See also Vol. III: METAL ORES.

METAL ORES, *see* COPPER MINING; MERCURY; TIN MINING; LEAD MINING; IRON ORE; PLATINUM; NICKEL; *see also* Vol. III: METAL ORES.

See also Vol. VIII: IRON AND STEEL.

METHYLATED SPIRITS, *see* INDUSTRIAL ALCOHOL.

MICA is a mineral which is easily split into thin flakes or leaves of about the thickness of a piece of stout paper. These can be bent without breaking. There are several varieties of mica, and these are called by different geological names. Most kinds are transparent, and some are of a whitish or neutral tint while others are coloured. The mineral is found principally in India, but also in the U.S.A., Brazil, Canada, and Ceylon. India is the main producer and exporter, the most important mines being at Hazaribagh and Nellore. Hazaribagh produces a reddish mica, and Nellore a mica of a greenish tint. Mica is very little affected by heat, and for this reason, and also because of its transparency, it is much used for the windows of stoves, lanterns, and industrial furnaces, for the chimneys of lamps and gas burners, and for the eyepieces of gasmasks and goggles. The ordinary kitchen hot-water boiler, or anthracite sitting-room stove, often has mica windows. In the past mica has been much used for window-panes in remote regions, as in parts of Russia, which were then far from industrial centres and where glass could not be bought.

The mining of mica is done in India by rather primitive methods, which often result in damage to the large sheets found underground. For many years these damaged portions were looked upon as useless and wasted, but in recent years uses have been found for ground and powdered mica. Ground mica is used in the manufacture of wallpaper and is used for giving the frosted effect to Christmas decorations and stage

Bodleian Library
AN INDIAN LEGEND OF QUICKSILVER
The metal was supposed to spring up from wells when a virgin passed. 18th-century Rajput painting

constantly sprayed with a chemical which corrects the poisonous effect of mercury, and makes it possible for men to work there.

Mercury is transported and sold in iron flasks containing 76 lb. of the metal. Since it expands or contracts a good deal on being heated or cooled, it is a useful liquid to use in THERMOMETERS (q.v. Vol. VIII), although alcohol thermometers must be used for POLAR REGIONS (q.v. Vol. III) or wherever very low temperatures are met with; even where mercury freezes, alcohol will remain fluid. Mercury is much used in metal refining, particularly in the refining of the precious metals, because it is able to absorb many of them and to form with them what are called 'amalgams'; for this reason it is also used in ASSAYING (q.v.). Until the cyanide process replaced it, mercury was used to separate the gold from the dross in GOLD-MINING (q.v.). A compound of mercury known as fulminate is much used in making detonators for setting off

scenery. Powdered mica is used in paint manufacture.

One important property of mica is that it is a very good electrical insulator. This is true even when it is split into extremely thin sheets; it is therefore of use in ELECTRICAL ENGINEERING (q.v. Vol. VIII), in the construction of electric motors and dynamos, in some types of condensers, in radio and television receivers, and electronic equipment.

An artificial mica has been produced in German and British research laboratories, but not cheaply enough for general use. The Americans have also undertaken research on artificial mica, for the U.S.A. is the biggest importer of natural mica from India, her own mines producing only a tiny fraction of her requirements.

See also MINING.

MICROFILM PHOTOGRAPHY, see PHOTOGRAPHY, HISTORY OF.

MILK PASTEURIZATION, see PASTEURIZATION OF MILK.

MILLING, FLOUR, see FLOUR MILLING.

MINING. As long ago as the Stone Age, men extracted minerals from the earth by mining. In Britain at that time the southern and eastern parts were regularly mined for flints (see CHALK). But no detail of how mining was done in those days has been handed down to us. The Greeks in the 4th and 5th centuries B.C. mined extensively in the silver-mines at Laurium, inventing mining tools and methods of SMELTING heavy ores (q.v. Vol. VIII). They used the silver to make the coins which were known all over the then known world (see COINS). The Romans developed mining wherever they could in those parts of the world which they conquered, for example in Italy itself, in Britain, and especially in Spain which at that time was rich in gold, silver, and lead.

Minerals in the earth occur either as seams or as lodes. A seam is a horizontal layer of mineral or mineral ore, usually at a good depth below the surface. Coal is practically the only mineral that occurs in seams; most others occur in the form of lodes. A lode is a streak or vein which may be found in the earth at all sorts of angles, varying from the horizontal to the vertical, according to the way in which the movements of the earth's crust have twisted it. Lodes are often called 'reefs', notably in South Africa. The angle of a lode is important: if it is vertical its presence may be missed, unless a borehole happens to be sunk right on top of it or unless it is found quite by chance.

In fact, throughout the history of mining, chance has played a very large part. The famous Bolivian silver-mines of Potosi were discovered because an Indian stumbled and held on to a bush, which came away in his hand and disclosed a deposit of metallic silver. It is only in the present century that chance has given place to science in the search for useful minerals. Searching for mineral deposits which are 'payable', that is, which will pay to work, is called 'prospecting'. The old-time prospector of the 19th-century adventure stories was a figure more romantic than scientific, although he had a good practical grasp of his trade. He had a working knowledge of geology, knew the appearance and properties of the different minerals, and was able to apply simple chemical tests to find out their precise nature. Nowadays he has been replaced by mining geologists trained in the new science of geophysics, who make use of modern methods and highly complicated instruments. But even to-day it is sometimes difficult to detect mineral lodes unless they are exposed on the surface as an 'outcrop', and chance still plays some part in mineral prospecting.

When prospectors think there is a mineral deposit in a piece of ground, they try to find it by drilling narrow boreholes deep into the ground. From different levels samples are brought up to the surface and tested or assayed (see ASSAYING). Often many years pass before a series of boreholes, 'sunk' at various points, proves the existence of an underground lode. If the samples disclose the existence of payable ore, mining is begun.

Mining can take four main forms. The first and simplest is open-cast mining; the lode is exposed on the surface or lies just beneath it, and can be worked after the top soil or 'overburden' has been removed. Methods of open-cast mining do not differ essentially from those used in STONE QUARRYING (q.v.).

The second form is alluvial mining (or 'placer mining' as it is called in America). Alluvial soil is formed by mud washed down the course of a river or stream (see ROCKS, Section 3, Vol. III). Alluvial mineral deposits are found in pockets

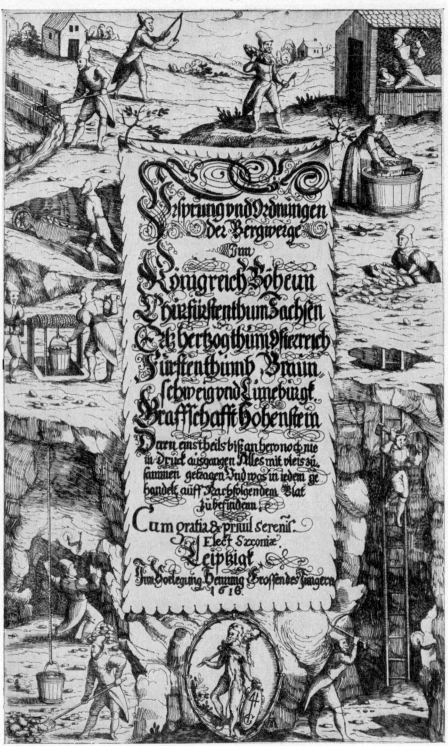

ALLUVIAL, DRIFT, AND UNDERGROUND MINING
Title-page of a German book on mining, 1616

Lawley Bros.

A LODE OF TIN IN A CORNISH MINE
The men are hand drilling by the light of an acetylene lamp

National Coal Board

OPENCAST COAL-MINING AT NEWMAN SPINNEY,
NEAR CHESTERFIELD

or pools in existing or ancient river-beds or watercourses. 'Diggings' of this kind still account for a small proportion of the gold and diamond production of the world.

Drift mining is the next form of mining. It involves driving towards the lode a slightly sloping tunnel or gallery, called an 'adit', usually from the side of a hill. In the early days of the British COAL-MINING industry (q.v.) many of the mines in Northumberland were drift mines. Drift mining has been started again in recent times by the National Coal Board in Scotland, Yorkshire, and Staffordshire.

The fourth form of mining takes place in underground workings, and accounts for by far the largest part of the world's metal mining. Underground mines at great distances below the surface are called 'deep levels'.

Once the existence of payable ores has been proved, the first three methods of mining are not difficult. The ways in which alluvial deposits of ore are dealt with are described in the article on GOLD-MINING (q.v.). Drift mining also is comparatively simple. Along the adit, or inclined plane driven below the surface, conveyor-belts or self-discharging trucks travelling on an endless cable keep up a continuous delivery of ore from the working 'face'. Underground mining, however, involves sinking main shafts before the lode can be reached and worked. Main shafts are usually big enough to provide sufficient room for skips or cages, used both for lowering men and materials to the working face and for hoisting ore to the surface. A section of the shaft is generally set aside for compressed-air mains, electric cables, and an upward discharge pipe by which underground water can be pumped away from the workings. To sink shafts and drive tunnels underground is very expensive. From the main shaft horizontal galleries or passages called 'levels' are driven towards the lode, usually about 60 feet apart. Unless the lode is absolutely vertical, these levels are seldom directly above each other, and each level is connected with the next by small shafts called 'winzes'. Very often, if the lode is irregular, 'raises' are driven upwards from one of the levels towards it. When the lode is reached, a 'stope' or big working-place is dug out, and this is often timbered (supported by wooden props) to hold up the roof and protect the workers at the face. From these stopes the ore is taken away, and this process is called 'stoping'. Holes are drilled in the rock, and filled with explosive and fired to bring down the ore. Drilling is usually done by rapidly moving compressed-air drills called 'jackhammers'. The ore is sent along the nearest convenient level to the shaft, in modern pits usually by continuous conveyors. At the surface the ore is crushed in a 'battery', consisting of several heavy iron 'stamps' that are raised by mechanical means and allowed to drop from a height on to the ore; sometimes a tube mill is also used for this purpose. The crushed ore, now in powder form, passes through chemical, mechanical, or heat processes; these either 'concentrate' it so that much metal is contained in small bulk for overseas shipment, or they smelt the metal out from the ore (*see* SMELTING, Vol. VIII). If there is enough fuel and labour on the spot, it is cheaper to smelt near the mine; otherwise the mineral is shipped as a 'concentrate' to the country where the smelting process will be carried out.

See also COAL-MINING; GOLD-MINING; SILVER-MINING; ASSAYING; MINING IN BRITAIN.

See also Vol. III: METAL ORES; COAL.

See also Vol. VIII: MINING ENGINEERING; PROSPECTING.

National Coal Board

ENTRANCE TO A DRIFT MINE IN FIFESHIRE

MINING IN BRITAIN.

To-day COAL-MINING and the mining or quarrying of IRON ORE (qq.v.) are almost the only forms of mining carried on in Britain. In earlier days many more minerals were mined in Britain. The records go back to the days of the Roman occupation, when the Romans did much to develop British tin and lead mining. A writer in the 1st century A.D. describes how smelted tin was exported from the island of Ictis—probably St. Michael's Mount in Cornwall—to Marseilles, then called Massilia. Lead was mined in considerable quantities, probably in the Mendip Hills and in Derbyshire, Flint, and West Shropshire. Pliny, the Roman writer, mentions the large supplies of lead pipes and sheeting from Britain that were imported into Rome for building. The Romans also mined copper in Anglesey—probably at Amlwch, where a little mining is still done— and in Shropshire.

Long after the Romans left, lead and tin mining continued on a large scale. In the 12th and 13th centuries lead was in great demand, particularly for the roofs and guttering of churches and monasteries. Some centuries later, mining was encouraged by Queen Elizabeth, who was anxious to make her country as self-

Canadian National Film Board

WINDING GEAR FOR LIFTING THE CAGES FROM A DEEP MINE IN MANITOBA

One of the 3,500 foot cables is attached to the cage and the other to a counterbalance. The gear is controlled by the man on the platform

supporting as possible. She brought many continental mining engineers to England. Two CHARTERED COMPANIES (q.v.) were formed to foster mining, the Mines Royal Society being the larger. CORNISH MINING (q.v.) much expanded after 1730, when the invention of a method of tinning steel plate was the beginning of the South Wales TINPLATE industry (q.v. Vol. VIII). About the same time an improved method of extracting zinc from its ores led to the opening in Bristol of the first British smelting-works. The ores came mainly from the Mendip Hills, and by the end of the 18th century nearly 100 zinc-mines were being worked.

Throughout this period the old Roman mines in Anglesey and Shropshire continued to produce copper, and newer mines in Devon and Cornwall were opened up. In the early 19th century Cornwall and Devon together produced about half of the world's copper. When immense supplies of rich copper ores were discovered in Chile and the U.S.A., the English mines ceased to pay. Mining for other non-ferrous metals (metals other than iron) has also declined. The peak period of British lead-mining was between 1850 and 1870, principally in Derbyshire, Durham, Cumberland, and Dumfries. There is no mining now in the last two districts, though there is a little in Flint, Durham, and Derbyshire, and also in the Isle of Man, where the ores are rich in silver. In 1939 the value of the lead produced in Britain was just under £400,000. Zinc production reached its peak in 1881, but has since greatly declined; and tin-mining is no longer an important Cornish industry.

Small quantities of other minerals are still mined in Britain. In some of the limestone areas, particularly in Derbyshire, the heavy minerals barytes and strontiamite are mined or quarried. These are used as filling material in high-class PAPER-MAKING (q.v.). Derbyshire also has deposits of fluorspar, which is used in some metal processes and is the base for producing hydrofluoric acid. This acid has the unique property of eating away glass, and it is therefore used for etching designs on glass. Nottingham-shire and South Durham have deposits of gyp-sum, a soft, chalky mineral which, when ground up and evaporated, becomes plaster-of-paris. To the west of Edinburgh there are deposits of oil-bearing shale (see SHALE OIL).

Gravel and sand are quarried on a large scale for use in building and in METALLURGY (q.v.

Vol. VIII). A special metallurgical sand, used for CASTING molten metal in metal-works (q.v. Vol. VIII), comes from Mansfield in Nottinghamshire. In some parts of the country there are sands, consisting mainly of quartz, that are very useful in GLASS-MAKING (q.v.). Many of these deposits have been exhausted, but those at Aylesford in Kent and Leighton Buzzard in Bedfordshire are still worked.

See also MINING; COAL-MINING, HISTORY OF.

MINTING COINS, see COINS; see also Vol. X: MINT.

MOHAIR, see HAIR TRADE.

MOLASSES, see INDUSTRIAL ALCOHOL.

MONEY. 1. Money came into existence to answer a need of mankind, but this need did not arise until civilization had grown beyond its earliest stages. Primitive man lived by hunting, each hunting only for himself and his family or tribe. At such a stage, when strangers were avoided or driven away, money and even trade were unnecessary. Later, when he had learned to domesticate wild animals, man lived a nomadic and pastoral life, constantly wandering as he drove his flocks and herds to new pastures. As the road to wealth was then the possession of beasts, money in its modern form was still not necessary, although the beasts themselves were really a form of money. It would suit what few craftsmen there were to be paid for their wares in cattle, and farmers and herdsmen to pay in that way. To this day some of the native people of South Africa still regard cattle as their money, and every bridegroom has to pay the bride's family a price in cattle for his wife.

When human communities began to settle down and cultivate the land, instead of wandering over it with their flocks and herds, the DIVISION OF LABOUR (q.v.) increased, and people specialized in crafts and trades. Most men specialized in growing or producing something, of which only a very small portion was necessary for their own wants. So they had to get rid of their surplus. In exchange for it they wanted something which would give them the power to choose what they wanted from the surpluses of other people. A few transactions might take place by straightforward exchange, or barter, but only certain things could be treated in this

THE MONEY CHANGER
German woodcut, 1539

way. It was unlikely, for instance, that a cobbler needing supplies of corn for his family from time to time would always find that the farmer would take shoes in payment. It would be more convenient if there were some other object that would always be useful to both the shoe-maker and the farmer.

Once people have agreed what this other object is to be, and once they are prepared always to accept it or to offer it in payment, then we have money in its primitive form. It is the go-between in all business transactions or, as the economists say, a 'medium of exchange'. We have seen that in the pastoral stage of human history cattle themselves were this generally acceptable commodity; it is therefore not strange that the Latin word for money, *pecunia*, comes from a similar Latin word, *pecus*, meaning cattle. In modern English we still use the adjectives 'pecuniary', meaning concerned with money, and 'impecunious', meaning having no money.

The trouble about cattle is that they are subject to disease, are easily driven away while their owners are asleep, require a lot of land on which to graze, and cannot easily be concealed. Worst

of all, they cannot be subdivided without being killed and so losing their value. The precious metals, such as gold and silver, do not suffer from any of these disadvantages. A small weight of gold has cost a good deal of labour and effort to produce, and so it is equal in value to other things that have taken about the same amount of labour and effort to produce. It can be buried and hidden away easily; it does not rust or lose weight through storage; it can be weighed out into quite small quantities without loss of value. Even some modern communities have used the precious metals by weight as their standard money, although they have used coins for pocket-money and for small change. For many years the standard money of China was the tael, which was not a coin, but a weight of silver; the dollar and the 'cash' were used for small change and minor transactions.

There are, however, disadvantages in using weighed quantities of these metals. Dishonest persons may mix them with less valuable metals of the same appearance and weight. In time, so many mixtures might then be passing from hand to hand that every business man would

MIDDLESEX TOKENS, HALFPENNIES 1795–6, THE UPPER ONE
SHOWING A LACE MAKER, AND THE LOWER ONE ANTI-SLAVERY
PROPAGANDA

In the 17th and 18th centuries there was such a shortage
of coins issued by the Royal Mint that token coins were
made for tradesmen and Local Authorities. These were
used for small payments in the district in which they
were issued. They were engraved with illustrations of subjects of topical interest

need to be accompanied by an assayer to test
and weigh every piece presented to him. The
obvious way out of this difficulty is for the State
to make coins of a standard shape, weight, and
fineness which are then called CURRENCY (q.v.)

Anything which passes from hand to hand as
money, and which is thus 'current', is called
currency, although in modern countries the
word is usually reserved for money issued by the
State. BANKING (q.v.) creates another kind of
money, in the form of bank accounts withdrawable by cheque. It is comparatively easy for a
powerful government to make certain of the
purity of its coinage, although, when governments were not powerful, the coinage often
got into very bad condition. This was so when
William III came to the throne in 1689, and
re-coinage was needed to put things right. A
strong government can also control the quality
and quantity of the bank-note currency; in
modern days the right to issue notes is usually
given only to a single State bank, called a Central
Bank. If the Central Bank is also given power
to control the extent to which the banks can

create bank money, withdrawable by cheque,
then the value of money in general may be
adequately controlled. For if the quantity of
money in a country, particularly bank-notes and
bank money, is allowed to increase without
check, money will follow the economic rule that
the more common a thing is, the less valuable it
will become.

2. CHANGES IN VALUE. Very serious social
results follow changes in the value of money.
A fall in its value is the same thing as a general
rise in prices; a rise in its value means a general
fall in prices. On the whole, rising prices are
good for trade. Manufacturers and merchants
can make or buy almost anything, in the certainty that its price will rise, and go on rising,
and that profits will be almost automatic. In
times of falling prices the possibility of loss
discourages enterprise, and leads to general
trade depression. But apart from these short-
period changes in the value of money, there are
the long-period changes. Wars cause prices to
rise and to stay high, and this has serious consequences. People with fixed incomes and
pensioners are particularly badly hit. It is
therefore the duty of a government to keep the
value of money as steady as possible.

There is a way of measuring changes in the
value of money. It is not absolutely perfect, and
must be used carefully. It is called a Price Index
Number. By means of an Index Number we
can compare prices now with what they were in
some earlier year of steady prices (known as a
'base year'), and we can measure from this the
percentage of change in the value of money
between one year and another, or even between
one month and another (*see* COST OF LIVING).

If a country's money is made out of some
precious metal, it will always be worth (by
weight) an equal amount of the money of
another country made from the same metal.
But the value of paper money depends upon
what one can buy with it if it is spent in the
country that issues it. The value may vary from
time to time within the issuing country; it is also
possible that when the value of one country's
paper money goes up, that of another country's
may go down. There is no certainty that the
values of different nations' moneys will always
keep level. The reasons for such variations are
discussed in the article on RATES OF EXCHANGE.

See also PRIMITIVE MONEY; EXCHANGE AND TRADE;
CURRENCY; BANKING; COINS.

MONEY MARKET. This is the name given to the activities of a number of banking firms dealing in money. In London, it has no special building of its own. 'Money' is not a very good name for what is dealt with in the Money Market, because its members are not buying and selling actual bank-notes: they are borrowing or lending money for various periods—generally for short periods.

In the London Money Market the principal lenders of money are the ordinary commercial banks. They lend money, usually from day to day, but sometimes on weekly agreements, to firms called Bill Brokers or Discount Houses. These firms earn their profits by investing the borrowed money for a short time in BILLS OF EXCHANGE (q.v.). Before the First World War, most of the bills arose from ordinary trading business, either within Britain or in connexion with international trade. Since 1914 most of the bills have been British Government Treasury Bills.

Rates of interest on loans to the Money Market, and rates of discount on bills of exchange, naturally depend on the amount of free money that the banks feel able to lend, and on the quantity of bills coming into the market for discount. Generally, money is lent at about $1\frac{1}{2}\%$ per annum below BANK RATE (q.v.), and bills are discounted at $\frac{1}{8}$ to 1% per annum above the borrowing rate, according to their quality and period. Discount rates on bank bills are always lower than on bills payable by ordinary merchant firms.

The Bank of England is the leader of the London Money Market. It is able fairly effectively to control the rates at which business is done, and also its extent.

SHARE CERTIFICATE IN A MONOPOLY GRANTED BY GEORGE I FOR MAKING OIL FROM SUNFLOWER SEEDS

MONOPOLY. The word 'monopoly' comes from two Greek words meaning 'a single shop' or 'a single seller'. A firm or group of firms or a State organization is said to have a monopoly when it is the sole manufacturer or seller of a product or the sole producer of some kind of service. Few firms possess a perfect monopoly, extending over the whole world. But there are many firms that have a monopoly within their own country. The National Coal Board, which is the only producer and seller of coal in the United Kingdom, is an organization of this kind. So is the Post Office, which has the sole right to carry letters and to carry out other services. There are to-day many public monopolies of this kind.

A monopoly is the direct opposite of free competition. In the middle of the 19th century competition in Britain was practically unrestricted; firms were small and numerous, and were keen rivals of each other. Competition kept prices down, which was, of course, often to the benefit of the consuming public. It was not long, however, before these numerous small firms began to form themselves into Trade Associations, bodies which laid down standard prices throughout the whole country and forbade price-cutting. This move had much the same effect on prices as if a single firm had possessed a monopoly to produce and distribute the article.

A firm possessing a monopoly is called a 'monopolist'. The object of a monopolist is to make his total profits as large as possible, and he can do this in one of two ways. If there is no real substitute for his product, he can probably raise its price without suffering any falling-off in sales (*see* SUPPLY AND DEMAND), and he can raise his price to that figure which will make the highest profits. He has another choice; he can decide to restrict output, and to sell only to his better-off customers who will pay a higher price. Usually a monopolist will make higher profits if he restricts output below what it might be if there were free competition.

A monopoly in the hands of private firms may, therefore, greatly injure a country's consumers, who are the ordinary members of the public; they may pay a higher price than they would pay if competition were free, and they may also find fewer goods to buy. In Britain, as industry has tended more and more towards large COMBINES (q.v.), consumers have agitated for some form of Government control of monopoly. In the U.S.A., many laws to prevent the growth of monopolies have been passed since the year 1900.

MORTAR, *see* CEMENT.

MOTOR INDUSTRY. The manufacture of motor vehicles, passenger and commercial, could not be said to have become an industry until just before the First World War. Until 1896, 'horseless carriages' as they were then called could not travel on British roads unless preceded by a man carrying a red flag, and it was not until this restriction was removed that any progress could be made (*see* MOTOR-CAR, HISTORY OF, Vol. IV.) Until 1914, the production of motor vehicles in Europe remained a small and modest industry, carried on in moderate-sized factories whose layout and methods differed little from those of the earlier coach-building works. Many British firms made chassis only, and left bodywork to firms that still called themselves coach-builders. In Britain, the leading makers were Lanchester, Rolls-Royce, Napier, and Thornycroft; in France, Citroën and Renault; and in Italy, the Fiat works in Turin. Even in the U.S.A. the annual production of passenger cars did not exceed 4,000 until 1900. Many of the present American makes were then being produced, but on a small scale and by the same general methods of production as in Britain and other European countries.

Just before the First World War Henry Ford began at Detroit (U.S.A.) the manufacture of mass-produced cheap cars. His first model became famous, and his example was soon followed by other makers in the U.S.A. In Europe, however, factories remained small and most of them had an annual output of only a few hundred cars. Some of the firms in the industry had begun as makers of bicycles in the bicycle boom of the 1890's (*see* BICYCLE, Vol. IV). A few of these firms, particularly Rudge-Whitworth, made motor-cycles only.

The First World War was only to a limited extent a mechanized war, and it did not hasten the concentration of motor vehicle production in very large factories. After the war there was a large demand for cars and lorries; new firms joined the industry, each producing a few hundred vehicles a year. The American motor industry had gone ahead rapidly during the first 3 years of the First World War when

MORRIS-OXFORD ASSEMBLY LINE

Internal trimmings are being fitted and final work done on the engine

America was still neutral; and so the U.S.A. was practically the only country represented in the growing world export trade in motor vehicles. General Motors Corporation, a big COMBINE (q.v.) embracing several producing plants whose scale was constantly increasing, was formed to organize the production of the medium-priced car, in much the same way as Ford had popularized the production of the cheaper model.

One reason for the success of the Americans was the way in which production was organized. Most of the big producers merely assembled cars from a number of component parts, including even engines, turned out by specialist firms on mass-production lines. In Britain an enterprising car-maker named W. R. Morris (who later became Lord Nuffield) was the first man to adopt this system, and the early Morris-Cowleys were similarly assembled from components, the original engine being a Hotchkiss. Between the two World Wars the Ford Motor Company, which at that time merely assembled American components at Trafford Park, Manchester, and Cork, Ireland, built a large works on the American model on the north bank of the Thames at Dagenham, near London. In spite of its American ownership and control, there were distinctive British features in the models turned out, and Dagenham produced not only passenger and goods vehicles but also agricultural tractors (see TRACTORS, Vol. VI). By the middle of the 20th century three firms—Ford, Morris, and Austin—had come to lead the British motor industry in quantity of production, although some of the smaller firms existing in the 1920's had survived: some firms with a long tradition. such as the Standard and Vauxhall companies, had survived as individual and much bigger concerns, while others had merged with larger firms. In Britain, fewer people can afford private cars than in America, and this has prevented the building-up of the industry on the same spectacular lines of mass-production, but in the world's production STATISTICS (q.v.)

Britain is the only country to approach the United States, and is far and away ahead of all the other countries of Europe. In the quality of the more expensive models, made to high standards of craftsmanship with bodywork by specialist coach-builders, no other country's manufacturers can equal those of Britain, and in the making of sports-cars and motor-cycles Britain has no serious rival.

See also TRANSPORT.

See also Vol. IV: MOTOR-CAR, HISTORY OF.

MULTIPLE SHOPS or 'chain stores' were opened in growing numbers in the U.S.A. and Britain towards the end of the 19th century, at a time when the population of big towns was growing fast. One of the earliest chains in Britain was the grocery and provision firm of Sainsbury, formed in 1869. Freeman, Hardy, and Willis, the boot and shoe distributors, were formed in 1876, and the 1880's and 1890's saw the opening of many grocery chains, such as the United Kingdom Tea Company, the International Stores, and Lipton's. These new firms were large concerns, and most of them were LIMITED COMPANIES with large CAPITAL behind them (qq.v.). Their usual policy was to expand by buying up other shops. By the beginning of the present century the whole country was covered with a network of multiple shops, in the grocery and provisions, tobacco, sewing machine, cheap tailoring, drug, bookselling, boot and shoe, china and glass, and meat trades. The Domestic Bazaar Company, a British concern, sold china and glass and household utensils at the fixed price of 6½d. each. The Woolworth 'variety chain stores' in the U.S.A. sold a much wider range of goods at 5 or 10 cents (then worth 2½d. and 5d.).

Before and after the First World War the multiple shops of Britain increased in number and variety. Woolworth opened many branches, later forming a British company. Marks and Spencer started a growing chain of popular multiple department stores, but without the low Woolworth limit of 3d. and 6d., as it then was. The war had increased the number of women at work earning independent incomes, and multiple firms selling women's shoes, hosiery and underwear, and millinery opened up in growing numbers. Later, firms of football pool promoters found a use for the growing amount of money in their hands by opening their own chains of multiple shops.

Big concerns of this kind can buy in very large quantities, and thus obtain from the manufacturer or wholesale merchant a lower price or a larger discount. The extension of multiple shops has lowered prices. The multiple department store of the Woolworth type can sell cheaply not only because it buys in immense quantities, but also because its operating costs are low (*see* COSTING). It comes very close to being a SELF-SERVICE STORE, with a big TURNOVER (qq.v.) and a small staff.

The head offices of the multiple shops exercise very close control over their branches. In many trades the branches are allowed to sell only for cash; and in those firms where credit is allowed, the branches must make to head office regular returns of unpaid bills and of the period for which they are owing. Usually the accounts of the branches are kept at head office, and it then becomes easy to control each branch, whose cash remittances to head office and unsold stock on hand must always equal the selling value of the stock received from head office. Branch accounts and results are closely analysed and compared at head office, and are used to estimate the efficiency of the various branch managers.

See also RETAIL TRADING.

N

NAVIGATION ACTS were laws passed in Britain and some other countries, from the 14th century onwards, to develop native shipping by allowing goods to be carried to and from that country in that country's own ships only.

In earlier years any increase in a nation's merchant shipping was linked with its strength in naval vessels; changing a merchant vessel into a naval one was a comparatively simple matter in those days of light weapons and absence of armour. The first English Act was passed in 1381, in the reign of Richard II, 'to increase the navy of England which is now greatly diminished'. The Act provided that 'none of the King's liege people do from henceforth ship any merchandise in going out or coming within the realm of England in any port but only in ships of the King's liegance'. Anxiety about the decay of the navy was continually being stressed. The first Navigation Act of Henry VII's reign in 1485 laments 'the great diminishing and decay that hath been now of late time of the navy'. This Act ordered that the wines of Guienne and Gascony in France, which were then coming to England in big quantities, should be imported only in English, Irish, or Welsh ships. Later, these ships were obliged to have English masters and mariners.

Henry VIII strengthened his father's laws, and this led to retaliation by other countries. Elizabeth, who wished to reduce her enemies to a minimum, tactfully repealed the Navigation Acts, adopting instead the principle that goods imported in foreign ships should pay higher customs duties than those carried in English ships.

Then came the famous Navigation Act of 1660, which remained in force for the best part of 200 years. It sought 'the encouraging and increasing of shipping and navigation', and ordered that 'no goods or commodities whatsoever shall be imported into or exported out of any lands . . . to his Majesty belonging or in his possession . . . in Asia, Africa or America . . . but in such ships or vessels as do truly and without fraud belong only to the people of England or Ireland, Dominion of Wales or town of Berwick-upon-Tweed . . . and whereof the master and three-fourths of the mariners at least are English'. This Act was aimed chiefly at the Dutch, with whom England was then beginning to dispute the mastery of the world's carrying trade.

There has been much argument as to whether the great increase of British shipping during the following 100 years was due to the 1660 Act, or would have taken place anyway. The figures are impressive. Between 1663 and 1774 the tonnage of British ships leaving Britain increased eight times, whereas the tonnage of foreign ships increased by only a half. Modern historians think this advance was due to other causes. During a long struggle between the Dutch and the French, British shipping took the lead. It is now believed that it was not the Navigation Acts that established Britain's lead, but her enterprising and aggressive policy of developing colonies.

It was a long time, however, before the Navigation Acts were finally repealed. The deep-sea traffic to and from British ports was thrown open to the ships of all nations in 1849, although the coastal trade around the British Isles remained reserved to British ships and British owners. In 1853 the British coastal trade was opened to the ships of any nation, largely in the hope (which was not fulfilled) that the United States would copy the British example and allow coastal competition in their own home waters. The growth of British shipping since then does not suggest that the repeal of the Navigation Acts was a mistake.

See also SHIPPING; TRADE, HISTORY OF.
See also Vol. X: ROYAL NAVY.

NEWSPAPER INDUSTRY. From a modest start this has reached in 50 years a leading position in British industry. British daily newspapers had a capital of £75 millions in 1946, and made a total profit in that year of £13,700,000, or more than 18%. A modern production unit, publishing one morning, one evening, and one Sunday paper, may employ 3,000 people and have a gross income of nearly £10 million a year.

A newspaper is an unusual industrial product in that its income comes from two very different sources. It costs more than the reader pays to produce a single paper, and unless the paper sells some of its space to advertisers it cannot pay its way Of the price paid by the reader—whatever that price may be—more than a third goes to the retail and wholesale newsagents. A tenth may be spent on transport—in 1949 British newspapers and magazines paid the railways £1,750,000. The most costly item is NEWSPRINT (q.v.), manufactured from imported raw materials. A national newspaper with a large sale may use over 300 tons of paper every night, and will then have to pay the railways over £1,000 a night to carry the printed copies. In one way and another it may cost about £100,000 a week to produce an important daily paper. A quarter of that sum, or about £4,000 a day, will be received back in the form of advertisement revenue.

The total money paid by readers and by advertisers is closely related, for advertisers find that it pays them to advertise in the papers with the largest numbers of readers. The cost of the advertisement, averaged over the number of readers who will see it, tends to be cheaper when the circulation is larger. For instance, an advertiser of bicycles might wish to hire an entire column of a newspaper for one day. A paper with a million readers might charge him £100, but a paper with two million readers would only charge him, say, £170. So his advertisement would be seen by twice as many people for less than twice the cost.

The development of newspapers to the status of a leading industry is quite recent. Although newspapers have a long history—some news-sheets or news-books began to appear regularly in 1622—for a long time they were merely one of the by-products of printers' shops. During the Napoleonic wars The Times consisted of a small sheet of paper, folded in two; fewer than 250 copies an hour could be printed on hand-presses. In 1814 a steam-engine made it possible to print 1,000 copies an hour. Newspapers were then heavily taxed, and few people could afford to buy them. Taxes were paid on all paper supplies and on advertisements, while each copy of a newspaper had to bear a stamp as well. In the 1830's a single copy of a newspaper might cost as much as sevenpence—a sum then worth several times its present value—and 5½d. of this

would represent taxes. By degrees Parliament reduced these taxes, and in 1861 the last of them was abolished. Until then, few daily papers had a circulation of 5,000 copies, and few dailies were published outside London. The Times was unique in selling 50,000 copies of each issue. With the removal of taxes the circulation of newspapers began to increase, and many new papers were established. In 1855 The Daily Telegraph was reduced to a penny, and it thus became the cheapest daily paper in London. Soon it was competing in circulation with The Times.

From the middle of the century, when it became worth while to print large numbers of papers, many technical improvements made fast printing possible. The rotary press, first devised in America, enabled both sides of an endless band of paper to be printed (see PRINTING, HISTORY OF, Vol. IV). A newspaper firm that could afford to install a number of rotary presses could print many hundreds of thousands of copies of a paper in a single night. Although this new machinery lowered the cost of each paper and made cheap newspapers possible, it was itself very expensive, and caused the total costs of production to rise very considerably. It cost as much to equip a newspaper office as to equip a large factory.

It was Alfred Harmsworth—later Lord Northcliffe—who first regarded newspaper production as a branch of manufacturing industry. At the age of 23, with hardly any money, he started a weekly magazine called Answers. It was first published in 1888, when many more people had been taught to read as a result of the recent compulsory Education Acts. Answers was very popular, and was soon selling a million copies a week. With his profits Harmsworth bought cheaply the goodwill and plant of an unsuccessful London paper, the Evening News, and caused it to be so brightly edited that it became profitable too. Then he used the printing-plant of the Evening News to launch the Daily Mail. Within 4 years the Daily Mail, which had an unconventional popular appeal, was selling nearly a million copies a day, which was more than any newspaper had ever sold before.

The cheap Press which quickly grew up in imitation of the Daily Mail was made possible by advertising. Most of the earlier newspapers had carried advertisements (see ADVERTISING AND PUBLICITY), but they had been rather restricted in quantity and appeal. As the nation prospered

Sport and General

FLEET STREET, THE CENTRE OF LONDON'S NEWSPAPER
PRODUCTION

policy of most newspapers to achieve the largest possible circulation, so as to possess an advantage over rival newspapers in obtaining advertising contracts. Circulation was important for another reason. Papers that received larger advertisement fees could spend much more money on development. They could install faster and better printing machines. They could set up branch works in big cities, and save the time of sending papers from London by train. They could pay famous authors large sums for writing articles, and they could send their staffs of journalists all over the world in search of exciting news. They could also print more copies than they would sell, so that there were always copies on view in every bookstall in the land, while hundreds of paid canvassers went round to people's doors, persuading them to take these papers regularly. Newspapers with smaller circulations received smaller fees from advertisers, and could not afford the money for this kind of development. Their circulations were slow to increase, or even shrank. Advertisers therefore turned away from them, and gave the bulk of their fees to the papers with the largest circulations. Many of the less successful papers went out of business.

The papers which secured the lion's share of the many millions of pounds spent on newspaper advertising made large profits for their owners. In the past, most newspapers had been owned personally by one individual; most newspapers were now formed into limited companies. As in other industries, the companies began to be associated in big groups and combines, which tended to become bigger still by absorbing other companies. In the 1920's various London groups began to buy up provincial newspapers. Where two rival newspapers had long been published in a provincial town, the purchase of one paper by a London group with large financial resources would sometimes be followed by the closing down of the competing paper which lacked such resources. Thus in the provinces, as in London, the reader's choice of papers was reduced. Within 26 years Britain lost forty daily papers.

See also Vol. IV: NEWSPAPERS, HISTORY OF.

NEWSPAPER PRODUCTION. The making of an issue of a newspaper is an act of team work strictly limited by space and time, and by the capacities of printing-machines. Tens of thousands of copies of each edition of a national

during the late 19th century, and the number of people with middle-class incomes increased, there were many more customers ready to spend their money in the shops, and shopkeepers became anxious to advertise their goods to them. The removal of the various newspaper taxes made it possible for more papers to be sold, and advertisers benefited by the greater number of customers who read their advertisements. In the course of time advertising by shopkeepers was partly replaced by advertising by manufacturers. A bicycle shop could spend a pound or two on advertising in a local paper, but a bicycle manufacturer supplying hundreds of bicycle shops could spend hundreds of pounds on a single advertisement in a national paper read all over Britain.

When the cheap Press began to grow early in the present century, the national newspapers set out to compete for advertisement fees. A paper selling 600,000 copies every day could charge larger fees than a paper which might have been much better edited, but only sold 300,000. In the 30 years that followed the first success of the cheap Press, it became the business

Home Counties Newspapers

THE MOULD OF A PAGE OF A NEWSPAPER

papers through London at any one time, requiring a permanent garage organization like that of a bus maintenance depot. Foreign correspondents may be costing the firm £2,000 a week, and bank credits have to be arranged in all the capitals of the world for the use of these correspondents and of cable companies serving the paper. Only when all these arrangements are in working order can the editor and his staff set about their daily work.

When the news has been prepared by reporters, sub-editors, and editors (*see* NEWSPAPER, Vol. IV), it is sent to the printing department in written or typewritten sheets, and there composed in metal type. No matter how important the news or how incomplete the information, an even flow of reports from the sub-editors must reach the printing operators throughout the evening, otherwise steady production would break down. After the type has been corrected for printers' mistakes, various senior journalists read the proofs to detect journalists' mistakes, and the proofs are often read by a lawyer also, to ensure that there are no LIBELS (q.v. Vol. X) or other wrongful statements about people, which might involve the paper in the payment of legal damages. Throughout the evening copies of all news are telegraphed on private TELE-PRINTER machines (q.v. Vol. IV), by means of trunk lines rented from the Post Office, to the paper's Manchester and Glasgow branches. Carbon copies of all reporters' work are available for this service, as well as all messages telephoned from correspondents. Proofs of every few inches of type are supplied by the printer as they emerge from every composing-machine. Local editors of Manchester and Scottish editions of papers controlled from London have a good deal of freedom to print local news in place of news supplied from London. The Manchester and Scottish offices, however, have to observe an equally strict production time-table in their printing departments.

Finally, in London (as in Manchester or Scotland) the metal type is assembled into the shape of pages, the news and pictures are fitted together according to a plan provided by the chief sub-editor, and the advertisements are placed as directed by the advertisement manager. If news items are too long to fit the space allotted after being composed in type, sub-editors indicate to the printing staff where the text may be cut. The responsibility for the composition, correc-

morning paper must be loaded on to trains which leave their railway stations at precise times. In the printing-works each page of metal type, completely ready for printing, must be passed to the machines at a given minute. In each column of every page, a precise number of inches is available for the journalists' work. Therefore the rigid industrial process involved in manufacturing a million or more copies of a morning newspaper in a printing-works every night governs the whole business of editing.

A London printing plant, which may produce a morning and evening and a Sunday paper, requires a vast organization. Printing plant must be maintained in central London (within easy reach of all the terminal railway stations) and in Manchester and sometimes also in Scotland. As many as 3,000 men and women may be employed by one newspaper firm. The editorial office may need to be equipped with 40 or more telephone lines to the exchange and perhaps 200 extensions within the office. Private telegraphic and picture transmission apparatus links the London office with its Manchester branch and with the Post Office telegraph system in London. A fleet of perhaps forty vans carries the firm's evening

NEWSPAPERS COMING OFF THE PRESSES
They are placed in piles on the conveyor-belt and carried along it to the delivery vans

tion, and accurate assembly of each page at the right time belongs to the manager of the composing department, who is always known as 'the printer'. When the pages are ready, moulds are taken, in which molten metal is cast to make the curved plates actually used for printing the newspaper (*see* PRINTING, Section 5, Vol. IV).

The heavy rotary printing-presses need firm foundations, and so are placed in the basements of newspaper offices. There the various reels of printing-paper (*see* NEWSPRINT), each containing a 4-mile strip, are in position, and the machines are started up. Each unit of machinery will print 30,000 to 40,000 copies an hour, and fold and count them in batches. A battery of 15 units on a big newspaper will thus turn out from 450,000 to 600,000 copies an hour. As the batches emerge from the machines, the packing staff tie the batches in large bundles, and paste on each bundle a label ready printed with the name of the wholesaler or town to which it must go. The bundles are carried on conveyor-belts to rows of waiting vans, which take them either direct to railway stations, or to wholesalers'

depots where they are parcelled again, with other morning papers, for distribution to various retailers.

The mechanical side of evening paper production is like that of morning papers, except that sporting results, which may arrive as each edition is going to press, have to be handled with great speed by the printer's staff. The pressure on sub-editors also is more intense.

See also NEWSPAPER INDUSTRY.

See also Vol. IV: JOURNALIST; NEWSPAPER; NEWSPAPER, HISTORY OF; REPORTER.

NEWSPRINT. This is the name given to the paper on which most newspapers are printed. This kind of paper—a paper of cheap quality—is made in larger quantities than any other kind, to provide for the enormous number of NEWSPAPERS (q.v. Vol. IV) printed every day. Wood pulp is the basic raw material used. Newsprint is generally made from about 85% of ground wood pulp, made by a mechanical process, and about 15% of sulphite pulp, made from spruce wood by a chemical process (*see* WOOD PULP),

China Clay (q.v.) is also added to make the paper more opaque and give it a smooth surface for taking print. Britain imports some newsprint, but makes very large quantities, and possesses the largest newsprint machine in the world.

If the newsprint mill is near the pulp mill, both kinds of wood pulp are kept in a slush form in separate tanks, and are then drawn off by pumps to the refining engines, as needed. But if the pulp has to be taken some distance, the chemical sulphite pulp is transported almost dry, and the mechanical ground wood pulp with about 50% moisture in it; and, on reaching the paper mill, the bales go into breaking engines to convert them again into slush form.

The paper-machine for newsprint is a very large Fourdrinier machine (*see* Paper-making, Section 1), of a width up to 26 feet. The pulp, or 'stuff', goes into the machine chest from which the paper-machine, is served. It is then strained to remove coarse lumps, and passed on to the paper-machine, which spreads it evenly over a fast-moving wire cloth so that the water can drain away. To draw out yet more water the pulp then passes over suction boxes and a suction roller, by which time the pulp is in a thin sheet, which, though still wet, can hold together. It is then carried on woollen felts to presses which compress it into a fairly smooth, even sheet of paper. To remove the rest of the moisture, it is passed over drying cylinders heated by steam, the wet web of paper being held against them by cotton felts. The paper is then rolled up, 'calendered' (that is, given a smooth shiny surface) if many illustrations have to be printed on it (*see* Paper-making, Section 2 *b*), and cut up into rolls of the required width. It is then ready to be sent to the printer.

See also Paper-making; Wood Pulp.
See also Vol. IV: Newspaper.

NICKEL was not discovered until the middle of the 18th century, when a new mineral called 'niccolite' was found in a Swedish mine. It was not until 1775 that there was any successful attempt to refine the pure metal from its ore. The world's earlier supplies of nickel were obtained from Norway, but these Norwegian deposits are no longer important. Nowadays

Central Press

THE FINAL STAGE OF THE NEWSPRINT MACHINE
The roll of newsprint is nearly ready to be taken off the machine

J. H. Stembridge

DRILLING IN A NICKEL MINE IN SUDBURY, ONTARIO

materials would therefore be very easily detected. Until the 1930's nickel was used for electroplating, but since chromium plating became more popular, nickel has been used only as the lower layer, the surface being finished off in chromium. Nickel silver, the metal out of which silver-plated table-ware is made, is neither silver itself nor any alloy of silver; it is an alloy of nickel, zinc, and copper.

NYLON. This is a synthetic fibre, which can be spun into a yarn for weaving, knitting, or other textile uses. It was discovered in 1930 by an American firm which was experimenting in such fibres. The firm produced nylon commercially by December 1939, and within a few years it became known to the public in many countries for the elegant and hard-wearing stockings that could be knitted from it for women's wear. Nylon is a yarn which derives from mineral sources, and is made chiefly of phenol or benzene (produced from coal-tar), water, and AMMONIA (q.v.). It is produced by much the same process as one of the rayon fibres: as a gluey liquid it is spun

Canada produces about nine-tenths of the total world output, and practically all the rest comes from New Caledonia, the French island in the south-west Pacific. The Canadian nickel mines are nearly all in the Sudbury district of Northern Ontario. Their ores are very rich in the metal, and the area is now the world's cheapest producer of nickel.

Nickel is mainly used in the steel and engineering trades. Nickel steels are used for motor and aero-engines, guns, and MACHINE TOOLS (q.v. Vol. VIII). An important alloy of nickel is cupro-nickel, made from nickel and copper; it is very resistant to salt-water corrosion, and is much used for marine condensers (*see* CONDENSER, STEAM, Vol. VIII). Cupro-nickel is now used for the British token coinage (*see* CURRENCY); all the coins that used to be made of silver are now made of this alloy. Pure nickel has never been a British coinage metal, but it has been much used for the coinage of the U.S.A., where a 'nickel' is the common word for a 5-cent piece. Nickel is an excellent coinage metal, for it resists wear and corrosion well, and is extremely tough; it is also magnetic, and any attempt to make counterfeit coins out of non-magnetic

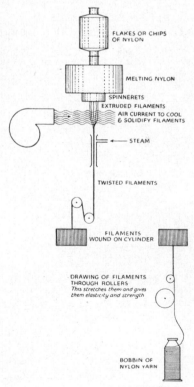

FLAKES OR CHIPS OF NYLON

MELTING NYLON

SPINNERETS
EXTRUDED FILAMENTS
AIR CURRENT TO COOL & SOLIDIFY FILAMENTS

STEAM

TWISTED FILAMENTS

FILAMENTS WOUND ON CYLINDER

DRAWING OF FILAMENTS THROUGH ROLLERS
This stretches them and gives them elasticity and strength

BOBBIN OF NYLON YARN

British Nylon Spinner

STAGES IN THE MAKING OF NYLON YARN

British Nylon Spinners

PREPARING NYLON YARN FOR TESTING
The yarn is wound in bobbins

their original length before going through further textile processes which make the yarn suitable for knitting and weaving.

Chemically, nylon fibre is an organic compound, of the same general composition as silk or hair, but artificially made, or synthetic. Nylon yarn, used for over 200 textile products, is knitted or woven into many articles of clothing previously made only from real silk or rayon. One of its principal advantages is that it is far stronger than rayon, and also far less liable to rot. It has great strength when stretched, and replaces cat-gut for making casts for dry-fly fishing, for the strings of musical instruments and of racquets for tennis and other games, and for threads to stitch wounds and cuts. When worked up into twine or rope it has a very high breaking-strain; ropes of a given strength may be thinner if made of nylon than of any other material. Nylon ropes are expensive, but they are more elastic and much more efficient, particularly for towing, mooring, and for the running rigging of yachts (*see* SAILING, Vol. IX). Since nylon is chemically inert, the organisms of decay such as MOULDS (q.v. Vol. II) do not easily grow on it, and it is taking the place of natural bristles for tooth and hair BRUSHES (q.v.). Household and industrial brushes are being made from it as well. It wears well as an insulating material for coating electric wires, for which molten nylon is allowed to form round the naked wire and solidify.

through tiny holes, and the slender strands or filaments thus formed become dry as soon as they meet the cool air. The filaments are gathered together to form a single strand, which is wound on to a cylinder. These strands are then stretched mechanically to about four times

O

OFFICE EQUIPMENT. Nearly all modern business is done in offices, and the bulk of office work consists of some form of communication. Reading, writing, talking, telephoning, and typewriting are essential forms of business communication. It is important to save time and labour over all this, as office expenses are not what is called 'productive' expenditure: that is, they do not lead directly to the production of goods. Office communications may be classified into two groups: first, the linking of people and things so that they can make contact easily, and the standardizing of written communications for the sake of speed and clarity; secondly, the compiling of information, and its rapid and ready presentation so that nothing is overlooked or lost.

   1. COMMUNICATION. The TELEPHONE (q.v. Vol. IV) is a vital link. Telephones within an office may be either part of the public Post Office system or private intercommunication telephones that may be bought or rented. Most business firms have switchboards for their exchange lines. In small firms these may be single, with two or three extension lines, watched by a clerk who also has other duties. Bigger firms may have a number of large switchboards, with perhaps 100 lines to the public telephone exchange and 300 or 400 internal extension lines running to various members of the staff. In a large modern business, and particularly in such a one as a big newspaper office, as many as eight or more full-time operators, usually ex-employees of the public telephone service, may be needed to work in shifts to maintain a telephone service of this kind; and a Post Office staff engineer may have a whole-time job supervising, repairing, and adjusting the lines of such a firm. Most of the private intercommunication telephone systems are of the automatic type and require no operator. Sometimes the head of a business or of a large department makes use of an instrument by which several members of the staff may be signalled and spoken to at the same time, either through linked telephones or loud-speakers. Short conferences of several people can thus take place without their having to come together. If a firm has offices in two or more distant parts of the country, a tie-line rented from the Post Office will provide constant telephone communication without the need to book trunk calls. The TELEPRINTER (q.v. Vol. IV) is also much used by large business firms with a central head office and many provincial branches, and teleprinter messages have the advantage that they provide a definite record of what has been said. In large offices rows of coloured lights on the walls or ceilings of corridors and other places are used to catch the attention of important officials and to warn them that they are urgently needed at some point in the building; different officials are identified by different combinations of lights. American experiments in saving time over internal communications have included the use of messengers on roller-skates for long journeys along the corridors of large buildings.

   Large shops, particularly DEPARTMENT STORES (q.v.), often have special means of communication to enable their sales staff to send customers' money to a central cash desk, from which change and receipts are sent back to the counters. Earlier in the century this was often done by placing the money in a hollow wooden ball which ran 'downhill', moved by its own weight, on gently sloping rails. Later, a small container, hanging from a wire, was 'shot' across the shop by a spring. Pneumatic tubes, in which containers are propelled by compressed air, are the more modern system. They are much used in newspaper offices to send 'copy' from the editorial to the printing departments, and to send other communications about the office. In Paris the principal post offices are linked by pneumatic tubes, through which express letters—called locally *bleus* or *pneumatiques*—can be sent for a special fee.

   Much time is saved in modern business by standardizing written communications, generally through the use of forms. All printed forms such as invoices and receipts are standard ways of communicating information in a quick, easy, and accurate way. Departments and branches

Ofrex Business Machines

AN 'AUTO-TYPIST' TYPING MACHINE

When the appropriate buttons are pressed, the machine automatically types standard sentences. Blank spaces are left
where necessary for details to be filled in by hand typewriter

of banks, shops, factories, and other large concerns keep their records by standardized means,
often on standard printed forms.

2. INFORMATION. In modern business the
compiling or recording of information has now
become very systematized and is often mechanized. Many documents that would be bulky to
handle are now filed in a compact and orderly
way by being photographed microscopically.
As with AIRGRAPHS (q.v. Vol. IV), a roll of film
1½ inches wide can carry a record of hundreds of
documents. When a document has to be consulted, it can either be viewed through an
enlarger or be projected on a screen in the same
way as a cinema film. Speech can be recorded
and stored on plastic discs like gramophone
records, on discs of toughened paper or paper
tape, or on a magnetized steel wire or steel
ribbon (*see* SOUND RECORDING, Vol. VIII).
Filing systems may be arranged alphabetically
or, like library catalogues, on a system of decimal
figures (*see* CATALOGUING AND INDEXING, Vol.
IV). Files are kept in cabinets, drawers, trays,
boxes, shelves, or folders, as may best suit their

use. Folders, leaves, and cards can be fitted with
coloured tabs, so that all information on a given
subject can be located at a glance and presented
at a touch of the finger. The presentation of
STATISTICS (q.v.) is made easier if the office is
equipped with the 'punched card' system described under ACCOUNTING, MACHINE (q.v.);
sorting-machines group the information contained on the cards according to any pattern
thought necessary, and deliver it automatically.

3. EQUIPMENT FOR LETTERS. In a small firm
little equipment except typewriters will be used,
but nowadays most large firms use a variety of
labour-saving machines, most of them in order to
save time over writing, dispatching, or even
receiving letters. Most business letters, except
those that are purely formal, need to be dictated
by a responsible member of the firm's staff, and
a dictaphone or similar machine—which is
really a recording gramophone—makes it
possible for letters to be dictated at any time
and typed when a typist is ready. Another
machine that saves much time in a busy office,
and retains the goodwill of the customers of a

business, is the automatic typewriter. One of the problems that many businesses have to solve is how to send out a letter that is really a 'form' or circular letter, but which must appear to the recipient as if it has been dictated and written especially for him. It is impossible to convey this impression if this kind of letter is prepared in quantities in advance, the name and address and the opening greeting being typed on to it afterwards. Even if the same typewriter which typed the original is used, the alignment and adjustment of the address and greeting can never be perfect. The automatic typewriter solves the problem. It works on much the same principle as the player-piano or PIANOLA (q.v. Vol. IX), typing automatically from a perforated paper record of the original that has been made beforehand. The typist loads the machine with a record of the appropriate form letter, types in the name and address and the opening greeting, and then switches on the machine, which completes the letter automatically.

For the preparation of ordinary circular letters which do not need such careful attention as this there are many efficient types of duplicator. One form makes use of a 'stencil', a sheet of paper coated with wax; this is inserted in a typewriter, the inking-ribbon of which is put out of action; when the typewriter keys are struck by the typist in the usual way, the sharp metal characters of the alphabet cut through the thin film of wax on the paper. Later, when the waxed paper is inserted in a duplicator, and ink is applied, the ink will only take effect where the wax has been cut; the principle is that involved in stencilling. Other forms of duplicator act more or less on the same principle as an ordinary printing-machine (see PRINTING). For the duplication of drawings, diagrams, specifications, and original documents the photostat process of copying by a camera is used. Another problem that arises in connexion with the dispatch of circulars is the addressing of large numbers of envelopes. If the same people are being written to frequently, it may pay to install an 'Addressograph' or similar type of automatic envelope-addressing machine. One type of machine works from thin metal stencil-plates that are cut mechanically, and can be stored in trays in alphabetical or any other desired order. A stack of envelopes and of plates is then placed in the machine, which delivers the envelopes automatically addressed. The 'window' type of envelope, with an opening covered with transparent paper, solves the problem in another way, provided that the letter, circular, or other enclosure being sent has the name and address already typed on it. The enclosure is then merely folded so that the name and address is visible through the 'window' in the envelope. The envelope-addressing machine may be used to put the names and addresses on the enclosures instead of on the envelopes.

Opening incoming letters and sticking the stamps on outgoing letters are tasks which can take up much time. There are now efficient machines that will open letters automatically at a high speed. The office boy who used to stick stamps on letters is now merely a memory in many large offices which have installed 'franking' machines. These automatically stamp envelopes passed through them, and have a counting mechanism attached which shows the total postage charge to put through the firm's accounts. Such machines are set and locked by officials of the Post Office, according to the amount paid over beforehand.

See also Vol. IV: COUNTING INSTRUMENTS.

OIL-CLOTH, see LINOLEUM.

OIL, MINERAL. The technical name for the mineral oil that comes from the depths of the earth is petroleum. Petroleum is a mixture of chemical compounds consisting almost entirely of hydrogen and carbon, and is therefore a 'hydrocarbon' oil. Mineral oil as it comes from the well is called 'crude oil', and contains many different substances, which boil at varying temperatures. And it is therefore possible by DISTILLATION (q.v.) to separate the crude oil into many different 'fractions', such as petrol (called 'gasoline' in the U.S.A.), lubricating oil, and asphaltic bitumen. The products of distillation can also be treated by further refining processes which alter their arrangement of molecules or 'molecular structure', and thus change them into entirely different substances (see OIL REFINING).

Bitumen was the earliest mineral oil product used by man. Seepages of crude oil escaping to the earth's surface had become weathered by sunlight and exposure, and had left deposits of bitumen—as in the famous Trinidad lake in the West Indies, which still produces important quantities of bitumen. Where the seepage oil remained in liquid form, other uses were found for it: the Red Indians of North America, for instance, used it as a medicine. In fact, almost all the early users of mineral oil made use of it in the form in which it was found naturally at the surface.

The modern mineral oil industry dates from 1859, when a well was bored at Titusville in Pennsylvania, U.S.A. (*see* OIL WELLS). The first efforts to convert this crude oil into other products were made by borrowing methods of distillation and refining from the SHALE OIL industry (q.v.), which had flourished (particularly in Scotland) since the middle of the 19th century.

In the year following the boring of the first well, the total production of crude oil in the world was under 80,000 tons, or about 18 million gallons, and most of this was produced in the U.S.A. By the outbreak of the First World War the world's annual production of crude oil had risen to 58 million tons; United States production accounted for almost two-thirds of this, and the rest came from many other countries, of which Russia, Mexico, Roumania, and Indonesia (then the Dutch East Indies) were the most important. By the end of the Second World War, world production of crude oil and natural gasoline had increased to more than 375 million tons.

Although some crude petroleum is found in many countries, most of the world's supply comes from a few regions where it is plentiful. These

are chiefly the U.S.A. (where Texas, California, Louisiana and Oklahoma are the leading oil-producing states), Mexico, the Caribbean region of South America (Venezuela, Colombia, and the island of Trinidad), and Persia, Saudi Arabia, Kuwait, Iraq, and other countries in the Middle East. The U.S.S.R. is also a large oil producer, and Indonesia and British Borneo are areas of some importance. The Commonwealth has comparatively few proven oilfields, the chief producers being British Borneo, Canada, and Trinidad. Vast reserves, especially in the Middle East, have not yet been drawn upon.

For about the first 50 years of the industry, lamp oil (paraffin or kerosene) was the most important product distilled from crude oil, though some lubricating oil was also produced. The remaining products of distillation, especially petrol, were regarded as a nuisance, and were burned or thrown away. About 1900 the early motor-cars were being made, for the INTERNAL COMBUSTION ENGINE had taken a practical form (q.v. Vol. VIII). Petrol ceased to be a waste product, and the oil industry began to find uses for many new substances refined from crude oil. The First World War increased the demand for petrol and lubricating oil, and for fuel oil to replace coal-firing afloat and ashore.

Until after the First World War the industry remained dependent on the range of products that could be obtained by simple distillation and

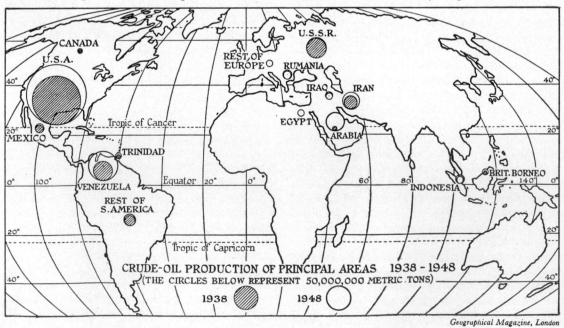

CRUDE-OIL PRODUCTION OF PRINCIPAL AREAS   1938 - 1948
(THE CIRCLES BELOW REPRESENT 50,000,000 METRIC TONS)

1938   1948

Geographical Magazine, London

refining. The thermal 'cracking' process, to increase the yield of petrol, was first used on a commercial scale about 1912. From about 1920 the cracking process became more efficient, and products in great demand (such as petrol) could be made by 'breaking down' other products (such as gas oil and fuel oil) in less demand.

By 1930 the high-speed DIESEL ENGINE (q.v. Vol. VIII) was becoming more used for buses and heavy lorries, and the demand for diesel oil rose rapidly. Developments of the aero-engine also called for improved lubricating oils and aviation spirit. Scientific discoveries responded very well to all these changes in the types of oil needed, and also satisfied the increasing demand of the chemical industry for special products and solvents.

See also OIL WELLS; OIL REFINING; OILS, VEGETABLE.
See also Vol. VIII: FUELS.

OIL REFINING. Crude oil (*see* OIL, Vol. III) contains many separate substances. Most of these are liquids which boil and turn into vapour, but they do not all boil at the same temperature. Some will turn to vapour at almost normal air temperature; others may have to be heated to more than 600° F. These various substances can be separated by gradually heating up the crude oil and condensing in different stages the various vapours that come from it. In the early days of the oil industry this DISTILLATION (q.v.) was done by heating the crude oil in a still and then passing the vapour from it through a water-cooled condenser. The liquid coming from the condenser changed from one product to another as the temperature in the still was raised. Nowadays a more efficient and economical method of distillation is used: a continuous flow of crude oil enters the plant at one end and the separated 'fractions' (*see* DISTILLATION) are drawn off at different levels. The crude oil is heated to a high temperature by passing it through tubes in a furnace. The hot oil then goes to the lower section of a large cylindrical steel vessel, called a 'fractionating tower', which may be as much as 120 feet high. This contains large metal plates or baffles (called 'bubble-trays') at intervals between 1 and 2 feet all the way up. The temperature in the tower is high at the bottom and becomes lower towards the top. The mixture of different vapours rises up the tower; as the temperature gets lower, more and more

Petroleum Information Bureau

PIPELINES CARRYING OIL FROM THE PERSIAN OILFIELDS TO REFINERIES AT ABADAN AT THE HEAD OF THE PERSIAN GULF

vapour condenses into liquid and is collected on the bubble-trays, from which it drains away through pipes to storage tanks. Each bubble-tray delivers a liquid with a different boiling-point: thus the liquids from the lower trays may be gas oil or lubricating oil, while that draining from the top trays will be kerosene. Petrol will generally be condensed with the vapours leaving the top of the tower. In practice, it is usual to employ several different fractionating towers, linked up in series so as to recover the full range of products by distillation and redistillation.

The raw products from this first distillation need further treatment, each being treated in a different way. Some processes involve 'cracking': this means creating new products by regrouping the atoms of a product into different molecular arrangements. Some forms of cracking require high temperatures and pressures of 1,000 lb. per sq. in. or more. There are also other special processes, such as hydrogenation.

A wide range of products is obtained from the raw materials of the oilfields and used in modern industry. The list includes synthetic or artificial rubber, explosives, anaesthetics, spirits and

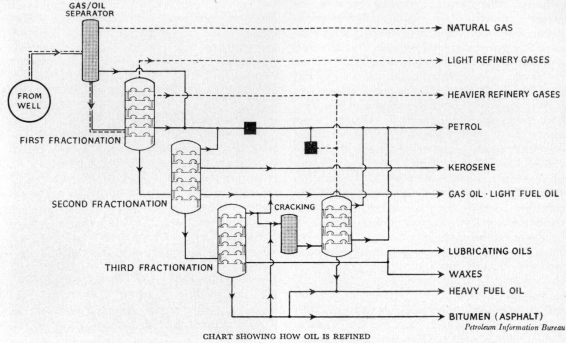

GAS/OIL SEPARATOR

FROM WELL

FIRST FRACTIONATION

SECOND FRACTIONATION

THIRD FRACTIONATION

CRACKING

→ NATURAL GAS

→ LIGHT REFINERY GASES

→ HEAVIER REFINERY GASES

→ PETROL

→ KEROSENE

→ GAS OIL · LIGHT FUEL OIL

→ LUBRICATING OILS

→ WAXES

→ HEAVY FUEL OIL

→ BITUMEN (ASPHALT)

Petroleum Information Bureau

CHART SHOWING HOW OIL IS REFINED

Further refining processes take place at the stages marked by black squares

solvents, insecticides, carbon black (used as a dye in the manufacture of printing inks, and also in RUBBER MANUFACTURE (q.v.)), asphaltic bitumen or asphalt, lubricating oils and greases, paraffin or kerosene (including medicinal paraffin), highly refined colourless and tasteless oils for lubricating machinery (used in the manufacture and packing of foodstuffs), paraffin wax, petroleum jelly, petroleum coke (much used for making carbon blocks and rods for electrical uses, such as electrodes in arc-lamps), and various forms of light and heavy fuel oils.

See also OIL WELLS; OILS, VEGETABLE.
See also Vol. VIII: FUELS.

OIL, SHALE, *see* SHALE OIL.

OIL WELLS. Nowadays immense quantities of oil are needed for making various FUELS (q.v. Vol. VIII) to drive ships, aircraft, and all forms of land transport, as well as for industry and agriculture. Those countries which have their own oilfields have an advantage over those which have not, although the world-wide operations of the international oil industry have made petroleum products available to all countries which can pay for them. The U.S.A. produces about half the oil supply of the world, and there

are extensive oilfields in Venezuela, the U.S.S.R., Persia, Saudi Arabia, Kuwait, Mexico, Indonesia, Roumania, Colombia, British Borneo, Argentina, Canada, and many other countries. In all, some forty countries produce oil.

Oil usually lies thousands of feet below the earth's surface, and is contained in the pores of rock strata (*see* OIL, NATURAL, Vol. III).

The earliest method of discovering this underground oil was simply to sink a well at a point where oil had seeped out on the surface, and to bore downwards until oil was found. Later on, this rather 'hit and miss' method was replaced by more scientific methods, based on a careful study of the geology of the region where oil was being sought. In particular, it was necessary to study what lay below the earth's surface, because oil occurs only in certain types of underground rocks and sands. The nature of the rock formation below the earth's surface could often be judged from 'outcrops' (where a ridge of rock broke through the surface) or from what could be seen on hill-sides or in river valleys or gorges. The invention of aerial photography helped these surveys a great deal. What are called 'geophysical' methods are now also being used, and most of them involve the use of delicate scientific instruments. Different rocks have different 'gravitational pulls': that is, the earth's force of gravity is not the same everywhere. By using very delicate instruments experts can measure these differences in gravitational pull, and estimate whether the rock-structure below the surface is of the type in which oil will probably be found. Another property of rocks is also made use of. Some types of rock reflect sound-waves differently from others; and by producing a minute artificial earthquake (through the explosion on the ground of a small charge of dynamite), and measuring how quickly the sound-waves are reflected from the different layers of rock below the surface, the rock most likely to yield oil may be discovered.

But the actual existence of oil in any area can be proved only by drilling boreholes or wells. While a well is being drilled, samples of the rock or sand below the surface at different levels can be obtained by using a 'drilling bit', which is rather like the sharp end of a carpenter's drill but on a much larger scale. It has a hollow centre, and the material from the earth which

collects in this centre is called a 'core sample'. After the well is drilled, an instrument that measures the electrical resistance of the rock-layer may be lowered down it: different rocks and sands have differing electrical resistance, and those that contain oil have a particularly high resistance. This process is called 'electric logging'. As more and more wells are drilled, it becomes possible to compare an increasing number of core samples and electric logs, and eventually a good plan can be drawn of the layer below the surface. By studying such a plan, geologists can often decide on the most likely direction in which to extend drilling, and on the depth to which wells should be sunk. The big steel framework structure over an oil well is called a 'derrick', and serves to raise and lower the drilling machinery and other instruments.

The diameter of an oil well varies. Very deep wells may have a diameter of 24 inches at the top, tapering to as little as 3 or 4 inches at the bottom. Many oil wells are very deep: oil has even been produced from a well nearly 3 miles deep. The world's deepest borehole, which was drilled in an unsuccessful attempt to find oil, went to a depth of almost 4 miles. At such depths the temperature of the oil is sometimes over 400° F., and the pressure may be as high as 3,500 lb. per square inch.

There are three stages in getting oil from a well. Firstly, the well must be started or 'brought in'. Then its flow must be controlled throughout the months or years during which oil continues to come from the well. This period is known as the 'life of the well'. Individual wells must not be allowed to flow too freely, or the output of other wells in the oilfield will decline very seriously; and care must be taken not to drill wells too close together, or one may 'steal' another's oil. Even when the natural flow of a well declines, and the oil has to be brought to the surface by pumping, only a portion of the oil will be recovered, the greater part remaining in the oil-bearing layer underground. The third and final stage is to bring some of this to the surface by what are called secondary recovery methods.

The force that pushes the oil up the well to the surface is called the 'drive'. This may arise from the pressure of natural gas dissolved in the oil, or from the pressure of the 'gas-cap' above the oil (see GAS, NATURAL, Vol. III); it may also

Petroleum Information Bureau

A TEST WELL SUNK IN SEARCH OF OIL IN SOUTHERN PERSIA

Lengths of drill stem are stored in the derrick for use as the shaft is sunk deeper into the ground

arise from the pressure of a layer of water below the oil; or it may arise from all these influences working together. Before it is decided to bring an oil well into production, the oil at the bottom of the well is kept under control by filling the well with a heavy mud. When it is decided to start production, this mud is thinned out or removed, so that the oil, forced by the 'drive', is free to rush up the well in a bubbling mass to the surface. When, as in some formations, the oil does not flow freely through the pores of the rock, production may be improved by various methods. For example, hydrochloric acid is often pumped down wells to dissolve limestone; and explosives are sometimes used to break up the rock formation at the bottom of the well, and so help the oil to flow more easily.

During the life of an oilfield the 'drive' loses its initial vigour, and the natural flow arising from the 'drive' gradually ceases. When this happens, the oil must be pumped to the surface. This is usually done by a pumping engine on the surface, which operates a plunger at the bottom of the well. Most wells to-day produce 'on the pump', because the natural flow generally ceases long before the life of an oilfield ends; but in some oilfields it is necessary to pump from the beginning. This applies to England's oilfields at Eakring in Nottinghamshire, which produce about 50,000 tons of oil every year.

See also OIL REFINING; OIL, MINERAL; OILS, VEGETABLE.

See also Vol. III: OIL, NATURAL.

OILS, VEGETABLE. 1. Oils are derived from practically every part of a plant, although not all plants yield oil. Most vegetable oils come either from the sap of trees or from seeds. They are widely used for making soap, perfumes, paints, and flavourings.

All vegetable oils consist of compounds of carbon and hydrogen. They fall into two main classes: the 'essential' or volatile oils, which give a distinct odour to the plants in which they are found, and evaporate easily; and the 'fixed' oils, which are greasy and do not easily evaporate. These include the oils which can be used in food ('edible' oils) and those used in paint manufacture, known as 'drying oils'. Some edible oils can also be used as drying oils.

2. VOLATILE OILS. The most important are the turpentines, which are made by distilling the resin of pine trees. In the paint industry the turpentines are used as thinners and solvents (see PAINTS AND VARNISHES). Essential oils are used in waxes and polishes (see CLEANING MATERIALS, Vol. XI). A volatile oil which is popular in the U.S.A. is wintergreen, which is used in medicine, in cosmetics, and for flavouring. A kindred oil is sweet birch, from the tree which grows in Canada and the northern United States. It is a rather heavy oil. From the mountains of India comes sandalwood, which is cultivated in dry open spaces. It is a parasite on the roots of trees, and, before it can be obtained, a tree has to be felled and the roots dug up (see PARASITIC PLANTS, Vol. II). The best grades of sandalwood are used in India for carvings and in making incense, but most of the wood is used for the distillation of sandalwood oil. The 'soft drinks' industry uses sassafras oil in their manufacture, and it is also used in medicine. Volatile oils used as flavouring include peppermint and anise. Other volatile vegetable oils are lavender, eucalyptus, and nutmeg (see OIL-BEARING PLANTS, Vol. VI, Section 2).

The usual way of isolating an essential oil from an aromatic plant is by distillation. The material is packed into a still, and water added. Steam is then injected, and the influence of the hot water and steam frees the oil from the glands in the plant tissue. Sometimes mixed liquids have to be separated by a process known as 'fractionation'. In earlier times flower scents were extracted with fats (see PERFUMERY); alcoholic washings of the perfumed fats were then blended with distilled essential oils to make perfumes. Some flowers continue to give out perfume after having been picked, and the oil is absorbed by cold fat. This method is known as *enfleurage*. Other flowers die on being picked, yielding no more oil than is in the flower at the time. Such flowers are immersed in hot fat, which dissolves all the oil from the glands of the flowers. This process is known as 'maceration'. Only in parts of India and the Grasse region of southern France is *enfleurage* still carried on, while maceration is little used. Solvent extraction is a more modern technique. The solvent, which is usually petroleum ether, penetrates the flowers and dissolves the natural perfume together with some waxes and colouring matter. The solution is pumped into an evaporator, and after the solvent has evaporated the concentrated

United Africa Co

PALM OIL STORAGE INSTALLATION AT PORT HARCOURT, NIGERIA
The oil is shipped in barrels or pumped straight from the storage tanks into tanker ships

flower oil remains. The solvent process has not, however, replaced distillation as a method of extracting essential oils. Distillation is simpler and cheaper, and can be carried on in remote parts of the world by the use of portable direct-fire stills.

3. EDIBLE OILS. These have always served mankind as important items of diet. They are basically compounds of organic acids and glycerine; they may also contain small amounts of other substances, including pigments and vitamins. Many vegetable oils are used for cooking. Several oils are used in the making of margarine, including cottonseed, coconut, soya bean, palm, and peanut (or groundnut) oils, together with flavouring materials. Corn oil is used as a salad and cooking oil, and in lard substitutes; it comes from maize. In the U.S.A. COTTON is a large crop, and refined cottonseed oil is used to make lard compounds, margarine, and cooking and salad oils. The kernels of the COCONUT palm yield coconut-oil, again used for margarine. The SOYA BEAN yields an oil which has been used for many years in the East for cooking. It is now used all over the world in the making of margarine and mayonnaise (qq.v. Vol. VI.)

Groundnut oil can be used for margarine and salad and cooking oils, and for cooking sardines when they are tinned. Schemes for growing GROUNDNUTS (q.v. Vol. VI) on a large scale

have been tried, especially in Tanganyika, for there is a demand for them in many countries.

The fruit of wild African palms and cultivated Sumatra palms yields two kinds of oil. From the fleshy part of the fruit palm oil is obtained, and it is the nut which provides palm kernel oil. Both these can be used in margarine. The seeds of Muscat grapes give us another edible oil called raisin oil. This is mainly used for coating raisins, to prevent their sticking together when they are packed. An important oil comes from the OLIVE (q.v. Vol. VI). Other edible oils are poppy seed oil, sunflower oil, and rapeseed oil.

4. DRYING OILS. The standard by which all drying oils are judged is linseed oil, which has been the mainstay of the paint industry and has great importance in the manufacture of soap and linoleum. The oils known as 'semi-drying' absorb sufficient oxygen from the air to dry to a tough, elastic substance, and are much used to add bulk to the more expensive linseed oil. Examples are sunflower seed, soya bean, cottonseed, kapok, and hempseed oils and—rather less well-known—tomato-seed and pumpkin-seed oil.

LINSEED (q.v. Vol. VI) is the oily seed of the plant whose fibres, known as flax, are woven to make linen cloth. Before 1939 the main producers of linseed were Argentina, the U.S.S.R., India, and the U.S.A., but the Second World War disorganized its production and distribution. The post-war shortage has been overcome by extensive production in the U.S.A., Canada, and Argentina, but the dollar shortage has limited exports from these countries to the sterling area. In Britain linseed has been grown sporadically for many years, and the Ministry of Agriculture has attempted to stimulate production by guaranteed prices to farmers. The pre-war cheapness of the imported product discouraged its growth in the United Kingdom.

After the First World War tung oil was developed as a substitute for linseed oil. It had long been used in China for painting and weather-proofing boats.

Although castor oil is a non-drying oil, it can be made by chemical processing to resemble tung oil in its drying properties. It is much used in making leathercloth.

The soya-bean is mainly grown for food, but its oil is used for lamp oil and soap making. In America it is used in paint. Candlenut, sunflower, safflower, and chia oils are other drying oils, less known and less important. Walnut, poppy, and hempseed oils have been used for artists' colours from very early times (see OIL BEARING PLANTS, Vol. VI, Section 1).

5. EXTRACTION. After the oil-seeds have been cleaned, they are prepared for extraction by being crushed, to break down the walls of the oil-containing cells. A typical crushing-plant consists of iron rollers ranged one above the other in an iron frame. The seeds are passed in turn between the first and second rollers, the second and third rollers, and so on, the pressure increasing each time. The seeds are then cooked, so that a clean separation will take place in the actual process of extraction.

There are three different methods. One is to 'express' the oil by subjecting the 'meal', which is obtained by cooking, to heavy pressure in a hydraulic press. Another is to expel the oil by subjecting the meal to increasing pressure in a screw-press working in a perforated cylinder. The most modern process is solvent extraction, by which a petroleum spirit, acting as a solvent, is brought into contact with the meal. The solution of oil in the solvent is run off, and the operation is repeated several times. The solvent is then removed by distillation. This method produces about one and a quarter tons of oil for every ton produced by pressing.

After the oil has been extracted by any of these methods it must be refined by heating, for it will still contain many impurities. On cooling, the impurities sink to the bottom and the oil is decanted.

See also OIL, MINERAL; OIL REFINING; MARGARINE; SOAP; PAINTS AND VARNISHES.

OPENCAST MINING, see MINING.

ORGANIZATION, see BUSINESS ORGANIZATION; FACTORY ORGANIZATION.

OVERDRAFT, see BANK ACCOUNTS.

OVERHEAD CHARGES, see COSTING, Section 2.

OVERSEAS TRADE. Before the Second World War Britain's overseas trade was almost entirely a matter for private enterprise, and Government departments had little direct share in it. Most of the goods dealt in were imported and exported in large quantities, on a wholesale basis (see WHOLESALE TRADING). As well as the goods exported from Britain, and imported for manufacture or consumption within Britain, there was also a large 'entrepôt' trade, that is, trade in imported goods which would later be re-exported to other countries. Such commodities as wool, tea, coffee, hides and skins, rubber, many metals and metal ores, and various spices and essences, figured in this 'entrepôt' trade, and London was the biggest centre of this trade in the world.

The largest firms engaged in overseas trade handled export, import, and re-export business. Typical firms of this kind were the big Eastern merchant houses, with offices in London and branches in India, Burma, Malaya, and China. There were similar firms in the Australasian and West African trade. Their overseas branches acted as managers and AGENTS (q.v.) for many local enterprises. The Indian merchant firms, for example, controlled and managed coalmines, jute mills, cotton mills, tea and coffee plantations, light railways, and river steamers. They exported produce to their British houses, and in return imported through them machinery and stores for their mines, mills, and plantations, as well as any other goods for which they could find a market.

The smaller firms of merchants or manufacturers usually handled exports or imports only. Export firms were organized in many different ways. Some firms opened overseas branches for

EUROPEAN 'FACTORIES' (TRADING HOUSES) AT CANTON, CHINA, ABOUT 1820
The trading houses of the various foreign companies fly their national flags. The goods are brought to the warehouses in Chinese native boats

the sale of their goods. Some were wholesale branches, and dealt in large quantities of goods in bulk; others were retail branches, selling through shops to the public. But many manufacturers and merchants did not sell enough in any single 'territory'—as any particular district or province of a country was called—to justify opening a branch in it. Such firms therefore often sent out members of their staffs as local REPRESENTATIVES (q.v.) in each important territory. A representative had to get as many orders as possible for his firm's goods, and to post or cable the orders to his head office in Britain, which then sent the goods ordered direct to the actual buyer. In some countries, and for some lines of goods, the resident representative system worked well, but very often it was found better to appoint for each territory a well-established local firm as 'sole AGENT' (q.v.). Usually the agreement signed between the home exporter and the overseas sole agent laid it down that the agent would not sell the products of any firms which competed with the exporter; it also stated the COMMISSION (q.v.) the agent was to receive on the orders. Many

firms working through sole agents appointed resident representatives as well: for example, a British firm exporting to Australia might have its own resident representative for the whole of Australia and sole agents for each of the States of the Commonwealth. It was the representative's duty to travel round the country at regular intervals and visit the sole agents, so as to satisfy himself that they were doing their best for his firm.

Sometimes a firm did such little business in any single territory that it was not worth while to appoint a resident representative or a sole agent. Such a firm usually worked through a manufacturer's agent or an export agent in London or one of the big provincial cities. These agents were in touch with overseas firms which sent orders to them direct, and they passed on the orders to the merchant or manufacturer they thought most suitable. The firm executing the order then dispatched the goods direct to the overseas buyer, and paid the export agent a commission on the value of the goods sent.

Many firms made a business of rendering special services to exporters. The largest exporting firms ran special departments of their own for all these services, but smaller firms found that it would not pay them to do this. One service consisted of the special packing of goods for export, to satisfy the strict requirements of the shipping lines and marine insurance companies, and to resist heat and insect pests. There were several specialist firms of export packers. The trade of shipping and forwarding agent was another speciality: these firms collected goods from exporting manufacturers or merchants, had them specially packed for export, and attended to all the details of shipment, including loading the goods into the ships and obtaining signed BILLS OF LADING (q.v.) from the ships' officers.

The organization of the British import trade was on much the same lines, although for many goods the organization at the non-British or export end was controlled by foreign firms. But Britain was so outstandingly the world's biggest importer, particularly of foodstuffs and raw materials, that the import trade often copied the export trade's system of resident representatives. Resident 'buying agents' were appointed in certain countries; sometimes these agencies were turned into local branches of the British import firm, particularly when the goods had to be processed in some way before they were shipped.

Britain's total overseas trade, including all exports and imports, exceeded £4,000 millions a year in value by early in 1950. But since the Second World War there have been changes in methods of conducting this trade. The organization of the export trade is still much as it was, but with few exceptions the import trade is now the direct concern of the Government, although the buying and merchanting organization that has taken so long to establish is still largely used for routine work. All overseas trade is under Government supervision by a system of Board of Trade import and export licences.

Overseas trade has always been complicated by official regulations. For example, many countries, including Britain, levy import duties or taxes on goods coming in from abroad (*see* TARIFFS), and when these duties are based on the cost of the goods, they can be largely evaded if INVOICES (q.v.) are made out for less than the true value. Certificates of value, called Consular Invoices, have therefore to be signed by the importing country's consul at the port of shipment. Some countries make their import duties lower for particular countries than for others, and the favoured countries are then said to enjoy a 'preferential tariff'. The true origin or place of manufacture of such goods has therefore to be vouched for in a document called a Certificate of Origin, signed by a responsible official of the exporting country.

See also INTERNATIONAL FINANCE; TRADE, HISTORY OF; SHIPPING.

OXIDATION. This is the name given to chemical reactions on which many important industrial processes are based. The simplest form of oxidation occurs when an element (*see* MATTER, Vol. III) absorbs oxygen from the air and thus forms what is called an 'oxide'. This may take place at ordinary temperatures, as with phosphorus, or at higher temperatures, for example, when coal is burned and the carbon of the coal goes up the chimney as carbon dioxide; or when metallic mercury is heated, and forms red oxide of mercury. Another form of oxidation takes place when a substance absorbs oxygen from another substance, and not from the oxygen of the air. In the BLAST FURNACE (q.v. Vol. VIII) oxide of iron, containing oxygen, gives up its oxygen to the coke with which it is mixed, and the carbon in the coke passes off as carbon monoxide or 'blast furnace gas'.

P

PAINTS AND VARNISHES. Paint consists mainly of two things—the colouring matter which is known as pigment, and a liquid which is known as the 'vehicle' because it carries the pigment.

1. PIGMENTS. The first pigments used were made of natural earth, which was easy to find. Stone Age man drew pictures with them on the walls of caves in southern France and northern Spain 20,000 years ago (see PREHISTORIC ART, Vol. XII). Examples of such earth colours are yellow ochre, siennas (dark yellows), and umbers (browns), all of which are earthy iron oxides. At a later date the Egyptians added lime and glue to their colours and used white chalk and charcoal, making the first cold-water paints.

Pigments are of two kinds, 'prime pigments' and 'extenders'. While extenders are merely cheap pigments, used to increase the bulk of a paint and thus reduce its cost, prime pigments must be completely opaque, or non-transparent, and must also have colour and brightness. They have to cover up the surface over which the paint is applied, and 'hide' it, or prevent its colour showing through. They must also protect the surface. For this they must have stability (resistance to chemical action), and must not dissolve in the oils and other liquids used to make paint.

The following are examples of prime white pigments. White Lead (basic carbonate of lead) has been widely used since Roman times; it makes a good surface to paint over, but collects dirt. Lithopone (zinc sulphide and barium sulphate) was in great demand from the end of the 19th century until recent times; it dries well but does not 'hide' other colours so well. Zinc Oxide, sometimes called Chinese White, dries into a hard film. Zinc Sulphide is very opaque. Titanium Dioxide, used for finish of high quality, is bright, very opaque, and keeps its colour well.

Natural pigment materials are mined or quarried, then ground up. Other pigment materials are prepared chemically.

2. VEHICLES. The fluid part of paint is a combination of 'drying-oils', resins, 'thinners', and 'driers'. A drying-oil must absorb oxygen from the air when applied as a thin film, and then dry into a tough and elastic substance. Such oils were not mixed with paints until the Middle Ages, when artists discovered their use. The oils come from oil-bearing seeds and nuts, and from plants, fish, and animals (see OILS, VEGETABLE). The seed of the flax crop yields linseed oil, which is widely used for house paints and for varnishes. In varnishes it has the disadvantages of turning yellow and of drying slowly, but it is the only oil that meets all needs in oil paints. Castor oil can be made into a drying-oil. Fish oils tend to remain sticky, even when dry. Soya-bean oil does not turn yellow. Tung oil, the best varnish oil for all purposes, comes from the Chinese tung nut, which is now also grown in the U.S.A.

Resins (see GUMS AND RESINS) help to 'bind' the paint together, make it easier to lay on with a brush, and hasten drying. They also make varnish stronger and more lasting.

'Thinners' are used to make paint less 'gluey', more even, and easier to put on; they are solvents which evaporate quickly, and include naphthas, turpentine, kerosene, pine oil, and various coal-tar hydrocarbons.

A 'drier' is a chemical which makes the paint dry quickly. Until modern times, litharge (monoxide of lead) was almost always used, but to-day compounds of lead, manganese, cobalt, and zinc are often used.

3. VARNISHES. These liquids are transparent or translucent (letting light pass through), and are meant to protect a surface and improve its looks. Varnish is made of resin, which provides the hardness and shine. The more resin in the varnish, the more brilliant but less lasting it will be; whereas the more oil, the tougher and more lasting it will be.

4. PAINT MANUFACTURE. The separate operations in paint manufacture are mixing, grinding, reducing and tinting, filtering, and packaging.

During mixing the vehicle is added to the pigment. Rotary mixers, in pairs and electrically driven, are generally used. Methods of charging mixers vary.

Grinding takes place mostly in a roller mill.

Ball-and-pebble mills are also used (*see* TUBE MILL, Vol. VIII). Hard pigments tend to scratch the rollers of roller mills, and there is also loss by evaporation. Ball-and-pebble mills require little labour and carry out mixing and milling in one step, but they are hard to clean. Tinting-pigments, having been ground into a paste with an oil, are now added by hand. Before passing into cans the paint is strained through sieves, and any 'skin' is removed.

5. TYPES OF PAINT. Of the many types of paint, the following are the most important:

(*a*) Priming paints are used for the first coating on unpainted surfaces. They usually consist of white-lead pigments in linseed oil vehicles. For painting on metal, red lead is used, because it prevents corrosion. For paints on cement or plaster surfaces, a tung-oil resin is usually favoured.

(*b*) Undercoats or flat paints are put on to hide the original surface; they have a large proportion of white pigments. They may be put on after the priming coat, or alternatively two coats of undercoating may be painted on.

(*c*) Gloss paints are finishing-paints, with a smooth surface. They contain heat-treated oils, which make the paint flow better, and varnishes to give brilliance and hardness to the surface. There are many kinds of gloss paints. 'Enamel' is a trade term for the more brilliant types of hard-gloss paint, though it must not be confused with the art of ENAMEL work (q.v.).

(*d*) Stoving finishes are used for metal articles. They usually consist of heat-resisting varnishes, with some pigment for colouring.

(*e*) Stone paints are used extensively for outside work, and dry with a surface like stone. They are mostly made with tung oil, and have sand or finely ground rock in place of a pigment.

(*f*) Anti-fouling paints contain materials poisonous to marine growths. They are painted on ships' hulls and on the underwater parts of bridges and similar structures to which living organisms are likely to become attached.

(*g*) Fungicidal paints, containing special chemicals, are used in such places as greenhouses and dairies, to prevent the growth of fungi in damp atmospheres.

Other special paints in common use are heat-resisting paints, fire-retarding paints, and aluminium or bronze paints, which contain metallic powder as a pigment. Luminous paints are of great importance in the instrument industry. They are usually composed of a special type of zinc oxide and barytes powder.

PALM OIL, *see* OILS, VEGETABLE. *See also* Vol. VI: PALM TREES.

PAPER-MAKING. Modern paper is composed of the fibres of wood, esparto grass, flax, cotton, straw, repulped waste paper, and rags, felted together into a pulp which is pressed and dried into a sheet. All these raw materials, or a mixture of them in varying proportions, produce different kinds of paper; the actual constituents of any particular kind of paper may also vary slightly according to the individual custom of the particular paper-maker.

1. HISTORY. The art of making paper was discovered by the Chinese 2,000 years ago. For raw materials they used such things as old rags and worn-out fishing-nets, which they made into a pulp by soaking them in water and then stamping them with a pestle in a stone mortar. When the soaking and stamping had reduced the rags to individual fibres, the fibrous pulp was spread thinly on to pieces of cloth and dried in the sun. These first sheets of paper were very rough; but soon the Chinese invented a better method. They used a bamboo mould, rather like a sieve, which they dipped into a tank or vat containing the fibrous pulp. When the mould

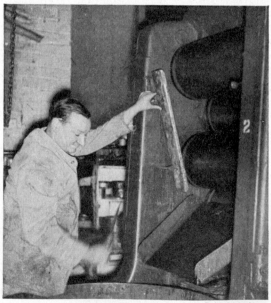

Paint Manufacture
TRIPLE ROLLER MILL FOR GRINDING PAINT

was lifted out, it was covered with the wet pulp, and, as the water drained through it, a thin sheet of pulp was left on top. This sheet, after being dried in the sun and polished with a smooth stone, made a much finer paper. The Chinese made very beautiful paper in this way, pieces of which survive to-day in perfect condition. They also made coloured papers which were 'sized' with a gummy substance to give them a surface on which it was possible to write with ink or paint.

It was not until the 8th century that the art of paper-making spread from China. Some Chinese paper-makers were captured by the Arab army at Samarkand, and, during their captivity, they taught the Arabs how to make paper. The art spread westwards through Bagdad, where there was a street of paper-makers in the 8th century in the time of Haroun Al-Raschid of *Arabian Nights* fame. Thence it came to Egypt, where many paper mills were set up in Cairo; and from Cairo the art spread along the shores of the Mediterranean to Fez in Morocco. The Moors brought it to Toledo in Spain in the 13th century; from there it spread northwards into Italy, France, Germany, and Holland, and finally it came to England in the 15th century. Water power began to be used for driving the stampers, or pestles, about the 12th century. Paper-making did not become established in Britain for a long time, and it was not until 1588, when John Spielman started his mill at Dartford, that the industry began to spread; although John Tate had actually made paper at Stevenage in 1490.

At that time paper was made entirely by hand, by methods very little different in principle from those used by the ancient Chinese. Indeed, some papers are still made by hand to-day in Britain and other countries: for example, the most beautiful papers for water-colour painting and drawing, and for banknotes. For making paper by hand a sheet of wire cloth is used as the mould, and this is dipped into the vat of pulp. If a watermark is to be put in the paper, a piece of wire or wire cloth bearing the device is stitched or soldered on the wire mould before dipping. When the mould is lifted out covered with pulp, the vatmen shake it from side to side and backwards and forwards to make the fibres mat evenly together and allow the water to drain through, until a wet sheet of paper has formed on the mould. The mould is then lifted, and the

Walmsleys (Bury) Ltd.

THE BEATER ROOM IN A PAPER MILL

Bales of dry pulp are ready to be put into the beaters in which wet pulp can be seen

wet paper deposited on a sheet of woollen felt. When a pile of alternate sheets of wet paper and felt has been assembled, the whole is squeezed in strong presses to remove the water. The paper sheets are then dried, sized with gelatine 'size' to prevent their being too absorbent (like blotting-paper), and calendered (that is, a form of ironing rather like being put through a mangle) to make them smooth.

At the beginning of the 19th century a paper-making machine was invented by a Frenchman, Nicolas Louis Robert, who brought it to England, where it was taken up by the Fourdrinier brothers. The modern paper-making machine is called the Fourdrinier machine after them, and the large modern machine, making, perhaps, 200 tons of paper a day, is simply a development of this original machine.

2. MODERN PAPER-MAKING. (*a*) *Raw Materials.* Until the middle of the 19th century the only raw materials used for paper-making were linen, hemp, and cotton. Paper was very scarce, as there was not enough of these materials to meet the demand. But in the middle of the 19th century esparto grass (*see* FIBRE CROPS, Section 8, Vol. VI) began to be brought from Spain and North Africa and used, as it is to-day, for very fine paper. There followed an even more important discovery—it was found that wood could be made into a pulp which could be used for paper (*see* WOOD PULP). The wood pulp used in British paper-mills is almost entirely imported

THE WET END OF A PAPER MACHINE

The pulp flows on to the machine at the left and is carried along the wire cloth to the rollers at the other end

from abroad, and in a condition ready to go into the beating-engines. But the linen, cotton, esparto grass, or straw are made into pulp at the paper-mill. To pulp them, they are boiled in water and chemicals to remove any colour, and impurities such as grease, from the rags; then they are washed in clean water, and put into a machine called a breaking-engine, which breaks up the bundles of fibres or rags into a pulpy mass.

As well as wood pulp and the pulp made from the other fibrous materials, a certain proportion of waste paper is repulped, purified, and used to make new paper. It is possible to make paper entirely from repulped waste paper, and most papers contain a good proportion of repulped waste paper, especially when wood pulp and other modern materials are scarce; so it is important to salvage waste paper.

(*b*) *Manufacture.* The pulpy fibrous mass first goes into a beating-engine, where it is circulated with water round an oval tank. In this it passes under a revolving roller fitted with steel knives, which carries it over stationary steel or bronze knives. These cut the fibres to the right length, treating them differently according to the kind of paper required. Then the majority of papers are 'loaded' with some mineral matter, usually CHINA CLAY (q.v.), which is added to make the paper opaque and its surface smooth; and resin 'size' is added to make the paper take ink without absorbing it like blotting-paper.

The fibrous mixture is next put into a storage chest, from which it is fed on to the paper-machine. The modern paper-machine consists of three main parts: the wire part, where the wet sheet of paper is formed; the press part, where the wet sheet is made firm by pressure and suction; and the dry part, where any remaining water is taken away by heat. Paper-making is a continuous process from one part to the next, the machines running for many hours without stopping.

When the pulp from the storage chest, diluted with water, is fed on to the machine, it looks rather like milk. It is carried along a moving belt of woven wire cloth through which the water drains, leaving the fibres on top. The wire belt is shaken mechanically from side to side to make the fibres in the pulp lie evenly in all directions and so 'felt' together. At the end of the wire cloth the pulp is firm enough to hold together in a sheet and to be lifted off and placed on a woollen felt, on which it is carried into the presses. There the fibres are squeezed together under high pressure, making a smooth, but still wet, sheet of paper. The sheet is then carried alternately between felt and hot cylinders until it is quite dry and can be wound upon a wooden or metal cylinder at the end of the paper-machine.

The paper is then treated in various ways according to the type of paper needed. If a highly polished surface is needed for printing or reproducing pictures, it is usually 'calendered': that is, it is damped and passed through a machine containing rolls, some of iron, some of paper, pressing against each other. If the paper is needed in rolls (which are usually narrower than the machine roll) for a printing press, the roll from the machine is cut up and rewound into smaller ones. If the paper is required in sheets, several machine rolls are put into a cutting-machine, and the paper is unwound into the cutter and chopped off to the right size. The number of sheets cut is usually counted on the cutter, and reams of the required number of sheets are kept separate by marking-tabs.

Central Press

SUPER CALENDER FOR PUTTING A HIGH GLOSS ON TO PAPER AFTER IT HAS BEEN MADE

Watermarking, when required, is done at the stage when the wet pulp is passing along the wire cloth. The name or device is sewn or soldered on to a revolving 'dandy roll', which disperses the fibres in the pulp when they reach it. This makes the paper thinner and leaves a clear impression when the paper is held to the light.

A kind of thick paper known as cardboard or folding boxboard is made on a different machine. This machine has a series of vats or tanks in which metal cylinders, covered with wire-cloth, revolve, picking up a layer of fibre and transferring it to the underside of a felt which is travelling along the top. Layers of fibres are pressed on to the felt until a thick paper is formed. The sheets of paper then go through presses and over drying-cylinders in much the same way as in the ordinary process. These boards are used for cartons and folding boxes for packing fruit, and so on.

Papers which are to be used for reproducing half-tone illustrations (*see* PROCESS REPRODUCTION) need to have a highly finished shiny surface. Art paper is a high-quality paper usually made from wood pulp and esparto grass, the surface of which is coated with a solution of white mineral matter such as calcium sulphate to give it a smooth, polished, and finely grained surface. The colour plates in this *Encyclopaedia* are printed on art paper. Imitation art paper is the same as art paper except that it has large quantities of china clay added to the pulp during manufacture, and not added as a coating after the paper is made. It is subsequently super-calendered to give it a highly polished surface. This *Encyclopaedia*, except for the colour plates, is printed on imitation art paper. There are many other varieties of paper, with different types of finish for different purposes.

See also WOOD PULP; NEWSPRINT; PRINTING.
See also Vol. IV: PAPER.

PARTNERSHIP. Firms jointly owned by two or more persons, unless they are private LIMITED COMPANIES (q.v.), are called Partnerships. They have the advantage over one-man businesses of being able to draw on, not only the capital, but also the brains and experience of more than one person.

Partnerships may be formed without the signing of any special agreement, and are then bound by the Partnerships Act of 1890, which lays down that all partners shall contribute and share equally and that the partnership shall be automatically ended by the death, bankruptcy, or retirement of any one of the partners. Partnerships formed by the drawing up of a Partnership Deed, however, are not bound by the provisions of the Act: capital can be provided, and profits or losses shared, in different proportions; interest on a partner's capital, and salaries for one or more of the partners, can also be paid.

But partnerships, being unlimited liability associations (*see* LIMITED COMPANIES), suffer from the disadvantages of this form of enterprise. For instance, if such a firm gets into difficulties and owes more than it possesses, a partner with spare money will have to pay up for those who have none. Early in the present century, therefore, Britain adopted the continental device of the 'limited partnership', by which partners may be classified as either general or limited partners. Limited partners contribute capital to the firm, and get a share of the profits or bear a share of the losses; but they may not take any part in the management of the business or withdraw any part of their capital without the consent of the other partners. Limited partnerships must be registered with the Registrar of Joint-stock Companies.

The great disadvantage of a partnership is that it becomes dissolved on the death of any partner, and a promising business may then have to be 'wound up' simply for lack of the capital lost in this way. So it is usual for partnerships whose business would be seriously affected by such an event to insure the lives of the partners for a sufficient sum of money to replace a deceased partner's capital (*see* INSURANCE). This allows the surviving partners to re-form the partnership with the same amount of capital as before.

See also CO-PARTNERSHIP; LIMITED COMPANIES.

PASTEURIZATION OF MILK. 1. NATURE OF PROCESS.
The value of heat for the preservation of foods has been known for thousands of years, but it was not realized until the 19th century that a very mild heat treatment, far below the boiling-point, made liquid foods such as milk keep much longer. The discovery followed the work of the French scientist PASTEUR (q.v. Vol. V) on wine and beer. The process, called after him 'pasteurization', is a carefully controlled mild-heat treatment. It was

Graham Enock

GRAVITY FLOW TYPE OF H.T.-S.T. PASTEURIZING PLANT
The casing has been opened to show the pipes through which the milk flows to be heated

found that the process served two purposes: it prevented the souring of milk, and it destroyed the dangerous disease germs which occur in some samples of milk. These germs include the bacteria causing tuberculosis, undulant fever, typhoid and paratyphoid fevers, dysentery, diphtheria, scarlet fever, and septic sore-throat (*see* BACTERIAL DISEASES, Vol. XI). It was known to bacteriologists that the tubercle bacillus was the germ which most strongly resisted heat treatment. To destroy this organism it is necessary to heat milk to about 140° F. for 15 minutes, and its destruction has always been taken as a way of testing the efficiency of pasteurization. A heat treatment of this kind destroys also about 99% of the common bacteria in milk, including nearly all those which cause milk to get sour—the lactic streptococci, the coli-aerogenes bacteria, and the staphylococci.

2. TECHNIQUE. To ensure the certain destruction of tubercular and other disease germs in milk, it must be held at a fixed temperature for a fixed time, and in 1923 these conditions were officially defined in Britain as 145° to 150° F. for 30 minutes. This became known as the 'holder' process. Properly carried out, it was a thoroughly reliable method, but for the dairyman it had

certain disadvantages. The raw milk had to be heated to just over 145° F., pumped into a tank, held there for half-an-hour, and then pumped out and cooled. This was a slow process and required a very bulky plant. For many years scientists and engineers experimented to try to devise a continuous-flow method by which the milk would only need to be held for a much shorter time; by 1949 a method known as 'high-temperature short-time', or H.T.–S.T., was officially recognized. Most of the milk now pasteurized is treated by this process, which involves the following stages:

(a) The heating of the cold incoming milk by the returning hot pasteurized milk in a 'heat-exchanger', in which the liquids are separated by a thin sheet of metal.
(b) Filtration or clarification.
(c) Heating by hot-water pipes to just over 161° F.
(d) The holding of the milk at this temperature for at least 15 seconds.
(e) The cooling of the hot milk by the cold incoming milk in the heat-exchanger.
(f) Further cooling by brine or chilled water outside the compartments which contain the milk.

A flow-control valve maintains a constant rate of flow of milk through the plant to keep the temperature precise. An ingenious device, known as the flow-diversion valve, makes it impossible for milk to pass through the plant unless it has been properly pasteurized. The bulb of a very sensitive thermometer is held in the milk at the end of the 15–seconds holding-pipe, and if the temperature of the milk at this point falls below 161°F., the flow-diversion valve is brought into operation by pneumatic or electrical control, and the under-pasteurized milk is diverted back into the raw-milk tank, ready to pass through the plant again.

In one type of heat-exchanger in use in Britain, the liquid to be heated flows in a thin film between two stainless steel plates, the heating liquid being on the other sides of the plates. Thus there are thin films of cold and hot liquids arranged alternately. In another type the pasteurized milk is finally chilled by an ammonia REFRIGERATION unit (q.v. Vol. VIII).

Efficient pasteurization may reduce the bacteria in raw milk from, say, one million to only a few thousand per cubic centimetre. The bacteria that are left are chemically mostly of the inert type: that is, they either do not sour milk at all, or sour it only slowly. In certain cases, however, pasteurized milk in a commercial plant may become contaminated by souring-bacteria in the tanks, pipe-lines, and bottle-filling machines; and unless these are most efficiently cleaned and sterilized, the advantages of pasteurization may be wasted. If milk is pasteurized in the bottle, with a securely fitted cap, contamination after pasteurization is impossible. Milk treated by this so-called 'in-bottle' method has an extremely good keeping quality, although the process involves serious practical difficulties.

See also DAIRY INDUSTRY; COLD STORAGE.
See also Vol. XI: BACTERIAL DISEASES; TUBERCULOSIS.

PATENTS. The word 'patent' is a contraction

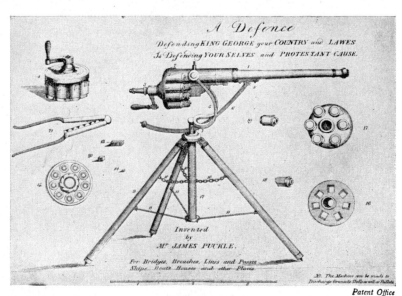

Patent Office

SPECIFICATION FOR PUCKLE'S MACHINE-GUN, PATENTED 1718
The gun is designed to shoot square bullets against Turks and round bullets against Christians

of Letters Patent, a document, signed by the King or someone acting on his behalf, conferring some right or privilege. Letters patent are still issued when commoners are raised to the PEERAGE or Governors are appointed to overseas COLONIES (qq.v. Vol. X). From the reign of Queen Elizabeth onwards, letters patent were granted by the Crown to many persons or companies, giving them a MONOPOLY (q.v.) to produce some kind of goods, or exclusive rights to trade and explore in overseas territories. By the time of James I the number had grown so big that laws were passed to abolish them, on the ground that they were 'grievous and inconvenient to the subjects of this Realm'. An exception, however, was made in favour of letters patent granted for the 'sole working or making of any manner of new manufactures'.

This exception is the origin of our modern patents, which are rights of monopoly granted to any person who invents a new machine or a new process, or the apparatus for carrying out the process. A patent cannot be granted for an idea, but only for putting an idea into practice.

Patents are granted by the British Patent Office, which is a government department, for a first term of 16 years. The person to whom a patent is granted is called a patentee. At the end of 16 years patentees may apply to the law courts for an extension, usually an additional 5 years, but sometimes an additional 10. Patenting an invention or process is a highly technical matter. To be worthy of a patent, an article or process must be something entirely new, which has never been the subject of a previous patent. For this reason there are firms called Chartered Patent Agents, who specialize in the law concerning patents and in the details of applications to the Patent Office; these firms are usually consulted by would-be patentees. British patents cover Britain only, and patentees who wish to prevent foreigners from copying their inventions abroad should take out patents in all other important countries, according to the laws prevailing there. A patent is a form of PROPERTY (q.v. Vol. X), and can therefore be bought or sold, or assigned or leased to other persons. Inventors of articles or processes, who do not wish to take the personal risk of developing them commercially or industrially, may allow other firms to use their patents under licence. The licensees may pay for this privilege in various ways: a lump sum, an annual rent, or a ROYALTY (q.v.).

A 19TH-CENTURY PAWNBROKER'S ADVERTISEMENT
From Ambrose Heal's *London Tradesmen's Cards* (Batsford)

PAWNBROKERS are persons or firms who are permitted to lend money against the security of goods deposited with them. Their methods of business are extremely ancient, and are rigidly controlled by law. The pawnbroker's sign is three golden balls: these have sometimes been held to be the arms of the Medici family of Florence, but this is denied by many historians, who consider the device to be the general sign of the bankers of Lombardy who came to England in the late Middle Ages (*see* BANKING).

Goods left as security with pawnbrokers are called 'pledges'. The interest that may be charged on loans is limited by law. On top of this, a halfpenny (or, on loans of over 10s., a penny) is usually charged for the pawnticket, which states the terms of the contract between pawnbroker and pawner. If the pawner has failed, by a certain date, to 'redeem' his pledge, that is to say, to repay his loan with the interest due, the pawnbroker can sell the goods left with him. For loans over £2 pawnbrokers may issue special tickets which usually give the pawner the right, if the goods have been sold, of searching the pawnbroker's books and claiming the difference between the amount due and the sum received from the sale.

In the 19th and early 20th centuries the pawn-broker's sign was frequently seen in Britain. People who suddenly needed money would take personal jewellery or household valuables to a pawnbroker in the hope that he would lend them the sum they wanted. Many poor people were regular customers of pawnbrokers, and would even pawn their clothes. To-day pawn-brokers' signs are much rarer.

PAYMENT. Coins and bank-notes are the usual means of payment between shopkeepers and customers when something is bought for cash, and not 'on credit'. Bank-notes can be used up to large sums for the payment of debts in general, whenever payment can be made in person, but there is a danger of theft if too many bank-notes are carried about.

For payment of larger sums cheques are a more suitable means of payment, although cheques have certain disadvantages. A cheque is unacceptable if the person giving it is not known to the person receiving it, as the value of the cheque depends on whether he has enough money in his bank account to meet it. This difficulty can be avoided through the use of what is called the 'certified cheque', a method once popular in Britain, which has since died out, although it is still an everyday method in

the United States and Canada. A person wish-ing to offer a certified cheque in payment of a debt would get his bank to certify it as 'good for the sum named'. The cheque would be charged to the customer's account forthwith, so that there would be no question of there not being funds to meet it when it was presented for payment.

British banks now prefer to issue bank drafts. A bank draft is simply a cheque 'drawn' (signed) by a banker himself, drawing on his banking account at some other bank, or at one of his branches. Everybody trusts a banker's signa-ture, and in these days the chance of failure of a British bank no longer exists, so the risk of accepting a bank draft is not worth worrying about. Bank drafts are a useful means of sending money from one town to another—and even from one country to another.

But everyone does not possess a banking account, and banks cannot waste time writing bank drafts for small sums. There are other means of payment. Bank-notes and coins may be sent by registered post, and the Post Office will pay compensation for losses up to £5 (or more if special insurance fees are paid). For quite small payments, 'postal orders' are convenient. The name of the person to whom the money is being sent, and the name of his nearest Post Office,

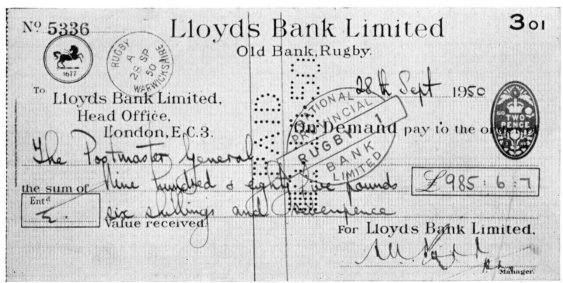

Lloyds Bank

A BANKER'S DRAFT FOR THE ACCOUNT OF A CUSTOMER OF LLOYDS BANK, RUGBY, IN FAVOUR OF THE POSTMASTER GENERAL
The customer's account is debited with the amount, and it is cleared through Lloyds Bank Head Office after the Post-master General has paid in the draft to his own banker, the National Provincial Bank

may be filled in before posting an order: there is thus some protection against theft if the letter should get into the wrong hands. For larger sums 'money orders' may be used. These are only paid across the Post Office counter if the receiver of the money can say who the sender is, and this is a great protection against fraud. If payment is urgent, money orders may be telegraphed. People who have an account with the Post Office Savings Bank can ask for a draft to be made out in favour of someone to whom they wish to send money.

As an extra safeguard, postal orders, money orders, cheques, and bank drafts may be 'crossed'. A 'crossing' consists of two parallel lines drawn obliquely across the face of the document. Sometimes the words '& Co.' (a relic of the days when all banks were private partnerships) are added at the right-hand end of the crossing; but a crossing consisting of two parallel lines is legally sufficient. No crossed cheque will be paid in cash across the counter: its value will only be paid to a banker, usually the banker of the person to whom it is made payable.

Greater protection can be given if the crossing is a 'special' instead of a 'general' crossing. Thus, if a cheque is crossed 'Account Payee only', the money may only be placed to the credit of the actual bank account of the person to whom it is made payable. Another form of special crossing is to write the name of the payee's bank between the lines of the crossing: the money then becomes payable only to the bank named. Another special crossing is the inclusion of the words 'Not Negotiable' between the lines; a person cashing such a cheque for someone who has stolen it cannot legally recover the money if he passes the cheque on to someone else.

Banks can arrange 'telegraphic transfers' of money, at home and abroad, and most international payments are made in this way. The table of foreign exchange rates in a newspaper will show that the rate for telegraphic transfers is slightly different from the rate for ordinary postal or 'mail' transfers. The time taken for letters to travel between the more distant cities of the world is so great that sometimes bank drafts are made payable several days, or even months, after the date on which they are drawn. Such drafts are really BILLS OF EXCHANGE (q.v.).

The technical business term for sending money by post, by the various methods described, is 'remitting', and the sums sent are called 'remittances'.

See also BANKING; CURRENCY.

PEDLARS AND HAWKERS. The street salesman has existed since very early times: he was, in fact, the earliest kind of shop. Though he no longer fulfils the important function he once did, he still survives; and in some countries, particularly in the East, a great deal of the normal day to day trading takes place in the street and at house doors. In Europe, from the Middle Ages until well into the 18th century, the streets of towns were full of street hawkers, sellers of flowers, fruit, fish, and various kinds of cooked food, besides menders of chairs, knife-grinders, and so on, many of them with a traditional cry or song to advertise their wares. Some of these, such as the muffin man with his bell, were to be seen in some parts in the 19th and even the 20th centuries, and the wandering rag-and-bone man is still a common sight in most towns. Mainly, however, street selling, apart from that of the regular STREET MARKETS (q.v.), is confined to flowers and fruit, though, in the streets of big towns there are still to be seen not only girls with baskets of flowers and the 'barrow boys', but also sellers of matches, bootlaces, and other small goods, and men who demonstrate clockwork toys on the pavement.

The pedlar, the wandering salesman of mixed wares, is a character rather distinct from these street vendors of the towns, though his ancestry goes back quite as far. Early names for him were 'huckster' (related to 'hawker', and still sometimes used of a 'huckster's store' where miscellaneous goods are sold) and 'chapman'.

White Yeoung parfnips Old Shoos bye any Broomes

Bodleian Library

EARLY 18TH-CENTURY LONDON STREET CRIERS

Bodleian Library

AN EARLY 19TH-CENTURY PEDLAR

The word 'pedlar' is probably derived from the old Scottish word 'ped', meaning the basket he carried. The verb 'to peddle' came later, and was derived from 'pedlar'. Pedlars were common in the Middle Ages, and valuable, since there were no shops where people could buy the household and other wares in which they dealt. Often, like Autolycus in Shakespeare's play *The Winter's Tale*, they sold BALLADS (q.v. Vol. XII), as well as trinkets of every kind. As with the street traders, there seems to have been no special legislation to govern pedlars, though they were no doubt included in the laws against vagrants. The earliest special reference to them in English law comes in a statute of Edward VI's reign, which insists that every 'pedlar, tynker, or petty chapman', selling such articles as 'pins, points (suspenders), laces, gloves, knives, glasses, tapes', should hold a licence issued by a J.P. In Queen Elizabeth's reign, when special laws were passed to clear the streets of vagrants, unlicensed pedlars were included in the list of vagabonds upon whom strict penalties were imposed (*see also* STREET ENTERTAINERS, Vol. IX).

Apart from GYPSIES (q.v. Vol. I), who generally sell goods they have made themselves, pedlars are rarely seen in the 20th century. They were common, however, until the end of the 19th century, and in 1871 a special Act, known as the Pedlar's Act, was passed to govern their position. This Act, which is still in force, defines a pedlar as 'any hawker, pedlar, petty chapman, tinker, caster of metals, mender of chairs, etc.' who 'without any horse or other beast bearing or drawing burden, travels and trades on foot and goes from town to town or to other men's houses carrying to sell or exposing for sale any goods, wares, or merchandise—or selling or offering for sale his skill in handicraft'. A tax of 5*s*. a year is imposed on him, entitling him to a certificate. He must be over 17 years of age, and able to produce references as to his character. His pack is subject to inspection by the police.

In 1888 a further act, the Hawkers' Act, was passed, which makes a legal distinction between a pedlar, who travels on foot, and a hawker, who is defined in this Act as anyone who 'travels with a horse or other beast of burden, selling goods, etc.'. The hawker, like the pedlar, must produce a certificate of good character signed by a responsible person, and must pay a tax of £2 before he is granted a licence. He must have the words 'licensed hawker' legibly written, painted, or printed on every box, package, and vehicle.

These two Acts, however, apply only to travelling salesmen dealing in their own wares. They do not cover the REPRESENTATIVES of firms, nor people who sell goods at STREET MARKETS (qq.v.); nor do they apply to vendors of food, or traders such as rag-and-bone men, who buy

R. Gorbold

A SELLER OF SWEETS IN BAGDAD

to sell again. Also exempt are all street traders who do not travel from place to place. Legally a trader who remains at a certain pitch is neither a pedlar nor a hawker, and does not need a licence unless this is required by a local bye-law in the place where he is working. There is, in fact, no special legislation to govern him, and such regulations as there are are purely local, being usually framed to limit the number of traders, and to prevent obstruction. In some towns, for instance, the by-laws may prohibit trading in the busiest parts of the town, or after certain hours at night. In London, where the numerous street traders have made tighter regulations necessary, trading is only allowed by those holding special street traders' permits.

See also STREET MARKETS.
See also Vol. VI. MARKETS.

PERFUMERY. This was originally the art of extracting the scented essences of plants and other fragrant substances and of combining them with other materials, such as grease, spirits, starch, and soaps, that had no odour or only an unattractive one. The art of the perfumer is very ancient. The Assyrians, ancient Egyptians, Phoenicians, and Persians made much use of perfumes. Tyre, on the shores of the eastern Mediterranean, was a famous export market for perfumes to be sent away by sea, and Babylon was an equally important inland market for supplying the country around. Perfumes were much used by the Greeks and Romans, and they used them in ways in which we do not use them to-day: for example, they perfumed their wines with roses, violets, and hyacinths, in much the same way as rosewater is now used in making Turkish coffee. Pliny, the Roman writer, gives many details of the trade in perfumes in ancient Rome. Like many other arts, that of the perfumer had come to Rome from Greece, and most perfumers in the time of the Roman Empire were Greeks. Their shops occupied a special quarter of the city, and were a favourite resort for fashionable loungers; they were supplied with perfumes from all parts of the then known world.

In the Middle Ages the use of perfumes spread from the southern and eastern Mediterranean towards the west. The Arabs introduced them into Spain, and France and Italy became the most important countries that made them. Many modern perfumes are mixed with alcohol, and perfumes of this kind are believed to have

Goya Ltd.

FILLING BOTTLES WITH PERFUME
The perfume is stored in large 'carboys', from which it is drawn into the bottles through rubber tubing. In the picture small phials are being filled.

been first made in the 14th century. Hungary Water, the earliest of which we have any record, was distilled from rosemary in 1370 by Queen Elizabeth of Hungary. Italy, the centre of culture and luxury of those days, was a leader in this new trade, but when Catherine of Medici left Florence for France in 1533 she took with her a famous perfumer, and ever since then the French have been the real leaders of the industry, in quality if not in quantity.

Fragrances are nowadays extracted from flowers and plants by four methods: DISTILLATION (q.v.), enfleurage, maceration, and solution. The details of each method are described in the article on OILS, VEGETABLE (q.v.). Modern stills for distillation can often take up to a ton of leaves or flowers, and may hold 1,000 gallons or more of liquid perfume. Enfleurage is now used mainly for jasmine and tuberose; the fragrant essence of the flowers is usually absorbed by a purified mixture of beef and pork fat. Fats charged with perfume by the enfleurage process are called *pomades*. Maceration means soaking the flowers in hot fat or oils at a temperature of about 150° F. Most flowers except jasmine and tuberose are now treated in

COLOUR PRINTING: FLOWER PIECE BY PAUL GAUGUIN, 1896

The four-colour print in the centre is made from the four surrounding blocks. The yellow is printed first,
then red over it (bottom left), then blue (bottom right). Finally, the black gives the finished print

this way. In the solution method the leaves or flowers are put into sealed containers with a solvent that evaporates at a fairly low temperature: petroleum ether is normally used. The solvent is then distilled away, leaving in the still what is called a 'concrete'. 'Concretes' contain unwanted waxes, which are got rid of by filtering and freezing. The solution of flower essence that is left after the waxes have been removed is then further distilled, until a residue is left which is the true essential oil or absolute essence of the flower. These essences are the most expensive raw material of the perfumery trade, and the highest classes cost many pounds per ounce. Over 1,000 tons of essence of jasmine alone are used in the world's perfume industry every year.

As well as flower extracts, certain animal extracts are used. The three most important are musk, which comes from the glands of the musk deer, a native of China; ambergris, from the sperm whale (*see* WHALING INDUSTRY, Vol. VI); and civet, which is a glandular secretion from the civet cat.

Natural flower extracts are no longer used by themselves, and synthetic or artificial perfumes are the basis of the modern industry. Most natural flower fragrances have been imitated synthetically, particularly violet, lily, lilac, hyacinth, narcissus, clover, may-blossom, orange blossom, carnation, heliotrope, **peach**, and gardenia. The cheaper perfumes **are** entirely synthetic. Better-class perfumes are a blend of synthetic essences, animal extracts, and certain gums and balsams. In all good perfumes a small quantity of natural flower essence is always used. In the making of perfumes, the synthetic essence or essences (for many perfumes **are** a blend of two or more fragrances) are first dissolved in alcohol. They are then 'toned' or blended with gums and balsams, which prevents too much evaporation and thus makes the finished perfume last longer. For the better-class perfumes natural extracts are added. The liquid is then allowed to mature in glass-lined tanks, often for many months.

The main world centres of modern perfume manufacture are Paris, London, New York, and the Mediterranean towns around Grasse in the south of France. Some of the most expensive perfumes are marketed by famous fashion houses in Paris.

See also OILS, VEGETABLE.
See also Vol. VI: OIL-BEARING PLANTS.

PERSONNEL, *see* FACTORY ORGANIZATION, Section 4; SCIENTIFIC MANAGEMENT.

PEWTER. This is a silvery-grey alloy, once much used for TABLE WARE (q.v. Vol. XI) and other domestic articles. It is composed principally of tin and lead, although lead is sometimes replaced by COPPER (q.v.) or antimony. The antiquity of pewter is shown by the reference made to it by the Hebrew prophet, Ezekiel, when the city of Tyre is said to have laid up riches of silver, iron, tin, lead, and copper, which were made into pewter vessels.

In England, pewter gradually superseded wooden platters and porringers during the Middle Ages. It supplied articles for the table for people who could not afford real silver. It went out of general use in the early 19th century when cheap china and EARTHENWARE (q.v.) became common, but it is still used to-day for such vessels as beer tankards.

The pewter-making industry was recognized by royal charters as early as the 13th century. Its chief centre was London, although the craft also flourished in York and Newcastle, and extended later to other towns. The reputation of English pewter on the Continent was second to none, although there were important centres of manufacture in France and Germany. The first written records of the Pewterers Company date from 1348.

In those days pewter consisted of tin with the addition of as much brass or copper as it would take up in the melting process—the proportion being about 4 parts tin to 1 part copper. This was called 'Fyne Peauter, No. 1', and from it were made such things as salt-cellars, platters, chargers, and ribbed or 'fluted' vessels. 'Fyne Peauter, No. 2', consisting of about 112 parts tin to 26 parts lead, was used for commoner household articles such as pots, pans, bowls, cruets, and candlesticks. This alloy is very similar to that used by the Japanese in the 17th and 18th centuries, and also to that prescribed by law for the manufacture of spoons and candlesticks in France to-day. The metal was worked either by hammering or casting. Craftsmen using the first method were called 'sadware' men ('sad' being used in the sense of 'heavy'— like 'sad cake'); those using the second were called 'hollow-ware' men. The two classes belonged to quite distinct crafts. It was the custom of those days for travelling pewterers **to** recast all worn-out and damaged pieces, and this accounts for the disappearance of much medieval pewterware.

To-day, pewter is still manufactured by casting and hammering. The pewter is melted in iron pots, and before it is ready to pour into the moulds it is stirred with a 'green' stick. This can be any piece of living shrub or tree, the theory being that the sap in the green stick generates steam when plunged into the melting pot and distributes oxygen throughout the molten metal, thereby purifying it. The green stick is also used to clear the dross from the top surface of the molten metal. The casting is generally done in gunmetal moulds. When the cast is removed from the moulds, the pewter has a white, frosted appearance. This is removed in the finishing processes, which are generally done on a lathe. Tankards and mugs are cast in two or three pieces; large dishes are made entirely by hand from rolled sheet metal which is hammered and fashioned on an anvil and on a metal pattern (a 'swage') covered with soft leathers. Some pewter vessels with roughened surfaces, particularly beer tankards, are first cast, and then finished by hand-hammering.

The old regulations of the Company laid down that pewter vessels should always be stamped, like

Topical Press Agency

PEWTER TRAYS BEING BEATEN INTO SHAPE ON TREE TRUNKS
On the left a start is made with a flat sheet of pewter; the man on the right is hammering the curved edge; and in the foreground is a finished tray

silver, with the maker's mark (*see* ASSAYING, Section 2), but the regulations seem to have been very often ignored. At one time the Pewterers Company used to lend out moulds to its members, and this accounts for articles of the same shape being found with different makers' marks on them. The Company still have some of these moulds, and moulds 300 years old are still in use.

PHOTOGRAPHY, HISTORY OF. Photography depends upon the action of light-rays focused through the LENS of a CAMERA (qq.v. Vol. VIII) on to a plate or film made chemically sensitive to light. The first definite step towards practical photography was taken in Germany in 1727, when it was found that light caused chemical changes in silver nitrate. But no apparatus existed for applying this piece of knowledge. Artists later experimented with lenses, and noticed that if they sat in a darkened room, or looked into a darkened box on one side of which was an opening with a lens, an image of the sunlit outer world would be projected at the opposite side. In the early 19th century this form of darkened chamber enabled Thomas Wedgwood to experiment in England on the action of light on silver nitrate: he coated a paper surface with the nitrate. Humphry Davy, the inventor of the miner's safety-lamp, experimented on the same lines: he discovered that silver chloride was more sensitive to light, and that the use of white leather instead of paper produced better pictures in a shorter period of exposure.

These early photographs quickly faded, because it had not yet been found possible to 'fix' the image so that it would not be affected by daylight; but in 1822 a Frenchman, J. Nicéphore Niepce, succeeded in making the first permanent photograph. In 1829 another Frenchman named Daguerre, who had been experimenting on his own, joined Niepce. By 1839 the result of their efforts was the daguerreotype, a photographic picture which was itself 'developed' and 'fixed' on to the silvered copper plate which we would now call the negative. Mercury vapour was used to develop or make visible the image. For many years the daguerreotype was the way in which photographs, usually portraits, were commercially produced, and many families still have early-Victorian daguerreotypes among their relics. In 1839 also, William Fox Talbot, a wealthy English experimenter, disclosed to the

Royal Society his 'calotype' process, which in many ways is the real basis of modern photography. Talbot used thin semi-transparent paper for his sensitized coating. Having first produced on this what we now call a 'negative' (a word first suggested by Sir J. Herschel in 1841), in which the bright parts of the original object appear dark, he obtained 'positives' or prints from it by contact printing on another piece of sensitized paper.

The later history of photography consisted mainly of improvements on Fox Talbot's work. Paper had disadvantages as a negative: it was always to some extent opaque, and light would,

AN EARLY CALOTYPE BY FOX TALBOT
From the Fox Talbot Collection, Science Museum, London

therefore, not pass through it easily. In 1843 Herschel suggested glass, and glass became the customary material for what were soon called photographic 'plates'. The photograph film was invented some years later, but plates are still used in professional photographers' studios, and also in printing-works (*see* PROCESS REPRODUCTION).

In 1848 F. Scott Archer first experimented with what became known as the 'wet collodion' process. This soon took the place of calotypes and daguerreotypes, and rapid improvements followed. In 1856 Parkes proposed and patented a flexible film instead of a glass plate, and shortly afterwards the manufacture of films on a commercial scale was started by Hyatt in the U.S.A. In 1873 Willis invented the platinotype process for printing positives, in which a paper coated with ferric oxalate and a salt of platinum and silver was used for making 'contact' prints. Until the middle 1870's the great drawback to photography was the length of exposure. A person whose portrait was being taken on a daguerreotype had to sit absolutely still for 30 minutes, with the back of his head held steady in a clamp. Fox Talbot's calotype process required 3 minutes. Scott Archer's process involved an exposure of only 10 seconds; but there was not a great deal of difference between 30

minutes and 10 seconds, as in either period only a very still object could be taken. In 1874 Kennett produced on a commercial scale the first successful 'dry' plate, which greatly increased 'speed', that is, diminished the period of exposure.

In 1889 George Eastman (later the founder of the Eastman Kodak Company of the U.S.A.) introduced a roll-film of celluloid, to be used in the first portable roll-film camera. In 1891 the Eastman Kodak Company improved this roll-film by a light-proof paper backing, so that it could be loaded into a camera by daylight. This was an important landmark in the history of photography. Not only did the portable camera make photography possible as a pastime, but it also helped the very early cinema experiments. Moving pictures had been first produced by Muybridge and Marey in the 1870's. Later Thomas A. Edison used the new Eastman roll-film for his first successful motion pictures. In 1882 paper coated with gelatino-chloride, which has since come to be known as printing-out-paper or P.O.P., came into general use. This paper can be seen to darken gradually, and so the quality of the printing can be watched as it goes on. Later came the so-called 'gaslight' or bromide papers, invented and improved since 1890, which require development to bring out the image.

Early in the present century a 'film pack' was invented, a store of flat films which could easily be inserted in the camera, and which made it unnecessary for photographers to carry a bulky batch of plates. In 1913 the autographic film was produced; after taking each picture the photographer wrote its title, with a metal point, on the red paper backing of the film, through a hole at the back of the camera; the writing 'scratched' the red surface of the paper, and light passed through, printing the writing on the film, which showed up when developed.

Improvements in colour photography made in the present century are based on the experiments of CLERK MAXWELL in 1861 (q.v. Vol. V). He discovered that different coloured objects had different effects on a photographic negative. This discovery was the basis of two lines of development. The earlier plates and films were sensitive only to violet and ultra-violet rays (see COLOUR, Vol. III); if an object containing blues, greens, and reds was photographed, the greens and reds came out darker in the photograph, and the blues lighter than they would appear if viewed by the human eye. This discovery led to colour photography, by means of different coloured light-filters; and also to the invention of the orthochromatic plate or film, by using which it was possible for photographs to reproduce far more faithfully the real colour values of the original. The Clerk Maxwell method of colour photography was developed by the Eastman Kodak Company and by the Gaumont Company for motion pictures.

Apart from pleasure, photography is important in science and industry. Without it the illustration of newspapers and magazines would be practically impossible. It has many scientific uses. It is the basis of the cardiograph, used by doctors for recording movements of the heart, and of radiography or X-RAY photography (q.v. Vol. XI). In seismography the recording of distant earthquake movements is done photographically. Aerial photography is not only of military value but also much used in SURVEYING (q.v. Vol. VIII).

Bodleian Library

MICROPHOTOGRAPH RE-
DUCED FROM A MEDIEVAL
MANUSCRIPT

The actual height of the page is 21¼ inches

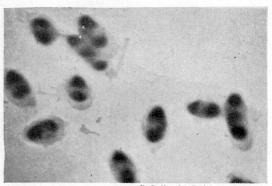

J. Smiles, Medical Research Council

PHOTOMICROGRAPH OF BACTERIA OF EPIDEMIC TYPHUS, ENLARGED 10,000

In 1916 the Royal Flying Corps, the forerunner of the R.A.F., first used a camera with a dummy machine-gun, which recorded photographically the accuracy of the aim taken by opposing fighter pilots. Photography provides the basis of the 'photostat' method of reproducing documents, plans, and legal records (see OFFICE EQUIPMENT). Microphotography is now an important branch of photography. A special lens is used in the camera so that a very small photograph of an object is produced. The earliest practical use of microphotography was in Paris during the German siege of 1870: very small photographs of letters and newspapers were sent out of the city on quills attached to the legs of carrier pigeons. Microphotography was found very useful in the Second World War when, owing to the risk of bomb damage to documents, microphotographic copies were made, and a vast quantity of information could then be stored in a very small space. If a very small object like bacteria is photographed through a microscope, a photomicrograph is obtained; this can enlarge the appearance of the object several thousand times. Photomicrography is also much used in metallurgy and engineering, for examining the quality and structure of metals and alloys.

See also Vol. IX: PHOTOGRAPHY.

PHOTOGRAVURE, *see* PROCESS REPRODUCTION.

PIECE-WORK, *see* WAGES.

PLANNING, INDUSTRIAL, *see* FACTORY ORGANIZATION, Section 5.

PLASTICS. 1. This term is given to all sorts of materials which can be moulded, squeezed, cast, or squirted into some desired shape. Many of these materials are not connected with one another in any way, nor are the various methods used in their manufacture. For instance, a tarry stuff called bitumen, taken from a lake in the West Indies, can be hardened and squeezed into the shape of the black stoppers that screw into beer bottles. The india-rubber material taken from trees in Malaya can be filled with air bubbles before it hardens, in order to make a sponge for the bathroom or a springy cushion for a bus seat; or a liquid chemical can be squirted through a small hole so that it dries in the form of a very thin filament, from which the yarn for knitting women's nylon stockings can be spun. All these things can be referred to as 'plastics'. The word 'plastic' itself is really an adjective meaning 'capable of being shaped by pressure'.

One advantage of plastic materials is that their properties may be altered in various ways, either by changing the mixtures or combinations of raw materials, or by changing the amount of heat or pressure used in manufacture. In such ways a plastic material may be given one or more of the following special qualities: hardness or softness; resilience (a springy or cushioning quality); insulation against electricity; transparency, or else its opposite, opacity; resistance to heat or cold; resistance to wear, blows, scratching, vibration, or other mechanical stresses; resistance to the effects of water, oil, chemicals, and various foods which might corrode a container.

From the earliest recorded times resinous and wax-like materials found in nature were collected and refined, for useful or decorative purposes. These natural products are too few for men's needs to-day, and in recent times intensive chemical research has led to new products. In the first half of the 20th century rapid progress was made in producing artificial materials. Plastics can therefore be classed in two main groups: natural and synthetic (artificial). A rigid division must not be drawn between the two, for natural and artificial plastics are sometimes combined. There is also a group consisting of natural materials that have been modified artificially by chemical means. Moreover, the synthetic plastics industry is dependent upon nature for its raw materials, such as coal, petroleum, and wood and other substances containing cellulose.

2. NATURAL PLASTIC MATERIALS. In this group there are four outstanding classes: the GUMS AND RESINS, the bitumens and waxes, RUBBER and gutta-percha, and the CLAYS (qq.v.).

Waxes are of animal and vegetable origin. Beeswax, paraffin and other waxes from petroleum, and the ozokerite, ceresin, and montan-earth waxes have long been used for waterproofing papers and textiles, for bottle-sealing, for polishes, and for moulding into shapes. The black stoppers for beer bottles and cases for electric batteries are examples of the use of bitumen as a plastic moulding material. Bitumens or pitches come from natural deposits, like the famous Trinidad lake (*see* ASPHALT, Vol. III); and they are obtained from petroleum and other oil residues, or by 'blowing' these oils with air. They also come from coal-tar (*see* BY-PRODUCTS).

Rubber was an early industrial plastic. In the mid-19th century the secret of combining sulphur with rubber was discovered, a process known as 'vulcanization', which makes it possible to increase the hardness of the final product by increasing the amount of sulphur used. The hard rubber, containing 20% to 30% of sulphur, is known as vulcanite or ebonite. The various qualities of rubber can be produced as rods, tubes, sheets, or mouldings, and have varied uses for electrical insulation, waterproofing, and chemical plant.

Clays are natural plastics, on which the potter's art depends (*see* POTTERY).

3. SYNTHETIC PLASTIC MATERIALS. The most important of the plastic materials used to-day are synthetic. For convenience they can be divided into the 'thermosetting' and 'thermoplastic' varieties. A thermosetting plastic is one based on a resin in which the process of shaping and moulding under heat creates a permanent change in the material; that is, it cannot be dissolved, melted, or moulded again. By contrast, a thermoplastic resin is one which can be shaped under heat, but which does not undergo an irreversible change; the article can be again rendered plastic by heat and re-shaped. There are also some synthetic plastics that fall outside these two groups.

(*a*) Thermosetting materials. The firm establishment of the plastics industry is probably due to phenolic resins, which were developed rapidly between the First and Second World Wars, after many years of preliminary research. Phenolic

A HUGE PRESS FOR MAKING THERMOSETTING PLASTIC BOARDS

resins are produced by combining phenol with formaldehyde. Phenol is a BY-PRODUCT (q.v.) of tar, which in turn is a by-product of coal; formaldehyde is made from wood alcohol, which is a product of the destructive DISTILLATION of wood (q.v.). In 1872 a hard resinous substance was first made by combining these two materials. Early in this century Dr. Leo Baekeland showed that this chemical process could be controlled to make useful commercial products. As a tribute to his work the word 'bakelite' is still used for this type of resin, for which 'phenolic resins' is the more correct technical name.

The phenolic resins are dark in colour. The demand for articles in pale and pastel shades led to the setting up of another group of thermosetting materials, known as the amino, urea, or 'beetle' plastics. Commercial production began in the early 1930's, and later a similar resin called melamine was made.

(*b*) Thermoplastic materials. The first important synthetic material of the thermoplastic group was based on nitrocellulose. Nitrocellulose was known in Switzerland in 1846, but the first cellulose plastic was not produced until an English scientist, Alexander Parkes, discovered in 1864 that a horn-like solid could be produced by combining nitrocellulose, camphor, and alcohol. Americans had similar success in searching for a suitable material for billiard balls. In this way the highly inflammable 'celluloid' came into use.

Research for a non-inflammable celluloid led to cellulose acetate in 1865; this was produced commercially by the end of the century. Acetate film was used in 1912 for photographic purposes; sheet, rod, and tube were available in 1927 for bending into certain shapes; powders were made by 1934 for moulding into more complicated shapes. It was, however, bulk production for spinning into 'acetate' RAYON (q.v.) that made this plastic so important. In more recent years two others, cellulose butyrate and cellulose propionate, have been produced; for some purposes they are superior to the acetate, as when an article has to resist damp. Ethyl cellulose is another thermoplastic material of this type.

Other important thermoplastic resins produced commercially include the acrylic, polystyrene, and vinyl resins. Polyvinyl chloride, or

P.V.C., is the most used of these products. Polythene, formed by the chemical treatment of the simple hydrocarbon ethylene under very high pressure, was available in 1937. NYLON (q.v.) is a recent thermoplastic.

The thermoplastics all soften when heated, but at a heat greater than 140 to 175° F. they risk being distorted. By treating ethylene with fluorine, and then using heat and pressure, a plastic is produced which will safely withstand temperatures of 400 to 480° F.

Plastics of a different class are the 'regenerated' celluloses. Purified wood cellulose is dissolved in one of several chemical solutions, and squirted through a small opening into another solution, where the cellulose takes form again as a thin strand which can be spun into viscose rayon yarn. Film of the 'cellophane' variety can be made in this way. Paper and pulp can be partially treated to produce 'hydrated paper', 'parchmentized paper' and 'leatheroid'; treated papers can be built up to yield 'vulcanized' or hard fibre, which is tough and leathery, and is used for making suitcases.

Another plastic material in a class by itself is hardened casein. This is made from milk with formaldehyde, and was once much used for such things as buttons, buckles, and handles, but it is affected by damp.

See also PLASTICS IN INDUSTRY; CHEMISTRY, INDUSTRIAL.

PLASTICS IN INDUSTRY. 1. MANUFACTURE.

Most PLASTICS (q.v.) are combined with other substances in the manufacture of plastic articles. To give it bulk, a plastic is often combined with a 'filler' or filling material, such as wood flour (sawdust), chopped cotton or fabric, inorganic powders such as CHINA CLAY, MICA dust (qq.v.), slate dust, or mixtures of these and also with colouring matter. Plastic moulding powders (thermosetting powders) are pressed in hot moulds and thus become rigid articles. Thermoplastic powders coalesce and soften when heated, and are injected into cool moulds, to set to the desired shapes. Plastic solutions can soak into paper or textile sheeting, and a number of layers can be built up and pressed hot, to make sheets or boards. Used in this way, the thermosetting resins produce hard, rigid boards which do not soften with heat and which are known as laminated from their layer-like formation. The phenolic resins can be cast into rods, sheets, and other shapes.

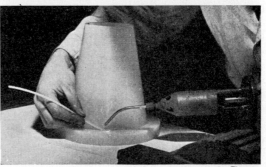

Tenaplas

MAKING OBJECTS OF THERMOPLASTIC POLYTHENE
Above, the polythene is being shaped by a lathe; and below, two pieces are being welded together

Thermoplastics can be 'extruded', that is to say, squeezed out through a narrow opening on the same principle as toothpaste leaving a tube. The hot material can be forced under pressure through a die of the required shape. It can also be extruded and hot-rolled into film or sheet. Film can be made in another way by continuous evaporation from solution fed on to rollers. Threads and fibres can be made by extrusion and spun into yarn or woven into fabric sheets. Many thermoplastics can be filled with air bubbles and expanded into light-weight sponge-like products, such as expanded rubber or 'Sorbo'.

2. ELECTRICAL ARTICLES. The electrical industry has greatly encouraged plastics because its needs are so exacting. Mouldings are used for insulators, boxes, and cabinets. In Britain the telephone hand-set is moulded in black bakelite or coloured beetle; in America, cellulose acetate butyrate or propionate is used for this. Cabinets for radio-receivers are moulded in bakelite or beetle. Polythene, which helped to make RADAR practicable (q.v. Vol. VIII), is used for insulating the cabling. The fluorinated poly-

thenes (PTFE) were essential to the development of ATOMIC ENERGY (q.v. Vol. VIII). Silicones enabled smaller transformers to be built for war-time aircraft. P.V.C. was substituted when rubber was short during the Second World War, and later came into use for cable insulation. Cellulose acetate film is an improvement on paper and fabric for coil insulation. Laminated phenolic resin paper or fabric is the main insulation in board form. Moulded bitumen compounds are used for battery cases. Grey vulcanized fibre is used in railway track insulation, and red fibre provides the fronts of switch-boards.

3. BUILDING INDUSTRY. Bakelite and urea-laminated sheets are used for panellings. The coloured and patterned walls of many milk bars are made from this material: their surface can imitate polished woodwork. It is used for counter-tops and table-tops, and also for furniture. Its qualities are permanence, freedom from damage by moisture and fungi, and great strength. Mouldings in bakelite or urea are used for knobs, handles, light-switches, and clock-cases. Coloured forms of P.V.C., cellulose acetate, or polythene, some of them patterned, embossed, or crinkled, make lamp shades, and the methacrylates are used instead of glass for transparent shades.

T. H. and J. Daniels

A 100-TON PRESS FOR MOULDING PLASTIC ELECTRIC SWITCHES

4. CHEMICAL INDUSTRY. Metal tanks are lined with polythene, P.V.C., or hard rubber to resist corrosion by chemicals. Tanks are also made entirely of hard rubber or mineral-loaded bakelite. The vinyls and polythene are used for containers, for pipe-lines and ducts, and for cocks and valves; and they can be fitted together by welding in much the same way as metals are welded. PTFE has become important in making gaskets, to prevent leakage of gases or liquids at joints; it plays a part in making fluorine compounds, such as uranium hexafluoride for atomic energy. Polythene bottles, beakers, flasks, and buckets are used in laboratories.

5. WRAPPING. Plastic films of regenerated cellulose (cellophane), cellulose acetate and butyrate, rubber hydrochloride (pliofilm), P.V.C., and polythene are used for wrapping and packaging. Polythene is particularly important for 'cold pack' foods, such as refrigerated fruits and vegetables. Various forms of closure for bottles, tubes, pots, and jars are moulded in bakelite or cellulose acetate, while beer-bottle stoppers are moulded in bitumen compound. Containers or boxes are moulded or shaped in transparent plastic. Firms packing goods for the tropics use polythene, heat-sealed, to give an airtight closure. Vinyl solutions can be sprayed to give a complete envelope around an article, and enable it to resist the weather. War stores were protected in this way when shipped during the Second World War from America to the Far East; aircraft were carried as deck cargo, and, when the plastic films were peeled off on arrival, the aircraft were ready to take the air.

6. CONSTRUCTIONAL. Wood joined together or 'bonded' with phenolic resin is a light but strong constructional material. It made the design of the Mosquito R.A.F. aircraft possible, and has been used for air gliders and small boats, such as canoes and motor launches, and even for aeroplane propellers. Synthetic resin adhesives enable waterproof plywood to be made, and are also used in aircraft construction for cementing light alloys together. This improves flying, for the joints are as strong as those made by riveting, and have less wind-resistance.

7. LIQUID USES. Solvent solutions form the basis of adhesives, cements, paints, varnishes, enamels, and coating materials. Practically all modern lacquers, varnishes, and enamels used in industrial finishing have a synthetic plastic base. Nitrocellulose yields lacquers and enamels,

Tenaplas

EXTRUSION OF P.V.C. PLASTIC

Grains of P.V.C. are fed from the hopper on the right to the barrel of the machine. The material is heated by electric elements until it is soft and then forced through a die or nozzle to give it the required shape. The shaped plastic cools and comes out of the barrel in a long strip at the lower right of the picture

including the finishing materials for furniture and other woodwork, and for metal surfaces such as motor-car bodies. Melamine resin enamels are used in making refrigerators. Cellulose acetate is used for the lacquers which protect the cores of CABLES (q.v. Vol. IV). The phenolics, ureas, and melamines form the basis of air-drying and stoving enamels and varnishes.

8. MISCELLANEOUS. Rubber, expanded rubber, and expanded P.V.C. are used for resilient cushioning blocks to mount the engines in more expensive motor-cars, to prevent the passengers from feeling vibration. Both polystyrene and poly-methacrylate are used for lenses, on account of their admirable optical properties. Spectacle frames are made from cast resin or from acetate.

PLATE, SHEFFIELD, *see* SHEFFIELD PLATE.

PLATINUM is almost invariably found in nature in metallic form, and not as a compound or ore (*see* METAL ORES, Vol. III). It is, however, never found in absolutely pure form, but generally in company with one or more of five other metals, which together with platinum are called the 'platinum metals'. These others are iridium, osmium, palladium, rhodium, and ruthenium. The platinum metals are found principally in Brazil, Central America, Russia, Australia, Borneo, California, and the Union of South Africa. Tasmania is now the chief source of osmiridium, a mixture of iridium and osmium.

The platinum metals are important in industry, mainly for two reasons: they are very little affected by heat, and do not melt until heated to very high temperatures; they also possess excellent powers of catalytic action, that is, they can speed up chemical processes without themselves being affected by them. Owing to their high melting-point, which enables them to glow brightly without melting, they were originally much used for electric bulbs, and the trade name 'Osram' was adopted because osmium was the principal constituent of the filaments used in these lamps. Platinum itself, usually reinforced with one or other of the platinum metals to give it added toughness, is much used for laboratory work in chemistry, because it resists ACIDS (q.v.). One of the main modern uses of platinum is in the JEWELLERY TRADE (q.v.). It is used either by itself, or in the form of an alloy called 'white gold', which is a mixture of gold with a small quantity of platinum or palladium. Platinum salts are also the basis of the platinotype process of photographic printing, which gives pleasing results in portraiture.

PLUMBAGO, *see* GRAPHITE.

PLYWOOD AND VENEERS. Before plywood was thought of, thin sheets or veneers of expensive and rare woods had been used as facings on less costly wood, particularly for furniture. This use of veneers is very old—archaeologists have found evidence of it in Egyptian sculptures dating from about 1500 B.C. How the original veneers were cut has not been discovered, but they were fixed with some kind of animal glue and weighted down with sandbags until the glue had set. After these earlier uses there was a long interval during which only solid wood was in general use; but veneering was revived in the late 17th century in France and Holland, whence the practice of the craft spread to England (*see* INLAY AND MARQUETRY). The exact date when ornamental

THREE-PLY

MULTI-PLY
(7 PLIES)

BLOCKBOARD

LAMIN BOARD

TYPES OF PLYWOOD

veneering suggested the idea of using plywood for more general purposes is uncertain; but in the second half of the 19th century plywood was used for tea-chests in the China tea trade, and for curved perforated seats for railway stations and tramcars.

Plywood in its simplest form consists of three thin layers or veneers of wood glued together so that the grain of one veneer runs at right angles to that of the next. This arrangement gives the piece of plywood equal strength in both directions. There are other advantages. Shrinkage is reduced to a minimum; there is little or no tendency to split; and as veneers can be cut from big logs at their greatest width, plywood can be made in large sizes. The so-called 'waterproof plywood' made with special glues is so resistant to the action of water that it will not come to pieces even if soaked or exposed to the weather for a long time. Plywood can also be moulded to various shapes and will keep them more or less indefinitely.

In the present century the development of commercial plywood has been rapid, and there are now several types. Three-ply is the simplest. Multi-ply may have any odd number of veneers. Blockboard has blocks of solid timber with thick veneers glued to each side. Diagonal plywood has the grain of each layer running at an angle of 45° to the grain of the next. Lamin board has a core of strips of wood glued together with the grain running at right angles to the veneers. Plywood may itself be faced on one or both sides with a decorative veneer, or even with thin sheets of metal such as steel, copper, or zinc.

Before the Second World War, European birch, mostly from Finland and Sweden, was the timber chiefly used for plywood. Other woods used were Canadian Yellow Birch, Douglas Fir or Oregon Pine, European Alder, and Gaboon from French West Africa.

Most veneers for plywood are cut from a log on a rotary cutting machine. This is a kind of giant lathe, in which a round log is revolved against a stationary knife, and the veneer comes off in a thin continuous sheet. This process is called 'peeling', and logs suitable for it are often called 'peelers'. Peeling is a highly skilled operation, for much good wood may be wasted if the knife angle is incorrect or the speed of rotation is wrong. After the veneer has been peeled off it is trimmed to size, and then dried in a drying-kiln, into which the damp veneer is fed at one end and from which it emerges dry at the other (see TIMBER INDUSTRY, Section 2).

There are two main ways of sticking the veneers together. An automatic glue-spreader may be used, looking like a clothes mangle with a trough of glue at the bottom. The rollers pick up glue from the trough and the veneer becomes covered with glue as it passes through the rollers. The other method requires 'glue film', which is thin paper impregnated with glue. This is put between the veneers and becomes liquid under heat in the presses. Veneers, when glued, are arranged in the necessary number of layers, and the panels of plywood are then carried to the press. This is usually a hydraulic press (see Vol. VIII, p. 213), and can press several panels at once; steel sheets or 'plattens' keep each panel separate from the next. Some glues require the pressing process to be cold; others require heat treatment, and the plattens are then heated by steam. Heat treatment reduces the setting time of certain synthetic resin glues from hours to a mere matter of minutes. On coming from the press the plywood boards have their edges trimmed and their faces surfaced by scraping or sandpapering; they are then inspected for defects, and graded. Large-sized boards are made by glueing several smaller boards together by long taper joints. This process is known as 'scarfing'.

Much of the success of modern plywood construction arises from improved glues. The early vegetable glues made from starch, and animal glues made from bones or skin, were apt to be spoilt by BACTERIA and MOULD (qq.v. Vol. II), and they failed to hold if the plywood got wet.

John Wright and Sons

A PEELING-MACHINE FOR CUTTING SHEETS OF VENEER FROM A LOG

Casein, made from milk, is still widely used; it resists water, but it can be affected by mould. Since 1930, synthetic resin adhesives have been used (*see* GUMS AND RESINS). There are two main types: the urea formaldehyde (or U.F.) resins, which are moderately, but not entirely, resistant to moisture; and the phenol formaldehyde (or P.F.) resins, which can be exposed to the weather, or even submerged in water for long periods, without being affected at all. The choice of glue naturally depends on the use to which the plywood is to be put. The P.F. resins are principally used for aircraft construction and for boat-building.

Plywood lends itself well to being moulded into various shapes. The simplest way to bend it is to press it while the glue is still wet against a solid block shaped to the desired curve, and to keep it there until the glue has set. This was the earliest method used, and it is still used for simple bends; but it will not work when bends in more than one direction are required in the same sheet of plywood. For this kind of bending or moulding a new technique has been evolved. A mould in the desired shape is made from wood or other materials, and the freshly glued plywood is placed upon it. The whole is then covered with a sheet of rubber or plastic, and put in a pressure chamber called an 'autoclave'. Here it is subjected to heat and air-pressure, by which the rubber sheet is forced against the plywood and the plywood against the mould. The heat hastens the setting of the glue. This process, which is often called the 'rubber bag' method, can be used for boat hulls, which can thus be made in one pressing.

Plywood is still used for tea-chests, and for boxes and packing-cases of all kinds. It is used in boat-building and ship-building for many purposes, from the hulls of small boats to the bulkheads of ships. In the building trade it is used for interior walls and partitions in shops, offices, and factories, and sometimes even for exterior walls, for floors, doors, kitchen cabinets and fitments, and as shuttering for the construction of concrete walls. It is used in the FURNITURE TRADE (q.v.), and for running up cheap buildings and sheds on farms. It is much used for the construction of railway carriages and wagons, and in the construction of certain aircraft. It is widely used for sports goods—table-tennis bats and laminated skis are examples—and also for making trunks and other baggage. Manufacturers of wireless and television sets make much use of it.

See also TIMBER INDUSTRY; FURNITURE TRADE; CABINET-MAKING.
See also Vol. VI: TIMBER.

POLICY, INSURANCE, *see* INSURANCE.

PORCELAIN. This term includes all POTTERY (q.v.) which is translucent, that is, through which light can be seen. Porcelain can be classified into three main types: the hard porcelain, sometimes called 'true porcelain', of China and of Europe; the soft porcelain of the 18th century, now no longer made; and the 'bone china' of England, which comes somewhere between the two. The term 'china' was first used for wares imported from China itself; these were greatly admired, and European potters tried to imitate both their texture and their decoration. The term properly means English porcelain, but it is now often used for any kind of table-ware.

The porcelain of the Far East was a development of STONEWARE (q.v.), from which it differed only in being whiter and more translucent. At first it was made in strong sculptural shapes; but gradually these became freer and lighter, and more and more painted decoration was used. A beautiful blue-and-white painted porcelain, which had a great influence on Delft ware (*see* EARTHENWARE) and early European

PORCELAIN JAR WITH 'FAMILLE VERTE' DECORATION
Chinese, period of K'ang Hsi

porcelain, was first made during the Ming dynasty of Chinese emperors (A.D. 1368–1644), and was at its best during the reign of K'ang Hsi (1662–1722). At the same time, delicate monochrome (one-colour) glazes were used in greens, blues, yellows, and the copper-red glaze known by the French name *sang-de-bœuf* (ox-blood). Later we find decoration in soft coloured glazes or 'enamels' painted all over the shapes, and known by the respective ground colours as *famille verte* (green), *famille noire* (black), *famille jaune* (yellow), and *famille rose* (pink). In the 18th century, Chinese porcelain reached that final stage of fragile delicacy and prettiness which was to impress itself on European wares for a long time.

The first successful attempts to produce hard porcelain in Europe were made near the German town of Dresden about 1709, and soon afterwards porcelain appeared at Vienna, St. Petersburg (Leningrad), and elsewhere. Meanwhile, other experiments in Venice and in France led to the making of soft porcelain, *pâte tendre* (soft paste), which was softer and quite different in composition, being really a kind of opaque glassy material. Much interesting work was done in soft porcelain, and to a French factory at Sèvres, under the patronage of the influential Marquise de Pompadour, we probably owe the form of our present-day cup and saucer. With the discovery of CHINA CLAY (q.v.) at Alençon (France), about 1758, *pâte tendre* was gradually replaced at Sèvres by *pâte dure* (hard paste).

In Britain soft paste was made before 1750. Meanwhile china clay and china stone (which gives porcelain its translucency) were discovered in Cornwall. Experiments were made at Plymouth, and later at Bristol and at North Stafford, but English potters never succeeded in making practical use of hard porcelain. Other experiments were being made at Chelsea, Derby, and Worcester, and these resulted in the discovery of 'bone china', which is made by adding ground and burnt animal bone to the china clay mixture. This distinctively English paste needed a lower heat to fire it than was needed for hard porcelain, and a soft glaze was applied to it. Josiah Spode the younger perfected the technique about 1800, and it is now the only kind of porcelain made in Britain. The decoration of early English china consisted chiefly of delicate overglaze painting, at first under the influence of Sèvres. During the 19th century it became

FLOWER BOWL OF ROSE POMPADOUR SÈVRES PORCELAIN,
DATED 1757
From the original in the Wallace Collection, by permission

over-elaborate and ornately gilded; but the 20th century has shown signs of a return to free yet restrained brush-work decoration.

See also POTTERY; EARTHENWARE; STONEWARE.

POTTERY is the general name given to all objects made of clay and certain other minerals when they have been 'fired'—that is, hardened by heat in the potter's kiln. When heated, clay undergoes chemical changes, and the resulting pottery is a substance quite different in its physical and chemical properties. 'Sunbaked' pottery is merely dried clay, not true pottery.

Pottery is one of the oldest crafts, practised as soon as man learned to control fire, and long before the smelting of metals. Prehistoric man made pots for storing and cooking food, for ritual vessels and large burial urns; and he also made pottery figures of men and animals. Pottery is thus very important to archaeologists, who sometimes find in this imperishable material the only record of a forgotten race (*see* ARCHAEOLOGY, Vol. I).

CLAY (q.v.) is the residue of the natural weathering of rocks, mainly granite and feldspar. White CHINA CLAY (q.v.), the Chinese 'kaolin', which in England is found only in Cornwall, is a 'sedimentary' clay—one which has remained on the site of the original rock. Surface clays are usually not pure enough to be good for pottery; but modelling clay may be of any kind that is sufficiently plastic, and it can generally be fired quite successfully at a low temperature. Plasticity is a quality that clay possesses more

than any other material; when moist, clay can be formed easily into any shape, and will retain that shape when dry. Potters' methods depend to a great extent on this quality of plasticity.

There are three principal ways in which objects can be made in pottery. The first is modelling: an object can simply be squeezed into shape from a lump of soft clay, using the fingers and palms of the hands, and can then be trimmed, if needed, by any simple tool, such as a knife or pointed stick. The second way is 'throwing': the soft clay is spun round on a potter's wheel, and is shaped by the hands while spinning round; this method can be used only for round objects, such as cups, bowls, or dishes. The third way is moulding: by this method, a pattern object is made, and then pressed into some soft substance which becomes moulded to its shape; the mould is made hard, and soft clay is then pressed into it and becomes a copy of the pattern.

Figure groups are either directly modelled or moulded, or are made by a combination of both methods. The delicate groups made in the 18th century at Chelsea and Derby, and the even more elaborate ones of continental manufacture, were partly moulded and partly built up by direct modelling. Pottery can be decorated by painting, incised ornament (knife marks), or modelled details. It is usually covered with a 'glaze', in one of the many available colours and textures, as described later on.

Brighton Museum

MODELLED POTTERY GROUP, STAFFORDSHIRE, 18TH CENTURY

THROWING A POT ON A WHEEL

The potter draws up the clay as the wheel revolves, shaping it with one hand outside and the other inside

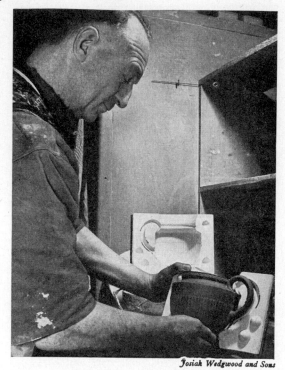

Josiah Wedgwood and Sons

REMOVING A TEA-POT FROM A MOULD

The plaster mould is made in several parts so that it can be removed without damaging the object

There are three main types of pottery: EARTHENWARE, STONEWARE, and PORCELAIN (qq.v.). The difference between them lies in the kind of clay and other materials from which they are made, and in the method of firing. The earliest pots were made by pinching, coiling, stroking, or otherwise shaping the clay with the fingers, or by pressing it into a basket, or even perhaps into a hole in the ground (see PREHISTORIC POTTERY, Vol. I). These pots were often very well made, quite 'true' in shape, and sometimes beautifully thin and light; some were so smoothly finished that one can only guess at the method employed. No one knows where or when the first potter's wheel was made; it probably developed slowly from the stone or mat on which a pot was slowly turned while being shaped by hand, and it may have developed independently in several parts of the world. The Chinese claim to have invented it, but so far the evidence points to Asia Minor, where the earliest wheel-made pottery yet found was unearthed at Ur of the Chaldees; it was under a layer of clay which is thought to have been deposited there at the

time of Noah's flood, about 5,000 years ago. Wheel-made pottery has been found also in ancient Assyria, in Egypt, Crete, and the Aegean—where very fine shapes were made in Homer's time, about 1000 B.C.—and later in Greece and Rome. The Romans introduced the potter's wheel wherever they settled; there was little if any wheel-made pottery in Britain before their occupation.

The potter's wheel is a horizontal disc of wood or metal, rather like the turntable of a gramophone, mounted on a pivot so that it can be made to revolve easily, either by its own momentum once started, or by some other means, such as a foot-treadle or a motor: for both the potter's hands must be free to control the clay. 'Throwing on the wheel' is not only the most characteristic but also the most interesting of all pottery processes. It makes the fullest use of the clay's peculiar quality of being both plastic and tensile (able to be pulled out or stretched). A lump of soft clay is placed on the wheel, and this is then made to spin quickly. The potter's wet hands smooth and control the clay till it looks like a spinning top. The lump is then hollowed out with the fingers into a cup shape; the cup is stretched up until it becomes a straight-sided cylinder; finally the cylindrical shape is further stretched into the springing curves typical of this process. All this is done within a few minutes while the wheel spins round. The term 'throwing' refers to the fact that the potter's hands guide the spinning clay against its 'throw' or centrifugal tendency to fly off the wheel. Wherever the wheel came into use, hand-building methods were largely abandoned; but until recently the wheel had not reached parts of Africa, Central America, or the South Seas.

When pottery is to be cast in a mould, the mould is usually made of plaster and clay, thinned down by water, is poured into it up to the neck of the mould. The clay nearest the mould dries quickest, so that when a sufficiently thick layer has been allowed to dry, the rest of the clay is poured out. In drying, the clay shrinks, and the cast comes away easily. Moulding came into general use in Britain in the 18th century, especially for non-circular shapes. At this time thrown shapes were afterwards turned with tools till they were thin and mechanically accurate. Cups, saucers, and plates are made, as in the past, on a machine known as a 'jigger and jolley'. This consists of a revolving wheel-head holding a plaster mould which shapes the inside of the article, and a metal profile suspended over it which can be brought down to trim the outside, the clay shape being made between the mould and the profile. Cup handles are moulded and applied afterwards. The typical shapes and proportions of modern household china were more or less settled during the 18th century (see CHINA, HOUSEHOLD, Vol. XI).

When the pots have been made, they are thoroughly dried, and are then ready to be fired in a kiln or furnace. Firing means gradually heating the ware to the temperature necessary to effect cer-

tain chemical changes in the clay, and an equally gradual cooling down. 800° C., a bright red heat, is enough for very 'soft' pottery; the harder kinds may need up to 1400°, a bright yellow heat. The time taken for firing pottery varies with the size and type of kiln and the temperature needed, the shortest being not less than 24 hours, while large kilns may take up to 2 weeks. The most primitive type of firing is just a bonfire of pots and brushwood, partly earthed over to make it burn slowly. Rather more elaborate is the covered trench hearth, with the pots piled up at the end in what is really a short up-draught chimney. The traditional English 'bottle kiln' or 'bottle oven' is a development of the up-draught chimney, and is sometimes as high as 30 feet, with four to six fire-mouths at the base. For firing in these kilns the ware is packed in oval or circular boxes made of heat-resisting fireclay (see FIRECLAYS AND REFRACTORIES, Vol. VIII). These boxes are called 'saggars'. The even firing of these large kilns needs great skill and judgement. But the bottle kilns which still dominate the landscape of the Potteries, in Staffordshire, where the industry is concentrated, are gradually being replaced. The modern system is one of continuous firing in tunnel kilns, through which the ware, mounted on trolleys, slowly passes from the cool end to the hot centre and on to the

Josiah Wedgwood and Sons

LOADING TRUCKS FOR FIRING IN AN ELECTRIC TUNNEL OVEN

Josiah Wedgwood and Sons

TAKING A PAPER PRINT FROM AN ENGRAVED PLATE
The pattern is transferred from the paper on to the pottery

cool farther end. These kilns are heated by gas or electricity, and are kept at a constant temperature.

After the first firing the ware is known as 'biscuit', and is now ready to be glazed. Glaze is a coating of glass which makes the surface of the pottery smooth and non-porous. Primitive wares were not usually glazed. Even Greek pottery was not really glazed; it had merely a slight sheen of a glassy kind, and must have been difficult to clean. Realizing this, the Greeks had definite and easily recognizable shapes for different purposes, so that wine would not be poured into the oil jar by mistake, or water into the wine jar. For certain kinds of glaze the raw materials of glass are ground together, mixed with water to a creamy consistency, and the ware is coated with the mixture by dipping or spraying. For other kinds, some or all of the materials are first melted together to form a kind of glass known as 'frit', which is then ground up and applied in the same way. The ware then has a second or 'glaze' firing, which melts the powdered glass material to a smooth, shining skin of glaze. Some kinds of glaze can be applied to the unfired pot, so that only one firing is needed.

Pottery can be decorated by marking the surface with the fingers or a tool; by applying a thin coating or 'slip' of clay of a lighter colour than the foundation, and cutting or scratching through this; or it may be painted with colours mixed with the glaze, or applied under or over it before firing. The pigments used for the painting—and in fact for colouring pottery in any way—are all derived from the oxides or salts of metals. Iron gives yellows and browns, or grey-green; copper, green or red; cobalt, blue; manganese, purple or brown; antimony, yellow; chrome (a recent addition) gives green or pink; tin, white; gold, pink. These pigments can also be mixed with the clay. The variety of colours obtainable from some of the metals is explained by the fact that these behave differently under different firing conditions, and in different glazes.

The potter has made an important contribution to the art of most countries. Almost the only record we have of Greek painting is in the decoration of their vases, which was often the work of famous artists. In China there were royal potteries at an early date, and exquisite stoneware survives from the Sung Dynasty (A.D. 960–1280) onwards. From the 17th century, when Chinese pottery was first imported into Europe, Western potters tried to copy both the texture and the designs, and the development of modern European pottery is largely due to the inspiration of the Chinese. By the end of the 18th century European pottery was fully developed; in the 19th century, as the process became more and more industrialized, the design of pottery became much poorer. The 20th century, however, has produced a new

Victoria and Albert Museum

EARTHENWARE LOVING-CUP DECORATED WITH COLOURED 'SLIP'

English, late 17th century

type of individual artist-potter who is redis-covering the old hand methods so as to produce vessels of individual beauty and character.

See also PORCELAIN; STONEWARE; EARTHENWARE.
See also Vol. XI: CHINA, HOUSEHOLD.

POULTRY AND GAME. 1. POULTRY. The rearing and marketing of turkeys, geese, ducks, and chickens has been a fast-growing industry during the present century; and the develop-ment of COLD STORAGE (q.v.) on land and sea has made it possible for countries to import poul-try from distant lands.

Norfolk is the traditional English centre for the raising of turkeys, but they are reared also in all parts of the United Kingdom. The eastern shires of Scotland and most parts of Ireland produce thousands of birds each year for the Christmas trade. Although chickens and ducks are seen on most farms and small-holdings, the Lancashire district around Preston and Blackpool has become noted in recent years for the number and quality of its chickens, whilst Yorkshire has come to the fore as a large-scale commercial producer of ducklings (*see also* POULTRY, Vol. VI).

Smithfield Market, in London, is the main marketing centre for the poultry trade. Each year it distributes thousands of tons of the table poultry that is sent to that market from many parts of the world, as well as from every county in the United Kingdom. Leadenhall Market, in the centre of the City of London, also plays a prominent part in the wholesale and retail poultry trade. There are other important dead-poultry markets at Manchester, Liverpool, Birmingham, Leeds, and Bristol; and there are scores of country markets, where the farmers sell their live poultry for dispatch to the big cities.

Northern Ireland sends nine-tenths of its poultry production to Britain, which is also the main market for exports from Southern Ireland. The United States and Canada were once leading poultry producers for the British market, but, owing to the shortage of dollars after the Second World War, Britain now imports more poultry from Australia and South Africa.

Poland and Hungary send large supplies. Under British guidance the Poles and Hunga-rians have modified their methods, and have succeeded in raising small turkeys for modern needs, some of them being varieties not bred in Britain. By careful packing and grading and

A 19TH-CENTURY POULTERER'S SHOP

the use of fast transport, Holland and Denmark are finding a ready British market. Before 1939 Britain imported large quantities of geese from Russia and ducks from China, whilst the Argen-tine accounted for a large share of our turkey imports.

The retail sale of poultry was once the exclusive right of the poulterer. The trade is now shared by the fishmonger, butcher, and provision merchant, and poultry finds a much larger place in the British diet than it did early in the century.

2. GAME. This is the word generally used to define pheasant, partridge, grouse, black-cock, moorhens, and hares, but various Acts of Parliament include bustard, woodcock, snipe, quail, landrail, and deer, among English game, and ptarmigan among Scottish. All these game animals are described separately in Vol. II. The Game Laws control the trade in game, and make a licence necessary to kill or deal in it. These laws differ slightly in their application to the four countries of the United Kingdom.

Game and wild birds may not be taken during the breeding season, and there are statutory 'close' seasons when they may not be killed or sold. The grouse season opens on 12 August, and is followed by partridge on 1 September and pheasant on 1 October. The close season for other birds is governed by the Wild Birds Pro-tection Act, and varies from county to county. Details can always be seen at the local police station (*see* GAME SHOOTING, Vol. IX).

As in the poultry trade, London is also the centre of the game trade. Buying and selling on Smithfield and Leadenhall markets fixes the day-to-day prices of game for the whole country. Prices sometimes change rapidly, as good or bad weather for shooting affects the ebb and flow of supplies.

There is not enough game in Britain to supply all her wants, and large quantities are imported. Before the Second World War many pheasants were imported from Manchuria. Thousands of partridges, packed in ice and wood-shavings, reached this country from Hungary and Poland, and game dealers were able to offer this class of game all the year round, as there are no restrictions on the sale of foreign game out of season. To-day Icelandic and Norwegian ptarmigan, Dutch wild duck, and Danish pheasants add to the supplies from abroad. Although rabbits are not strictly game, they are one of Britain's chief imports from Australia. All these importations play an important part in the negotiation of trade agreements between Britain and other countries, especially those that are chiefly agricultural.

Grouse are Britain's only export of game birds, since the British red grouse is not to be found anywhere else. The United States are willing buyers at all times. Britain also exports a large number of hares to France, for in Paris they realize twice the price the game dealer can obtain in London.

See also Vol. II: GROUSE; PHEASANT; TURKEY; GEESE.
See also Vol. VI: POULTRY.
See also Vol. IX: GAME SHOOTING; DUCK SHOOTING.

PREFABRICATION, see Vol. VIII: PRE-FABRICATION.

PRESERVATION, FOOD, see Vol. XI: FOOD PRESERVATION.

PRICE, see VALUE AND PRICE; SUPPLY AND DEMAND.

PRIME COST, see COSTING, Section 2.

PRIMITIVE MONEY. 1. Aristotle, the Greek philosopher, summed up the four chief qualities of money some 2,000 years ago. It must be lasting, and easy to recognize, to divide, and to carry about. In other words, it must be 'durable, distinct, divisible, and portable'. When we think of money we picture it either as round, flat pieces of metal which we call coins, or as printed paper notes. But there are still parts of the world to-day where coins and notes are of no use for they will buy nothing, and a traveller might starve if he had no native 'money' to exchange for food.

A collection of primitive money from all parts of the world will show hundreds of different objects of differing materials, shapes, and sizes. There are the feather coils of the Santa Cruz Islands, the 'millstones' (some of them 10 to 12 feet high) from the Caroline Islands, the copper plates of British Columbia, the 'drums' of Indonesia, the 'tin hats' of Malaya, the brick tea and squirrel skins of Siberia, the boars' tusks of New Guinea, the dog, porpoise, or fish teeth of the Solomons, the silver 'fishhooks' of the Persian Gulf, or the 'mat-money' of West Africa, the New Hebrides, and Polynesia.

Among backward peoples, who are not reached by traders from outside, commerce usually means barter (see EXCHANGE AND TRADE). There is a direct exchange of fish for vegetables, meat for grain, or various kinds of food for pots, baskets, or other manufactured goods, and money is not needed. But there is often something that everybody wants and everyone can use, such as salt to flavour food, shells for ornaments, or iron and copper to make into tools and vessels. These things—salt, shells, or metals—are still used as money in out-of-the-way parts of the world to-day.

2. SALT. Salt seems a rather uninteresting thing to us. But it is rare in the inland parts of Africa, and wherever the food of the people is mainly vegetable there is a desperate craving for it. African carriers and road-makers are often paid in salt, which they can exchange for food in the markets, although some of the lump may be licked away before it gets there! Until recently salt bars were the ordinary money of Abyssinia, and bars of exact weights had definite values. Cakes of salt, stamped to show their value, were money in Tibet; and cakes of different sizes, worth from a penny to a shilling, still buy goods in Borneo.

2. SHELLS. Cowrie sea-shells have been used as money over the greater part of the Old World. They were collected mainly from the beaches of the Maldive Islands in the Indian Ocean, and were traded to India and China. Here they were used either singly as coins or, for larger sums,

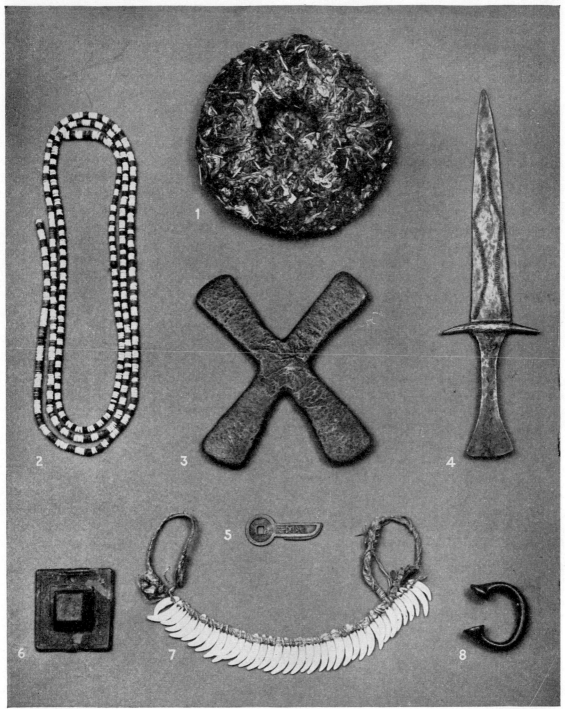

Pitt Rivers Museum

PRIMITIVE MONEY

1. Brick of tea made in Yunnan, China.   2. String of shell and coco-nut discs, New Guinea.   3. Copper ingot, Congo Free State.   4. Copper dagger, Congo Free State.   5. Knife, China.   6. Tin hat, Siam.   7. Dog's teeth necklace. 8. 'Manilla', West Africa.   (about ⅓ size)

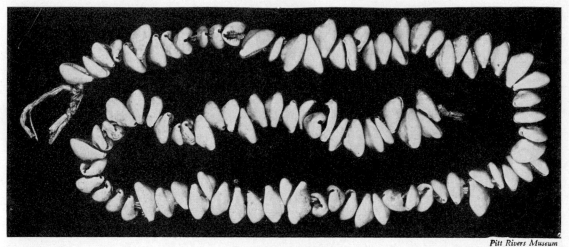

COWRIE SHELL MONEY
A string of 100 shells from Uganda

were weighed up into bags. In India, in the 19th century, they were accepted by traders in payment for goods, and by Government in payment of taxes. Four or five thousand went to the rupee (about 1s. 6d.) yet revenue was still collected in cowries. Huge buildings were needed to store them, and fleets of boats to float them down river to Government headquarters, then at Calcutta.

In Africa cowries were traded right across the continent from east to west. The 'cowrie counter' was a necessary official in the Sudanese markets, where he had to count many thousands daily in fives, with fingers and thumbs. Four or five thousand went to the Maria Theresa dollar, an Austrian silver coin which had become accepted as currency in many parts of Africa. Cowries were used for large payments as well as small. When the Arabs brought the first cowries to Uganda they were so highly prized that two cowries were worth a woman, or four to five cows. But cowries very like the Indian ones could be picked up on the East African shores, and millions more were brought in by merchant ships. They soon became too common to be worth much in the market, and when small coins were introduced cowries were no longer used as money.

They lasted longer as money in West Africa. In Nigeria during the present century cowries could still be seen in the markets, although a thousand were worth only about sixpence; and a woman on her way to market, seeing a cowrie

in the sand, would pick it up with her toes and add it to her store. In up-country districts, off the trade routes, cowries are still in use and the people often prefer them to coins.

In the islands of the Pacific Ocean, from New Guinea to New Caledonia, cowries are used here and there in place of money. In some inland parts they are very valuable, ten cowries being the price of a capable young woman or a full-grown pig in Dutch New Guinea, while many useful objects can be bought with a single shell of the right size and shape. Travellers tell of inland natives coming down as carriers to the coast and hunting for shells in the sand as eagerly as gold-miners hunt for lumps of gold.

But the native money of the Pacific islands is usually made of different shells which are broken up, ground down into discs, and threaded on strings like beads. The strings are sometimes short, in bunches; more often they are long, and measured by the fathom (6ft.). They are usually made in the outlying islands where food is scarce, and used for trading with the mainland. They may be coarse or fine, and are of many colours. The red are usually more valued than the white (perhaps because the red shells are less common), and each island has its own preferences.

The best known shell money, the *diwarra* of New Britain in the Bismarck group of islands, is not strung. The little cowrie-like shells are pierced, and forced on to a stiff piece of cane. They are evenly spaced and do not touch each other; any desired number of shells can thus be counted and the cane broken off. *Diwarra* is used widely. A hundred to two hundred fathoms buy an expensive object such as a wife or a canoe, half a fathom buys a fowl, and only two or three shells have to be paid for a purchase of vegetables.

Wampum is an example of shell money from America, and it was used by the colonists as well as by the native Indians. Long cylindrical beads were cut out of white and purple clam shells (like oyster shells) and strung together; these strings were 'legal tender' (*see* MONEY). But when wampum began to be manufactured by the white man, who could make fifteen to twenty strings a day on a lathe, its value as money came to an end.

3. METAL. Metal, valued by weight, preceded coins in many parts of the world. Iron in lumps, bars, or rings is still used instead of money over parts of Africa. It can be exchanged for goods, or made into tools, weapons, or ornaments by the smith. West coast 'manillas', 'Kissie pennies', Congo spears, and Fan 'axes' are examples in collections of primitive money, and may still be seen sometimes in local markets. Copper crosses are used in place of, or together with, coins in the Congo and Northern Rhodesia.

The early money of China, apart from shells, was of bronze, in the shape of spades, knives, hoes, and other familiar objects, and also in flat round discs with a hole in the middle, which we know as 'cash'. The date of the earliest of these is uncertain, but some are believed to be between 3,000 and 4,000 years old—older than the earliest coins of the eastern Mediterranean.

Metal lumps and bars formed the primitive money of prehistoric Europe before the coming of coins, although wealth was commonly counted in cattle or slaves, as in Greece in Homeric times. 'Currency bars' were of iron, copper, or bronze, and gold rings—sometimes in a series of definite weights—were used in trade as well as for gifts. Greece in early times had its 'talents' of copper and bronze as well as of gold, and also rough lumps and bars, which could be broken in pieces. In the course of time these rough bits became more shapely, and when stamped may properly be called coins. These early examples, whether from the Greek island of Aegina or (as Herodotus reports) from the Lydian coasts of Asia Minor, are held to be the models from which European coinage is derived (*see* COINS).

In the civilized world coins and notes have taken the place of all the picturesque forms of primitive money. In the less civilized parts the beads, cloth, and tobacco of the trader are often preferred to the native money, and drive it out of use. Although it is still often hoarded for ceremonial occasions such as weddings and funerals, examples of primitive money will soon be found only in museums.

See also MONEY; COINS.

PRINTING. 1. This is a method of making many copies of a design. The design may consist of letters, words, and sentences, or of a picture, or some sort of decoration. Printing may be applied to books, newspapers, showcards, wallpaper, materials, chocolate wrappings, tins of food, and so on.

The broad term 'printing' involves two operations which are entirely distinct. First, the pattern to be printed has to be made and assembled; this pattern may be a page containing hundreds of words, or it may contain mainly pictures. The second and quite separate operation consists of inking that pattern and pressing it on the paper. Strictly speaking, the first operation is that of 'composing' or 'setting' type, while the second alone is the act of printing, and is known as 'presswork' or 'machining'. The craftsmen engaged in both operations are called printers, however, because in the past the entire work was carried out by one man or a small team of men. These two operations are now so distinct that they can even take place in two different countries. A magazine, the type of which is assembled by Americans in Chicago, can be printed by Frenchmen in Paris, for sale in Britain. In fact, however, very often both operations are carried out by different departments in the same printing-works.

All printing is done from an inked pattern. There are three main methods of printing, and each is distinguished by the different kind of surface used.

The first method is Letterpress, Relief or Typographic Printing: in this case the design (whether letters or a picture) is made into a raised surface, which may be raised ridges or dots or large raised areas (Fig. 1A); ink is spread on the raised

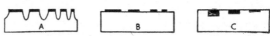

FIG. 1. DIAGRAM OF BLOCKS SHOWING METHODS OF PRINTING
A. Letterpress; B. Lithographic; C. Engraving or photo-gravure

surface only, and this is then pressed against the paper or other substance to be printed. This has been by far the most usual form of printing for some centuries. The whole of the *Oxford Junior Encyclopaedia*, both words and pictures (including the coloured plates), is printed by this means.

The second method is that of Engraving. Hollow spaces to represent the design are cut in some flat surface, either by a tool such as a knife, or by acid. Then the whole surface is covered with printing-ink, which is carefully wiped off again, leaving the flat surface dry, but the grooves full of ink. If paper is pressed on the pattern, the design will be printed on it from the inky grooves (Fig. 1C). This method is the basis of photogravure, the means used for the mass-production of many popular illustrated magazines.

The third method is that of Lithography or chemical printing. This does not depend on either a raised surface or a sunken groove; a completely flat surface is used. On this is transferred the design, which consists of markings in some greasy chemical which will mix with printing-ink (itself a greasy substance) but not with water. When water is applied to the whole surface, the actual markings of the design, being greasy, are not wetted by it. Then, when a roller of printing-ink is run over the whole surface, the greasy ink sticks to the greasy markings of the design, but is repelled by the water on the rest of the surface. If a paper is then pressed against the surface, the inky design will be printed on it (Fig. 1B). This method is much used for printing coloured posters. With photo-lithography, almost anything can be copied and printed.

All three methods are used for printing words and sentences, but in all three the letters of the alphabet must first be assembled or composed in lines.

2. TYPE-SETTING BY HAND. Although composing is now mainly mechanical, many of the traditions and terms, as well as some actual materials, of the days of hand-composing have continued among printers. For more than 4 centuries the craft of composing type was based on hand-setting, that is, the putting together by hand of pieces of metal, each having the shape of a letter, until an entire book or newspaper had been hand-set, page by page or column by column (*see* PRINTING, HISTORY OF, Vol. IV).

In hand-set type, the individual letters consist of thin rectangular pieces of metal, each eleven-twelfths of an inch in length (*see* diagram in PRINTING-TYPE, p. 362). The pieces of type are made of a metal mixture which is mainly lead, and are given their shape in a mould into which the molten metal has been poured. At the upper end, or 'face', of each piece is seen a letter of the alphabet, and this face, when coated with ink, is the part of the type which is pressed against the paper. The width of the letters varies, 'i' and 'l' being narrow, 'm' and 'w' being wide, and 'o' and 'n' being of medium width. All other dimensions of the letters are carefully standardized for each particular size or kind of alphabet (*see* PRINTING-TYPE).

Words and sentences are formed, as shown in Fig. 2, by assembling the letters side by side. For hand-setting a compositor stands in front of two large trays called 'cases', and picks out the letters he requires from the various open compartments in which they are stored on the trays. The letters are kept loose in each compartment, rather like the nails in a carpenter's box. The largest compartment always contains the letter 'e', the letter which occurs most frequently in the English language. The compositor holds in his left hand a small metal frame (called a 'stick') in which he assembles the lines of type

FIG. 2. HAND COMPOSING
The compositor arranges the letters in the 'stick'

as he composes them. The width of this frame is adjustable to suit the width of any page or column. With his right hand he picks up the letters he requires, one at a time. As he picks up each one he is able, by feeling the nick in the letter, to turn it the right way up before placing it with the lines of type which he has already assembled. In the large trays there are other pieces of metal which are shorter than the rest, and which have no 'faces' of letters on them. They are used to fill out the blank spaces between words. As these pieces are of many different widths, the compositor is able to wedge them between the words so that each line is filled out exactly to the end. Otherwise printed lines, like typewriting, would be irregular in length. Of the two trays (or cases) in front of him, which rest on supports, the upper one always contains capital letters, and the lower one the small letters —hence the printer's habit of calling the small letters 'lower-case' letters. When the compositor has filled the small frame in his hand, he empties it by transferring the lines of type to another receptacle; then he continues to compose as before. A good compositor will 'set' about 1,500 letters an hour. Until recent times all the books and newspapers in the world were made in this way.

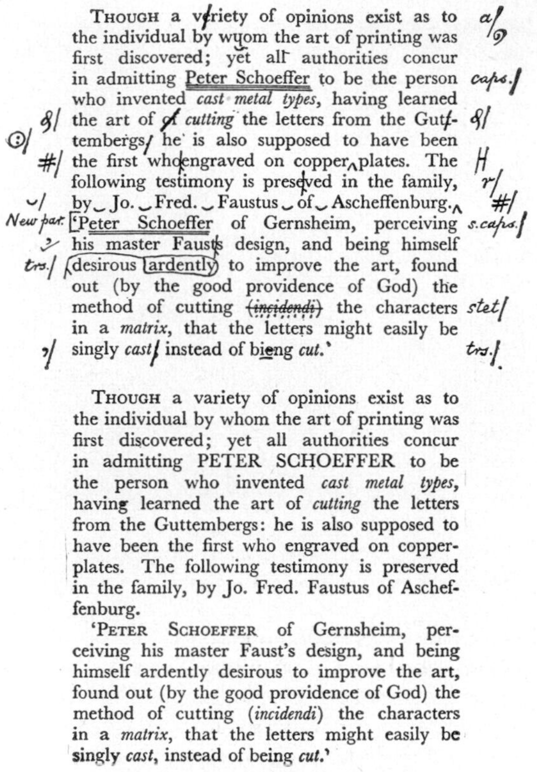

THOUGH a vriety of opinions exist as to the individual by wyom the art of printing was first discovered; yet alr authorities concur in admitting Peter Schoeffer to be the person who invented *cast metal types*, having learned the art of of *cutting* the letters from the Gutt-tembergs he is also supposed to have been the first whoengraved on copperplates. The following testimony is presved in the family, by Jo. Fred. Faustus of Ascheffenburg. 'Peter Schoeffer of Gernsheim, perceiving his master Fausts design, and being himself desirous ardently to improve the art, found out (by the good providence of God) the method of cutting (*incidendi*) the characters in a *matrix*, that the letters might easily be singly *cast* instead of bieng *cut.*'

THOUGH a variety of opinions exist as to the individual by whom the art of printing was first discovered; yet all authorities concur in admitting PETER SCHOEFFER to be the person who invented *cast metal types*, having learned the art of *cutting* the letters from the Guttembergs: he is also supposed to have been the first who engraved on copper-plates. The following testimony is preserved in the family, by Jo. Fred. Faustus of Aschef-fenburg.

'PETER SCHOEFFER of Gernsheim, perceiving his master Faust's design, and being himself ardently desirous to improve the art, found out (by the good providence of God) the method of cutting (*incidendi*) the characters in a *matrix*, that the letters might easily be singly *cast*, instead of being *cut.*'

FIG. 3. THE CORRECTION OF PROOFS

Above is a proof with corrections, and below the corrected proof

3. CORRECTING PROOFS. After composition, the lines of type are placed in a long and narrow metal tray. Printer's ink, which is a sticky substance unlike writing ink, is then applied to the face of the type with a roller, and a strip of paper is pressed against the inked type with a heavy weight, so that the words become printed on it. The piece of paper thus becomes a 'proof', and is examined by a printer's 'reader', an expert whose duty it is to mark for correction any mistakes the compositor may have made. After correction the type is prepared for printing; it is fixed tightly in a strong framework of steel, so that it will stand high pressures.

4. MECHANICAL SETTING. Almost all composing to-day is done by machine, the two main methods being represented by the Monotype and Linotype machines. Both are operated by striking the keys of an alphabetical keyboard with the fingers, and both make use of molten metal, which is forced into a tiny mould to make each letter.

Monotype setting is done in two operations. First a compositor strikes the keys of a machine like a typewriter, which causes holes to be punched in a long strip of paper, the pattern of the holes indicating the letters of the alphabet. When holes representing some hundreds of words have been punched, the strip is removed and inserted in a casting-machine, which contains a supply of molten metal and a set of moulds for all the letters of the alphabet. As the strip of paper passes through the machine, the holes indicate mechanically which letters are required, and an electric motor moves the moulds so that these letters come in turn to a point at which molten metal is forced into them. The letters emerge in lines, as in hand-setting, and proofs for correction are taken in the same way. As each letter has been cast singly, one advantage of the Monotype is that a wrong letter can be replaced easily by hand with the right letter during correction. (*See* Figs. 4 and 5.)

The Linotype allows quicker setting, and is widely used for newspapers. No punched holes are needed for this machine. As the compositor touches each key, a tiny piece of brass, containing a hollow mould of the letter required, falls

FIG. 4. A MONOTYPE KEYBOARD

The copy to be printed is on the left, and the paper
punched by the striking of the keys is at the top

FIG. 5. A MONOTYPE CASTER

The punched paper is at the top right-hand corner; at the
bottom left the cast type is coming out of the machine

down into a rack. When enough moulds are in
position to form a line, molten metal is forced
into all of them at once, so that the line of type,
which hardens in a few seconds, is a solid bar
of metal. Linotype can be cast very quickly, and
the solid lines of type can be handled with more
speed than the lines of single letters, which easily
become disarranged. But the correction of a
mistake in one letter involves re-setting the whole
line.

5. MACHINING. Many books, leaflets, and
posters are printed from the actual type assembled
by composition; but much modern printing is
done by means of stereotype 'plates', each plate
being a copy, in a single piece of metal, of an
entire page or series of pages of compositors'
type. Stereotype plates are usually made in
Britain by pressing a layer of papier-mâché (a
moulded paper pulp) against pages of type, so
that it becomes deeply indented with the shape
of the type; molten metal is then poured over
the papier-mâché, and solidifies into a printing
surface. The first edition of a book is usually
printed from the actual type, and then moulds
are made, for these are much easier to store than
masses of type; when later editions are to be
printed, plates are cast from the moulds.
Newspapers, however, which are printed on
high-speed machines, requiring the printing
surface to rotate rapidly, are usually printed
from plates only (*see* NEWSPAPER PRODUCTION).
Plates for books are generally made, not by

casting in a mould, but by an electro-chemical
process (*see* ELECTRO-PLATING, Vol. VIII).
Another method of reproducing a book, provided that a printed copy is already in existence,
is to photograph each of the pages and to make
new copies by photo-lithography (*see* PROCESS
REPRODUCTION).

Although plates for printing books are used
flat, the plates required for newspapers have to
be cast in a curve, so that they can be attached
to cylinders which will rotate for very fast
printing (*see* PRINTING, HISTORY OF, Section 2,
Vol. IV). Newspaper rotary presses print on a
continuous strip of paper, about 5 miles long,
which unwinds from a spool. One Sunday
newspaper, printed mainly in London, uses
700 rolls of this kind for every issue, weighing
525 tons and wound with strips of paper totalling
3,500 miles in length.

See also BOOKBINDING.

See also Vol. IV: PRINTING, HISTORY OF; BOOK; NEWS-
PAPER.

PRINTING TEXTILES, *see* TEXTILE PRINT-
ING.

PRINTING-TYPE. Characters of the alphabet
used in printing are called 'type'. They are
almost always of metal, although very large
letters made of wood are still sometimes used for
posters. From the word 'type' (Greek for an impression or stamped mark) comes 'typography',

HISTORIC DESIGNS

ROMAN INSCRIPTIONAL
24 PT. BEMBO CAPS

Chancery italic c. 1500   Old Face *c.* 1670
24 PT. BEMBO ITALIC   FELL DOUBLE PICA

Modern Face *c.* 1780   𝕭𝖑𝖆𝖈𝖐 𝕷𝖊𝖙𝖙𝖊𝖗
22 PT. BODONI   24 PT. OLD ENGLISH TEXT

DECORATED
30 PT. BELL ORNAMENTED

REGENCY TYPES
10 PT. FIGGINS SHADED

TYPES OF TO-DAY

Contemporary bold   *& Script*
18 PT. GILL EXTRA BOLD   30 PT. RONDO

SHADOW   TITLING
24 PT. ROCKWELL SHADOW   24 PT. ALBERTUS

NEWSPAPER TITLING
18 PT. TIMES TITLING

TEXT TYPES

In a strict sence, a good Compositer need be no more than an English Scholler, or indeed scarce so much; for if he knows but his Letters and Characters he shall meet with in his Printed or Written Copy, and have otherwise a good natural capacity, he may be a better

MONOTYPE PERPETUA

Compositer than another Man whose Education has adorn'd him with Latin, Greek, Hebrew, and other Languages, and shall want a good natural Genius: For by the laws of Printing, a Compositer is strictly to follow his Copy. *From* MOXON, 1683.

LINOTYPE CALEDONIA

FIG. I. EXAMPLES OF TYPE FACES, RULES, AND 'FLOWERS' (DESIGNS IN THE BORDER)

which used to mean simply 'printing'; now it usually means the art of making the best and most pleasing use of printing materials. To-day good PRINTING (q.v.) is a practical art of importance. The production of books, periodicals, and posters requires the careful choice of a well-designed type, laid out with simplicity, using balanced sizes of lettering, surrounded by carefully proportioned margins, and printed on paper of pleasing texture and colour.

The kinds of type in use differ greatly in size and in style. These may range from

type as small as this, which is known as 5-point

up to such sizes as this

one, called 24 point.

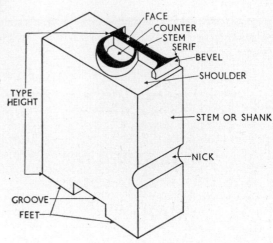

FIG. 2. A PIECE OF TYPE

In measuring, a printer reckons 72 points to an inch, the points indicating the depth of the metal body of the letter. All the letters of one design of type, whatever their size, have the same general form, the same proportion of thick and thin lines, and the same kind of 'serifs' if any (Fig. 2). Some type, such as THIS, has no serifs.

Letters of exactly the same size of body give impressions which may vary a great deal in size and design, as is shown by these lines:

This sentence shows some of the various styles of letters cast on the same size of body.

There are many hundreds of type designs, and they vary in fashion from one generation to another, and one country to another. During the 19th century, when the printing industry was expanding fast, many printers used a jumble of ugly type faces; but recently there has been a much higher standard of typography. Fig. 1 shows specimen letters from some of the better-known type faces, the main groups of which are known as 'families'.

The basis of modern type, of which there are many varieties, is the roman letter. This derives from the inscriptions (in what we now call capital letters) which were carved on the stone monuments of ancient Rome. These letters show the effect of writing (with quill pen or brush) as the upward strokes are thin, the downward strokes thick, and the middle of curved strokes tends to thicken. The small, or 'lower-case', letters now used in the roman printed alphabet were

originally imitations of the conventional writing of the best Italian scribes of the later Middle Ages. Practically all roman alphabets, as supplied for the use of printers, are accompanied by an italic alphabet of the same size. *Italic lettering, in which this sentence is printed, is a sloping lettering, and is chiefly used for contrast.* It was first devised by Italian printers, and is also based on handwriting.

Some roman type faces, based on the shapes evolved when types were first made, are known as 'Old Face'; others, with greater distinction between thick and thin strokes, are called 'Modern Face'. Some entire families of type faces are associated with the name of a great printer or typefounder of the past, such as the Englishman Caslon, or the Frenchman Garamond.

𝔗𝔥𝔢 𝔤𝔬𝔱𝔥𝔦𝔠, 𝔬𝔯 𝔟𝔩𝔞𝔠𝔨-𝔩𝔢𝔱𝔱𝔢𝔯, an ancient style of type now rarely seen, is based on the style of writing in northern Europe in the Middle Ages, and was used by Caxton in printing the first English books. It survived in Germany until recent years, but now is confined everywhere to merely ornamental uses.

Apart from the basic roman and italic, and the rare gothic, many other kinds of face have been designed in modern times. The *Oxford Junior Encyclopaedia* is printed in 10 point Baskerville.

Besides using letters of the alphabet, figures, and punctuation, printers often carry out artistic work with pieces of ornamental metal, known as 'rules' and 'flowers'.

See also PRINTING.
See also Vol. IV: PRINTING, HISTORY OF; BOOK.

PROCESS REPRODUCTION. 1. This is the reproduction for printing purposes of various kinds of illustrations for newspapers, books, and posters. The term 'process engraving' is often applied to this, although other methods than engraving can be used. Designs or pictures are reproduced by three different basic methods, as described in PRINTING, Section 1. They are: Relief printing, in which the design stands up in relief; Engraving or Intaglio printing (after an Italian word first applied by jewellers to engraved gems), in which the design consists of similar grooves filled with ink; and Lithographic or Planographic printing, in which the printing is done from an absolutely smooth or plane surface, the design or picture being defined by chemical rather than mechanical means.

2. AUTOGRAPHIC PROCESSES. Apart from mechanical and photographic methods, printing surfaces for designs or pictures may be prepared autographically, that is, by the hand of the artist who composes the picture or design. Designs are engraved or cut in wood or metal or 'bitten' by acid into metal, or drawn on stone (see WOOD-ENGRAVING AND WOODCUTS, ETCHING AND ENGRAVING, LITHOGRAPHY, Vol. XII), and prints are taken from them in a printing-press. But work of this kind, done by hand, takes time and much skill; it is costly and otherwise unsuitable for commercial production in large quantities. For example, the wooden blocks by means of which wood engravings are printed would certainly wear out before a large enough number of prints had been taken.

Although most modern methods of reproduction are based on photography, some autographic methods can be adapted for mass production. Wood engravings, for example, can be reproduced in large quantities if 'electrotypes' of the original are made on copper. A mould is made from the wood block upon a thin sheet of plaster softened by heat. After it has been cooled the block is withdrawn, and the mould sprayed with a solution of silver nitrate. It is then hung in a liquid solution through which an electric current is passed. In the same solution there is a piece of copper, and the current causes a layer of tiny particles of copper to be deposited on the surface of the silvered mould (see ELECTROLYSIS, Vol. VIII). Then the mould is taken out, and the thin copper layer or shell peeled from it. The copper shell is next backed by a softer metal and planed to produce a 'plate' of even thickness.

It is then strong enough to be used for making more prints than could have been made direct from the wood engraving; even larger numbers may be taken if a coating of nickel is deposited upon the copper face. In the same way, original engravings made by an artist on copper plates can be given a steel or nickel face.

3. RELIEF PROCESSES. For most modern purposes, process engraving has taken the place of the older autographic methods. All designs to be reproduced fall into two broad classes: (a) those made up solely of lines and other solid areas of ink, such as pen-and-ink sketches, engineering drawings, and statistical diagrams; (b) those made up of tones, such as photographs and oil paintings, watercolour drawings, pastel sketches, and any other pictures or patterns which are mainly without sharp lines and which convey their effect by gradual changes of tone—some parts being white, some light grey, some darker grey, and some black. The surfaces from which these two classes of design are printed are called Line Blocks and Half-tone Blocks, since printers use the term 'block' for any lump of wood or metal from which an illustration is printed.

(a) Line Blocks. To make a line block, the original black-and-white drawing is photographed, and a clear negative obtained (see PHOTOGRAPHY, Vol. IX). The negative is then photographically printed by strong artificial light on to a plate of polished zinc coated with a layer of emulsion sensitive to light. The light passes easily through the transparent parts of the negative (the dark lines of the original drawing), and, where it reaches the zinc plate, hardens the emulsion on it. The thick black parts of the negative (the white or blank parts of the original drawing) allow no light through, and so the emulsion underneath them on the zinc plate remains comparatively soft. The plate is then covered with ink and soaked in water, when the softer emulsion, which has not been affected by the light, dissolves. The plate, after being dried, is dusted with finely powdered resin, which sticks to the inked parts where the emulsion has not been dissolved. The plate is then put into a tank or bath of acid, and the parts unprotected by resin (representing the blank white parts of the original drawing) are etched or eaten away by the acid. Etching goes on until the etched parts of the plate have become fairly deep hollows. Thus, when printing takes place later, those parts will not be

1. HALF-TONE REPRODUCTION OF A LINE BLOCK. 2. PRINT FROM THE LINE BLOCK IN (1). 3. ENLARGEMENT OF THE HALF-TONE BLOCK FROM WHICH (1) IS PRINTED

touched by the inked rollers, nor will they touch the paper that is being printed on (*see* Fig. 1).

(*b*) Half-tone Blocks. Since the 'line block' method described above is not suitable for pictures which have graded tones, these must be reproduced by the 'half-tone' method. First, the original picture must be photographed through a 'screen'. A screen is prepared from two sheets of plate glass, each marked with extremely close parallel lines. There may be 100 lines or more to every inch in the glass. The two sheets are fixed at right angles to each other with transparent cement, forming a screen like trellis-work with tiny square 'windows' of glass. Each window may be only one-hundredth of an inch across. In that case there would be 10,000 dot-like windows to every square inch of the screen. Half-tone blocks in a newspaper will have a screen of 60 or 80 lines to the inch, that is to say, 3,600 to 6,400 windows to a square inch, while those in a book or art magazine will have 133 or more lines to the inch, making more than 17,000 windows to a square inch. This half-tone screen is placed in the camera in front of the photographic plate; the original picture is then illuminated and photographed through the screen. From those parts of the original which are dark in tone, no light will pass through the square windows of the screen, and so the photographic plate will not be affected. But where the original is pale in tone, the light will pass through the square windows. When the light passes through a window, it tends to fan out to form a cone; thus it reaches the photographic plate in the form of a round dot: the stronger the light, the bigger the dot. The sensitive, photographic emulsion on the plate will register these dots of varying sizes which will

even run into each other where the light is strongest; in this way the plate or negative will show masses of solid black where the original picture is lightest. The half-tones of the original will become smaller dots, varying from black to grey, and becoming smaller where the original is darker. When the negative is developed, all these varying sizes of dots will be clearly seen: as, in fact, they can be seen if a magnifying glass is held over a newspaper photograph. From this negative a block or zinc plate is then prepared in the same way as for line blocks. That is to say, from the negative a 'positive' is photographically made in zinc, and this is etched in a bath of acid. Photographs make very good originals for half-tone blocks, particularly those on glossy paper.

4. INTAGLIO PROCESSES. The only commercially important intaglio process is photogravure (*see* Section 1). As in the half-tone form of relief process, a screen is used, which breaks up the design into tiny squares. When the negative of the original picture is photographed on to the zinc plate, the darker parts of the original are reproduced on the zinc in the form of fatter dots than the lighter parts. The plate is given a coating which protects it from acid (except where the dots occur); it is then etched in a bath of acid. The darkest parts are eaten away most by the etching process, and the lightest parts least. The parts immediately under the cross-lines of the screen have not been affected at all by light, and therefore during the etching process they remain untouched by the acid. Thus, after etching, the plate consists of a series of tiny ridges and of countless tiny hollows between the ridges. When the printing takes place an ink scraper on the printing-machine wipes the ridges clear of ink. The deep-etched hollows (the darks of the original) hold much ink and the shallow ones (the lights of the original) hold little or none. Therefore, when the plate is pressed against the paper, the dark and light tones of the picture are printed exactly as they were in the original. A great advantage of the photogravure process is that it can be used not only for the reproduction of pictures but also for the printed words of books or periodicals. The process can be speeded up by the use of flexible plates which can be bent round cylinders in rotary printing-presses (see PRINTING, Section 5). This is called 'rotary photogravure' or 'rotogravure'.

5. PLANOGRAPHIC PROCESSES. These are worked on the chemical principle that grease and water will not mix. The earlier lithographs were done on limestone, a porous stone which absorbs grease. The design was drawn direct on the stone by the artist, with a greasy black 'chalk' or with a pen and greasy lithographic ink. The stone was then moistened with water, and a roller of greasy printing-ink passed over it. This ink was absorbed by the greasy portions of the stone but it left no mark on the wet portion on which there was no design. From this stone numbers of sheets of paper could be printed. For modern lithographic work stones have now been replaced by thin pliable metal plates, usually of zinc; these can be used in rotary presses, and are therefore suitable for rapid reproduction in large quantities. A printing-plate of this kind is still called a 'stone' in a printing works. The image to be printed is put on to it photographically, as in the line and half-tone processes, and the process is called

DRAWING ON A LITHOGRAPHIC STONE
On the right is a print taken from the stone

Odham's Press

photo-lithography. A variant of it is photo-litho-offset, usually called 'offset', in which the image on the plate is first impressed on to the rubber surface of a cylinder, and from that is pressed against the surface of the printing-paper.

Collotype is a process which has been developed from the water-and-grease principle of lithography. The image to be printed is photographically transferred to a film of hardened gelatine on a sheet of plate-glass. When water is applied, the 'light' parts of the image absorb more moisture than the dark parts. Then, when ink is applied, the driest parts take most ink and therefore print heaviest. Only about 1,500 copies can be taken from a collotype plate, but as no screen has to be used there is no dotted 'screen grain' on the prints, which come out as very faithful reproductions of the original. It is an ideal process for reproducing works of art. Collotypes can make very good colour copies.

6. COLOUR PRINTING. Reproduction of coloured originals depends on the principle that all colours are varying combinations of the three primary colours of pigment—red (magenta), blue, and yellow (see COLOUR PLATE, p. 96, Vol. III). The original is photographed in turn through three different colour 'filters', pieces of high quality glass coloured each with one of the three complementary primary colours of light—green, red, and violet. Each filter cuts out its complementary colour, and the plate in the camera is affected by the other colours. A positive print is made which reverses this, and so shows only those places where the complementary colour was in the original. For example, if a photograph were taken of an object whose colour was orange (a combination of the primary colours red and yellow), a violet filter would be used to make a photograph of where the yellow was, and a green filter of where the red was. Separate 'blocks' would be made, one for the yellow colour and one for the red. Two successive printings, one from each block, would then reproduce the true orange colour of the object. If a colour of an original object or picture were a combination of three primaries, that object or picture would, of course, need to be photographed through three filters, and three separate blocks would be made. In practice, three blocks are made in nearly all cases. Just as all colours on the original can be analysed or 'split' into the three primaries, so successive printings in each of the primaries cause a synthesis or 'build-up' into the original

colour. This process is called the 'three-colour' process. Sometimes a fourth filter is used for black, and if so a fourth block in black will be prepared. The order of printing is yellow, red, blue, black; some printers take black third and blue last (*see* Colour Plate, opposite p. 336).

See also PRINTING; ENGRAVING.
See also Vol. IV: ILLUSTRATION.
See also Vol. IX: PHOTOGRAPHY.

PRODUCTION. **1.** THEORETICAL. The economic life of mankind depends upon the production of goods and services. To produce either of these things, use must be made of land and human labour, and also of at least a modest amount of CAPITAL (q.v.) with which to buy tools and raw materials. Moreover, as all except very primitive production depends on teamwork by several people, there must be someone to manage or co-ordinate production. Land, labour, capital, and management are therefore the four things concerned in practically all production, and economists call them 'the factors of production'. To the manager or co-ordinator of any act of production, economists have given the technical name 'entrepreneur', which is a French word from which comes the English word 'enterprise'.

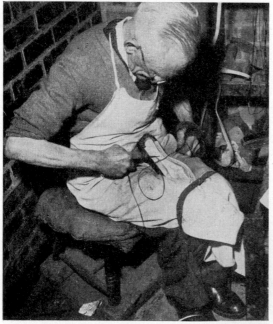

JOB PRODUCTION: THE HAND CRAFTSMAN
A shoemaker sewing on the welt of a shoe

Norman Wymer

Just as so many processes in industry depend on the correct mixture of ingredients, so efficiency of production depends very much upon the way in which the quantities of land, labour, and capital are combined or mixed together. The most efficient mixture or combination— called by economists the optimum (or best) combination of the factors of production—is that which reduces the cost of production to the lowest possible figure. At any given moment the best combination depends on the price of each 'factor'. At certain times, land may be relatively more expensive than capital or labour. For example, in some countries land and labour are plentiful and cheap, but capital is scarce and can be borrowed only at a very high rate of INTEREST (q.v.). Such countries use much land and labour, and very little machinery. Other countries may find it more profitable to make great use of capital and to reduce the amount of labour to a minimum. One such country is the U.S.A., where the WAGES (q.v.) of labour are extremely high, and capital extremely cheap because the people are well off and much money is saved. In the amount of machinery used Britain does not approach the U.S.A., but she is far ahead of many other countries of the world.

2. PRACTICAL. In a practical sense production takes three forms: job production, batch production, and continuous or mass production. 'Job production' means producing a single article, usually specially ordered: for example, a suit from a West End tailor, or an architect-designed house from a builder. SHIP-BUILDING (q.v.) is mainly job production. 'Batch production' is, as the name suggests, the production of a batch of articles, all of the same type, size, and design. Production in the textile industries, for example, is often batch production, certain weaves or patterns of cloth being run through the loom for days on end. Batch production is naturally cheaper than job production. 'Continuous production' may take two forms. Production of pig iron in a steel-works, or of glass in a glass factory, is truly continuous, because work goes on during the whole 24 hours and only ceases for a time when furnaces have to be relined or repaired. The term is often applied, however, to continuous production of the same pattern—for instance, in the MOTOR INDUSTRY (q.v.)—although work is interrupted at the end of the usual 8-hour day. There is continuous production of models of the same type, and the work moves from worker to

E. K. Cole Ltd.

FLOW PRODUCTION: ASSEMBLING RADIO SETS
Each worker does her job on the set as it comes to her along the conveyor belt between the benches

worker and process to process, often along a conveyor (*see* FACTORY ORGANIZATION). 'Flow production' is another and perhaps better term for this kind of production. 'Mass production' is a term in common use for what is very often merely line or continuous production. Strictly, the term should be used only for such production at a rapid rate and on an immense scale.

See also LABOUR; FACTORY ORGANIZATION.

PRODUCTION COSTS, *see* COSTING, Section 1.

PROFIT SHARING, *see* CO-PARTNERSHIP; PROFITS; WAGES.

PROFITS. A business man's profits are either 'gross' or 'net'. If he sells goods, he must first find what the goods have cost him. That cost includes not only the actual purchase price of the goods, but the expenses of their being taken to the WAREHOUSE (q.v.), any customs duties or taxes, and the wages bill and expenses for unloading and arranging the goods in the warehouse. Gross profit is the difference between what the goods have cost and what is received from their sale. Net profit is gross profit less all the 'overhead' expenses (*see* COSTING) such as

ADVERTISING, travellers' COMMISSION, and office salaries (qq.v.). A manufacturer usually makes a distinction between his profit on manufacture and his profit on trading.

To the economist, profit is what is left to the owners of any business after they have paid for land and labour (rent and wages) and INTEREST on borrowed CAPITAL (qq.v.). Profit to the economist is, therefore, much the same thing as the merchant's or manufacturer's net profit. If profits are made, they are the reward to the owners for successfully taking on the risks of production. In modern business, which is conducted mainly by LIMITED COMPANIES (q.v.), the owner who assumes the risks of trading or manufacturing is really the body of persons holding ordinary shares, whose DIVIDEND (q.v.) fluctuates with the profits earned.

See also ECONOMICS; BOOK-KEEPING; COSTING.

PROMISSORY NOTE, *see* BILLS OF EXCHANGE.

PROSPECTUS, *see* ISSUING HOUSES.

PROVISION TRADE, *see* GROCERY AND PROVISIONS.

PUBLIC UTILITY COMPANIES. These provide services such as gas and electricity, necessary to all the inhabitants of a city or area. To carry out their business they have to have powers to interfere with the private rights and property of ordinary citizens; and so most public utilities are not ordinary LIMITED COMPANIES (q.v.), but are incorporated by special Acts of Parliament. Before NATIONALIZATION (q.v. Vol. X) the railways were a good example of public utility companies, for in order to lay their tracks they had to be given compulsory powers to acquire land. Similarly gas, electricity, and water undertakings have to break up public and private roads to lay their mains; when the 'grid' electricity system was organized (*see* POWER STATIONS, Vol. VIII), the Central Electricity Board had to be given permission to carry overhead cables across the countryside. Most public utilities possess a MONOPOLY (q.v.), having been given exclusive rights in their areas by Acts of Parliament. It would be an impossible situation, for instance, if roads were constantly being broken up by a succession of competing gas companies.

Some public utilities are national: the British BROADCASTING CORPORATION (q.v. Vol. IV) is an example. Others are local: of these the best examples are the dock authorities, such as the Port of London Authority and the Mersey Docks and Harbour Board. Another local public utility is the Thames Conservancy, which is responsible for the Thames from Teddington Lock upwards. The majority of local public utilities (which are not usually referred to as 'companies') obtain their capital by successive issues of BONDS or DEBENTURES bearing fixed rates of INTEREST, or of STOCK entitling the holders to DIVIDENDS payable out of earned profits (qq.v.). But there are some utilities which adopt the ordinary limited-company method of finance: that is, they have a fixed authorized capital.

When consumers have to buy their services from a monopoly, they are largely at its mercy, because it has no competitors to whom they might go if dissatisfied. So the parliamentary charters of public utilities usually contain restrictions which enable the State to look after the interests of the public. Sometimes maximum charges or rates are laid down, and these must not be exceeded without reference to a Minister, or to some neutral body such as (in the days before nationalization) the Railway Rates Tribunal. A maximum rate of dividend is often fixed, and this can only be exceeded if the price of the service concerned is lowered at the same time.

A nationalized or State-owned industry is simply a public utility on a grand scale. The National Coal Board, formed in January 1947, is the largest public utility in Great Britain at the present time. The greatest in the U.S.A. is the T.V.A., or Tennessee Valley Authority, which was organized by President Franklin Roosevelt's administration as part of the unemployment relief programme in the great period of depression which preceded the Second World War. This was an immensely ambitious scheme of development for a vast tract of land in the Southern States of the U.S.A., including among much else the building of great dams and electric power-stations, and the reclamation of hundreds of thousands of acres for agriculture and forestry. (*see* SOIL EROSION, Vol. III.)

See also COMPANIES.
See also Vol. X: NATIONALIZATION.

PUBLISHING. It is only recently that publishing became a separate trade. Early publishers (for example, the existing firms of Longmans and John Murray, both founded in the 18th century) opened up as booksellers, but later found it profitable to arrange for the publication of works of their own choice. The trade in books is now shared by the publisher, the printer and binder (who are often firms distinct from one another), and the bookseller; each of these is an independent branch of the trade. The publisher takes the commercial risk on the production of the book; the printer prints the book to the publisher's order; and the bookseller distributes it to the buying public. There are both wholesale and retail booksellers. The wholesale booksellers receive a larger discount than the retailers, because they buy in big quantities and usually supply the large and steady demand of the public libraries, schools, and colleges.

Some books are written by their authors in the hope that a publisher may be found for them; many are 'commissioned', or ordered by publishers themselves. The creation of a book is described in detail in the article BOOK in Vol. IV. In the early days of publishing, publishers usually bought authors' works outright for a lump sum, which very often was extremely small. It has been said that Milton received only £5

THE AUTHOR AND HIS PUBLISHER
A satirical drawing by Thomas Rowlandson (1756–1827)

for *Paradise Lost*. The usual arrangement nowadays is for the publisher to finance the production of the book and to pay the author a percentage ROYALTY (q.v.) on the sales. But sometimes authors merely use publishers as AGENTS (q.v.) for the production and distribution of their works, the publisher merely receiving a COMMISSION (q.v.) on the sales. For many years George Bernard Shaw arranged for the publication of his own works in this way.

When a publisher has decided to publish a work, he signs the contract with the author, and usually instructs a firm of printers to produce the actual book. Some publishers print their own works, but these are few. After batches of the book have been bound in quantities decided by the publisher (*see* BOOK-BINDING), they are distributed to firms of booksellers. Until 1900, when a Net Price Agreement was signed, there was much under-selling and price-cutting among retail booksellers. This agreement laid down

that every book should be sold at the exact price which had been decided by its publisher and advertised by him, and not at any lower price, and that publishers would not supply books to retailers who refused to sign the agreement. The Net Price Agreement was largely due to the persuasion of two large firms in the trade, Dent and Macmillan. Dent's brought out the 'Everyman's Library' series, originally sold at a shilling a copy, and were the pioneers of the modern cheap book. Within a few years the principle of the net price became generally accepted.

Announcements of books which are due to be published are made in *The Bookseller*, which is the trade journal of the publishing world. These announcements contain what is known as the 'blurb', or the publisher's own opinion of the merits and attractions of his books. These announcements are usually made before the books are printed, and publishers are prepared to take orders from booksellers immediately. Such orders are called 'subscription orders', and booksellers who give the orders receive a larger share of the selling-price, as they are then to some extent sharing the risk of production with the publisher. The average share or 'discount' allowed to booksellers is about 30%.

Publishing is a highly speculative business. First novels, by unknown authors, are the most speculative books of all, and one in nine is unprofitable. No one has yet discovered what it is that makes a 'best-seller', and those publishers who bring out best-sellers are fortunate. Most publishers bring out a mixture of profitable and unprofitable books. Some books, such as expensive and scholarly works with a limited appeal, are bound to be unprofitable, but as their publication adds to a publisher's reputation, he is often prepared to bring them out, and to cover his loss by his profit on more popular works. Unsuccessful books are often 'remaindered' when sales have dropped to a low figure: that is, the unsold copies are sold in bulk, usually at a very low 'knock-out' price; they are then often 're-pulped' to make new clean paper from them (see PAPER-MAKING).

Book publishing is not only a speculative trade, but is also one of the first to suffer when bad times come, for books seem to be one of the first things on which people economize.

Publishers' costs are almost impossible to set out in a hard-and-fast way, as they vary so much with types of books and even individual books, and with different editions of one book. Broadly speaking, it may be said of a new book with a moderate sale that about a third of the price paid by the public is kept by booksellers, about a third is paid by the publisher for printing, binding, and warehousing, and the remaining third is left for advertising, for the general working expenses of the publisher's office, for his own profit, and for the author's royalty. In order to avoid the discount paid to booksellers, some firms in the trade began from 1900 onwards to sell expensive works, sometimes in fortnightly parts, direct to the public through newspaper advertisements.

See also PRINTING; BOOK-BINDING.
See also Vol. IV: BOOK.

PUNCHED CARD SYSTEM, *see* ACCOUNTING, MACHINE.

Q R

QUARRYING, *see* Stone Quarrying.

QUICKSILVER, *see* Mercury.

QUOTAS. A quota (which is a Latin word meaning proportion) is a means used by governments to protect home producers of goods against foreign competition. For example, British flour mills may be ordered by the government to mill a quota of 40% of English wheat in every 100 tons of wheat they mill. Or the importation of foreign steel may only be allowed up to 80% of the total imported in some previous year. Quotas have the effect of giving the home producer an assured sale for his goods, or of so limiting the quantity of imports from abroad that his interests cannot be damaged.

During and after the Second World War, quotas were used as a means of rationing certain things that were very scarce. For example, public houses, wine merchants, and hotels were restricted to a quota of the whisky supplies that they had been receiving in 1939.

RAILWAYS, *see* Industrial Revolution; Transport; Clearing Houses; *see also* Vol. IV: Railway Systems; Railways, History of.

RATES OF EXCHANGE. In the days before bank-notes and banking accounts became general, money used to be made of gold or silver; and, although coins of one country would not usually circulate in another country, they could always be melted down and recoined. So the 'rate of exchange' between one country's money and another's would be roughly the ratio of the weights of gold or silver in their coins; and the rate of exchange between any two moneys made from the same metal would only alter whenever one of the countries altered the weight of metal in its standard coin.

Nowadays there are few countries with their standard money in the form of coins made of the precious metals; most money to-day is made of paper. The rate of exchange between the paper moneys of two countries depends mainly upon the purchasing power of the money within its own country. Trade is, of course, the main reason why paper money is exchanged between citizens of different nations. Obviously the value put upon the money will vary according to what it will buy in the way of goods and services. If, for instance, owing to the raising of all wages and costs, the prices of all goods in a certain country became double what they were before, then the value of that country's money would be halved in the eyes of another country whose prices had remained steady. If wages and costs remain steady in two countries, the rate of exchange between the two paper moneys will settle down at a figure at which one country's money will buy in the other country roughly the same as it will buy at home. The reason statesmen so dislike rising wages and costs is that these always make their own country's money worth less in other countries.

Rates of exchange are arranged between dealers in the foreign-exchange market, and are simply the prices at which the brokers acting for the banks find themselves able to buy and sell. Rates of exchange are quoted each day in certain newspapers—but not always in a very clear manner. If the rate for American dollars is quoted as being 2.79⅞–80⅛, it means that a person having pounds and wanting to buy dollars would receive 2.79⅞ for each £, and a person with dollars wanting to buy pounds would pay 2.80⅛ for each £. But the rate of exchange between London and Calcutta might be quoted the opposite way round—as 1s. 5¹⁵⁄₁₆d.– 1s. 6¹⁄₁₆d. per rupee. This means that a person with sterling who is a buyer of rupees would have to pay 1s. 6¹⁄₁₆d. for each rupee, while a buyer of sterling with rupees would only get 1s. 5¹⁵⁄₁₆d. for every rupee.

The two prices quoted are the market's buying and selling prices, and the difference between them is the market dealer's profit.

Sometimes the governments of States take action to control the rate of exchange to prevent inflation; and this is described in the article on Currency Control in Vol. X.

RAYON is the name that has been used in the textile industries since 1924 for what was earlier called 'art silk', short for 'artificial silk'. The idea of making artificial silk was discussed by scientific writers long before any process became commercially practicable. Dr. Robert Rooke published in England in 1664 a book called *Micrographia*, which seems to be the first mention of the idea that a synthetic silk might be a possibility. Nearly 100 years later a French scientist, René Réaumur, in his *Histoire des Insectes*, commented on Rooke's earlier ideas, and considered that there was no reason why they should not eventually be put into practice. Both these writers were struck by the gummy

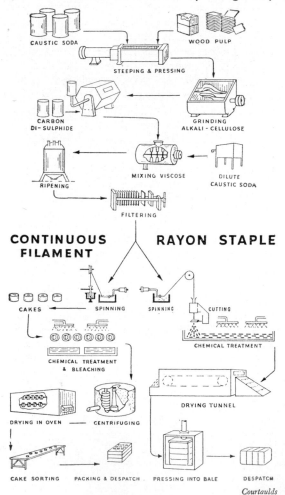

CONTINUOUS FILAMENT

RAYON STAPLE

HOW VISCOSE RAYON IS MADE

Courtaulds

The filaments of viscose drawn through the spinnerets are either made up in 'cakes' to be wound on bobbins as a continuous yarn, or are cut into short lengths (staple) to be spun like the fibres of cotton and wool

nature of raw silk in the cocoon (*see* SILKWORMS, Vol. VI). If an artificial gum could be manufactured, they thought, it might be just as easy to spin it into yarn as to spin the threads of real silk from the cocoons.

The first artificial silk made was exhibited at the Paris Exhibition of 1889 by Count Hilaire de Chardonnet, who had begun his preliminary research and experiments some 10 years earlier. The chemical basis of his product was nitrocellulose (*see* PLASTICS). His artificial silk fibre was very weak and brittle, and the textile machinery of that time was able to do nothing with it, so his experiments had no commercial success. But scientists noted the details; quite early in the 19th century it had been discovered that cellulose was present in all vegetable matter. Many natural woods contain an average of 40% to 50% of cellulose, and when natural wood has been chemically treated and converted into WOOD PULP (q.v.) it becomes practically pure cellulose.

At the end of the 19th century a method for making rayon by the viscose process was invented and used commercially by the British firm of Courtaulds. The raw materials for the viscose process are water, sulphuric and acetic acids, wood pulp, carbon disulphide, and other ingredients, including titanium dioxide or similar lustre-diminishing chemicals, and bleaching substances. A gummy liquid is produced, which is then filtered. This is squeezed out under pressure through very tiny nozzles or 'spinnerets'; it emerges as a solid, and can be dried and wound on to bobbins. From these it is later spun into yarn. The yarn and fabrics had a considerable sale, but for many purposes the viscose rayon was at first an unsatisfactory substitute for real silk, because of its exceptional sheen or lustre. In 1926 Courtaulds incorporated petroleum jelly into the solution from which the rayon threads were spun, and were able to produce a rayon yarn without the disadvantage of excessive lustre. Other improvements have been made since. A by-product of the viscose rayon process is the transparent wrapping material known as 'cellophane'.

The manufacture of rayon by another process —that of cellulose-acetate—ranks commercially next in importance to the viscose process; it was developed to a successful stage between the First and Second World Wars. Cellulose acetate itself was first produced in 1869 by a French chemist, who heated acetate anhydride and cellulose together in a sealed vessel with the air excluded. Not for another 30 years was it found possible to spin cellulose acetate filaments successfully. The process was taken up by the brothers Dreyfus, of Switzerland, and during the First World War their cellulose acetate solution was used as a 'dope', or varnish, for coating the wings of aircraft, which were then made of unbleached linen; the brothers were invited to England by the British Government, and set up a large dope factory at Spondon, near Derby. The process was not used for textile fibre until a few years after the war. Camille Dreyfus was then successful in producing acetate rayon yarn on a commercial scale, and this and the fabrics made from it were marketed under the trade name of 'Celanese'. His success was delayed because none of the dyeing materials then in existence was able to give fast colours to the new material. This difficulty was solved, and acetate rayon has now as large a range of uses as the viscose product. The raw materials of the acetate process are purified cellulose, either from cotton waste or wood pulp, sulphuric and acetic acids, acetone, acetic anhydride, and water, with titanium dioxide as the lustre-dulling substance.

There are two other important methods of making rayon—the cuprammonium process, and the casein process. In the cuprammonium process the gummy solution from which the filaments are eventually squeezed out and spun is obtained from a mixture of cellulose (usually in the form of bleached and purified cotton waste), copper sulphate, and a solution of liquid ammonia. The cotton is first soaked in a hot caustic solution under pressure until it becomes almost pure cellulose, and the other chemicals are then added. The process is German, and was invented at the end of the 19th century, but it was not commercially developed until after the First World War by J. P. Bemberg. The big German Dye Trust, I. G. Farbenindustrie, shortly afterwards began to use the process on a large scale. Bemberg himself later opened up plants in other countries, notably in Britain, Japan, and Italy, and also founded the American Bemberg Corporation in the U.S.A.

The casein process was developed by the Italian rayon company, Snia Viscosa. The advantage of casein rayon is that it is more like wool than any other synthetic textile fibre. For

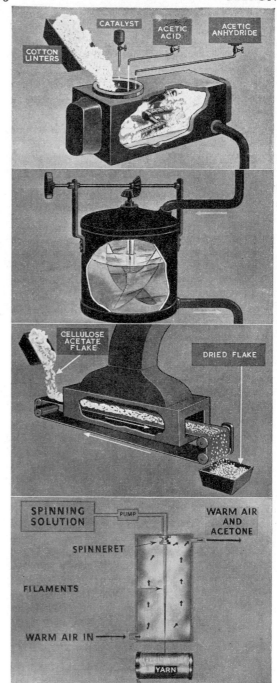

British Celanese

THE CELLULOSE-ACETATE PROCESS OF MAKING RAYON

1. Cotton waste (linters) is treated with chemicals. 2. The solution is 'refined' and cellulose acetate flakes are formed. 3. The flakes are dried and dissolved in acetone to form the syrup-like spinning solution. 4. Filaments are made by pumping the solution through spinnerets and drying them in warm air

this reason it is frequently mixed in with viscose rayon, to give a woolly effect to the mixed fabrics, and the British firm of Courtaulds uses the process for this purpose. Before the Second World War the annual output of the product by Snia Viscosa in Italy was 30 million lbs. The casein used, which occurs in CHEESE (q.v. Vol. XI), was obtained from milk-processing plants. The percentage of casein in skimmed milk is so small that it would not pay to send it direct from the farms to the rayon factories.

Rayon has now as many commercial and industrial uses as real silk. For men's wear it is used for the linings of suits, for socks, pyjamas, dressing-gowns, and underwear, for tropical suitings, and for ties. For women's wear it is used for hosiery, underwear, dress fabrics, bathing suits, linings, and ribbons. It has many uses in household furnishing, particularly for curtains and bedspreads. For electrical insulation work it is more efficient than any other real or synthetic textile material, with the possible exception of glass fibre.

See also NYLON; PLASTICS; TEXTILE FIBRES AND FABRICS; SILK INDUSTRY.

RECEIPT, *see* INVOICE.

REFINING is a word used to describe many different industrial processes. In metallurgy it means purifying or separating metals from dross or dirt or other unwanted matter; converting impure metals, such as pig-iron or unrefined copper, into a purer form; and separating a metal from an alloy or mixture of two or more metals, as for example the separation of silver from lead. The term is also used for any process of purifying or clarifying a substance: for example sugar (*see* SUGAR REFINING), or fats for MARGARINE (q.v.). It is also applied to the series of processes by which crude mineral oil is converted into petrol, paraffin, and other products (*see* OIL REFINING).

See also ASSAYING.

REFRIGERATION, *see* COLD STORAGE; *see also* Vol. VIII: REFRIGERATION.

REMITTANCES, *see* PAYMENT.

REPRESENTATIVES. This is the modern term for 'commercial travellers'. The word is also used for any person acting on behalf of his own employer, even if he is selling nothing; thus, an insurance company may send round its 'representative' to inspect the wreckage of the sitting-room carpet after an accidental fire. This article deals with representatives concerned with the sale of goods.

The way in which representatives do their work differs in different trades. In some trades they have to carry bulky samples about with them; in other trades they need no more than an order book in which to write up orders and get them signed by their customers. In trades where samples are necessary, the old-fashioned method was for the representative to travel by rail with a collection of large baskets or cages, called 'skips', in the luggage van. When he got to his destination, these skips would be taken up to the sample room of his commercial hotel, and next day their contents would be put out on trestle tables. The local firms in which he was interested would have previously received invitations to this display. There he would take and book his orders from their buyers, and in the evening he would post off the originals to his firm, keeping the duplicates in his own book for record purposes.

This old-fashioned method still exists. But since motor-cars became cheap it is not so common as it was. Goods are more standardized nowadays than they used to be, and a great deal of business can be done without showing samples at all, but if samples are necessary, the representative takes them with him in either an ordinary car or a specially fitted van. In this case he does not usually organize a show in a hotel sample room, but drives direct to the premises of the firm where he hopes to do business, bringing in samples as and when he needs them.

Large firms with many representatives make each one responsible for a definite 'territory' or section of the country. Firms marketing several 'lines' of goods in widely differing branches of commerce may have a few representatives for each line going round the country on a pre-arranged programme, details of which are sent in advance to their customers. Representatives may be either permanently employed by a single firm or 'free-lance' representatives working for quite a number of firms. The second of these types is really a travelling AGENT (q.v.).

Most representatives are real salesmen, with a thorough knowledge of the goods they are selling and the class of customer likely to be most interested in them. Modern firms realize that their representatives are their most important and regular contacts with their customers, and that by their representatives they themselves will be judged. Most large firms therefore take a great deal of care in choosing them, and run classes and even special schools for their training.

In paying their sales representatives, most firms rely on some form of 'payment by results'. Wholesale houses and manufacturers usually pay a moderate fixed salary, either a fixed monthly travelling allowance or the actual travelling expenses incurred, and a COMMISSION (q.v.) on the value of the orders booked. There are, however, many firms, particularly those selling 'specialities' direct to householders, which pay no salary at all or only a nominal one, and remunerate their representatives entirely or mainly by commission. The representatives of such firms are, in effect, in business on their own account, although financially backed and assisted by the firms they serve.

See also AGENT; BROKER; BUSINESS ORGANIZATION; MARKET RESEARCH.

RESINS, *see* GUMS AND RESINS.

RESTAURANTS, *see* CATERING INDUSTRY.

RETAIL TRADING. This is the branch of commerce which distributes goods into the hands of the people who finally buy them. Retail trade is not restricted to actual shops. Everybody who sells goods to the final customer is a retail trader. Kerbstone men, hawkers, and barrowmen (*see* PEDLARS AND HAWKERS) are also retail traders just as much as the shopkeeper himself.

Modern retail trade includes those firms—prominent in the U.S.A.—that specialize in selling by post direct from their warehouses to the public (*see* MAIL-ORDER TRADING). One branch of retail trade includes canvassers who pay personal visits with their firms' wares to the homes of people to whom they hope to sell. Another branch includes automatic delivery-machines, better known as 'slot machines'; when a coin is inserted, a tray is released, and a small packet of some foodstuff or other commodity can be drawn out.

All the same, shopkeeping is the branch that distributes most goods. Shopkeeping has always been necessary since man gave up a wandering life, settled down to agriculture, and began to live in villages and towns. As the years have passed and the population has increased, the number of shops has increased as well. It is therefore probable that in the United Kingdom there is now a shop for every eighty people; or,

A 15TH-CENTURY SHOP
Painting from the manuscript *Les Chroniques de Jérusalem*

EARLY 19TH-CENTURY HABERDASHER'S SHOP
Engraving on the cover of a letter-file

putting the average family at four people, there is a shop of some kind or other for every twenty families in the country. There might seem to be far too many shops for a very small number of people, but it is perhaps not so excessive when the yearly requirements of an average family are added up and the great variety of what they buy is considered.

Shops may be classified as specialist shops, selling a single line of goods, and compound shops, selling a variety of different goods. On the whole, the tendency to-day is for specialist shops to decrease and compound shops to increase. Even butchers' shops now mostly also sell poultry, tinned soups and vegetables, sauces, stuffings, and other sundries which formerly had to be bought elsewhere. But certain trades still keep to the specialist shop, in particular the boot and shoe, jewellery, and furniture trades. Craftsmen's shops, run by electricians, plumbers, and painters and decorators, sell materials for anybody to buy and use, but they also offer the trained services of the craftsman proprietor or manager, or of his assistants.

Shops may also be classified, not by the goods they sell, but by the type of shop that sells them: the small personal or family business, the chain store or MULTIPLE SHOP, and the DEPARTMENT STORE (qq.v.). In Britain, the typical and most numerous shop is the small personal business, staffed by the proprietor and his wife and family, with perhaps one or two paid outside assistants if the business grows. Between the small family business and the multiple shop comes the small local chain of shops; this may have grown up because a single parent shop has done so well where it was first opened that its owner has opened other branches nearby on which he can keep a personal eye. There are many more of these small local chains than is generally realized. The most highly developed forms of modern shopkeeping, however, are the multiple shop and the department store.

Contrary to common belief, it is not easy to succeed in shopkeeping. Statistics show that in no branch of British commerce is the percentage of business failures or bankruptcies so great as in retail trading. Although such modern techniques as MARKET RESEARCH (q.v.) make the problem of shopkeeping better understood, there are still many risks involved in opening a new shop in an unknown district. There are often right and wrong streets, and even a right and a wrong side of the same street. Wrongly sited shops may do a reasonable business, but may not handle a sufficiently large TURNOVER (q.v.) of goods to enable them to buy goods cheaply from manufacturers and WHOLESALERS (q.v.) who will only cut prices for those who can place big orders. The success of a shop does not depend very much on cutting prices below those of rivals. Even in the same locality, retailers' prices for the same article differ considerably. Success depends much more upon such things as the volume and speed of turnover, efficiency in buying, and building up a large body of customers loyal to the shopkeeper through personal satisfaction rather than through low prices. Successful shopkeeping therefore depends largely on the personality of the shopkeeper himself and his assistants.

See also SELF-SERVICE STORES; DEPARTMENT STORES; MULTIPLE SHOP; WHOLESALE TRADING.

ROPE-MAKING. 1. HISTORICAL. No one knows who first twisted strips of hide, hair, or other materials to make rope. References occur in the Bible and in classical histories. Crude ropes were used in China about 2700 B.C., and early followers of BUDDHISM (q.v. Vol. I) used ropes made of women's hair while building temples. In the tombs of ancient Egyptian kings ropes have been found made of flax, date-palm fibre, halfa grass, bulrushes, and camel-hair. The most ancient rope yet discovered was found in an Egyptian tomb, and is now in the Cairo Museum in an almost perfect state of preservation. It is made of flax, and is about 5200 years old.

Ropes were being made commercially in Britain 500 years ago, and until the second half of the 19th century they were still being made by hand, in long narrow alleys called 'rope-walks'. One man, with the raw fibre wound round his waist, would pay out this fibre, walking backwards down a rope-walk that was anything up to a third of a mile in length. Meanwhile, another man or boy would turn a wheel with hooks to which the fibre was fastened, and in this way the ropes would be spun. Rope-walks are still in use, but the process is now a mechanical one.

2. RAW MATERIALS. The raw material of the rope-maker is fibre, and nowadays this is almost always vegetable or synthetic. Vegetable fibres are classed as either hard or soft. The hard fibres include manila, sisal, henequen, New Zealand, and coir. Soft fibres are hemp, cotton, flax, and jute (see FIBRE CROPS, Vol. VI). The principal synthetic fibres are nylon, rayon, saran, and fibre glass.

Manila (*Abaca* or *Musa textilis*) is derived from a plant like the banana plant which is a native of the Philippine Islands, although plantations have been developed in Central America in Panama, Guatemala, Costa Rica, and Honduras, and in the East Indies in Borneo. Sisal (*Agave sisalana*) is obtained from a plant rather like a cactus, and comes mainly from British East Africa. Henequen (*Agave fourcroydes*) comes from a plant resembling the sisal plant, and is grown mainly in Mexico, but is not used much outside that country and the U.S.A. *Phormium tenax* is obtained from a plant that is native to New Zealand, but is also grown in St. Helena. It is not unlike sisal, but it has a brownish tinge, whereas sisal is white. Coir (see COCONUTS, Vol. VI) is made up of very short

A 19TH-CENTURY ROPE-WALK

fibres extracted from the husks of coconuts in India, Ceylon, and the Philippines.

The principal soft fibre for rope-making is hemp (*Cannabis sativa*), a crop grown in many parts of the world. The highest quality of hemp is cultivated in Italy; it is also grown in Russia, India, Hungary, Yugoslavia, Chile, and the U.S.A.

Much experimental work has been carried out on the production of man-made fibres. The most successful of these is NYLON (q.v.), which has a pulling or 'tensile strength' which is about twice that of the highest-quality vegetable fibre ropes, and is also extremely elastic. It is ideal for use where resistance to sudden jerks is important, as in towage at sea, or in glider towing. It is also used for mountain climbing, for belting for driving machinery, and for many other purposes. RAYON (q.v.) is used in conditions of extreme heat. Synthetic ropes are much more expensive than other fibre cordage, but for many purposes their advantages outweigh the increased cost.

Until the middle of the 19th century soft

hemp was used almost exclusively by British rope-makers, and the bulk of the material came from Russia. The outbreak of the Crimean War put an end to this source of supply, and the rope trade was forced to turn to manila hemp. Manila had been little used in Britain, although recognized in the Far East as a reliable cordage material; so satisfactory did it prove, and so much better than soft hemp for use at sea, that it soon became the most important material of this kind. It remained so until, once again, war affected supplies.

from the Philippines, and sisal from Java, were completely cut off in 1941 when the Japanese occupied these countries. Sisal from British East Africa and Mexico then became the most important cordage material available to the Allied Nations. Certain treatments were developed to make it last and to resist water, so that it could be used more successfully at sea.

The comparative strengths of some of the more important rope-making materials are given in the table below. Rope, by the way, is always measured by circumference and not diameter.

Size Circumference in inches	Weight (lb. per 100 ft.)	Sisal Breaking load (lb.)	Yacht Manila Breaking load (lb.)	Nylon	
				Weight (lb. per 100 ft.)	Breaking load (lb.)
1	3½	1,064	1,344	3	2,000
1¼	4¾	1,400	1,736	4½	3,200
1½	7¼	2,100	2,632	6¾	4,600
2	13	3,976	4,984	11¾	8,200
3	28½	8,960	11,200	26½	17,920

The First World War caused British rope-makers to experiment with other materials. Attempts were made to use British East African sisal, and, although it never became popular for rope-making, it was much used for binder-twine and cord. The Second World War had a more decisive effect, because supplies of manila hemp

G. M. McLean

SLIVERS OF ROPE BEING FED INTO DRAWING-MACHINES TO BE COMBED TO PRODUCE FINER SLIVERS

A 3-inch rope is about 1 inch in diameter, and so on, proportionally.

3. MANUFACTURE. Rope-making is a series of spinning or twisting operations. After the raw fibre has been prepared and combed into 'sliver', there are three operations. The sliver is twisted from left to right to spin the yarn. The yarns are twisted from right to left to form the strand. The strands are twisted from left to right to 'lay' the rope: this results in what is known as a 'right-hand laid' rope. Occasionally the process of twisting is reversed, to form a 'left-hand laid' rope, but opposite twists must be given at the different stages.

The fibres are received in bales, consisting of bundles (or 'heads' as the rope-maker calls them), which have to be separated before the mechanical process can commence. The bundles, or heads, of fibre are fed into machines with sets of chains, or screw-operated fuller bars, fitted with hackle pins or steel spikes. These comb and clean the fibre. The fibre leaves these machines in a continuous ribbon or 'sliver'. This process is repeated several times, to produce still finer slivers. The spinning is done on automatic spinners, which convert the slivers (or fibres lying parallel to one another) into yarns (slivers with a pre-determined twist according to size). These yarns are wound on to bobbins.

The finished rope is made by drawing the yarns from the bobbins and forming them into

G. M. McLean

ROPE YARN BEING SPUN INTO STRANDS

strands by machinery. There are two chief methods: in one, the machine which draws the rope runs on rails down a long straight building, which is still called a rope-walk. By a second method, instead of the newly made rope stretching the full length of a rope-walk, it is coiled, ready for dispatch, as soon as the strands are formed.

4. DEFINITIONS. The following definitions are generally accepted in the trade:

'Cordage' is the word used to describe all ropes and twine, of whatever size.

'Fibre' is the raw material as it reaches the rope-maker. It is combed into long ribbons or slivers, and then spun to form yarn.

'Yarn' is a number of fibres spun together.

'Twine' is one or more yarns twisted together (this also describes cord and string, although these two words are not always used in quite the same way by the rope-maker and by the general public.)

'Rope' is cordage over 1 inch in circumference, and consists of more than six yarns formed into three or more strands. For example, two yarns are spun together to form a strand; three or

Hawser lay, 3 strand

Cable lay, 3 or 4 strand

Shroud lay, 4 strand.

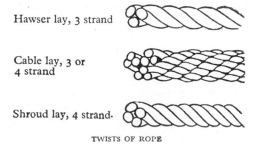

TWISTS OF ROPE

more such strands are spun together to form a rope.

'Hawser-laid rope' is three strands twisted together to form a rope; this is the general construction, and the strongest.

'Cable-laid rope' is rope made of three or more hawser-laid ropes twisted together. The cable has greater flexibility, but has not the strength of a hawser-laid rope of equal size.

'Shroud-laid rope' is four strands twisted together to form a rope. Surface wear is more evenly distributed than in a hawser-laid (three-strand) rope.

Rope is dealt in commercially by weight, and not by length.

See also Vol. IV: KNOTS.
See also Vol. VI: FIBRE CROPS.

ROYALTIES. These are a form of payment-by-results; royalties are paid for the use of land for mining, or for the use of some special process or machine (*see* PATENTS). The word is also used for payments made by publishers to their authors, and by play promoters to playwrights.

In many countries, particularly the U.S.A., the owner of land owns the mining or mineral rights below the surface as well, and mining companies pay a royalty to the ground landlord (*see* PROPERTY, Vol. X) for the privilege of mining beneath his land. British mineral rights were owned by private landlords until the passing of the Coal Mines Act of 1938. The State then arranged to buy out the royalty-owners for a cash compensation of £66,450,000; it also became the owner of all future mineral rights: not only for coal, but also for other metallic ores, china and other clays, and slate and building stone. The most general arrangement for mining royalties is a payment either on the tonnage mined or, if the mineral is coal, on the acreage and thickness of the coal seam being worked (*see* COAL-MINING). The average royalty paid to landlords for coal-mining in Britain before the 1938 Act was just under 6*d.* a ton. This payment included what are called 'wayleaves', or the right of access to the mine across the owner's land.

Royalties are still frequently paid for the use of secret or patented processes, or for the use of special machines with which to carry out the processes. In the history of British industry one of the earliest arrangements of this kind was made in the early 19th century by Boulton and

Watt, of Birmingham, for James Watt's steam-engines. Boulton and Watt could not make in their own works all the engines the world needed; they therefore allowed other engineering firms to make them, under licence, provided that they paid a royalty on each engine turned out. Similar licences are often granted by owners of patent processes to other firms that make use of them. Sometimes a fixed annual payment is made for the use of the process; sometimes a percentage royalty is paid on the goods manufactured and sold. Royalties are also often paid to inventors. The firms that take up the inventions often have to spend much money on making them profitable, and the usual arrangement is that the inventor is paid a royalty on every machine produced and sold. As actual sales are the only proof of the commercial success of an invention, such an arrangement is fair to both parties. For much the same sort of reason, royalty arrangements are the customary way in which publishers pay their authors (see PUBLISH-ING), and theatrical promoters those who write their plays. Neither in the publishing nor in the theatrical world is it possible to estimate accurately in advance what the revenue from a book or a play will be.

RUBBER MANUFACTURE. Rubber is obtained by cutting the bark of various tropical trees. It comes out in the form of a milky liquid

Dunlop Rubber Co.
MIXING RUBBER WITH SULPHUR IN AN OPEN MILL

Dunlop Rubber Co.
MOULDING AND VULCANIZING TIRES
The rubber is heated and softened by steam while in the heavy press

called 'latex' (see RUBBER, Vol. VI). Rubber was first heard of by Europeans in the 16th century, when the Spanish settlers in South America saw the natives playing with rubber balls and using rubber to make their clothes waterproof (see WATERPROOFING TEXTILES).

Before shipment, the latex is first made to set solid by adding acetic or formic acid (see ACIDS). It is then rolled, pressed, and dried. The rubber can be made either into 'smoked sheet', dark brown in colour, by being hung in a smoke-house and 'smoked' by wood fires. Or it can be made into 'crêpe', with a surface like corrugated paper, by being passed between heavy rollers and dried in the air.

The most important step in the history of the rubber industry was the invention in 1839 of the 'vulcanization' process by Charles Goodyear, an American, whose name is still given to the well-known Goodyear motor tires. In vulcanization, SULPHUR (q.v.) is mixed with the rubber; the mixture is then heated, and this alters the nature of the material. Tiny grains of sulphur can be seen in rubber that has been vulcanized. The texture and properties of vulcanized rubber depend largely on the proportion of sulphur mixed with it. Soft rubbers are mixed with $2\frac{1}{2}\%$ to 10% of sulphur, and hard rubber, such as that used for motor tires, with 10% to 50%. Early processes of vulcanization were rather slow, but now it can be done quite quickly:

whereas formerly it took about 3 hours to vulcanize a motor tire, nowadays less than an hour is needed. Vulcanized rubber is much stronger, and resists changes in temperature. It is also resilient: if twisted out of shape it returns to its original form. In the final stages of manufacture the vulcanized material is treated with 'anti-oxidants' to prevent the rubber from perishing when used or stored.

Rubber has many uses in modern life, for example, tennis balls, hose-pipes, and crêpe soles of shoes. But it was above all the invention of the pneumatic tire for wheels of cars that caused the industry to expand. To make tires, rubber is 'built' on to the basis of the tire, which is a cord fabric made of cotton. The tires are then vulcanized in steel moulds. Some rubber goods (ordinary indiarubber, for example), are made by 'extruding' or thrusting them out like toothpaste through a nozzle, and then cutting them to the right shape.

A substitute for rubber is now made artificially. The earliest experiments were made in Germany, when that country was blockaded during the First World War and could not obtain supplies of natural rubber. The synthetic product then turned out was not very satisfactory. Improvements have been made since then, and when, during the Second World War, natural rubber was again scarce, the output and quality of synthetic rubber increased considerably. Synthetic rubber is now made from three principal raw materials: crude oil, acetylene,

U.S. Information Service

TESTING TIRES IN A PRESS WHICH CAN EXERT UP TO 600,000 LB. PRESSURE

and INDUSTRIAL ALCOHOL (q.v.). It is most satisfactory in use when mixed with natural rubber.

See also Vol. VI: RUBBER.

RUBBERIZING, *see* WATERPROOFING TEXTILES.

RUGS, *see* CARPET MAKING.

S

SACKCLOTH, *see* JUTE INDUSTRY.

SALES, *see* AUCTIONS; COMMISSION; RETAIL TRADING.

SALT MANUFACTURE. The world has almost inexhaustible supplies of SALT (q.v. Vol. III), which has always been one of man's important necessities, for himself and his animals as well as for his industries. Supplies exist in two main forms—rock-salt and sea-water. Sea-water contains a large percentage of soluble salts, but the proportion of sodium chloride or 'common salt' (the kind used with food) is only 3%. In earlier days most salt was usually obtained by

I.C.I.

SALT PANS AT WINSFORD, CHESHIRE
The brine, which is pumped from below the ground, is evaporated by heating in a large, shallow, open pan

allowing sun and wind to evaporate sea-water in shallow pans or 'salterns' constructed by the side of the sea or estuaries. This system is still followed in warm countries, particularly in India and China, and on the shores of the Mediterranean and the Red Sea. Evaporation of the water leaves the salts concentrated as a solid, and this is collected usually once a year. A drawback to the evaporation of sea-water is that pure 'common salt' is not left behind; it is mixed with other salts. The bulk of the present world production of salt is therefore rock-salt.

This is either dug out by mining, or pumped as brine from underground workings. There are large deposits of rock-salt in Europe, North America, Russia, and India; Polish mines near Cracow have been worked since the 13th century. Stassfurt in Germany, where much natural potash is produced (*see* ALKALIS), has deposits of rock-salt also. The largest British deposits are in Cheshire, around Middlewich, Northwich, Nantwich, and Winsford; this area contains reserves sufficient for several centuries. At Winsford the salt is only about 200 feet below the surface and is mined. In other parts of Cheshire, and also in Droitwich and elsewhere, the salt is produced by pumping brine.

Where rock-salt is mined, ordinary mining methods are followed, as in COAL-MINING (q.v.). Pillars of rock-salt are left unhewn, to support the roof. There are no poisonous or explosive gases; the mines are electrically powered and lighted, and working conditions are safe, cool, and comfortable. If mining is impossible, there are two ways of pumping brine. Sometimes natural water has trickled down from the surface of the land towards the salt deposits, and natural or 'local' brine is already present below. This merely has to be pumped to the surface. If there is no natural water below, some must be led down through shafts or boreholes. This water dissolves the salt, and is left for some time to settle before it is pumped to the surface again as brine. The brine must then be evaporated.

Some 2,000 years ago the Romans mined the Cheshire salt deposits, and mining has been continuous ever since. They got solid salt by evaporating the brine in open pans over furnaces. Nowadays the vacuum process is generally used: that is, the evaporation takes place at less than normal atmospheric pressure and therefore at a lower boiling-point (*see* DISTILLATION). Whichever method is used, as the water boils the salt crystallizes, falls to the bottom of the evaporator, and is removed.

Cheshire rock-salt is about 95% pure and, like most rock-salt, is a light reddish-brown, owing to the presence of iron. Most rock-salt, whether mined or evaporated, is disposed of in unrefined form as a solid, but liquid brine is also sent in tanks from Cheshire salt-works to the chemical works of Cheshire and Lancashire. Purity is increased by REFINING (q.v.). Salt, particularly in refined or powdered form, is very liable to get damp in an ordinary atmosphere; table-salt is therefore usually mixed with about 1% of magnesium carbonate, which prevents it from caking. Apart from the large quantities consumed by the chemical industry (*see* ACIDS and ALKALIS), salt is used for many industrial purposes, including the preserving of hides and skins and of foodstuffs.

SANDSTONE, *see* Vol. III: SANDS AND SAND-STONES.

SAVINGS, *see* CAPITAL; *see also* Vol. **X:** NATIONAL SAVINGS.

SCIENTIFIC MANAGEMENT. 1. This means using scientific methods in the management of business firms. The need for scientific management only became clear when the old DOMESTIC SYSTEM (q.v.) of industrial organization had developed into our modern factory system.

Management was a comparatively simple matter when industry was in the domestic stage. Workers were then their own managers, and worked in their own homes; although an employer controlled the pattern and design of the goods turned out, and provided the materials for making them, he did not in our modern sense 'manage' those who worked for him. Management remained fairly simple in the early days of the INDUSTRIAL REVOLUTION (q.v.), when the factory system was just beginning. Most of the employers of the period were practical working-men who had risen in life; and, as they often worked side by side with their workers and were in close daily contact with them, the problems of management solved themselves by 'give and take' as they arose. Now that factories are much larger, with an orderly array of managers and foremen controlling large bodies of workers, the problems of management are much less simple, and the need has arisen for a scientific technique.

This branch of scientific management, which deals with human beings at work, is called 'personnel management'. It makes much use of the modern science of INDUSTRIAL PSYCHOLOGY (q.v.).

There are other aspects of scientific management. No business can go on providing work, even for the most contented workers, unless it is fully efficient in other ways. Unless it happens to have a MONOPOLY (q.v.), every business has to meet the competition of rivals at home and abroad, and must constantly be trying to speed up output and reduce its cost of production. Management, therefore, is largely concerned with costs of production, output, and sales, and makes much use of such scientific techniques as BOOK-KEEPING, COSTING, STATISTICS, and MARKET RESEARCH (qq.v.). But the main part of scientific management is what we might call 'factory science'. This includes measuring and assessing the jobs to be done, and fixing rates of payment for them (*see* WAGES); the simplifying of goods and processes, so that the cost of production can be reduced to a minimum; TIME AND MOTION STUDY (q.v. Vol. VIII), that is, observing the motions which workers go through in doing a job, planning the least fatiguing and most efficient motions, and calculating the 'standard' or ideal times that various tasks should take; and the organization of a factory so that those employed there may work as efficiently and contentedly as possible.

2. HISTORY. Modern scientific management owes more to an American engineer, Frederick Winslow Taylor, than to anyone else, but there were pioneers of modern management in Britain long before Taylor's ideas were published. Boulton and Watt, the famous Birmingham engineering firm of the early 19th century, was one of the first to work out a scientific costing system. Personnel management goes back as far as Robert OWEN (q.v. Vol. V), the father of the co-operative movement, who discovered over 100 years ago that if workers were treated well their work improved. Richard ARKWRIGHT (q.v. Vol. V), who invented the water-frame for textile spinning, was also a clever manager and organizer. Even time and motion study is not an entirely modern idea, for Charles Babbage, a Cambridge mathematician and the inventor of the Babbage calculating-machine, wrote about it over 100 years ago, and also made some important suggestions about costing.

Taylor, however, was the first to see clearly that the principles of management could be worked out by studying industry in general, and that such principles could be applied to all industries and not merely to one. On the whole, his observations were restricted to firms in the engineering and allied trades, but his principles were worked out so soundly that later on they were found to apply equally well to other industries, and even to firms that merely traded in goods and did not manufacture them. Taylor emphasized that there must be good relations between management and employees, and he suggested that there would have to be in the future a scientific study of the causes that led human beings at work to think and act in the ways they did. He stressed the importance of selecting workers for particular jobs, and of transferring 'misfit' workers from jobs that did not suit them to others which they might perform brilliantly. Years before such a science came into existence, Taylor clearly foresaw the necessity of what is now called industrial psychology. He was also the first to emphasize the importance of what we now call 'work measurement', that is, the careful definition of what each individual in a factory has to do, and the calculation of the rate that will be paid for doing it. Taylor improved upon Babbage's ideas about time and motion study, and was the first to work out 'standards' of work and performance which all workers in a factory should attain. He also made important suggestions for drawing up what are now called 'organization charts' (*see* BUSINESS ORGANIZATION), giving the detailed chain of responsibility from the top of a business downwards, and defining the duties of each person or group of persons in the chain. Finally, the very term 'scientific management' was invented by Taylor and his assistants. They did not claim too much for it. They believed that management was not a science but an art: an art, however, that could be more effectively acquired if various scientific techniques—such as organization, accounting, costing, statistics, time and motion study, and industrial psychology—were used also.

3. SCIENTIFIC MANAGEMENT TO-DAY. Taylor's ideas date from the early years of the present century, and they have been much enlarged and improved upon since his death in 1915. Motion study has been elaborated, and such details as the shape of tools, the height of work-benches,

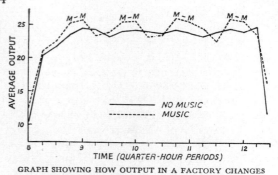

GRAPH SHOWING HOW OUTPUT IN A FACTORY CHANGES WHEN MUSIC IS PLAYED AT QUARTER-HOUR INTERVALS (M-M)

From *Fatigue and Boredom in Repetitive Work* by permission of the Controller, H.M.S.O.

the way that workpeople stand or sit at their work, have all received careful thought. Methods of factory control and inspection have been improved. Financial control of business has been assisted by such techniques as BUDGETARY CONTROL (q.v.). Market research is being more and more used to find out in advance whether what it is proposed to produce can be profitably sold, and in what quantity. Industrial psychology has not only done much to avoid waste of effort through 'misfit' workers, but has made a more definite contribution towards good management by working out the scientific foundations of a healthy 'climate of work'. Scientific management now has its own specialists, and there are firms of business consultants or business efficiency experts that are prepared to advise manufacturers on what should be done to increase the efficiency of their businesses.

See also BUSINESS ORGANIZATION; FACTORY ORGANIZATION.

SECURITY. This word is often used in the world of finance, and has two meanings. By its more important meaning it is some kind of document, stating that the person named in it is the owner of stock or shares in a limited company (*see* STOCKS AND SHARES), or is entitled to receive interest on a LOAN (q.v.) made to an industrial concern, to a government, or to a local authority. Such 'securities' can be bought and sold on the stock exchanges, and are called 'negotiable' securities.

The other meaning of the word is some form of guarantee given to a lender of money that the promise to repay it will be carried out. This may take the form of negotiable securities deposited with the banker or lender, so that if

NORWICH MARKET-PLACE

Painting by John Sell Cotman (1782–1842). The market has changed little since the 19th century

the loan is not repaid he may sell the securities and repay himself the amount due. But sometimes bankers are quite satisfied if they receive written guarantees, signed by responsible persons, that they will themselves repay the loan if the original borrower fails to do so. Title-deeds of houses and of Property (q.v. Vol. X), life-insurance policies, and other documents are often put up as security to bankers and other lenders. Such security is called 'collateral'.

See also Banking; Debentures.

SELF-SERVICE STORES. For some time this kind of shop has been a feature of Retail Trading (q.v.), particularly in Sweden and the U.S.A. It is also developing rapidly in Britain. In the U.S.A. the larger types of self-service stores are called 'super-markets'.

The self-service store differs greatly from the Woolworth type, in which there is only a little self-service. In the true self-service store, the customer, on entering, picks up one or two baskets which she can slide along on runners, as in many British cafeterias (see Catering Industry). All goods are displayed within the customer's reach, and, as she passes the various stands, she fills her baskets. Rails prevent movement in all but one direction. After passing round the store and completing her shopping, the customer passes through what are called 'check-out lanes'. Here the goods are taken out of the baskets by a cashier-assistant, counted and priced, and paid for. The customer then puts

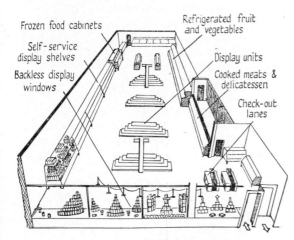

LAYOUT OF A SELF-SERVICE STORE
Customers take what they want from the shelves and pay at the desk as they go out

Frozen food cabinets
Self-service display shelves
Backless display windows
Refrigerated fruit and vegetables
Display units
Cooked meats & delicatessen
Check-out lanes

the goods into her own shopping-bag and passes through the exit.

In most countries, this sytem has been adopted so far principally in the grocery trade, which is particularly suitable for it. The display stands where the goods are stacked are kept continuously stocked with fresh articles. The very small staff employed is an advantage of this type of shop, which requires only the assistants who keep the stands filled with stock, and the cashiers who work the cash registers in the check-out lanes.

See also Multiple Shops; Department Stores.

SHALE OIL comes from oil shale, a type of rock (see Clays and Shales, Vol. III). The deposits most worked are in Scotland, Estonia, and the Transvaal in South Africa; others are in Canada, Sweden, and Australia. The Scottish deposits are principally in West Lothian, Midlothian, and Fife. The U.S.A. has large deposits which are little used because petroleum is cheaper to produce (see Oil, Mineral). One of the earliest shale-oil industries is that of France, which was started in 1830, but the first large-scale works was opened in Scotland in the 1840's.

Oil shale is mined in much the same way as coal, either in open-cast workings or by underground mining (see Coal-mining). Chemically, oil shale contains both organic and inorganic compounds (see Chemistry, Vol. III); the inorganic portions turn to ash when heated, and the organic portion (known as the 'kerogen') decomposes into crude oil. The mined shale is crushed into small pieces, put into large cast-iron retorts similar in principle to those used in Gas Manufacture (q.v. Vol. VIII), and heated to a high temperature. The 'kerogen' decomposes into crude oil and what is called 'retort gas'; from this gas some crude petrol can be obtained. The process produces a large quantity of Ammonia (q.v.), which is treated with sulphuric acid to form sulphate of ammonia, a valuable soil fertilizer. The crude oil is then distilled and refined into various products, including solvent spirits, petrol, paraffin or kerosene, and paraffin wax (see Oil Refining).

SHARES, see Stocks and Shares.

SHEFFIELD PLATE. This silver-plated ware, which included mainly articles for domestic use, such as dishes, tea-caddies, biscuit-boxes and

18TH-CENTURY LABEL OF A SHEFFIELD PLATE
MANUFACTURER

snuff-boxes, decanter-stands, and candlesticks, was made by a special process that was practised for about a century, and then died out. The general level of taste and design in England stood very high during that particular period—from the middle of the 18th century onwards. Sheffield plate possesses a beautiful quality of its own, which is absent in articles silvered all over by the process of ELECTRO-PLATING (q.v. Vol. VIII) which took its place.

Silversmiths had long looked for a way in which wares made of cheap metal or alloy could be 'plated', or given a coating of silver, so that they should appear to be made of the solid metal. Two methods were widely practised: 'amalgamation', a chemical process, and 'French plating', in which thin silver-leaf was made to adhere to the copper or brass underneath it by means of heat and friction. The first of these methods gave rather a poor effect, and the second required immense labour if a thick enough layer were to be built up by repeated heating and burnishing. In 1752 Thomas Bolsover, a Sheffield workman, while mending a knife handle made of copper and silver, discovered that by accidentally overheating it he had fused the two metals so closely together that no later working could part them. He began the manufacture of what came to be called Sheffield plate, though he confined himself to small articles, which he first made in base metal and then plated. The method finally adopted was to produce first of all a strip or small ingot of copper and brass alloy, about 12 inches by 3, and about an inch thick. It was carefully filed and scraped dead flat and clean on its upper face, great care being taken to prevent any dirt—even a fingermark—from

reaching it. On this was placed a slightly smaller piece of silver, the under surface of which had been similarly cleaned and flattened. The thickness of the silver was between about 1/16 and 3/16 of an inch, according to the thickness of plating finally required. A sheet of iron, washed with whiting to prevent its sticking during heating, was then placed over them, and the three pieces of metal were bound tightly together with iron wire. Finally, the edges of the silver were painted round with borax ground to a paste, and the whole was put into a small furnace and brought to a red heat. As this temperature was approached, the edges of the silver (helped by the borax) began to show signs of melting; and just at that moment the metals were taken from the furnace and laid aside to cool. It was on the great precision of this that the chief success of the process depended; for, if correctly done, it made so perfect a join between the silver and the base metal that no subsequent operation, however violent, could separate them. To reduce the twin ingot to sheet-metal of the required thickness, it was passed repeatedly through iron rollers (not unlike a mangle in operation), being 'annealed' (or softened by being reheated) as necessary (see HEAT TREATMENT, Vol. VIII).

In early Sheffield plate only one side of the alloy was silvered, the other being usually tinned; later on, both sides were plated. In each case there remained the raw copper edge, which had to be concealed. This was done by soldering silver wire over it or along it. Various ornamental sections of wire were used, and at times they were further treated by being hammered so as to overlap above or below. Articles were further decorated by having mounted on them ornaments either of solid silver or of silver filled with pewter. These, too, were soldered into place. The presence of these joints, beautifully concealed as they are, is one of the features distinguishing Sheffield plate from electro-plate, in which the covering of silver is deposited uniformly everywhere; another is the pleasant characteristic texture and colour of the metal itself, the result of the process of manufacture.

For some years the makers of early Sheffield plate were forbidden to stamp their 'mark' on it, as was done with solid silver, but in 1784 the right to mark plate was granted by law. Marking is by no means a sure guide to the genuineness or quality of Sheffield plate, because many of the finest specimens carry no mark at all.

Sheffield plate was made not only in Sheffield, but to a very large extent in London and Birmingham also. Birmingham used a copper base, which was not only softer, but shows as a much redder metal where the silver has been worn or polished away. From 1850 onwards the commercial manufacture of Sheffield plate ceased, but the method is occasionally revived for special orders.

See also GOLD AND SILVER WORK.

SHELLAC is one of the natural resins (*see* GUMS AND RESINS). The natural resins are divided into two classes: those of woody origin, obtained as a rule from tree-tapping, and those of insect origin. The insect group includes the lac resins, of which shellac is the best known.

There are about sixty varieties of trees which act as hosts to the grubs or larvae of the lac insects, a variety of the SCALE INSECT (q.v. Vol. II). These larvae feed on the sap of the trees, and produce a kind of resin which they then exude to protect themselves from weather and enemies. The larvae encase themselves in

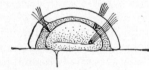

LAC INSECT IN ITS RESINOUS COVERING

The mouth parts point downwards into the plant. Three sets of breathing tubes pass through gaps in the resin

resinous shells, allowing only a narrow tube to protrude for breathing. The trees become covered with the lac, which at the proper season is collected by rolling and sifting. It is called 'sticklac' in the crude form and is purified by being kneaded in warm water and 'fused' over a fire.

Resins of insect origin occur chiefly in India, where shellac is first recorded as being used. In the 16th century shellac lacquerwork and shellac varnishes were widely known in India. Since then the uses of shellac varnish and sealing-wax have increased throughout the world. About 95% of shellac still comes from India, the remainder coming from Burma, Siam, and Indo-China.

Besides yielding resin, shellac also contains some dyestuffs and waxes. There are two types of colouring matter in shellac, of which only one is a true dye.

Shellac is chiefly needed for making varnishes, lacquers, inks, wax emulsions, sealing-wax, and 'fillers' or filling-material for certain woodwork. In the United States alone some 14 million lbs. of shellac varnish is used on wood floors every year. Varnishes account for 60% of the known uses of shellac; shellac mouldings, mostly in the form of gramophone records, account for 30%; shellac cements and adhesives use 2% of the world's output; the remaining 8% is useful for many purposes, ranging from fireworks to the chocolate industries. Although synthetic materials, such as cellulose acetate and vinyl chloride, have been used increasingly in recent years for gramophone records, shellac is still the most important material for this industry.

See also GUMS AND RESINS; PAINTS AND VARNISHES.

SHIPBUILDING INDUSTRY. The records of the past, before the days of writing, show that from the earliest times men have been building ships, and that some of them were quite large. Oars and sails were the only methods of propulsion. Wood was the chief material used, and there is evidence that the early builders of boats and ships had a good deal of practical skill (*see* PRIMITIVE SHIPS, Vol. IV).

At the close of the Middle Ages, when we begin to have more plentiful records, ships were still being built of wood and were propelled by sails. Vessels were built usually at ports where there were banks suitable for building and launching, and very large forests in the background to provide the wood. Some of the sites of these early ship-yards were on such narrow waters that launching had to be done sideways. In Queen Elizabeth's time London was a great shipbuilding centre, and every effort was made to preserve the forests of Kent and southern England, so as to keep up the supply of oak. The arsenal at Woolwich on its present site dates from the days of Elizabeth. The shipyards were higher up the river, at Deptford; there were anchorages at Greenwich, and a gun park—to which the naval armament was taken for repair—at Woolwich. In those days masts and spars were imported from Scandinavia, and also such things as resin and tar, needed for caulking seams. Each busy port around the coasts of Britain and other countries had its own ship or boat building yard, and each district produced its own local designs, to suit the particular work the ships had to do.

The same kind of activity went on in North America after colonization had begun, and it was on the Atlantic seaboard, near to the timber forests, that a shipbuilding industry first became estabished there. By the 18th century world trade was increasing. Competition between the nations meant calls for better and faster ships, and shipbuilders had to keep up with the enlarged demands that were being made upon them. The sturdy traders of Canada and New England, in north-eastern America, began to build fast ships, at least as good as those built elsewhere, and often better. These vessels were still of wood, and if they had to withstand the SHIP-WORM (q.v. Vol. II) of the tropics, their bottoms were sheathed with copper. As skill and mathematical knowledge increased, and more experience of handling and operating larger and faster ships was gained, designs improved.

The standards of design and construction of the wooden ship reached their height about the middle of the 19th century. This was the period of the great CLIPPER SHIPS (q.v. Vol. IV), graceful, almost alive, with their towering mass of sails and their carved figureheads and bowsprits—vessels capable of holding their own even against the early steam-driven ships. But advances in knowledge were not confined to ships. Men were learning more about the SMELTING and working of iron (q.v. Vol. VIII); the steam-engine was invented and began its gradual process of improvement; and—very slowly at first—the use of iron for ships' hulls began. It was no longer necessary to have one's shipyard near supplies of timber; instead it should be near the iron foundries, the forges and mills, and the new engineering centres (see STEAMSHIPS, HISTORY OF, Vol. IV).

By the beginning of the 19th century there was a steady drift of the industry away from southern England. There was still a good deal of shipbuilding on the Thames, but new centres opened up on the Clyde, the Tyne, the Wear, the Tees, the Mersey, and Belfast Lough, and the outlines of the modern location of the industry were appearing. Glasgow, Newcastle, Sunderland, and Liverpool were the first of the new centres, and they had behind them the coalfields of the midland valley of Scotland, of the north-east coast of England, and of Lancashire, and the furnaces and foundries where the iron was made.

The new techniques were at first almost entirely British, but they spread slowly to Europe and North America. In the early days of iron almost all ships were still driven by sail, and the use of this new material did not involve any great changes in hull design. Thus, at first, little advantage was taken of the properties of iron for the creation of entirely new designs. But Britain, a fairly small island, with an enormous overseas trade, was well placed to become the world's leader in shipbuilding. She had the knowledge and the raw materials (coal and iron), and needed ships more than other nations did.

In 1856 Henry Bessemer showed the world how to make steel cheaply and in large quantities, and steel began to replace iron (see IRON AND STEEL, Vol. VIII). In its early years steel remained rather an experimental material for shipbuilding, but later its use was better understood, and old-fashioned methods of construction, differing little from those of the wooden ships, were gradually given up.

By 1867 LLOYD's Register of shipping (q.v. Vol. IV), a body which concerns itself with the standards to which ships are built, accepted steel as a standard material, while such companies as the Cunard already had steel vessels. In the new steel construction Britain took the lead, and also taught other nations. British shipbuilders were among the founders of what became famous shipyards at Gothenburg in Sweden, at Copenhagen in Denmark, and in Belgium. Among the emigrants to the United States and Canada were many British shipwrights and mechanics skilled in the modern techniques.

By 1890 the United Kingdom built about four-fifths of the world's shipping, and owned about three-fifths of it. Many firms were in the industry, and it had become almost a general rule for each yard to build only one kind of ship. The larger yards usually engined their own ships, but many yards did not build marine engines themselves. In the last quarter of the century there was a great trade depression (see TRADE CYCLE), which came about when other countries were beginning to challenge Britain's industrial leadership. The depression hit the British shipbuilding industry very hard, and one of its most serious competitors was Germany, where a large and important shipbuilding industry was being set up. London had once been a great centre of the shipbuilding industry in earlier days, and had continued to build iron and steel ships in spite of the great distance from raw materials. But in these new days of intensified competition this was no longer possible, and in

John Brown

A PASSENGER-CARGO SHIP ON THE CLYDE

1911 the Thames Iron Works launched its last big vessel, the battleship *Thunderer*.

The outbreak of the First World War in 1914 thus saw the end of the Thames as a centre for the building of any but smaller craft. During that war the ships of all nations were sunk in great numbers by the German submarines or 'U-boats' (*see* SEA WARFARE, MODERN, Vol. X), and all countries had to set about building new ships. Even the United States, whose shipbuilding had hardly recovered at that late date from the consequences of the Civil War of 1861–5, set up shipyards and later outstripped the production of any other nation. Under the stress of war Britain could spare neither the time nor the materials to build for any foreign owners as she had previously been doing, and foreign yards were opened or enlarged all over Europe, and also in Japan.

Thus the end of the First World War saw many more shipyards throughout the world than ever before. Shortly after the war there was work for them all, because ships that had survived the war were nearly worn out and there were also all the war losses to make good. This great activity fell off within a few years, and during the years before the Second World War broke out, shipbuilders had a very hard time. In Britain many yards were closed, and many workers were unemployed. The same thing was happening abroad, for there were more shipyards than the peace-time world could fully use. But this was not a period during which the science of shipbuilding stood still. Welding was being introduced to replace or to supplement riveting; ships became faster, as more efficient engines and hull designs were produced (*see* MARINE ENGINEERING, Vol. VIII), and special ships were designed and built for special kinds of cargo.

Thus, in spite of hard times, the British shipbuilding industry was well up to date, and was able to play its part in a fresh war effort. From 1939 onwards, as in the earlier war, every naval vessel or merchantman that could be built was needed, and once again all the world's shipyards were busy. The use of welded construction was extended, particularly in the United States, where a manufacturer named Henry Kaiser developed a process which almost amounted to the mass production of ships. Instead of assembling small, shaped parts of a ship one by one in the yard itself, large sections were welded together in workshops, often far from the yard; these sections were then transported to the yard, lifted into place by powerful cranes, and welded together until the complete hull was ready for launching. Similar processes were developed in Britain, and machines were invented for automatic welding. These new methods made it necessary to reorganize the layout of the yards, and to use more powerful cranes and equipment.

After the Second World War the world was again busy replacing its war losses, and Britain's share in this work was considerable. Increased demand for ships, and insistence on quicker delivery, led to the development of new methods. On the Clyde one yard invented a system of building ships in vertical instead of horizontal stages, beginning with the stern and working towards the bow. This was a rather revolutionary departure from the time-honoured method of laying the keel first, and building upwards from it the ribs and frames and plating until the decking stage was reached. Between 1945 and 1950 Britain built nearly as many ships as the rest of the world put together. Many of these ships were for British owners, but there was hardly an overseas nation that did not come to Britain for at least some of its ships.

See also Vol. IV: SHIP; PRIMITIVE SHIPS; CLASSICAL SHIPS; SAILING SHIPS; STEAMSHIPS, HISTORY OF.

See also Vol. VIII: MARINE ENGINEERING.

SHIPPING. The history of SHIPS (q.v. Vol. IV) is very closely bound up with the history of trade, for it is cheaper to carry goods by sea than by land. Britain's greatness as a mercantile power has depended very largely upon the efficiency and size of her merchant navy. By the end of the 17th century the English had succeeded the Dutch as leaders of the world's carrying trade by sea. They improved upon this lead in the 18th and 19th centuries; and, although in the 20th century competition from other countries became very keen, the largest part of the world's seaborne trade is still carried in British ships.

This position has taken centuries to reach. In the Middle Ages the seaborne trade of the western world was chiefly restricted to the Mediterranean, the Channel, and the North Sea, and was largely in the hands of the Venetians and the HANSEATIC LEAGUE (q.v.), the ships of the League being based on north German ports such as Lübeck and Hamburg. In the north the

National Maritime Museum

SHIPS LOADING TIMBER IN A NORTHERN EUROPEAN PORT
Painting by H. C. Vroom, 1566–1640

Viking pirates had ceased to exist, and it was reasonably safe to cross the seas. But in the Mediterranean the famous Barbary pirates, from what are now the Algerian and Moroccan coasts, were still a menace to shipping, and compelled the Venetian galleys to travel in convoy (*see* PIRATES, Vol. IV). The arrival of these galleys in Spithead and the Solent was a great spectacle every year.

It took a long time for England to get a start as a merchant-shipping nation, and longer still to achieve a leading position. The start was made during the later Middle Ages, when the ships of the MERCHANT ADVENTURERS (q.v.) began to challenge the supremacy held by the Hanseatic League. By the 15th century the Venetians were being so much occupied by troubles at home— by wars with other Italian republics such as the Genoese, and by the attacks of the Turks—that they were no longer serious rivals. At the end of the 15th century English shipping was firmly established in north European waters; but by that time the Portuguese and the Spaniards had begun to voyage into the remoter and unknown waters of the world.

England's Tudor rulers had foreseen the coming struggle with Spain and they encouraged seafaring, not only in home waters but also abroad; even before the defeat of the Spanish Armada in 1588, the number of English ships on the more distant seas was considerable. After this defeat Spain was so crippled that the sea-faring people of the Netherlands, who had struggled under Spanish domination, succeeded in their fight for independence. For a time the Dutch fleets were occupied with overcoming the Spanish and Portuguese fleets, and this gave England an opportunity to build and man more ships and to send them all over the world. But as soon as the Dutch had settled with their other enemies, they turned their attention to England; and there began a long period of Dutch–English rivalry at sea, which occasionally resulted in open war, and which never really came to an end until a Dutch prince, William III, became King of England in 1689. But Britain even then could not fully consider herself 'mistress of the seas' until TRAFALGAR (q.v. Vol. X) had been fought in 1805.

After the Battle of Waterloo Britain enjoyed nearly 100 years of freedom from wars in western Europe, when she could develop her industry at home and her shipping abroad. The owners of her diverse fleet of sailing-ships found themselves in a favourable position to run their ships cheaply in competitition with the rest of the world, and so to make a good profit. In a country where few towns were, on the average, more than 40 or 50 miles from the sea, the sea was in the people's blood. The fishing industry and a series of naval wars had bred a magnificent force of trained seamen, whose skill and knowledge were handed down from generation to generation.

By the beginning of the 19th century, the pattern of British shipping organization had become established, and it did not in fact alter greatly when steamships began to replace sailing-ships. There were famous lines of fast and well-found ships trading regularly between British and overseas ports, and there were also the sailing 'tramps' which picked up cargoes when and where they offered themselves, and which ran on no regular schedules. There was also a large fleet of coasting vessels, using the smaller ports.

Towards the end of the sailing-ship period competition began to be serious, particularly from Finland, Sweden, Norway, Denmark, and Holland. The crews of these foreign ships were prepared to work for lower wages and under less attractive conditions than British crews. To counter this, many British shipowners put British officers, boatswains, and quartermasters in charge of foreign crews from these northern countries. But this undercutting of freight and passenger rates by foreign competitors might have seriously injured Britain's supremacy in the world's seaborne carrying trade, had not the coming of the steamship saved the situation. For Britain was at this time so much in the lead in the production of iron, steel, and machinery, that she had an overwhelming advantage in the building of STEAMSHIPS (q.v. Vol. IV).

There were, however, many British and American shipowners who did not believe in steam for long deep-sea voyages. They argued that steamships would have to carry so much coal that there would be little space for a paying load of cargo; also that, if sailing-ships could be redesigned for speed and given the fine lines of yachts, they might hold their own against steam. Although in the end these arguments proved unsound, especially as steam technique improved, for a while they were believed in, and in consequence there followed the magnificent period of the CLIPPER SHIPS (q.v. Vol. IV). But in spite of spectacular performances, and of frequent daily runs of between 350 and 400 sea-miles in the areas of the trade winds, the clippers could not hold their own; and the owners who had pinned their faith to steam were justified.

The local geographical advantages possessed by Britain, such as coal and iron fields (and therefore steelworks) on the shores of tidal estuaries, gave her a lead in building and running steamships which on the whole has not been lost. The old distinction between the 'line' of ships plying regularly between port and port, and the tramp ship, picking up cargoes wherever they offered, became more marked in the age of steam. LINERS (q.v. Vol. IV) may carry passengers only, cargo only, or mixed cargo and passengers; their voyages are planned and advertised beforehand, and they run, as trains do, to a time-table, regularly and punctually. The TRAMP-SHIP (q.v. Vol. IV) leaves Britain with a cargo for a particular destination and then picks up whatever cargo is offered; it is possible that a tramp voyage may last a year or more without a call at a home port. Another difference between the cargo liner and the tramp is that the cargo liner carries a variety of goods in small consignments; the tramp is loaded with a single bulk cargo for an overseas port, and there picks up another full cargo. The ownership and management of cargo liners remains permanently in the hands of the owning company; the management of the tramp remains always, of course, in the hands of the owning company, but a kind of temporary ownership of the vessel is given to the shipper of the cargo (or charterer) by a document called a 'charter party'. Arrangements for chartering are usually made on the Baltic Exchange in the City of London.

Towards the end of the 19th century Britain's leading position in world shipping was again challenged by the merchant fleets of other nations, Japan in particular. Many governments gave SUBSIDIES (q.v.) to shipping companies, helping them to build and run ships of a higher speed than would normally have been profitable, so that they would be useful as auxiliary CRUISERS (q.v. Vol. X) if war came. For instance, in Germany, big subsidies were paid to the Hamburg-Amerika and the Norddeutscher-Lloyd lines. The Austrian Government followed the German example, and subsidized the Austrian-Lloyd on the Eastern run. The Russian Government went even further: it organized as a State enterprise the Russian Volunteer Fleet, officered and manned by reservists, and intended to be useful in war-time as fleet auxiliaries and armed merchant cruisers.

Against this kind of State-assisted competition there was not much that British statesmen could do, believing as they then did in free trade and the freedom of business enterprise from government intervention. To some extent concealed SUBSIDIES (q.v.) were given, in the form of in-

British Railways

CARS BEING LOADED INTO A SHIP FOR EXPORT TO SOUTH AFRICA

creased payments by the Post Office to liner companies for carrying the mails. However, British shipowners had some big economic advantages on their side. Britain then had a large exportable surplus of cheap coal. British ships could go abroad full of coal, and come back full of bulky cargoes such as wheat, rice, jute, cotton, nitrates, iron-ore, and manganese. British shipowners, therefore, had the considerable advantage of operating full ships both outward and homeward bound. Foreign owners were not so fortunately placed. On the other hand, cut-throat competition among the various owners made the British shipping industry much more unstable than foreign State-controlled shipping. The leading owners partly combated this competition by amalgamating themselves into bigger groups; the P. & O. group, for instance, included the P. & O. Company, the British India Company, and the New Zealand Shipping Company. But this could not altogether control the constant cutting of freight rates, particularly by the smaller owners. Under the leadership of the more important lines, associations or 'conferences' were therefore formed in order to fix standard rates for freight and passenger transport, to which all members of a conference had to conform. Between the First and Second World Wars, many successful attempts were made to co-operate with foreign lines and to form international conferences.

In spite of losses in two wars, and great economic changes in the world as a whole, British shipping still stands well in the lead. Coal does not rule the situation as it used to do, for many ships now use other fuels such as oil; and the exportable surplus of British coal is neither as big nor as cheap as it used to be. But the inherited skill and knowledge of the past still enable British builders to construct ships that are as modern in design as those of other countries, and British owners to run them profitably. The earnings of her ships are still the most important 'invisible' item of Britain's export trade (*see* INTERNATIONAL TRADE).

See also SHIPBUILDING INDUSTRY.

See also Vol. IV: SHIP; MERCHANT SHIPPING; PORTS AND HARBOURS.

SHOES, *see* BOOT AND SHOE MAKING.

SHOP, see RETAIL TRADING; MULTIPLE SHOP; DEPARTMENT STORES; SELF-SERVICE STORES.

SILK, ARTIFICIAL, see RAYON.

SILK INDUSTRY. 1. According to Chinese legend, the breeding of SILKWORMS (q.v. Vol. VI) for their silk thread goes back more than 4,000 years. For centuries the Chinese kept their knowledge of this craft to themselves. A silk industry existed in India by 1000 B.C. or even earlier, but it is very likely that 'wild' silk was used, produced by the tussah-moth and not by specially bred silkworms. This tussore silk, as it is now called, is still made in India. Silk goods do not appear to have been brought to Europe until 320 B.C., when Alexander the Great returned from his campaign against the Persians; whether the goods were of Chinese or Indian origin is not certain. Nearly 300 years later silk was being imported into Rome, and silk garments were worn by the wealthy. They probably came overland by camel caravan from China. In the third century silkworms and the art of weaving silk were introduced into Japan. During all this time European merchants bought silk goods but knew nothing of how they were made. The Roman Emperor Justinian (A.D. 483–565) is believed to have introduced the silkworm to Europe. It is said that two Persian monks who had travelled in China told Justinian about the silk industry, and that he sent them back to China with instructions to bring out its secrets. They are reported to have returned about A.D. 550 with a collection of silkworms' eggs hidden in a hollow bamboo staff. In any event, in the later years of Justinian's reign silk manufacture became a MONOPOLY (q.v.) of the Emperor, and weaving looms were set up in part of his palace. By the 8th century A.D. the knowledge of silkworm breeding (or sericulture, as it is sometimes called) had spread to countries which were then under the influence of the MOORS (q.v. Vol. I), including Sicily and Spain. By the 12th century silkworms were being bred in Italy, and by the end of the 13th century in France also. The climate and vegetation of many countries were not suitable for silkworms. In the 16th century the Spanish conqueror Cortez took silkworms to Mexico, as well as the mulberry trees which are their natural food. But nothing came of this. Later attempts elsewhere in North and South America had no greater success, and the chief modern producers of silk on a commercial scale are still the countries that were producing in the Middle Ages—China, Japan, Italy, and France. By far the largest producer is Japan.

The threads spun by silkworms and by spiders are very much alike; in fact, spider-silk is used where silkworm-silk would not be fine enough, as for marking the centre line of lenses in optical instruments, such as those used for surveying or for directing gunfire in war. Attempts have been made, notably in the U.S.A., to 'farm' spiders on a commercial scale.

2. MANUFACTURE. The silkworm spins the silk round itself in the form of a cocoon, and the manufacturing processes begin with the reeling of the silk from the cocoons; this takes place in a silk-reeling establishment, or *filature*. (The words used in the industry are largely French, as for centuries the city of Lyons has been the centre of the European industry.)˙ The cocoons are first boiled and then sprinkled with cold water. They are brushed, and the brush fibres catch up the end of the thin thread of the cocoon. This end is then picked up by hand. Series of threads, sometimes six or more, are reeled into a single stronger thread; this is known as the 'raw silk', the form in which the material is usually exported. If a thread breaks, the natural gumminess of the silk makes it possible to press the broken ends together. During the brushing a good deal of fluff or floss is caught up from the cocoons by the brushes. This is silk waste, and is later made into what is called 'spun silk'.

Before manufacture the reeled silk is soaked in oil or in an emulsion of soap. This softens the thread and reduces, but does not entirely remove, the natural gumminess which is a feature of the silk. The reeled silk is then wound on to bobbins and is ready for the process called 'throwing'. Reeled silk does not have to be spun. Spinning, in which short slender fibres have to be drawn out straight and twisted together to form a continuous yarn or thread, is peculiar to cotton and wool and similar fibres (see WOOL SPINNING). Reeled silk is already a continuous thread, although a very thin one, and 'throwing' either gives a twist to the single thread or twists several threads together. The word 'throw' is probably derived from the Anglo-Saxon *thrawan*, meaning to turn or twist. A silk-thrower is called a 'throwster'. Not all silk is thrown; some fabrics are made from unthrown silk.

After throwing, there follow the various

weaving or knitting processes by which fabrics are made from the yarns. The fabrics then go through the usual textile finishing processes, such as bleaching, dyeing, and printing, although sometimes the yarns are bleached and dyed before being worked up into fabrics (*see* BLEACHING, DYES, TEXTILE PRINTING). 'Weighting' is a finishing process peculiar to the silk industry. Many silk fabrics, if not weighted or 'filled' in some way, might be too light and flimsy for practical use, or to satisfy the demands of fashion. Some substances, particularly some of the metallic oxides, are absorbed and held by silk, even up to two or three times the weight of the silk itself. A common weighting process is to soak silk fabrics in an acid solution of tetrachloride of tin, which causes particles of oxide of tin to be left in the fabric.

A silk thread is found to be very strong if pulled or stretched (tensile strength); it is also very elastic. Much of the silk produced is used for hosiery (*see* HOSIERY AND KNITWEAR). Stockings of this natural or real silk hold their shape well, do not bag at the ankle and knee joints, and after being worn they soon return to their original shape. Silk is a poor conductor of heat, and therefore a very warm and cosy material for stockings and undergarments. Like wool, silk can absorb perspiration and yet not feel clammy. It has many military uses, particularly for wrapping up the charges of explosive which fire big guns, as it breaks up thoroughly on explosion into a very fine ash.

3. SILK WEAVING IN BRITAIN. Since synthetic fibres such as RAYON and NYLON (qq.v.) have been produced, the British silk industry has become less important. Its most prosperous days were the 18th and 19th centuries, when there were no artificial substitutes, and when men as well as women sometimes wore silk outer garments (*see* CLOTHES, HISTORY OF, Vol. XI). As with other British industries, silk owes much to foreign immigrants, and particularly to those from France and Flanders. In the 16th century Flemish weavers made bombazines, of mixed silk and cotton, in Norwich and Colchester. They settled also in Sandwich and Macclesfield, and made silk ribbons in Coventry. The knitting-frame was invented in the 17th century (*see* HOSIERY AND KNITWEAR) and Nottingham and Derby began to make quantities of silk stockings for wear by men and women. Many French Protestants or HUGUENOTS (q.v. Vol. I) were

PICKING UP THE LEADING THREADS OF THE COCOONS WITH A BRUSH WHICH MOVES MECHANICALLY

Silk and Rayon Users' Assn.

REELING SILK FROM THE COCOONS
The threads are passed through spindles and wound on a reel

driven from France by the loss of their religious rights in 1685, and those who were skilled in silk weaving settled in Spitalfields, which was then a suburb just outside the City of London, and already an important centre for woollen fabrics.

By 1700 silk weaving was one of England's most flourishing industries, and Spitalfields had become its principal centre. From 1713 onwards, the industry was encouraged by protective TARIFFS (q.v.) imposed by the Government to keep out silk fabrics woven abroad. The reeled or thrown silk used in England was imported, principally from the eastern Mediterranean, India, and Italy. The technique of silk throwing was not known to British manufacturers until John Lombe, of Derby, brought the knowledge of it from Italy in 1717. He is believed to have disguised himself as a workman and to have worked in an Italian throwing-mill, where he could make drawings of the machinery. Soon after his return the Huguenot family of Courtauld, now famous in the rayon industry, began silk-throwing at Braintree in Essex; throwing-mills were opened later in Malmesbury, Sherborne, and Taunton, in the west of England.

The industry reached its highest prosperity in the first half of the 19th century. In Spitalfields weaving was organized largely on the DOMESTIC SYSTEM (q.v.), and hand-work was the rule. As machinery was invented and applied to the many processes, there was less work for Spitalfields and neighbouring parts of London, but in Macclesfield and other towns of northern England mechanical weaving increased. In 1857, Lister of Bradford rendered the industry a great service by discovering a method of spinning silk waste. During most of the processes, from reeling onwards, much fluff or waste was brushed or rubbed off, and there had hitherto been little or no use for it. The West Riding of Yorkshire became the centre of waste-silk spinning, and for weaving plain and mixed 'spun silk' fabrics. In 1860 the Government tariffs were removed. British makers could no longer compete with imports from France, and the industry gradually declined. The present main centres of manufacture are Macclesfield and Congleton in Cheshire, and Leek in Staffordshire. Plushes and upholstery cloths are woven in Bradford. Brighouse is the main centre for spinning waste silk.

See also RAYON; NYLON.
See also Vol. VI: SILKWORM.

SILVER-MINING. Silver is the whitest of all metals and, like gold, does not oxidize or scale when heated. Unlike gold, however, it combines with SULPHUR (q.v.) and therefore rapidly tarnishes in industrial atmospheres, in the fumes from gas or coal fires, and when kept near vulcanized rubber.

Native silver is not nearly as common in the earth's crust as gold (see METAL ORES, Vol. III), but scattered deposits have been found in central Africa, Spain, Armenia, Norway, and North and South America. The palace decorations of the ancient cities of Tyre, Nineveh, and Babylon, and the silver used for coinage in countries between the Indus and the Nile many centuries B.C., were possibly made from silver collected from such sources. The Athenians obtained silver from silver-mines at Laurium, from which they made silver coins used all over the known world (see COINS).

Silver also occurs in many parts of the world in the form of a black, soft ore called Argentite (silver sulphide), and the wax-like Kerargyrite or Horn Silver (silver chloride), as well as other more complex minerals. As long ago as 1500 B.C. the Babylonians and Myceneans found that it was possible to obtain metallic silver from these ores. They used the process known to-day as 'cupellation', which is still practised for refining some types of impure bullion. In this process the ores were heated with lead on a shallow hearth, where they formed a lead-silver

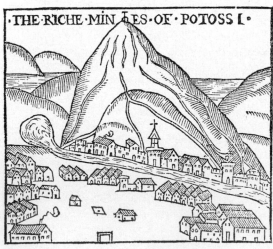

POTOSI, BOLIVIA, WHERE THERE WERE SILVER MINES IN THE 16TH CENTURY

Woodcut from the title-page of Augustin de Zarate's *History of Peru*, 1581

ALLOY (q.v. Vol. VIII). Heating was then continued with free access of air. In these circumstances the lead oxidized to form molten lead oxide (litharge), which was run off from the top of the bath (*see* OXIDATION). After some hours all the lead oxidized (as well as any copper, iron, and other base metal impurities, whose oxides dissolve in the litharge); and, on raising the temperature, a pool of molten silver, which might be as much as 99·8% pure, was left on the hearth or 'cupel'. The silver was ladled out, and poured into moulds.

This simple method was practised universally until early in the 16th century, when Mexico became the foremost source of silver. In many Mexican districts fuel and water are scarce, and in 1557 an 'amalgamation' method—a modification of the process used for recovering gold from ores (*see* GOLD-MINING)—was devised, using mercury, common salt, and 'magistral'—an impure form of copper sulphate. Salt was mixed with damp copper ore, and crushed by mules walking round a yard paved with flagstones, to tread the materials together. The next day magistral was mixed with the mass in the same way. The salt and magistral set up a chemical reaction with the silver sulphide in the ore, converting it to silver chloride with some metallic silver. Then, when mercury was added on the third day, and the mass trodden daily, or every other day, for 2, 3, or 4 weeks, the greater part of the silver slowly dissolved in the mercury to form silver amalgam. Finally, the mass was mixed with water in large tubs and the amalgam collected. This was heated in retorts, from which the mercury was distilled away and collected for use over again (*see* DISTILLATION), the silver being left behind. As years went on, improvements were made in details. Cast-iron pans, fitted with mechanical means for grinding the ore and mixing it with mercury, took the place of paved yards and mules, and some ores were roasted before treatment; but until about 1905 the amalgamation process remained the most important method of recovering silver from its ores.

Early in the 20th century the cyanide process (*see* GOLD-MINING) was introduced in South Africa for recovering gold from its ores. It soon became apparent that, with few modifications, the process would prove just as economical for treating silver ores. Before many years, all the principal Mexican mines, which then produced more than half the world's output, were using

Fresmillo Co.

A SILVER-REFINING PLANT IN MEXICO
In the foreground are cyanide tanks

weak solutions of sodium cyanide to dissolve the silver from the crushed ores, the pulp being agitated with the cyanide solution for about 3 days. The silver was subsequently removed from the solution by adding powdered zinc, and was then collected for melting and refining.

Mexico has remained the chief source of straight silver ores, but by the middle of the 20th century about three-quarters of the world production of silver was obtained, not from silver-mines, but as a BY-PRODUCT of the extraction of LEAD and COPPER (qq.v.). It has been estimated that of the world's production of silver only 20% is derived from straight silver ores; 45% is recovered from lead-zinc ores, 18% from copper and copper-nickel ores, 15% from gold-silver ores, and 2% from tin ores. The important producers of silver are still in the New World—Mexico, the 'Silver' States of America—Montana, Idaho, Colorado, Utah, Nevada, California, Arizona, and New Mexico—and South and Central America. But these producers are now essentially large base-metal refiners, each of which has perfected special methods for recovering the traces of silver present in the products dealt with.

Pure silver is the best known conductor of electricity, and in industry very large quantities are used for electrical contacts. As silver resists corrosion by food acids and many chemicals, it is used to line machines used in food-processing and in the manufacture of such chemicals as acetic acid (*see* ACIDS). Its best-known alloy is standard or sterling silver, containing $7\frac{1}{2}\%$ of copper. This was used for the British silver coinage from the reign of Henry II until 1920, and has been the material out of which silver-ware of all kinds has been made for hundreds of years.

See also ASSAYING; MINING.
See also Vol. III: METAL ORES.

SILVER WORK, *see* GOLD AND SILVER WORK.

SLATE INDUSTRY. Slate, which in Britain is mainly quarried in North Wales, was formerly much used for the roofs of houses and factories. But during the present century, coloured tiles, made of clay or concrete (*see* BRICKS AND TILES), have proved cheaper and more popular, and the output of slate has fallen.

1. DEPOSITS. Slate began as a muddy sediment deposited on the bottom of the sea (*see* ROCKS, Section 4, Vol. III). During later geological ages these beds became deeply buried under other layers. The resultant pressure and heat forced the particles in the sediment into parallel positions (*see* MINERALS, Vol. III), with their broader sides lying all in the same direction, and altered them into hard slate rock which could be easily split. Owing to the chemical composition of the sediments, and the combined effects of pressure and heat, most slates are proof against the decomposing action of the acid-laden atmosphere of big industrial towns. It is this quality of exceptional durability, and the capacity of being split into thin but very strong sheets, that make slate so good a roofing material.

The presence of slate in certain areas is the joint result of movements in the earth's crust—when the slate beds were crumpled into alternating arch-like and trough-like folds—and the natural process of DENUDATION (q.v. Vol. III). Slate beds that were once horizontal, and buried thousands of feet down, are now often steeply inclined or even vertical, and are exposed on the earth's surface. Where the beds are fairly vertical, and 'outcrop' on level ground or at the bottom of a valley, they are worked in deep open quarries. If they outcrop on a steep mountain-side, quarrying is done in a series of terraces or galleries, and there may sometimes be as many as twenty of these, each providing a working face about 20 yards high. Where the slate beds are not so vertical, open quarrying soon becomes unprofitable because of the cost of removing the increasingly thick layer of useless rock on top of the slate, and it is found cheaper to work it in underground mines. A slate-mine consists of a series of long parallel chambers—which are in effect underground quarries—divided by pillars of slate rock, left in place to support the roof of hard rock covering the slate bed. Most of the slate in Britain is produced in open quarries.

In North Wales the two main quarries, the Dinorwic Quarry, Llanberis, and the Penrhyn Quarry, Bethesda, are linked by private railways with their own miniature ports in the Menai Strait; together they produce more than half the total British output. Practically all slate is sent to market by rail, but before 1850 all Welsh slate was shipped coastwise, and even in 1900 half of it was still being sent by sea. The other main centres of production in Wales are the Nantlle district of Caernarvonshire, and the slate mining area of Festiniog, in Merioneth. In England production is concentrated in the Lake District and the Cornwall-Devon-Somerset area. In Scotland the only commercially important slate region is Argyllshire.

2. TECHNIQUE. The first step in the production of slate is to get the blocks out of the rock face and cut them to a size convenient for transport. 'Rockmen', using pneumatic drills, make holes for blasting. The blasting dislodges large blocks, and these are further split and 'pillared' into smaller ones. (Slate rock will fracture at right angles to the line of cleavage). The small blocks of slate are transported along inclined planes or aerial cableways to 'sheds'. Here they are split into slabs, and then sawn by circular saws into blocks, of a convenient size for making into roofing slates by the 'splitters' and the 'dressers'. Splitting is invariably done by hand, and is a difficult task that calls for great skill and long experience. Using steel chisels and wooden mallets, the splitters divide each block into sheets of the required thickness, which are then trimmed to rectangular shapes. There are three methods of trimming: by hand, by a foot-operated machine acting on the principle of a printer's guillotine, or by mechanically-driven

SPLITTING SLATE IN A CORNISH QUARRY

Graphic Photo Union

rotating blades. There are some thirty standard sizes of trimmed slates, and there are other colours than the dull blackish grey so well known in England. The Dinorwic quarry, in particular, produces a variety of colours, including attractive greens.

3. USES. About 97% of the total output of the industry is roofing slates. The remainder of the output consists of slabs and BY-PRODUCTS (q.v.). Slate slabs are used for monumental work, such as gravestones or memorial panels, billiard-tables, brewery and chemical vats, laboratory benches, dairy and pantry slabs, blackboards, and enamelled mantelpieces. There is a growing demand for slabs for use as electrical switchboards. The Penrhyn quarry produces slate granules and 'flour' out of crushed slate waste. This may be used as a filler or filling material to give bulk to gramophone records, and to such products as plastics, rubber, linoleum, paints, and insecticides. Its main use is as a filling material for the tarry coating given to prefabricated road surfacings. The Dinorwic quarry has produced a kind of mineral wool out of waste rock.

The peak of British slate production was reached in 1898, when 634,000 tons were produced and 19,600 people were employed. In the next 50 years the industry contracted greatly, the output in 1937 being 268,000 tons and the number employed 9,700. Output in 1950 was barely half what it had been 10 years earlier, and it is unlikely that the industry will recover its earlier importance.

See also BRICKS AND TILES; STONE DRESSING; BUILDING INDUSTRY.

SLAVE TRADE. A slave is someone who is not free, who is deprived of rights enjoyed by others, and who is compelled to obey a particular master under fear of punishment (*see* SLAVERY, Vol. X). An extensive trade in human slaves went on from the earliest times until the 19th century. Even in 1935 there was evidence that the trade was still going on in some of the more distant parts of Africa, and in the remotest parts it may still survive even to this day. The earliest slave-markets mentioned in historical records were those in the cities of Greece and Asia Minor, around the Aegean Sea. Most of the slaves sent to these markets were people conquered in war: 150,000 slaves are said to have been sold in 168 B.C. after the defeat of Perseus of Macedon. Dealings in slaves regularly took

Parker Gallery

H.M. BRIG 'BLACK JOKE' ENGAGING A SPANISH SLAVE SHIP OFF THE WEST AFRICAN COAST
Coloured engraving, 1829

place in the days of ancient Rome. Later, during the DARK AGES (q.v. Vol. I), many slaves were sold in the markets of Spain, and most of these were of Slav race, from beyond the eastern frontiers of Germany. A big trade in these Slavonic captives (from whose name comes the word 'slave') flourished in continental Europe during the Middle Ages, mostly under the control of Jewish dealers. Lyons and Verdun in France, Civita Vecchia and other towns in Italy, Kiev in Russia, and Constantinople (Istanbul) were the main European markets; there were also many markets in Africa, where slavery, which had existed from time immemorial, was widespread.

Slavery as an institution died out in western Europe with the passing away of the FEUDAL SYSTEM (q.v. Vol. X), at the close of the Middle Ages, but the trade in African Negro slaves continued. At first it was merely an internal trade, supplying Africa itself and adjoining Moslem countries. But after the period of the 'Discoveries', when Portuguese and Spanish navigators explored Africa and other new lands (*see* EXPLORATION, Vol. IV), European dealers entered the African trade. The Portuguese were the first, and they drew their supplies of slaves from the west coast of Africa. There were big

slave-markets in Benguela and Loanda, from which Negro slaves were shipped to Brazil and to the Spanish possessions in the West Indies and South and Central America. By agreement with the local African chieftains the Portuguese at first had a MONOPOLY (q.v.) of this trade. This was disputed by other nations, and in 1563 the English navigator, Sir John Hawkins, carried out a successful raid, and made a profitable shipment of slaves to the West Indies. Later, Dutch and English dealers entered the trade in large numbers, and in the 18th century it reached its peak. These were the days of the famous 'triangular trade' out of the ports of Bristol and Liverpool. Ships went out with gin and cheap finery to the West Coast of Africa, voyaged with cargoes of slaves from Africa to the West Indies and the British colonies in North America, and did the homeward voyage to Bristol with sugar and tobacco. In those days the prosperity of Bristol and the growth of Liverpool were largely founded on this triangular trade, for it was very profitable. The price of the slaves was trifling, and they were sold in the West Indies and on the American mainland at an average price of about £25 per head. During the 18th century nearly 2 million were imported into the British colonies in America. Towards the end of the 18th century a great agitation against the cruelties of the slave trade grew up in Britain, and in 1807 an Act of Parliament introduced by William WILBERFORCE (1759–1833) (q.v. Vol. V) made it unlawful to deal in slaves. Other European nations, and also the northern States of the American Union, soon copied the example of Britain. Until the close of the American CIVIL WAR (q.v. Vol. X) slavery continued in the Southern or Confederate States; in 1832 the price of a young Negro fit for active work on a Southern plantation was well over £100. This rise in prices was largely the result of reduced supplies, for British and other European dealers no longer took part in the trade. But Arab dealers still continued to deal in African slaves. Zanzibar, off the coast of East Africa, was the big central market; thousands of slaves were sold there every year, and distributed through various other markets all over the Moslem world. At last an agreement was made with the Sultan of Zanzibar, by which his territory ceased to be the centre of the African slave trade; but it still persisted on the mainland of Africa, and was only gradually abolished as the various European nations occupied more territory.

See also Vol. I: AMERICAN NEGROES.
See also Vol. X: SLAVERY; PRISONERS OF WAR.
See also Vol. XI: DOMESTIC SERVICE.

SOAP MANUFACTURE.

Soap in a crude form, made from the same basic ingredients as we use to-day, was known to the ancient Romans, but it was not manufactured by them in any quantity. The making of soap became an important industry in Italy and Spain in the 8th century, and in the 13th century the industry was started in France. Marseilles became the main centre, for the principal raw material was olive-oil, and olives grew close by. Soap works are mentioned in the 14th century as having been started in England, but soap does not appear to have been made in London itself until the 16th century.

Soap is made when animal or vegetable fats or oils are combined chemically with caustic soda or potash (*see* ALKALIS). Until the 19th century, methods of manufacture were rather haphazard, but the industry was then put on a much more scientific basis after research into the chemistry of oils and fats. The raw materials of modern **soaps** are tallow and grease, among animal oils; coconut, cotton seed, soya, palm kernel, and olive oils, among the vegetable oils; and fish and whale oils, now that the discovery of the hydrogenation process makes it possible to harden them and remove their unpleasant smell. Apart from the true soaps, there are many modern 'detergents' or artificial soaps, and some of these are made from mineral oils. In the manufacture of the latherless or brushless shaving creams, only a small proportion of true soap is used.

'Saponification' is the technical name given to the process of making soap from fats and caustic alkalis. Soft soap is the simplest soap to make, and is produced by boiling oil with water and caustic potash, or with a mixture of caustic potash and caustic soda, until saponification takes place. Hard soaps are made either by the 'cold process' or by boiling. For the cold process the materials are well mixed together and slightly warmed, when soap soon begins to form. As

Lever Bros

POURING LIQUID INTO THE SOAP PAN

soon as a small quantity has been formed, it speeds up the rest of the mixture into becoming soap, and this is accompanied by a rise in temperature. The cold process can be used only with coconut or palm kernel oils, but it is extremely cheap: most of the heat needed comes from the chemical process in the mixture itself, and outside heat is only necessary to start the process going. The disadvantage of the cold process is that impurities cannot be removed, and there can be no recovery of the glycerol (a chemical which is important for many industrial purposes), which remains as part of the soap. The boiling process, which involves three or more stages, makes it possible to remove impurities and recover glycerol, the sale of which cheapens an otherwise expensive process.

Household soap is made by cooling boiled soap and then cutting it to shape. To make soap flakes, a thin film of soap is run on to a cold steel roll, and the sheet coming from the roll is slit into ribbons and dried. The dried ribbons are rolled out into a very thin sheet, and cut into tiny sections. For toilet soaps, perfume is added to the dried ribbons, which are then pressed through a nozzle, and the continuous rod that emerges is cut into correct lengths and stamped into shape.

See also OILS, VEGETABLE.
See also Vol. VI: OIL-BEARING PLANTS.
See also Vol. XI: CLEANING MATERIALS.

SODA ALKALIS, *see* ALKALIS.

SOFTWOODS. The word 'softwoods' is used by the timber trade to mean wood coming from the trees called conifers, such as pine, fir, and spruce (*see* TREES, CONIFEROUS, Vol. VI).

The softwoods of the world are distributed in a fairly well-defined belt running from the northern part of the British Isles and the Baltic countries to the northern half of Russia and Siberia, and continuing across the Bering Strait to the northern half of North America. Although softwood trees are not common in tropical countries they are often found there at a high elevation in the mountain ranges, where the climate is permanently colder. The world's two great reserves of softwoods are in Canada and other parts of North America, and in Russia and Siberia; in each of these localities there are coniferous forests so vast that great areas of them are still untouched.

Only two of our principal softwoods come from European countries. The first of these is the European Redwood, also called Red Deal, Yellow Deal, and other names depending upon the exact source of origin. Trees producing this timber grow in Britain, where they are known as Scotch Pine. The second is the European White-wood, also called White Deal; it is the product of a spruce-tree which in this country is known either as Common or Norway Spruce. Most of the timber from Europe comes already sawn into boards and planks; but there is a considerable proportion of pitprops and round poles, most of these being telegraph poles.

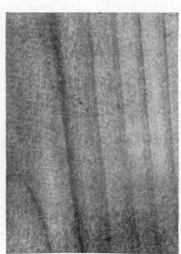

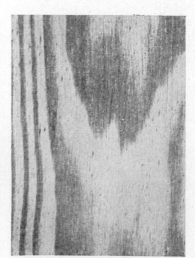

Timber Development Assen.

COMMON SPRUCE   EUROPEAN LARCH   DOUGLAS FIR

Softwoods are bought and sold commercially by the 'standard'; a standard is 165 cubic feet of timber, and the term is used for softwoods only. Before the Second World War a small house would use up about two-and-a-half standards of timber, equivalent to nearly a mile of timber, 12 inches wide and 1 inch thick. It is reckoned that at that time a quarter of British imports of softwoods went to the building-trade. A still larger fraction was used up in the

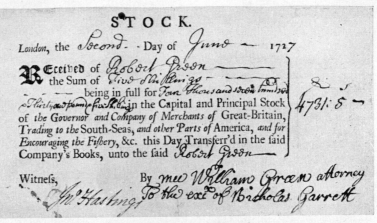

RECEIPT FOR AN INVESTMENT IN SOUTH SEA STOCK, DATED 1727

manufacture of boxes and packing cases, largely for the export trade. The coal-mines also used large quantities of softwood pit-props; the comparatively damp and sluggish atmospheric conditions in deep mines caused them to rot quickly, and a constant supply of fresh ones was needed. The railways consume large quantities of softwoods, principally for sleepers. These are usually made of redwood from the Baltic, although Canadian timber is also used. Sleepers are thoroughly treated with creosote before being laid on the track, and for that reason have quite a long life. Softwood poles are much used for overhead electric transmission by the Post Office telegraph and telephone services, for the cargo derricks of ships, and for the masts and spars of yachts; and softwood planks and baulks are used as shuttering for concrete construction, and also in dock and harbour work.

See also TIMBER; HARDWOODS.

See also Vol. VI: FORESTRY; TREES, CONIFEROUS.

SOUTH SEA BUBBLE. 'Bubble' is a word that used to be applied to SHARES of COMPANIES (qq.v.) when they were pushed up to unjustified prices by wild promises and speculative rumours —'blown up by the air of great words' (*see* SPECULATION). The name was first used in 1636, when there was a big boom in Dutch tulips. Tulips were bought and sold in Amsterdam like mining shares, and rose rapidly in price, only to collapse equally rapidly later on.

'South Sea Bubble' is the name given to the speculation in the shares of the South Sea Company and other concerns in the early 18th century. The Company was formed in 1711 as a CHARTERED COMPANY (q.v.), its objects being (according to its charter) 'trading to the South Seas and other parts of America and encouraging the Fishery'. The South Seas meant Central and South America, and 'fishery' referred to whaling. The original stock or CAPITAL (q.v.) issued was increased in 1714 and 1717, and speculative dealings in the Company's shares began in earnest in 1719, when the directors of the Company suggested that they might take over the responsibility of gradually paying off Britain's NATIONAL DEBT (q.v. Vol. X). They offered the Government £7 millions in cash (to be subscribed by the Company's stockholders) for this privilege, and, as the Government had greatly increased the National Debt by the cost of the War of the Spanish Succession, they accepted the proposal eagerly. A Bill was passed through Parliament in 1720, with Government support, and before it reached the House of Lords each £100 of the Company's stock was being dealt in at a price of £400—four times its nominal value. The support given to the project by the Government, over-optimistic calculations of profits, and wild rumours led to still further speculation, and the stock rose in the end to ten times its nominal value. At the height of the boom Change Alley and Cornhill in the City of London were almost impassable. The directors of the Company, taking advantage of this boom, issued a further £1 million of stock at three times its nominal value, and another £1 million worth at four times its nominal value, the second offer being all bought up in a few hours. The speculative fever that attacked the investing public, and the general feeling of optimism that came from the rapid rise in the Company's stock, led to the starting-up of other concerns. Some only lasted for a few days; one promoter advertised in a newspaper for subscriptions 'to a certain promising or profitable design, which will hereafter be promulgated'. On this extremely vague prospectus, the promoter of the enterprise sold in a few hours 1,000 £1 shares for £2 each, and then disappeared and was never heard of again.

When such a feverish stage is reached, booms of this kind usually collapse. The South Sea Bubble soon 'burst', and the prices of the Company's stock and of the shares of other companies collapsed. Thousands of speculators were ruined, and the directors of the Company had to meet big claims out of their own private estates. The South Sea trade gave few opportunities of profit, and the Company turned its attention to the whaling fishery. But after eight successive annual voyages the Company had made no money out of whaling, and in 1750 an arrangement with Spain deprived the Company of any advantage in the South American trade. In 1807 the Company's exclusive trading rights were formally taken from it by Parliament, and after some years it was finally wound up.

See also SPECULATION; STOCKS AND SHARES.

SOYA BEAN, *see* OILS, VEGETABLE.

See also Vol. VI: SOYA BEAN.

SPECIALIZATION, *see* DIVISION OF LABOUR.

SPECULATION. In one way all commerce and industry is speculative; there is always a risk that goods will not sell at a profit. But by speculation we usually mean market dealings (buying or selling) by persons who are neither manufacturers nor merchants, and who are merely out to make profits for themselves. There is obviously nothing to be said for the unintelligent gambler; but the intelligent speculator has had his place and his use in the world of business.

An example may make this clear. Let us suppose that a speculator has made a careful study of the production and consumption of plantation rubber all over the world, and that he forms the opinion that there is likely to be serious overproduction. He sells fairly large quantities of rubber (which he does not yet possess) by promising to deliver it on the London market a year ahead (*see* MARKET). His action in selling such

large quantities causes the price to fall, as it always does when there appears to be too much of any commodity for sale. Other people join in the selling movement, and lower the price still further. A year later, when he has to buy rubber to fulfil his earlier contract to deliver, he can therefore buy it more cheaply than he sold it—and so he makes a good deal of money.

During the year, as the result of his action and that of other people, the price of rubber has been steadily dropping; and this may have had two effects. It may have stopped someone planting still more rubber-trees; and it may have led business men to buy rubber for some useful purpose which could not have been afforded at the earlier high price. It is true that the overproduction of rubber would have produced these results in time, without the action of the speculator, but he has helped to hasten the changes.

The markets in 'futures', in which goods can be bought or sold for delivery many months ahead, can be useful to merchants and manufacturers, and could not be so easily or freely organized if there were no speculators. For example, a miller can buy wheat on 1 January in order to mill it into flour during the next 3 months. But during that time the price of flour may fall. So the miller, on 1 January, promises to sell a quantity of wheat for delivery on 1 April. If by 1 April wheat has fallen in price, the price of flour will also have fallen in sympathy; so the miller must sell his flour more cheaply, and make a loss on his milling. But what he has lost on milling will be made up by what he gains when, on 1 April, he buys cheap wheat to fulfil his earlier contract to deliver. Dealings of this kind are called 'hedging' contracts.

A dangerous form of speculation is that in 'foreign exchange' or CURRENCY (q.v.). Speculation in commodities or in STOCKS AND SHARES (q.v.) is subject to certain natural economic checks: in the long run prices are bound to come back to what the goods or the shares are really worth. But speculation in foreign money is quite different. If an international ring of speculators were to put down the value of British money (the pound sterling) from 2 dollars 80 cents to only 2 dollars, by selling large quantities of pounds, the result would be that all imports to Britain from the United States, and from countries financially connected with the United States, would cost about one-third more in British

Neck or Nothing, or the downfall of y. Missippi Company.

FIAT JUSTITIA　　RUERUNT REGNA

Should Law be just to unjust Laws,
And all his proud Directors,
The Law must hang up Laws, becaufe
The vileft of Projectors,
Let this invite you to behold
Their decent Execution,
Who bafely, for the fake of Gold,
Have brought us to confufion—
A Sermon you fhall also hear,
From Perry's Lamentation
To comfort Suff'rers that appear
Upon this fad Occafion.
The words appointed for the Text are
Lamentations Chap. iv. verses the 5 & 15.
They that did feed delicately are become defolate in the Streets They
that were brought up in scarlet, embrace dunghills They hunt our
Steps that we cannot go in our Streets our fond is near; our days
are fulfilled for our end is come

Engrav'd by Monf. Duchange Engraver to the Missippi Company in France.　　*Sold by y Printfellers of London & Westminster Price 6*

AN 18TH-CENTURY PRINT SHOWING THE FATE DESERVED BY THE PROMOTERS OF SPECULATIVE COMPANIES
The figure of Justice presides over the execution of the promoters

money. Wages paid in Great Britain would then buy less, and there would be trade union pressure to have them raised; this would cause an increase in the prices of our exported goods, and so the new and lower value of the pound in foreign countries, being now economically justified, would become permanent (*see* RATES OF EXCHANGE). Speculation of this sort must therefore be suppressed. The method adopted by Great Britain in 1932, when this kind of speculation was increasing, was to give the Bank of England a fund of sterling, gold, and foreign currencies big enough to break any 'ring' of speculators in the world. This fund is still being used.

See also INTERNATIONAL FINANCE.

SPINNING, *see* WOOL SPINNING; COTTON MANUFACTURE; LINEN INDUSTRY.

STANDARD OF LIVING. The 'standard of living' of any country means the average person's share of the goods and services which the country produces. A country's standard of living, therefore, depends first and foremost on its capacity to produce wealth. 'Wealth' in this sense is not money, for we do not live on money but on the things that money can buy: 'goods' such as food and clothing, and 'services' such as transport and entertainment.

A country's capacity to produce wealth depends upon many factors, most of which have an effect on one another. Wealth depends to a great extent upon a country's natural resources, such as coal, gold, and other minerals, water-supply, and so on. Some regions of the world are well supplied with coal and minerals, and have a fertile soil and a favourable climate; other regions possess perhaps only one of these things, and some regions possess none of them. The U.S.A. is one of the wealthiest regions of the world because she has vast natural resources within her borders, her soil is fertile, and her climate is varied. The Sahara Desert, on the other hand, is one of the least wealthy.

Next to natural resources comes the ability to turn them to use. China is perhaps as well off as the U.S.A. in natural resources, but has suffered for many years from civil and external wars, and for this and other reasons has been unable to develop her resources. Sound and stable political conditions, and freedom from foreign invasion, enable a country to develop its natural resources peacefully and steadily, and to produce more wealth than another country equally well served by nature but less well ordered. Another important factor is the technical efficiency of a country's people. Old countries that have, through many centuries, trained up numerous skilled craftsmen and technicians are better placed to produce wealth than countries whose workers are largely unskilled. Wealth also begets wealth. As a country becomes wealthier, its people have a larger margin for saving, and can put their savings into factories and machines which will help workers to turn out more goods in their working day.

A country's standard of living does not only depend upon the wealth that is produced and consumed within its own borders, but also upon what is indirectly produced through INTERNATIONAL TRADE (q.v.). For example, Britain's wealth in foodstuffs and other agricultural products would be much less if she had to depend only on those grown at home. Trade makes it possible for our surplus manufactured goods to be traded abroad for the agricultural products that would otherwise be lacking. A country's wealth is, therefore, much influenced by its manufacturing capacity, provided that other countries can be found ready to accept its manufactures.

Population is also an important influence. A country's population may be, to start with, too big or too small for the best use of its resources. Countries such as India and China are generally thought to be overpopulated. Their immense populations put a great strain upon the available natural resources, particularly agricultural land. There are so many people growing foodstuffs on a limited quantity of land, and foreign trade and manufacturing are so underdeveloped, that the standard of living of the masses of the population is extremely low. A smaller population would make it necessary to farm only the more fertile land, and there would consequently be a larger average share of food for each person. But a country may even have too small a population for the full development of its natural resources. If, for example, the population of North America were only one-tenth of what it is to-day, the much smaller market for goods would make it impossible to manufacture them cheaply on mass-production lines, and the standard of living of the average American—particularly in such things as motor-cars and labour-saving household goods—would be far lower than it is to-day.

But it is not only the quantity of a country's population that influences its wealth. The quality of the population needs also to be taken into account. Skill and craftsmanship have been already mentioned as important, but a great deal depends upon what proportion of the population is engaged in useful work. Other things being equal, less wealth will be produced in a country with a large non-working class than in another where most people work. For example, the average standard of living in 18th-century France was very much lower than it is to-day; and the high standard of living of the U.S.A. owes much to the long-standing tradition that even the sons and daughters of the rich should work. The proportion of young people to old people affects considerably the number of a country's workers. If the population of any country is gradually getting larger, it will have a smaller proportion of old people than one whose population is falling; and old people who are no longer fit to work must be supported by the work of those who are younger.

To calculate the average standard of living of any country, one divides its 'national income' by the number of people in it. 'National income' means the total of goods and services produced for consumption in a year. Measured in money, the national income of the United Kingdom in 1950 was about £10,000 millions. As there were about 50 million people to share this, the average standard of living of each person was £200 worth (at current prices) of goods and services every year. Averages, although convenient to use, do not always show clearly the true facts (see STATISTICS), and some groups of our population receive more than £200 per person, and other groups less. Tradition and habits influence the standard of living of different kinds of people, and once a group has got used to a certain standard of living, it does not like to give it up. Just as there are varying standards of living for different groups within a country, so also there are varying standards between different countries. Britain's standard of living, for example, is below that of the U.S.A., but it is higher than that of south-eastern Europe, the U.S.S.R., and the countries of the East.

See also Cost of Living.

STATEMENT, *see* Invoices.

STATISTICS. 1. The object of statistics is to find out information about groups of people or things by collecting facts about them, and arranging these in an orderly way. Those who compile the figures, and make a scientific study of them, are called statisticians.

Statistics are very important to business men, as well as to statesmen and government officials. A merchant who buys and sells goods is interested particularly in comparing past and present trading results, and often in trying to forecast future trends (*see* Market Research). He may also want to compare the results of one branch with those of another, or of one department with another's. Manufacturers are also interested in knowing how the sales of some products are progressing as compared with the sales of others, and also in checking the quality and standard of the goods turned out.

Some businesses use statistics for more definite purposes. Insurance (q.v.), for instance, is really based upon the belief that the future will follow fairly closely the pattern of the past. For example, a life insurance company must know the number of people who die in any given year compared with the total number of the population, and also the average ages at which death has taken place. From statistics of past experience they can make fairly accurate estimates of the future, and can construct what are called 'mortality tables'. Similarly, companies insuring against accidents at sea or on land, or against other events (such as rain on a Bank Holiday), must know what lessons the past has to teach before they can work out how much they must charge for insuring against such risks in the future.

2. Methods of Presentation. Statistics can be set out in a number of different ways. One method is to tabulate the figures in several sets of columns. Figures presented in this way, however, do not very easily draw attention to the really important points; the eye and the other senses do not quickly take in their meaning.

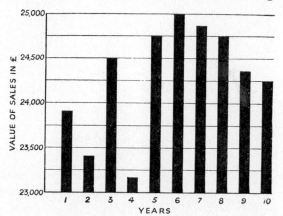

FIG. 1. A FIRM'S YEARLY SALES SHOWN IN A BAR DIAGRAM

Figures are therefore often more effective if they are expressed in the form of diagrams. The 'bar' diagram is one of the most useful. Thus we could represent a firm's sales on a bar diagram (*see* Fig. 1).

This diagram arranges the history of the firm's sales over the past 10 years in a way that hits the eye, and enables anyone studying the diagram to take in at a glance the years that have been most or least successful. The diagram could also be used to build up a curve showing the up-and-down movements of sales over the 10-year period.

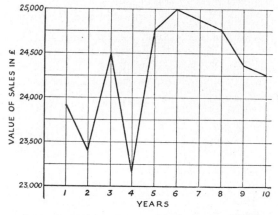

FIG. 2. THE SAME YEARLY SALES SHOWN IN A GRAPH

If we join the tops of each of the bars by a connected series of lines, we get an up-and-down curve, rather like a hospital patient's temperature

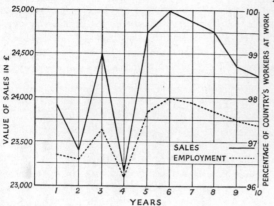

FIG. 3. THE YEARLY SALES (AS IN FIG. 2) COMPARED WITH
EMPLOYMENT

chart (see Fig. 2). We can then, if we wish, plot
on the same graph any other figures which may
help to explain the changes in sales. The percentage of insured workers employed in any year
would be a useful figure, as sales in general
would be very likely to vary with the total of
workers' money incomes (see Fig. 3).

The employment curve in this diagram follows
the sales curve very closely: as indeed it should.
If there are big differences between the sales
curve and the employment curve in particular
years, then very probably the fault lies with the
business. When two or more sets of figures are
compared in this way, their relationship to each
other is called a 'correlation'. The closeness of
this relationship is called the 'coefficient of correlation'. Fig. 3 shows a very close correlation
between the two sets of figures.

Statistics can also be presented in the form of

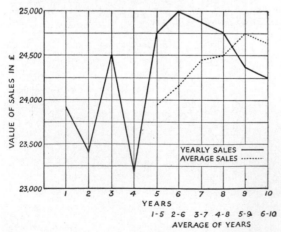

FIG. 4. THE YEARLY SALES (AS IN FIG. 2) AND THE AVERAGES
OF SALES OVER PERIODS OF 5 YEARS

pictures. We could thus compare, say, the
average output per man in one country with that
in another, or the average output per man of one
factory in a big business with that of another.
Diagrams to show these might take the form of a
black-shaded or coloured picture of a worker,
drawn to scale in such a way that the taller the
man the greater is the output represented. This
method is much used in government posters and
publications, particularly those connected with
matters of production and output, and designed
to appeal to the ordinary man or woman. Care
must be taken in the preparation of such diagrams, and in the scales used. For example, if
comparative figures are represented by circles or
squares, it must be remembered that a circle and
a square of the same width will have different
areas.

Only limited information can be given in
simple statistics of this sort. For example, a
curve, showing the movement in average sales
over a series of years, does not take account
of changes in circumstances which may have
affected sales in certain years. The CAPITAL
(q.v.) of the firm, for instance, may have increased, the number of factories at work may be
larger, or the total number of workers may have
grown; for such reasons the average yearly sales
are likely to go up in any case. What is really
wanted is a diagram which will show, not the
average yearly sales, but the way in which the
average itself is moving. If we worked out for
each year the average sales for, say, the past
5 years, each time dropping the first year and
substituting the last, we should obtain what is
called a 'moving average'. Using the figures of
Fig. 2, and plotting a curve from them, we
should obtain the diagram shown in Fig. 4, which
gives more complete information.

3. THE MODE. There are other business problems which statistics may help to solve. To take
an example, a boot and shoe manufacturer is
interested in knowing how many pairs there
ought to be of each different size out of, say,
every hundred. It is not possible for him to send
REPRESENTATIVES (q.v.) into every household in
the country, and to take a sort of census of sizes
and fittings. Statistics can help here, by using
what is called 'the law of statistical regularity'.
If a reasonably large number of items is chosen
at random from a very much larger number of
items, the difference between what an analysis of
the smaller number can tell us, and what we

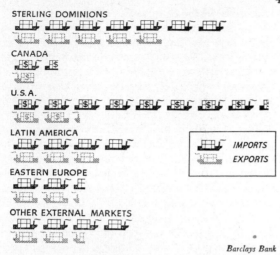

STERLING DOMINIONS

CANADA

U.S.A.

LATIN AMERICA

                       IMPORTS
                       EXPORTS

EASTERN EUROPE

OTHER EXTERNAL MARKETS

Barclays Bank

FIG. 5. PICTORIAL DIAGRAM OF WESTERN EUROPE'S TRADE
WITH EXTERNAL MARKETS, JANUARY–MARCH, 1950

should learn if we examined the whole, is likely to be extremely small. Our boot-manufacturer could therefore solve his problem by taking several 'random samples' of the population (say, 100 families in each of ten different districts of the country), and then assembling and arranging the result. Naturally, success would largely depend on the random way in which the instances had been chosen. All kinds of social groups and classes must be more or less equally mixed together in each sample. The results of such an investigation might be: size 6, 109 pairs; size 7, 141 pairs; size 8, 343 pairs; size 9, 232 pairs; size 10, 134 pairs; size 11, 41 pairs.

Our manufacturer would be interested in working out the average size of shoe worn. A layman might say that the average size of shoe, calculated from the above figures, would be $8\frac{1}{2}$: that is, the various sizes added up, and divided by 6, which is the number of different sizes. This is called the 'arithmetic average', and is useless for our purpose, if there is no such actual size as $8\frac{1}{2}$. It is more important for our manufacturer to know which is the size that most frequently occurs out of the whole thousand samples taken. This is obviously size 8, and statisticians would call size 8 the 'mode', or 'modal' size: namely, that size likely to be most frequently met with in actual practice. The 'mode' is, therefore, of more use to the manufacturer than any average, because he could arrange to manufacture more pairs of the modal size than of other sizes, and by applying mass-production methods to their

manufacture to reduce their cost, and thus to reduce the average selling price of shoes in general.

The 'mode' is being found of increasing use in business statistics. For instance, in comparing the trading results of a MULTIPLE SHOP organization, it might be found useful to find out the 'modal' profit expressed as a percentage of TURN-OVER (qq.v.): that is, the figure which is attained by the largest number of branches. It would then be possible to investigate 'sub-modal' branches, so as to find out why they did not do so well; and the 'super-modal' branches might also be studied, so as to find out what made them more efficient than the others. In a manufacturing industry, using large numbers of similar machines, a modal output for a machine could be established; this could be used to detect and check inefficiency, and to increase efficiency by discovering what features there were about the super-modal machines that made their performance so outstanding.

Modern statistical technique also assists manufacturers in another way. Most factories have an inspection department, which examines the products to see that they are of a standard quality and finish. This department cannot, of course, examine every single article produced; it must work by the 'random sampling' method, described above. An analysis of such results will establish the modal size and finish. It may then be necessary to work out to what extent goods can be allowed to be inferior to the mode.

4. THE INDEX NUMBER. This is another statistical device used in the modern world. It is much used in government and other economic statistics, particularly those which show changes in wholesale and retail prices and in the COST OF LIVING (q.v.). A mass of figures for different articles would convey little information; and, for any cost-of-living graph, the number of items appearing in an average person's normal weekly list of purchases would be so immense that the number of lines and curves would merely create confusion. But if a representative collection of items were priced in any year, and the result called 100 (which would be the index for that year), the same collection of goods could be priced at later periods and the cost expressed as a percentage of the cost in the standard year. For instance, if goods became slightly cheaper in one year, the index number might fall from 100 to 94; if, in a later year, prices rose a good deal,

the index number might become 110 or more. The index number has been found so useful in practice that, in certain industries, wages are regulated upwards or downwards according to the movement of the cost-of-living index.

See also SCIENTIFIC MANAGEMENT.
See also Vol. X: VITAL STATISTICS.

STEEL INDUSTRY, *see* Vol. VIII: IRON AND STEEL.

STOCK EXCHANGES are regular associations of dealers in STOCKS AND SHARES (q.v.). An association was not formed in London until late in the 18th century, although dealings had previously taken place among bankers, brokers, and financial houses. The members of the new association met regularly at a coffee-house in Change Lane, known as 'Jonathan's', and early in the 19th century they acquired a building of their own. The New York Stock Exchange had even humbler beginnings, for at the end of the 18th century it started as a street market under a spreading tree in Lower Wall Street.

Early dealings were limited mainly to Government loans or gilt-edged securities (so called because of the gold-bordered paper on which they were printed) and the stocks of the larger CHARTERED COMPANIES (q.v.). As the INDUSTRIAL REVOLUTION (q.v.) went on, dealings began to

Graphic Photo Union

SCENE OUTSIDE THE STOCK EXCHANGE DURING A BOOM IN GOLD SHARES

Members continue business in the street after the Stock Exchange has closed

take place in the shares of the unlimited liability companies (*see* LIMITED COMPANIES) which came on to the market in growing numbers. The limited liability companies which followed the Companies Acts of 1855 and 1862 greatly helped the development of the London Stock Exchange, and in America Wall Street began to develop at the same time.

The organization of the London Stock Exchange is different from that of other stock exchanges and of the continental exchanges or 'bourses'. In London there is a rigid division of membership into those who act as jobbers or dealers and those who act as BROKERS (q.v.); in most other stock-markets all members carry on both functions. In London the jobber or dealer is really a kind of shopkeeper in securities. Just as there are different shops for different commodities, so there are different firms of jobbers in different markets. Usually a firm of jobbers specializes in one market, such as the gilt-edged market, the miscellaneous industrial market, or the 'Kaffir' market (which is the market in South African mining shares). The broker is just an intermediary between the jobbers and the outside public, since non-members are not admitted to the 'House', as the Stock Exchange is called.

A broker, wishing to deal for a client, goes down to the House and asks perhaps several jobbers what prices they are 'making' in the shares concerned. The price quoted by any jobber will actually be a pair of prices, such as $5-5\frac{1}{16}$. This means that if the broker's client wants to sell the shares named, the jobber will buy them at £5 each; but if the client wants to buy them, the jobber will arrange to sell them at £5. 1s. 3d. The difference between the two prices is the jobber's 'turn', or profit. A broker may approach several jobbers before deciding where he can get the best terms for his client. The 'bargain', as it is called, is entered in the jobber's book, and the broker posts off that evening to his client a Contract Note, which gives details of the transaction at the price arranged and also includes the broker's commission or brokerage. If the client is a buyer, he has to pay Government transfer stamp duty (in 1950 this was £2 per £100 of market-price) and a small transfer fee to the company (if he is buying other than Government securities) for a new share certificate. All the routine details of settlement are arranged through the Stock Exchange Clearing Department.

Before the Second World War, dealings on the London Stock Exchange, except in gilt-edged securities, took place 'for the Account': that is, accounts would be settled on fortnightly (or occasionally three-weekly) Account Days, authorized by the Stock Exchange Committee. At that time it was possible, also, to arrange before Account Day to 'carry over' purchases of shares which speculators did not wish to pay for in cash. It was also possible for speculators who had sold shares to postpone delivering them. Sometimes such payment or delivery could be postponed over a long series of Accounts. 'Bulls' (persons who had bought shares in the hope that they would rise in price) would have to pay a rate of interest, or 'contango', for the privilege of postponing payment. 'Bears' (who had sold shares which they did not really possess, hoping later on to buy them in at a lower price before they had to deliver them) might receive a rate of interest, called 'backwardation', as compensation for postponing delivery.

These arrangements encouraged speculators, especially as shares carried over from one account to another did not involve the 'bull' in the payment of stamp-duty or transfer fee. During the Second World War, dealings 'for the Account' were suspended, and payments had to be made as soon as one received the transfer deed. The system of Account Days was restored soon after the war; but carrying-over facilities were not restored until quite recently, and then not so extensively as before the war. If a 'bull' speculator cannot carry-over his purchases, he is obliged to pay stamp-duty and transfer fee, so his shares must have to rise very considerably in price before he could be certain of making a profit.

Stock Exchanges are useful to business in that they provide a free market in stocks and shares, and offer a means by which the worth of investments can be valued. Capital for industry would not be found so easily if investors did not feel that they could sell their shares when they wanted. In recent years the Government and the Stock Exchange Committee have done much to prevent reckless SPECULATION (q.v.).

See also FINANCE; STOCKS AND SHARES.

STOCKING MANUFACTURE, *see* HOSIERY AND KNITWEAR.

STOCKS AND SHARES. These are investments that can be bought and sold on Stock Exchanges. Formerly the word 'stock' nearly always meant an investment on which a fixed rate of interest was paid, and 'share' meant an investment receiving a dividend paid out of profits which varied from time to time. But the keeping of a Stock Register, as laid down by law, means less office work than the keeping of a Share Register, and so many shares nowadays are being converted into stock, and the old distinction no longer holds good.

Whether a company calls its capital 'stock' or 'shares' is of no real importance. A share is a fractional part of the capital of a company. Thus a company with a capital of £100,000 might arrange for its capital to be in 100,000 shares of £1 each, or it might arrange for it to be in 20,000 shares of £5. On the other hand, it might decide that its capital should be in stock. A person with 1,000 £1 shares in a company with a capital of £100,000 in £1 shares owns a one-hundredth share in the prosperity or misfortune of the company; a person owning £1,000 worth of stock is in exactly the same position.

Government LOANS (q.v.) are usually stocks which are transferable from one investor to another in multiples of £1. The older Government stocks, such as 2½% Consols, can be transferred in multiples of a penny. The loans of foreign governments and the capital of overseas railways are mostly stocks, and nearly all DEBENTURES (q.v.) are stocks. The bulk of the capital of other concerns dealt in on the Stock Exchange is in shares.

Stocks and shares may be of different classes: that is, the legal and voting rights and the interest or dividend rights of the various stockholders and shareholders may vary. Debentures, and the priority rights of their holders, are explained in the article DEBENTURES. (In any case, debentures are not shares in the fortune of a business, but loans made to it against the security of its assets). Apart from debentures, stocks and shares can be divided into two main classes, 'preference' and 'ordinary', although there is a variety of names for each class. A preference share gives the holder the first right to be paid a dividend out of the earned profits of a company before any dividend is paid to a non-preference shareholder, that is, an owner of ordinary shares. The limit of a preference dividend is stated in the title of the share. This might be, say, a 5% or 6% preference share, which means that earned profits will first be used for paying the preference shareholders their 5% or 6%, as the case may be, and that any profits then left over will be divided among the ordinary shareholders, as the directors decide.

Naturally, preference shares are a steadier kind of investment than ordinary shares, and are not so liable to changes of price on the Stock Exchange. There are various types of preference share. The most solid is the 'cumulative preference' share: if the fixed dividend due to the holders of these shares cannot be paid in any one year because there are not enough profits, the amount which is left unpaid becomes 'cumulative', that is to say, it accumulates as a debt and has to be paid out of the profits of later years. After a long trade depression, one sometimes reads that certain cumulative preference dividends are 3 or 4 years in arrear, but they may one day be paid, whereas a 'passed' ordinary dividend is not paid later. Another type is the 'participating preference' share, which entitles the shareholder to a fixed preference dividend and also to a 'participation' or share-out with the ordinary shareholders in what is left over, according to the terms on which the shares were issued.

Ordinary shareholders are entitled to dividends paid out of earned profits after the dividends due to the preference shareholders have been paid. Ordinary shareholders are said to own the 'equity' of a company: that is, the whole of its earning power after all fixed obligations have been met. Usually the rates of interest on debentures, and the fixed rates of dividend on preference shares, are lower than the percentage a good company can earn on its ordinary shares. If this is so, the equity owned by the ordinary shareholders becomes very valuable, and they may receive high dividends. Companies with a large amount of debentures or preference shares in proportion to ordinary share capital are said to have their capital structure 'highly geared'. Just as there are many types of preference share, so there are different types of ordinary share. 'Preferred ordinary' shares are really another name for preference shares. In some companies there are 'deferred' shares, which do not receive a dividend until the ordinary shares have received a fixed maximum. This device really turns the ordinary shares into preference shares, and the deferred shares become the real equity shares of the concern.

The market-prices of stocks on the STOCK EX-CHANGE (q.v.) are quoted on a percentage basis. Two prices are given, the lower being that at which jobbers (or dealers) are prepared to buy stock from investors who wish to sell, the higher being the price at which brokers (who work for outside clients) can buy from the jobbers. Thus, $2\frac{1}{2}$% Consols might be quoted in the Stock Exchange Official List at 69–$69\frac{1}{2}$, and $3\frac{1}{2}$% War Loan at $92\frac{1}{2}$–93. These prices mean that a buyer of Consols would pay £69. 10s. for £100 nominal value of that stock on the Register of the Bank of England, and a buyer of $3\frac{1}{2}$% War Loan would pay £93 for £100 of War Loan stock on the Register. A seller, however, would receive the lower of the figures quoted, the difference between them being the jobber's profit. What is really being bought by the investor in Consols for his £69. 10s. is the right to an annual income of £2. 10s., and the buyer of the War Loan is paying £93 for an annual income of £3. 10s.— since a $3\frac{1}{2}$% stock simply means that a holder of such stock receives an annual income of £3. 10s. for every £100 of stock standing in his name on the Register, even though he has only paid £93 for it.

The market-price of a stock therefore depends on the rate of interest on money invested which will satisfy the investing public. If people thought that just over £2. 10s. on every £100 actually invested was a reasonable rate of interest, they might be prepared to pay nearly £100, say £96, for £100 of stock at $2\frac{1}{2}$%; but they would only pay £48 for a $1\frac{1}{4}$% stock, which at that price would give them the same income as a $2\frac{1}{2}$% stock standing in the market at double the price. But if the investing public considered that not less than £5 on every £100 invested would satisfy them, they would be prepared to pay only £50 for £100 of stock at $2\frac{1}{2}$%. In this case we should find $2\frac{1}{2}$% Consols standing at a market price of £50. The investor in Consols, however, would be earning 5% on every £100 he invested in them.

Some shares, as explained above, are preference shares or preferred ordinary shares receiving a fixed rate of dividend. If this is so, their market-prices will vary on the same general lines as Government stocks, which also pay fixed rates. The only difference will be that the method of quotation will be different. Thus, a $6\frac{1}{2}$% preference share might be quoted in the market at 35s. for the £1 share. The rate of $6\frac{1}{2}$% means that on every £100 of nominal value an annual

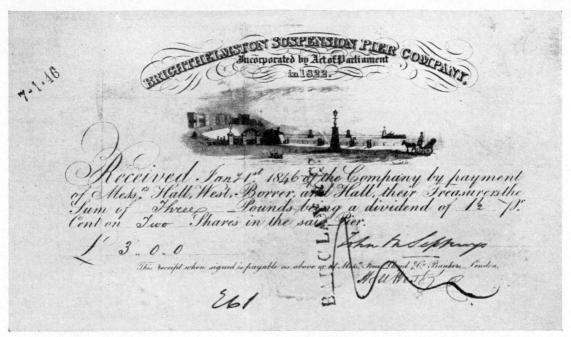

RECEIPT FOR A DIVIDEND ON SHARES IN THE BRIGHTON PIER COMPANY, 1846

income of £6. 10s. is received. At the price of 35s. for the £1 share, £100 of shares could be bought for £175, and the yield would be £6. 10s. multiplied by 100 and divided by 175, or £3. 14s. % on money invested. Such a share would stand in the market at a price which gave an investor in it a 'higher yield', or larger percentage on money invested, than he would obtain on Consols. This difference exists because people feel that there is a greater risk in investing in industry than in stocks guaranteed by the British Government.

If no profits are earned by an industrial firm, its ordinary shares, whatever might be their nominal value, may become worthless and almost unsaleable. Let us take an opposite case—one of high profits. If a company is able to pay the high dividend of 24% on its £1 ordinary shares, it is quite possible that these £1 shares might be quoted in the market at £6 each, for even at that price the yield on money invested would still be 4% per annum. It is, therefore, impossible to obtain any idea of what the market price of an ordinary share ought to be unless one knows what rate of dividend the company is paying, and what rates it is likely to pay in the future.

Another factor which affects the value of a share is what is called the 'break-up' value of the company, or what would be left in cash if the company's assets were disposed of and all liabilities settled. The shares of companies which cannot pay dividends are often valued in the market simply on their break-up value; but the shares of dividend-paying companies are more often valued solely on the basis of their yield, as explained above.

Certain technical terms may be explained here. The word 'par' means the nominal value of a share of stock. Thus a 3% stock standing in the market at £100 would be said to be quoted at par. If the price is below £100, say £95, then the stock is said to be standing 'at a discount'. If a stock is standing at over £100, it is said to be 'at a premium'. The same terms are applied to shares.

See also STOCK EXCHANGES: DEBENTURES; DIVIDEND; SPECULATION.

STONE DRESSING. This ancient industry forms a branch of masonry and is one of the building 'trades'. Nowadays the hand dressing of stone on a bench or 'banker' has been largely superseded by machinery. The machines are so large and costly that they either adjoin the

SAWING AND PLANING STONE
Drawing by W. H. Pyne, 1802

quarries or are found only in workshops belonging to building contractors.

Building in stone is one of the most cherished traditional crafts in Britain, creating her greatest monuments of architecture, cathedrals, abbeys, parish churches, colleges, and mansions, as well as some of her most beautiful old cottages. One finds these especially along the belt of fine limestone that runs from Dorset to Lincolnshire, including the Cotswold country that has given this distinctive style of rural building its name. But the mason's craft is dying. Even in the Cotswolds it is cheaper to build cottages of imported brick or of concrete than to use the cream-coloured stone that lies beneath the soil. In 1949 Italian workmen had to be brought to Britain to carry out the masonry of a new dam in South Wales, for the number of skilled British masons was then only half of what it had been in 1938. The greatly increased use of machinery for stone dressing has led to a saving in skilled manual labour, and so has the use of 'reconstructed stone' in place of natural stone. Reconstructed stone is really concrete, usually mixed in the proportion of 4 parts gravel to 1 part of Portland cement (see CEMENT) and then faced with chips of stone or stone dust from the works at the quarry. Reconstructed stone, therefore, looks very much like the natural stone with which it is

faced, and there is no need for dressing, either by machinery or by hand.

Natural stone is quarried in large blocks. Bath stone blocks average 4 to 6 feet long, and weigh from 2 to 3 tons. The blocks are first cut into parallel slabs of convenient thickness by a horizontal frame-saw. This has a swinging frame, into which are wedged a series of large steel blades, continuously fed with sharp grit, steel shot, and water. The next process is sawing the slabs into blocks of the required size by a vertically fixed circular saw, fitted either with diamonds set into dovetailed sockets or with a carborundum rim (this is an abrasive mineral with a cutting edge which is hard enough to go through stone). This gives the block its final finish, assuming that a plain 'ashlar' finish is desired. Water is used to keep the stone and saw wet. Other machines, very elaborate in design, are capable of planing the blocks when a very smooth finish is needed, or of producing stone mouldings. Large masonry workshops, whether at the quarry or at the contractor's own premises, have a battery of these great machines, arranged in an orderly sequence. Machinery seems to have been first used for working stone as long ago as 1730, at the Aberdeen granite works, but the dressing of hard granite differs considerably from that of the relatively soft limestones, such as Bath and Portland stone. Granite, like MARBLE (q.v.), is often polished. This is done by machinery. Shot, sand, and water are first used to produce a smooth surface; a felt disc then does the polishing, or 'glassing' as it is called.

All ornamental work—including carving and curved mouldings—must be done by hand, even when machinery is used for shaping the plain blocks; and, if a special finish is desired for the blocks, hand work is also needed. Apart from dressing, the processes of cutting which involve precise geometrical accuracy, such as the stones of a Gothic traceried window, are known as 'stereotomy', a word of Greek derivation meaning 'solid cutting'. The masons who actually fix the stones in position on a building are called 'setters' or 'wallers'.

See also STONE QUARRYING; BRICKS AND TILES; SLATE INDUSTRY.

STONE QUARRYING. 1. BUILDING STONE. Stone for building is generally one of five kinds —granites, sandstones, limestones, slates, and marbles (see SANDS AND SANDSTONE; LIMESTONE;

Rocks, Sections 2 (*b*) and 4, Vol. III). Many building stones are also used to make rollers for paper-making machines and for grinding-mills. Building stones are usually identified by the names of their type, sometimes varying from one locality to another; and knowledge of where they come from is very useful to the builder or architect, in judging the purposes for which they can best be used. The chief building granites come from Cornwall, North Wales, and Scotland, and limestones from Bath and Portland. Among the British marbles, Purbeck is the best known.

Large regular lumps of stone are required for building, preferably with parallel faces. Rocks, in their natural form (q.v. Vol. III), are divided by cracks or fissures, which are known in the trade as 'joints'. These joints often enable quarrymen to separate masses of stone with their faces roughly parallel to each other. Some types of stone, known as 'freestones', can be cut easily in any direction. Bath and Portland stones are of this type.

If the stone which is to be quarried shows above the surface of the ground, as an 'outcrop', or exposed at the edge of a cliff or the side of a valley, direct quarrying work can be begun. But more often the useful stone is covered by debris or by inferior stone, called the 'overburden', which must be removed before the good stone is reached. The best stone is often found at lower depths, and quarries are therefore often deep. To get down far enough, Mining (q.v.) is sometimes necessary, but the methods of working underground are very like those used in surface quarries. Some of the softer stones can be removed, in the required sizes and shapes, by the use of wedges and crowbars; but the normal method of releasing blocks of stone from the face of the quarry is more complicated. A row of holes is made with a pneumatic drill, and two steel plugs, each of a semi-circular section, are inserted in each hole. A long thin steel wedge,

U.S. Information Service

QUARRYING GRANITE IN VERMONT, U.S.A.
Wedges or 'feathers' being driven into the drill holes to split the stone

known as a 'feather', is driven between the flat surfaces of the two plugs (*see* picture). The feathers are gradually driven farther in, until the pressure breaks away the stone. Sometimes the pressure is applied by water-power (*see* Hydraulic Power Transmission, Vol. VIII). In some quarries each individual bed of stone may be cut through with a wire-saw, which is really an endless thin wire rope passing over pulleys. The rope is driven by steam or electric power, and is forced against the stone to be cut. Where the constantly moving rope touches the stone, a mixture of abrasive sand and water is fed on to the rope, and this enables the rope to eat its way gradually into the stone. The lumps of stone, when broken away from the face to about the right size, are lifted by cranes and sent to the dressing-sheds, where they are shaped more exactly (*see* Stone Dressing). Lumps of building stone may weigh several tons, and if the dressing-sheds are far away, the stone is often taken to them by aerial cableway, in skips or containers running on a rope.

There is still a demand for the best quality stone for use in building work. Clipsham stone from Rutland has been used for the new House of Commons. Granite is in demand for harbour walls, and was used for the new London embank-

OLD LIMESTONE QUARRY ON THE DORSET CLIFFS
The stone was let down the cliff face into boats

ment on the south bank of the Thames. So far, no manufactured substitute has been found for granites or marbles. A very fair substitute for Bath, Portland, and similar stones is now produced in concrete. This substitute is usually called 'artificial stone', and can be worked in the same way as natural stone and at much lower cost.

2. Broken Stone. In Britain this is mostly either granite or limestone, but it seldom comes from the same localities as building stone. There is very little stone to be found east of a line drawn from Lyme Regis in Dorset to Flamborough Head in Yorkshire. Good deposits of granite are found in Devon and Cornwall, and in the Midlands and many parts of the North. There are scattered deposits of granite in South Wales, and some large granite quarries in North Wales. In the north of Scotland some of the finest granite in the country is found, particularly in Aberdeenshire. Limestone is more widely distributed. There are small deposits in Devonshire, and a good deposit of carboniferous limestone in the Peak District of Derbyshire. As this is near the centre of the chemical industries, the limestone is mainly used in the chemical and steel trades. There are large deposits of limestone from Yorkshire northwards, up to the Scottish Border, and there are scattered deposits of limestone in Wales. There is also a fair amount in the lowlands of Scotland.

Broken stone ranges in size from 12-inch lumps to dust. Dust has many uses in modern industry. Granite and the harder stones are used almost exclusively as road metal or railway ballast. Limestone is used to some extent for the same purposes, but in much greater quantities in chemical manufacture, and as a 'flux' for smelting iron-ore and for certain processes of steel manufacture. A good deal of limestone is also converted into lime by being burned in kilns.

The methods of quarrying broken stone are different from those used in quarrying building stone. After any overburden present has been removed by scrapers, excavators, bulldozers, and similar equipment, the stone itself is blasted with explosives to loosen it. There are three main methods of blasting, and the nature of the quarry decides which shall be used. By the first method a compressed-air drill is used to drill holes in the rock, from $1\frac{1}{2}$ to $2\frac{1}{2}$ inches in diameter and up to 20 feet deep. These holes are filled with explosive to within about 2 feet of the face. This space of 2 feet is then filled with 'stemming', consisting of dust or clay. The explosive is fired from some distance away by means of an electric wire, and the stone is blasted away from the face of the quarry. A second method, which is finding favour in large quarries, uses the 'churn' drill. This drill makes a vertical hole, of from 5 to 9 inches diameter, to any depth up to about 250 feet. A series of holes is drilled some feet back from the existing face, and parallel to it. These holes are then filled, to about 10 feet from the top, with a quantity of explosive, and the 10-foot space is filled with 'stemming'. The explosive is then fired: The advantages of this method are that the explosive is well distributed in the rock, and a large quantity of well-fragmented stone is brought down at a time. A third method, which also produces larger quantities, is the system of tunnel-blasting. This can be used if the stone is fairly well broken up beforehand into thin layers. A small tunnel, about 3 feet by 2, is driven in at right angles to the face of the quarry. When some way in, the tunnel is turned again at right angles, and continued parallel to the face. The tunnel is driven as far as required, and a series of sinks or cavities are made in it for the explosive. When this is in position, the tunnel is filled with loose stone as 'stemming' before the charge is fired.

Usually the blasting produces large pieces of stone, which have to be again drilled and blasted before they are small enough to be taken to the breaking-plant. It is only comparatively recently that the old system of breaking down stone on the quarry floor with a sledge-hammer has ceased. The big lumps were thus broken down to the size a man could handle—about a hundredweight. The stone was then loaded by hand into 'trams', or small trucks. But in a modern quarry the stone is loaded by mechanical 'navvies' into railway wagons, lorries, or dump wagons, and taken to the breaking-plant to be broken up by machines known as primary crushers. Mechanical handling enables much larger lumps to be dealt with. Lumps of stone weighing from 3 to 5 tons can now be handled by the primary crusher, whereas before the use of handling-machines the size of a lump was limited to what a man could lift. If the stone is required for chemical-works or steel-works, it is broken by the crusher into lumps about the size of a 4-inch cube. For railway ballast or road metal, it is broken down to about $2\frac{1}{2}$ inches. The stone is sorted into various sizes by screening, and each size is stored in a separate bin.

See also STONE DRESSING; MINING; SLATE INDUSTRY; MARBLE AND ALABASTER.

See also Vol. III: LIMESTONE; SANDS AND SANDSTONE; ROCKS, Sections 2 (b) and 4.

See also Vol. VIII: QUARRYING MACHINERY.

Brighton Museum

SALT GLAZED STONEWARE JUG MADE AT FULHAM ABOUT 1720

STONEWARE is hard POTTERY (q.v.)—physically hard, and cannot be scratched with a knife. It has been fired to a temperature sufficient to 'vitrify' the clay; its texture is therefore no longer earthy, but vitreous, that is, of the nature of glass, and consequently non-porous, as distinct from EARTHENWARE (q.v.). It is also opaque. There are two main types: the salt-glazed stoneware of Europe, and that of the Far East, which in some respects resembles PORCELAIN (q.v.).

Salt-glaze stoneware originated in the Rhineland in the Middle Ages, and has been made there ever since. The glaze was produced by throwing common salt into the kiln when it reached its greatest heat (about 1,200° C. or over). The salt volatilized, or turned into gas, decomposed, and attacked the clay of the pots, forming on their surface a thin skin of very hard glaze, with an 'orange-peel' texture. These wares, blue-grey, buff, or dark brown, were often decorated before firing with incised (knife-cut) patterns or with applied 'low reliefs', that is, ornaments modelled in clay and stuck on to the pot. The only colouring pigments used were cobalt blue, manganese purple, and iron brown.

Dr. Dwight of Fulham, about 1670, was one of the first to make stoneware in England; it was made later at Nottingham, and also in North Stafford, where from about 1720 it became a flourishing industry. Astbury, Whieldon, and others, using Dorset clay and flint, produced English white or cream salt-glazed ware in the first half of the 18th century. But the smooth cream earthenware perfected about 1750 by Josiah WEDGWOOD (q.v. Vol. V) had many advantages over white salt-glaze, and eventually drove it out of production. The coarser kinds of salt-glazed stoneware continued to be made for certain purposes, such as sewer pipes and sanitary and bathroom fittings. In the 19th century, stoneware was given a new importance by the firm of Doulton of Lambeth, who made a wide range of stoneware, from drain-pipes to heat-proof dishes. Large articles, such as drain-pipes, are made by squeezing a continuous length of plastic clay through a wide nozzle. In the centre of the nozzle is a steel disc, whose diameter is the same as the interior diameter of the pipe.

See also POTTERY; EARTHENWARE; PORCELAIN.

STREET MARKETS. A street market is usually held once a week, although some street markets are open daily. 'Street market' is the term gener-

The Times

BERWICK MARKET, LONDON, AT NIGHT

ally used for a market in groceries and provisions, fish, fruit and vegetables, clothing, and household necessities; weekly markets for the sale of livestock are now usually held on properly regulated market grounds, and are called 'fairs' or 'marts' (see MARKETS, Vol. VI). The large-scale market held once, or at most two or three times, in the year is also called a 'fair' (see TRADE FAIRS).

Some periodical markets held in the streets and squares of British towns are centuries old. They are survivals from an age when agriculture and stock-raising were the main industries of the country (see AGRICULTURE, HISTORY OF, Vol. VI), and when country folk visited their nearest town once a week for shopping, as they still do in many parts of Britain to-day. Some of our British street markets are so old that the original rights or charters under which they are held cannot be traced. Others are more recent, and their rights are based on a Royal Charter or special Act of Parliament. Since 1847 the authority of Parlia-

ment has been necessary to start any new market. Some street markets in Britain are not properly constituted markets of this kind, but are merely selected 'pitches' where numbers of hawkers or barrowmen stand their barrows and trade with the passers-by. Lewisham High Street in southeast London is a hawkers' market of this kind. Hawkers have to take out a licence as such, whether they trade singly or in groups, whereas traders in a regularly organized market, held in a street or any similar public place, need no licence. They may, however, have to pay a 'stallage' or rent to the owner of the land, or to the local authority, for the privilege of running a market stall, which is usually a horse-drawn or motor van that can be opened out into a booth where goods may be displayed and sold.

'Petticoat Lane' (Middlesex Street) in East London is one of the most famous London street markets, and another important though less well-known market is that in Brewer Street,

Soho, not far from Piccadilly Circus. Street markets are not as numerous as they were even 50 years ago. Owing to the growth of motor traffic and the congestion of town streets, many of them have been shifted to enclosed sites, either in the open or under cover. Most of these sites have been provided by the local authorities, and the markets have thus become ordinary municipal markets.

See also PEDLARS AND HAWKERS.

STRIKE, *see* TRADE UNIONS.

SUBSIDIES are payments made by the government of a country to a particular industry. Their purpose may be to protect an industry from foreign competition. For instance, the growing of SUGAR-BEET (q.v. Vol. VI) was subsidized after the First World War, when Parliament decided that Britain must never again be as dependent on imported sugar as she had been. Since British farmers could not grow sugar-beet profitably against the free competition of imported sugar, a subsidy was necessary. In 1925 a temporary subsidy was given to the coal industry because it would otherwise have been forced to reduce the miners' wages.

Subsidies can also be used to help the export of goods which might be too expensive to sell abroad at their normal market-price. If, say, foreigners were unable to buy British coal at the prices ruling, the difficulty might be overcome by making a subsidy on exported coal of, say, £1 for each ton sold. Such a subsidy, added to what the National Coal Board could get from foreign buyers, might pay for the cost of production of exported coal.

During and after the Second World War the Government adopted the policy of subsidizing the market-prices of certain essential foodstuffs. This meant that the public could buy food such as bacon and butter in the shops for less than it cost the importers or manufacturers. These firms were paid a subsidy of so much per lb. so that they could still do business without losing money. The cost of these subsidies was met from taxation, and at one period was at the rate of over £400 million a year.

See also QUOTA; TARIFFS.

SUGAR CONFECTIONERY. This is the trade name for sweets, for sugar (sucrose) forms the main part of the ingredients. Sweetmaking was perfected in France before the art was brought to Britain, and the word 'confectionery' comes from a French word meaning 'to make up', or 'to manufacture'. The making of sweetmeats goes back to the earliest days of man's history, when it was practised with such natural things as honey, fruits, nuts, and eggs.

1. MODERN METHODS. Sucrose is a crystalline substance, and, like all crystalloids, will revert to its original crystalline state unless other ingredients are added; the most usual is confectioner's glucose, or corn syrup, a cereal starch converted to a syrup by the chemical process known as 'acid hydrolysis'. The cereal mostly used is maize, but potatoes can also be used. The starch is extracted, and is then turned into a clear syrup by first boiling it with a strong acid and water, and then by neutralizing the acid and evaporating some of the water. The chemically pure glucose known as dextrose is a different product from confectioner's glucose, which prevents the sucrose from recrystallizing in the products manufactured. It was discovered only in the second half of the 18th century, and thus did not affect the methods used in the early manufacture of confectionery.

Sugar and liquid glucose remain the basic ingredients; others also used to-day include treacle, molasses, honey, and 'invert' sugar, as sweetening materials; starches; fats, such as butter and cream; hardened vegetable oils (*see* OILS, VEGETABLE); gelatine; gum, both arabic and tragacanth (*see* GUMS AND RESINS); pectin from fruits, used for jellying; isinglass from seaweed, also for jellying; egg albumen; milk; dried and fresh fruits; nuts; flavourings and colourings. All ingredients must be eatable, and they should preferably be soluble in water. The amount of water remaining in any sugar solution depends on heat. Every solution has a boiling-point; the higher the concentration of sugar in a solution, the higher is the boiling-point. Water in a solution can be evaporated down to 2% and the product will set in a hard, clear mass. While it is still in a plastic condition, flavour and colour can be introduced and the mass formed into individual pieces by pressing it through rollers in which shapes are cut. The sweets called 'drops' are made in this way. If larger percentages of water are left in the sugar solution, a softer texture of product is obtained. This will usually be too soft to set firmly so as to form individual

Keystone

MAKING BOILED SWEETS

On the left colouring and flavouring are kneaded into boiled sugar. On the right the mixture is pressed into shape by rollers before being cooked

pieces, and other materials are therefore included to prevent the pieces from collapsing. Thus, gelatine, pectin, or isinglass is used to make the syrup set as a jelly. Gum, when it dries out in the sugar solution, forms a fairly hard sweet. Fat and milk set when cold, and make a caramel or toffee.

In some other types of confectionery the tendency of sugar to form into crystals is important. As soon as a supersaturated syrup is made, the excess sugar starts to crystallize, and the temperature at which the syrup is held will have a distinct bearing upon the rate of growth of the crystals. When the syrup is hot and concentrated, the crystals form much more rapidly than when it is cold. If a syrup is made and poured on 'centres' in a revolving pan, the crystals as they form will adhere to these centres and will make a crust round them. Such sweets are known as 'pan goods' and include sugared almonds and aniseed balls. The centres can be of almonds, or anything similar which will not break or distort during the sugaring process. Nonpareils are made in the same way, the centre being a grain of sugar. The size of the finished sweet naturally depends on the quantity of syrup deposited on the centre.

With some sweets it may be necessary to pre-

vent the sugar from recrystallizing, and so varying proportions of glucose are added. More liquid glucose is used for a perfectly clear product than for a product such as fondants, which are made from a solution of water, sugar, and liquid glucose, agitated to form a fine crystal. A fondant is not clear, but clouded or opaque; this is the result of the crystal formation and the mixing with air which takes place during agitation.

Some sugar confectionery is prepared without first boiling a sugar solution. Lozenges are a good example; their basis is sugar finely ground and made into a stiff dough with a gum solution. The gum dries out the dough hard, after the lozenges have been shaped by machinery.

2. THE CONFECTIONERY INDUSTRY has developed to its present stage mainly during the last 100 years. Even 50 years ago hand methods were still the rule, but machinery has since been introduced for most processes. Some of the firms in the industry to-day have been producing confectionery for 200 years, but their methods and products have greatly changed.

Before the Second World War caused a shortage of sugar, Britain's yearly output of sugar confectionery was 499,000 tons, valued at nearly £50 million, equal to 7 oz. weekly for each person of the population. For this, the industry used 296,000 tons of sugar, 96,500 tons of glucose, 18,000 tons of oils and fats, 77,000 tons of milk, 4,200 tons of dried fruits, and 18,500 tons of nuts. About 82,000 people were employed in actual manufacture.

The normal distribution of confectionery is from manufacturer to wholesaler; the wholesaler then distributes to shops. A few very large manufacturers have depots in most of the big industrial areas, and deliver their products direct to the shops. Most chain stores or MULTIPLE SHOPS (q.v.) buy in big quantities direct from the manufacturer. A few large manufacturers have their own chains of shops.

There is no particular district of Britain where the manufacture of sugar confectionery is concentrated, although most of the factories are in the industrial areas, where labour is easily obtained. Most of the employees do not need to be highly skilled.

A recent feature of the industry is the tendency to pack confectionery in unit-containers, which hold a stated quantity and do not need to be weighed.

See also COCOA AND CHOCOLATE; GROCERY AND PROVISIONS; SUGAR REFINING.

SUGAR REFINING. In earlier days few who used sugar bothered about its colour, but during the Italian RENAISSANCE (q.v. Vol. I) in the 14th and 15th centuries people became more particular and the idea of white or 'refined' sugar became attractive. The practice of importing raw sugar (*see* SUGAR-CANE, Vol. VI) and refining it started in Venice about 1400. In England the first refinery was opened in the 16th century.

An essential part of refining is the large use of charcoal (made if possible from animal bones rather than from wood) to remove the brown colour and certain impurities from the sugar. The raw sugar is first washed in a centrifugal machine, from which comes out washed sugar together with some syrup. The washed sugar, dissolved in water, is passed through charcoal filters as a brown fluid, and comes out of these as a white fluid of refined sugar. The syrup may be refined in the same way into brown sugar, which may be later melted and refined into white sugar. The 'char filters', through which the washed sugar passes, are vertical cylinders containing about 30 tons of animal charcoal, through which the dissolved sugar is allowed to flow. When the charcoal has been in use for some time, it loses its power of removing the brown colour from the sugar. Therefore it must be removed, burned once more and purified, and it can be then used again. The liquid sugar after coming from the charcoal filters is crystallized, that is, it is boiled until the water evaporates, leaving more or less pure sugar. The quality is improved if boiling takes place at a fairly low temperature; this can be achieved if the boiling takes place in a 'vacuum pan', from which some air has been withdrawn, so that the pressure, and therefore the temperature, is lower. Further evaporation during stirring causes the sugar to 'granulate' to the size of the grains in which it appears on the breakfast table. Cube or loaf sugar is a pressed mass of small crystals, with a certain amount of refined syrup to bind the crystals together.

See also SUGAR CONFECTIONERY.
See also Vol. VI: SUGAR-CANE.

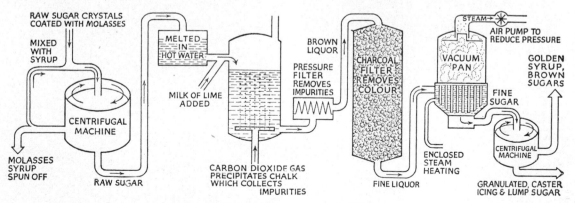

STAGES IN THE REFINING OF SUGAR
The process starts on the left

TERRA SVLPHVRATA PVTEOLANA

THE CRATER OF SOLFATARA, ITALY, WHERE SULPHUR WAS FOUND IN THE 17TH CENTURY
The sulphur was prepared in the huts. Sick people came to be cured by the sulphur fumes

SULPHUR or brimstone (from Anglo-Saxon words meaning 'fiery stone') is a MINERAL (q.v. Vol. III), which burns easily. It is yellow and brittle, and is found in a more or less pure state in regions near both active VOLCANOES and extinct ones (q.v. Vol. III). There are deposits in Italy, Iceland, Mexico, the U.S.A., New Zealand, and Japan. On the Pacific island of Vanus Lava in the New Hebrides there is a mountain of almost pure sulphur, nearly 2,000 feet high. For many years Italy produced most of the sulphur used in the world's industries, but in the late 19th century supplies began to come from big underground deposits in Louisiana and adjacent American States. Sulphur is mainly used in the manufacture of the important industrial chemical, sulphuric acid (see CHEMISTRY, INDUSTRIAL), and of sulphite WOOD PULP (q.v.).

It is also used in medicine, and as 'flowers of sulphur' in substances used for killing insects, moulds, and other fungi and parasites. Sulphur plays a big part in the vulcanizing processes of RUBBER MANUFACTURE, and a gas made from sulphur is used for BLEACHING (qq.v.).

The choking fumes and unpleasant smell given off by sulphur when burnt have impressed man's imagination for centuries. Some of the ancient philosophers believed that it was one of the prime elements out of which all things were made (see CHEMISTRY, HISTORY OF).

SULPHURIC ACID, see ACIDS.

SUPPLY AND DEMAND. The expression 'demand', expressed in terms of money, means the wish of a number of people to buy certain articles. 'Supply' is the quantity of articles put on sale to satisfy these wants.

The prices of goods in the market move upwards and downwards in accordance with changes in supply and demand (*see* VALUE AND PRICE). The supply of any commodity is not always constant, and changes in supply come often from causes outside human control. Climatic and seasonal influences, for example, may affect the supply of foodstuffs and other agricultural products. The world price of wheat alters greatly from one year to another, falling when harvests are good and rising when they are poor. Fish is another commodity whose supply changes considerably because of changes in the weather. The supply of manufactured goods is more constant than that of natural products such as wheat and fish, and tends to rise or fall as people want more or less of them. If supply and demand are sensitive to alterations in prices, they are said to be 'elastic'; if not, they are called 'inelastic'. As a general rule, the supply of manufactured goods is elastic, and of natural products inelastic. If the price of some manufactured article goes up, and its manufacture therefore becomes more profitable than it was, it is usually fairly easy for its manufacturers to turn out more of it, and thus to increase the supply coming on to the market. But, in the short run at any rate, it is not easy to increase the supply of, say, wheat or meat. More wheat will only be forthcoming if more is sown, and, even if more is sown, there is an interval of months before it can be harvested, always provided that the weather is favourable to the crop; and an increased supply of meat may only be possible after many years.

In normal times, demand does not alter as much as supply. People's tastes and preferences remain very much the same, and do not greatly depend on changes of climate and seasons, although of course there are many things whose demand depends on the weather. Changes in demand arise mainly from changes in people's incomes, and we must not forget that changes in supply may alter these incomes. North American business men, for example, are well aware that the demand for many of the things they sell depends on the incomes of the farmers of the Prairie Provinces and the Middle West; and these incomes depend in their turn on the supply of the crops they have grown and livestock they have bred and sold. UNEMPLOYMENT (q.v.) is another great influence on demand, for the demand for all kinds of goods decreases very much when millions of people, perhaps, are out of work.

The demand for most necessities is so urgent that upward or downward changes in price (coming, perhaps, from changes in supply conditions) are likely to have little influence on the quantity demanded or bought. Bread is an example. If its price were doubled, there would be greater economy in its use, and demand might decrease slightly; but it is almost certain that demand would not be halved or anything like it. Similarly, if its price were halved, it is very unlikely that people would want twice the quantity of bread; demand might increase by a fraction, but little more. The demand for necessities is, therefore, generally inelastic. On the other hand, the demand for luxuries, and for other things that most of us can do without if forced to, is elastic. This is particularly true of such things as books and theatre and cinema seats, and very true of things such as fruits and flowers out of season and such purely luxury goods. Whether a rise or fall in the price of any article will cause demand to alter very much depends, therefore, on the elasticity or inelasticity of the demand for that particular thing.

See also COMMERCE; EXCHANGE AND TRADE; VALUE AND PRICE.

SWEET MANUFACTURE, *see* SUGAR CONFECTIONERY.

SYNTHETIC PRODUCTS, *see* PLASTICS; CHEMISTRY, INDUSTRIAL; DYES; RUBBER MANUFACTURE; OIL, MINERAL; TEXTILE FIBRES.

T

TANNING. 1. This is, strictly speaking, only one of the processes of leather manufacture, but the term as used in the trade means the art of converting animal skin into leather. Tanning makes skins and hides supple and elastic, and protects them from damp and decay. In a rather primitive form, the art of tanning goes back more than 15,000 years in the history of mankind.

Leather manufacture has three distinct stages. There are, first of all, the 'wet-work' processes. In these, the corium or true skin is separated from the hairy outside layer (the epidermis) and the fleshy inside layer (*see* HIDES AND SKINS). Next come the tanning processes proper, in which chemical treatment makes the corium proof against damp and against the growth of BACTERIA and MOULDS (qq.v. Vol. II). Finally there are the finishing processes, which improve the appearance of the leather and make its outer surface more fully waterproof.

2. WET-WORK. These processes vary with the type of skin or hide, but the treatment of ox-hides for shoe soles provides a good example. They are first soaked in water to remove dirt and blood and any salt that may have been used in 'curing' the hides for preservation, and also to restore any moisture in the hide which had been lost in curing. To loosen the hair and epidermis, the hides are then steeped in a chemical solution chiefly composed of lime. This treatment takes place in rectangular pits of wood, brickwork, or concrete, sunk into the ground. After a few days in this liquid, the hides are taken out and the loosened hair is scraped off by machine. Next comes 'fleshing', or cutting away the loose underlayer of the hide, also by machine. 'Scudding', or working over the grain of the hide with a blunt tool to force out dirt, is then done by hand or machine. The corium or central layer of the hide has now been separated, as a flat white sheet. The shoulder or foremost portion,

and the two bellies or side portions, are cut off to be tanned separately for such uses as straps and cycle-saddles. This is called 'rounding'. The central portions, or 'butts', are treated with a little weak boric or lactic acid to kill any lime left in the surface, and are then ready for tanning.

After the wet-work processes, it may be necessary to divide the skins or hides horizontally into two or more layers. This is done in a splitting machine in which the skin is pressed, edge on, against the sharp edge of a travelling band-knife, a thin, ribbon-shaped blade that goes round and round like a bicycle chain. Sheepskins are often split; the uppermost layer, or grain, is vegetable-tanned for fancy leathers known as 'skivers'; the lower layer, or flesh, is oil-tanned for chamois leather. Cattle hides are also often split, when the whole thickness of the hide would be too great for such uses as upholstery leather or shoe uppers.

3. TANNING CHEMICALS. These fall into five main classes. (*a*) Vegetable tannins are extracted by water from the bark, leaves, roots, and other parts of certain plants. Oak-bark is the traditional English material, but is now very scarce and little used. Important modern materials are chestnut wood from France and Italy, oak wood from Yugoslavia, quebracho wood from Argentina and Uruguay, mimosa or wattle bark from Natal, myrobalan nuts from India, valonia acorn-cups from Turkey and Greece, and sumac leaves from Sicily. Vegetable tannins produce

Kenneth H. Cole

HAIR BEING REMOVED FROM THE HIDE BY MACHINE

leathers varying in colour from pale cream to reddish-brown. (*b*) MINERALS (q.v. Vol. III) provide such tannins as salts of aluminium, chromium, and zirconium. ALUM (q.v.) is one of the oldest tannins, and produces a white leather which is not very waterproof. Chrome tanning was introduced in 1884, and produces a greenish-blue leather, extremely waterproof. The use of zirconium is recent; it produces a white leather suitable for gloves, handbags, and sports shoes. (*c*) Fish oils, of which the most used is crude cod-liver oil, produce the well-known wash-leather or chamois. (*d*) Formaldehyde, made from wood alcohol, produces a white washable leather, much used for gloves. (*e*) The modern synthetic tannins made from coal-tar products (*see* CHEMISTRY, INDUSTRIAL) produce leathers resembling in many ways those made with vegetable tannins. Sometimes more than one tannin is used—chrome after vegetable, for example, giving semi-chrome leather.

The details of the tanning process, the time taken over it, and the chemicals used vary with the class of leather being prepared. A typical process is the treatment of ox-hide butts for vegetable-tanned sole leather. The butts are hung in a tanning pit to soak in the 'liquor', and are moved every day to a pit containing a slightly stronger liquor. Later soakings last one week and two weeks. In the end, a pit of strong liquor is filled with alternate layers of butts and tanning material. This stage of the process takes a month. Tanning is completed by 'hot pitting' the hides for a week in a warm strong liquor. Contrasted with this lengthy process is chrome tanning, used for the two chief types of shoe upper leather: box calf, and glazed goat or kid. The unhaired limed skins are first washed and the lime removed with a weak acid, such as boric. Then comes a cleansing process called 'bating', or steeping in a mixture of ammonium chloride and digestive juices from animal pancreatic glands. The bated pelt is then 'pickled' in a solution of salt and sulphuric acid. The pickled skins are placed in a revolving drum with salt and water, and green chrome liquor (basic chromium sulphite) is fed through the hollow axle of the drum. Tanning is complete in about six hours.

4. FINISHING PROCESSES. These are varied, and include washing, the introduction of lubricating oil, dyeing, drying, and glazing or giving a high gloss. Some leathers, for special uses, have to go through a process of CURRYING (q.v.).

Barrow, Hepburn, and Gale

A TAN YARD

'Split' hides (used for upholstery, &c.) and 'dressed' hides (used for harness, etc.) are tanned here

Much sheep leather is embossed or stamped with the grain patterns of rare and expensive skins, such as lizard, crocodile, and python, and is dyed to the right colours. Parchment and vellum are made respectively from sheep or calf skins, without tanning (*see* PAPER, Section 3, Vol. IV). Morocco leather is goat skin, sumac-tanned by a special method, with a pattern produced by graining in several directions. Glacé kid for women's gloves is made by treating prepared kid skins with a mixture of alum salt, flour, and egg yolk. The leather is not proof against water, and this process is called 'tawing' rather than tanning. Suède and velvet leathers are made by holding the leather against a rapidly revolving wheel covered with carborundum, a gritty substance which teases up the fibres of the leather. Upholstery leathers are mostly made from cattle hides split into two or more layers. The top layer is vegetable-tanned. It may be merely stained and given a plain finish; or it may be stained, embossed, and otherwise worked up to give antique and other effects. Patent leather is made by varnishing leather with boiled linseed oil or with cellulose lacquers.

See also HIDES AND SKINS; BOOT AND SHOE MAKING; UPHOLSTERY; LEATHER.

TAPESTRY. This is a textile with a woven

pattern, and it is generally used for wall hangings. The pattern is not applied after the cloth has been woven as in EMBROIDERY (q.v. Vol. XI); it is made by the weft threads themselves (*see* WOOL WEAVING). Sometimes the two crafts are confused; the famous BAYEUX TAPESTRY, for instance (q.v. Vol. XII), which was made soon after the Norman Conquest, is actually an embroidery of wool on a linen foundation. The tapestry method of weaving is very early in origin, and small pieces of tapestry used for garments and wrappings have been found in ancient Egyptian tombs (*see* EGYPTIAN CIVILIZATION, Vol. I). But we know little about the craft until the Middle Ages. Tapestry hangings then began to be made chiefly for rich people; sometimes the hangings were meant for religious or decorative use, and sometimes to keep rooms warm by covering the damp stone walls and stopping the draughts (*see* CURTAINS AND HANGINGS, Vol. XI).

Tapestry, like other weaving, is done on a frame or 'loom'. The warp is either upright or horizontal, and the warp threads, usually of a dull neutral colour, are completely covered by the weft threads which form the pattern. These, which are in various colours, are not thrown completely across the warp, but are woven backwards and forwards, each colour across the appropriate part of the warp (*see* picture). In this way is built up a pattern that may be of a simple geometrical kind, or a complicated picture with figures. The original design (called a 'cartoon') is worked out in detail on paper, and the weaver follows it closely. This design is seldom the work of the weaver, being usually commissioned from an artist. In the early tapestries illuminated manuscripts were often used as sources of inspiration, and usually tapestry follows the style of painting of its own times. The range of subjects in the early tapestries is very wide—biblical or mythological scenes, romances, history, hunting, games, sport, landscapes, heraldry, and decorative panels of all kinds. In the early work the range of colours is small, little more than a dozen shades being used; but by the 18th century several hundred might be used in a panel.

As tapestries have always been very expensive to produce, they are found usually only in churches, public buildings, and great mansions. They were often kept for special occasions, such as state ceremonies, pageants, and festivals, when they were used to enliven the buildings and the streets.

Many of the best tapestries have come from the Netherlands (now Holland and Belgium). Their craftsmen emigrated to all the European countries and strongly influenced all tapestry weaving except that of Scandinavia. Arras, in northern France, was so famous a centre of this craft in the 14th and 15th centuries that in England and Italy all tapestries came to be called 'arras'. In the 16th century Brussels became the centre of importance, and for two centuries dominated the whole field of tapestry production, after which it declined.

In France, until the 17th century, there were many small workshops which were much influenced by Flanders, the western part of the Netherlands; but in 1662 the famous Gobelins factory was inaugurated in Paris under royal patronage. It is here that most of the finest

Ashmolean Museum

DETAIL OF TAPESTRY CUSHION COVER MADE BY WILLIAM SHELDON IN THE 16TH CENTURY
The warp runs horizontally and is covered by the weft threads whose different colours form the design

French tapestries have been woven. Beauvais, in the north, and Aubusson and Felletin in central France, have also been important centres for hundreds of years, and are still flourishing, producing good tapestries of modern design.

William Sheldon established a small English factory in Warwickshire in the 16th century. This lasted for about 100 years, and produced some fine maps and heraldic tapestries. About 1600 a factory was founded at Mortlake (now part of south-west London), and weavers were brought over from the Netherlands. During the 19th century William MORRIS (q.v. Vol. V) started a small factory at Merton, south of London, and this is still in existence.

Early German tapestries show little foreign influence. They are very simple, having as subjects old legends or fanciful scenes. Later tapestries, chiefly woven in Berlin, imitate the French style.

In Italy the foundation and progress of tapestry-making were largely due to Flemish weavers, the Italians' greatest contribution being in the design of the cartoons. Famous artists, including LEONARDO DA VINCI and RAPHAEL (qq.v. Vol. V), designed tapestries that were sometimes woven in Flanders.

See also WOOL WEAVING; UPHOLSTERY.
See also Vol. XI: UPHOLSTERY, HISTORY OF.

TARIFFS. A tariff is a list of duties or taxes on goods imported, and is published by the government of a country for the information of international traders. The word 'tariff' is also commonly used to mean an individual tax in this list.

Some governments impose a tariff purely for revenue purposes—that is, to collect money to meet their normal costs. If this is the purpose of the tariff, duty will be charged on goods in the list even if they are produced inside the country

The Edinburgh Tapestry Co.

WEAVING H.M. THE QUEEN'S COAT OF ARMS
The weavers work from the back of the warp. The original design for the tapestry is at their left

itself. Duties imposed on such home-produced goods are called Excise Duties.

Some countries may impose a tariff in order to protect home industries against foreign competition (see INTERNATIONAL TRADE). The tariff of Britain is arranged both for revenue and for protective purposes. The tariff on imported tobacco is for revenue only, because there is no tobacco-growing industry in Britain. But the British import duties on clothing manufactured abroad are mainly protective, although they are also useful in providing some revenue.

Import duties may be either 'specific' or *ad valorem*. A specific duty is a duty of so much per ton, gallon, bushel, or whatever the measure of weight or size may be. An *ad valorem* duty is one of so much per cent. on the money value of the goods imported. If the money values of imported goods subject to *ad valorem* duties were declared at a false figure, the country's revenue would suffer; and so invoices for such goods must be certified by a British Consul abroad as representing fair and reasonable market values in the country from which they come. Such invoices are called Consular Invoices, and must be shown before the goods can be cleared through the Customs.

Import and excise duties are collected by the Board of CUSTOMS AND EXCISE (q.v. Vol. X).

See also QUOTA; SUBSIDIES.

TEA TRADE. Chinese legend suggests that tea was first grown and drunk in that country about 3,000 years before our first written record, which belongs to the 9th century. It was grown in Japan from the 9th century A.D. onwards. Centuries passed before it was known and appreciated in Europe. In the early 17th century some officers in the distant stations of the EAST INDIA COMPANY (q.v.) in Japan and the Philippines in the Pacific introduced tea to the Indian stations of the Company. At the end of the 17th century the Company made a trial shipment of a small quantity to England. This was green China tea, of the type generally drunk in China and Japan to-day. This first consignment was sold in London at about £8 a pound. Even at this immense price many liked the new beverage, and other small shipments followed. The tea was brought direct in Chinese junks to the Company's trading stations, or 'factories', in India, and was then re-exported. As the taste for tea increased, the Company decided that the tea trade had a promising future, and set up in Amoy, in China, a buying depot for direct purchases of tea from that country. As the trade developed, the demand for tea in

Tea Bureau

TEA FERMENTING ON TRAYS IN KENYA

London grew with it, and towards the end of the 18th century the average price had fallen below 20s. This was still high, but the Company had a monopoly of the new trade, and at that time there was no known source of supply outside China itself. By the beginning of the 19th century the annual consumption of tea in Britain had risen to over 2 lb. per head of the population.

It was obvious to London merchants that sales of tea could be considerably increased if supplies came forward in greater quantities at a reduced price. The Company agreed to look into the possibility of growing tea locally in India itself. In 1813 the Company was forced by Parliament to give up its MONOPOLY (q.v.) of Indian trade and commerce, but it still retained its monopoly of the China trade. Its officers believed that by selling a comparatively small quantity of China tea at a high price, more profit could be made than by encouraging the growth of the plant in India and selling larger quantities at a more popular price. The experiments in transplanting Chinese tea-bushes in India were therefore rather half-hearted. But between 1823 and 1834 the tea plant was discovered growing wild in the Assam province of north-east India (*see* TEA, Vol. VI). Calcutta business men were anxious to develop Indian tea-gardens, and in 1834 the Governor-General set up a committee to arrange for the cultivation of tea in India on a commercial scale. The first consignment of Indian tea reached the London market in May 1838, and was sold at an average price of just over 20s. a pound. Indian tea-gardens were established not only in Assam, and the Sylhet and Darjeeling districts adjoining, but also in Travancore and the Nilgiri Hills. The finest teas came from the Darjeeling district. India became the most important producer of tea for the British market, and for 30 years shared with China the export tea trade of the world. Other countries then turned their attention to tea-growing, but the world market was steadily expanding and the prosperity of the Indian tea industry was not affected. By 1875 India was exporting to Britain alone 25 million lb. a year, and by the outbreak of the Second World War the quantity was not far short of 500 million lb.

In 1869 the coffee plantations of the island of Ceylon were largely ruined by blight. Through the combined energies of the Government, which helped financially, and the planters themselves, the ruined coffee estates were replanted with tea. By the end of the 19th century there were over 300,000 acres of tea-gardens in Ceylon. Tea seed from Assam had also been planted in the Dutch East Indies, now Indonesia, and a big local industry was established. Since the beginning of the present century other countries have entered the industry; of these the most important growers are Uganda, Kenya, and Nyasaland in East Africa.

Three main varieties of tea now enter into the world's commerce: black tea, green tea, and Oolong. Black tea forms the bulk of the output from India, Ceylon, the East Indies, and Africa, and is the type of tea drunk almost exclusively in Britain. The small quantities of China tea drunk in Britain are fermented black tea. To make black tea, the green leaf is subjected to several manufacturing processes, the most important of which are the fermentation of the leaves and their subsequent drying by hot air. Green tea, which is unfermented, is produced mainly in China and Japan. Its consumption in Britain had been declining steadily before the outbreak of the Second World War, and now it is no longer imported, but considerable quantities are consumed in the U.S.A. and Russia. In the form of small 'bricks' green tea is exported in large quantities from China to the U.S.S.R. by camel caravan. It is widely drunk throughout the whole of Central Asia and Tibet, and is even used as a form of currency. Oolong tea stands halfway between green tea and black tea. It is semi-fermented, and the principal centre for its growth and manufacture is the island of Formosa which is off the south-eastern coast of China. It is not much drunk outside China and Japan, but it has a small market in the U.S.A. Before the First World War attempts were made to popularize it in London, and for some years the Formosa-Oolong Tea Rooms were open in Piccadilly. It is now on sale again in London grocers' shops.

Tea is packed for export in plywood chests lined with aluminium foil and hermetically sealed: this was one of the earliest known uses of PLYWOOD (q.v.). Before the Second World War black tea, mainly from India and Ceylon, accounted for the bulk of the tea trade of the world. The largest markets were Calcutta and London. Regular auctions were held in Calcutta during the export season, which lasted for about 8 months of the year, but a good deal of tea was

Tea Bureau
A TEA-TASTER

sold direct from the gardens. In London, regular auctions were held at the London Commodity Exchange in Mincing Lane. When war broke out in 1939 the Ministry of Food adopted the system of BULK PURCHASE (q.v.) direct from growers and merchants in India, Ceylon, and the African producing countries. However, the pre-war auctions were subsequently resumed, and are now held at Plantation House in the City of London.

See also GROCERY AND PROVISIONS.
See also Vol. VI: TEA.

TERYLENE, *see* TEXTILE FIBRES AND FABRICS.

TEXTILE FIBRES AND FABRICS. The word 'textile', from the Latin *texere* 'to weave', is generally applied to all clothes, carpets, or other materials made of textile fibres or with yarn spun from such fibres.

1. FIBRES. These are the raw materials, such as wool, flax, or silk, from which the threads or yarns are spun before weaving or knitting can take place. The researches of archaeologists suggest that man first discovered and acquired the art of spinning during the New Stone Age, perhaps about 5000 B.C. Long before textile yarns were woven into cloth, rushes or osiers were plaited or woven into baskets, mats, and screens, and were used to make nets. The earliest homes of primitive man were screens of woven rushes or slender branches joined up into the form of circular huts. Later, man made use of the more slender textile fibres that lent themselves to the spinning. Of these, the most important were the vegetable fibres, such as flax and cotton, and the animal fibres, such as wool and silk. Flax was probably the first to be used by man, and from it he spun linen thread and wove linen cloth. Scraps of linen have been found among the ruins of the dwelling-places of earlier peoples—in particular the making of fine linen cloth was developed in ancient Egypt.

The next natural fibre to be used was probably wool. There are records of the existence of a wool-weaving industry in Mesopotamia about 4000 B.C. Cotton is another of the earlier fibres used. It has a long history in India, although it was some time before it was introduced into Europe. Silk is perhaps almost as ancient. Legend suggests that its use in China dates from about 2700 B.C.

The four fibres mentioned are the most important in human history, but many other natural fibres have been used. Hemp is a vegetable fibre, and the Scythians are believed to have used it for the making of ropes and nets as early as 500 B.C. To-day, hemp is used as well as jute for coarse fabrics, sacking, and some furnishing materials. The fibre of the stinging-nettle plant was used quite early in Sweden for ropes and sailcloth, and its use was also known in southern Europe during the Middle Ages. In South America and in the Philippine Islands fibre from the leaves of the pineapple plant has been much used. Many textile yarns are also spun from the hair of various animals (see HAIR TRADE). Even feathers have been spun into yarn, although only the downy feathers of birds can be used in this way, as the quills of the stronger feathers would damage spinning machinery.

In the present century man has added to these natural fibres by fibres of his own making. Of these artificial or synthetic fibres the most important are the RAYON group (q.v.). Although rayon fibres are made synthetically, the basis of most of them is the chemical compound called cellulose, a product of natural textile fibres such as cotton. Three of the four main methods of making rayon are based on cellulose, and the other is based on casein, which is a chemical constituent of milk. Synthetic fibres have also been made from soya-beans and peanuts.

Paper is largely made from WOOD PULP (q.v.), which contains cellulose. During the First World War Germany and Austria were closely blockaded, and could not import wool, raw cotton, and jute. Experiments were made in spinning paper yarn as a substitute for these natural textiles. Webbing equipment worn by soldiers and sandbags for trench warfare were successfully woven out of paper yarns. Towards the end of the war clothing fabrics were also being woven from paper yarns that had been treated by WATERPROOFING (q.v.). Paper fabrics have been used in Britain and on the continent of Europe as a backing for rugs and carpets; they are much used in the cheap-furniture trade of the U.S.A. NYLON (q.v.) has recently been added to the long list of synthetic textile fibres. Its production on a commercial scale began only in 1940. The most recent synthetic fibre is Terylene. The raw materials from which it is made are produced during OIL REFINING (q.v.). Terylene has already been used to make a variety of things—for example, rope and fishing lines, lace and curtains, women's underwear, and men's tropical suits.

Perhaps the most remarkable synthetic fibre is glass. It was not until 1936 that it became possible to spin glass fibre into yarn that would resist breaking, and from it to weave fabrics that would stand a reasonable amount of hard treatment. The perfection of the process is the result of American research and enterprise, and in Britain the material is known as 'fibre glass'. Its use is less advanced in Britain than in the U.S.A., where tablecloths, lampshades, curtains, and bedspreads have been made from it. An interesting use has been its mixture with real silk or rayon for men's ties, as fibre glass does not easily crease. It is also used for electrical insulation. Fibre glass has the same properties as ordinary glass, and will break in time if it is bent or folded too much. Therefore, the fibres out of which the yarns are spun are specially lubricated during manufacture, to prevent them from cutting each other. An outstanding advantage of fibre glass is that the colours given to it are absolutely fast, that is, will not fade. The temperature at which it melts is higher than that of natural textile fibres, and in consequence, in Britain, it has been used for making firemen's helmets.

2. FABRICS. Textile fabrics are in everyday use for clothing, furnishing, floor covering, and other domestic and industrial purposes. They are woven, knitted, crocheted, or sewn. Until the development of mechanical power at the end

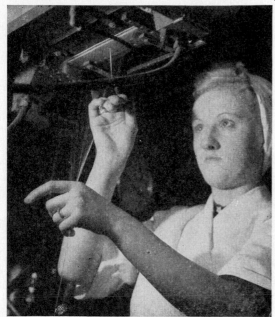

Fibreglass Ltd.

DRAWING GLASS FILAMENTS FROM THE FURNACE TO BE SPUN
AND WOVEN INTO TEXTILES

of the 18th century cloth was always woven by hand, and hand-weaving is still practised to a certain degree in most countries. Whether spinning and weaving are done mechanically or by hand, the principles remain the same (*see* Wool Spinning and Wool Weaving). Power-spindles and power-looms are much larger than the corresponding hand machines; they have complicated mechanism to produce different weaves and patterns; and they turn out material much more quickly.

Textiles can be decorated in many different ways. Patterns may be woven by using threads which have already been dyed in different colours, or the yarns used may be of various textures and thicknesses. If the threads go uniformly across the fabric, the result will be an even pattern of lines or checks. The patterns in Tapestry (q.v.) are arranged by taking each colour across portions of the fabric only, instead of right across from one side to the other. In Carpet Making (q.v.) additional threads are knotted into the weave in order to make a pile or nap that stands out on top of the original weave. Velvet also is made by weaving into a fabric additional threads which stand up to form the pile.

Another way of decorating textiles is by printing (*see* Textile Printing). This is done after the cloth is woven.

A third form of decoration is Embroidery, in which patterns are stitched on to the surface of the fabric. Silk, wool, cotton, or linen thread are chiefly used; sometimes gold and silver thread and beads or precious stones are added (*see* Embroidery, Vol. XI).

Weaving is not the only method of making textile fabrics. They may also be knitted or crocheted (*see* Hosiery and Knitwear, and Lace-making). These processes were originally carried out by hand, but are now adapted to machinery. Knitting and crochet are crafts or arts that are not as ancient as weaving, and we have no records of their having been practised by peoples of the ancient civilizations. Lace was probably not made before the 16th century.

See also Wool Spinning; Wool Weaving; Cotton Manufacture; Linen Industry; Silk Industry; Rayon. See also Vol. XI: Clothes, History of.

TEXTILE PRINTING is the quickest and cheapest way of decorating fabric. It is not known who invented the process, nor when it was first used.

Until the 18th century hand-block printing was the only method known, and it is still used for certain classes of work. For this the design is drawn or traced on a block of wood (generally

Council of Industrial Design

HAND-BLOCK PRINTING

SILK-SCREEN PRINTING
Photowork Ltd.
Men are pressing the colour through the screens

sycamore, plane, or pear wood), and the parts not to be coloured are cut away to a depth of about a quarter of an inch, leaving the rest of the design standing up in relief. Details too fine for woodwork may be built up by brass or copper strips driven edgeways into the wood. The block is then pressed on a pad covered with pigment or dye; next, it is placed on the cloth, and given a blow with a heavy mallet to make sure that the design is pressed hard against the cloth. A separate block has to be cut and used for each colour in the design. The pattern cut on the block is called a 'repeat', and the whole design on the cloth is made by printing the 'repeat', over and over again. Pins, set at each corner of the blocks, are used to ensure that designs and colours produce a pattern without gaps or overlaps.

In the 18th century textile printers began to use engraved copper plates instead of wooden blocks; in this way they did much finer and more delicate work. Before long, however, the textile trades became mechanized. Machines for printing from engraved copper rollers instead of flat plates were invented in 1783 and 1784. This process greatly speeded production, and made printed materials much cheaper; it is still the basis of modern textile printing. Yet the old hand craft is still practised, not only in the studios of craftsmen-designers, but also within the industry itself. The cost of engraving rollers

is very great, and it is more economical to produce by hand small quantities of the more experimental designs. In this way good artistic standards are maintained. One form of printing which is more akin to dyeing is 'batik' (*see* DYES).

Textiles are also decorated by the silk-screen process which is a form of stencilling rather than true printing. Colour is pressed on to the cloth through a screen made of fine silk gauze stretched on a framework. The pattern is made by covering parts of the screen with a substance through which the colour will not pass. Different screens are used for each colour.

The silk screen process is usually done by hand but mechanical methods are being developed in America. It is not only used for textile printing, but for wallpapers, posters, and coloured labels and advertisements.

See also COTTON INDUSTRY; LINEN INDUSTRY; WOOL INDUSTRY, MODERN.
See also Vol. XII: DESIGN.

TICKET AGENCIES, *see* ENTERTAINMENT INDUSTRY.

TILES, *see* BRICKS AND TILES.

TILES, ORNAMENTAL. These are thin sections of baked clay, generally glazed, which are principally set into floors, walls, and fireplaces. They are usually 5 or 6 inches square, and $\frac{1}{4}$ to $\frac{1}{2}$ inch thick. Larger sizes than these are difficult to keep flat during the drying and baking or 'firing' processes.

Ornamental tiles are very ancient. Wall tiles with coloured glazes and relief ornament have been found in the ruins of ancient Egypt, Assyria, and Babylon. The Louvre Museum in Paris contains parts of two magnificent friezes of tiles from the palace of Darius, the great Persian king, at Susa (700 B.C.). They are glazed

Ashmolean Museum
13TH-CENTURY PERSIAN TILES

Victoria and Albert Museum

FOUR 17TH-CENTURY DUTCH TILES

in several colours, and decorated with life-size figures of men and animals in relief.

The Near East seems to have been a centre for glazed and painted tiles, and Persia in the 13th century produced some of the finest. These were usually not squares, but were hexagons, stars, and crosses: in fact, almost any shapes that would fit together into a repeating pattern. They were enriched with painting in various colours. China was another country which made great use of glazed and ornamental tiles, not only for walls and floors but also for the roofs of important buildings. By placing at gable ends or elsewhere matching figures (such as dragons) in glazed earthenware, their artistic effect was enhanced.

The art of making ornamental tiles travelled to Europe. The MOORS (q.v. Vol. I) introduced it when they conquered and occupied Spain, and it spread from there to Italy and northward. Some of the finest English tiles of the Middle Ages were made for a monastery at Chertsey, on the Thames. Both in England and in France the floors of many churches in the Middle Ages were paved with glazed tiles of elaborate design, inlaid, embossed, or incised. Fragments of these lovely old tiled floors can still be seen in old churches. The tiles varied in colour from golden brown to dark chestnut, through the use of different local clays.

In the 17th century the potters of Delft and other places in the Netherlands produced a large range of ornamental tiles, which found their way into every house of importance in the country. The paintings of Dutch artists, particularly VERMEER (q.v. Vol. V), show that they were used on the skirtings of walls as well as in fireplaces and elsewhere. These Delft tiles were imported in vast quantities into England, and were soon being made in this country at Lambeth (London), Bristol, and other places. They were usually about 5 inches square, and were made by pressing clay into wooden moulds. They were then dried, fired, coated with glaze, and painted over the unfired glaze. Sometimes a little transparent glaze was spread over the painting, and the tiles were then fired again. The earlier Delft tiles were patterned all over in lines and curves in several colours. The later tiles were pictorial, and were painted usually in blue or purple.

Modern ornamental tiles are mostly machine-pressed from almost dry materials. The machine-pressing process was invented in the 19th century. They look harder and more mechanical than hand-made tiles. A certain number of artist-potters still survive, and produce in their own studios tiles decorated with hand-painted designs, in pleasing colours and glazes.

See also POTTERY; BRICKS AND TILES.

TIMBER INDUSTRY. 1. Before the Romans came to Britain the country was thickly forested, and there was more than enough timber for the needs of the people. As population grew, many of the woodlands had to be cleared to make room for arable and pasture land (*see* AGRICULTURE, HISTORY OF, Vol. VI). Then industry, when it began to be at least as important as agriculture, itself used a tremendous amount of timber; in fact, the Sussex iron industry, which smelted its ores with CHARCOAL (q.v.), completely changed the original face of Sussex. The result has been that Britain has imported increasing quantities of timber from overseas. When Samuel Pepys, the famous diarist, was Secretary to the Navy in the 17th century, the importing of timber had become well established. He was responsible for buying SOFTWOODS from Scandinavia and HARDWOODS (qq.v.) from other sources. Softwoods are the woods of the coniferous trees such as pine, fir, spruce, and larch; while hardwoods are such woods as oak, teak, beech, and mahogany. In the timber trade a strict distinction is made between the two classes.

Between 1918 and 1939 Britain was the largest

YUGOSLAVIAN BEECH-WOOD SEASONING

Wm. Mallinson and Sons

and South America, and also from Central Europe.

2. SEASONING. Most of this timber is imported in an unseasoned or semi-seasoned condition. Newly cut timber contains a great deal of moisture, and, if used in this state, will shrink unduly, and may split and warp. Seasoning is a carefully controlled process of drying out the surplus moisture. This increases the strength of the wood, and seasoned timber is therefore less likely to decay. It is also easier to work and to finish with polish or paint, and can more easily absorb preservatives. Timber left in the open will have from 18 to 23% of moisture in it, according to the state of the weather; but the moisture content of furniture in a warm, dry house will be as low as 10 to 12%.

There are two main methods of seasoning: air seasoning and kiln drying.

The traditional method is that of air seasoning. Boards coming from the sawmill are arranged in a large stack, built up on piers about a foot or more off the ground; each layer of boards is separated from the next by 'piling sticks' or 'stickers', which are rectangular softwood timbers, usually an inch square and as long as the pile is wide. These sticks are spaced 2 to 4 feet apart and vertically above one another. Their object is to allow air to circulate freely through the pile and to reach both faces of every board, thus drying the wood thoroughly. The stack is roofed to protect it from heavy rain or very hot sun.

Softwoods are best piled in the spring, and boards 1 inch thick will dry to 20% moisture content ('air dry') in from 2 to 3 months. Hardwoods require to dry out more slowly than softwoods, and if they are piled in winter they will dry more slowly at first because of the cold, damp weather conditions. Hardwood boards 1 inch thick, piled in autumn, are usually down to 20% moisture content by the following summer. Only in very dry weather does timber in the open dry below 18 to 20% moisture content.

Kiln drying is a modern process. Its objects

timber importer in the world. She imported about nine-tenths of all the timber she used. In quantity her imports were about 10 million tons, and their value about £40 million, which was more than one-third of the cost of Britain's total imports of all raw materials.

During the First World War it became difficult to import timber, and it became necessary to fell the home woodlands rather ruthlessly. In the Second World War tree fellers had to be still more ruthless. Although in 1943 Britain's home production was just under 4 million tons she was still very short of timber; rigid economy became necessary, as well as the use of substitutes whenever possible.

The need for softwoods is always greater than for hardwoods, and before 1939 Britain imported on the average five times as much softwood as hardwood. Finland was then the biggest single supplier, sending a quarter of the softwood imports; Russia sent a fifth, Canada and Sweden each about a sixth, and the rest came from other countries, principally Latvia and Poland. The Second World War and its consequences altered the regular channels of trade. Canada has become Britain's principal supplier, and only comparatively small quantities now come from other sources. The range of countries from which hardwoods are imported is much wider; they come from Commonwealth countries, from North

are to reduce the drying time and to control the moisture content more exactly. A kiln consists essentially of a brick room with heating pipes in the ceiling or below the floor, a number of steam jets, and fans to circulate the air. A pile of timber is made as for air seasoning, but usually smaller, and is set on a trolley so that it can be run into the kiln. When the pile is in the kiln, and the large airtight door has been closed, air and steam are circulated through the pile by the fans. The temperature is raised only slightly at first; gradually it is raised higher, and the steam jets are turned off, reducing the dampness of the air, until at last the timber is seasoned to the desired moisture content. From time to time samples of the wood are removed to test their moisture content.

There is much prejudice against kiln-dried timber, based on the bad condition of timber treated in the early days of the process, when efforts were made to speed up the drying too much. There is no real difference in the quality of timber treated by either method of seasoning, if each is correctly used. Kilning is a necessity when timber is to be used in centrally-heated buildings, for the moisture content may then have to be as low as 10% if no undue shrinkage is to take place. Air seasoning, however long it is allowed to take, will never reduce the moisture content much below 20%.

Several new methods of seasoning have been tried, but most of them have not yet passed the experimental stage. These include drying by high-frequency electricity: this has the advantage of drying the core of the wood first, instead of the outside as in ordinary drying. In 'solvent drying' the wood is treated with a water-absorbing solvent (usually acetone) at a high temperature; the moisture is later separated from the solvent, which is then used again.

3. PRESERVING. Even the most careful seasoning will not prevent wood from deteriorating if it is exposed to adverse conditions. Deterioration is principally caused by the attacks of wood-destroying insects or fungi. Several preservatives are used to defeat the attacks of these pests, the most widely used being creosote, a heavy, tarry oil much used for railway sleepers, telegraph-poles, and the gate-posts and gates of farm fences. The smell and oiliness of creosote make it unsuitable for the preservation of wood used indoors; for such timber there are several chemical preservatives.

Seaboard Lumber Sales, Canada

CUTTING TIMBER INTO BOARDS IN ONE OPERATION WITH A POWER-DRIVEN SAW

Timber is not used solely in its natural state. Many important commercial products are made from it or extracted from it. Among these are CHARCOAL, wood-alcohol, resins (*see* GUMS AND RESINS), turpentine, RUBBER, and TANNING-extracts (qq.v.).

See also HARDWOODS; SOFTWOODS; PLYWOODS AND VENEERS; WOODWORK, HISTORY OF.

See also Vol. VI: FORESTRY; TIMBER; TIMBER MEASUREMENTS.

TIME AND MOTION STUDY, *see* Vol. VIII: PRODUCTION ENGINEERING, Section 4.

TIN, one of the metals in bronze, was much used in prehistoric times during the Bronze Age. Tin is not found in nature as a free metal, but only as an ore (*see* METAL ORES, Vol. III). The most important ore is tinstone or cassiterite, which is dioxide of tin. Five-sixths of the world's tin now comes from alluvial or river-bed workings, but underground mines are still worked in Cornwall and Bolivia, and in the Waterberg district of the Transvaal, in South Africa. Until about 1870 Cornwall was the world's leading producer of tin (*see* CORNISH MINING), but tin

19TH-CENTURY TIN DRESSERS AT A CORNISH MINE

The tin ore, mixed with water, flowed along the central troughs and down the sloping 'decks'. The heavy ore stuck to the decks and was swept up by the women, who were called 'bal maidens'

was then discovered in Malaya, and the production from that region has since increased steadily. Malaya produces about one-third of the world's tin, Bolivia about one-eighth, Indonesia about one-fifth, and Nigeria about one-twentieth.

Tin has many industrial uses. It is used for lining iron cooking-pots, stills for DISTILLATION (q.v.) and other such devices, particularly those that have to deal with foods. Tinfoil is much used for wrapping chocolates, confectionery, and some forms of cheese; it is made by beating out thin sheets of tin with a wooden mallet.

Tin plays a part in several important ALLOYS (q.v. Vol. VIII). Solder consists of equal parts of tin and lead. Tin and copper in varied proportions make different types of bronze, such as gunmetal and the bronze used for coinage (see COINING). Tin alloys are much used in engineering for making bearing metals (see BEARINGS, Vol. VIII). Various types of bell metal, out of which church bells and other big bells are cast, contain 16 to 20% of tin. A large quantity of tin is used in making TINPLATES (q.v. Vol. VIII), whose main use is for packing preserved foods.

TINNED FOODS, see CANNING INDUSTRY.

TOBACCO INDUSTRY. 1. MANUFACTURE. There are three main varieties of the *Nicotiana* leaf, and some forty sub-varieties (*see* TOBACCO, Vol. VI). The three main varieties are these:

Nicotiana tabacum: originally found in America, and cultivated extensively there.

Nicotiana rustica: grown in Turkey and the Levant, and known by different names—Indian, Syrian, Turkish. This is mild in flavour and makes excellent cigarettes, but burns too quickly for the pipe.

Nicotiana persica: Persian tobacco, which makes a delicate smoke in a hookah or water-pipe, but does not burn well enough to be used in the form of cigars.

When gathered, the leaf must first be cured. After being plucked the leaves are dried, either in the sun, or under cover by the artificial process known as 'flue-curing'. The drying-houses look rather like cabins or huts, in which the tobacco leaves, after being cut, are exposed to heat spread through flues. After 4 or 5 days, when the leaves have become brittle in a temperature of 170°, the main stalks are stripped from the leaves, and the leaf tobacco is sorted according to quality. The leaves are then made up into bundles, and fermented for about a month (*see* FERMENTATION, Vol. II). At the end of this time the curing process is complete, and the leaf is ready for the auction sales.

The packed leaf is imported into the country of manufacture in casks called 'hogsheads', or in bales. After being removed from its packings, it is first steamed and picked free of stalk, sprayed for flavouring if that is required, and cut by machinery into coarse or fine tobacco. This is then treated in stoves, where its moisture is reduced and the aroma developed. For flake tobacco, the leaf is pressed into a hard slab, which is cut into bars. Shags are made by moulding loose leaf into slabs, which are baked before being cut. Roll or twist is made by feeding coils of leaf into a spinning machine. 'Cavendish' and 'negrohead' tobaccos are prepared by adding liquid sweetening matter. The name 'Cavendish' comes from the Elizabethan admiral who invented the process. Many pipe mixtures contain a certain amount of strong dark latakia leaf, a leaf grown in Asia Minor, getting its particular flavour from being cured in heat produced by fires of dried camel dung.

Tobaccos used for cigars are varieties of

Nicotiana tabacum, and undergo much the same processes of curing as other tobaccos. The cigar originated in the Spanish West Indies, and was first manufactured in Britain at the beginning of the 19th century. After 1840 there was a considerable increase in demand and production, and in the second half of the 19th century cigars became the most popular type of smoke among the upper and middle classes. The Havana is considered the finest of all cigars, but from the time of the Second World War importation into Britain was prohibited to save dollars, and the Jamaican cigar took its place.

2. CIGARETTES. The cigarette is a comparative newcomer in the history of British smoking. It is believed to have originated during the Turco-Egyptian war in 1832, and to have been introduced to England by British troops serving some 20 years later in the Crimea. The first cigarette manufacturer to establish himself in London was a Greek named Theodoridi, who had been a captain in the Russian army. In 1861 he brought from Odessa to London a staff of one hand-cutter and several skilled cigarette-makers, and started a business in Leicester Square. These early cigarettes were made of Turkish tobacco, and had cardboard mouth-pieces an inch long. Theodoridi later introduced the Woronchoff cigarette, which had one end turned in on itself, but no mouthpiece. This was a further stage in the evolution of the modern cigarette, which did not make its appearance until 1865. It was first made by another Greek, Arramachi, who opened premises in Regent Street, London. The earlier cardboard mouth-pieces were superseded by tips made of all sorts of materials, among them amber, gold leaf, silver, bronze, aluminium, glass, silk, rose-leaf, and violet-leaf. By the 1870's British cigarette-makers had become masters of this new craft, and some of them went out to the United States to teach their methods to the Americans. A few years later American cigarettes, made of Virginian tobacco, began to appear on the British market. Turkish cigarettes began to lose favour, and were gradually largely displaced by the new Virginian cigarettes, which had a greater uniformity of flavour.

3. MODERN INDUSTRY. The founders of modern cigarette manufacture were two sons of Henry Overton Wills, a Bristol dealer in cigars, who was born in Bristol in 1761. The sons so expanded the father's small business that, by the

W. D. and H. O. Wills

CONDITIONING TOBACCO LEAF

The dried leaf has to be softened by steam before it is cut

time the cigarette habit began to gain ground, they were able to take a lead in manufacture. At first, all cigarettes were made entirely by hand. The mechanization of the industry followed the invention of the cigarette-machine by Bernhard Baron at the end of the 19th century. Baron was then working in a tobacco factory in New York, and when he had invented his machine he offered it to several American manufacturers. They rejected it, and he brought his machine to England. His early attempts to get British manufacturers interested in it were equally unsuccessful. After many rebuffs in London, he prevailed on William Yapp, who owned a tobacco shop in Wardour Street and traded under the name of Carreras, to put up £1,000 for a practical test of the new machine. Within a short time the two partners were producing cigarettes at a cost of less than a farthing each, and by dint of strenuous advertising were selling them at the rate of 20 millions a day. From this time onwards the mechanization of the industry was rapid.

There had, however, always been rivalry between British and American manufacturers. In 1901 the British industry was suddenly faced with a crisis. James Duke, the leader of the American tobacco trade, had formed the Tobacco Trust, which acquired almost a MONOPOLY

CUTTING TOBACCO FOR CIGARETTES

The leaves are compressed and cut by rotary knives. The cut tobacco is examined before passing on conveyor belts to be cooled and dried

W. D. and H. O. Wills

MAKING COILS OF 'TWIST'

The leaves are spun into ropes and then baked in steam heated presses to make the tobacco black

(q.v.) in the U.S.A. He tried to do the same in Britain, after buying a British firm. He placed immense financial resources behind his campaign, flooded the country with cheap cigarettes, and adopted all kinds of devices to help his sales. He was the first to introduce picture-cards into packets of cigarettes, and he offered handsome bonuses to retail tobacconists who would handle his products. The British firms were compelled to take similar action. They cut down prices, sometimes even below the actual cost of production, and offered to retail tobacconists bonuses equal to those offered by Duke.

Duke's campaign was eventually brought to an end by the incorporation of thirteen of the leading British firms into what became known as the Imperial Tobacco Company, with a capital of £15 millions. With these large financial resources behind it, the Imperial Tobacco Company was able to win over the retailers. Within 2 years of its formation, Duke called a truce, and undertook to withdraw from the British trade. The two antagonists agreed jointly to form the British-American Tobacco Company, to acquire and conduct the export business of both countries. Other manufacturing firms later joined the Imperial Tobacco Company, which now controls some 75% of the British output.

See also Vol. VI: Tobacco.
See also Vol. XI: Smoking, History of.

TOKEN CURRENCY, *see* Currency.

TOURIST INDUSTRY. The religious Pilgrimages of ancient and medieval times (q.v. Vol. I) were often organized by agents, but no details are known of how they ran their businesses. In those days, and indeed down to the coaching days of the 18th and early 19th centuries, travel was looked upon generally as an unavoidable necessity and not as a recreation, although a few pleasure trips were organized, such as the 'grand tour' of the cities of Europe and excursions to such beauty spots as the English Lake District. But until the time of the railway and the steamship, the organization of travelling cannot be said to have become a proper industry.

At first the beginnings of this new industry were slow. Its pioneer was Thomas Cook, a young man who organized the first railway excursion in 1841, and who later founded the firm of Thomas Cook and Son (*see* Travel Agencies, Vol. IV). The railway companies paid Cook a share of the fares actually charged to the passengers. No other arrangement would have been legally possible, as the railway tickets, being legal contracts between company and passenger, could not have been issued by Cook himself at his own price. A share of the passenger fare, or a COMMISSION on it (q.v.), is still the way in which Cook's and other travel agencies are paid for their services. Originally the parties of passengers who took part in 'Cook's Tours' were in charge of leaders or 'couriers', who could usually speak several languages. The charge to the traveller for the whole tour was fixed and paid in advance, previous arrangements having been made with innkeepers on the route for food and accommodation at fixed prices. From the innkeepers and restaurant proprietors, as well as from the railway and steamship companies, Cook received a commission or discount on the actual charge to the traveller. Later, Cook established 'inclusive independent travel'. His agency quoted an inclusive charge for travel, food, and accommodation for a fixed period over any chosen route; and the traveller, having paid his money, made his own way independently. At first independent tourists were restricted in each town to a single hotel or restaurant with which arrangements had been made in advance; but in 1866 'inclusive independent travel' was made easier by Cook's invention of the 'hotel coupon'. A traveller, when he booked his tour, received detachable coupons in a counterfoil book, each coupon being valid for a meal or a night's lodging at any one of a large number of hotels and restaurants on Cook's list.

Cook had many imitators, at home and abroad, and the firm he founded is now only one of a large number. Since the later years of the 19th century, the only important development in the travel industry has been the increase in its size. Nowadays there is more time and money for pleasure travel. New means of travel have also become available—air travel, PLEA-SURE CRUISES (q.v. Vol. IX), and inland and continental motor-coach tours. Cultural societies and organizations now promote tours of their own, particularly to such countries as Italy and Greece; some of these promoters make their own arrangements, while others rely on the ordinary travel agencies. Some begin as cultural societies and end by becoming travel agencies themselves.

For many years economists have known the tourist industry to be an important factor in a country's balance of payments (see INTERNATIONAL TRADE). A country such as Switzerland lives largely on foreign tourists, for almost as much of her foreign currency is earned that way as by the export of actual goods. Until recent years British Government policy was not greatly concerned with the tourist industry. After the Second World War, however, Britain's economic difficulties made it necessary not only to diminish foreign travelling by British tourists, particularly to the HARD CURRENCY countries (q.v.), but also to increase greatly the number of foreign visitors to Britain. In 1946, therefore, the Government set up the British Tourist and Holidays Board, to raise Britain's earnings of foreign currency. In 1950 the Board was amalgamated with the Travel Association, a private organization which had for many years encouraged the general growth of the tourist industry.

See also Vol. IV: TRAVEL AGENCIES.

TRADE, *see* EXCHANGE AND TRADE; INTERNATIONAL TRADE; OVERSEAS TRADE; TRADE, HISTORY OF.

TRADE CYCLE. This is the name given to the up-and-down movements of business activity, from good times to bad times, that have been a feature of economic life since the early 19th century. The typical cycle begins with a general collapse of business activity, followed by depression and UNEMPLOYMENT (q.v.). There follows a gradual recovery from depression, beginning at first very slowly and acquiring momentum as the years go on. At the end of the recovery phase, business activity increases more swiftly, and there is a good deal of speculation in goods and raw materials on the commodity markets, and in STOCKS AND SHARES on the world STOCK EXCHANGES (qq.v.). Later still, speculation and business activity increase to a feverish height, which another general collapse brings to a sudden end. This series or cycle of events then repeats itself.

The average period of the cycle has been about 10 years. For example, 1825, 1837, 1847, 1857, and 1866 were years in which active, or 'booming', business conditions suddenly came to an end. The passing of over a hundred years seems to have made little difference to this average 10-year period, and nearer our own times 1920 and 1929 were both years in which boom conditions suddenly collapsed. Before the outbreak of war in 1939 there were signs that the normal pattern of the cycle would be repeated, but the money spent on rearmament and war preparations succeeded in checking the tendency towards depression.

Serious unemployment is a feature of the trade

of the plant and machinery of nationalized enterprises; also, that at the same time governments should assist private enterprise by making loans and capital freely available, if necessary by government guarantee. Further, taxation should be increased, and a budget surplus built up, in years of active business; and taxation decreased,

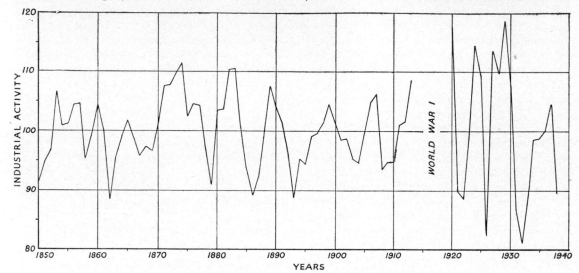

CHART OF INDUSTRIAL ACTIVITY IN BRITAIN, 1850–1938

100 is taken as the average activity. Boom years are indicated by the crests and depressions by the troughs.
From Beveridge's *Full Employment in a Free Society*

cycle, which is thus intimately linked with the welfare of those who earn their living in industry and commerce. Professional economists have studied the cycle very carefully, in order to find out its causes and possible cure. Its regular rhythm, and its recurrence about every 10 years, are the strangest things about it, and these are just the features that many of the theories fail to explain. All schools of thought, however, are in general agreement that during the 'boom' phase of the cycle people are spending too much and saving too little, and that during the 'depression' phase they are spending too little and saving too much. The real differences between economists lie in their explanations of the remoter causes of this alternation of overspending and underspending.

Most modern economists now agree that a possible cure for the trade cycle may be found in government intervention. It is suggested that at the beginning of any depression the business 'pump' should be 'primed' by government expenditure on public works, house building programmes, and modernization and renewal

and the budget surplus allowed to run off, in years of depression. Government intervention would thus work in a direction exactly opposite to that of the cycle itself.

This plan was the basis of the 'full employment' policy adopted by the British Government after the Second World War. Whether such measures can be effective depends to some extent on events in other countries. Similar measures taken in the United States, to check a tendency towards depression in 1948 and 1949, appear to have been reasonably effective, and it is possible that the trade cycle, as past generations knew it, has now become a thing of the past.

See also UNEMPLOYMENT; ECONOMICS.

TRADE DISCOUNTS, *see* WHOLESALE TRADING.

TRADE FAIRS arose in past centuries just as much for religious as for commercial reasons, and, in the German language, the word *Messe* is used for both a religious SACRAMENT (q.v. Vol. 1) and for 'fair'. In Europe, fairs were at

LEIPZIG FAIR IN THE 18TH CENTURY
Merchants discuss business while pedlars sell their wares to the women

first held on days that were important festivals of the Christian Church, when many people gathered together in some cathedral city or other shrine of the faith. Merchants and traders saw in such gatherings good opportunities of doing business, and either petitioned local Church dignitaries for permission to set up stalls in the cathedral square or on Church lands, or obtained a municipal or Royal charter granting a similar privilege. Gradually these fairs came to be associated not only with religion and business, but also with entertainment and amusement (*see* FAIRS, Vol. IX). Fair days began with religious services, continued with business, and often ended at night-time in rather riotous gaiety. Many fairs of this kind now survive only for purposes of amusement. The annual 'Mop Fair' at Stratford-on-Avon is one of these.

Fairs of the mixed religious and commercial kind go back a long way in the history of most countries. Sidonius Apollinaris, who wrote in the 5th century, mentions fairs then being held in Champagne and Brie, in France. The big Mohammedan fair at Mecca dates from the early days of ISLAM (q.v. Vol. I), and the Hindu fair at Hardwar, in India, is of very long standing. By the 10th century fairs were being held regularly in western Europe, notably at Provins and Troyes in France. The number of English fairs increased after the Norman invasion in the 11th century: one of the most famous was Stourbridge Fair, which was first held in 1211. These fairs continued to flourish for many centuries, but gradually changed their character. Some, which were held at first only on Church feast-days, became street or municipal markets, held weekly, as the population and trade of their district expanded (*see* STREET MARKETS). Others, held in large towns or cities, became in time international trade fairs. Leipzig, for instance, began as a local fair at the end of the 12th century, but soon became a large annual market in furs, hides and leather, glassware, and linens and woollens. At the end of the 17th century the *Ostermesse*, or Easter Fair, at Leipzig became the annual gathering of the merchants and agents interested in the German book trade, and later this fair became the main European centre for

The Times

THE LONDON MOTOR SHOW AT EARLS COURT IN 1950

dealings in Russian and East European furs (*see* FUR TRADE). The big Russian fair at Nijni-Novgorod was founded in the 17th century, and other important European trade fairs are those of Lyons and Prague.

These large international trade fairs are still held, although improvements in communications and in trade organization have greatly changed their character. In trades that are seasonal, such as books and furs, a fair such as Leipzig is still largely what it once was: a centre for the actual sale and purchase of goods. But, in general, trade fairs are nowadays organized advertising displays on a large scale, where manufacturers and merchants may see the latest designs in goods, and in machines with which to manufacture them. As at the earlier fairs, however, large orders are often booked and much actual business done. The British Industries Fair (B.I.F.) is a modern trade fair of this kind, and is held every year simultaneously in London and Birmingham, London housing the general exhibits and Birmingham the engineering section.

See also EXHIBITIONS.

TRADE, HISTORY OF. 1. The beginnings of trade in the primitive days of mankind are difficult to trace, for the only evidence we have is from digging by archaeologists. For example excavations in the early CHALK workings (q.v.) in south-eastern England and discoveries elsewhere have shown that, even in the New Stone Age (about 2500–2000 B.C.), there was a widespread trade in flints and stone axes, and an axe workshop in Cumberland supplied axes as far away as the Oxford region. This period was the beginning of agriculture and close settlement, which favoured the growth of trade. But it was a long time before trade became organized along regular routes, and developed by systems of MONEY, BANKING, and CREDIT (qq.v.). These things belong to a later period, when man began to live in towns and cities.

2. THE ANCIENT WORLD. The trade about which we first know something definite is the caravan trade across the Asiatic deserts, to and from the cities of Mesopotamia, Egypt, and Arabia (*see* TRADE ROUTES, Vol. IV). In those days traders could rely on protection from robbery or murder only when near the cities, as is the case in parts of Asia to-day. Caravans had to carry not only their cargoes, but also fodder for the animals and food for the drivers, merchants, and guards, for foodstuffs were not easy to find or buy in the lands they travelled through. As the space left for merchandise was not large, the goods carried by the merchants tended to be light and yet valuable: that is, luxuries and not necessities. The oases along these routes became first of all trading depots, and later big commercial centres. Mesopotamia, particularly the valleys of the Tigris and Euphrates rivers, and north-east Africa, particularly Egypt, became in those days the main trading regions of the known world.

A big advance was made when, in some parts of the world, sea-borne trade became usual. The Phoenicians of north-east Africa are usually thought to have been the first to have developed sea-borne commerce, but this is not certain. It is quite possible that about 3,000 years ago the coastal trade of China was equally important, but we have no records that can prove this. The Phoenicians traded from ports in North Africa and Syria to Crete, Cyprus, Rhodes, and other Greek islands, and later to the western Mediterranean and beyond. Carthage was the capital, and Tyre and Sidon were other important commercial towns. The Phoenicians were manufacturers. The outward or export trade was mainly in manufactured goods, notably metal ware, glassware, and textiles. These were traded for raw materials, principally metals, and especially tin, copper, and silver (*see* PHOENICIAN CIVILIZATION, Vol. I). This trade was mainly in luxuries, for the sea was no safer from marauders than the land, and ships were small. The western peoples with whom the Phoenicians traded were primitive and uncivilized, and had not adopted the regular use of money. The basis of these Phoenician dealings was the direct exchange of goods for goods, or barter (*see* EXCHANGE AND TRADE).

The Phoenicians were contemporary with the Greeks and the Romans. The Athenians were the most advanced of the Greeks in the matter of trade. In their trading relations the Athenians looked east and the Phoenicians west, and there was no real conflict of interest between them. Athens was the first big commercial city of the European mainland, and its importance was assisted by sound money and an efficient banking system. Athens itself was not a seaport, but not very far away was the port of Piraeus. Athens was the first community to import necessities in any quantity. Grain came in for its increasing population from the shores of the Black Sea, then called the Euxine, and her exports included figs, olive oil, honey, pottery, metal ware, and textiles. Athens lost the political leadership of the Greek world after the Peloponnesian War (about 400 B.C.), but her trade was not greatly affected. When ALEXANDER THE GREAT (q.v. Vol. V) gained the leadership of the Greek peoples and fought his way into Asia, the trade of Athens and Piraeus increased, and they are still commercially important cities. Alexander's marches into Persia, Mesopotamia, Central Asia, and India opened up more of the caravan trade, and Antioch and Alexandria became big commercial cities. Many inland caravan routes converged on Antioch, which had a port, Seleucia, not far off. Alexandria was a base for sea-borne trade. The trade of both cities was mainly in luxuries, principally in spices, drugs, and silks.

The Roman Empire was the next big trading community. The city of Rome produced little; it was a political capital and the financial centre of the Empire. Before Rome could expand, Carthage had to be reckoned with; for Carthage controlled the cornlands of North Africa, which were vital to the growing population of the city of Rome, and was an influential sea-power which could endanger Rome's communications. So, before the Empire was founded, the two Punic Wars were fought, which ended in the destruction of Carthage in 146 B.C. Rome's rise to the rank of the world's leading power did not much affect the nature of trade, nor the main centres where it was carried on. Increasing

British Museum

ROMAN POTTERY, CALLED 'SAMIAN WARE', MADE IN GAUL AND EXPORTED TO BRITAIN IN THE 1ST CENTURY A.D.

Bodleian Library

EUROPEAN MERCHANTS AT AN INDIAN COURT

Members of Sir Thomas Roe's embassy to the Emperor Jehangir, 1616–17. Detail from a Mogul painting (MS. Douce Or. B. 3. f. 21)

quantities of luxuries were imported from the East and from North Africa. These imports were what we should nowadays call 'unrequited imports': they did not have to be paid for by exports, but were the tribute paid to Rome by the various peoples she conquered. Most of the trade tended to come from the Eastern Mediterranean, as can be seen from the number of Jews and Greeks in the business life of the Roman Empire. These races are still the merchants of the eastern Mediterranean to-day.

In the 5th century A.D. Byzantium, rebuilt and renamed Constantinople (and to-day called Istanbul), became the political capital of the Roman Empire, and remained the world's commercial capital from the beginning of the Dark Ages until the time of the Crusades (*see* BYZANTINE EMPIRE, Vol. I). The commercial importance of Constantinople was founded on solid hard work, and the surrounding district was a busy manufacturing centre. Textiles, leather-work, armour, pottery, and artistic metal work

were manufactured and exported. Imports included not only the raw materials of these trades, such as wool, metals, wax, furs, and amber, but also a considerable amount of grain. Big TRADE FAIRS (q.v.) were held annually at Constantinople and Thessalonica. The leadership of Constantinople in world trade rested largely, like that of Athens many centuries earlier, on a sound system of currency and banking. The standard Byzantine coin, the 'bezant' (*see* COINS), kept up its international value, and it became the currency of European business. The use of BILLS OF EXCHANGE (q.v.) for making payments in distant countries (without the risk of carrying coin over routes infested with bandits and pirates) was developed to a high degree. The Emperor Justinian made the SILK INDUSTRY a State MONOPOLY, and joint-stock COMPANIES (qq.v.) were formed by groups of private traders and manufacturers. A good deal of the commerce of Constantinople was done by sea, and risks were greater than they are to-day. So the Byzantine merchants invented a very efficient system of marine INSURANCE (q.v.).

3. THE MIDDLE AGES. Many foreign merchants, principally those of Venice and Genoa, took part in Byzantine trade. In 1453 the Turks conquered Constantinople, and made trade with the west difficult. The Venetians and Genoese succeeded the Byzantines as the world's leading traders. Venice was well placed to be the main European commercial centre. There were overland routes to southern Germany, the Rhineland, and the Netherlands, and there was, of course, the sea. It was by sea that imports arrived from the East, and from the early 14th century onwards a fleet of galleys (*see* SHIPPING) took exports once a year to north-west Europe. Bruges, in Flanders, was then a port capable of berthing the largest ships, and was the main objective of these annual voyages; Southampton, Sandwich, and London were also visited. The exports were mainly luxuries, principally spices and silks. Raw materials, particularly wool, hides, and metals, were imported from the West, worked up in Venice and the interior of Italy, and re-exported to the East as manufactured goods: particularly Florentine cloths and silk fabrics from Lucca. The Venetians improved on the Byzantine banking system, and developed the science of double-entry BOOK-KEEPING (q.v.). In northern Europe in the Middle Ages the HANSEATIC LEAGUE (q.v.)

PLATE MADE IN CHINA FOR THE DUTCH MARKET

It illustrates the destruction of Rotterdam in 1693 during the French wars. In the 17th and 18th centuries large quantities of blue and white porcelain were exported from China to Europe

occupied much the same position as Venice in the south, the depots or 'factories' of the League extending as far east as Nijni-Novgorod in Russia and as far west as London.

4. THE MODERN WORLD. All this trade of the late Middle Ages remained predominantly a luxury trade, although cloth, which was a necessity, figured in it to an increasing degree. World trade could not grow into its modern pattern until people had more knowledge of the world itself; the period when this knowledge was acquired is known as the 'Age of Discoveries' or 'Navigations' (*see* EXPLORATION, Vol. IV). Spaniards and Portuguese made voyages more or less as State projects: in fact, one of the kings of Portugal at this time acquired the name of HENRY THE NAVIGATOR (q.v. Vol. V). Britain and other countries of northern Europe countered by forming big CHARTERED COMPANIES (q.v.), each being given a certain part of the world as its exclusive domain. The new companies penetrated into distant lands and brought back their products, many of which were new and unknown. The Russia Company, for instance, opened up a route into the very south of Russia, from Archangel in the north and thence southward by land and river. The Levant Company, operating in the eastern Mediterranean, was the first to introduce the currant into

Britain. But Spain and Portugal, particularly Spain, rather scorned trade. They merely imported silver and gold from Mexico and Peru, and bought the goods they wanted from the trading nations; and so they helped to make their enemies more wealthy and powerful. By the 17th century the Dutch and English dominated the world's trade, which was becoming more and more a trade in necessities. Both nations opened up the tropical and sub-tropical lands of the East and West Indies, and imported into Europe sugar and tobacco, and tea and coffee, which gradually ceased to be luxuries and became the necessities of the masses of the people. The long political struggle between the British and the Dutch ended in their sharing the trade of the world between them.

During the following century, the 19th, the INDUSTRIAL REVOLUTION (q.v.) led to greater production, and the pattern of world trade started to become what it is to-day. Luxuries still entered into world trade, but formed a smaller and smaller part of it. North-west Europe—Britain, Belgium, France, Germany, Sweden, and Switzerland—became a concentrated manufacturing region, to which raw materials came from all parts of the world, and whose growing populations came to rely more and more on imported foodstuffs. In the present century the U.S.A. has also become an important trading nation, but her trade within her own borders

PUNCH BOWL MADE IN BRISTOL TO COMMEMORATE THE ARRIVAL THERE OF THE SWEDISH MERCHANT SHIP 'VIGILANTIA' IN 1765

is vastly greater and more important than her external trade. Practically the whole of the world's trade is now in articles of necessity, although what would now be considered necessities would have been the undreamed-of luxuries of even a few centuries ago.

See also INTERNATIONAL TRADE.

TRADE MARKS are distinctive names or designs applied to goods manufactured or sold by the owners of the trade mark. A trade mark is carefully protected by law; the right to it is obtained through the Government Patent Office in London, where it must be registered, in much the same way as a PATENT (q.v.). Under the rules a trade mark will be granted for a representation of the name of the individual or company in some 'special or particular manner': for example, in Gothic lettering, or in some symmetrical pattern of differently-sized letters. A signature can also be used, such as, for example, the signature 'King C. Gillette' on a packet of Gillette razor-blades. The most successful and well-known trade marks rely on an invented word or words, for example 'Bovril', 'Kolynos', or 'Glaxo'. But any ordinary word in general use will satisfy the regulations, provided that it does not refer to the character or quality of the goods, and is not a geographical name; for instance the word 'skipper' is lawfully applied to 'Skipper' sardines. A trade mark will also be granted for the use of a 'distinctive mark', such as the drawing of a swan on a 'Swan' fountain-pen. In this case the trade mark contains not only an ordinary word ('swan') but also a distinctive mark.

Many trade marks, when granted, become valuable pieces of property. If a trade mark is an invented word (such as 'Bovril') or a clever design (such as 'Mr. Peek and Mr. Frean'), it may lend itself to very successful ADVERTISING (q.v.) and lead to big sales of the product. It is for that reason that owners of trade marks are protected by law against any infringement of their rights by other firms. The owner of a trade mark may sell it to someone else, but the new owner cannot use it for any other article than that for which it was first granted. The trade mark 'Bovril', for example, could not be sold for use with a toothpaste.

Goods sold under a trade mark are called 'branded goods', or 'brands'. It is fairly easy to advertise a brand successfully, if it has a short and 'catchy' name or a clever design. Since trade became highly competitive in the second half of the 19th century, more and more of the goods sold in British and American shops have been branded goods bearing registered trade marks.

See also PATENTS.

TRADE SIGNS. In the days before most people could read, shop fronts did not display the names and trades of the shopkeepers, and it was their custom to indicate their business by some sort of emblem. This practice certainly goes back to the days of ancient Rome, for many of these old

THE WRAPPER OF AN EARLY SALMON TIN
The illustration is the trade mark of the manufacturer

signs have been dug up by archaeologists. The signs were sometimes painted, but more commonly were made of stone, or stamped on *terra cotta* or baked clay, and embedded in the walls, usually above the entrances. In the days when the goat, and not the cow, was the more usual source of the household milk (as it still is in many Mediterranean countries) the dairyman's sign was a goat; the baker showed a mule driving a flour mill, the surveyor a measuring rule, the tavern-keeper a bunch of grapes.

In the same way medieval shops proclaimed their business by models of what they sold, or by tools and utensils, or by signboards painted to represent such objects. As long as trade was limited, a simple device was enough for each tradesman. The cutler displayed a knife, the tailor a pair of scissors, and the hosier usually a carved wooden shape painted to look like a stocking. Later, when there were several people of the same trade doing business together in the same part of a town, they might find it necessary to adopt some sign to distinguish, say, Brown the Tailor from Green the Tailor. Brown might, therefore, exhibit a signboard showing a brown bear, and Green a signboard with a green dragon. Brown's address would come to be known generally as 'at the sign of the Brown Bear'; Green's address, similarly, would be 'at the sign of the Green Dragon'. A tradesman could choose any sign he liked: animal, vegetable, or mineral; but often he would advertise his name by a pun or 'rebus' (*see* PUZZLES, Vol. IX), Mr. Haywood's sign being a haystack and a bundle of sticks, and Mr. Hancock's a hand and a cock.

As trade rivalry increased and town life developed, painted signs became more elaborate and beautiful. Not only were the designs themselves artistic, but the ornamental ironwork on which they hung reached a high level of craftsmanship.

As more people learned to read, signboards became fewer, and the practice of numbering houses and shops in streets increased. A few tradesmen's symbols still survive. The best known are the barber's pole and the three brass balls of the PAWNBROKER (q.v.). The merchants from Lombardy, in northern Italy, who settled in England in the 15th and 16th centuries as pawnbrokers and money-lenders, brought this symbol with them as the sign of their trade. It may have represented three gold coins, al-

London Museum

18TH-CENTURY GOLD-BEATER'S SIGN

London Museum

18TH-CENTURY SIGN FROM A TOBACCONIST'S SHOP

A FRENCH GLASS-BLOWER'S SIGN

Musée Carnavalet, Paris

though the real origin of the sign is obscure. The barber's pole was once commonly seen, striped in red and white, and sometimes in blue as well. Before 1745 barbers were members of the Barbers and Chirurgeons (Surgeons) Company, and also practised blood-letting, tooth-pulling, and rather rough surgery; the stripes round the pole indicated the material used for bandaging.

TRADE MARK OF THE BOWATER PAPER CORPORATION
It is registered for use in Great Britain only

Some of the private bankers of the City of London, whose businesses were founded in the 17th or 18th centuries when trade signs were more usual than numbers, remained true to the old tradition, and in Lombard Street the golden grasshopper of Martins Bank and the anchor of Glyns, the Admiralty agents and bankers, still hang to-day. The newer bankers have followed this old custom, and Lombard Street is full of symbols or heraldic signs such as the prancing horse of Lloyds Bank, or the full coats-of-arms of other houses (*see* picture, p. 34).

See also Vol. IV: INN SIGNS; SYMBOLS.

TRADE UNION HISTORY, BRITISH.
Trade unions are essentially associations of wage-earners, unlike the CRAFT GUILDS (q.v.) of the late Middle Ages, which included all persons engaged in a trade, and not wage-earners alone. The guilds were joint associations of masters, workers (then called 'journeymen' because they were paid by the *journée* or day), and apprentices in any particular trade. When industry began to form itself into larger units, most of the craft guilds split up into two separate bodies: companies of masters, and associations of workers or journeymen. There is no real historical continuity between these early workers' guilds and modern trade unions.

In the reign of Elizabeth the Government took over the functions of both the masters' and the workers' guilds. The workers' guilds largely disappeared. The masters' guilds gradually transformed themselves into livery companies (*see* CITY COMPANIES). The Government took over the duty, hitherto performed by the craft guilds, of regulating wages and conditions of work and apprenticeship. The Statute of Artificers (or the Statute of Apprentices—both words appear in the title) laid down conditions in 1563 in regard to working hours, standards of work, and the period of apprenticeship, and also made the local JUSTICES OF THE PEACE (q.v. Vol. X) responsible for fixing the wage-rates of the various trades in their districts.

Such of the journeymen's or workers' guilds as survived became mere benefit or FRIENDLY SOCIETIES (q.v. Vol. X). They did not exist to bring pressure against employers to grant concessions in regard to hours and wages, and they thus had little in common with modern TRADE UNIONS (q.v.). It was not until the local justices began to disregard the duties laid upon them by the Act of 1563 that any movement towards the modern trade union began. During the 18th century fewer and fewer people accepted the old view that the regulation of working conditions and wages was rightly a matter for the King's Government or the local justices. By the end of the century the Justices of the Peace were still carrying out their bare duty of fixing wages, but all that they attempted to fix was the maximum wage which might not be exceeded. No attempt

EMBLEM OF THE AMALGAMATED SOCIETY OF ENGINEERS, 1852

The goddess of Fame stands in the centre on the cornucopia of Plenty. A smith refuses to repair the sword of Mars, the god of War, but an engineer accepts a design from Clio, the Muse of History. The kneeling figures represent Aesop's fable of the bundle of sticks, showing that unity is strength. The busts are Samuel Crompton, James Watt, and Sir Richard Arkwright. The branches of the Iron Trade are depicted below

N.U. of General and Municipal Workers

CELEBRATING THE REDUCTION OF THE WORKING DAY TO 8 HOURS IN 1889
Invitation to a breakfast given by the Amalgamated Society of Gas Workers and General Labourers at Birmingham

was made to fix minimum wage-rates, below which no worker could legally be engaged. This favoured the employer and not the worker.

By the 19th century the general view was that wages and hours should work themselves out by what Adam SMITH (q.v. Vol. V) had called 'the higgling and bargaining of the market'. The 18th century had been, on the whole, a time of expanding trade and increasing prosperity, but there were periods of bad trade, and many unions of workers were formed. Strikes were not unknown. All these new unions had no real legal status, and as early as 1721 a Combination Act was passed which made associations of workers illegal. Similar Acts were passed in 1726 and 1749. The effect of these Acts was to drive the budding trade union movement underground.

In 1793 war broke out with France. The British Government became frightened of secret societies, which might possibly be working against the safety of the State. An Act was therefore passed in 1797 which prohibited seditious or subversive societies, and forbade any society whatever to administer oaths to its members

which would bind them not to inform or give evidence against fellow members. This Act was followed by the Combination Acts of 1799 and 1800, which made associations of workmen generally illegal, whether seditious or not.

War against Napoleon made labour scarce and wages high. It was not until after Waterloo that times began to get bad and the movement towards trade unionism began to grow again.

In 1824 and 1825 the Combination laws were repealed. This was largely due to the influence of Francis Place, himself a journeyman tailor of London and a pioneer leader of the movement to organize working people. The Act of 1797, forbidding criminal societies and oaths of secrecy, was left on the Statute Book. Between 1825 and 1834 many more small unions were formed. On the whole, these were years of business activity and general prosperity, and the new movement made quiet headway without worrying either employers or government. In 1834, however, one incident touched the conscience of the nation. Some workers at Tolpuddle in Dorset had formed a 'Friendly Society of Agricultural Labourers', and although the ban on such societies had now been removed, it was found possible to prosecute under the Act of 1797 for 'administering an illegal oath'. Six of its members were tried at Dorchester, found guilty, and sentenced to TRANSPORTATION (q.v. Vol. X) to an overseas penal settlement for 7 years.

There was general sympathy throughout the country with the victims of this prosecution, which took place during the rise of another workers' movement—Chartism. The repeal of the Combination Acts in 1824 and 1825 meant that trade unions were no longer 'criminal associations', as they had been hitherto. No precise legal status, however, had been conferred on them, and the law gave them no rights, even against their own officials if they happened to be dishonest. In spite of this, however, and in spite of the harsh treatment of the six Dorset labourers (they became known as 'the Tolpuddle Martyrs', and were reprieved in 1836), there was a considerable expansion of trade unionism after 1834. In 1841 the Miners' Association of Great Britain and Ireland was formed. In 1851 one of the most famous of the early trade unions came into being—the Amalgamated Society of Engineers. This union was on a 'new model', and the title was applied to others similarly formed. The new union embraced a number of hitherto separate unions of blacksmiths, fitters, pattern-makers, machinists and others, and was from the first large and influential. The 'new model' unions were the first to cover the whole country, and also the first to amalgamate into one society separate crafts, each sharing in the same general activity. The engineers were followed in 1861 by the Amalgamated Society of Carpenters and Joiners. Other important unions of the time were the Iron Founders, the Bricklayers, and the Boot and Shoe Workers. These new and powerful unions elected a directing committee, called a 'Junta', and now embarked on an organized fight for the recognition of trade unionism by the law of the land.

The fight was successful, and Acts were passed between 1871 and 1876. The Act of 1871 made trade unions legal associations, and gave their funds legal protection. 'Picketing' of works where a strike was in progress became lawful (see TRADE UNIONS, MODERN), provided that it did not go as far as intimidation or violence. The law also made clear that striking, or any similar combined action, would no longer be regarded as a conspiracy against the security of the State. Shortly after 1871 the Trades Union Congress was formed, a body representing most of the leading unions.

From 1871 onwards, further changes in the law strengthened the legal position of the unions, although there were occasional setbacks. In 1906 an Act was passed protecting union funds against legal actions brought by employers for compensation for losses caused by strikes. In 1906 the Labour Party was founded (see POLITICAL PARTIES, Vol. X). In those days Members of Parliament received no salary, and most of the larger unions supported financially those of their members who found seats in Parliament, and also the Labour Party itself. The right of the unions to do this was challenged in the law courts in 1907 by W. V. Osborne, a member of the Amalgamated Society of Railway Servants (later the National Union of Railwaymen), who was not a member of the Labour Party. In 1909 the judges of the House of Lords decided in his favour. What has since been called the Osborne Judgement threw a doubt upon the lawfulness of trade union activity in politics. In 1913 an Act was therefore passed allowing the unions to spend money for political purposes, but providing that unsympathetic members not wishing to pay the 'political levy' would be entitled to 'contract out' without prejudice to their general membership of the union.

In 1926 a general strike took place in Britain, a form of activity used in foreign countries for political purposes. The British General Strike was an attempt by all the great industrial unions to force the Government to intervene in a long-drawn-out mining dispute. British industry, including transport, was practically at a standstill; volunteers drove trains and buses, and troops guarded dumps of food in the parks. After nine days the strike collapsed. As a result, in the next year, the Trade Disputes and Trade Unions Act was passed. This reversed the Act of 1913, and made it necessary for members who wished to pay the 'political levy' to 'contract in' by an agreement in writing. The Act of 1927 was reversed in 1945. Since then the trade union movement has been entirely free, not only to press for improvements in wages, hours, and labour conditions, but also to engage in politics.

See also TRADE UNIONS, WORLD; WAGES.
See also Vol. X: INDUSTRIAL WELFARE; FACTORY INSPECTOR; ARBITRATION.

TRADE UNIONS, MODERN. Members of a trade union generally form branches in various towns or districts, and elect certain members as officials (such as branch secretary or treasurer). Delegates are also elected to national and regional committees or councils of the union to look after the members' interests. Every member of a union pays regular subscriptions to meet the cost of running his union and to provide a fund to help members whose wages cease if they 'strike' against the employers or are 'locked out' by them.

Trade unions can be classified as craft, industrial, and general labour unions. The members of a craft union, such as the Pattern-makers, practise a single skilled craft or trade. An industrial union includes several different types of craftsman, all working within the same industry: the National Union of Railwaymen is a typical union in this class. A general labour union includes members, usually unskilled or semi-skilled, working in several industries: for example, the Transport and General Workers Union. In 1948 the total membership of the unions affiliated to the T.U.C. (Trades Union Congress) was nearly 8 millions, and there were a few influential unions that were not affiliated. Trade union membership in Britain is, therefore, not far short of 10 millions. The largest individual union is the Transport and General Workers, with a membership of over 1,250,000.

British trade unions on the present-day lines were formed in the middle of the 19th century (*see* TRADE UNION HISTORY), and have been generally successful in attaining their main object, which was to raise the STANDARD OF LIVING (q.v.) of their members. This success is largely due to their having replaced 'individual bargaining' by 'collective bargaining'. Before trade unions became lawful in the 19th century, wage-rates and working conditions were decided by bargaining between each employer and each workman. If a workman thought the wages offered were too low, he had two choices: to continue to work discontentedly at that wage; or to leave his work, which usually meant leaving his home and district and taking his chance elsewhere. He could not apply much pressure on his employer, especially in times of serious UNEMPLOYMENT (q.v.); he could only hope to persuade his employer that he was a valued and almost indispensable employee, as he usually had no money to fall back on if he decided to stop working. Moreover, it would be too big a risk for all the workers of an employer to agree to stand together, without the backing of a trade union and of the money it could pay the members as 'strike pay'.

This situation was completely changed when wages and other conditions (such as hours of work) came to be negotiated between employers and unions. Employers were then faced with the chance that all the workers in a trade or industry might stop working, or 'strike', if they were not satisfied with the wages and conditions offered. Sometimes the threat of a strike was sufficient to force employers to raise wages, but often it was not; and, if the union felt itself strong enough, an actual strike might take place. A strike could not achieve its aim unless all the members of

Protection
FOR THE
INDUSTRIOUS
Weavers.

INFORMATION having been received that a great number of industrious Weavers have been deterred by threats and acts of violence from the pursuit of their lawful occupations, and that in many instances their Shuttles have been taken, and their Materials damaged by persons acting under the existing Combinations:

Notice is hereby Given,

That every Protection will be afforded to persons so injured, upon giving Information to the Constables of Stockport: And a Reward of

FIFTY GUINEAS

Will be paid, on conviction, to the person who will come forward with such evidence as may be the means of convicting any one or more of the offences mentioned in the Act of Parliament, of which an Extract is subjoined: And a Reward of

TWENTY GUINEAS

Will be paid, on conviction, to the person who will come forward and inform of any person being guilty of assaulting or molesting industrious and honest Weavers, so as to prevent them from taking out or bringing in their Work peaceably.

PETER BROWN, ⎱ CONSTABLES.
Stockport, June 17th, 1808. T. CARTWRIGHT, ⎰

By the 22nd, Geo. 3, C. 40, S. 3.

It is enacted, " *That if any person enter, by force, into any House or Shop, with intent to Cut and Destroy any Linen or Cotton, or Linen and Cotton mixed with any other Materials, in the Loom, or any Warp or Shute, Tools, Tackle, and Utensils, or shall Cut or Destroy the same, or shall Break and Destroy any Tools, Tackle, or Utensils, for Weaving, Preparing, or Making any such Manufactures, every such Offender shall be guilty of FELONY, without Benefit of Clergy".*

J. CLARKE, PRINTER.

ANTI-COMBINATION NOTICE, 1808

A local order under an anti-combination law to protect mill-workers in Stockport

the union (or of the branch concerned) joined in it, and unless the majority of workers in the industry belonged to the union. Therefore, when a strike took place at a factory, the strikers appointed some of their members as 'pickets'; their task was to stand near the factory gate and to persuade members of the union who wanted to work, and often non-union men also, to change their minds and join the ranks of the strikers.

What is called a 'General Strike' is rare in Britain. This is a stoppage of all work in all or many industries throughout a country. It is generally more political than industrial in nature. A general strike occurred in Britain in 1926 (*see* TRADE UNION HISTORY).

Collective bargaining led to a slow yet steady improvement in the welfare of the worker, which individual bargaining would not have achieved. Once a higher wage-rate had been agreed upon, in a district or in a whole industry, it became very difficult for employers to reduce it. If the union members would not agree to lower wages, employers sometimes decided on a 'lock-out', a weapon which they used in the same way as their workers used a strike. A lock-out meant that an employer or group of employers shut down the works, and lost money for the time being, so that the workers would earn no wages and would be forced in the end to accept the conditions offered by the employers. Usually a lock-out was only declared when general trade depression or foreign competition made the prevailing wage-rate in an industry too much for the majority of employers to pay.

Wages have seldom been the only concern of the trade unions. Hours of work and general working conditions have long been matters of negotiation between unions and employers, and in recent years holidays with pay have been added to these. The unions are also vitally interested in the technical efficiency of their members and in keeping a balance between skilled workers and unskilled people who may join them, whether as learners or otherwise. The rules for APPRENTICESHIP (q.v.) and training in the skilled trades are drawn up with the help of the unions. These rules may be relaxed when new entrants to the trade are falling off, or when the trade itself is expanding. At other times the rules for the admission of learners are tightened up, the unions being anxious that wages and conditions shall not suffer. To deal with disputes promptly, in the actual workshops where they

arise, union members in most works elect a 'shop steward' as their spokesman in all negotiations with the management, and as the link between themselves and the executive committee of the union.

British trade unions are registered under the FRIENDLY SOCIETIES Acts (q.v. Vol. X), for they are in a true sense friendly or 'mutual benefit' societies for their members. During a strike that is officially ordered by the union committee, the union pays out 'dispute benefit' or strike pay. If a member is unemployed, his union usually pays him money, which is additional to the unemployment benefit paid by the State (*see* UNEMPLOYMENT INSURANCE, Vol. X). Unemployment benefit is not paid by the State during a strike. Most unions also pay sickness and disability benefit, in addition to the payments now made by the State under the NATIONAL HEALTH SERVICE (q.v. Vol. X). Most unions also pay out a lump sum for the funeral expenses of members who die, and many have pension schemes to supplement the pensions paid by the State. Another important function of British unions is the giving of free legal advice to their members, and the payment of solicitors or counsel if a case has to go to court. A union is generally prepared to fight a member's case as far as the House of Lords, the highest Law Court in the land, whenever it involves a point of law vital to the interests of the union (*see* APPEAL COURTS, Vol. X).

By the end of the Second World War British trade unions had become powerful, and although problems of wages were still important, direct negotiations on wages had ceased to be the main concern of most unions. After wages boards or wages councils for many industries had been set up by law from 1909 onwards, the chief responsibility of many unions in the matter of wages was to sit as joint representatives with the employers on these councils or boards (*see* ARBITRATION, Vol. X). The unions began to concern themselves more with the efficiency of industry, on which they had already had a great influence. Every time a union successfully pressed for higher wages or better working conditions (either of which would cost employers more money), the less well-managed firms had been driven towards greater efficiency in order to maintain their profits, and the hopelessly inefficient firms had been driven out of business entirely. In regard to actual output or pro-

*N.U. of **General** and Municipal Workers*

BANNER OF THE NORWICH BRANCH OF THE NATIONAL UNION OF GENERAL WORKERS
This union amalgamated with another in 1924 to become the National Union of General and Municipal Workers

ductivity, however, the interest of British unions rather lagged. It is only comparatively recently that the connexion between increased productivity and the welfare of workers has been stressed. An earlier view was that if productivity increased, that is, if more goods were turned out by a given number of workers in a given time, some of the workers might be dismissed. This actually happened in individual factories and individual districts, and caused much distress (*see* LUDDITES). These experiences led the unions to take a view which, if applied to industry as a whole, was economically false, and came to be called the 'lump of work' fallacy: that is, the idea that there is in the world at any time only a limited amount of work to be done and goods to be turned out. In actual fact the human demand for goods can practically never be satisfied, provided that their cost and selling price can be reduced. The American trade unions had always thought differently, believing that increased productivity meant cheaper goods, and that

cheaper goods would mean bigger sales, greater output, and a demand for more labour. The economic difficulties of Britain after the Second World War made it generally clear that increased productivity was the only road towards a higher standard of living, not only for trade unionists, but for all. In 1949 a team of British trade unionists visited the U.S.A., and in 1950 the British Trades Union Congress published their report, which proved the American view to be the correct one, and recommended the adoption of American methods as far as possible.

Following the Second World War, these tentative moves towards increased productivity in industry were not checked by 'official' strikes, or strikes sponsored by the executive committees of the unions; but there were 'unofficial' or local strikes, contrary to union policy and instructions. These unofficial strikes were actually against the law of the land. To save any damage to the country's war effort, a Government Order was made under an Act of Parliament in 1939

Picture Post Library

A MEETING OF THE TRADES UNION CONGRESS AT SOUTHPORT IN 1940

(and agreed to by the Trades Union Congress) laying down that any dispute on wages or conditions should go before a Court of Arbitration, composed of equal numbers of employers' and union representatives, and presided over by an impartial chairman. This 'standstill' agreement to withhold the use of the strike weapon by the unions themselves, or of the equivalent employers' weapon of the lock-out, continued in force for some years after the war.

The principle of the 'closed shop' has long been favoured in many British unions, although not always practised; it is based on the idea that every worker in a factory or an industry shall be a union member, in order to place the union in a stronger position to negotiate. In the years that followed the Second World War a movement developed among many trade unionists in favour of the 'closed shop' policy being made compulsory by law; it was claimed that non-unionists, who paid no subscriptions, should not in fairness benefit from the better wages and conditions that the unionists had achieved after years of effort.

See also TRADE UNION HISTORY; TRADE UNIONS, WORLD; WAGES.
See also Vol. X: INDUSTRIAL WELFARE; SOCIAL INSURANCE.

TRADE UNIONS, WORLD. Trade unions have a long history in many other countries besides Britain, and in most cases have had similar struggles to become recognized by law. In most countries the earliest unions arose among skilled craftsmen, usually serving as benefit societies all the time, and uniting into larger groups occasionally, for a campaign in defence of wages and conditions of work. In both France and Germany their history goes back to the 18th century, but they did not gain great influence until the second half of the 19th century. In France they were suppressed by law after the Revolution of 1789, and, though they revived, were given no legal recognition until 1884. In Germany they were active in the mid-19th century, chiefly among skilled craftsmen, but became highly organized only towards the end of the century. The Roman Catholics of Germany organized a rival Christian Trade Union movement, open to both Catholics and Protestants, especially in the Rhineland and Ruhr, and this remained separate until 1933, when Hitler's Nazi Government suppressed both movements. Separate Christian Trade Union movements exist to-day in Belgium, France, Holland, and Italy, often working in friendship with the larger movements which are non-religious. Where, as in France and Italy, the main trade union movements are largely under Communist leadership, the Christian unions are very hostile to them. In France and Italy there are also anti-Communist trade unions loosely associated with the Socialist Parties. The French movement, in spite of its strong Communist leadership, remains highly localized, with weak central organization, whereas the Germans have a tradition of strong centralization. Trade unionism in Spain was suppressed when General Franco came to power in the 1930's. The Scandinavian countries and Finland have strong trade union movements, fairly closely associated with the Socialist Parties.

In Russia trade unions were vigorously suppressed until the Revolution of 1917; but in the U.S.S.R. they now have a very big membership, though they are in effect part of the machinery of State, with no power of independent action. They are entrusted by the Government with many functions of social administration and inspection, and they run extensive social services for their members. The same situation has arisen in most of the Communist-controlled countries of Eastern Europe. All over Eastern Europe trade unions, except on a very small scale, are of recent growth, for they were allowed little scope before 1945. Only Czechoslovakia and the former German part of Poland have trade union movements of long standing, and these have now passed under Communist control and are, therefore, no longer independent trade unions as the term is understood in western Europe.

In the United States, trade unions have made rapid progress in recent years. They were largely set up by emigrants from Europe in the early 19th century. To-day the movement is sharply divided into two main groups. The American Federation of Labour, founded in 1881, has its main strength among skilled workers and in the older industries; the newer Congress of Industrial Organizations, founded in 1936, has enrolled mainly workers in the growing mass-production industries; (such as steel, oil, motor-cars, and rubber). Both groups, and also most of the independent unions associated with neither (such as Railroad Brotherhoods), are strongly anti-Communist, and the once considerable Communist element in the C.I.O. has been driven out of the leadership.

Trade unionism in Canada is largely in the hands of the United States unions. Latin America has its own movements, strongest in Mexico, but highly unstable. Australia and New Zealand have well-organized movements; that of South Africa is weaker because of the division between white and African workers. India's movement is developing, and in recent years there has been a rapid growth of trade unions in the colonies (Jamaica, Malaya, West Africa, and elsewhere). China had many unions, with little central organization before a Communist Government took control of the country in 1949.

There are two rival movements which try to bring together the unions of many nations. The Communist-dominated World Federation of Trade Unions was founded in 1945 as successor to the rival pre-war Communist and non-Communist Internationals. The International Confederation of Free Trade Unions was founded in 1949, when the West European and American movements (hostile to Communism) left the World Federation in protest. There are also International Federations of workers in particular trades or industries (such as miners and transport workers), and in some cases rival bodies cover the same occupations. The first Trade Union International was founded in 1913, after a series of international conferences which began in 1901.

TRAINING, see APPRENTICESHIP; FACTORY ORGANIZATION, Section 4.

TRANSPORT is often a costly item of expense to a manufacturer or merchant, and he tries to reduce it as much as possible. To some manufacturers, using large quantities of bulky raw materials, the cost of their transport would otherwise be so great that the factory is located near the source of the principal raw material. This is particularly true of iron and steel works, which are usually built near ironstone mines or deposits, or on a coalfield (see LOCALIZATION OF INDUSTRY). If a firm's raw materials come in by sea, transport charges can be reduced if the factory stands at the waterside, with wharves or jetties for unloading sea-going ships of deep draught. A site of this kind is still more economical when the goods manufactured are for export and can be sent away from the factory by sea. The Ford Works at Dagenham, on a deepwater reach of

Lever Bros.

OIL FOR MAKING SOAP BEING PUMPED FROM A BARGE INTO A STORAGE TANK AT PORT SUNLIGHT

the Thames, is ideally sited for these purposes. Freight charges by sea, particularly for cargoes in bulk, are so much cheaper than railway charges that a distant waterside site involving long journeys often proves cheaper than a much nearer inland site. Canal sites have the same general advantages as sea or river sites. Canal communications are slow but, unlike railway goods services, they provide a form of transport that is free from shocks and vibration. The heavy and bulky raw materials used in the Staffordshire pottery industry, and the brittle nature of the finished articles, had much to do with the decision to build a canal to serve this area (*see* CANALS, BRITISH, Vol. IV). If, however, a firm decide to rely on railways, it may be cheaper to place the works in open country, and to build private sidings connecting it with the main line, than to pay the cost of road transport to and from a railway station.

Most light industries, and nearly all trading businesses, need not consider transport charges quite so seriously. But to handle their goods they must choose one of three methods of transport: (*a*) public-service transport (railway or publicly run road services); (*b*) their own road vehicles;

(*c*) hired road vehicles. The decision can only be made when the comparative costs have been carefully worked out for that particular business, for a method that would suit one business would not necessarily suit another, even in the same trade or industry. A firm deciding to run its own vehicles must then decide which type of vehicle suits its requirements best.

The transport problems of the retail trader are simpler, for his goods are usually delivered to him from a manufacturer or wholesaler, or other central depot. Many retailers do not have to deliver goods to their customers, while others, such as large DEPARTMENT STORES (q.v.), may have a large fleet of delivery vans.

See also Vol. IV: MOTOR TRANSPORT; GOODS TRAIN; SHIP; CANALS; AIRCRAFT, SPECIAL USES; HORSE TRANSPORT.

TRAVEL AGENCIES, *see* TOURIST INDUSTRY.

TRUST, *see* COMBINES.

TRUST HOUSES, *see* HOTEL INDUSTRY.

TURNOVER. 1. The 'turnover' of a business

is the value of its 'net' sales during any chosen period, say a month or a year: that is, its 'gross' or total sales, less the selling price of any goods returned by customers as unsatisfactory. The only way by which a business can increase its net profit is usually by increasing its turnover. In most businesses the gross profit (*see* PROFITS), or difference between the selling price and the cost price of the goods sold, remains much the same. Many overhead charges (*see* COSTING) also remain much the same: for example, rent, lighting and heating, and office salaries. The advantage of a high turnover can be seen from a comparison of the trading results of a business in two distinct periods, one showing a low turnover and the other a high turnover. In the following example the proportion of gross profit remains the same; half the overhead charges remain the same, or are 'constant'; the other half (for instance, delivery charges and stationery and printing) rise as turnover increases, and form the variable overheads. The advantage of a higher turnover can be seen from these figures. Not only has the net profit risen from £5,000 to £13,000, but it has risen from being 10% of turnover to 13%.

PERIOD I—TURNOVER £50,000

	£		£
Cost of goods sold	40,000	Net Sales .	50,000
Gross profit .	10,000		
	£50,000		£50,000
Constant overheads	3,000	Gross profit .	10,000
Variable overheads	2,000		
Net profit . .	5,000		
	£10,000		£10,000

PERIOD 2—TURNOVER £100,000

	£		£
Cost of goods sold	80,000	Net sales .	100,000
Gross profit .	20,000		
	£100,000		£100,000
Constant overheads	3,000	Gross profit .	20,000
Variable overheads	4,000		
Net profit . .	13,000		
	£20,000		£20,000

2. STOCK TURNOVER. The word 'turnover' is also used in business for the number of times a year the average stock of goods on hand is sold or 'turned over'; this is usually called the 'stock turnover'. Different trades vary greatly in this respect. If a jeweller's or furniture dealer's stock turnover were 1, that is, if he just managed to sell within the year the stock with which he started, he would consider himself reasonably fortunate, for in these trades the sales are slow. But a fishmonger or butcher might worry seriously if his stock turnover fell much below 50, or a complete turnover of stock about once a week; and a milk retailer would naturally expect a stock turnover of 365. Other things being equal, a high stock turnover will enable a trader to cut his 'profit margin': that is, his gross profit, or difference between cost price and selling price; it is, of course, equally possible that cutting the profit margin, and thus lowering the selling price, may lead to a higher rate of stock turnover than before. Stock turnover and sales turnover are usually closely connected with each other, and move together; sales turnover is nearly always encouraged when the price to the public is lowered.

TYPE, *see* PRINTING-TYPES.

U

UNDERWRITER, *see* INSURANCE; ISSUING HOUSES.

UNEMPLOYMENT. In more primitive days, before industry had become highly organized, unemployment was much less serious. Workers then mostly worked at home (*see* DOMESTIC SYSTEM). Some grew or made things for their own families, and would naturally never throw themselves out of work. Others, who made goods to sell, could always cut their prices and be content with a smaller 'wage', rather than become unemployed. In those days there was also less DIVISION OF LABOUR (q.v.) or specialization in one type of job; all except highly skilled craftsmen could easily adapt themselves to other jobs, moving from one to another as the demand for goods changed.

In modern industrial countries there are four main types of unemployment: seasonal, technological, transitional, and cyclical. Much unemployment is due to two or more of these causes acting together.

1. SEASONAL UNEMPLOYMENT. This may be of two kinds. The first arises from the fact that some occupations can be carried on only at certain seasons of the year. Boatmen, yacht hands, and others engaged in the seaside holiday industry are examples of people following seasonal occupations. The only way in which they may avoid prolonged unemployment is to combine a summer with a winter occupation. Many persons following seasonal occupations do so merely to supplement retired pay or pension or earnings from running a business. The Scots girls engaged ashore during the British herring fishing season regard this employment as a part-time activity only. The second type of seasonal unemployment arises from weather conditions, and particularly affects those engaged in the building trades: wet weather, or hard and pro-

longed frost, make some kinds of work temporarily impossible.

2. TECHNOLOGICAL UNEMPLOYMENT may also be of two kinds. The first, which is less serious, arises from the occasional necessity to re-equip a factory with new or improved machinery. While Henry Ford, the American motor-car manufacturer, was redesigning and re-equipping his works in Detroit for the manufacture of a car of an entirely different model, a great deal of technological unemployment took place in that city. The more serious type of technological unemployment arises when the demand for some particular article falls off, or ceases entirely, and when the management of the factory concerned have failed to foresee this and to switch over to the production of something else. There was a good deal of technological unemployment of the first type during the first two years following the Second World War, while factories were

ALL
UNEMPLOYED
SHOULD ROLL UP
ON
WEDNESDAY NEXT, the 13th,
FOR THE
THIRD GREAT MARCH

....

We are going to see the Chairman of the L.C.C. to inquire why they do not push on with their works faster. Rates are being saved while men are starving for want of work, which could and should be done.

Don't forget that JACK WILLIAMS is at home to the Unemployed on TOWER HILL every Monday, Wednesday, and Friday (bar the 13th, of course) at 12.30.

Contingents should assemble from all parts every Friday.

....

We are going to St. Paul's, Sunday, 17th.
COMING?
MEET AT TRAFALGAR SQUARE AT 2, AND MARCH TO THE CATHEDRAL.

Twentieth Century Press, Ltd. (T.U. and 48 Hours), 37a, Clerkenwell Green, E.C.

Daily Herald

UNEMPLOYED MARCH NOTICE, 1905

Daily Herald

UNEMPLOYED MEN MARCHING FROM JARROW TO LONDON IN 1936
Jarrow, County Durham, was one of the 'depressed' areas badly hit by the slump of the 1930's

being rearranged for peace-time production after having been occupied for many years with war-time orders.

3. TRANSITIONAL UNEMPLOYMENT. A worker is transitionally unemployed when he has left one job and has not yet started on a new one. This kind of unemployment is less serious than other forms, and the transitionally unemployed formed the largest part of the persons registered as unemployed in Britain in the years immediately after the Second World War. The average period of transitional unemployment is not more than 2 or 3 weeks.

4. CYCLICAL UNEMPLOYMENT. The most serious kind of unemployment is cyclical: so called, from the Greek word for 'circle', because it tends to come round again every time business becomes slack in what is known as the TRADE CYCLE (q.v.). Unemployment of this kind tends to last a long time; it usually begins with the 'heavy' industries (such as iron and steel, and shipbuilding) and spreads to others. The men dismissed have less to spend; this creates further unemployment in the industries turning out goods for which the demand has thus decreased. Cyclical unemployment is therefore cumulative; during the worst year of the depression of the 1930's it rose in Britain to over 2,600,000, in Germany to nearly 7,000,000, and in the U.S.A. to 10,000,000. Preventing unemployment on this tragic scale involves preventing the trade cycle from recurring as it did before the Second World War.

See also TRADE CYCLE.
See also Vol. X: SOCIAL INSURANCE.

UPHOLSTERY is the covering of furniture, such as chairs, couches, and beds, with springs, padding, or other materials, so that they become comfortable to sit or lie on.

The earliest British form of upholstery, known at least as far back as the 14th century, consisted simply of strips of leather stretched across the top of a kind of X-shaped camp stool, with strips of the same kind across the back. For 3 centuries this was the only kind of upholstered chair used until about the middle of the 17th century, when padded upholstery of the modern type gradually came into use. Steel springs were used later to give added resilience.

The traditional upholstering method was a combination of steel springs and padding, and this method is still very commonly used. The steel springs, usually in the shape of a cone, or a

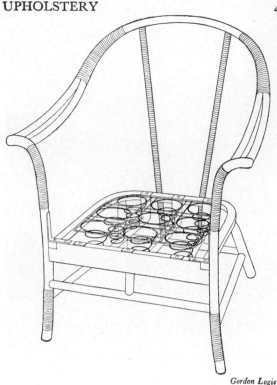

Gordon Logie

FIG. I. THE SPRINGS OF AN UPHOLSTERED CHAIR SEAT

bones of the pelvis, compressing the skin and muscle below these bones: this is felt if one sits on a hard wooden seat for any length of time. The object of upholstery is to give side support and to spread the area of muscle taking the load so as to reduce the amount of compression. The load on the pelvis can also be reduced by tilting the seat and back of a chair; this throws the body backwards and spreads the load on to the lower part of the back and the thighs. The seats of the coaches on the London Tubes, in passenger aircraft, in luxury motor-coaches, in modern theatres, and other places are designed in this way, and are very comfortable.

In addition to the old traditional methods of upholstering with springs and padding, new methods have come into use. One is the use of horizontal springs. These are slung like a hammock from the front of the seat to the back, and support a cushion filled either with small conical springs or with some springy material such as rubberized hair. Another modern method is the use of sponge rubber, or more correctly 'latex foam', which is cast in the form of complete seats and backs. The top surface of the rubber is shaped to the curve of the body, while the underside is cut out in a deep honeycomb. This saves rubber, and gives a deeper spring than a solid section would give. The amount of spring can be increased or reduced by varying the spacing of the walls of the honeycomb (Fig. 2). Sponge rubber has also been used for bed mattresses and for underlays to carpets (*see* RUBBER MANUFACTURE).

double cone, are joined to each other by wire clips or fabric, and rest on a network of canvas tapes fixed to the bottom of the chair. Similar tapes hold the springs in position at the top. The tapes form a basis on which padding is sewn (Fig. 1).

A designer of upholstered furniture should take into account the anatomy of those who are going to sit in it. When someone sits down, the weight of the body is carried on the points of the

Modern upholstery sometimes makes use of compressed air in the form of the pneumatic cushion, which is simply a rubber bag filled with air. It has been used for the seats of motor-cars and aeroplanes.

See also FURNITURE TRADE.
See also Vol. XI: FURNITURE, HISTORY OF.

USURY. Nowadays this means lending money at an excessive rate of INTEREST (q.v.), but in medieval times it meant not only moneylending of any kind, even at very low rates of interest, but also a good many commercial transactions that are regarded to-day as normal and reasonable. Aristotle, one of the famous philosophers of ancient Greece, considered money itself, as distinct from goods, to be 'unproductive', and he condemned as immoral not only money loans but also the earning of interest on them. Many

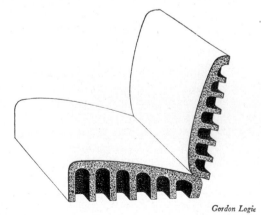

Gordon Logie

FIG. 2. THE CONSTRUCTION OF FOAMED LATEX UPHOLSTERY

of Aristotle's ideas were later adopted by the Schoolmen, or medieval philosophers of the Catholic Church, who at first condemned the lending of money at interest as usury, just as Aristotle had. But they were living in a period of rapidly expanding business and enterprise, and gradually their earlier ideas became changed. At first they condemned not only moneylending but also trading; it was lawful, they argued, to buy goods in order to manufacture or fashion them into something else, but unlawful to buy goods merely in order to resell them at a profit, which was only one degree better than usury. As trade enlarged and specialization developed, the Schoolmen adapted their views to the changing times, and St. Thomas AQUINAS (q.v. Vol. V), the greatest of the Schoolmen, admitted that there was such a thing as 'trading for the public good'. Gradually, in place of the complete condemnation of trading and moneylending, there grew up the theory of the 'Just Price', under which trading became lawful provided that the trader made no more profit, and charged no higher selling price, than would enable him to maintain himself in his own station in life. Later, some new ideas were put forward on the vexed question of moneylending. The Church, which in those days had immense influence, began by removing its previous objection to the earning of profits by persons who put up CAPITAL (q.v.) for a trading or manufacturing venture; it was now accepted that these people were merely partners with the trader or manufacturer himself, and shared his risks; but it was still held to be wrong to charge a fixed interest on money loans which involved no trading or manufacturing risk. Business, however, was advancing still more rapidly, and at last the Church agreed that interest on money loans was morally justified on two grounds: first, that the lender would be deprived during the period of the loan of the opportunity of using the money profitably for his own business purposes; secondly, in order that he might be compensated by those who repaid him for the losses he might suffer from those who did not repay their debts.

Once the morality of charging interest had been accepted, commercial loans became a normal feature of trading; but interest rates rose to very high figures—sometimes as much as 60% per annum. The shortage of capital may have

National Gallery

TWO BANKERS OR USURERS
Painting by Marinus van Reymerswael, 1497–1567

had much to do with this. The Church's earlier view on the immorality of interest in any form was dropped, and what was now condemned as usury was only a rate of interest that was excessive. When, after the Reformation, the State became the sole law-making power in the country, laws were passed to limit rates of interest, and in Britain the maximum rate permitted until early in the 19th century was 5%. These laws were known as the Usury Laws.

They have now been repealed, and the only laws in force concerning rates of interest are those in connexion with loans by licensed moneylenders. By the Money Lenders Act of 1927 any rate of interest over 48% per annum is considered excessive, and contracts at rates above this figure are liable to be set aside by the law courts as 'harsh and unconscionable'. Rates of interest as high as this are not met with in normal business, but arise only on loans from moneylenders against types of security that would not be accepted as safe enough by a banker.

See also LOANS; INTEREST.

V

VALUE AND PRICE. Using the word 'value' in its economic sense, the value of anything is the amount of some other thing that can be obtained in exchange for it. If a hundredweight of coal can be exchanged for 4 pounds of mutton, we might say that the value of a pound of mutton was a quarter of a hundredweight of coal, or the other way round. In the modern world MONEY (q.v.) is the general medium of exchange, and values are more conveniently measured in money. The price of an article is its 'exchange value' in money.

It used to be thought that the value of anything depended solely on what it cost to make. David Ricardo, the British economist, argued in the early 19th century that the comparative values of different articles depended on the 'quantities of labour' that had gone to make them. Thus, if it took 100 man-hours to make article A, and 200 man-hours to make article B, article B would be twice as valuable as article A, and one B would exchange in the market for two As. Ricardo's theory held the field for quite a time. It was the foundation on which Karl MARX (q.v. Vol. V) built his own theory of value many years later, but by that time an important objection had been raised to Ricardo's theory. If equal amounts of labour had gone to the making of something that was very useful, and of something that was quite useless, would each have the same exchange value, or fetch the same price? Marx got over this difficulty by introducing the idea of 'socially necessary labour'; but this suggested that society—that is, people themselves—had a great deal to say on the question of values and prices.

Towards the end of the 19th century some economists, including W. S. Jevons in England, approached the problem from a different angle. In the main, their views are still held by modern economists. They suggested that the value of anything depends upon what the buyer is prepared to pay for it, and that he will value articles, or 'price' them, according to their scale of usefulness to himself. He might put an equal value upon a hundredweight of coal and 4 pounds of mutton, because each of these quantities of things represented to him an equal amount of usefulness—or 'utility', which is the word that economists have come to use.

Naturally, any individual purchaser may put different values upon the same things at different times or in different places, and even at the same time and in the same place the valuations put upon the same things by different purchasers may not be the same. Prices are therefore likely to change when demand changes. But prices are just as likely to be influenced by the available supply of the article—by the fact that it is plentiful or scarce. For example, if bad harvests in Canada make wheat scarcer, it is likely that the price of wheat will rise, for in order to get enough of it buyers will have to raise their 'bids' in the market. Goods made of materials of which there is a very limited supply in the world, such as sable fur coats or diamond necklaces, will always, therefore, have a high value. Their actual price at any given time depends mainly on the amount of money people have to spare after buying the necessities of life. Prices are therefore really dependent upon the joint influence of SUPPLY AND DEMAND (q.v.).

VARNISHES, *see* PAINTS AND VARNISHES.

VEGETABLE OILS, *see* OILS, VEGETABLE.

VEGETABLE TRADE, *see* GREENGROCERY.

VENEERS, *see* PLYWOODS AND VENEERS.

W

WAGES. 1. These are payments made to workers in return for their labour. Wage-rates are now usually fixed by Wages Boards or Wages Councils which have been set up by law, or else they are settled by direct negotiation between employers, or employers' federations, and TRADE UNIONS (q.v.). 'Time-rate' and 'piecework' are the two main methods of wage payment, but there are also various bonus or 'incentive' systems that are combinations of the two main methods.

Time-rates are based on the number of hours worked. An ordinary hourly rate of pay is agreed on, and this is increased by a quarter or a half, or is sometimes even doubled, for 'overtime' put in by the worker after normal working hours or at week-ends or on public holidays.

On piecework wages the worker is paid an agreed rate for the quantity of material he produces: for example, a miner may be paid so much per ton of mineral ore dug out and sent to the surface. In most modern industrial processes men work in groups and not singly, and piecework payments are worked out for the group or gang and shared among its members. In COAL-MINING (q.v.), for example, a 'check-weighman' at the pithead weighs the loads of coal sent up by the different gangs.

Most bonus systems of wage payment are based on a 'standard' or minimum performance by the worker; extra payments are made, on a sliding scale, for what is produced above that standard. There are many practical difficulties in working out bonus systems, as the individual performances of the various workers in a group or gang are liable to differ widely from each other.

The wage-rate that any industry can afford to pay depends on the price at which the product of that industry can be sold. If the earnings of an industry fall, the wage-rate will be reduced in the long run. To begin with, the employer will dismiss his least productive workers. The trade union to which they belong will then have to pay out union unemployment benefit, and it is likely that the union subscriptions of the unemployed workers will soon fall into arrear. If the depression in the industry continues, and unemployment in it increases seriously, the executive committee of the union may soon be ready to agree to a reduction of the wage-rate. Sometimes the selling price of a product falls because it is losing popular favour: as, for example, when horse-carriages were being replaced by the early motor-cars; the wages of coachbuilders then fell, in sympathy with the fall in the price of their product. At other times the selling price of a product falls because it is being made more cheaply abroad, and if this is the case the wage-rate can only be maintained in two ways. One way is for the Government to impose an import duty or TARIFF (q.v.) on the foreign product; this will make the price quoted by foreign competitors artificially higher, so that their product will not undersell the home-made article. Another way of maintaining the wage-rate is by altering by law the value of the home country's currency in comparison with that of other countries (*see* RATES OF EXCHANGE). This happened in Britain in 1949, when the Government 'devalued' the £ sterling from its previous dollar value. If neither of these things is done, and if wages (particularly in the industries manufacturing for export) are allowed to fall, there may be a difference between the low wages in the 'unsheltered' or export industries and the comparatively high wages in the 'sheltered' industries manufacturing mainly for the home market. In Britain such a difference was a feature of the years that followed the First World War.

In a country in which people are free to find what work they can, changes in wage-rates cause workers to move from one employment to another in accordance with the changing tastes and preferences of the public who buy the goods the workers make. The prices of goods for which the demand exceeds the supply will rise; the wage-rates in these industries will rise also, and more workers will thus be attracted towards them. In the same way workers will be encouraged to leave industries whose products are over-abundant, and are falling in price.

Differences (or 'differentials', as the trade

unions call them) between wages in different occupations, and between different grades of worker in the same occupation, are also necessary, so as to secure a proper balance between skilled and unskilled workers, and between foremen and managers and their subordinate workers. Unless this differential is a reasonable one, there is no reward for the hard work, time, and study involved in acquiring knowledge or skill, or for the risks of taking responsibility.

Wage payments to the 'black-coated' or non-manual workers, such as clerks, are usually fixed at an annual figure, and are called 'salaries' and paid monthly. In the long run, salaries tend to rise and fall for the same reasons as the wages of manual workers, although salaries are generally slower to rise than wages.

2. 'REAL' WAGES. Changes in 'money wages' and changes in 'real wages' are not always the same thing. 'Money wages' is the term given by economists to the actual pounds, shillings, and pence received. But 'real wages' is the term which indicates how many goods and services those pounds, shillings, and pence will buy. For instance, some workmen may receive 10% more money from their employer in a given year than in the previous year. This means an increase of 10% in their 'money wages'. But if the prices of food, clothes, and bus fares have also gone up by 10%, they cannot buy any more than they could the year before. Therefore their 'real wages' are not changed. The welfare of workers depends not on a rise in money wages, but on a rise in real wages. Workers in any particular industry may receive a rise in real wages if that industry increases its productivity, or if the price of the product rises while the general COST OF LIVING (q.v.) remains stationary; they may then receive a rise in money wages which will mean a rise in real wages as well. For the community as a whole, a rise in real wages can only result from a general increase of productivity in all industries.

See also TRADE UNIONS.

WALLPAPER, *see* Vol. XI: WALLPAPERS, HISTORY OF.

CARGO AWAITING EXPORT IN ONE OF THE WAREHOUSES AT SOUTHAMPTON DOCKS

British Railways

WAREHOUSES. Since the earliest days of dock development, warehouses have always been a help to traders. In modern docks some warehouses are built and operated by the dock authority itself. Others are built by the dock authority and leased, more or less permanently, to shipowners and forwarding agents.

In dock areas of extensive acreage, land is often available on which private warehouses may be erected, the constructors paying the dock company a ground rent for the use of the land. All these warehouses are of great commercial service. Goods for export can be sent down to the docks and stored to await a convenient ship. Manufacturers and merchants do not have to build such storage space at their own business headquarters. For import cargoes, warehouses fulfil a similar purpose: ships can be emptied straight away, reloaded, and dispatched without having to wait a long time until importers are able to come and withdraw their cargoes. Warehouses also assist trade by making possible the sampling of goods. Sampling or inspection orders, or delivery orders for small quantities, may be given to merchants possibly interested in buying the goods, and sampling and inspection can be done in the dock warehouses.

A special kind of warehouse is the bonded warehouse. This is licensed by the Board of CUSTOMS AND EXCISE (q.v. Vol. X) for the storage of imported goods that are subject to Customs duty. Importers of dutiable commodities, such as wines, spirits, and tobacco, may save much expense by storing their goods in a bonded warehouse until they withdraw them in small parcels on payment of duty.

See also Vol. IV: DOCKS.

WATERPROOFING. **1.** For countless centuries men of many nations have tried to protect themselves and their possessions either from falling rain or the general dampness of a climate. In particular, their clothes, their living-tents, and their ropes and fishing nets have been in danger of rotting away if they could not be guarded from wet. The skins of beasts have been used as outer garments (*see* CLOTHES, HISTORY OF, Vol. XI); the thickness and natural greasiness of sheep's wool will keep off rain, whether used as a garment or as the covering of a tent. In man's more advanced stages he has used hides and skins without their hair or wool, and has preserved them and made them fairly waterproof by CURRYING (q.v.). The leather jerkin of the Middle Ages was made in this way. But it has been more difficult to keep water out of TEXTILE FIBRES AND FABRICS (q.v.): woven and knitted materials, as well as ropes and cords.

2. CLOTHES. In modern times, clothes have been made more or less waterproof by coating them with rubber, by varnishing them, or by filling the tiny air-spaces between the threads with particles of various solid substances.

(*a*) Rubber-coating. Rubber is one of the most important of the natural GUMS AND RESINS (q.v.) used for waterproofing. The Spanish colonists who settled in South America in the 16th century found that the native Indians used rubber 'latex' (*see* RUBBER MANUFACTURE) for waterproofing their clothes. The Spaniards copied them, and it is recorded that in 1615 their soldiers in Mexico spread this 'tree-gum' over their capes to protect themselves from rain. The export trade in rubber-waterproofed garments may have begun when the King of Portugal was sent a suit of waterproof clothes from the province of Para, in what was then the Portuguese colony of Brazil. For a couple of centuries little could be done with rubber, because the gum became hard soon after it was taken from the tree; men did not know how to make it sufficiently fluid when it reached Europe, to enable them to coat their clothes with it. Many attempts were made to find suitable solvents, that is, spirits which would dissolve the rubber into a liquid solution, and which would then evaporate after the coating was done, leaving only a layer of rubber. At last, in 1819, success was achieved by Charles Macintosh, after whom the macintoshes we wear to-day are called. He used certain BY-PRODUCTS (q.v.) from coal tar to manufacture a rubber solution which dried to a sticky film when spread on a fabric. He overcame this stickiness by sandwiching the rubber between two layers of fabric. Later the method was made more practicable by kneading the rubber between rollers, a process known as 'mastication'. Because of this, the rubber could be more easily dissolved in the solvents and a thicker coating could be spread on the cloth.

Like natural rubber, these materials did not resist extremes of heat and cold, and tended to become sticky. But in 1839 the process of 'vulcanization' was discovered, which converts the raw rubber into a much more useful substance (*see* RUBBER MANUFACTURE). In course of time, the early heavy, cumbersome macintoshes gave place to lighter and better-looking garments, which would last for a long time.

Putting on the rubber, or 'rubberizing', takes place in several stages. Substances such as oil and grease are first removed from the fabric. The rubber is masticated and mixed with solvent, with the right amounts of sulphur (for vulcanization), colours, and other compounds. This solution is spread over the fabric in a thin even layer. Fresh layers continue to be spread until the right thickness has been built up. After each layer has been put on, the solvent is evaporated by passing the coated fabric over heated rollers. Double-texture material may be used, each fabric being rubber-coated separately, and the combination pressed together by the machines. Finally, the fabric is vulcanized or 'cured' by wrapping it tightly around a drum, and baking it in an oven under controlled heat. Some materials are 'cold cured'.

(*b*) Filling air-spaces. The method of waterproofing which consists of filling up the 'pores' of a fabric (the air-spaces between threads) with solid particles, to keep the rain from soaking in, is much used for raincoats or 'shower-proof' coats. The particles must be of a substance which will not dissolve in water, and they are inserted in the fabric by a simple chemical process. The fabric is first soaked in a chemical solution (generally aluminium acetate); then it is dried by heating. During the drying, the chemical changes into two substances: a compound whose solid particles remain in the fabric, and acetic acid which evaporates. Fabrics treated in this way are useful as light-duty waterproofs. They do not resist driving rain very well, and they tend to lose their waterproof property in course of time.

(*c*) Varnishing. This method of heavy-duty waterproofing is used for oilskins worn at sea and in severe tropical weather. The fabric, which may be cotton or silk, is first treated with a coating of starch. Then the varnish is put on in repeated coatings until it is thick enough; it contains plenty of drying-oil such as linseed oil, or preferably china-wood or tung oil (*see* PAINTS AND VARNISHES), and a small proportion of gum. Varnished cotton and silk cloths (sometimes called 'oiled') can be very flexible, and give good protection in severe rain. The normal colours are transparent yellowish-brown or opaque black, though opaque coloured materials are also widely made. The black varnished cloths are exceptionally good, because the varnish used contains a proportion of bituminous resin, which greatly increases their resistance to water and makes them last longer.

3. OTHER ARTICLES. Many articles besides clothing need waterproofing, including tents, groundsheets, tarpaulin sheets (for lashing across ships' hatches, over the tops of open lorries and railway wagons, and over goods stacked in the open), fishing nets and lines, all nets and cord for outdoor use, and especially ships' ropes and hawsers. The heavy fabric used in the manufacture of tarpaulins is treated with black varnish containing bituminous resin as described in (*c*) above. The varnish coating on tarpaulins needs to be very flexible, as they are continually being folded and pulled over the sharp corners of packing-cases or trucks.

For some purposes, plastic coatings have replaced oil varnish, but they have not yet shown the same hard-wearing qualities. The first of these to be used was nitrocellulose, to which castor oil and solvents were added. Fabric coated in this way is called LEATHER-CLOTH (q.v.). Another coating recently developed is polyvinyl chloride (P.V.C.) which is spread on to the fabric in paste form (*see* PLASTICS). In another process, the material to be waterproofed is first soaked in a solution of gelatine, glue, or size (all of which are of the same general nature) and then in a solution which will harden it. The second solution makes the gelatine insoluble in water and fixes it inside the structure of the fibre. The gelatine thus makes the fibre able to resist water. Chemicals such as alum, bichromate of potash, or formalin are used for hardening. Tents, sailcloth, awnings, and thick blankets are treated in this way. A similar process, using aluminium resinate instead of gelatine, is applied to yarns and canvas, particularly the canvas used for satchels and sports-bags.

Waxes, bitumens, and tars are used to waterproof such things as cordage, ropes, hawsers, fishing lines and nets, and sackings, especially when these things have to be used in water, or exposed to continuous rain, or have to stand in puddles or pools. These materials do not give a waterproof covering as rubber or varnish do to macintoshes and oilskins, but they fill up the spaces in the fibres and thus make them much more difficult to wet; if the fibres do get wet,

fermented liquor, but is distilled in a patent or Coffey still, invented by Aeneas Coffey over 100 years ago. The features of the patent still process are a continuous instead of intermittent operation, and the extraction of the alcohol from the fermented liquor by means of steam. The grain whisky made in the patent still is much lighter than the heavy malt whisky made in the pot still, with which it is blended.

Scotch whisky is an important item in Britain's export trade, especially as much of it is paid for in American dollars (*see* HARD CURRENCY). The flavour of whisky, like that of wine (*see* WINE TRADE), owes much to local soil and local materials, and attempts to imitate abroad the peculiar aroma and bouquet of Scotch whisky have not been successful.

See also INDUSTRIAL ALCOHOL.
See also Vol. XI: WINES AND SPIRITS; LIQUEURS.

WHOLESALE TRADING. A wholesaler is a shopkeeper who keeps a shop for the benefit of other shopkeepers who sell goods to the consumer by RETAIL TRADING (q.v.). An ordinary customer finds it convenient to deal with a few shops rather than with dozens of manufacturers; so does the retail shopkeeper. The word 'wholesaler' is used for firms dealing in widely used products and in branded or proprietary goods. The word 'warehouseman' is generally restricted to wholesale houses dealing in drapery, fashion goods, millinery, and haberdashery.

Wholesalers are a great convenience to the retail shopkeeper. By dealing with them, he can keep a smaller stock of goods in his shop than would otherwise be necessary—a great advantage in the case of commodities that are perishable or likely to lose their quality if kept too long. Also, wholesalers are usually large firms with a good deal of CAPITAL (q.v.); so they can grant extended CREDIT (q.v.) to the shopkeeper often long enough for him to be able to sell his goods and collect the cash for them before he has to pay for them himself.

Wholesalers are also of service to manufacturers. There is a good deal of competition in most manufacturing trades, and few manufacturers would be content to sit down in their factories and to wait for retail shopkeepers to call upon them: they would probably have to send out travelling REPRESENTATIVES (q.v.) to call on retail shopkeepers and to take their orders. This would mean a series of car or van journeys from most manufacturers to every shop in the country, and much overlapping and waste of transport in getting goods distributed. If manufacturers want to avoid making use of wholesalers, as some do, they must be prepared to organize their own wholesale departments, and it is not always true that an efficient manufacturer will be an equally efficient wholesaler.

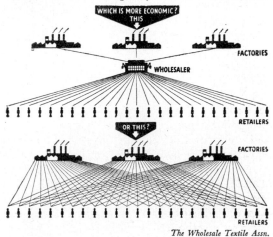

The Wholesale Textile Assn.

THE ADVANTAGES OF BUYING FROM WHOLESALERS

The main reason why most manufacturers avoid doing their own wholesaling is that they specialize in a single limited line of goods, and so the expense of organizing a force of travelling representatives to get orders from retailers is not worth while: travellers' calls are only profitable if they can obtain large orders for a selection of mixed goods.

Price policy and methods of trading differ in the various branches of the wholesale trade. Firms dealing in staple products such as iron and steel, building materials, grains, farmers' feeding-stuffs, and so on, usually add on to the producer's price an additional margin or 'mark up' which will cover expenses and leave them a satisfactory profit. Then from time to time they send to their retail customers price-lists, which are amended as manufacturers' prices alter. Warehousemen in the textile trade do the same thing. But wholesalers of branded or proprietary goods, of which cigarettes and tobacco are good examples, usually give the ordinary retail selling-prices in their catalogues, and allow their shopkeeper customers a trade discount which is comparatively low on small orders, but which rises with orders for larger quantities.

See also RETAIL TRADING.

WINDOW DRESSING, *see* ADVERTISING AND
PUBLICITY.

WINE TRADE. 1. CLASSIFICATION OF WINES.
Wine is the natural fermented juice of freshly
gathered grapes (*see* FERMENTATION, Vol. II),
and the only strictly manufacturing process is
the pressing out of the juice. Even this is not
mechanically done in some districts, where the
primitive system of pressing the grapes with the
feet still persists. The world trade in wines is
very ancient. Samian and Falernian wines are
mentioned frequently in Greek and Roman
classical literature: by the Roman poet, Horace,
for example. Those countries that have been
favoured by nature with the warm, dry, and
sunny climate that suits the grape have always
produced their own wines, and others not so
favoured have relied on importing it. In the
Middle Ages, England imported much wine
from France, as she does to-day, although in
those days the grape vine was often cultivated in
England in the sheltered walled gardens of
monasteries. From time immemorial the Mediterranean and adjoining countries have been
great producers of wine, and France, Portugal,
Spain, Algeria, Italy, Greece, and some of the
Balkan countries are still important. In more
recent years countries much farther afield have
become included in the list. Wine is now produced in large quantities in the State of Cali-

fornia in the U.S.A., in Chile and Argentina, in
Australia, and in the Union of South Africa.

Wines can be classified in many ways. There
is first the distinction between white and red,
and there are gradations of colour in between.
The varying colours of wine depend upon the
colours of the grape skins: white wines are made
from white grapes, and red wines from black.
There is next a distinction between still and
sparkling wines. Still wines are put into bottle
when the process of fermentation is complete and
when there are no longer bubbles of gas in the
wine. Sparkling wines can be made either
naturally or artificially. Those made naturally,
by what is called the 'champagne process', are
put into bottle while fermentation is still going
on. During fermentation carbon dioxide gas is
produced; and, if the wine is bottled before fermentation is complete, this gas becomes dissolved
in the wine. It is the gas that gives the wine its
sparkle. Fermentation after bottling produces
an undrinkable sediment, which must be removed before the wine is sold. This is done by
placing the bottles cork downwards in a refrigerator. The sediment drops down towards the
neck, and is frozen. The cork is then removed,
the frozen ice and sediment are forced out by the
pressure of the gas in the bottle, and the wine
is quickly recorked. Artificial sparkling wine
is made in the same way as mineral water:
carbon dioxide gas is introduced mechanically
into a bottle of still wine, which is then immediately corked.

All wines may be further classified as 'fine'
wines, 'beverage' wines, and 'dessert' wines.
Most of the fine wines of the world come from
famous estates, although a particularly good
season may accidentally produce a really fine
wine from quite an ordinary vineyard. The
quality of wines generally regarded as in the
highest class is not constant from year to year,
and a wine of a particularly good year is known
and identified by its year of growth. A good
year is called a vintage year, and a fine wine of
such a year a 'vintage' wine. Fine wines are
rare, and most of the wines produced in the
world are beverage wines of ordinary quality.
Wines drunk before or after a meal, such as the
ports and sherries, are generally classified as
dessert wines. These wines are strengthened
with spirit to increase the amount of alcohol in
them and to make them keep longer. For the
best dessert wines this fortifying spirit is brandy,

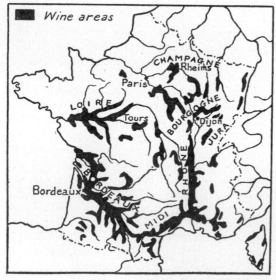

MAP OF FRANCE SHOWING THE WINE AREAS

MAKING WINE
16th-century engraving

which is itself distilled from wine. Another classification is into 'dry' and 'sweet'. With the exception of the dessert wines, most still wines are 'dry'. During fermentation practically all the grape sugar in the juice is converted into alcohol, and the wine therefore lacks any sweetish taste. The dessert wines, being fortified with brandy before fermentation is complete, are comparatively sweet.

2. WINES OF THE WORLD. France has been for centuries the leading wine country of the world. Of the French wine districts the most important are Champagne, Bordeaux, and Burgundy, which give their names to the wines that come from them (*see* Map). According to French law, no wine may be described as 'champagne' that does not come from the area which was once part of the old French province of Champagne. The principal towns are Rheims and Epernay, and all true champagne from this area is made by the process described. Sparkling wine made in France by any other than the true champagne process is called *vin mousseux*. Some very good wines made by the champagne process are made outside the Champagne district, notably in the valley of the River Loire at Saumur, and in the Vouvray district of Anjou, north-east of Tours. The country inland from Bordeaux, in the valley of the Gironde, is the home of the Bordeaux wines, or clarets. The ordinary beverage clarets are mostly transported and sold in cask and are bottled by merchants, but the finest wines are 'château-bottled'. The word *château* (literally 'castle') is applied in France to many of the more important country residences; in the wine trade the word is applied to any large estate where grape vines are grown and wine is made. The clarets fall into four main groups: Médoc, St. Emilion, Graves, and Sauternes. There are three sub-divisions of the Burgundy district. The most important is the Côte d'Or ('Golden Ridge') district, south-west of Dijon

Picture Post Library

PRESSING WINE IN A VILLAGE IN CENTRAL FRANCE

A traveller by road from Dijon to Le Creusot would pass through many villages that have wines named after them, such as Nuits St. Georges, Beaune, Pommard, and Volnay. South of the Côte d'Or is the country where the Beaujolais wines are grown; north-west of Dijon is the Chablis district. Some good sparkling burgundy is made by the champagne process in Nuits St. Georges and Beaune. Château Yquem, a sweet Sauternes, is perhaps the most renowned of the Bordeaux wines, and Clos de Vougeot of the burgundies. (The word *clos* means a walled or enclosed vineyard.) North-east of Bordeaux is the town of Cognac, which is the centre of a big vine-growing district, whose wines are chiefly distilled into the finest brandy.

Next to France, Germany is the largest European producer of table wines. German wines are classified as hocks or moselles. The hocks come from the Rhine valley around Coblenz, and the moselles from the valley of the Moselle between Trèves and Coblenz. Coblenz is therefore an important wine-making centre, although Mainz is the commercial headquarters of the German wine trade. Spain, Portugal, Greece, Italy, Cyprus, and Hungary produce a good deal of table wine, but, with the exception of Italian Chianti and Hungarian Tokay, little is sold on the British market.

Spain and Portugal have been for years the biggest exporters to Britain of her dessert wines. Sherry comes from the district around Jerez de la Frontera, in the south-west of Spain, which is the centre of the trade. By British law the word 'port' may not be applied to a wine unless it has been grown in Portugal and shipped from Oporto. Imitations of port are usually described as of 'port type'. The Canary Islands produce Madeira, which is a good dessert wine, and another dessert wine, Marsala, comes from Sicily. Wine grapes have been grown in Australia since the end of the 18th century, and the climate is well suited to them. There are few European wines that cannot be closely imitated in Australia, although in quality and aroma ('bouquet') they do not come up to those of Europe. There has been for a long time a big export trade from Australia to Britain in wines of the port and burgundy types. The vine was established in South Africa in the 17th century. The chief wine district in the Union to-day is in the Western Province, not far from Cape Town. The principal centres are Constantia, Stellenbosch, and Paarl. Most of the European types of wine are produced in these districts, some particularly good wines of the hock type coming from Paarl.

From the Middle Ages until comparatively recently there cannot be said to have been a British wine industry, and even now this industry does not make wine from home-grown grapes naturally fermented. The British wine industry, more truly a manufacturing industry than natural wine-making, was developed between the First and Second World Wars. Its raw material is unfermented grape juice imported from abroad. As grape juice will ferment naturally if left to itself, it has to be sterilized before it is shipped; on its arrival in Britain fermentation is started up artificially by the addition of sugar and yeast. Such wines, although quite palatable, do not possess the flavour and bouquet of natural wine, and indeed do not claim either.

See also Vol. XI: WINES AND SPIRITS.

WOOD, see TIMBER INDUSTRY; FURNITURE INDUSTRY; PLYWOOD AND VENEERS; WOODWORK, HISTORY OF; HARDWOODS; SOFTWOODS.

See also Vol. VI: TIMBER.

Picture Post Library

BOTTLING WINE WHICH HAS MATURED IN BARRELS

WOOD PULP. This is the most important material from which paper is made at the present time, and a variety of wood pulp is also used in the manufacture of RAYON and PLASTICS (qq.v.) and for EXPLOSIVES (q.v. Vol. VIII). It also forms part of many of the building boards used in modern building work.

Wood pulp is made from many different kinds of trees, most of them belonging to the coniferous group—spruce, pine, and balsam fir (*see* TREES, CONIFEROUS, Vol. VI)—which are found in northerly countries, especially in Canada, the U.S.A., Scandinavia, Germany, and Russia. Deciduous trees such as poplar and aspen are also used. Some trees may be 40 years old before they are cut for pulp. The mills in which the logs of wood are made into pulp are usually situated on rivers near the forests; and the logs are floated down the rivers to the mills and into large pools, where they are sorted (*see* LOGGING, Vol. VI). At the mills the logs are cut up into manageable lengths, the bark removed and used as boiler fuel, and the knots, which could make blemishes in the paper, taken out.

There are several kinds of wood pulp, made for different purposes. The simplest form is called 'mechanical wood', and this consists of coarse sawdust 'ground' from the logs, which are held against rough circular grindstones, revolving at a very high speed in water. The wet sawdust, or pulp, is then carried away from the grindstones by the water and passed over screens which take out any big lumps. The pulp is then put through a machine which thickens it by removing excess water, until it is thick enough to hold together, and cut off in 'laps'. Then, if it has to travel a long way to the paper-mill, the thick wet mass is made into bales and called 'moist mechanical wood pulp' or ground wood. This mechanical wood is not very durable; it soon loses its colour and in course of time breaks up. It is used principally in the making of NEWSPRINT (q.v.), wallpapers, and other cheap printing-papers which do not have to last a long time; all these papers tend to go yellow and, after some long period of exposure to air, to crumble away. The other pulps made from wood are all called 'chemical pulps', because they are treated with chemicals to remove everything from the wood except the cellulose fibres, which are felted into a pulp from which the paper is made. To make chemical pulp,

LOADING LOGS INTO THE GRINDER FOR PREPARING
MECHANICAL PULP

The moving belts on either side press the logs on to the
grindstones

MECHANICAL PULP BEING THICKENED READY TO BE MADE
INTO NEWSPRINT

the logs are more carefully stripped of bark, and
the knots more thoroughly removed, than for
mechanical pulp. The logs are then taken to a
chipping-machine which cuts them up into
small, regular-sized chips; these are blown into
large vertical digesters, or boilers, where they are
boiled with bisulphite of lime or other chemicals
to remove any resin, lignin, or other impurities
in the wood. These chemical pulps are known
as 'sulphite pulp' or 'soda pulp', according to
the chemicals used. The different types of pulps
are used to produce different types of paper.

If the pulps are required for white papers,
they are subsequently bleached by chlorine gas,
then treated with caustic soda, and finally
bleached with hypochlorite of lime, or other
chemicals, to bring them up to a good white
colour. Some of these pulps, however, are left
in their natural colour, and not bleached. These
are generally called 'strong pulps' if treated by
the sulphite process, or 'kraft pulps' if treated
by the soda or sulphate process.

Chemical pulps, whether bleached or not, are
carefully strained to remove lumps and big
pieces of badly broken-up fibre. They are then
passed on to a machine which works on the same
principles as an ordinary paper-machine, and
dried either in a vacuum drier or over cylinders,
in much the same way as paper is dried (see
PAPER-MAKING, Section 2). As the pulp comes
off the machine it is cut up into sheets, which are
then made up into bales weighing about four
hundredweight each. The pulp is then ready
for export.

Chemical pulps are used for a great variety of
papers. Strong sulphite pulp forms about 15%
of the wood pulp used in the manufacture of
newsprint; it is also used for wrapping-paper,
envelope papers, and other strong papers.
Bleached sulphite pulp is used for fine writing-
papers, typewriting-papers, and (together with
esparto grass) for printing-papers and papers for
illustrated magazines. Brown kraft pulp is used
for strong, brown wrapping-papers, and bleached
kraft pulp is also used for a variety of papers,
including fine tissues. The pulp mostly used
for the manufacture of rayon and plastics, and
also for explosives, is the bleached sulphite pulp.

See also PAPER-MAKING; NEWSPRINT.

WOODWORK, HISTORY OF. From earliest
times men have turned to wood for making the
things they needed in the everyday business of

Bowaters

MAKING SULPHITE PULP IN A 'DIGESTER' IN WHICH WOOD
CHIPS ARE BOILED WITH CHEMICALS

The pulp is blown out of the valves at the bottom

Bowaters

SULPHITE PULP COMING OFF THE THICKENING MACHINE
BEFORE BEING DRIED

living. There was a plentiful supply of it in the forests; it was one of the most easily worked materials, being softer than stone or iron; and it was strong and lasting enough for most purposes.

No very early woodwork remains, for wood cannot, like stone, resist exposure for an unlimited time. Of British woodwork, little remains that is earlier than the 14th century, and there is not very much of that; but it is clear that in the Middle Ages carpentry was a highly developed trade, and the uses and drawbacks of wood were well understood (*see* CARPENTRY AND JOINERY). Much of what has survived is in churches and cathedrals, for in houses there was a greater risk of fire, or of dispersal when the owner died. In the early Middle Ages the technique of woodwork, like that of all crafts, was fostered in the monasteries. But, as the towns grew, woodworkers set up their shops, and their craft was organized by their CRAFT GUILD (q.v.). For the most part, what they made was structural: that is, it was an essential part of the building, such as the main framework, the roof, staircase, and so on.

The woodworker considered the essential structural importance of his work first; if it lent itself to decoration, he would then enrich it with carving, or later with inlay (*see* INLAY AND MARQUETRY). Because of this, the decoration was always appropriate, and served to emphasize the beauties of the structure. Later on, men came to regard the decorative features as of more importance, and sometimes adapted the construction to suit them. For instance, in true half-timbered buildings the beams are an essential part of the structure; but almost all the imitation 'beams' decorating modern half-timbered houses could be removed without affecting the stability of the house in the slightest degree.

The nature of wood greatly affects the design and structure of woodwork. It is a natural growth and a splendid ready-made material, so long as it is used with some thought for the way it has grown. It is not like metal or plastics, which can be worked or moulded into any shape that may be needed. Wood has to be used as it is; the most the woodworker can do is to cut it into smaller sizes or to join bits together. There is a limit to the length of individual pieces of timber that can be used; this limit is fixed by the average height of trees, while the width is fixed by the girth of a tree trunk.

Another point is that as wood 'seasons' or dries out, it shrinks across the grain, but remains much the same in length. This is most important, because it means that to make a piece of work strong in both length and width, it must be constructed so that the grain runs both ways. Early craftsmen got over the difficulty in an ingenious way. They evolved what is known as the 'frame and panel' system, in which the strength was provided by the framework, the panels being little more than a filling. The members of the framework were fixed together with strong joints, and grooves were cut round the inner edges to house the panels. So the panels could shrink along the grooves without affecting the over-all size of the work. Nothing can stop wood from shrinking, and, if it is fixed rigidly across its grain to an immovable groundwork, it will either split or else distort the groundwork. The frame-and-panel system avoids both drawbacks, and was the basis of woodwork design for centuries. It is only within the past few years that the use of plywood, which shrinks neither in length nor width, has enabled a new method of construction to be worked out (*see* PLYWOOD AND VENEERS).

The width to which wood panels can conveniently be cut is obviously limited by the girth of trees; in early years, therefore, panels were made in comparatively small sizes, no wider than could be cut from average logs. Thus we find that a feature of early panelling is the small size of the panels. Later, when glue came to be used, craftsmen learned to join boards together, and then the size of the panels increased.

A woodworker's life in the old days was a hard one; everything had to be done by hand, with such comparatively crude tools as the smith could make. After the felling of the tree, the log had to be sawn into beams or boards with a two-man saw. This was several feet long, with a handle at each end, and was used upright. The log was laid across a strong framework or over a pit. One man, the 'top-sawyer', stood on the log and worked the top handle. His duty was to guide the saw accurately along the line to be cut. The other man was in the pit below, and he simply supplied additional energy, and by pulling strongly downward prevented the saw from buckling. (The remains of an old saw-pit can sometimes be found in the woods to-day.) It was a laborious procedure; but there was no other way, except for some woods like oak, which could be riven or split. To do this, wedges were driven into the log at end and sides, causing the log to split open. This had the advantage (apart from being quicker) of splitting the wood exactly along the grain, so that the planks would be stronger than sawn boards. On the other hand, they were seldom straight, because the grain of a tree undulates along its length. This accounts for the irregularity of much old woodwork.

To trim the work after being riven or sawn, the adze was used. This is rather like an axe, but has the cutting edge running at right angles to the shaft, instead of in line. It is a tool still much used in a yacht and boat-builder's yard.

16TH-CENTURY PANELLING AT HATFIELD HOUSE (LEFT) AND 18TH-CENTURY PANELLING IN CLARE COLLEGE HALL, CAMBRIDGE
The earlier panels are much smaller than the later ones

THE HOUSE AT STRATFORD-ON-AVON IN WHICH SHAKESPEARE WAS BORN
The beams have been shaped with an adze

The craftsman stood astride the wood and swung the adze downwards and towards his feet, removing the wood in chips. This produced a series of facets which made the surface approxi-

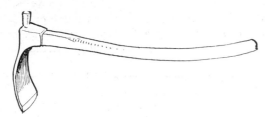

AN ADZE

mately true and smooth. The craftsmen became extremely skilful in its use, and could make an uneven piece of wood extraordinarily true. Adzed work has a characteristic and rather pleasant finish, the slightly undulating facets catching the light at each mark of the tool.

Old illuminated manuscripts and carvings tell us much about the tools men used in early days. Chisels and gouges date from earliest times and, except for being comparatively crude, were much like those in use to-day. The plane, too, has an ancient history. Naturally, all wooden tools from so early a date have long since perished, but a metal plane of Roman origin is still in existence. Boring tools, squares for testing wood, and hammers, must all have been in daily use, and their general construction scarcely varied until machines became general in the 19th century. Gradually more tools were invented, such as the LATHE (q.v. Vol. VIII), on which chair legs and other round parts could be turned. Nowadays, most of the processes—from sawing tree-trunks into planks to polishing the surface of the wood—can be, and are, done by power-driven machinery (see WOODWORKING MACHINERY, Vol. VIII).

Just as in early times woodwork developed as a separate craft, so later the craft of woodworker

Tate Gallery

CHRIST IN THE HOUSE OF HIS PARENTS

Painting by Sir John E. Millais, 1829-96. The painter made studies of an English carpenter's shop for the background

began to separate into sub-crafts. The carpenter was the man responsible for the structural woodwork in houses; the fittings, such as doors and window-frames, were made by the joiner (*see* CARPENTRY AND JOINERY). The joiner was so called because he 'joined' pieces of wood together to make, say, one long table top, replacing the loose planks previously used. The cabinet-maker —the man who made furniture—began to work separately at his trade during the second half of the 17th century (*see* CABINET-MAKING). There is little doubt that other woodworking trades had also become detached by this time: for instance, that of the wheelwright and wagon-builder, and that of the cooper or barrel-maker. In the villages, the carpenter probably was still prepared to tackle all things in wood; but in the towns, where there was scope for it, the separate trades developed.

The splitting-up of trades, or DIVISION OF LABOUR (q.v.), has continued right up to the present time—indeed, at no earlier time has there been so much specialization. The all-round carpenter often does little more than assemble or fit work that other men have made. One firm makes nothing but doors, while another produces only window-frames. The same story is true of practically every branch of woodwork. In one respect this leads to efficiency, for one man can install all the plant he needs for his own special trade; but it robs the general woodworker of a lot of experience.

It was during the 19th century that machines began to be widely used, and their development has had an immense effect on the woodworking craftsman. To-day one of the most highly skilled woodworkers is the machinist: though even here there is frequently a further subdivision, each man specializing in using one particular kind of machine.

The old-time craftsman with his huge chest of tools who made everything by hand is gone; many a woodworker to-day can go to his job carrying everything he needs in a small attaché case. A few craftsmen carry on the old tradition; and the amateur who learns to love wood and use his tools well can do much valuable carpentry in his home, as well as make furniture worthy of the fine tradition of British craftsmanship in wood.

See also CARPENTRY AND JOINERY; CABINET-MAKING; FURNITURE INDUSTRY; TIMBER INDUSTRY.
See also Vol. XI: FURNITURE, HISTORY OF.

WOOL INDUSTRY, MEDIEVAL. 1. England was the great wool-producing country of the Middle Ages, and English wool was looked upon as better than any other. The fact that the Lord Chancellor sits on the Woolsack in the House of Lords is a symbol of England's early dependence on wool for her riches and commercial prosperity.

The wool trade connected England with the Continent. The wool-growing areas of Wiltshire and the Cotswolds were linked up with the cloth-producing region of the Low Countries on the other side of the Channel. English sheep supplied about four-fifths of the money value of all English exports. The Netherlands was by far the most important market in English foreign trade, and its importance led to the setting up of the selling organization called the 'Staple' (*see* MERCHANTS OF THE STAPLE), in the interests partly of the merchants' convenience, and partly of royal finance. For it was not only the wool merchants who had a special interest in their business. The Government also had a direct interest in the trade. It was a useful lever in diplomatic negotiations, and produced valuable customs duties which formed a large part of the revenue.

There were many types of English sheep in the Middle Ages, all different from the breeds of to-day. The best wool came from Shropshire and Herefordshire, especially the famous 'Lemster Ore' of the Leominster district, the Golden Fleece of England. Next in value came the high-priced wool of Lincolnshire and the Cotswolds (*see* SHEEP, Vol. VI).

Sheep-farming was in the hands both of large landowners and of small tenant farmers. Many of the monasteries owned large sheep farms, which were the biggest economic units of the Middle Ages. At the time of Domesday Book, Ely Abbey had 13,400 sheep on its estates, spread over six counties. There was a further growth in the size of stock holdings in the 12th and 13th centuries, and on the Bishop of Winchester's estate there were about 29,000 sheep in the 13th century. Large-scale production slackened off in the 14th and 15th centuries, and sheep-farming passed into the hands of the tenant farmers. This was the age of the small man, who sold his wool to a middleman dealer.

The story of English sheep farming is buried in a mass of local records, but it is still possible to catch a glimpse from them of the romance of wool production. Shakespeare writes in *The Winter's Tale* of the sheep-shearing feast which always ended the successful sale of the 'clip'. The SHEPHERD (q.v. Vol. VI) was a most important person, and many rules were laid down as to how he should look after his sheep. 'It is a token of the shepherd's kindness if the sheep be not scattered abroad but browse around him in company. Let him provide himself with a barkable dog and lie nightly with his sheep.'

Home-produced wool got into the hands of the merchants in two different ways. The wool that was produced by the big landowners was usually sold direct to an export merchant. The exporter or his agent would ride round to the monasteries or big houses, look at the fleeces as they grew, and contract to buy the clip in advance. The wool of the small man went through a more complicated process of collection. Sometimes agents

British Museum

MEDIEVAL WOMEN PREPARING WOOL FOR WEAVING
In the foreground the wool is being combed (right), carded, and spun; at the back the warp is being put into the loom. 14th-century illumination (*Roy. MS. 16 G.v. f. 56*)

G. C. Mills

FAIRFORD CHURCH, GLOUCESTERSHIRE, BUILT 1490–1500
BY THE CLOTH MERCHANT, JOHN TAME

—wool gatherers—would go around gathering it together. At other times the big landowners would deal with it. Eventually middlemen grew up in the industry, collecting wool and then selling it to exporters for the international markets. As wool production by small farmers grew in relative importance in the 15th century, these middlemen or woolmen became as rich as the export merchants themselves. The greatest of them lived in the Cotswolds, the chief wool centre at this time. The village of Northleach, on the top of the wolds, was a celebrated centre of the trade, as we can still tell from its impressive church and the brasses of its wool men. Some of the wool men acknowledged their indebtedness to the sheep for the whole of their riches:

'I praise God and ever shall
It is the sheep hath paid for all.'

Some of the middlemen lived not in the Cotswolds, but in London. They would sometimes buy the wool from the Cotswolds' wool men and sell it to the clothmakers or exporters. They would buy the wool by samples, and thus a great deal of responsibility fell on to the shoulders of the wool-packer, who was also the valuer of the wool: he had to mark each sample with its place

of origin, and to grade it either as good or as middle-quality wool. The welfare of the wool trade depended upon the wool-packers, just as the care of the sheep depended upon the shepherds. The work of the middlemen would have been impossible if it had not been for this careful grading and valuation of the clips.

At first the export of wool was in the hands of foreigners—Italians, Germans, and Flemings. Later (from the 13th century onwards) it was in the hands of the MERCHANTS OF THE STAPLE (q.v.). From 1363 the Staple was centred in Calais, which at that time was in the hands of the British, and was a good gateway to the Low Countries and to the manufacturing districts of France.

The wool was carried by pack-horses from the shearing centres to the ports, divided among several ships to cut down risk of loss, and safely deposited in Calais, where it was examined by representatives of the Staplers. We can build up a clear picture of the organization of the medieval wool industry from a collection of letters and papers which still survives and which belonged to a firm of wool merchants, Cely and Sons. They were London merchants with offices both in London and in Calais. They dealt largely in Cotswold wool, and young Richard Cely, the son who did the buying in London, would ride down frequently from London to Gloucestershire to select Cotswold wool to ship to his brother in Calais. Most of the dealings of the Celys were carried out on CREDIT (q.v.); indeed, this applied to the wool trade as a whole. Wool dealers in the Cotswolds would buy on credit from the sheep farmer; the Celys in London would buy on credit from the dealers; and Dutch and Flemish customers in Calais would buy on credit from the Celys. BILLS OF EXCHANGE (q.v.) would be given for the debts incurred, and an all-round settlement would be made when the Celys collected their money 6 months after they had sold the wool at one of the great fairs in the Low Countries. They would transmit the money back to England—they did not try to buy goods overseas with it—and after that the various other debts would be paid. This highly organized trade shows that the trade of the Middle Ages was not merely a matter of local production. Wool was a truly international industry, and commercial contacts were many and wide.

2. CLOTH MANUFACTURE. Towards the end of this period, cloth began to take the place of raw wool as England's most important export. Cloth manufacture grew up in certain specialized industrial districts. About half the woollens were made in the West Country: that is, mainly in Gloucestershire, Wiltshire, and Somerset. The best broad-cloth for export was made in Wiltshire. Another branch of the wool industry was in East Anglia. In the Norfolk village of Worstead a new sort of manufacture grew up, which finally took over for itself the name of the village. It used long-fibred wool, and made a smooth and very durable cloth which is now chiefly associated with Yorkshire (see WOOL SPINNING, Section 3). At the end of the Middle Ages the West Riding of Yorkshire was beginning to be a rising centre of manufactures, with industry spreading up the dales as far as Kendal in Westmorland.

The organization of the cloth industry differed from place to place. In some places there were small local craftsmen working at home. In other places great 'clothiers', as they were called, put out raw materials to be spun by cottagers, and then collected the finished work. There were many important families—for example those founded by John Tame of Fairford, and Thomas Spring of Lavenham—which prospered by providing raw materials for others to manufacture (see DOMESTIC SYSTEM).

Exports of English cloth became of great importance during the 15th century. As early as 1265, English cloths, known as 'Stamfords', were being imported into Venice, but it was not until the 15th century that cloth exports began to challenge wool exports in weight and value. In the early 15th century, nearly half the English export trade in cloth was in the hands of foreigners, about a fifth of it being in the hands of the German HANSEATIC

National Buildings Record

CARVINGS ON A BUTTRESS OF A CHAPEL IN CULLOMPTON CHURCH, DEVON, BUILT IN 1526 BY THOMAS LANE, WOOLSTAPLER

Above, a ship symbolizes the export of wool and below are shears for cutting cloth

LEAGUE (q.v.). Later on in the century the share of cloth exported by the English Company of MERCHANT ADVENTURERS (q.v.) greatly increased; but there was a long struggle between the rival groups, which did not end in favour of the Adventurers until the early 17th century.

Most of the national economic policy in the Middle Ages was bound up with the wool industry. It far outstripped all other trades in importance. Wool was important first of all as a source of TAXATION (q.v. Vol. X). The wool tax was one of the chief sources of the royal revenue at the end of the 13th century. Many of the struggles between king and merchants revolved round the problem of the tax, and it was not until the middle of the 14th century that a compromise was reached: the king was left in possession of a high subsidy on wool; Parliament was left in control of taxation—a most important privilege; and the wool exporting company, the Merchants of the Staple, was left with what was to all intents and purposes a MONOPOLY (q.v.) of raw wool export.

There were attempts also to work out a national policy to deal not only with wool but also with cloth. As early as 1258, Parliament prohibited the export of raw wool. But the policy of stimulating the native clothing industry had few results at this time, and indeed the industry showed signs of decay in the early 14th century. Edward II made real attempts to revive it, and Edward III offered even greater protection, encouraging many cloth-workers to come to England from overseas; and these brought new life to the industry. Later, Henry VII and Henry VIII did much to encourage the cloth industry and to discourage the export of raw wool; and the most important figures in the English wool industry at the

4852 7

end of the Middle Ages were not the wool dealers but the great clothiers.

History is written in stones as well as in books, and this is particularly true of the wool trade. Some of the most impressive parish churches in England are those of the wool towns, such as Lavenham in Suffolk, Boston in Lincolnshire, and Rotherham in Yorkshire. The south aisle of Cullompton Church in Devon, at the edge of the sheep-rearing country, is decorated with carvings of the instruments used in the wool trade. The church at Cirencester in Gloucestershire has a three-storeyed south porch, in whose upper rooms the CRAFT GUILDS (q.v.) used to hold their meetings. John Tame built a magnificent church at Fairford. Defoe has written that the Cathedral at Salisbury—the town of the famous 'Salisbury Whites'—was believed to rest on a foundation of woolpacks.

Such monuments in stone are testimonials to the wealth of the dealers in wool and the makers of cloth, but they show also that business in the Middle Ages was not entirely a matter of self-advancement.

See also WOOL SPINNING; WOOL WEAVING.
See also Vol. VI: SHEEP.

WOOL INDUSTRY, MODERN. 1. RAW MATERIALS.

In the modern wool trade, there are three main types of wool: merino, crossbred, and carpet. Merino is fine, crossbred is medium, and carpet is coarse; the first two are grown mainly for clothing. Nearly 4,000 million lb. of wool are produced in the world every year, and of this about 35% is merino, 45% crossbred, and 20% carpet wool. Australia alone provides over 1,000 million lb.: a large proportion of all the merino wool grown in the world. New Zealand, by contrast, is the largest grower of crossbred wools, while the biggest growers of carpet wools are the U.S.S.R., India, and Pakistan.

The chief properties that make wool so generally useful are strength, durability, and elasticity. Other properties are its low inflammability and its capacity to absorb moisture. A single fibre of wool is as strong as a thread of gold of the same thickness. Wool fibres can be bent repeatedly without breaking—an important property when we consider how often we bend our knees or elbows during the life-time of a wool garment. A wool fibre will return to its original length after being stretched almost double; wool clothing, therefore, crushes less easily than other fabrics, and soon recovers its original shape and appearance. Wool does not easily burn; if it does catch fire it tends merely to smoulder, and then to go out. The capacity of wool to absorb moisture is important to health. Dry wool will absorb water vapour equal to half its own weight; the moisture is absorbed into the actual structure of the fibre, and does not cause the garment to feel wet. While absorbing moisture, the wool fibres generate heat, and the moisture that is absorbed is given off again only very slowly. These properties make wool clothing useful in preventing chills. A good deal of air is also held in the spaces of wool fabrics; this acts as an insulator, and so wool clothing feels warm in cold or damp weather and cool in hot weather.

Chemically, wool is a protein, consisting of carbon 50%, oxygen 22%–25%, nitrogen 16%–17%, hydrogen 7%, and sulphur 3%–4%. Treatment of wool with appropriate chemicals has led to many important developments. Thus, by treatment with chlorine, or with an enzyme or ferment called 'papain'—obtained from the tropical paw-paw tree—the scales covering the wool fibre may be smoothed down, and the wool prevented from matting or 'felting'. Since felting is the main cause of shrinking, unshrinkable socks and other woollens can now be made.

2. MARKETING. Each of the three main types of wool can be distinguished from the others by many subtle differences, such as differences in fineness and length of 'staple', or fibres. For accuracy in commercial dealings, these three types are given quality numbers in the trade, on a scale ranging from about 20 to over 100—the finer the wool fibre, the higher the number, and (generally speaking) the dearer the price. In the following table the widths of the fibres are given in microns (1 micron = 0·001 millimetres), because this unit of measurement better emphasizes the differences in their widths.

Wool	Average width of fibre (microns)	Length range (inches)	Quality number
Merino	19	0·5–5	60s–100s (called sixties and hundreds)
Crossbred	28	2·5– 6	36s–58s
Carpet	41	5 –17	22s–34s

The value of raw wool also depends not only on fineness and length of fibre but also on 'yield'—in other words, on the percentage of

AN AUSTRALIAN WOOL AUCTION

Fox Photos

clean wool remaining after the raw wool has been washed free from grease and dirt. Raw wool may contain from 25% to 70% of natural grease and other impurities, and for this reason its trade name is 'greasy wool' or 'wool in the grease'.

The raw wool is taken from the sheep farms to the nearest big port or other large city, where it is generally sold by Auction (q.v.). As the wool in each bale has been carefully classed at the farm by an expert, the buyers bid for the wool after having inspected samples only. In the old days a bale offered in the auction room did not always match the sample; sometimes it contained not only wool, but also horseshoes, bricks, stones, and sand to make up the weight.

A big problem of the modern wool industry is fluctuation in raw wool prices. The supply of wool is relatively steady; so changes in the demand for it, which are frequent and often violent, are the main cause of price changes, which are sometimes spectacular, even over short periods. These ups and downs in demand, and hence in price, are due largely to general economic changes in the world of industry and commerce, demand naturally being high in good times and low in periods of depression and unemployment (*see* Trade Cycle). The demand for wool, and therefore its price, are also much affected by changes in fashion and in the public taste.

Prices have also altered considerably over longer periods, as a result of changes in the purchasing power of money. As many as 300 British sheep sold in 1762 for as little as £17; earlier still, in the 17th century, van Riebeck, the founder of Cape Town, was able to buy a sheep from the Hottentots for a plug of tobacco or a piece of copper wire about as long as a sheep.

3. Production. The wool industry in Britain is organized in several separate and distinct sections, each producing a different kind of wool fabric. (*a*) What is called the woollen industry produces fabrics such as blankets and thick socks that are woven from fuzzy yarns (wool threads) the fibres of which are spun in a higgledy-piggledy fashion. (*b*) The worsted industry makes smooth cloth, much used for suitings,

Crown Copyright reserved

WOOL CARDING (LEFT), DRAWING (RIGHT), AND ROVING (BACK) IN 1835
Engraving in the Science Museum, London

from selected smoother yarns, the fibres of which lie parallel to one another (*see* WOOL SPINNING, Section 3). (*c*) The knitting industry makes fabrics from one continuous yarn (which may be either woollen or worsted) as distinct from the warp and weft threads from which woven materials are made. (*d*) In the carpet industry the yarns are woven so that they project on one side of a backcloth (*see* CARPET-MAKING). (*e*) In the FELT industry (q.v.) the wool fibres are intermingled at random and compressed into a thick sheet.

All these great branches of the wool industry began as home crafts during the period of the DOMESTIC SYSTEM (q.v.). Under the influence of the inventions of the INDUSTRIAL REVOLUTION (q.v.) they became mechanized and transferred to factories. The factory system now dominates the wool industry of Britain, although there is still a considerable production of homespun and hand-woven materials in the remoter districts.

In the 18th century, when conditions were favourable, a brilliant series of technical inventions transformed British life and British industry. Although these inventions could be applied to

both cotton and wool, almost all of them were first taken up for cotton-making. For this industry, based on raw cotton imported from American plantations, was entirely new; and, having no ancient traditions to draw upon, it readily adopted the new machinery. The wool industry, on the other hand, based on long-established methods, was less willing to try new ideas.

The first of the great new inventions was the flying shuttle, which John Kay patented in 1733. This is a small appliance, containing a bobbin of thread, which moves backwards and forwards in the loom, carrying the thread with it (*see* WOOL WEAVING). The flying shuttle (used first in wool and not in cotton) enabled one person to operate a broad loom, where previously one man had been needed to throw the shuttle from one side of the loom to the other, and another to throw it back again. In 1769 Richard Arkwright improved on earlier ideas and invented the water-frame method of spinning. The water-frame got its name because it was worked by water-power (a water-mill with a wheel turned by the flow of a stream). Its basic

A MULE SPINNING FACTORY IN 1835

The mule on the right is extended and that on the left is drawn back. Children who had to sweep the floor were in danger from the moving parts. Engraving in the Science Museum, London

idea was to draw out the wool, through sets of rollers, into a strand ready for spinning. Six years later Arkwright invented his 'carding machine' of revolving spiked cylinders, for unravelling the tangles in raw wool (see WOOL SPINNING, Section 2).

Other inventors were working on spinning methods at the same time. James Hargreaves had invented his famous spinning-jenny about 1764. This was a wheeled device which enabled one person to spin several threads at once. It was a much lighter apparatus than Arkwright's, did not need power, and could be operated at home; but it was suitable only for soft yarns.

By 1780 Samuel Crompton had designed a machine (the 'mule') which combined the ideas of the water-frame and the jenny, and took the place of both. Woollen yarns are still spun to-day on an improved form of mule.

In 5 years Edmund Cartwright, a country clergyman, had invented the power-loom, first worked by oxen. Later it was worked by steam, for James Watt had discovered in 1781 how to use a steam-engine to produce circular motion

(see STEAM-ENGINE, HISTORY OF, Vol. VIII). Later, Cartwright invented a combing-machine, by which the best fibres are picked out and smoothed to make worsted.

4. LOCALIZATION OF THE INDUSTRY. All these earlier inventions, which reduced for a time the demand for labour, were fiercely opposed by the workers. Trouble began with blows and violent demonstrations, and went on to the burning and smashing of machinery and the LUDDITE riots (q.v.). But the growth of the power-driven machine and of the factory system was inevitable, and in consequence the greater part of the wool industry tended to gather in the West Riding of Yorkshire. There were exceptions, however; knitted goods were made more and more in Nottingham and Leicester; and the industries of the West Country and the Tweed valley, though continuing where they were, reduced their output and began to specialize in high-quality goods only. The East Anglian wool industry, which had given birth to British worsteds, disappeared altogether.

The population of the West Riding more than

SORTING RAW WOOL INTO ITS DIFFERENT QUALITIES

doubled between 1801 and 1851. A keen competitive spirit was aroused in Yorkshire manufacturers by the vigorous new cotton industry in Lancashire. The Yorkshiremen had the foresight to produce high-quality goods, for which the markets were expanding, instead of the poorer stuffs for which the West Riding had been previously known. Finally, Yorkshiremen were helped by the existence, almost on their doorsteps, of the necessary coal for power, and of the soft water needed for washing and dyeing. To-day, over nine-tenths of the worsted, and two-thirds of the woollen industry of Britain, are still located in the West Riding.

By 1850, as the result of the modern tendency to specialize, Dewsbury, for example, had ten times as many people employed in woollens as in worsteds, whereas Keighley was almost entirely given over to worsted. These differences persisted as time went on. To-day such places as Dewsbury, Batley, and Morley are woollen towns; Keighley, Halifax, and Huddersfield are famous for worsteds, the last town also for fine woollens. Bradford—the centre of the British wool trade—is mainly concerned with wool commerce, combing (to make worsted yarns), and dyeing and finishing. With the help of skilled immigrants from eastern and central Europe, Leeds has become one of the most important centres for making up wool cloth into clothing. In general, worsted manufacture is located to the west and north, woollen to the east and south of the West Riding. There has been no clear-cut division into spinning and weaving districts, but rather into woollen areas and worsted areas.

The woollen mills are mostly organized on the 'vertical' system: that is, all stages of manufacture, from the raw wool to the finished cloth, are carried out by the same firm. The worsted industry is organized on the 'horizontal' system, that is, the various stages of manufacture are divided amongst a number of separate and specialized firms. One firm will convert the raw wool into 'top' by combing out the short fibres; a firm of spinners will convert the top into yarn; another will weave the yarn into cloth; while dyeing and finishing the cloth may be carried out by a fourth firm.

But Yorkshire does not stand alone. The West of England also has an important woollen industry, producing specialities of high quality such as billiard-cloths, blankets, flannels, hunting cloths, serges, and overcoatings. Another important woollen area is the Border country of Scotland, where Galashiels, Selkirk, and Hawick produce tweeds. In the far North (from the islands of Harris and Lewis, and other parts of north-east Scotland, as far as Shetland), world-famous tweeds and homespuns are made. Ireland produces Irish tweeds and other special cloths, mostly woollen. Felts are produced at such places as Bury, Denton, Hyde, and Stockport in the north-west of England, and Luton and London in the south. The North Midland centres, which have coal and soft water, produce chiefly knitwear. In this area Leicester, Loughborough, and Nottingham are very important, but there are also mills in Cheshire and Derbyshire. Kidderminster, which is noted for carpets, is probably the only English survival of the formerly prosperous Midland wool industries of the Severn Valley. Kilmarnock and Halifax also make carpets, and other pile fabrics such as plush.

See also Wool Industry, Medieval; Wool Spinning; Wool Weaving.

WOOL SPINNING.

1. Raw wool, straight from the sheep's back, is not a good material to make into clothing. It is dirty, greasy, lumpy, and matted, and it must go through several processes before it can be woven into fabric. It must be cleaned; opened out, so as to get rid of the lumps as far as possible; pulled or drawn out into thin strands; and the strands must then be twisted so as to bind the wool fibres together in a regular fashion, rather like the strands of a rope. At the end of all these processes the wool becomes yarn, and the drawing out and twisting processes are known as spinning. Yarns, once made, can be knitted or woven to make the various garments and materials that we are familiar with.

Wool in the raw state is not only dirty and lumpy, but it is not all of the same length and fineness and colour. It must first be sorted, according to the purpose for which it is to be used. Next it must be cleaned, and this is done in much the same way as a housewife's weekly wash: with soap and water and a little washing soda. In the factories the wool is passed through several tanks of warm, soapy water, and finally it is rinsed in clean water, a process called 'scouring'. The clean wool, still lumpy, is then dried.

Although scouring removes all grease and dirt, some vegetable matter, such as seeds and burrs, may still remain in the wool. These must be removed, either by a weak solution of sulphuric acid which is harmless to the wool but reduces the impurities to dust, or by crushing them

mechanically into a fine powder. Whichever process is used, the dust remaining is automatically shaken out afterwards.

Valuable By-products (q.v.) are obtained from the spent fluids (known as 'liquors') left after the scouring of wool. The most important of these is lanolin, which is used in the manufacture of such diverse things as adhesive plasters, disinfectants, cosmetics, polishes, inks, rust preventatives, veterinary preparations, emulsions, and soaps.

2. Carding. Wool fibres in the raw state are tangled together, and the loops have to be teased out by tugging at them. This is known as 'carding'. A carding-engine is a sort of mangle, with several pairs of rollers of different sizes, instead of a single pair. Unlike the smooth rollers of an ordinary mangle, those of the carding-engine are covered with short, thin, wire spikes, rather like the bristles of a hair-brush. The lumpy washed wool goes through these rollers just as washing goes through a mangle. All the fibres of the wool are pulled apart by the wire spikes, and the lumps largely disappear. In the early days carding was done by hand. One

Fox Photos

SPINNING WOOL ON A SPINNING-WHEEL

The wheel, which is turned by a foot pedal, turns the spindle on which the wool is wound. This twists the wool as it winds it

can make a hand-card by shaping a flat, square piece of wood with a handle, like a hair-brush, and studding it with fine nails, the points all sticking out on the same side. If one took two cards of this kind, one in each hand, placed some wool between them, and stroked the cards away from each other, the wool would gradually become carded.

The carding delivers the material as a belt or veil of fluffy wool, almost ready to be spun into yarn (compare picture, p. 138).

3. COMBING. There are two basic types of yarn in the wool industry: woollen yarn and

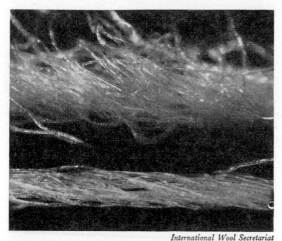

International Wool Secretariat

PHOTOMICROGRAPHS OF WOOLLEN (TOP) AND WORSTED
YARNS

worsted yarn. The difference between the two is easily seen if the two yarns are inspected under the microscope. In woollen yarn, the individual wool fibres are thoroughly intermingled and lie more or less higgledy-piggledy. In worsted yarn the individual fibres have been combed straight and made to lie roughly parallel to each other. The difference between the yarns can be seen with the naked eye. For some wool garments the fluffiness and fuzziness of woollen yarn are desirable; for others, the smoothness of worsted yarn is essential. Worsted yarn goes to make the smooth even cloths from which men's finer suitings are made up. Smoothness in such materials is considered so essential that the cloths, when woven, are often cropped or mown in much the same way as the grass on a lawn, in order to shear off the tiny ends of fibres that the worsted spinning process cannot entirely eliminate (*see* WOOL WEAVING). Worsted yarn was first made

at Worstead in Norfolk, from which it gets its name.

As far as the carding process, both woollen and worsted yarns are made in the same way. After carding all the wool fibres are still lying in a rather irregular way, and there are a lot of short, broken fibres mixed up with the long ones. To make worsted yarn, these irregularities must be smoothed out, and the best and longest fibres chosen, all more or less of a standard length. So the belts of wool from the carding-engine are combed in much the same way as one combs one's hair—although, of course, by machinery. This makes all the individual wool fibres lie parallel to one another, while all pieces of broken and short wool are combed out. These last are called 'noil', and the long, parallel wool fibres that remain are called 'top'. It is this 'top' that is spun into worsted yarn.

Various kinds of machines, known as 'combs', are used for this. In earlier days hand-combs shaped rather like a garden rake were used, but they had five or six sets of teeth instead of one. There were two combs: one was fixed to a post and the wool was placed on it, while the other was pulled several times over it. To keep the wool flexible, the combs had to be heated by charcoal stoves called 'comb-pots'. As the fumes of these stoves were poisonous, wool-combing was then an unhealthy occupation.

4. SPINNING. This process involves pulling (or drawing) and twisting the wool so that it comes out as one long thread. This cannot be done with the belt of wool that emerges from earlier processes, as the result would be a yarn almost as thick as rope. The belt of wool is therefore first split up into a series of thin strips, called 'slubbings'. Each of these is then pulled and twisted into yarn on the spinning-frame.

Our modern power-driven spinning-frames are very complicated improvements on the primitive spinning-wheel. With the early wheel, the thread or ribbon of wool was kept in tension and drawn out to a greater length, while the wheel or spindle gave a twist to it. The modern spinning-frame also draws out the wool into a thin thread, twists it, and winds it on to a bobbin. Machine-spinning has great advantages over the old system of hand-spinning. The amount of stretch, or tension, is arranged mechanically; it is therefore constant and regular, instead of being dependent on the uneven hand of the operator; this makes for a constant size and

International Wool Secretariat

COMB FOR WORSTED YARN

Combed wool is fed into the machine and pushed down on to circular revolving rows of pins by the brush. The longer fibres or 'top' are drawn off the pins in slivers—one of which can be seen on the left—and the short fibres or 'noil' are kept back

quality in the yarn being spun. The whole process is now very rapid, and many threads or yarns are spun at one time on the same frame.

A final stage in spinning is sometimes the manufacture of two-ply, three-ply, and four-ply yarns; such multi-ply yarns are often sold for hand-knitting. These yarns simply go through a second process which twists the required number of single yarns together. A modern spinning-mill is a maze of long lines of quickly revolving spindles, among which the dyed yarns make a gay mixture of colour.

See also COTTON MANUFACTURE; WOOL WEAVING; TEXTILE FIBRES AND FABRICS.

WOOL WEAVING. This is one of the processes that take place after WOOL SPINNING (q.v.).

The simplest kind of woven fabric is made by interlacing threads over and under each other, as in darning. Threads, called the 'warp', are stretched on a frame; other threads, called the 'weft', are darned to and fro across the warp, running over and under alternate threads to make a web.

Weaving is done on a device called a loom. In the simplest looms, the warp is held in crude wooden frames, and the warp threads are lifted by a needle, by sticks, or by loops of cord to allow the weft to be woven in. Such looms are still used by primitive people; but weavers began to make improvements centuries ago to increase speed, and to weave finer cloth with more intricate designs. Looms may vary in size from small ones on which scarves or other narrow fabrics can be woven, to those capable of turning out wide lengths of cloth.

All cloth was woven by hand until the invention of the power-loom, which was introduced at the end of the 18th century, though steam looms became common rather later. Power did not alter the basic principles of weaving; it merely mechanized them and speeded them up. Even after the power-loom was in general use for cloth-production on a large scale, hand-weaving still remained an important craft in most parts of Europe and Asia, but it very nearly died out in Britain. William MORRIS (q.v. Vol. V) tried to revive an interest in hand-crafts in general, including weaving, and there are now quite a number of hand-weavers in Britain. Hand-woven cloth has a quality all its own, with an individuality that is lacking in machine-made fabric, and the weaver can experiment freely in designs and colours. Hand-weaving has this importance in the modern textile factory: a textile designer will often build up a sample of his design on a hand-loom, as this gives him the opportunity of experimenting with texture, weave, and colour, and then, when the pattern is finally approved, it is woven in bulk on a power-loom.

The machine-weaving process is the same for both woollen and worsted yarns. The design is first drawn on squared paper, on which it is possible to reproduce each single warp and weft thread, and to show clearly how the intersection of warp and weft, and the colour pattern, are to be arranged. Most modern designers then weave an actual sample of their design on a handloom, so that any defects in the drawing show up

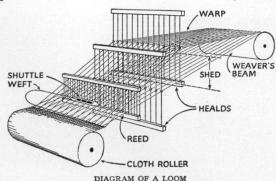

DIAGRAM OF A LOOM

The warp is wound on the weaver's beam at the back of the loom and threaded through the healds and reed on to the cloth roller in front. By pulling down one heald a space or shed is made between the warp threads through which the shuttle containing the weft is passed. By reversing the position of the healds another shed is formed so that the shuttle next passes over the threads which were beneath and under those which were above. The reed presses the weft tightly together

clearly, and can be corrected before the cloth is manufactured on a large scale.

In a modern factory the yarns that are to form the warp are wound on to a 'warping mill', a large revolving drum on which the warp threads are built up to receive the weft threads. The latter are passed alternately over and under the warp by means of a shuttle containing a bobbin, from which the weft thread gradually unreels. There must be a means of raising some of the warp threads, and depressing others, so as to form a 'shed' or opening through which the shuttle can pass. This is arranged by passing the warp threads through eyelets on wires, called 'healds', fixed in a moveable frame: when the loom is in motion, one set of healds moves up as the other moves down. The shuttle is 'flicked' automatically from side to side through the shed formed by the movement of the healds. As each successive weft thread is passed into the warp, it is automatically pressed hard against its predecessor. As the finished cloth is produced, it is wound on to a roller, and fresh lengths of warp are unwound off another roller. The process is therefore continuous while it lasts, and the lightning motion of the shuttle, and the rise and fall of the healds, combine to make the noise of a loom quite rhythmical.

If a pile fabric is required, the pile threads are looped around flat steel rods that are inserted during manufacture and then withdrawn when the fabric is close-woven and tight. This process leaves a series of projecting loops that will not

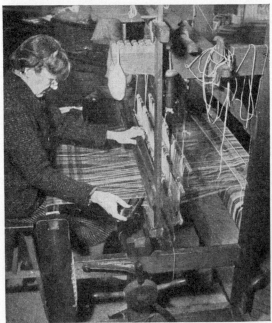

Norman Wymer

WEAVING ON A HAND LOOM

International Wool Secretariat

A WARPING-MILL

Threads from bobbins in the frame on the right are wound on to the weaver's beam, so that they lie side by side

come loose. If the pile is to be cut, the rods carry a knife-edge, and the cutting is automatic.

It is often said that it is the dyeing and finishing of the cloth that really make it saleable, for it leaves the loom in a very dirty and unattractive condition, and requires much further attention.

It is first thrown over a roller and examined for faults, such as burrs, knots, and missing threads—an inspection called 'perching'. Highly skilled women, in great demand in the trade, sew in by hand any broken or missing threads. They are called 'menders', and their craft is the same as that of 'invisible menders' who can sometimes be seen at work in shop windows.

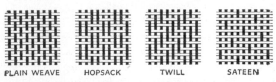

PLAIN WEAVE   HOPSACK   TWILL   SATEEN

PILE FABRIC *(SECTION)*

DIAGRAM OF DIFFERENT KINDS OF WEAVE

The cloth must next be washed or scoured. Worsteds are scoured in soap solution, but woollens usually need only weak soda, as the oil they contain mixes with the soda to form a natural SOAP (q.v.). The cloth shrinks during the scouring, and this has to be allowed for in the design and the weaving, as the finished cloth will come out smaller than the design.

If a woollen cloth requires a matted or felted surface (*see* FELT), it is lubricated with a soapy solution, and then put under mechanical pressure. For many cloths, particularly worsted suitings, where a smooth surface is wanted, the protruding fibres are clipped off in a 'cropping' machine, which has revolving knives like those of a lawn-mower, an improvement on the primitive shears that were once used. If a fluffy, raised surface is required, as in blankets, the cloth is passed over rollers covered with small, prickly 'teazles', which brush up the surface fibres. This machine is called a 'teazle gig'.

Wool may be dyed at any one of a number of stages in its manufacture. It may be dyed loose, or at various stages of the spinning process, or as

AN AUTOMATIC LOOM

International Wool Secretariat

finished yarn, or as cloth 'in the piece'. The dyes used depend upon the stage at which dyeing is considered desirable, for dyes differ in their resistance to fading. Wool that is dyed in the loose state—'dyed in the wool'—absorbs the dye well into every separate fibre, but the dye then has to withstand the rigours of all the drastic manufacturing and finishing processes that follow. Only dyes with a high resistance to such treatment can therefore be used when the wool is dyed loose. Wool to be spun into woollen yarn is usually dyed loose; worsted wool is usually dyed after the combing process (*see* WOOL SPINNING). Fabrics dyed after weaving—dyed 'in the piece'—have to withstand only rather mild finishing processes. Bright, light colours and pastel shades can then be used, most of which would not be 'fast' enough to resist more severe treatment (*see* DYES).

The use to which cloths will be put has also much influence on the timing and nature of the dyeing. Woollen cloths for women's garments may only have to last until fashion changes, but worsted cloths for men's suits and for overcoats have to last during many years of exposure to sun and wet.

After all these processes, the finished cloth is mechanically pressed and folded; this is how it is seen in the tailor's shop.

Some modern cloths are woven from yarns made up of both wool and alginate rayon (threads made from seaweed). The alginate rayon dissolves in a solution of soap and soda, leaving behind an ultra-lightweight wool fabric. In the same way, raised fancy patterns can be formed, and also wool lace.

In the past much damage has been done to wool clothing by moth larvae. To-day, wool can be effectively moth-proofed by a chemical treatment which is not removed by washing.

See also WOOL INDUSTRY, MODERN; WOOL SPINNING; COTTON MANUFACTURE.

WORSTED, *see* WOOL SPINNING, Section 3.

Z

ZINC MINING. Zinc is found in nature in the form of ores that are compounds of zinc (*see* METAL ORES, Vol. III), and most zinc ores are usually found together with those of LEAD (q.v.). The principal commercial zinc ores are zinc blende, which is more or less pure sulphide of zinc, and calamine, consisting mainly of zinc carbonate. Zinc was known and used in ancient times, principally as an ALLOY (q.v. Vol. VIII) with copper to form brass and, in the form of zinc compounds, for use in medicine as ointments. Nowadays zinc ores are mined in the U.S.A., Canada, Australia, Mexico, Russia, Poland, Italy, and (in smaller amounts) in many other parts of the world. Zinc ores are smelted in most industrial countries, including Great Britain. A very important by-product of zinc smelting is sulphuric acid (*see* ACIDS).

The principal industrial use of zinc is in the making of brass. Another important use of metallic zinc is for galvanizing articles made of iron, such as buckets, agricultural fencing-wire, dust-bins, and cattle-troughs, to prevent their rusting. Zinc plates are much used in the printing industry (*see* PROCESS REPRODUCTION). Zinc is also often used nowadays instead of tin, in making metal alloys with low melting-points for lining engine BEARINGS (q.v. Vol. VIII). Nickel silver, the material out of which much electro-plated tableware is made, is an alloy

ZINC SMELTING IN ANCIENT CHINA

The Chinese were among the first to isolate the metal zinc. Sealed pots containing zinc were heated with charcoal. The zinc was driven off as a vapour which solidified on cooling. Woodcut from a Chinese book printed in 1637, reproduced from Li Ch'iao-p'ing's *The Chemical Arts of China* (Journal of Chemical Education)

of copper, zinc, and nickel. The most important compound of zinc in industry is zinc oxide, or zinc white. This is much used as a pigment in making PAINTS AND VARNISHES (q.v.), and also for medicines and COSMETICS (q.v.). Lithopone, another zinc compound, is used in the manufacture of distempers, paints, and rubber articles.

PRINTED IN
GREAT BRITAIN
AT THE
UNIVERSITY PRESS
OXFORD
BY
CHARLES BATEY
PRINTER
TO THE
UNIVERSITY